*Induced Innovation*

# INDUCED INNOVATION

*Technology, Institutions,
and Development*

HANS P. BINSWANGER AND VERNON W. RUTTAN

*with Uri Ben-Zion, Alain de Janvry, Robert E. Evenson,
Yujiro Hayami, Terry L. Roe, John H. Sanders,
William W. Wade, Adolf Weber, and Patrick Yeung*

THE JOHNS HOPKINS UNIVERSITY PRESS
BALTIMORE AND LONDON

The Johns Hopkins University Press, Baltimore, Maryland 21218
The Johns Hopkins University Press Ltd., London
Library of Congress Catalog Card Number 77-23387
ISBN 0-8018-2027-8

Library of Congress Cataloging in Publication data will be found on the last printed
page of this book.

A change in the relative prices of the factors of production is itself a spur to invention, and to invention of a particular kind—directed to economising the use of a factor which has become relatively expensive.—J. R. Hicks, *The Theory of Wages*

# Contents

# Tables

# Figures

*Preface*

THE interpretation of technical and institutional change as endogenous rather than exogenous to the economic system—that is, as induced by economic as well as by social forces—is a relatively new development in economic thought. Economists have traditionally viewed both types of change as subject to cultural and intellectual influences that are not easy to analyze within an economic framework.

In this book we attempt to accomplish four objectives. First, using the induced innovation framework, we wish to relate the historical analysis of the sources of technical change to the normative process of research resource allocation and planning. Second, we want to combine the several different approaches to the analysis of the rate and direction of technical change into one investment framework. Third, we propose to expand the concept of induced innovation to include institutional as well as technical change. Fourth, we intend to explore the implications of the concept of induced innovation for development theory and policy.

The book is based on a set of interrelated studies that were initiated at the University of Minnesota. Several chapters are revisions of papers that were presented at either the Trade and Development Workshop, conducted by the University's Department of Economics, or the Agricultural Development Workshop, held under the leadership of the Department of Agricultural and Applied Economics.

Most of the empirical tests and case studies of induced innovation were drawn from agricultural development experience. However, the theory of induced technical and institutional innovation and the methodology of the tests of induced innovation have broad general application. The theory and methods employed in the studies presented in this book will be useful to students of technical change and economic development regardless of their sectoral interest.

We are indebted to Uri Ben-Zion, Alain de Janvry, Robert E. Evenson, Yujiro Hayami, Terry L. Roe, John H. Sanders, William W. Wade, Adolf Weber, and Patrick Yeung not only for contributing their time and effort to the preparation of several of the book's chapters but for providing their research data and findings as well. Comments by Richard R. Nelson and John P. Lewis, both of whom read the entire manuscript, were extremely helpful in enabling us to combine the views and the research findings of several different authors into an integrated, meaningful statement. Our many debts to other reviewers are acknowledged in individual chapters. We are particularly grateful to Virginia O. Locke, who served as copyeditor for the book. She made a major contribution to the clarity with which the ideas developed in the book have been presented.

Much of the research on which this book is based was supported by grants made by the Rockefeller Foundation and the Agency for International Development to the University of Minnesota Economic Development Center. The book was completed while both authors were members of the staff of the Agricultural Development Council.

HANS P. BINSWANGER

VERNON W. RUTTAN

*Induced Innovation*

# ONE

# Introduction

HANS P. BINSWANGER AND VERNON W. RUTTAN

THE 1970s have been a period of renewed uncertainty with respect to the long-run prospects for economic growth and human welfare. In the early years of this decade, scientific opinion and ideological perspectives converged to suggest that the world was fast approaching both the physical and the cultural limits to growth. There is a continuing concern that advances in man's capacity for scientific and technical innovation have not been matched by the institutional innovations needed to enable him to manage and direct this capacity for his own welfare. The theme that "progress breeds not welfare but catastrophe" has again emerged from the underworld of social thought as a serious issue in scientific and philosophical inquiry.[1]

The tools of the economist are relatively blunt instruments with which to confront the grand theme of epochal growth and decline. Until a few decades ago comparative statics was the most powerful theoretical tool available to the economist as a guide to empirical knowledge. Even modern neoclassical growth theory has been based primarily on an application of the tools of comparative statics to the analysis of alternative steady growth paths. In the simple Harrod–Domar–Mahalanobis models that dominated growth theory in the 1950s, increases in the capital–labor ratio were seen as the only source of increase in per capita income. This view continued to be embodied in the policy assumptions of planning commissions and budget bureaus long after intellectual debate had widened the scope of growth models and growth accounting.

Even in the more sophisticated models that became available to us in the 1960s, the growth of output was narrowly determined by increases in the labor force and in physical capital, by technical change, and by improvements

[1] J. B. Bury, *The Idea of Progress: An Inquiry into Its Growth and Origin* (New York: Dover, 1955; reprinted from the 1932 Macmillan edition). Bury traces the development, in Western thought, of reactions against the idea of progress.

1

in the quality of human capital. With few exceptions, technical change was treated as exogenous to the economic system, and institutional change was not dealt with at all in formal growth theory.

Substantial progress has been made in the effort to interpret the process of technical change as endogenous rather than exogenous to the economic system. In the early 1960s, the theory of induced innovation emerged as an important theme and focus of considerable professional debate in the literature on economic growth. An initial empirical test of the theory of induced innovation against the history of agricultural development in Japan and the United States, carried out by Yujiro Hayami and Vernon W. Ruttan, confirmed the power of this theory to add significantly to our understanding of historical development experience.[2] The Hayami–Ruttan analysis also suggested the importance of extending the induced innovation framework to the interpretation of the process of institutional change.

### Induced Technical and Institutional Innovation

Within the constraints imposed by existing natural resources, technology, and institutions, economic growth results from the accumulation of physical and human capital and from improvements in the efficiency of resource utilization.

Traditionally, growth-oriented economic policy has focused on improving efficiency in resource utilization and on modifying savings and investment behavior. In the absence of successful efforts to achieve more rapid rates of technical and institutional innovation, the effects of efficiency gains and of modifications in savings and investment behavior can be only transitional. But the processes by which technical and institutional change are induced are less well understood than are the conditions for achieving efficiency in resource allocation or the procedures for altering savings and investment behavior. Both technical and institutional change have long been employed as conscious instruments of development policy. The allocation of resources to these particular instruments, however, has traditionally been guided more by intuition and passion than by analysis.

A major limitation on the capacity of a firm or a nation to improve the efficiency with which it allocates resources to modify the rate or direction of technical change has been the lack of a solid microeconomic theory of induced technical innovation. A major contribution of this book is the development of an investment model of induced technical change. The model integrates

[2] Yujiro Hayami and V. W. Ruttan, "Factor Prices and Technical Change in Agricultural Development: The United States and Japan, 1880–1960," *Journal of Political Economy* 78 (September–October 1970): 1115–41; Yujiro Hayami and Vernon W. Ruttan, *Agricultural Development: An International Perspective* (Baltimore: The Johns Hopkins University Press, 1971).

and extends earlier work on the economics of research and development and on the theory of induced technical change.

The demonstration that technical change can be treated as endogenous to the development process does not imply that the progress of either agricultural or industrial technology can be left to an "invisible hand" that directs technology along an "efficient" path determined by "original" resource endowments or by the growth of demand. First, the way resource endowments and final demand express themselves in terms of relative prices is determined by existing income distribution, and change in the distribution of income may itself represent a specific policy goal. Second, the production of the new knowledge that leads to technical change and the embodiment of this new knowledge in new processes and new products are themselves the result of institutional innovation and development. But even fewer attempts have been made to understand the process by which resources are brought to bear to alter the rate and direction of institutional innovation and development than have been made to understand the processes leading to technical change.

A second major contribution of this book is the attempt to develop a theory of induced institutional innovation analogous to the theory of induced technical innovation. We will argue that the sources of demand for both technical and institutional change are essentially the same. Both types of change are induced by shifts in relative factor prices or by the changes in resource endowments and income distribution that are associated with economic growth. We will also argue that shifts in the supply of both technical and institutional change are produced by advances in knowledge in science and technology and that the costs of institutional innovation are reduced by advances in knowledge in the social sciences and related professions such as law, business, social service, and planning.

The development and testing of an induced innovation model of technical and institutional change, if successful, would represent a significant achievement. Many of the major issues that face both the developed and the developing economies center around the management of science and technology. Clarification of the nature of the impact of institutional factors on the rate and direction of technical change is essential for the development of science and technology policy. It is of equal importance to clarify the nature of the role that technology plays in determining the rate and direction of institutional change.

An attempt such as we make in this book—to treat both technical and institutional change as endogenous rather than exogenous to the development process—may seem, at least on the surface, to leave little scope for the role of policy in determining the future course of technical change and institutional development.

We do not imply that either technical or institutional change can be treated as entirely endogenous to the economic system. There is in science and technology an autonomous thrust toward the accumulation of knowledge. Furthermore, nature imposes some constraints on what can be discovered. And changes in the evolution of ideas in the general culture also influence the path of institutional change.

We explicitly reject the view that man's activity can be neatly partitioned into distinct sets of "economic" and "noneconomic" activity. Rather, we adopt the notion that both economic and noneconomic sources of behavior may condition any and every dimension of man's activity. We also insist that some of the goals that societies set for themselves are not achievable in the foreseeable future through any combination of technological and institutional changes.

There can be little argument, however, with the proposition that the viability of technical innovations depends on the economic environment into which they are introduced. Nor can one seriously question that the viability of institutional changes depends on the cultural environment into which they are introduced. History precludes absolute freedom in the choice of either technology or institutions. We are all familiar with the fate of both technical and institutional innovations that have been in advance of "their time."

The effort to achieve a clear understanding of the sources of technical and institutional change is designed to increase man's control over history. By increasing his understanding of how particular economic and cultural environments act to induce particular paths of technical and institutional change, man will strengthen his ability to allocate the resources that are available to him in such a way as to achieve viable technical and institutional innovations.

The most powerful force that man can command to alter the direction of technical or institutional change is his capacity for innovation. If he is to deploy his innovative effort effectively, man must learn as much as he can about the complex matrix within which technical and institutional change interact with each other and with the physical and cultural endowments of a particular society.

### Innovation Frontiers

The process of development involves the movement of three distinct *frontiers*, or levels of technological achievement. The first of these is the *scientific frontier*, which describes the set of the most efficient techniques that could be developed with unlimited research resources, given the existing state of knowledge in the basic sciences such as physics, chemistry, biology, and psychology. The scientific frontier shifts as advances are made in these basic sciences. The achievement of rapid advances in the scientific frontier requires an institutional framework, or institutional change, that provides for the most efficient allocation of resources to the various basic research activities.

Below the scientific frontier lies the *technology frontier*, or *metaproduction function*, which describes the set of techniques that have actually been developed in the most advanced countries and that are used by the most advanced firms. This frontier is always below the scientific frontier. Indeed, as we will discuss in chapter 4, it almost never makes economic sense to carry out enough applied research to push the metaproduction frontier to the scientific frontier because of diminishing returns to applied research. But the rapid movement of this frontier, like that of the scientific frontier, depends on an institutional framework within which resources can be allocated efficiently to applied research or to institutional change.

Below the technology frontier lies the *achievement distribution*, or distribution of levels of achievement, which represents the actual levels of technology achieved by individual countries or firms. (For the most advanced firms in the advanced countries, the achievement level is located on the metaproduction function.)[3] The development of countries and firms that have not yet reached the technology frontier requires more than just the rapid diffusion of available technology. To achieve effective use of research and technology, it is necessary to utilize existing knowledge of individual and institutional behavior. Agricultural and rural development, industrialization and urban development, physical and human capital investment and planning —all play an important role in economic advancement below the technology frontier.

In this book we will not examine the policy instruments that derive from the several fields mentioned above or the institutional requirements for the efficient use of these instruments. We will focus, rather, on movements of the three frontiers and, particularly, on the movement of the third of these—the achieved position of a country or firm—toward the second—the metaproduction function—through technical and institutional innovation. This is not to deny the importance of other sources of changes in the achievement distribution, account of which must be taken in any full view of the development process. And, as we will see, the theories of institutional change developed in the last part of this book have strong implications for the design of policies and institutions that affect these comparatively neglected sources of innovation.

## An Overview of the Book

This book is organized in four major parts. In part I (chapters 2 and 3), we introduce the concept of induced technical change and document its

[3] For the concept of *achievement distribution*, we are indebted to A. T. Mosher; see his *Lectures on Agricultural Extension* (Kandy: University of Sri Lanka, 1974).

significance for the process of agricultural development. In part II (chapters 4 through 6), we review and extend the theory of induced technical change. Part III (chapters 7 through 11) presents five cases of development that test the theory of induced technical change against historical experience. In part IV (chapters 12 through 14), we extend the theory of induced innovation to include the processes of institutional innovation and development.

In chapter 2, Hans P. Binswanger presents a review and evaluation of the literature on induced innovation. As he points out, the induced innovation hypothesis was first suggested by Sir John Hicks in the 1930s.[4] Hicks argued that there was no inherent labor-saving bias in technical change. Rather, he said, rising wages could be expected to induce entrepreneurs to seek out labor-saving innovations in order to offset rising labor costs. The Hicks position was generally accepted until the late 1950s, when W. E. G. Salter argued that firms are motivated to reduce total costs, not particular factor costs.[5] Since the early 1960s there has been renewed interest in the theory of induced technical change. However, neglect of the economics of the research and development process constitutes a major limitation on the models presented in the literature to date. Neither Syed Ahmad nor Charles Kennedy make any attempt, in their seminal papers, to show how, in the process of research and development, resources are used to influence the direction of technical change.[6]

In chapter 3, Vernon W. Ruttan, Hans P. Binswanger, Yujiro Hayami, William W. Wade, and Adolf Weber test the induced technical change hypothesis against the historical experience of the agricultural sectors in Japan, Germany, Denmark, France, the United Kingdom, and the United States during the period 1880–1970. We first establish the plausibility of the induced innovation hypothesis along the lines employed by Hayami and Ruttan in their earlier work on Japan and the United States.[7] We then try out the model, using a new test, in an effort to determine whether the observed changes in factor ratios of the late nineteenth century and the changes that have emerged over time are consistent with movement along a common production function or whether they were generated by nonneutral shifts in production functions among countries.

The results indicate that the United States has followed a more labor-saving path of technical change than have the four European countries. Since the 1950s, however, the paths followed by the United States and Japan have

[4] J. R. Hicks, *The Theory of Wages* (London: Macmillan and Co. Ltd., 1st ed. 1932; 2nd ed. 1963).

[5] W. E. G. Salter, *Productivity and Technical Change* (Cambridge: Cambridge University Press, 1960), pp. 43–4.

[6] Syed Ahmad, "On the Theory of Induced Invention," *Economic Journal* 76, no. 302 (June 1966): 344–57; Charles Kennedy, "Induced Bias in Innovation and the Theory of Distribution," *Economic Journal* 74, no. 295 (September 1964): 541–7.

[7] Hayami and Ruttan, *Agricultural Development*.

converged somewhat as the extreme labor intensity that characterized Japanese agriculture in 1880 has been modified to some degree. It also seems clear, from the data presented in chapter 6, that differences in the rates of growth in demand for agricultural products have played a significant role in inducing differential rates of technical change. This effect of demand seems particularly strong in the cases of France and Germany.

In chapters 4 and 5, Binswanger develops a microeconomic theory of induced innovation. His model incorporates the effects on the amount and direction of scientific and technical effort at the individual firm level of factor prices, scale of operation, interest rates, final demand, and exogenous advances in basic and applied knowledge. The model confirms the impact of these economic variables on the rate and direction of technical change, but it also leaves open the possibility that there are fundamental or exogenous biases in technical change. In these chapters, Binswanger considers the effects on the inducement process of market imperfections, including the inability of innovating firms to capture a significant share of the social benefits that stem from innovating activity. He also reviews some of the controversies in the literature on induced innovation from the viewpoint of the investment model of research and shows that it may be impossible to develop entirely satisfactory long-term equilibrium growth models that incorporate endogenous technical change in any meaningful way.

In chapter 6, Hans P. Binswanger and Robert E. Evenson integrate theories of research resource allocation, induced innovation, and diffusion of technology, bringing them jointly to bear on the problems of technology transfer. They show that the capacity for adaptive research is essential for efficient technology transfer and that the investment model of induced innovation is broad enough to include the "search" activities involved in the process of such transfer. They also utilize an index of *environmental sensitivity* to test the transferability of agricultural technology across microclimatic regions. The results of this test indicate that environmental constraints on technology transfer are such that very high priority must be given to investment in experiment station capacity to generate location-specific technology that is adapted to the physical and economic environment of each ecological region. Furthermore, the transfer of technology among regions and countries is responsive to essentially the same inducement processes that generate the research and development that lead to technical change within a particular agroclimatic, or ecological, region.

A basic limitation of the empirical test of the induced innovation hypothesis we employ in chapter 3 is that it is a two-factor test that involves substitution between labor and land. In chapter 7, Binswanger develops a multifactor test that measures biases directly instead of making inferences about them from changes in factor prices and factor ratios. This model involves the measurement of factor-using bias for five factors—land, labor, machinery, fertilizer, and "other" inputs—in United States agriculture for the period 1912–1968. The results indicate that very strong price-induced biases in technology affected the use of fertilizer and labor. Some of the advance in mechanical technology, however, reflected the working out of fundamental biases in innovation possibilities.

In chapter 8, Patrick Yeung and Terry L. Roe report the results of an effort to develop a modified *constant elasticity of substitution* production function that will permit the measurement of both the rate of technical change and the effect of factor prices on factor augmentation.

The formal models of induced innovation contained in the literature to date have focused primarily on shifts in the direction of technical change that are induced by changes in relative factor prices. In chapter 9, Uri Ben-Zion and Vernon W. Ruttan extend the modeling of induced innovation to include the effects on the rate of technical change of the rate of growth in aggregate demand. The authors test the model against aggregate data from the United States for 1929–1969 and find that the rate of technical change does respond to changes in the rate of growth in demand with a lag of three to seven years.

In chapter 10, John H. Sanders and Vernon W. Ruttan analyze the effects of overvalued exchange rates and subsidies to mechanization on technical change in Brazilian agriculture. They conclude that the distortion in factor prices that resulted from these policies has affected both the choice of available technology and the direction of technical change. The consequences have included more rapid mechanization and less rapid growth in the demand for labor in rural areas than would have occurred in the absence of governmental manipulation. The primary beneficiaries of these policies appear to be the larger farmers of the South. An additional effect has been the widening of income disparities among regions.

In chapter 11, Alain de Janvry shows that in Argentina structural imperfections in economic and political organizations have resulted in failure to translate the latent demand for biological and chemical technology into effective demand. The dominant economic and political role of the large landowners has prevented the factor endowments that characterize the smaller landholders from becoming an effective source of demand for biological and chemical technology.

In chapter 12, Ruttan attempts to expand the induced innovation hypothesis so as to incorporate the process of institutional change. He proposes a model in which institutional change may be induced by (a) a demand for more effective institutional performance that arises out of the shifts in relative factor and product prices and the changes in income distribution that are associated with economic growth or (b) advances in the supply of knowledge about social and economic organization, behavior, and change. Imperfections in economic and political structure that constrain the translation of latent to effective demand for institutional change are examined. The model suggested in chapter 12 opens up the possibility of the more effective direction of scientific and technical resources toward varieties of institutional change that are suitable to the resource and cultural endowments of a particular society.

In chapter 13, we use the induced innovation model to interpret the process of technical and institutional change that has occurred in agriculture's *green revolution* in a number of developing countries beginning in the mid-1960s. Our analysis illustrates the dialectical interaction between technical and institutional change during the process of agricultural development. The analysis also suggests that the new seed–fertilizer technology weakened the potential for revolutionary change in political and economic institutions in rural areas in many parts of the developing world in the late 1960s and early 1970s. By the mid-1970s, the productivity gains that had been achieved during the previous decade were coming more slowly. It is possible that the revolutionary changes in rural institutions that were anticipated in the radical literature on rural development may occur as a result of increasing immiserization in the rural areas of many developing countries in the next decade.

In chapter 14 we suggest that it is possible to outline the sources of alternative paths of institutional change and that the process of change is dialectical rather than linear. Technical and institutional innovations that generate new income streams can be expected to induce further institutional innovations that weaken communal and social control over the allocation and use of resources. Conversely, a period of relative stagnation or decline can be expected to induce institutional innovations that give society greater social control over the allocation and use of resources. This greater control then enables society to direct its energies to the generation of technical and institutional innovations that open up a new period of growth and development.

# I

*Induced Technical Change
and Development*

TWO

# Induced Technical Change:
# Evolution of Thought

HANS P. BINSWANGER

M ODELS of induced innovation and empirical tests of such models are an attempt to discover the roles played by factor prices, goods prices, and other economic variables in determining the rate and direction of technical change. The models and their empirical tests are thus part of a wider effort to understand the process of technical change—including the diffusion of change—as endogenous to the economic system. This effort has gained intensity since the publication, in 1957, of the results of Robert Solow's study measuring the rate of technical change in the U.S. economy. Solow reported that between 1909 and 1949, "gross output per man hour doubled over the interval, with $87\frac{1}{2}$ percent of the increase attributable to technical change and the remaining $12\frac{1}{2}$ percent to increased use of machines."[1] These findings shifted attention from investment to technical change as the main engine of growth and led to the construction of many new models and to a vast amount of empirical research aimed at achieving a better understanding of the entire process of technical change.

## Endogenous Technical Change and Economic Policy

The development of technical change is resource using, and technical innovation itself greatly influences the income of the owners of human and physical resources. Consequently, an empirically verified theory of endogenous

---

[1] Robert Solow, "Technical Change and the Aggregate Production Function," *Review of Economics and Statistics* (1957): 312–20. Although the size of the contribution of technical change has since been shown to be lower, there is now widespread agreement among economists that technical change accounts for a major proportion of growth in per capita income.

technical change should help us answer the following questions about the utilization of resources, the answers to which will strongly affect economic policy.[2]

First, what quantity of resources should be allocated by a society to the generation and diffusion of technical change in order to maximize the growth of per capita consumption? How should such allocation of resources be apportioned between basic and applied research, between development and diffusion of new technology, and among different sectors of the economy?[3]

Second, will a market economy produce an optimal allocation of research resources? If it will not, what changes in institutions, incentive structures, and economic policy are necessary to bring about such an optimal allocation? This problem has troubled policy makers and economists for a long time. As one can easily see, the nature of the output of the research process is such that an individual firm in an atomistic, competitive industry would have no incentive at all to do research.

The output of research and development is information, in the form of blueprints, chemical formulae, new seed varieties, and scientific or technical laws. Unlike ordinary inputs, information is neither used up nor depreciated in the production process. Its production is expensive, but its distribution is cheap. Although (as we will see in chapter 6) users may have to incur transfer costs, they can enjoy the benefits of information without having to incur the costs of its production. This is the classic free-rider problem associated with public goods. As Kenneth Arrow points out, social optimality requires that information, once produced, be made available to all potential users for the small, marginal cost of its distribution.[4] Under this condition, because he will not be compensated for his effort by the users, the potential producer of innovation will have no incentive to produce. It will be optimal for everyone to wait until someone else produces the information.

Arrow argues that the optimal arrangement is a total separation between the compensation of the innovator and any charge to the user of the innovation. In such an ideal arrangement, the innovator's compensation depends on the total social benefits that derive from his innovation. In fact, societies have moved in this direction in several situations. Most prominent is the case of basic scientific research, in which the researcher is paid primarily by

[2] The concept of induced innovation is just one building block of a theory of endogenous technical change. Some other building blocks are the theory of diffusion, the theory and methods of research resource allocation, and the principles of research management.

[3] It should be noted that in the last twenty years very few growth models have addressed this question. Instead they have concentrated on the consequences of various forms of technical change.

[4] Kenneth J. Arrow, "Economic Welfare and the Allocation of Resources for Invention," in *The Rate and Direction of Inventive Activity*, ed. Richard R. Nelson (Princeton: Princeton University Press, 1962).

government or other nonprofit organizations.[5] Particularly relevant to the present discussion is the case of biological and agronomic research in agriculture. Here, research often does not lead to a commodity, such as a pesticide or a tractor, whose price can be increased (through patent protection or product differentiation) to make the user pay for the use of the innovation. The agricultural experiment station is the institutional innovation whose essential purpose was to overcome the lack of incentive for private biological–chemical research in agriculture. The divorce of compensation to the researcher from charge to the user is almost complete also in fields of very risky research, such as defense or aerospace, which in most countries is carried out almost exclusively under government contract.

Patent and licensing laws are the other institutional means for compensating inventors and researchers. However, these methods have the disadvantage of impeding the socially optimal application of an invention by granting its inventor a monopoly right to its use for a specified number of years. There is now a substantial body of literature on the issue of optimal length of patent protection and on the general merits and demerits of patent laws—their effectiveness in protecting the innovator's rights and in calling forth new inventions as against their damaging restriction of the use of such inventions.[6]

Within this second set of questions economists have also looked at the effect of market structure on the rate of technical change. Joseph Schumpeter argues that large, monopolistic firms will achieve higher rates of productivity growth than will small, competitive firms and that this advantage outweighs any comparative static advantages of competition.[7] Large, monopolistic

[5] There are two reasons for this institutional arrangement: the uncertainty of potential benefits and the impossibility of assessing them. Basic research is usually much riskier than applied research. The probability of achieving stated research goals is less than it is for applied research. Moreover, the benefit of the expected research output cannot be measured because all possible future applications of this output cannot be known at the time research is begun. Benefits may occur in fields unrelated to the area of initial investigation. And often they are not immediate but depend on future research of a more applied character. Indeed, it is best to visualize the benefit of basic research as an input into applied research whose benefits, in turn, are new processes and products. Later in the book we will show that the state of the basic sciences can be regarded as determining and creating the potential payoffs for applied research. For a further discussion of these issues see Richard R. Nelson, "The Simple Economics of Basic Scientific Research," *Journal of Political Economy* 67 (1959): 297–306.

[6] See, for instance: Arrow, "Economic Welfare"; William D. Nordhaus, *Invention, Growth and Welfare* (Cambridge: Massachusetts Institute of Technology Press, 1969); idem, "The Optimal Life of a Patent: Reply," *American Economic Review* 62 (1972): 428–31; F. M. Scherer, "Nordhaus' Theory of Optimal Patent Life: A Geometric Reinterpretation," *American Economic Review* 62 (1972): 422–7; Morton I. Kamien and Nancy L. Schwartz, "Patent Life and R & D Rivalry," *American Economic Review* 64 (1974): 183–7.

[7] Joseph A. Schumpeter, *Capitalism, Socialism and Democracy* (New York: Harper & Row, Publishers, Inc., 1942). For a recent review of the literature on the role of market structure in technical change see Morton I. Kamien and Nancy L. Schwartz, "Market Structure and Innovation: A Survey," *Journal of Economic Literature* 13 (1975): 1–37.

firms have more incentive to produce inventions because they can more easily appropriate the benefits of such inventions. Furthermore, economies of scale make large research establishments more efficient in producing technical innovations. These economies derive from the effective functioning of a staff of highly specialized personnel and from the lower risks associated with a diversified research portfolio. Finally, large firms have an advantage in the financial market and can borrow more easily for research purposes than can small firms. Schumpeter's hypothesis continues to stimulate argument, and we will return to this issue in chapters 4 and 5.

A theory of endogenous technical change should enable economists and policy makers to answer a third question: How do economic variables affect the nature of technical change? Technical change generally has specific consequences for the distribution of income among industries, factors of production, and regions and countries. If these consequences are judged undesirable, policy makers will want to know whether they can be avoided. Can technology be guided into a more desirable direction by changing institutions, incentive structures, and economic policies? Or, will compensatory income distribution measures be more effective in dealing with the consequences of technical change?

The initial interest in biased technical change and in induced innovation clearly stemmed from interest in income distributional policy questions. To the casual observer, technical change seems clearly associated with a steadily increasing use of machinery in comparison with labor. On this view, it is natural to ask whether technical change is inherently biased in a labor-saving direction and, if so, to what extent technical change will result in unemployment problems or in a reduction of labor's share of total income. To economists of the 1930s, among whom under-consumption pessimism was widespread, this notion of technical change was particularly troublesome.

Sir John Hicks argued, however, that there was no inherent labor-saving bias in technical change but that rising wages motivated entrepreneurs to seek out specifically labor-saving innovations to offset the rising labor costs.[8] This conception implies not only that technology is malleable but that increases in productivity can be achieved through changes that have relatively few labor-saving implications. Presumably public policies can be found to counteract the entrepreneur's tendency to seek labor-saving innovations, and thus, theoretically, income growth that is based on technical change can be achieved without the adverse social effects of unemployment or of a decreasing labor share. And if wage rates fail to rise over a prolonged period, the labor-saving bias of innovation should disappear spontaneously.

The issues raised by these differing views did not lead to the development of a well articulated theory of induced innovation during the 1930s. The

[8] J. R. Hicks, *The Theory of Wages* (London: Macmillan and Co. Ltd., 1st ed. 1932; 2nd ed. 1963).

development of Keynesian economics and its successful application to the prevention of under-consumption crises after the Second World War reduced the threat of unemployment caused by labor-saving innovations, and the problem ceased to preoccupy economists and policy makers.

Kindled by efforts to build growth models consistent with U.S. economic history, interest in induced innovation reemerged in the early 1960s. The shares of both capital and labor in output had appeared to remain stable until the 1950s despite a rapidly growing capital–labor ratio.[9] This apparent contradiction may be explained either by an aggregate production function with constant unitary elasticity of substitution (Cobb–Douglas) or by a production function with less than unitary elasticity of substitution and a labor-saving bias just large enough to offset the tendency of the labor share to rise as a result of the growing capital–labor ratio. But how could such a precisely offsetting bias arise?

This question led to the development of the Kennedy version of induced innovation, which we will discuss in greater detail later in this chapter. Kennedy's mathematical theory has been refined and built into many growth models. It is a very aggregative theory which does not spell out a microeconomic foundation of the behavior of an innovating firm. As we shall see, it has run into many problems owing precisely to this lack of a microeconomic foundation.

It was not only growth theory that aroused interest in induced innovation. Development economics also led to renewed interest in induced innovation as well as in the problem of choice of technology.[10] Less developed countries (LDCs) are often characterized by extreme scarcity of capital relative to labor. Most modern technology, however, is capital intensive. If it is true that the high capital intensity of production typical of western market economies came about spontaneously in response to rising labor prices, then perhaps the less developed countries can evolve modern labor-intensive technologies that will offer cheaper sources of growth than those provided by the developed countries' (DCs) capital-intensive methods. Thus if the induced innovation hypothesis is valid, development policies and models that propose to

[9] "The inspiration of much theoretical work is the assumption that income shares are constant over long periods. . . . Various explanations of the mystery have been found—without exception interesting, but strange to the extent that the share of labor is in reality not constant. It fluctuates and moreover displays a rising trend." Jan Pen, *Income Distribution* (Harmondsworth: Penguin, 1971), p. 159.

[10] In the field of development economics, the choice of technology literature stems primarily from the work of A. K. Sen in "The Choice of Agricultural Techniques in Underdeveloped Countries," *Economic Development and Cultural Change* 7 (1959): 279–85; *Choice of Techniques* (Oxford: Basic Blackwell, 1962); and *Employment Technology and Development* (London: Oxford University Press, 1975). The induced innovation perspective was introduced by Yujiro Hayami and Vernon W. Ruttan, in *Agricultural Development: An International Perspective* (Baltimore: Johns Hopkins University Press, 1971).

fill the technological needs of less developed countries by the simple and cheap transfer of western technology are misguided. This hypothesis formed the starting point for the empirical tests of induced innovation performed by Hayami and Ruttan, and their work, in turn, has inspired most of the theoretical and empirical work of this volume. It is quite clear that conclusions about development policy based on the induced innovation hypothesis require a better understanding, at the micro level, of how firms or research establishments are motivated to take factor prices or factor scarcities into account in making their research resource allocation decisions. And this understanding can be achieved only through rigorous empirical tests of the theory and a precise theoretical framework.

A fourth question that must be addressed is how economic policies whose goals are unrelated to technical change may nevertheless affect the rate and direction of such change. If the rate of technical change in an industry is responsive to the price of that industry's output, then policies that alter prices of the output of one sector of the economy will affect the rate of technical change of that sector and of the sectors that produce substitutes.[11] For example, it would have been useful to both producers and consumers to know how strongly and how fast technology would move in a petroleum-saving direction in response to the rise in petroleum prices in the early 1970s. Further, an evaluation of minimum-wage legislation and of subsidies or taxes on capital depends crucially on whether changes in relative factor prices induce biases in technical change and on whether such induced biases are small or large.

We have presented the foregoing questions at this point in order to underline our belief that the building of a solid theory of induced innovation and a thorough testing of this theory is an important task of economics. In this chapter we review the development of the theory. We do not provide an exhaustive review of the literature on induced innovation; rather it is our goal here to set the stage for the further model-building of part II and for the empirical testing of part III of this book. In part II we will return to the above questions and will consider the success of the theory of induced innovation in providing answers to them.

### Problems of Definition

In this book we will use the term *technical change* to refer to changes in techniques of production at the firm or industry level that result both from

---

[11] G. Edward Schuh, for example, argues that the overvalued exchange rate of the U.S. dollar has tended to depress the price of agricultural output in the United States and that this has strongly influenced the rate at which new production technology has been adopted. Schuh suggests that this action of the exchange rate has also affected the way in which the gains from technical change have been distributed between U.S. producers and consumers and, ultimately, between the U.S. economy and the world at large. G. Edward Schuh, "Exchange Rate and U.S. Agriculture," *American Journal of Agricultural Economics* 56 (1974): 1–13.

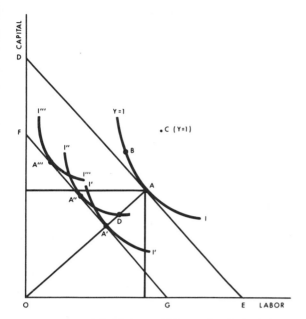

FIG. 2–1. Rates and biases of technical change.

research and development and from learning by doing. The term *technological change* will be used to refer to the result of the application of new knowledge of scientific, engineering, or agronomic principles to techniques of production across a broad spectrum of economic activity. We specifically exclude from the definition of technical change those shifts in individual factor productivities that result in choices among known techniques or from changes in commodity mix brought about by changes in the relative prices of factors or products.[12]

There are two distinct ways of measuring the technical change brought about by innovation. One is to measure the increase in output achievable with given inputs after a technical change has occurred. For example, we can measure the yield increase obtained with a new plant variety and given resources. The disadvantage of this approach is that the old input combina-

[12] This definition is generally consistent with that employed in the literature although a few authors have extended the definition of technical change to include choice of technique along a given macroproduction function and resulting from changes in relative factor or product prices. See, for example, Jacob Schmookler, *Invention and Economic Growth* (Cambridge: Harvard University Press, 1966), pp. 1–10. Other authors have restricted the concept of technical change to only those changes that result in new scientific knowledge. These authors have treated all possible designs based on existing scientific knowledge as factor substitution. In this connection, see W. E. G. Salter, *Productivity and Technical Change* (Cambridge: Cambridge University Press, 1960); pp. 14–16.

tion may not suit the new technology. For example, a new wheat variety may be superior only with a considerably greater application of fertilizer than was optimal for the old variety. Thus, output increase measured in this way may be misleading.

Because of the ambiguity of the above approach, technical change is usually defined as the proportional decrease in costs of production achievable by the innovation when both the old and the new techniques operate at their optimal input combination and when factor prices are held constant. Figure 2–1 shows this graphically. Let $I$ and $I'$ be the unit isoquants before and after the technical change respectively. The slope of the line $DE$ is the ratio of factor prices. A firm which produces output at the point $C$ is technically inefficient. If it moves from $C$ to $B$ it becomes technically efficient: it no longer makes a technical error. This movement is sometimes termed *reduction in slack*. However, at $B$ the firm still makes an error of allocation because costs can be reduced further by moving to point $A$, which is the economically efficient point.

Any inward movement of the isoquant is a technical change. When the isoquant moves from $I$ to $I'$, costs (not including research or adoption costs) are reduced by the amount of $GE$, in terms of labor, or $FD$, in terms of capital. The relative resource saving due to technical change is $GE/OE$ or $FD/OD$. Note that in terms of relative resources saved, the three new technologies $I'$, $I''$, and $I'''$ are identical. What differentiates them is the factor-saving bias of the technical change.

One source of frequent confusion is the common description of technical change as either labor saving or capital saving. In an absolute sense, the technology $I'$ saves both capital and labor. Requirements *per unit of output* of both of these factors are reduced at $A'$. The same is true for $A''$. Indeed, the most likely outcome of most technical change is that, at constant factor prices, the absolute amounts *per unit of output* of all cooperating factors are decreased. Of course, exceptions are possible, both conceptually and in the real world. $I'''$ is such an example: labor use in absolute terms has decreased, but capital use per unit of output has increased at the optimal point $A'''$.

In the literature, however, the terms *labor using* and *labor saving* (in the Hicksian sense) do not signify changes in absolute factor requirements per unit of output; they indicate which input requirement is reduced in the greatest proportion. The theory of biased efficiency gains in the Hicksian sense asks how the economically efficient point moves inward over time *at a constant factor price ratio*. If it moves inward along the ray $OA$ to $A'$, the efficiency gain is said to be Hicks-neutral. If it moves to $A''$ or $A'''$, the change has been labor saving. More specifically, efficiency gains are said to be labor saving, labor neutral, or labor using depending on whether, at constant factor prices, the labor–capital ratio decreases, stays constant, or increases. This can be expressed as follows, where $Q$ is the bias of technical change.

$$Q\big|_{\text{relative factor prices}} = \frac{\partial(K/L)}{\partial t}\cdot\frac{1}{K/L} \gtreqless 0 \rightarrow \begin{cases} \text{labor-saving} \\ \text{neutral} \\ \text{labor-using} \end{cases} \qquad (1)$$

The definition can be transformed immediately into a definition in terms of factor shares at constant factor prices, because a decrease in the labor–capital ratio will result in a decrease in the labor share also at constant factor prices.

As we have just seen, efficiency gains are labor saving, labor neutral, or labor using according to whether the labor share decreases, stays constant, or increases *at constant factor prices*. This definition generalizes easily to the many-factor case and will lead to one single measure of the biases for each factor.

The rate of the factor $i$ bias is defined and measured as:

$$Q_i\big|_{\text{relative factor prices}} = \frac{dS_i}{dt}\cdot\frac{1}{S_i} \gtreqless 0 \rightarrow \begin{cases} i\text{-saving} \\ i\text{-neutral} \\ i\text{-using} \end{cases} \qquad (2)$$

where $S_i$ is the share of factor $i$ in total costs. Alternative definitions are discussed in more detail in the appendix to this chapter. Here we will use definition (1) or (2) depending on the case under discussion.

When several techniques coexist in one or more economies, one must be careful to specify which technique one is comparing with a given innovation. Consider figure 2–2. Suppose country $A$ produces with a capital-intensive fixed-proportion technique $A$ and experiences a technical change to $A'$. For country $A$ this is clearly a neutral technical change. Suppose country $B$ produces with a labor-intensive technique $B$. Further suppose country $B$ adopts the technique $A'$, as it probably would with factor prices $CD$. With

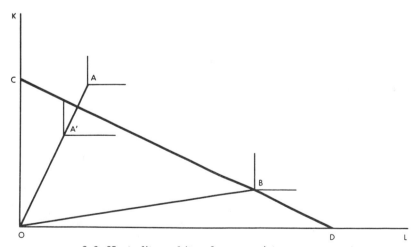

FIG. 2–2. Neutrality and its reference point.

respect to this country's own technique $B$, this is not a neutral but an extremely labor-saving technical change. This distinction is very important in discussions of technology transfer, and we will return to it later.

All models of induced innovation have been concerned exclusively with process innovations that reduce resource requirements for the production of existing goods. Because private-sector research institutes classify most of their work as product research, it would appear at first glance that new goods fall outside the scope of the induced innovation theories. On consideration, however, we see that this depends on one's point of view. The chemical industry would classify a new pesticide as a new product. To the agricultural producer, however, the new pesticide is a process innovation. Thus, since all development of new intermediate products can be viewed as process innovation from the standpoint of final production, the emphasis on process innovation is clearly appropriate.

Hicks, in his *Theory of Wages*, was the first to use the term *induced innovation* in the context of induced biases of technical change.[13] He argued that changes in factor prices induce biases which save the progressively more expensive factors. However, he did not specify the mechanism by which this would occur.

Since its introduction by Hicks, the term *induced innovation* has been used primarily by those authors interested in biased technical change. However, because biases and rates of technical change are determined simultaneously, we prefer to use the term for all theories that are concerned with explaining rate and bias of technical change as endogenous to the economic system. For the sake of clarity, we will retain the distinction between rate and bias and will discuss each subset of theories separately.

### Models of Induced Technical Change

Because innovation is a resource-using activity that leads to benefits which occur over a period of years, we may most appropriately consider it an investment problem.

The rate of technical change depends on the amount of resources that are invested in research, and the bias depends on whether the research investment portfolio contains more labor-saving or more capital-saving research projects. Both the amount of research undertaken by an "investor" and his choice of projects will then depend on the benefits expected to derive from the various projects.

The benefit of a research project is the discounted sum of the cost savings achievable by an innovation in each year of its lifetime. In each period the cost saving is the sum of the reductions in the requirements for all factors of

---

[13] Hicks, *Theory of Wages*.

production, each factor weighted by its corresponding (expected) price. Because prices (as well as the interest rate) enter as weights into the determination of the cost savings, it is quite natural to expect that prices will influence the allocation of resources to different research projects. Similarly, benefits from an innovation will be higher if the innovation is used for a larger rather than a smaller volume of output. The size of a sector or market in which innovations are used can therefore also be expected to influence rates of technical change.

As a result of the foregoing, from the standpoint of benefits we would like to include at least factor prices, interest rates, and size of output among the determining factors of rate and direction of technical change. However, we must remember that technological possibilities are not unlimited. The physical, chemical, and biological properties of the world and the state of basic sciences at any moment in time will limit the set of technologies which can be achieved with a given quantity of research resources. Moreover, theoretical argument continues as to whether the physical, chemical, and biological properties of the world are such that it is inherently easier, or cheaper, to develop labor-saving rather than capital-saving technologies. Thus the rate and bias of technical change will be conditioned by at least some factors that are exogenous to the economic system. Given the investment framework outlined in the opening paragraphs of this section, the question of whether or not the rate and direction of technical change depends on economic factors quickly becomes an empirical rather than a theoretical question. The answer is a function of the strength of the constraints imposed on technology by nature and the degree to which advances in production technology depend on advances in basic research.[14]

On the basis of his outstanding empirical investigation of U.S. patent statistics and of hundreds of important inventions in four industries, Jacob Schmookler concludes that the rate of return to inventions is of far greater importance in stimulating inventive activity than is the state of knowledge.[15] He shows that it is the action of market forces, not the availability of all necessary elements of basic-science knowledge, that triggers inventions. Although the availability of such basic knowledge may be a necessary condition, it is evidently not a sufficient condition. Schmookler found no instance where knowledge alone brought about an important invention. Moreover, in most of the cases reported, the necessary basic knowledge was available decades before the innovation was actually made.

[14] If advances in production technology at any given time can occur only after increases in basic-science knowledge (if in the terminology of part II of this book, applied sciences catch up with or exhaust advances in basic sciences), then the rate of technical change depends more on advances in supporting and basic sciences than on the amount of resources invested in applied research. In addition, if basic research is unresponsive to economic incentives, then the rate of technical change becomes exogenous.

[15] Schmookler, *Invention and Economic Growth*.

R. E. Lucas has considered investment in technical change at an aggregate, economy-wide level.[16] He specifies an aggregate production function of the form

$$Y(t) = A(t)f(X_t^1) \qquad (3)$$

where $X_t^1$ is a vector of inputs used in final goods production. $Y(t)$ is output of final goods, $A(t)$ is a neutral shift parameter, and $[dA(t)/dt] \cdot 1/A$ is the rate of neutral technical change. Changes in $A(t)$ are the result of a separate production process that uses the same resources as $Y$ and is specified as

$$\frac{dA(t)}{dt} = g[X_t^2, A(t)] \qquad (4)$$

where $X_t^2$ are resources devoted to invention. Lucas then builds this basic specification into various control theory models in which the discounted consumption stream of the economy is maximized. One feature shared by different versions of Lucas's model distinguishes them from models of exogenous technical change: the rate of technical change varies negatively with the interest rate $r$ and the wage rate $W$. Lucas uses quarterly time-series data for the U.S. manufacturing sector covering the period 1947 to 1960 and regresses the measured rate of productivity growth on wage rate, user cost of capital, interest rate, and capital stock variables lagged by one period (and/or their first differences). Confirmation of the theory derives primarily from the coefficients of the cost of capital variables.

Chapter 9 will continue this line of inquiry, using a different model. It will be seen that Schmookler's, Lucas's, and the Ben-Zion and Ruttan research all support the position that the determinants of the rate of technical change are endogenous to the economic system.

The theories of induced bias in technical change have been aimed primarily at explaining the puzzling observation that during the first half of this century labor shares failed to rise in the U.S. economy despite a continuing rise in the capital–labor ratio. Unless one accepts the Cobb–Douglas form as an aggregate production function, this failure of the labor share to rise is inconsistent with a rising marginal productivity of labor. The theories of induced bias are still very controversial. The primary reason for their controversial nature, according to William Nordhaus, is their lack of a microeconomic foundation.[17] It may be that such a foundation has never been worked out because of the strong macroeconomic focus of the theories.

As we have already noted, Hicks, although he did not specify the induce-

[16] R. E. Lucas, Jr., "Tests of a Capital-Theoretic Model of Technological Change," *Review of Economic Studies* 34 (1967): 175–80.

[17] William D. Nordhaus, "Some Skeptical Thoughts on the Theory of Induced Innovation," *The Quarterly Journal of Economics* 87 (1973): 209–19.

ment mechanism, argued that changes in factor prices induce biases which save the progressively more expensive factor.[18] (Of course, the biases themselves will influence the factor prices.) W. E. G. Salter criticized this price-induced innovation hypothesis. He distinguished between fundamental, or basic, and applied knowledge and argued that no firm could be induced to develop new fundamental knowledge. According to Salter, the theory of induced biases must be rejected:

> If...the theory implies that dearer labor stimulated the search for new knowledge aimed specifically at saving labor, then it is open to serious objections. The entrepreneur is interested in reducing costs in total, not particular costs such as labor costs or capital costs. When labor's costs rise, any advance that reduces total costs is welcome, and whether this is achieved by saving labor or capital is irrelevant. There is no reason to assume that attention should be concentrated on labor-saving techniques, unless, because of some inherent characteristic of technology, labor-saving knowledge is easier to acquire than capital-saving knowledge.[19]

Salter goes on to say that engineers, on the basis of fundamental knowledge, design machines to use optimal amounts of factors, given existing factor prices. But, he insists, this is not induced innovation. In effect, he has defined induced innovation away. The mechanisms by which engineers respond to existing factor prices in the design or development stage must also affect choices made at the research stage.

Salter also confused marginal adjustments in factor use with the factor saving that can be achieved through a given research investment. Suppose an entrepreneur has a choice between two research activities: one reduces capital requirements and the other reduces labor requirements, in each case by an equal proportion for a given research investment. The benefit of each research activity is the reduction in factor requirements multiplied by the price of each factor. Clearly, a rise in the wage rate relative to the capital rental rate increases the benefit of the labor-saving research activity relative to that of the capital-saving activity, although it leaves the costs of both research endeavors unaffected. As a consequence, entrepreneurs will be more likely to choose the labor-saving activity after the rise in wage rate than before it. This approach to induced innovation forms the basis of the models discussed in chapters 4 and 5.

Ever since it first appeared, Salter's criticism has haunted the induced innovation literature and has definitely slowed the development of these theories. There is hardly a major article in this literature which does not refer to Salter's position and take it very seriously. It sounds so reasonable that

[18] Hicks, *Theory of Wages.*
[19] Salter, *Productivity and Technical Change,* p. 43.

even after fifteen years many people working in this area are not entirely sure whether Salter was not right after all.[20]

William Fellner dismisses Salter's criticism, stating that it is not rising factor prices per se that induce biased innovations. Rather, he says, it is the *anticipation* of a continuous future rise in the price of the progressively scarcer factor that brings about a given bias.[21] It is not clear which level of innovation he meant. Entrepreneurs learn from past experience and seek to develop technology that will be optimal at future factor prices. This proposition is also misleading, however, as will be shown in chapter 4.

THE HICKS–AHMAD MODEL OF PRICE-INDUCED TECHNICAL CHANGE. Syed Ahmad has developed a very careful exposition of the idea of price-induced biases.[22] He uses the concept of a historic *innovation possibility curve* (IPC), defined as follows. At a given time there exists a set of potential production processes to be developed. This set of processes may be thought of as determined by the state of the basic sciences. Each process in the set is characterized by an isoquant with a relatively small elasticity of substitution, and each of the processes in the set requires that a given quantity of resources be developed to the point where the process can actually be used. The IPC is the envelope of all unit isoquants of the subset of those potential processes which the entrepreneur might develop with an exogenously given amount of research and development expenditure.[23] The determination of the rate of technological change, therefore, is not considered in this model. Figure 2–3, adapted from Ahmad's paper, explains the model.

For time $t$ the process $I_t$ was developed. The IPC corresponding to it is $IPC_t$. Given the relative factor prices of the line $P_t P_t$, $I_t$ is the cost-minimizing process. Once $I_t$ is developed, the remainder of its IPC becomes irrelevant because, for period $t + 1$, the IPC has shifted inward to $IPC_{t+1}$ and because it would take the same amount of expenditure to go from $I_t$ to any other technique on $IPC_t$ as to go from $I_t$ to any technique on $IPC_{t+1}$. If factor prices remain the same, entrepreneurs will develop the process $I_{t+1}$ for the next period. If the IPC shifts neutrally, the technical change will be neutral. (But Ahmad recognizes that the IPC may shift inward nonneutrally, which would result in biases even at constant factor prices.) If, however, factor prices change to $P_{t+1} P_{t+1}$, then it is no longer optimal to develop $I_{t+1}$

[20] For an example, see Paul A. David, *Technical Choice, Innovation and Economic Growth: Essays on American and British Experience in the Nineteenth Century* (Cambridge: Cambridge University Press, 1975), pp. 33–9.

[21] William Fellner, "Two Propositions in the Theory of Induced Innovation," *Economic Journal* 71 (1961): 305–8.

[22] Syed Ahmad, "On the Theory of Induced Invention," *Economic Journal* 76 (1966): 344–57.

[23] Nordhaus develops a similar model but with research expenditures introduced more explicitly. Nordhaus, "Some Skeptical Thoughts."

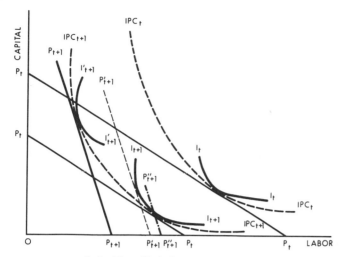

FIG. 2–3. Ahmad's induced innovation model. [Adapted from Syed Ahmad, "On the Theory of Induced Invention," *Economic Journal* 76 (1966), Figure 1, amended.]

and instead the process corresponding to $I'_{t+1}$ becomes optimal. In the graph, $P_{t+1}P_{t+1}$ corresponds to a rise in the relative price of labor. If the IPC has shifted neutrally, $I'_{t+1}$ will be relatively labor saving in comparison to $I_t$.

As we will show in part II, this graphic demonstration of the induced innovation process remains attractive as an illustration of a one-period microeconomic model in which a firm or research institute has a fixed exogenous budget constraint and in which market-structure problems do not arise. Once research budgets are no longer fixed, a two-dimensional graphic representation of the problem becomes almost impossible, and it is easier to tackle the problem mathematically.

Using Ahmad's graph, it is easy to show how economic factors become unimportant when nature or limited basic-science knowledge impose strong constraints on the degree of choice of technology. This situation is shown by IPCs with only slightly less curvature than the isoquants $I$ and $I'$ of the individual technologies. More formally, if the elasticity of substitution of the individual technologies is not much smaller than the elasticity of substitution of the IPC, the bias will be almost entirely exogenous to the economic system and will follow closely the bias of fundamental innovation possibilities.

An induced innovation framework similar to Ahmad's is used by Yujiro Hayami and Vernon Ruttan.[24] However, these authors introduce resources specifically to achieve efficiency increases. Consider figure 2–4, which shows the land and labor coefficients of agriculture in different countries in 1965 in double-logarithmic scale. (The logarithmic scale has the advantage that

[24] Hayami and Ruttan, *Agricultural Development.*

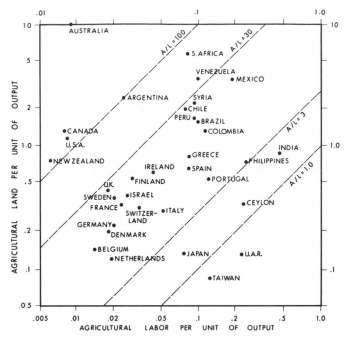

FIG. 2–4. Input–output ratios and land–labor ratios in agriculture, 1965. [Adapted from Yujiro Hayami and Vernon W. Ruttan, *Agricultural Development: An International Perspective* (Baltimore: The Johns Hopkins University Press, 1971), Table 4–2, p. 73. Note: Output is measured in wheat units. $A/L$ = land–labor ratio.]

efficiency differences of the same proportions are at equal distances at all points on the scales. The diagonal lines are points of equal land–labor ratios; zero inputs are at minus infinity.) Two observations can be made. First, the developed countries, whose input combinations are closer to the lower left-hand corner, are more efficient. Second, there exist huge differences in land–labor ratios which cannot be explained by ordinary factor substitution. For example, in the early 1960s, the U.S. had a land–labor ratio of 141 hectares per worker while Japan's ratio was 1.74 hectares per worker: the U.S. ratio exceeded the Japanese ratio by a factor of 81. However, Japan's land–labor price ratio exceeded the U.S. ratio by a factor of less than 30 during the same period. To explain the difference in factor ratios by factor price effects, the elasticity of substitution between the two factors would have to be 3 or more, which is a highly unrealistic value.[25] A simple empirical test of induced innovation based on this reasoning is presented in chapter 3, where we return to this data set.

Hayami and Ruttan note that many of the highly productive countries

[25] For empirical evidence see chapters 3 and 7.

have a long history of agricultural research, extension, and schooling, while the less efficient countries have accomplished little in these areas. Furthermore, countries with factor endowments and prices at one extreme or another have developed technologies designed to save the relatively scarce factors. The U.S. and Canada have high labor prices and high land–labor ratios. Taiwan and Japan, on the other hand, have extremely low land–labor ratios and use labor very intensively. The European countries, whose factor prices lie somewhere between these examples, tend to employ technologies that result in less extreme land–labor ratios.

Hayami and Ruttan hypothesize the existence of what they term a *meta-production function*. This function relates output to land ($A$), labor ($L$), physical capital ($K$), human capital ($HC$), and cumulative research capital ($RC$):

$$Y = f(A, L, K, HC, RC) . \tag{5}$$

In the $A/L$ space the production point shifts inward with higher levels of $K$, $HC$, and $RC$. To obtain efficiency increases, countries must invest in these three categories and particularly in research because much of agricultural technology is location specific. Given that such investment takes place, however, there is a wide choice in technology with respect to the capital–labor ratio. And, just as in Ahmad's framework, factor prices determine which technique is optimal. The higher the labor prices the higher the optimal land–labor ratios (and, by extension, the optimal capital–labor ratios).

The model developed by Hayami and Ruttan is consistent with an extensive body of cross-sectional and time-series observations. Their work, which is extended in chapter 3, has inspired much of the empirical work described in other chapters of this volume.

NELSON AND WINTER'S EVOLUTIONARY MODEL. The evolutionary models of economic behavior and technical change developed by Richard Nelson and Sidney Winter were not initially intended to be induced innovation models. Nevertheless, even their earliest models contain a simple induced innovation mechanism.[26]

In these simulation models, firms produce with fixed-proportion techniques in any given period of time. No distinction is made between substitution or moving along a production function and technical change. If profits fall below a certain margin, firms start to search for new techniques of

[26] The early versions of the models are described in Richard R. Nelson and Sidney G. Winter, "Towards an Evolutionary Theory of Economic Capabilities," *American Economic Review* 63 (1973): 440–9; Richard R. Nelson, Sidney G. Winter, and Herbert L. Schuette, "Technical Change in an Evolutionary Model," *Quarterly Journal of Economics* 40 (1976): 90–118; Richard R. Nelson and Sidney G. Winter, "Neoclassical vs. Evolutionary Theories of Economic Growth: Critique and Prospectus," *Economic Journal* 84 (1974): 886–905.

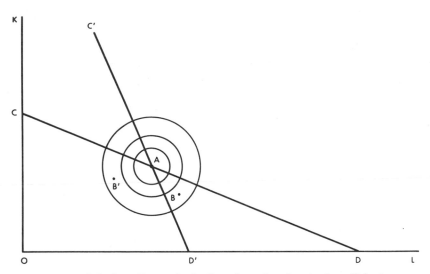

FIG. 2–5. Sampling and selection of new input–output coefficients.

production—that is, they change the decision rule with respect to their production process. The models assume that in this search the firms draw samples from a distribution of input–output coefficients as in figure 2–5. If $A$ is the present input combination, then potential input coefficients are distributed around it such that there is a much greater probability of finding a point close to $A$ than of finding one far away. Search is local. Once the firm finds a point $B$ it makes a profitability check: If costs are lower at $B$ than at $A$, the firm adopts the point $B$ and stops searching. Otherwise, search continues. Thus the point $B$ will be accepted if labor is relatively cheap, that is, if relative prices are such as $CD$. But with expensive labor, such as $C'D'$, the firm will reject point $B$ and continue to search until it finds another point, say $B'$. This point, however, will be labor saving relative to $B$.[27]

The mechanism is built into a model with many competing firms. All profits over and above a "normal" dividend are invested, so that the successful firms grow faster than the unsuccessful ones. The capital stock of the economy is determined by total investment by all firms. In addition, the model assumes that the labor supply is inelastic. Starting from an initial point where all firms are equal, Nelson and Winter let a simulation run its course. The model determines endogenously the output of the economy, the wage–rental rate, and the capital accumulation rates. After a while, firms

[27] Nelson and Winter's search model for new processes also contains an imitation component which is not shown here. And in certain versions of the model, labor-saving innovations have a higher probability than capital-saving innovations; that is, innovation possibilities are biased in labor-saving directions.

produce with many different techniques, but on the average these techniques tend to move in a labor-saving direction.

According to Nelson and Winter:

When firms check the profitability of alternative techniques that their search processes uncover, a higher wage rate will cause certain techniques to fail the "more profitable" test that would have "passed" at a lower wage rate, and enable others to pass the test that would have failed at a lower wage rate. The latter will be capital intensive relative to the former. Thus a higher wage rate nudges firms to move in a capital-intensive direction compared with that in which they would have gone. Also, the effect of a higher wage rate is to make all technologies less profitable (assuming, as in our model, a constant cost of capital) but the cost increase is proportionately greatest for those that involve a low capital–labor ratio. Since firms with high capital–labor ratios are less adversely affected by high wage rates than those with low capital–labor ratios, capital-intensive firms will tend to expand relatively to labor-intensive ones. For both of these reasons a higher wage rate will tend to increase capital-intensity relative to what would have been obtained.[28]

This responsiveness of the capital–labor ratio is very striking because, except for the profitability check, research outcomes are random in this model. The inducement mechanism comes about through competition, survival, and growth of the successful firms, not through an elaborate maximization scheme.[29] The inducement mechanism must therefore be very robust, as it can be demonstrated with only these minimal assumptions.

The Nelson–Winter model also underlines the fact that, even if research is carried out by capital-goods producers who compete for customers, and without direction from the customers themselves as to optimal capital–labor ratios, it is the elimination of capital goods with inefficient capital–labor

---

[28] Nelson and Winter, "Theories of Economic Growth," p. 900. An obvious error in the second sentence of this quotation has been corrected. The original read: "The former will be capital intensive relative to the latter."

[29] David, *Technical Choice, Innovation and Economic Growth*, pp. 50–91. David has developed a model of induced innovation that is similar in some respects to Nelson and Winter's model. David's model, which is discussed in some detail in chapter 8, is concerned primarily with the interaction between learning by doing and ordinary price-induced changes in production techniques. In his model, a firm has essentially no choice but to accept a technical innovation it has developed. David posits a *dynamic irreversibility* which carries technical change in the direction established by an initial innovation and which can be altered only by a dramatic change in relative factor prices. As a result, in order to make technical change responsive to factor prices, David must resort to restricting the set of potential innovations with so-called elastic barriers within which advances are sought. Since it is difficult to see how such elastic barriers could come about, this is a kind of implicit theorizing. In fact, David would not need these elastic barriers if he allowed his firm to choose among a set of several technical advances on the basis of a profitability check even if, as in his model, such advances come about in a random manner. The Nelson–Winter model shows that such a choice mechanism is sufficient to obtain both the price responsiveness of technical change and the technological paths on which much of David's reasoning depends.

ratios in the market place that guides observed capital–labor ratios in the direction of saving the economy's scarce factors. Neither randomness of research outcome nor divorce of the user of research from its producer will break this mechanism.

The early Nelson–Winter model was subject to one criticism. It states that firms start to do research only when profits fall below a certain level. It thus predicts that an increase in demand for the product of an industry, although it leads to greater profitability of every firm in that industry, will also lead to a reduction in research effort. This is not consonant, however, with empirical observation, and indeed, Schmookler presents strong evidence to the contrary.[30] An increase in demand leads to more innovation, not less.

Later versions of Nelson and Winter's approach to technical change explicitly introduce directed research.[31] These authors continue to emphasize the difficulty of distinguishing ordinary factor substitution from changes in factor proportions that are caused by technical change, and they stress the nonroutineness of the research response to economic incentives.

KENNEDY'S INNOVATION POSSIBILITY FRONTIER. Among induced innovation models, the most formally developed are the growth versions of Charles Kennedy, Paul A. Samuelson, and E. M. Drandakis and E. S. Phelps.[32] These models take into account the relative importance of factors and their prices. The basic idea of the models can best be explained with an example. Suppose it is equally expensive to develop either a new technology that will reduce labor requirements by 10 percent or one that will reduce capital requirements by 10 percent. If the capital share is equal to the labor share, entrepreneurs will be indifferent between the two courses of action. Half will choose one and half the other. The outcomes of both choices will be neutral technical change. If, however, the labor share is 60 percent, all entrepreneurs will choose the labor-reducing version. If the elasticity of substitution is less than one, this will go on until the labor and capital shares again become equal, provided the induced bias in technical change does not alter the trade-off relationship between technical changes that reduce labor requirements, on the one hand, or capital requirements, on the other.

Thus it would appear that shares can be stable even if the capital–labor

[30] Schmookler, *Invention and Economic Growth*.

[31] Richard Nelson and Sidney G. Winter, "Factor Price Changes and Substitution in an Evolutionary Model," *The Bell Journal of Economics* 6 (1975): 466–86; idem, "In Search of a Useful Theory of Innovation," *Research Policy* 6 (1977): 36–76.

[32] Charles Kennedy, "Induced Bias in Innovation and the Theory of Distribution," *The Economic Journal* 74 (1966): 541–7; Paul A. Samuelson, "A Theory of Induced Innovation along Kennedy, Weizsäcker Lines," *Review of Economics and Statistics* 47 (1965): 343–56; E. M. Drandakis and E. S. Phelps, "A Model of Induced Invention, Growth and Distribution," *The Economic Journal* 76 (1966): 823–40.

ratio changes historically. This implication of share stability is what interested the authors of the Kennedy-type models. They were not really interested in research resource allocation questions but rather in finding ways to simulate technical change in growth models.

In the following paragraphs we will discuss the assumptions of the growth models in detail as well as the objections that have been raised against them. The models assume the following production function with factor-augmenting technical change:

$$Y\left(\frac{K}{a}, \frac{L}{b}\right) = 1 \tag{6}$$

where $a$ and $b$ are augmentation coefficients.[33] The production function is homogeneous of degree one. Unit costs are $U = KR + LW$, where $W$ is the wage rate and $R$ is the capital rental rate. The instantaneous proportional rate of reduction in unit costs can be written

$$d \ln U/dt = \frac{\dot{U}}{U} = -S_K a' - S_L b' + \text{terms involving price changes}[34] \tag{7}$$

where $S_K$ and $S_L$ are the factor shares, and where $a' = -d \ln a/dt$ and $b' = -d \ln b/dt$, that is, $a'$ and $b'$ are the instantaneous rates of reduction of $a$ and $b$. Now assume:

1. given factor prices,

2. an exogenously given budget for research and development of new techniques, and

3. a fundamental trade-off between the rate of reduction in labor requirements, $a'$, and the rate of reduction in capital requirements, $b'$.

---

[33] For a discussion of factor augmentation, see Robert M. Solow, "Some Recent Developments in the Theory of Production," in *The Theory and Empirical Analysis of Production*, ed. Murray Brown, Studies in Income and Wealth, vol. 31 (New York: National Bureau of Economic Research, 1967). The production function in factor-augmenting form is

$$Y = f[(X_1/a_1), (X_2/a_2, \ldots, (X_n/a_n)]$$

where $(X_1/a_1)$ is the effective quantity of factor $X_1$. A decrease in $a_1$ has the same effect on output as an equiproportional increase in $X_1$ would have had prior to the decrease in $a_1$. Therefore, with factor augmentation, technical change cannot alter the form or the parameters of the production function. Technical change enters by changing the quantity of effective factor supply. Whether effective factor supplies can be measured is immaterial, because producers will react to changes in marginal productivities of the factors and will alter input quantities according to the unchanged parameters of the production or cost function. It is important to note, however, that an increase in the quality of factor $i$ not only raises the augmentation coefficient of factor $i$ but may affect the $a$'s of all cooperating factors. For a discussion of the relationship between factor augmentation and bias, see the appendix to this chapter.

[34] For derivation see Samuelson, "Theory of Induced Innovation."

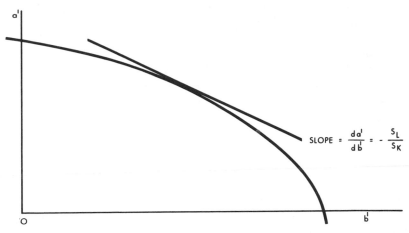

FIG. 2–6. Kennedy's *innovation possibility frontier*.

Assumption 3, which is an assumption about the underlying possibilities of technical change, can be written as:

$$a' = h(b')$$

or

$$H(a', b') = 0 . \tag{8}$$

If this transformation function—or as Kennedy called it, this *innovation possibility frontier* (IPF)—has the usual characteristic of such functions, namely, $da'/db' < 0$, $d^2a'/d(b')^2 < 0$, it will look like figure 2–6.

Given equations (7) and (8), one can set up a maximization problem. Maximize the rate of instantaneous unit-cost reduction subject to the trade-off relation of factor augmentation of equation (8). (Because the rate of unit-cost reduction is negative, this is a minimization problem.)

$$\min d \ln U/dt = -S_K a' - S_L b' + \lambda(a' - h(b')) \tag{9}$$

The solution is completely analogous to the solution of the similar system of minimizing cost subject to a given output, where $S_K$ and $S_L$ now have the same role as factor prices. Hence, the rate of cost reduction is minimized at a point where

$$\frac{da'}{db'} = -\frac{S_L}{S_K} \tag{10}$$

The slope of the IPF must be equal to the inverse ratio of the shares (see figure 2–6). Hence, the higher the labor share, the higher $b'$ will be in relation to $a'$, or the greater the extent to which technical change will be labor augmenting. Change will be labor saving if, in addition, $\sigma < 1$. (See appendix equation A-5.)

This is the comparative static solution to the model. This solution explains why, when an economy's capital–labor ratio rises in response to exogenous influences, forces should be set in motion to maintain share stability.

Drandakis and Phelps as well as Samuelson have built this model into a neoclassical growth model with a constant savings ratio.[35] An excellent exposition of that model is given in Wan, who also discusses in greater detail some of the criticisms we will offer next.[36]

The essential conclusion from the growth model with constant savings ratio is that, if the elasticity of substitution is less than one, there exists a stable asymptotic golden age equilibrium growth path with constant factor shares even if capital grows faster than labor. Along this growth path, technical change is Harrod-neutral.[37]

But remember that a neoclassical growth model without a Kennedy frontier also has an asymptotic golden age equilibrium growth path with capital growing faster than labor and Harrod-neutral technical change in which shares are stable. What then is gained by the Kennedy frontier?

The gain claimed for the frontier by its authors is that, in the induced innovation formulation, Harrod-neutral technical change comes about by the "working of economic forces, and not by postulation," as Wan puts it.[38] But obviously the Kennedy frontier is a postulation which must be examined. It must be consistent with some research process and competition; otherwise, as Nordhaus points out, neoclassical growth model assumptions are not warranted.[39]

First, note that in the model technical change comes about without cost. This observation is usually countered by the model's proponents with the remark that the frontier comes about as the result of a fixed budget constraint on research resources. But this cannot be the case in the growth model, since

[35] The Kennedy frontier has been used by many other authors in growth models of various complexities. However, because the model has come under sharp criticism (as discussed both in this chapter and in chapter 4), these other versions are not considered here.

[36] Henry Y. Wan, Jr., *Economic Growth* (New York: Harcourt Brace Jovanovich, Inc., 1971), pp. 215–26. See also David, *Technical Choice, Innovation and Economic Growth*, pp. 44–57.

[37] Harrod-neutral technical change is purely labor-augmenting technical change, that is, $a' = 0$, and $b' > 0$. This implies that the marginal product of capital remains unchanged when the capital–output ratio is unchanged. Harrod-neutral technical change will not be used much in this book. A good discussion of the concept can be found in James E. Meade, *A Neoclassical Theory of Economic Growth* (London: Unwin University Books, 1962), pp. 55–60.

[38] Wan, *Economic Growth*, p. 223.

[39] Nordhaus, "Some Skeptical Thoughts."

all savings go to investment in physical capital and none to investment in research.[40]

Even if one were to accept the budget constraint notion, the IPC still is a very problematic device. Nordhaus discusses some of its difficulties in the following paragraphs.

It is implicitly assumed that the level of research is independent of the size of the firm, for otherwise the size of the firm would enter the maximum problem. But since constant returns to $K$ and $L$ are assumed by all authors, cost per unit output, or $(wL + rK + R \& D)/Y$, will be a decreasing function of output of the firm. Competition will break down. One could, it is true, dream up ways to preserve constant costs and competition, but this would only come at the expense of realism, since technical change is endogenous and is produced by the firm.

In fact, about the only microeconomic framework that preserves competition is one in which a book of new blueprints falls from the sky every period—the new techniques given according to the IPC—and the entrepreneur chooses the best technique. In this case it would be quite misleading to say that technical change is induced. Rather, the IPC gives the technical possibilities at a point of time. The model is then just a disguised version of the neoclassical model with exogenous technical change.

The next step is to realise that if we cannot sustain competition, except in what is equivalent to the exogenous case, the behavior equations of the descriptive

[40] Nordhaus has constructed a growth theoretical model of a planned economy in which the position of the frontier depends on the amount of labor allocated to a research activity that shifts the IPC neutrally and derives optimum allocation decisions for labor. William D. Nordhaus, "The Optimal Rate and Direction of Technical Change," in *Essays in the Theory of Optimal Economic Growth*, ed. Karl Shell (Cambridge: Massachusetts Institute of Technology Press, 1967). John Conslick also has developed an interesting alternative to the IPC. A productivity sector, to which both labor and capital are allocated explicitly, creates augmented labor and augmented capital increments. Additional allocations of capital and labor to the productivity sector shift the trade-off frontier between augmented capital and augmented labor neutrally. Conslick then postulates two saving ratios, one for capital $s_1$ and one for labor $s_2$, which determine aggregate savings and capital–labor ratios in both the final goods and productivity sectors. These two savings ratios $s_1$ and $s_2$ and the ratio of creation of augmented capital to augmented labor $b$ are assumed to be functions of the economy's aggregate capital–labor ratio. John Conslick, "A Neoclassical Growth Model with Endogenously Positioned Technical Change Frontier," *Economic Journal* 69 (1969): 348–62.

In Conslick's model, "The allocation magnitudes $s_1$, $s_2$ and $b$ are allowed to vary only with the ratio $K/L$; this preserves degree-one homogeneity in the model, which is a quite conventional and almost essential assumption in a long-run growth model which is to have at least the possibility of a balanced asymptotic path. Some fairly weak assumptions about the form of the $s_1$, $s_2$ and $b$ functions will be introduced below. Nothing will be assumed about the precise origin of the functions. They may be the determinations of a central planner; they may be the reduced form of a competitive system; they may be something else." (ibid., pp. 351–2). This means that there is no microeconomic rationalization at all for the crucial allocation mechanisms in Conslick's model. Although his description of invention possibilities is very attractive, the model built with it represents implicit theorizing on the basis of assumptions whose only justification is mathematical convenience.

model are incorrect. A monopolist would minimize cost according to actual relative share, not competitively determined relative shares that add up to greater than unity. He must then consider the elasticity of supply and demand. The theory becomes much more complicated, and the hope of getting some kind of steady state is dim.[41]

Wan brings out the further point that the technical change frontier must be *ex ante* in character, that is, the entrepreneurs must know what it is.[42] But the *ex ante* frontier must also be identical to the actual innovation possibilities: unless the entrepreneurs know the innovation possibilities with certainty, the approach breaks down.

As we shall see in chapter 5, the most damaging assumption about the frontier is that it is stable over time and independent of achieved $a$ and $b$ levels. This implies that exponential increases in efficiency are forever possible in all directions regardless of the past history of technical change. Continuous labor augmentation does not exhaust the innovation possibilities in that direction.

Attempts to remedy this unrealistic assumption lead nowhere, as Nordhaus has shown in his critique of the frontier.[43] Nordhaus introduces some natural drift into the innovation possibilities as follows:

$$a' = h(b', a, b, \alpha, \beta) \tag{11}$$

where $\alpha(t)$ and $\beta(t)$ are the smallest (most efficient) values that $a$ and $b$ can take on at any time with infinite amounts of research resources. Nordhaus further assumes that it becomes more and more difficult to decrease $a$ and $b$ the closer they are to the limiting values, and he rewrites

$$a' = h\left(b', \frac{a - \alpha}{\alpha}, \frac{b - \beta}{\beta}\right) \tag{12}$$

such that $h_1 < 0$, $h_2 > 0$, $h_3 > 0$. He then shows that under these assumptions a balanced growth equilibrium is possible only if the natural drift of technology is Harrod-neutral at all times:

$$\frac{\partial \alpha(t)}{\partial t} = 0 \quad \text{and} \quad \frac{\partial \beta(t)}{\partial t} < 0 \tag{13}$$

However, this assumption does not differ in substance from the simple assumption of neoclassical growth models that technical change be Harrod-neutral at all times, and technical change is just as exogenous here as it is in a model without a technical change frontier! Chapter 5 will provide added

[41] Nordhaus, *Rate and Direction of Technical Change*, pp. 64–5.
[42] Wan, *Economic Growth*, pp. 219–20.
[43] Nordhaus, "Some Skeptical Thoughts."

strength to this criticism by showing that no real-world research process can lead to a Kennedy frontier that is independent of achieved $a$ and $b$ levels.

Another criticism of the growth model versions of induced innovation is that maximization of the instantaneous rate of unit-cost reduction may not be optimal in the first place. This view has been discussed by Samuelson and by Drandakis and Phelps.[44]

Given all the foregoing problems of its framework, it seems clear that the Kennedy approach to induced innovation has run into a cul de sac. In particular, it is very difficult to conceptualize an empirical counterpart of the innovation possibility frontier. This may account for the fact that almost no empirical work has been done using the IPF. The failure of the Kennedy approach clearly is a consequence of the theory's lack of a microeconomic foundation.

RADNER'S BEHAVIORAL MODEL OF COST REDUCTION. Radner's approach to induced innovation is behavioral, and he considerably enriches the Nelson–Winter approach while he maintains some similarity to the Kennedy model.[45] He uses a fixed-proportion technology with many inputs and describes innovation possibilities as follows: At time $t$, input $i$ is characterized by an input coefficient $R_i(t)$ (per unit of output). If at any time the firm manager (or researcher) concentrates his attention on one input, the input requirement $R_i(t)$ *may* be reduced by a fraction $\rho_i$. This proportional reduction is independent of time. The probability of the reduction occurring is $\theta_i$. On the other hand, if the manager does not pay attention to the input, $R_i(t)$ may increase by a fraction $\delta_i$ with probability $\psi_i$. Because the innovation possibilities are uncertain, we cannot trace the long-run development of input coefficients and factor shares precisely but must trace them in terms of their limiting probability distributions as time goes to infinity.

Radner then investigates these limiting distributions under the decision rule of *putting out fires*, under which "the manager's behavior is to allocate, at each date, all of his effort to cost reduction for an input that promises the largest possible expected cost reduction."[46] He shows that the limiting distribution of factor shares is independent of factor prices. However, the limiting distribution of the ratios of the input coefficients does depend on factor prices, that is, the basic induced innovation result is demonstrated.

Intuitively, this mechanism can be illustrated as follows: As the cost of each input is $P_i R_i$, where $P_i$ is the input price, it is clear that the higher $P_i$ (relative to prices of other inputs and given $R_i$ and $\rho_i$), the higher the chance

[44] Samuelson, "Theory of Induced Innovation"; Drandakis and Phelps, "Model of Induced Invention."

[45] Roy Radner, "A Behavioral Model of Cost Reduction," *The Bell Journal of Economics* 6, no 1. (Spring 1975): 196–215.

[46] Ibid., p. 198.

for the particular input to be the one that promises the largest expected cost reduction. A price rise thus induces faster technical change in the particular input until shares again follow the limiting probability distribution.

The model is a considerable improvement on the Kennedy model. For the first time (except for the Nelson and Winter model), the innovation possibilities are based on real activities that are resource using. Nevertheless, some of the criticisms of Kennedy's innovation possibility frontier remain. The research budget is fixed (one manager or researcher) and does not depend on expected payoff or the size of the firm. Furthermore, innovation possibilities are inexhaustible and independent of past history because $\rho_i$ and $\theta_i$ are independent of time. Finally, as will be discussed further in chapters 4 and 5, it is doubtful that real world research processes reduce only one of the input–output coefficients and leave the others unaffected, that is, that such processes are orthogonal.[47]

FELLNER'S EMPIRICAL EVIDENCE ON INDUCED BIASES. Economists have long been puzzled by the fact that factor shares in the U.S. economy have appeared stable for a considerable period of time even though the capital–labor ratio has risen rapidly. William Fellner points out that, as long as factor shares remain stable, it is impossible to choose among the following three hypotheses:

(a) Neither the rising capital–labor ratios of Western economies nor the character of their inventive activities tends to change the functional distribution of income, and hence we may incorporate into our macro-models unitary elasticities of substitution along with neutral inventions.

(b) Rising capital–labor ratios tend to raise the relative share of labor, while the character of the inventions tend to reduce it, and hence we may incorporate into our models smaller than unitary elasticities of substitution along with labor-saving inventions in Hicks's sense.

(c) Rising capital–labor ratios tend to reduce the relative share of labor, while the character of inventions tends to raise it, and hence we may incorporate into our models greater than unitary elasticities of substitution along with capital-saving inventions in Hicks's sense.[48]

Without specifying the mechanism of induced innovation, Fellner goes on to show that hypothesis (b) has the following corollary, which is not shared by either hypothesis (a) or (c):

[47] Radner is interested primarily in the effect of various decision rules, which are simpler than the overall optimization. His model is perfectly capable of being generalized to the nonorthogonal case by postulating fractional allocation of a manager's time to the different input coefficients. However, Radner shows that the model then loses its behavioral aspects and becomes more like a full optimization model. Some of the generalizations he sketches in his paper are shared by the models of chapters 4 and 5.

[48] William Fellner, "Empirical Support for the Theory of Induced Innovation," *Quarterly Journal of Economics* 85 (1971): 580–604.

TABLE 2–1. Capital intensity, productivity gains, and share of labor

|  | 1920–29 | 1929–48 | 1948–57 | 1957–66 |
|---|---|---|---|---|
| *Annual Comparative Rates of Increase* | | | | |
| Capital–labor ratio | 1.39 | 0.13 | 3.69 | 1.92 |
| Total factor productivity | 2.32 | 1.68 | 2.31 | 2.57 |
| Output per unit of labor input | 2.72 | 1.68 | 3.03 | 2.92 |
| *Labor Shares, First and Last Year of Each Period* | | | | |
| Kuznets[a] | 67.7 | ... | ... | ... |
| 1920 weights | 67.0 | ... | ... | ... |
| Kuznets[a] | 65.2 | ... | ... | ... |
| 1929 weights | 64.2 | ... | ... | ... |
| Commerce[b] | ... | 59.9 | 61.0 | 65.5 |
| 1929 weights | ... | 61.0 | 65.5 | 65.5 |
| Commerce[b] | ... | 60.6 | 62.9 | 67.0 |
| 1966 weights | ... | 62.9 | 67.0 | 67.1 |

Source: William Fellner, "Empirical Support for the Theory of Induced Innovation," *Quarterly Journal of Economics* 85 (1971): 587.

Note: All figures are in percents.

[a] Based on S. Kuznets, *National Income and Its Composition, 1919–38* (New York: National Bureau of Economic Research, 1941).

[b] Based on figures compiled by the Department of Commerce.

"Usually" the joint effect of rising capital–labor ratios (henceforth $K/L$) and of induced labor-saving innovations reflects the smooth working of an innovational shares-adjustment mechanism, in that pretax distributive shares remain reasonably stable; but an "unusually" steep increase of $K/L$, in conjunction with the corresponding change in the ratio of input prices, is apt to have a net labor-share-raising effect. That net effect comes through because the induced labor-saving character of the innovational process is not capable of fully offsetting the labor-share-raising influence of an "unusually" steep increase of $K/L$, as indeed the same result would presumably develop from a significant lowering of the rate of innovation given the "usual" rates of increase of $K/L$.[49]

To test this corollary, Fellner then examines aggregate "real" capital–labor ratios, factor shares, and rates of technical change for the private domestic U.S. economy (see table 2–1). It turns out that the only period in which there occurred a significant increase in the labor share was the period 1948 to 1957 and it was during this period that the capital–labor ratio rose at an especially rapid rate in comparison with all other periods. The rise of the capital–labor ratio was also exceptionally steep in comparison with the rates of increase in total factor productivity and in the output–labor ratio $Q/L$.

These findings are consistent with Fellner's corollary to hypothesis (b) and hence with that hypothesis itself, which is based on the concept of induced innovation. During most of the overall period 1920 to 1966 the labor-saving

[49] Ibid., p. 582.

bias of innovation was apparently sufficient to keep shares stable even though the capital–labor ratio rose, but it was not sufficient to keep them stable when the exceptionally sharp rise of $K/L$ occurred in the 1950s.

Fellner's evidence is thus consistent with induced innovation. But it is also consistent with an alternative hypothesis:

> When the aggregate elasticity of substitution is less than one, neutral technical change will lead to a rise in the labor share. However, technical change is determined exogenously and has a fundamental labor-saving bias which normally is sufficient to keep shares stable despite a rise of $K/L$. But when $K/L$ rises at an exceptionally rapid rate, the bias is not sufficient to maintain share-stability.

This hypothesis is one of exogenous bias. Fellner's data provide no final proof for the induced innovation hypothesis, because both his corollary and the hypothesis of purely exogeneous biases are consistent with those data.

### Conclusions

We have examined a wide variety of models of induced innovation, and we have described some empirical evidence that is consistent with that theory. With the exception of Nelson and Winter's approach, the models do not describe how firms choose among alternative research processes so that they end up generating technical changes that save the expensive resources. And in Nelson and Winter's model this process is reduced to a very elementary rejection rule. However, the models provide a good description of the repercussions of induced innovation at the macroeconomic level.

In chapter 4 an attempt will be made to fit the approach of the research resource allocation literature into a framework of induced innovation. We will construct a micromodel of an innovating firm capable of tracing the effects of factor prices, scale, interest rates, and exogenous technical change possibilities on the amount and direction of research pursued by the firm. The model should help to provide the microfoundation for a more aggregate model of induced bias and induced rate of technical change. We will not at this point attempt to construct a full, dynamic macromodel.

Before we proceed to the above extension of the theory of induced innovation, we will examine the experience of productivity growth in the agricultural sectors in Japan, Germany, Denmark, France, the United Kingdom, and the United States. Chapter 3 should thus provide the reader with the historical background necessary to understand the importance of the induced technical change problem in the development of six countries with widely different factor endowments.

APPENDIX 2–1

*Hicks-Neutral Technical Change: Definitions*
*and Relationship to Factor Augmentation*

In this chapter we have defined biases differently from the way in which Hicks originally defined technical change bias. Indeed, as shown in equations (A–1), (A–2), and (A–3) below, there are three ways in which one can define Hicksian biases. The spirit of all the definitions is the same, but they differ in numerical magnitude.

HOLDING FACTOR PRICES CONSTANT

In terms of factor shares, with many factors:

$$Q_i|_{\text{relative factor prices}} = \frac{\partial S_i}{\partial t} \cdot \frac{1}{S_i} \gtreqless 0 \rightarrow \begin{cases} i\text{-saving} \\ i\text{-neutral} \\ i\text{-using} \end{cases} \tag{A–1}$$

The bias measures the proportional change in shares due to technical change.

In terms of factor ratios, and 2 factors only:

$$Q'|_{\text{relative factor prices}} = \frac{\partial (K/L)}{\partial t} \cdot \frac{1}{K/L} \gtreqless 0 \rightarrow \begin{cases} L\text{-saving} \\ \text{neutral} \\ L\text{-using} \end{cases} \tag{A–2}$$

The bias measures the proportional change in capital–labor ratio due to the technical change.

HOLDING THE FACTOR RATIO CONSTANT

$$Q''|_{\text{constant factor ratio}} = \frac{\partial (f_K/f_L)}{\partial t} \cdot \frac{1}{(f_K/f_L)} \gtreqless 0 \rightarrow \begin{cases} L\text{-saving} \\ \text{neutral} \\ L\text{-using} \end{cases} \tag{A–3}$$

where $f_K$ and $f_L$ are the marginal products.

The bias measures the proportional rate of change in the marginal rate of substitution at constant $K/L$ ratio. Hick's original definition would be stated as follows: In figure 2–1, $I''$ is a labor-saving technical change because at the point $D$ (constant factor ratio) the marginal rate of substitution between land and labor has increased as compared to point $A$.

At the microeconomic level it is more useful to use definitions of holding factor prices constant because the prices are given to a firm and because these definitions are more easily visualized. At the macrolevel, where factor endowments are frequently assumed to be exogenous, the definition of holding the factor ratio constant is often more useful.

However, what is held constant does not matter very much in substance because it can be shown that the measures $Q'$ and $Q''$ are related as follows jn the two-factor case.

$$Q' = \sigma Q'' \qquad (A-4)$$

where $\sigma$ is the elasticity of substitution of the production function. Hence $Q'$ and $Q''$ differ only by a scalar multiple.

In the many-factor case, both $Q'$ and $Q''$ are inconvenient because for each factor there are $n - 1$ factor pairs to consider. Therefore, the definition in forms of factor shares, which leads to one measure of bias per factor, is preferable in that case.

In forms of a factor-augmenting production function, the biases can be expressed as follows:[50]

$$Q' = (1 - \sigma)(a' - b') \qquad (A-5)$$

where $\quad a' = -\dfrac{d \ln a}{dt} \quad$ and $\quad b' = -\dfrac{d \ln b}{dt}$

that is, $a'$ and $b'$ are the instantaneous rates of factor augmentation. This equation shows the important fact that relatively labor-augmenting technical change need not be labor saving. Three cases exist:

(1) $\sigma = 1$ Technical change is always neutral.
(2) $\sigma < 1$ Technical change is labor saving if $b' > a'$; it is capital saving if $b' < a'$.
(3) $\sigma > 1$ Technical change is labor saving if $b' < a'$; it is capital saving if $b' > a'$.

That relatively labor-augmenting technical change $b' > a'$ is labor using for $\sigma > 1$ can be explained as follows. The increase in efficiency of labor allows entrepreneurs to reduce the amount of labor used. But with higher marginal product at a constant price, there is now an incentive to substitute labor for capital. The elasticity of substitution is sufficiently large—that is, the marginal product of labor declines so slowly—that the incentive to use more labor owing to its increase in efficiency overrides the initial saving made possible by that increase.

[50] See Solow, "Some Recent Developments."

# THREE

# Factor Productivity and Growth: A Historical Interpretation

VERNON W. RUTTAN, HANS P. BINSWANGER, YUJIRO HAYAMI,
WILLIAM W. WADE, AND ADOLF WEBER

WITHIN the framework of the theory of induced innovation, economic development can be interpreted as a dynamic process of technical and institutional change that is initiated and propelled by the growth of demand, differences in resource endowments, and changes in relative factor and product prices. In this chapter, in order to illustrate this process, we draw on the agricultural history of Japan, Germany, Denmark, France, the United Kingdom, and the United States during the period 1880 to 1970.

First, we review the differences among the several countries in basic factor productivities and factor endowments and in the changes that have occurred over time in agricultural output, factor productivities, and factor endowments. Then, through a statistical analysis of the relationships between changes over time in relative factor use and relative factor prices, we establish the plausibility of the induced innovation theory. Using a test developed by Binswanger, we next determine whether differences in factor ratios observed in the six countries are due to the effects of real differences in the factor intensities on the production functions of each of the countries or whether they are brought about simply by price substitution effects along a common production function. Then we use the same test to discover whether the changes in factor ratios within these countries over time are consistent with neutral technical change or whether they were generated by nonneutral shifts in the production function of each country. In the final section of this

We are indebted to Rondo Cameron, Folke Dovring, William Newell, and Philip Raup for their review and criticism of an earlier draft of this chapter. We also wish to express our appreciation to Mr. Yun Wing Sung, graduate student at the University of Minnesota, for causing us to rethink some of our earlier conclusions regarding the direction of bias in technical change in Japan.

chapter, we explore the possibility that the differential rates of growth in factor productivity among countries were induced, in part, by differential rates of growth in demand.

There are several excellent reasons for testing the induced innovation hypothesis against the experience of the six countries we have chosen. In the first place, among countries with highly productive agricultural systems, Japan and the United States represent the extremes in terms of resource endowment: Japan has little land and much labor, and the United States has a great deal of land but very expensive labor.[1] Second, the countries of Germany, Denmark, France, and the United Kingdom fall somewhere between Japan and the United States in respect to resource endowments and thus provide us with a continuum. Finally, the four European countries' varying responses, in terms of institutions and technology, to declining grain prices in world markets since 1870 have continued to puzzle economic historians and agricultural policy analysts.[2] Our discussion, therefore, not only will demonstrate the power of the theory of induced innovation to interpret the process of technical change in a wide range of settings but will shed some light on the confusing picture of recent European agricultural development.

## Induced Innovation and Factor Substitution in Agriculture

In agriculture it has appeared consistent with the technical conditions of production to consider growth in land area per worker and in output per worker as "somewhat independent [of each other], at least over a certain

---

[1] The first attempt to test the induced innovation hypothesis against empirical evidence was made by Yujiro Hayami and Vernon Ruttan, who examined and compared the Japanese and United States experiences. See Yujiro Hayami and Vernon W. Ruttan, "Factor Prices and Technical Change in Agricultural Development: The United States and Japan, 1880–1960," *Journal of Political Economy* 78 (September–October 1970): 1115–41; Yujiro Hayami and Vernon W. Ruttan, *Agricultural Development: An International Perspective* (Baltimore: Johns Hopkins University Press, 1971), pp. 111–35.

[2] The classic discussion of this matter is by C. P. Kindleberger, in "Group Behavior and International Trade," *Journal of Political Economy* 50 (February 1951): 30–46. According to Kindleberger, the "differences in European responses to the decline in the world price of wheat in the 1870's and 1880's may be summarized as follows: In Britain agriculture was permitted to be liquidated. In Germany large scale agriculture sought and obtained protection for itself. In France...agriculture...successfully defended its position with tariffs. In Italy the response was to emigrate. In Denmark grain production was converted to animal husbandry" (p. 37). For an attempt to test the Kindleberger hypothesis see William W. Wade, "Institutional Determinants of Technical Change and Productivity Growth: Denmark, France and Great Britain, 1870–1965" (Ph.D. diss., University of Minnesota, 1973). For a comparative analysis of institutional change in modern European agrarian history, see Folke Dovring, *Land and Labor in Europe in the Twentieth Century* (The Hague: Martinus Nijhoff, 1965).

range."[3] Increases in land area per worker can be achieved through advances in technology that permit the worker to cultivate a greater amount of land. Typically, such advances replace or supplement manpower with sources of power that are economically more efficient (animal, mechanical, electrical), or they provide additional power sources per worker. For purposes of exposition, it is useful to refer to these technologies, which substitute for labor, as *mechanical technology*.

Increases in output per worker can be achieved also through increased land productivity, but only if the rate of increase in output per hectare exceeds the rate of change in the number of workers employed per hectare. It is useful to refer to technologies which increase output per hectare as *biological technology*.

The process of induced technical change can be described in terms of a series of shifts of and along innovation possibility curves.[4] In figure 3–1 (left)

---

[3] Zvi Griliches, "Agriculture: Productivity and Technology," *International Encyclopedia of the Social Sciences*, vol. 1 (New York: Macmillan and Free Press, 1968), pp. 241–5.

The two partial productivity measures are linked through the ratio of land area per worker. Thus

$$Y/L = (A/L)(Y/A)$$

where $Y$ = output, $L$ = labor, $A$ = land area, $Y/L$ = labor productivity, $A/L$ = land area per worker, and $Y/A$ = land productivity.

[4] As a result of the theoretical advances made in part II of this book, we no longer use the term *metaproduction function* to describe the *innovation possibility curve* (IPC), as was done by Hayami and Ruttan in their empirical work (see Hayami and Ruttan, *Agricultural Development*). We now define the metaproduction function as the envelope of the production points of the most efficient countries. As a consequence, the metaproduction function can be measured econometrically. It describes a technological frontier that countries now lying within its borders can definitely reach by borrowing or by adaptive research, as appropriate, and by investing in human capital, in extension and in rural infrastructure.

The innovation possibility curve, on the other hand, can be regarded as the envelope of all *neoclassical production functions* that might be invented, given the existing state of scientific knowledge. *In the short run*, in which substitution among inputs is circumscribed by existing capital and equipment, production relationships can be described by an activity that has relatively fixed factor–factor and factor–product ratios. *In the long run*, in which the constraints exercised by existing capital and equipment disappear and substitution becomes a function of available technical knowledge, including all possible factor–factor and factor–product combinations, production relationships can be described by the neoclassical production function. *In the secular period* of production, in which constraints are further relaxed so as to admit potentially discoverable production possibilities, production relationships can be described by a set of IPCs that describe all potential technologies that might be invented, given the current state of scientific knowledge. Each member of a set of IPCs corresponds to a given budget, and the larger the budget, the closer the IPC lies to the origin of the isoquant map. The IPC that corresponds to an unlimited research budget is the *scientific frontier*. Because of diminishing returns to research, however, it is unlikely that applied research will ever be carried to that frontier. The scientific frontier shifts with advances in the basic sciences, and each such shift carries with it a shift in the entire set of IPCs but not in the metaproduction function itself. However, shifts in the scientific frontier and in the IPCs make shifts of the metaproduction function easier, or less costly, to achieve.

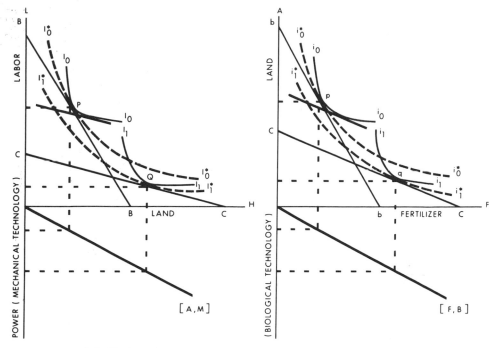

FIG. 3–1. Factor prices and induced technical change. [Adapted from Yujiro Hayami and Vernon W. Ruttan, *Agricultural Development: An International Perspective* (Baltimore: Johns Hopkins University Press, 1971), p. 126.]

for example, $I_0^*$ represents the land–labor isoquant of the metaproduction function (MPF) at time zero; it is the envelope of less elastic isoquants such as $I_0$ that correspond, for example, to different types of harvesting machinery. $I_1^*$ is the innovation possibility curve of time period 1. A certain technology—a reaper, for example—represented by $I_0$, is invented when the price ratio $BB$ prevails for some time. When this price ratio changes from $BB$ to $CC$, another technology—such as the combine—represented by $I_1$, is invented. Analogous inventions in the livestock sector might be, for instance, a succession of more highly automated animal feeding systems.

The new technology represented by $I_1$, which permits an expansion in land area per worker, is generally associated with higher animal or mechanical power inputs per worker. This implies a complementary relationship between land and power, which may be illustrated by the line $[A, M]$. It is hypothesized that mechanical innovation is responsive to a change in the wage rate relative to the price of land and machinery and involves the substitution of land and power for labor.

The process of advance in biological technology is illustrated in the right-hand portion of figure 3–1. Here $i_0^*$ represents the land–fertilizer isoquant of

TABLE 3–1. Agricultural output, factor productivity, factor endowments, and factor price ratios in six countries, 1880–1970

| Ratio | Year | Japan | Germany | Den- mark[a] | France | United Kingdom | United States |
|---|---|---|---|---|---|---|---|
| Agricultural output | 1880 | 100 | 100 | 100 | 100 | 100 | 100 |
| index ($Y$) | 1930 | 223 | 192 | 279 | 146 | 111 | 204 |
| | 1960 | 334 | 316 | 422 | 235 | 185 | 340 |
| | 1970 | 428 | 412 | 459 | 334 | 236 | 403 |
| Agricultural output | 1880 | 1.89 | 7.9 | 10.6 | 7.4 | 16.2 | 13.0 |
| per male worker | 1930 | 4.60 | 16.0 | 24.1 | 13.2 | 20.1 | 22.5 |
| in wheat units | 1960 | 8.41 | 35.4 | 47.5 | 33.4 | 45.3 | 88.8 |
| ($Y/L$) | 1970 | 15.77 | 65.4 | 94.4 | 59.9 | 87.6 | 157.4 |
| Agricultural output | 1880 | 2.86 | 1.25 | 1.19 | 1.06 | 1.10 | 0.513 |
| per hectare of | 1930 | 5.06 | 2.47 | 2.95 | 1.50 | 1.18 | 0.555 |
| agricultural land, | 1960 | 7.44 | 4.01 | 4.65 | 2.48 | 1.94 | 0.811 |
| in wheat units | 1970 | 10.03 | 5.40 | 5.27 | 3.70 | 2.61 | 0.981 |
| ($Y/A$) | | | | | | | |
| Agricultural land | 1880 | 0.659 | 6.34 | 8.91 | 6.96 | 14.7 | 25.4 |
| per male worker, | 1930 | 0.908 | 6.46 | 8.18 | 8.80 | 17.0 | 40.5 |
| in hectares | 1960 | 1.131 | 8.83 | 10.21 | 13.44 | 23.3 | 109.5 |
| ($A/L$) | 1970 | 1.573 | 12.20 | 17.92 | 16.19 | 33.5 | 160.5 |
| Days of labor to buy | 1880 | 1,874 | 967 | 382 | 780 | 995 | 181 |
| one hectare of | 1930 | 2,920 | 589 | 228 | 262 | 189 | 115 |
| arable land | 1960 | 2,954 | 378 | 166 | 166 | 211 | 108 |
| ($P_A/P_L$) | 1970 | 1,315 | 244 | 177 | 212 | 203 | 108 |

Source: Data are from appendix 3–2.

Note: One wheat unit is equivalent to one ton of wheat. The method of constructing output measures in terms of wheat units is described in Yujiro Hayami and Vernon W. Ruttan, *Agricultural Development: An International Perspective* (Baltimore: Johns Hopkins University Press, 1971), pp. 308–25.

Definitions of agricultural land are not strictly comparable among countries and over time, but in general they include all land in farms, including cropland used for crops, pasture, and fallow, plus permanent pasture.

[a] In Denmark, land price includes the value of agricultural land and buildings.

the metaproduction function. The metaproduction function is the envelope of less elastic isoquants (for example, $i_0$) that represent advances such as crop varieties characterized by different levels of fertilizer responsiveness. A decline in the price of fertilizer is seen as inducing plant breeders to develop more fertilizer-responsive crop varieties—which might be described by the isoquant $i_1$ along the IPC $i_1^*$—and as inducing farmers to adopt the new varieties as they become available.

The complementary relationship between biological technologies and fertilizer use, represented by the line $[F, B]$, extends also to the protective chemicals (insecticides, herbicides) and to the institutional innovations associated with the marketing and delivery of chemical inputs and services. Similarly, in livestock production a decline in the price of concentrated feedstuffs (e.g., oilcake, fish meal, urea) induces animal nutritionists and breeders both to direct their efforts to the development of feedstuffs that incorporate a higher percentage of the lower cost proteins and to select and breed for lines that gain more rapidly when fed the new rations. Breeders and nutritionists again may have similar aims in developing biological and chemical technologies to improve animal health.

In the next section, we illustrate the process of induced technical change that we have described above, using data drawn from the historical experience of agricultural development of the six countries mentioned above.

## Resource Endowment and Productivity Growth

Data that illustrate the differences among countries and changes over time in output and in factor productivity, endowments, and prices for the agricultural sectors of Japan, Germany, Denmark, France, the United

TABLE 3-2. Annual rates of change in agricultural output, factor productivity, and factor endowments in six countries, 1880–1970

| Time Period/Ratio | Japan | Germany | Den-mark[a] | France | United Kingdom | United States |
|---|---|---|---|---|---|---|
| *1880–1970* | | | | | | |
| Agricultural output ($Y$) | 1.63 | 1.59 | 1.71 | 1.35 | 0.96 | 1.56 |
| Output per worker ($Y/L$) | 2.39 | 2.37 | 2.46 | 2.35 | 1.89 | 2.81 |
| Output per hectare ($Y/A$) | 1.40 | 1.64 | 1.67 | 1.40 | 0.96 | 0.72 |
| Land per worker ($A/L$) | 0.97 | 0.73 | 0.78 | 0.94 | 0.92 | 2.07 |
| *1880–1930* | | | | | | |
| Agricultural output ($Y$) | 1.62 | 1.31 | 2.07 | 0.76 | 0.21 | 1.44 |
| Output per worker ($Y/L$) | 1.79 | 1.42 | 1.66 | 1.16 | 0.43 | 1.10 |
| Output per hectare ($Y/A$) | 1.15 | 1.37 | 1.83 | 0.70 | 0.14 | 0.16 |
| Land per worker ($A/L$) | 0.64 | 0.04 | −.17 | 0.47 | 0.29 | 0.94 |
| *1930–1970* | | | | | | |
| Agricultural output ($Y$) | 1.64 | 1.93 | 1.25 | 2.09 | 1.91 | 1.72 |
| Output per worker ($Y/L$) | 3.13 | 3.81 | 3.47 | 3.85 | 3.74 | 4.98 |
| Output per hectare ($Y/A$) | 1.73 | 1.97 | 1.44 | 2.28 | 2.00 | 1.43 |
| Land per worker ($A/L$) | 1.38 | 1.60 | 1.98 | 1.54 | 1.71 | 3.50 |
| *1930–1960* | | | | | | |
| Agricultural output ($Y$) | 1.36 | 1.67 | 1.39 | 1.60 | 1.72 | 1.72 |
| Output per worker ($Y/L$) | 2.03 | 2.68 | 2.29 | 3.14 | 2.75 | 4.68 |
| Output per hectare ($Y/A$) | 1.29 | 1.63 | 1.53 | 1.69 | 1.67 | 1.27 |
| Land per worker ($A/L$) | 0.73 | 1.05 | 0.74 | 1.42 | 1.06 | 3.37 |
| *1960–1970* | | | | | | |
| Agricultural output ($Y$) | 2.51 | 2.69 | 0.84 | 3.58 | 2.45 | 1.71 |
| Output per worker ($Y/L$) | 6.49 | 6.35 | 7.11 | 6.02 | 6.82 | 5.89 |
| Output per hectare ($Y/A$) | 3.03 | 3.02 | 1.26 | 4.08 | 3.01 | 1.92 |
| Land per worker ($A/L$) | 3.35 | 3.29 | 5.79 | 1.88 | 3.69 | 3.90 |

Source: Data are from appendix 3–2.

Note: One wheat unit is equivalent to one ton of wheat. The method of constructing output measures in terms of wheat units is described in Yujiro Hayami and Vernon W. Ruttan, *Agricultural Development: An International Perspective* (Baltimore: Johns Hopkins University Press, 1971), pp. 308–25.

Definitions of agricultural land are not strictly comparable among countries and over time, but in general they include all land in farms, including cropland used for crops, pasture, and fallow, plus permanent pasture.

[a] In Denmark the land price includes the value of agricultural land and buildings.

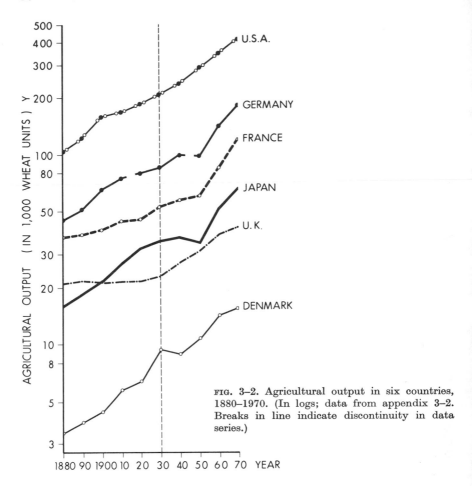

FIG. 3–2. Agricultural output in six countries, 1880–1970. (In logs; data from appendix 3–2. Breaks in line indicate discontinuity in data series.)

Kingdom, and the United States for 1880–1970 are summarized in tables 3–1 and 3–2 and in figures 3–2 through 3–7. The more detailed data on which these tables and figures are based are presented in appendix 3–2.

In 1880, agricultural land per male worker ranged from 0.66 hectares in Japan to 25.4 hectares in the United States. The prices of land and labor varied inversely with resource endowments. In the United States, 181 days of labor, at hired farm-labor wage rates, were required to earn enough to purchase one hectare of arable farm land; in Japan 1,874 days were required.[5]

---

[5] Definitions of agricultural land are not strictly comparable among countries and over time, but in general they comprise all land in farms, including cropland that is used for crops, pasture, and fallow as well as for permanent pasture. Arable land is generally considered to include only cropland that is used for crops, pasture, and fallow. Over

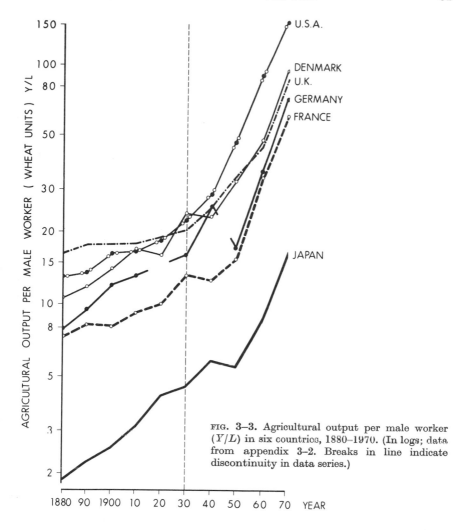

FIG. 3–3. Agricultural output per male worker ($Y/L$) in six countries, 1880–1970. (In logs; data from appendix 3–2. Breaks in line indicate discontinuity in data series.)

In Germany and the United Kingdom land, in comparison with labor, was approximately half as expensive as it was in Japan, and it was even less expensive in France and Denmark.

time, the amount of arable land in a given area may be increased by investment in clearing, drainage, terracing, irrigation, and fencing. In 1880, such investments were much more intensive in Japan, Germany, Denmark, France and the United Kingdom than in the United States. In general it is useful to think of agricultural land as a factor created by investment rather than as an original factor of production. Data on agricultural land area are more generally available than are data on arable land area. Data on prices are more generally available for arable land.

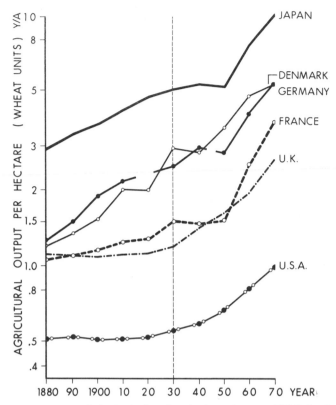

FIG. 3–4. Agricultural output per hectare $(Y/A)$ in six countries, 1880–1970. (In logs; data from appendix 3–2. Breaks in line indicate discontinuity in data series.)

Variations in output per hectare among countries were negatively related to land per worker and positively related to the price of land per hectare. Output per hectare was approximately 0.5 wheat units per hectare in the United States, 1.1–1.3 wheat units per hectare in the four European countries and 2.9 wheat units per hectare in Japan. Variations in output per hectare were sufficient only to partially offset the variations in land per worker. Output per male worker varied directly with land area per worker, ranging from 1.9 wheat units in Japan to 16.2 in the United Kingdom and 13.0 in the United States.

Limitations in resource endowments were apparently not a major constraint on growth of agricultural output over the period 1880–1970, even in countries with the most limited land resource endowments. The most rapid growth was experienced in Denmark, where output grew from an index of 100 in 1880 to 459 in 1970, and the slowest in the United Kingdom, where, during the same period, output rose from an index of 100 to 236. Japan, Germany, and the United States experienced roughly comparable rates of growth in output.

In *Japan*, agricultural output grew at 1.6 percent per year during the period 1880–1930 and at approximately the same rate between 1930 and 1970. During the earlier period, growth in output per hectare accounted for approximately 70 percent of the growth in total output and for over two-thirds of the growth in output per worker. After 1930, increase in land area per worker became a more important source of growth in output per worker than in the earlier period; between 1960 and 1970 it became a more important

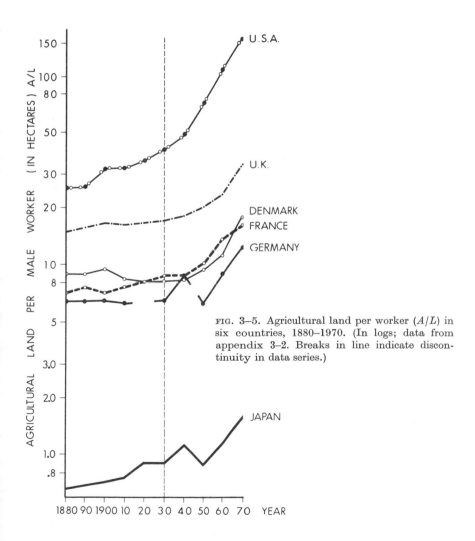

FIG. 3–5. Agricultural land per worker ($A/L$) in six countries, 1880–1970. (In logs; data from appendix 3–2. Breaks in line indicate discontinuity in data series.)

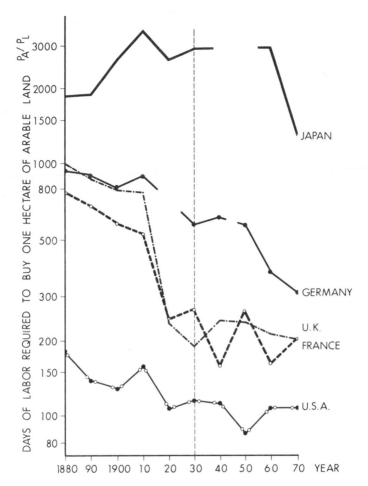

FIG. 3–6.  Days of labor required to buy one hectare of arable land ($P_A/P_L$) in six countries, 1880–1970. (In logs; data from appendix 3–2. German prices are for agricultural land. Breaks in lines indicate discontinuities in data series.)

source of growth in output per worker than were increases in output per hectare.[6]

In *Germany* agricultural output grew at approximately 1.3 percent per

[6] For a detailed analysis of the sources of agricultural productivity growth in Japan, see Yujiro Hayami, in association with Masakatsu Akino, Masahiko Shintani, and Saburo Yamada, *A Century of Agricultural Growth in Japan* (Minneapolis and Tokyo: University of Minnesota Press and University of Tokyo Press, 1975). See also Saburo Yamada and Yujiro Hayami, "Agricultural Productivity Growth in Japan, 1880–1970," in *Agricultural Growth in Japan, Taiwan, Korea and the Philippines*, eds. Yujiro Hayami, Vernon W. Ruttan, and Herman Southworth (Honolulu: The University Press of Hawaii, 1978).

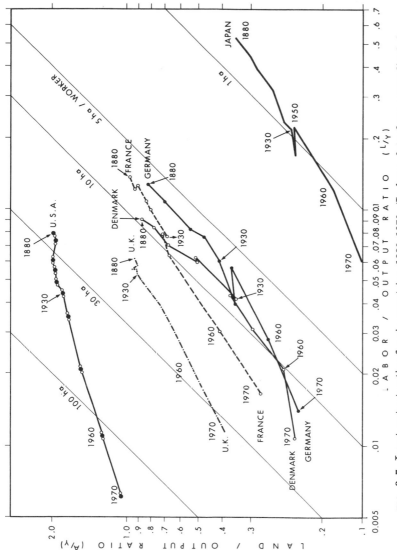

FIG. 3-7. Input-output ratios for six countries, 1880-1970. (In logs; data from appendix 3-2. Diagonals are land-labor ratios.)

year during the period 1880–1930 and at 1.93 percent per year from 1930 to 1970. Growth in output per hectare accounted for the entire increase in output between 1880 and 1930, and during the same period, it also accounted for most of the increase in output per worker. After 1930, increases in land area per worker that resulted from declining agricultural employment contributed significantly to output per worker.[7]

Among the six countries, the rate of growth of both total agricultural output and output per hectare between 1880 and 1930 was highest in *Denmark*. Denmark was also the only country that experienced a decline in land area per worker. Output per hectare rose more rapidly than output per worker but slightly less rapidly than total output. Again, Denmark was the only country in which output per hectare rose less rapidly during the period 1930–1970 than between 1880 and 1930. Output per worker continued to rise relatively rapidly, however, as a result of a reduction in the number of workers employed in agriculture.[8]

*France* experienced the most dramatic transition of any of the six countries between the periods of 1880–1930 and 1930–1970. During the earlier period, French agriculture was essentially static. Agricultural output grew at less than 0.8 percent per year and output per hectare at 0.7 percent per year.[9] Both output and productivity growth accelerated after World War II. Between 1960 and 1970, France achieved a 3.6 percent annual rate of growth in agricultural output, which was the highest among the six countries during that period.

[7] For an extensive review of the literature on agricultural growth in Germany, see Adolf Weber, "Productivity of German Agriculture, 1850 to 1970, with Comparisons to the Development of Japan and the United States," in *Rural and Development Economics*, ed. Paris Andreau (Nairobi: East African Literature Bureau, 1977), pp. 201, 277. Also, Adolf Weber, "Faktorpreise, Faktorenproduktivität und Technologie in der amerikanischen, europäischen und japanischen Landwirtschaft von 1880 bis 1965," *Zeitschrift für Wirtschafts und Sozialwissenschaften* 93 (1973): 197–226; Eckert Schremmer, "Wie gross war der technische Fortschritt während der Industriellen Revolution in Deutschland, 1850–1913," *Vierteljahrschrift für Sozial- und Wirtschaftsgeschichte* 60 (1973): 433–58.

[8] For a very useful review of Danish agricultural policies over the hundred-year period between 1870 and 1970, see Karen J. Friedman, "Danish Agricultural Policy, 1870–1970: The Flowering and Decline of a Liberal Policy," *Food Research Institute Studies* 13 (1974): 225–38. During the early part of this period, Denmark was shifting rapidly from a crop-based to an intensive, livestock-based system of agriculture. The classic study of agricultural development in Denmark is that by Einer Jensen, *Danish Agriculture–Its Economic Development* (Copenhagen: J. H. Schultz Forlag, 1937). For a more recent treatment see Svend Hage Hansen, *Okonomisk vaekst i Danmark*, 2 vols. (Copenhagen: København Universitet, 1972).

[9] These figures apparently represent a decline in the rate of growth of agricultural output; according to Newell, total output grew at approximately 1.1 percent per year during the sixty-year period prior to 1880. See William H. Newell, "The Agricultural Revolution in Nineteenth Century France," *The Journal of Economic History* 33 (December 1973): 710.

The *United Kingdom* experienced the slowest rates of growth of agricultural output and of output per worker among the six countries during the period 1880–1930.[10] From a rate of 0.2 percent per year in that period, growth in agricultural output rose to a rate of 1.9 percent per year between 1930 and 1970. Over the same time span, output per worker rose from 0.4 to 3.7 percent per year, and output per hectare rose from 0.1 to 2.0 percent per year. By the 1960s the United Kingdom was beginning to make a fairly successful transition from the period of relative stagnation that began with the decline of high farming, after 1870, to the modern era of higher growth rates in output and productivity. However, the United Kingdom has been somewhat less successful than France in making this transition to modern growth rates in the agricultural sector.[11]

The *United States* has been on a growth path that is quite distinct from that followed by the other five countries throughout the period 1880–1970. The United States rate of growth in total output lagged in comparison both with the rates in Denmark and Japan between 1880 and 1930 and with the rates in Germany and France from 1930 to 1970. Output per worker grew less rapidly than in any of the other countries except Great Britain during the period 1880–1930 but more rapidly than in any of the other five countries between 1930 and 1970. Output per hectare lagged in comparison with that of all other countries except Great Britain from 1880 to 1930 and in comparison with that of all countries other than Denmark during the period 1930–1970. The distinguishing feature of U.S. agricultural development has been its primary reliance on growth in land area per worker as a source of growth in output per worker over the entire period 1880–1970.[12]

The selection of the periods 1880–1930 and 1930–1970 for the data presented in tables 3–1 and 3–2 is not ideal for all countries. Some of the distortions that result from choosing the year 1930 as the dividing line between periods compared can be seen by reviewing figures 3–2 through 3–6, in which the data were plotted by decades (each point represents a five-year average centered on the decade year shown). For example, in some countries— particularly Germany, France, and Japan—a considerable acceleration in growth followed a long period of relative stagnation that did not end until

---

[10] The rates of growth in output and productivity in United Kingdom agriculture were apparently more rapid between 1815 and 1880 than they were from 1880 to 1930. See F. M. L. Thompson, "The Second Agricultural Revolution, 1815–1880," *Economic History Review* 21 (January–April 1968): 62–77.

[11] See Wade, "Institutional Determinants." For a useful comparison of the French and British experiences see P. K. O'Brien and O. Keyder, "Economic Growth in Britain and France from the Revolution to the First World War," mimeographed (Oxford: St. Anthony's College, 1974).

[12] Wayne D. Rasmussen, "The Impact of Technological Change on American Agriculture: 1862–1962," *The Journal of Economic History* 22 (October–December 1962): 578–91. See also Hayami and Ruttan, *Agricultural Development*, pp. 111–22, 139–42.

after World War II. However, selection of the year 1950 as a comparison base would have introduced similarly significant distortions.

In figure 3–7 we have brought together in a single illustration the long-term trends in the three ratios between land and output, between labor and output, and between land and labor. The diagonal lines represent constant land–labor ratios. Movements of land–output and labor–output ratios toward the lower left-hand corner represent improvements in the two partial productivity ratios that result from yield-increasing (or biological) and labor-saving (or mechanical) technology (see figure 3–1). An isoquant drawn through the input–output ratio points for the year 1970 describes what might be regarded as a metaproduction function (MPF). The innovation possibility curve (IPC) that describes potential technology, given existing scientific and technical knowledge, would stand farther to the left. In order to make the productivity ratios described by the 1970 metaproduction function accessible to farmers in countries whose productivity ratios fall to the right of that function, technical and scientific knowledge about improved crop varieties, animals, chemicals, and equipment must be made available through investment in experiment-station and industrial capacity.

Several general conclusions may be drawn from the data presented in tables 3–1 and 3–2 and in figures 3–2 through 3–7.

*First*, it is clear that there were enormous differences in factor endowment ratios among the six countries in 1880 and that these differences remain substantial in 1970. Yet all six countries have experienced an overall decline in labor intensity, whether this is measured in terms of labor per unit of output or in terms of land per worker. During the entire 1880–1970 period only Denmark experienced a sustained decline in land per worker that is comparable to the decline being experienced in many developing countries today.

*Second*, throughout most of the period 1880–1970, the countries whose land area per worker was relatively limited at the beginning of that period depended primarily on increase in output per hectare as a source of growth in agricultural output. The increases in land area per worker that have come about in these countries in recent decades have been associated more often with declining numbers of agricultural workers than with increases in actual land area.

*Third*, the countries whose land area per worker has been relatively limited have been able to achieve rates of growth in total output and in output per worker that have been roughly comparable to the rates achieved by countries with more favorable resource endowments. Limitation on land per worker apparently has not represented a critical constraint on capacity for growth in agricultural output.

*Fourth*, the growth rates of agricultural output, of output per hectare, and of output per worker have risen sharply in most of the six countries since

1930. In some countries these higher growth rates represent the acceleration of trends that were already evident. In others they represent a sharp transition from earlier experiences. In contrast to pre–1930 growth rates of output and productivity, typically less than 2 percent per year, modern growth rates range in the neighborhood of 2 to 4 percent per year for output, 5 percent per year for output per worker, and 2 to 4 percent per year for output per hectare.

## Factor Prices and Factor Use

In this section we explore, more formally than in the preceding section, the relationships between factor prices and the patterns of factor use associated with growth in both output per hectare and output per worker in the six countries.

BIOLOGICAL TECHNOLOGY. The model of biological technology outlined earlier in this chapter (figure 3–1) suggests that a decline in the price of fertilizer relative to the price of land can be expected to induce a rise in fertilizer use per hectare as a result of a movement to the right along the short-run production function ($i_0$). Such a decline can also be expected to induce advances in crop technology, such as the development and introduction of more fertilizer-responsive crop varieties, which can be characterized by a new short-run production function to the right of and below $i_0$, along the innovation possibility curve (IPC) $i_1^*$, such as $i_1$. A strong negative relationship is hypothesized between the price of fertilizer relative to the price of land ($P_F/P_A$) and fertilizer use per hectare ($F/A$).

Changes in the price of labor relative to the price of land are also expected to affect the level of fertilizer use per hectare. As the price of labor rises in relation to the price of land, farmers can be expected to attempt to reduce labor input per unit of land by substituting fertilizer—and other chemical inputs such as herbicides and insecticides—for more labor-intensive husbandry practices. A decline in the price of fertilizer can also be expected to result in the substitution of chemical fertilizers, produced by the industrial sector, for farm-produced fertilizers, such as animal or green manures. Thus a positive relationship is hypothesized between the price of labor relative to the price of land ($P_L/P_A$) and fertilizer use per hectare ($F/A$).

The strong negative relationship between the fertilizer–land price ratio and fertilizer use per hectare for all six countries is confirmed in table 3–3. Given the enormous differences among these countries in the cultural and physical environments in which farmers operate and produce their crops and the great differences in the levels of technology and in the kinds of social organization that have characterized each country, the similarity of the response coefficients in table 3–3 is truly remarkable. These data imply not only that farmers of all the countries have responded in a roughly comparable manner

TABLE 3-3. Relationships between fertilizer use per hectare and relative factor prices in six countries

| Country | Time Period | Coefficient of Price of | | Coefficient of Determination $(R^2)$ | Standard Error of Estimate $(S)$ | Degrees of Freedom |
| | | Fertilizer in Relation to Land $(P_F/P_A)$ | Labor in Relation to Land $(P_L/P_A)$ | | | |
|---|---|---|---|---|---|---|
| Japan | 1880–1960 | −1.274* (0.057) | 0.729* (0.220) | 0.974 | 0.081 | 14 |
| Germany | 1880–1913 | −1.806* (0.009) | 0.083 (0.515) | 0.943 | 0.289 | 13 |
| | 1950–1968 | −0.377* (0.098) | 0.799* (0.093) | 0.954 | 0.100 | 15 |
| Denmark | 1910–1965 | −1.120* (0.348) | 0.958* (0.430) | 0.87 | 0.310 | 9 |
| France | 1870–1965 | −0.950* (0.332) | −1.375*# (0.362) | 0.56 | 0.776 | 17 |
| | 1920–1965 | −0.664* (0.259) | 0.485 (0.733) | 0.386 | 0.538 | 7 |
| United Kingdom | 1870–1965 | −1.130* (0.025) | 1.010* (0.080) | 0.92 | 0.218 | 17 |
| United States | 1880–1960 | −1.357* (0.102) | 1.019* (0.168) | 0.970 | 0.083 | 14 |

Source: For Japan: Yujiro Hayami and Vernon W. Ruttan, *Agricultural Development: An International Perspective* (Baltimore: Johns Hopkins University Press, 1971). For Germany: Adolf Weber, "Productivity in German Agriculture: 1850 to 1970," Staff Paper P73-1 (St. Paul: University of Minnesota, Department of Agricultural and Applied Economics, August 1973), p. 23. For Denmark: William W. Wade, "Institutional Determinants of Technical Change and Agricultural Productivity Growth: Denmark, France and Great Britain, 1870–1965" (Ph.D. diss., University of Minnesota, August 1973), p. 128. For France: Ibid., pp. 134, 136. For the United Kingdom: Ibid., p. 149. For the United States: Hayami and Ruttan, *Agricultural Development*, p. 132, regression (W 15).

Note: Equations are linear, in logarithms. Parentheses enclose standard errors of the estimated coefficients.

\* Significant at $P = 0.05$ (one-tail test).

\# Inconsistent with simple induced innovation hypothesis.

to similar factor-price ratios but that farmers have been able to respond thus as a result of comparable shifts in short-run production functions. This, in turn, implies that research institutions in the several countries responded in a similar fashion, by making more fertilizer-responsive crop varieties available to farmers.

The positive relationship between the price of labor relative to the price of land and fertilizer use per hectare hypothesized above is also confirmed in table 3-3. The relationship appears to have evolved later in France and Germany than in the other four countries.

It seems reasonable to hypothesize that the model outlined in figure 3-1 can be applied to the analysis of the livestock as well as the crop sector. In some respects, feed concentrates—particularly the protein meals, such as soybean, copra, and cottonseed meal—play a role in animal husbandry that is analogous to that played by fertilizer in crop production. There has been an increasing tendency, as the price of feed concentrates has declined over time, to substitute these products for forages, hay, and other roughages. The availability of lower-cost concentrates has led to the development of husbandry practices and to the selection and breeding of animals to achieve earlier maturity and more rapid rates of weight gain per day and per feed unit. Where land resources are limited, as in Western Europe and Japan, concentrates are usually imported; this reinforces their role as land substitutes.

The data presented in table 3–4 confirm the hypothesis that the ratio between the price of concentrates and the price of land is negatively related to the use of concentrates. Although the estimated relationships are not entirely comparable among countries, it is clear that the increasing use of feed concentrates per hectare in Germany, Denmark, and the United

TABLE 3–4. Relationship between use of feed concentrates per hectare and factor prices

| Country | Time Period | Coefficient of Price of | | Coefficient of Determination $(R^2)$ | Standard Error of Estimate $(S)$ | Degrees of Freedom |
| | | Concentrates in Relation to Land $(P_C/P_A)$ | Labor in Relation to Land $(P_L/P_A)$ | | | |
|---|---|---|---|---|---|---|
| Germany[a] | 1880–1913 | −3.333* (0.569) | 3.974* (1.221) | 0.712 | 0.337 | 31 |
| | 1950–1968 | −1.567* (0.254) | 2.381* (0.255) | 0.973 | 0.337 | 15 |
| Denmark[b] | 1880–1925 | −0.680* (0.300) | 0.494* (0.124) | 0.590 | 0.030 | 7 |
| United Kingdom[c] | 1870–1965 | −3.642* (0.331) | 3.634* (0.331) | 0.970 | 0.137 | 17 |

Source: For Germany: Adolf Weber, "Productivity Growth in German Agriculture: 1850 to 1970," Staff Paper P73–1 (St. Paul: University of Minnesota, Department of Agricultural and Applied Economics, August 1973), p. 23. For Denmark: William W. Wade, "Institutional Determinants of Technical Change and Agricultural Productivity Growth: Denmark, France and Great Britain, 1870–1965" (Ph.D. diss., University of Minnesota, August 1973), p. 128. For the United Kingdom: Ibid., p. 149.

Note: Equations are linear, in logarithms. Parentheses enclose standard errors of the estimated coefficients.

[a] Net oil cake imports.
[b] All imported concentrates per hectare.
[c] All concentrates per hectare.
* Significant at $P = 0.05$ (one-tail test).

Kingdom has been closely associated with a continuing decline in the price of concentrates relative to the price of land. It also seems clear that as the price of labor has risen in relation to the price of land, farmers have substituted imported concentrates for labor-intensive systems of livestock feed production at home.

MECHANICAL TECHNOLOGY. The model of mechanical technology outlined earlier suggests that the use of land per worker rises as the price of land declines relative to the price of labor. In constructing the model, we assumed that, over the long run, expansion of the area cultivated per worker was dependent on increased use of machinery and power per worker. Thus technical changes that lead to a decline in the price of machinery relative to the price of labor should also contribute to an increase in the amount of land cultivated per worker. Drawing on the model, it is hypothesized that land area per worker ($A/L$) is negatively related to (a) the price of land relative to the price of labor ($P_A/P_L$) and to (b) the price of machinery relative to the price of labor ($P_M/P_L$). Similarly, it is hypothesized that the use of power (or machinery) per worker ($M/L$) is negatively related to (a) the price of land relative to the price of labor ($P_A/P_L$) and to (b) the price of machinery relative to the price of labor ($P_M/P_L$).

The results of the empirical tests of these hypotheses are not as clear-cut as were the results of our tests of the hypotheses relating to biological technology (see tables 3–5 and 3–6). The hypothesis that land area per worker is negatively related both to the price of land relative to the price of labor and to the price of machinery relative to the price of labor is confirmed in the historical experience of only Germany after 1950, the United Kingdom before 1925, and the United States. In all six countries, except Germany during the period 1880–1913, land area per worker is, as hypothesized, negatively related to the price of machinery relative to the price of labor. The hypothesis that power per worker is negatively related both to the price of land relative to the price of labor and the price of machinery relative to the price of labor is confirmed for all countries except France before 1920 and Denmark.

In both of the above tests the price of land relative to the price of labor performed less well than the price of machinery relative to the price of labor. Moreover, where the test was run for both an early and a late period, the results tended to be weaker for the early period.

A closer look at these equations reveals the following: For the power-per-worker equations, 14 of the 16 coefficients are negative, and 10 of these are significant. Only two of the 16 coefficients have an inconsistent, positive sign and only one of these is significant.

The land-per-worker equations have produced the most puzzling results. Of the 18 coefficients, 6 are positive, although only 2 are significant. (Of the 12 negative coefficients, 8 are significant.) Furthermore, 5 of the 6 positive

TABLE 3–5. Relationship between land per worker and relative factor prices in six countries

| Country | Time Period | Coefficient of Price of | | Coefficient of Determination $(R^2)$ | Standard Error of Estimate $(S)$ | Degrees of Freedom |
|---|---|---|---|---|---|---|
| | | Land in Relation to Labor $(P_A/P_L)$ | Machinery in Relation to Labor $(P_M/P_L)$ | | | |
| Japan | 1880–1960 | 0.159# (0.110) | −0.219 (0.041) | 0.751 | 0.016 | 14 |
| Germany | 1880–1913 | −0.264* (0.066) | 0.066*# (0.018) | 0.393 | 0.012 | 31 |
| | 1950–1968 | −0.177 (0.139) | −0.476* (0.087) | 0.975 | 0.083 | 15 |
| Denmark | 1910–1965 | 0.148# (0.084) | −0.357* (0.072) | 0.910 | 0.030 | 9 |
| France | 1870–1965 | 0.398*# (0.202) | −0.088 (0.141) | 0.323 | 0.189 | 17 |
| | 1920–1965 | 0.050# (0.226) | −0.498* (0.166) | 0.460 | 0.164 | 7 |
| United Kingdom | 1870–1925 | −0.129* (0.033) | −0.139* (0.070) | 0.610 | 0.041 | 17 |
| | 1925–1965 | 0.279# (0.159) | −0.065 (0.256) | 0.440 | 0.110 | 6 |
| United States | 1880–1960 | −0.451* (0.215) | −0.486* (0.120) | 0.828 | 0.084 | 14 |

Source: For Japan: Yujiro Hayami and Vernon W. Ruttan, *Agricultural Development: An International Perspective* (Baltimore: Johns Hopkins University Press, 1971), p. 131: Land per worker (W7); Power per worker (W9). For Germany: Adolf Weber, "Productivity Growth in German Agriculture: 1850 to 1970," Staff Paper P73–1 (St. Paul: University of Minnesota, Department of Agricultural and Applied Economics, August 1973), p. 24: Land per worker, regressions (6) and (7); Power per worker, regressions (4) and (5). For Denmark: William W. Wade, "Institutional Determinants of Technical Change and Agricultural Productivity Growth: Denmark, France and Great Britain, 1870–1965" (Ph.D. diss., University of Minnesota, August 1973), p. 128. For France: Ibid., pp. 134, 136. For the United Kingdom: Ibid., p. 149. For the United States: Hayami and Ruttan, *Agricultural Development*, p. 130: Land per worker (W1); Power per worker (W5).

Notes: For Japan, Denmark, France, and the United Kingdom, "land" is defined as arable land per male worker: for Germany and the United States it is defined as agricultural land per male worker.

Equations are linear, in logarithms. Parentheses enclose standard errors of the estimated coefficients.

* Significant at $P = 0.05$ (one-tail test).

# Inconsistent with simple induced innovation hypothesis.

coefficients are coefficients of the land–labor price ratio. This raises a question as to whether some systematic irregularity prevents this particular price effect from manifesting itself in the expected manner. Such behavior might have been caused by an exogenous labor-saving bias in the process of technical

TABLE 3–6. Relationship between power per worker and relative factor prices in six countries

| Country | Time Period | Coefficient of Price of | | Coefficient of Determination $(R^2)$ | Standard Error of Estimate $(S)$ | Degrees of Freedom |
|---|---|---|---|---|---|---|
| | | Land in Relation to Labor $(P_A/P_L)$ | Machinery in Relation to Labor $(P_M/P_L)$ | | | |
| Japan | 1880–1960 | −0.665* (0.261) | −0.299 (0.685) | 0.262 | 0.219 | 14 |
| Germany | 1880–1913 | −0.238* (0.070) | −0.607* (0.020) | 0.978 | 0.069 | 31 |
| | 1950–1968 | −0.234 (0.329) | −1.358* (0.207) | 0.979 | 0.213 | 15 |
| Denmark | 1910–1965 | 1.494# (1.010) | −3.180* (0.861) | 0.830 | 0.370 | 9 |
| France | 1870–1965 | 1.704*# (0.880) | −0.705 (0.614) | 0.160 | 0.810 | 17 |
| | 1920–1965 | −0.443 (0.976) | −2.460* (0.715) | 0.550 | 0.705 | 7 |
| United Kingdom | 1870–1965 | −1.120* (0.295) | −1.090* (0.527) | 0.810 | 0.075 | 17 |
| United States | 1880–1960 | −1.279* (0.475) | −0.920* (0.266) | 0.827 | 0.187 | 14 |

Source: For Japan: Yujiro Hayami and Vernon W. Ruttan, *Agricultural Development: An International Perspective* (Baltimore: Johns Hopkins University Press, 1971), p. 131: Land per worker (W7); Power per worker (W9). For Germany: Adolf Weber, "Productivity Growth in German Agriculture: 1850 to 1970," Staff Paper P73–1 (St. Paul: University of Minnesota, Department of Agricultural and Applied Economics, August 1973), p. 24: Land per worker, regressions (6) and (7); Power per worker, regressions (4) and (5). For Denmark: William W. Wade, "Institutional Determinants of Technical Change and Agricultural Productivity Growth: Denmark, France and Great Britain, 1870–1965" (Ph.D. diss., University of Minnesota, August 1973), p. 128. For France: Ibid., pp. 134, 136. For the United Kingdom: Ibid., p. 149. For the United States: Hayami and Ruttan, *Agricultural Development*, p. 130: Land per worker (W1); Power per worker (W5).

Notes: "Power" is defined as horsepower per male worker except for Germany, where it is defined as machinery investment per worker.

Equations are linear, in logarithms. Parentheses enclose standard errors of the estimated coefficients.

\* Significant at $P = 0.05$ (one-tail test).

\# Inconsistent with simple induced innovation hypothesis.

innovation, particularly in Japan, France, and the United Kingdom. This could have resulted from the biased borrowing opportunities available to these countries from countries that had more favorable land–labor ratios, such as the United States.

The analysis presented in this section supports the hypothesis that changes in factor use in each of the six countries have been responsive to changes in relative factor prices. Fertilizer use per hectare has been responsive to the price of fertilizer and to the price of labor relative to the price of land. And the two complementary inputs—power per worker and land per worker—have been responsive to the prices of land and of machinery relative to the price of labor.

These results are consistent with the induced innovation hypothesis, but they do not represent an adequate test of this hypothesis. The analyses presented thus far do not enable us to determine (a) whether the historical changes in factor use reflect the response of farmers to the rising economic value of land in relation to the price of fertilizer or to the increasing cost of labor compared to the cost of machinery along an unchanging, neoclassical macroproduction function, or (b) whether the production function available to farmers in the six countries has itself shifted to the left as a result of scientific and technical efforts made by scientists, engineers, and inventors in response to changing factor price relationships. The magnitude of the shifts in relative factor prices and in factor use, as shown in tables 3–1 and 3–2 and in figures 3–3 to 3–7, strongly suggests that the induced innovation process has been involved. The results of the statistical analyses alone, however, are consistent with either or both hypotheses. In the next section we present a simple two-factor test of the induced innovation hypothesis using data from the six countries. We will present a more definitive, many-factor test of the induced innovation hypothesis for United States agriculture in chapter 7.

## An Induced Innovation Test

It is useful at this point to restate the problem that must be solved in any test of induced innovation. In figure 3–1 (left), assume that the labor–land factor ratio in Japan can be represented by a line from the origin through $P$ and that the labor–land factor ratio in the United States can be represented by a line from the origin through $Q$. Assume also that the slope of the line $BB$ represents the factor price ratio in Japan, where land is expensive in comparison with labor, while the slope of $CC$ represents the factor price ratio in the United States, where labor is expensive in relation to land. If the substitution possibilities of the available agricultural technology can be represented by an isoquant map with little curvature, such as $I_0^*$ and $I_1^*$, the differences in factor ratios between Japan and the United States may be explained by simple substitution owing to factor-price change along a common production function. If, however, the possibilities of substitution between labor and land are represented by $I_0$ in Japan and $I_1$ in the United States, the points $P$ and $Q$ would not represent alternative factor combinations along production functions with equal factor intensity characteristics.

TABLE 3–7. Test of differences in technological paths: Necessary elasticity of substitution to explain differences in land–labor ratio by price ratio differences

| Item | 1880 | 1930 | 1960 | 1970 |
|------|------|------|------|------|
| *U.S. vs. other countries* | | | | |
| Japan | 2.08* | 1.35* | 1.95* | 3.12* |
| Great Britain | 0.29 | 1.47* | 2.50* | 2.70* |
| France | 0.87 | 1.96* | 5.79* | 4.13* |
| Germany | 0.80 | 1.16 | 2.49* | 4.00* |
| *Japan vs. Europe* | | | | |
| Great Britain | 7.01* | 1.21 | 1.24 | 2.04* |
| France | 3.26* | 0.92 | 0.79 | 1.39* |
| Germany | 4.13* | 1.29 | 1.00 | 1.28 |
| *Great Britain vs. Continental Europe* | | | | |
| France | a* | 2.47* | a* | 17.12* |
| Germany | a* | 0.98* | 1.71* | 5.72* |
| *Continental Europe* | | | | |
| France vs. Germany | 0.46 | 0.38 | 0.50 | 2.02* |

Source: Table 3–1.

Note: Critical value to reject hypothesis of equal technology is 1.34, that is, twice the value of $\sigma$ for equiproportional changes in $P_A$ and $P_L$.

$$\sigma_N = \frac{(A/L)_i - (A/L)_j}{(P_L/P_A)_j - (P_L/P_A)_i} \times \sqrt{\frac{(P_L/P_A)_i(P_L/P_A)_j}{(A/L)_i(A/L)_j}}$$

a Denotes cases where the country with the higher land–labor ratio also has the higher land price ratio. Such behavior is possible only if the country with the higher land–labor ratio employs a more land-intensive technology, that is, the hypothesis of equal technology is rejected. No common isoquant maps can be constructed through points $P$ and $Q$ in figure 3–1.

* The paths of the two different countries differ significantly in land–labor intensity.

The basic problem, therefore, is to break down any changes in the land–labor ratio $(A/L)$ over time or any cross-sectional differences between countries at a particular time into two components. The first such component is the result of ordinary substitution along a given production function in response to a change in the relative prices of labor and land. The second component is the change in the labor–land ratio that results from technical change.

This analysis can be accomplished if factor-demand elasticities or pairwise elasticities of substitution between land and labor are available or can be estimated. In appendix 3–1 we present a two-factor test for induced innovation, developed by Binswanger, that utilizes the concept of pairwise elasticity of substitution. The results of applying this test to the above analysis are presented in tables 3–7 and 3–8.

In table 3–7 we list the elasticities of substitution that would be necessary to explain the entire difference in the observed factor ratios between the two countries by ordinary factor substitution. If this elasticity exceeds a critical value of 1.34, we conclude that the two countries were on production functions characterized by different factor intensities. In table 3–8 we show the elasticities of substitution that would be necessary to explain the entire difference in the observed factor ratios between two time periods (within each country) by ordinary factor substitution. We reject the hypothesis of neutral technical change when this value exceeds the critical value of 1.34.

The analysis presented in tables 3–7 and 3–8 and in appendix 3–1 enables us to make a clear distinction between four historical paths of technical change. In 1880, the United States and the European countries were apparently on essentially the same production function. Thus, starting from a position quite similar to that of Europe, United States agricultural technology developed in a strongly labor-saving direction, particularly after 1930.

Great Britain also experienced strong labor-saving technical change after 1930, but its technology remains much more labor intensive than United States technology.

Continental Europe experienced almost neutral—possibly slightly labor using—technical change until the 1960s, when productivity growth in France and Denmark became strongly labor saving.

Japan started from an extremely labor-intensive position and has stayed on an essentially neutral path of technical change with the possible exception of the period 1930–1960, when it may have experienced labor-saving

TABLE 3–8. Necessary elasticity of substitution to explain the interperiod changes in land–labor ratios by price effects within each country

| Time Period | United States | Great Britain | France | Germany | Denmark | Japan[a] Land-Price Basis | Japan[a] Land-Rent Basis |
|---|---|---|---|---|---|---|---|
| 1880–1930 | 1.03 | 0.16 | .20 | .04 | b | ... | ... |
| 1890–1930 | ... | ... | ... | ... | ... | c* | .33 |
| 1890–1910 | ... | ... | ... | ... | ... | c* | .33 |
| 1910–1930 | ... | ... | ... | ... | ... | 1.09 | .34 |
| 1930–1960 | 16.5* | c* | .90 | .70 | .70 | c* | ... |
| 1960–1970 | d* | 9.43* | c* | .74 | c* | .40 | ... |

Note: The critical ratio to reject the hypothesis of neutral technical change is $\sigma = 1.34$.

$$\sigma_N = \frac{\text{Percentage change in land/labor ratio between two periods}}{\text{Percentage change of labor price/land price ratio}}$$

with geometric means as a basis for the two percentage changes, that is:

$$\sigma_N = \frac{(A/L)_{i+1} - (A/L)_i}{(P_L/P_A)_i - (P_L/P_A)_{i+1}} \times \sqrt{\frac{(P_L/P_A)_{i+1}(P_L/P_A)_i}{(A/L)_{i+1}(A/L)_i}}$$

where $i = 1880, 1930, 1960, 1970$.

    [a] Data for 1890–1930 are taken from table 3–10 and data for 1930–1960 from table 3–1.
    [b] Land–labor ratio declined very slightly, but price declined as well.
    [c] Price ratio and land–labor ratio rose, which implies labor-saving technical change. (No common isoquant map can be constructed through P and Q in figure 3–1 in this case.)
    [d] No price change; technical change labor saving.
    * Significantly labor saving.

technical change. Japanese agricultural technology remains much more labor intensive than United States, British, and French technology.

What do these findings imply for the theory of induced innovation? The simplest version of this theory implies that innovation possibilities are neutral and that the direction of technical change will be biased in such a way as to save the progressively more expensive factor. The data examined in the previous sections of this chapter and the tests of the induced innovation hypothesis presented in this section generally support this proposition. Each of the countries whose history we have examined has developed along a technological path that has been consistent with the country's particular resource endowments at the time the modernization process began and responsive to changes in relative factor prices within the country over time.

On the other hand, we can observe some phenomena that are not consistent with the simple induced innovation hypothesis. Japan may have experienced labor-saving technical change in the face of a rise in the land–labor price ratio between 1930 and 1960. The same possibility holds for Great Britain during that time period and, in the 1960s, for France and Denmark as well. Furthermore, the decline in the price of land compared with the price of labor was less in the United States than in Europe. Yet technical change in the United States was more labor saving than it was in the four European countries.

There are several factors that may account for the less than complete consistency between the induced innovation hypothesis and the observed difference in factor-price and resource-use ratios. First, the two-factor test used in this chapter clearly lacks precision. Second, it is possible that there are fundamental biases in innovation possibilities in the labor-saving direction that were sometimes only partially offset by the technical change induced by rising relative prices of land. A third possibility is that the effect of rising relative prices of land on the direction of technical change was offset by the low cost of borrowing labor-saving technical change from countries that had lower land–labor price ratios. Finally, differential rates of growth in demand may induce technical change through changes in the factor-product price ratios.

Transferring or borrowing technology from a country whose factor-price and factor-use ratios are very different from one's own may have a considerable impact on the borrower. For example, if a country begins the process of modernization from an extremely labor-intensive position, as Japan did in the 1870s and 1880s, the only technologies that it can transfer or borrow from other countries will be more labor saving than any that would be induced by the country's own factor endowments and price ratios. In such a situation, it is unlikely that the inducement process will be able to more than partially offset the combination of fundamental bias and transfer bias during periods of intensive technology transfer.

The possibility that such transfer biases operate—and particularly in respect to mechanical technology, which is less location specific than biological technology—may also explain the several findings of a positive relationship between the ratio of land price to labor price and land area per worker that are reported in table 3–5. Somewhat like Japan, Great Britain from 1930 onward and France after 1960 experienced strong labor-saving biases that were associated with the transfer of United States mechanical technology and that may have overpowered any simple price effects.

We are not able, on the basis of the material presented in this chapter, to provide quantitative estimates of the effect of the fundamental and transfer biases. The problem is addressed, however, by Evenson and Binswanger in chapter 6 and by Binswanger in chapter 7.

## Growth of Demand and Productivity Growth

The model of induced innovation outlined earlier in this chapter focuses primarily on the role of factor prices in directing technical change along alternative factor-intensity paths. No attempt has yet been made to explain the rate of growth of the several partial productivity ratios. In this section we present data that suggest that differential rates of growth in the demand for agricultural commodities among countries have been associated with differential rates of partial productivity growth.

Japan and the United States experienced essentially similar rates of growth in output over the 1880–1970 period. There were, however, substantial differences in rates of growth in output among the four European countries (table 3–2). In 1880, in Germany, France, and the United Kingdom land was almost as expensive in relation to labor as in Japan. These three countries have relied almost entirely on growth of output per hectare as a source of growth in total output, particularly in the years prior to 1930.

Denmark presents a major exception to the general pattern outlined. In 1880, land in Denmark was considerably less expensive in relation to labor than in the other three countries. Yet increases in output per hectare have been at least as important a source of growth in total output in Denmark as in the other three countries. This suggests that the explanation for Denmark's unusual behavior must be sought not so much in factor–factor price relationships as in a more rapid rate of growth in total output than that of the other three countries. The liberal trade policies pursued by both the United Kingdom and Denmark permitted Danish agriculture to respond to the rapid growth in demand for animal products in the United Kingdom.[13] An examination of the German experience suggests that rapid growth in demand has been an important factor in accounting for the more rapid growth of output in German agriculture.

[13] Friedman, "Danish Agricultural Policy."

During the period 1880–1930, relatively high rates of growth in output were associated, in Denmark and Germany, with relatively rapid rates of growth in both output per hectare and output per worker. During this same period, low rates of growth in output were associated with slower rates of growth per hectare and output per worker in France and the United Kingdom. In both Denmark and Germany land area per worker changed very little during this period. The rapid increases in labor productivity in Denmark and Germany resulted from a rate of growth in land productivity that exceeded the rate of growth of the agricultural labor force. The extent to which the more rapid rate of growth of agricultural output in Denmark and Germany, as compared with France and the United Kingdom, was the result of constraints on the demand or the supply side cannot, however, be inferred from the data presented thus far.

In table 3–9 data are presented which permit a comparison between the rates of growth in agricultural output and the estimated rates of growth in domestic demand that have resulted from growth in population and per capita income in the four European countries. In Germany and Denmark, domestic demand and output grew at a relatively rapid rate between 1880 and 1960. In France and the United Kingdom, demand and output grew at

TABLE 3–9. Rates of growth of population, per capita product, agricultural demand, and agricultural output in Germany, Denmark, France, and the United Kingdom, 1880–1960

| Time Period/Category | Germany | Denmark | France | United Kingdom |
|---|---|---|---|---|
| *1880–1960* | | | | |
| Population | 1.07 | 1.06 | 0.20 | 0.70 |
| Per capita product | 1.59 | 1.73 | 1.35 | 1.04 |
| Agricultural demand | 1.54 | 1.58 | 0.61 | 1.01 |
| Agricultural output | 1.45 | 1.82 | 1.08 | 0.77 |
| *1880–1930* | | | | |
| Population | 0.97 | 1.18 | 0.12 | 0.85 |
| Per capita product | 0.95 | 1.77 | 1.47 | 0.80 |
| Agricultural demand | 1.28 | 1.76 | 0.61 | 1.11 |
| Agricultural output | 1.31 | 2.07 | 0.76 | 0.21 |
| *1930–1960* | | | | |
| Population | 1.23 | 0.85 | 0.33 | 0.46 |
| Per capita product | 2.67 | 1.67 | 1.15 | 1.44 |
| Agricultural demand | 1.90 | 1.27 | 0.62 | 0.82 |
| Agricultural output | 1.67 | 1.39 | 1.60 | 1.72 |

Source: For population and per capita product: Simon Kuznets, *Economic Growth of Nations: Total Output and Production Structure* (Cambridge: Harvard University Press, 1971). Data, which are for ten-year periods centered on 1880, 1930, and 1960, were computed from Kuznets' working tables. For agricultural output: table 3–2 in this chapter. Figures for agricultural demand were estimated on the basis of population and income data from Kuznets, *Economic Growth*, assuming an income elasticity of demand of 0.33 for 1880–1930 and of 0.25 for 1930–1960.

relatively slow rates. The effects, on Denmark and the United Kingdc
these differential rates of growth in domestic demand were further rein:
by Denmark's role as a supplier of livestock and dairy products to the E...g....
market.

From the data presented in table 3–9 and from our earlier discussion, it is
possible to draw some inferences concerning the role played by constraints
on both the demand and the supply sides in the rate and direction of agricultural productivity growth in the four European countries. On the basis
of the data it seems reasonable to hypothesize that in France the most
serious contraints on both output and productivity growth between 1880 and
1930 were associated with the slow growth in domestic demand for the output of French agriculture. In the United Kingdom, productivity growth was
apparently inadequate to permit home agriculture to compete effectively
with imports from Denmark, Eastern Europe, and the new continents.
Agricultural output expanded even more slowly than did growth in demand.

In Germany, a more rapid growth in domestic demand was sufficient to
press against the domestic capacity to produce in spite of relatively rapid
growth in land productivity. And in Denmark, it seems likely that growth in
domestic demand and in overseas markets, particularly in the United
Kingdom, was sufficiently rapid for constraints on the supply side to limit
the rate of growth of agricultural output.

During the period 1930–1960 several new patterns emerged. In the United
Kingdom, agriculture began to respond to the growth of domestic demand.
Increases in output per hectare and per worker permitted the rate of growth
of agricultural output to rise more than twice as rapidly as the rate of growth
in demand. After World War II, French agriculture made a dynamic response
to the opportunities for growth opened up by the liberalization of trade after
World War II and by the formation of the European Economic Community
(EEC), and responded particularly to the rapid growth in demand for
agricultural commodities in Germany. In Denmark, the rate of growth of
total output and the rate of growth of output per worker fell below the rates
achieved during 1880–1930.

The data examined in this section suggest that differential rates of growth
in demand and in output have induced differential patterns of productivity
growth. The case for this argument is most clear-cut in the case of France. It
has been argued that during most of the nineteenth century the static nature
of French agriculture was a major source of retardation in overall French
economic development.[14] However, it seems very likely that during the

[14] See Newell, "Agricultural Revolution," p. 698; Tom Kemp, "Structural Factors
in the Retardation of French Economic Growth," *Kyklos* 15 (1962): 326–50; A. Whitney
Griswold, *Farming and Democracy* (New Haven: Yale University Press, 1948), pp. 86–
127. See also O'Brien and Keyder, "Economic Growth in Britain and France"; "Fundamental differences between British and French farming are not to be found in yields per

period 1880–1930, the primary retardant of growth in output and productivity in French agriculture was the slow growth in domestic demand for such output that was associated with slow expansion of employment in the industrial sector. During this period the "inefficient" French peasant increasingly provided the urban-industrial sector with more food per capita at lower real prices with little help from public investment in either physical or institutional infrastructure in rural areas.[15] The data presented in tables 3–1, 3–2, and 3–9 clearly cast considerable doubt on the structural explanations that have been offered for the slow growth in French agriculture after 1880. As soon as the constraints on demand were released after World War II, the structural constraints that had been associated with small-scale peasant organization ceased to be a serious barrier to rapid growth of output and productivity.

The data presented in this chapter do not represent a sufficient test of the role of demand in the process of induced innovation. They do suggest that if the induced innovation hypothesis is to be tested adequately against historical data, it must be extended to include the effects of changing differential rates of growth in demand in addition to the effects of differential resource endowments. Except for the work of Jacob Schmookler and Raymond Vernon, the induced innovation literature has generally focused on the effects of differences in resource endowments and of relative factor prices.[16] However, factor proportions are technically independent of factor–product price ratios only if the production function is linear and homogeneous or if all factor supply functions have similar elasticities.[17]

---

acre or techniques of cultivation or indeed in capital output ratios but between an institutional framework flexible enough to hold labor with a relatively low marginal product and the British system of tenant farming which compelled redundant and underemployed labor to migrate to towns." (p. 56)

[15] Wade, "Institutional Determinants," pp. 224–43.

[16] Jacob Schmookler, *Invention and Economic Growth* (Cambridge: Harvard University Press, 1966), pp. 66, 67, 176; Raymond Vernon, "International Investment and International Trade in the Product Cycle," *Quarterly Journal of Economics* 80 (May 1966): 190–207.

[17] The impact of the growth of demand on the rate of technical change is explored more formally for the U.S. economy in chapter 9.

APPENDIX 3–1

*A Two-Factor Test of Induced Innovation*

The basic task in designing a test for induced innovation is to divide any change in the labor–land ratio over time or any cross-sectional difference between countries at a particular time into (a) a component that results from ordinary price substitution and (b) a component that is the result of technical change. This can be done if factor demand elasticities (or elasticities of substitution) of the production processes are available or can be estimated.

The argument is as follows: First, differentiate the labor–land ($A/L$) ratio totally with respect to factor prices.

$$d\left(\frac{A}{L}\right) = \left(\frac{1}{L}\frac{\partial A}{\partial P_A} - \frac{A}{L^2}\frac{\partial L}{\partial P_A}\right)dP_A + \left(\frac{1}{L}\frac{\partial A}{\partial P_L} - \frac{A}{L^2}\frac{\partial L}{\partial P_L}\right)dP_L$$

$$+ \left(\frac{1}{L}\frac{\partial A}{\partial P_M} - \frac{A}{L^2}\frac{\partial L}{\partial P_M}\right)dP_M \qquad (A–1)$$

where $A$ = land, $L$ = labor, and $M$ = machinery. If there are more factors of production, then each additional factor will add a price-change term of the same form as the term in $dP_M$.

Converting (A–1) into elasticities leads to

$$d\log\left(\frac{A}{L}\right) = (\eta_{AA} - \eta_{LA})\,d\log P_A - (\eta_{LL} - \eta_{AL})\,d\log P_L$$

$$+ (\eta_{AM} - \eta_{LM})\,d\log P_M \qquad (A–2)$$

In equation (A–2), $d\log(A/L)$ gives the change of the land–labor ratio that results from the changes in prices. However, the total change in this ratio is $d\log(A/L)^*$, which includes the effect of technical change. This total change in the factor ratio can be decomposed as follows:

$$d\log\left(\frac{A}{L}\right)^* = \partial\log\left(\frac{A}{L}\right) + R \qquad (A–3)$$

where $R$ is the residual change of the factor ratio due to technical change. If $R > 0$, technical change has been labor saving and if $R < 0$, change has been land saving. $R$ can, of course, be computed as

$$R = d\log\left(\frac{A}{L}\right)^* - d\log\left(\frac{A}{L}\right) \qquad (A–4)$$

In undertaking the present test we confront the problem that only land and labor prices are available on an internationally comparative basis. As a result, the test will be based only on changes in $P_A$ and $P_L$ rather than on changes in all factor prices. How serious will be the biases that result from neglecting other prices? No bias will occur if the production function is separable between $A$ and $L$, on the one hand, and all other factors, on the other, that is, if the following condition holds:[18]

$$(\eta_{Ai} - \eta_{Li}) = 0 \qquad \text{for} \quad i \neq A, L \tag{A-5}$$

Clearly we cannot expect this to hold, and the estimates of factor demand elasticities of U.S. agriculture presented in table 7–5 of chapter 7 provide evidence that the agricultural production function is not separable in this way. However, as long as the differences in factor demand elasticities with respect to $P_A$ and $P_L$ are much larger than those with respect to other prices, the bias will be small.

From table 7–5 (chapter 7, appendix 7–2) we obtain the following values:

$$
\begin{aligned}
\eta_{AA} - \eta_{LA} &= -.3664 & \eta_{AM} - \eta_{LM} &= .0536 \\
\eta_{LL} - \eta_{AL} &= -.9722 & \eta_{AF} - \eta_{LF} &= .1634 \\
& & \eta_{AO} - \eta_{LO} &= .8234
\end{aligned}
$$

where $F$ stands for fertilizer and $O$ for all "other" inputs, such as pesticides, buildings, intermediate agricultural products, and the like.

Indeed, the own price factors are much larger than those for machinery and fertilizer. This is not the case for "other" inputs, whose price, therefore, could have a strong influence on the factor ratio.[19]

However, it is almost impossible to make price comparisons for "other" inputs on an international basis. Because of the possibility that the biases may be large, a very wide confidence interval has been adopted in the test that follows. We consider the test to be a fairly blunt instrument, incapable of making very fine distinctions. In chapter 7 a more powerful, many-factor

---

[18] E. R. Berndt and L. R. Christensen, "The Internal Structure of Functional Relationships: Separability, Substitution and Aggregation," *Review of Economic Studies* 40 (1973): 403–10.

[19] It may appear contradictory that machinery and fertilizer prices should have so little impact on land–labor ratios as is implied by the small differences in the factor demand elasticities, particularly because in figure 3–1 we hypothesize *mechanical technology* to have a strong impact on the land–labor ratio. However, the lack of impact that results from near fulfillment of the condition in equation (A–5) refers to the impact of a change in machinery prices on the land–labor ratio along a *static production function*, whereas the relationship hypothesized in figure 3–1 relates to changes in land–labor ratios brought about by a change in mechanical technology. And we have no doubt that mechanical technical change pulls the isosurface of the production function in a labor-saving direction regardless of the substitutability relationship along a given production function. Similarly, biological technical change will generally pull the isosurface in a neutral or labor-using direction regardless of whether the fertilizer price has a strong impact on the land–labor ratio along a given production function.

test for the U.S. is developed that takes all factor prices into account in the manner of equation (A–2). Data are not available, however, to utilize the many-factor test of chapter 7 for the cross-sectional analysis.

Equation (A–2) is expressed in terms of logarithmic changes of absolute prices. However, in an international comparison we can only compare relative prices, and therefore it is necessary to use the concept of a pairwise elasticity of substitution rather than of elasticities of factor demand. Mundlak[20] gives the expression

$$\frac{\partial \log A/L}{\partial \log P_L/P_A} = \sigma_{AL} = \frac{(\eta_{AA} - \eta_{LA}) \, d \log P_A - (\eta_{LL} - \eta_{AL}) \, d \log P_L}{d \log P_L - d \log P_A}$$

$$(A\text{--}6)$$

which is simply the first two terms of equation (A–2) divided by the logarithmic change of the relative price ratio. A test based on the pairwise elasticity of substitution is thus clearly equivalent to the general framework of such tests based on factor demand elasticities.

The elasticity of substitution test is somewhat complicated by absolute efficiency differences between periods or countries. Consider figure 3–1 (left). Assume that $P$ and $Q$ represent the input–output combinations in two different time periods in the same country (or in two different countries at the same time). Further assume that $BB$ and $CC$ represent the respective factor-price ratios in the two time periods (or the two countries). $Q$ has both a higher land–labor ratio than $P$ and a lower relative land price. Now, construct a homothetic isoquant map which is tangent to $BB$ at $P$ and tangent to $CC$ at $Q$. These would be the two production functions if the factor ratio change between $P$ and $Q$ could be explained by ordinary factor-price substitution and neutral technical change over time (or equality of factor intensities of the production functions in two countries at a given time). The pairwise elasticity of substitution on this isoquant map can be measured from the factor ratios and factor-price ratios (see notes to tables 3–7 and 3–8). These elasticities indicate the *necessary elasticity of substitution* $\sigma_N$ to explain factor ratio differences by factor-price ratio differences. Suppose now that we have an econometric estimate of an elasticity of substitution for agriculture $\hat{\sigma}$, and that isoquants with $\hat{\sigma}$ tangent to $BB$ at $P$ and to $CC$ at $Q$ would look like $I_0$ and $I_1$ instead of $I_0^*$ and $I_1^*$. The shift of $I_0$ to $I_1$ represents a labor-saving technical change over time (or true factor-intensity differences between two countries at a given time). Hence, if $\sigma_N$ is sufficiently larger than $\hat{\sigma}$ we can reject the hypotheses of neutral technical change or equal factor intensities.

Estimates of a pairwise elasticity of substitution between land and labor

[20] Yair Mundlak, "Elasticities of Substitution and the Theory of Derived Demand," *Review of Economic Studies* 35 (April 1968): 225–36.

TABLE 3–10. Divergent land–labor ratios obtained on basis of land-price or land-rent data, Japan, 1890–1940

| Year | Male Wage Rate (Yen) (1) | Land Price (Yen per *tan*) (2) | Land Rent (Yen per *tan*) (3) | Land Price/ Daily Wage [(2)/(1)] Absolute (4) | Land Price/ Daily Wage [(2)/(1)] Index (5) | Land Rent/ Daily Wage [(3)/(1)] Absolute (6) | Land Rent/ Daily Wage [(3)/(1)] Index (7) |
|---|---|---|---|---|---|---|---|
| 1890 | 0.172 | 37.4 | 5.09 | 217.4 | 100 | 29.6 | 100.0 |
| 1900 | 0.371 | 81.84 | 7.19 | 220.6 | 101 | 19.4 | 65.5 |
| 1910 | 0.469 | 150.0 | 10.24 | 319.8 | 147 | 21.8 | 73.7 |
| 1920 | 1.470 | 372.3 | 23.87 | 253.3 | 117 | 16.2 | 54.7 |
| 1930 | 1.098 | 297.5 | 14.00 | 270.9 | 125 | 12.8 | 43.2 |
| 1940 | 1.736 | 398.2 | 24.71 | 229.4 | 106 | 14.2 | 48.0 |

Source: Kazushi Ohkawa, Miyohei Shinohara, and Mataji Umemura, eds., *Estimates of Long Term Economic Statistics of Japan Since 1868*, vol. 9 (Tokyo: Toyo Keizai Shinposha, 1966). For column (1): Table 34, col. (3); five-year average, centered on the years shown, except for 1890. For column (2): Table 34, col. (9), price of paddy fields, and col. (10), price of upland fields, weighted by proportionate amounts of paddy and upland fields in total arable land as shown in Table 32, cols. (13) and (14); five-year moving averages, except for 1890 and 1900. Prices differ slightly from those shown in table 3–11 of this chapter because in the present table the same source is used for both land-rent and land-price data, and price is expressed per *tan* rather than per hectare. For column (3): Table 34, cols. (12) and (13); computed by the same procedure as for column (2) but based on paddy and upland field rents. Prior to 1890, neither land-price nor land-rent data are available; after 1943, only land-price data are available.

are not available in the literature. However, estimates of a full set of factor demand elasticities for the U.S. are available in Binswanger,[21] and we can use Mundlak's formula (A–6) to compute the pairwise elasticity of substitution from the elasticities of factor demand.[22]

[21] Hans P. Binswanger, "A Cost Function Approach to the Measurement of Factor Demand Elasticities and Elasticities of Substitution," *American Journal of Agricultural Economics* 56 (May 1974): 377–86. See also chapter 7, appendix 7–2.

[22] As can be seen from equation (A–6), given factor demand elasticities, the size of $\sigma_{ij}$ depends on the extent to which the factor-price ratio change comes from a change in $P_i$ or a change in $P_j$. Table 7–5 (chapter 7, appendix 7–2) gives the following values for the factor demand elasticities of $A$ and $L$:

$$\eta_{AA} = -.3356 \qquad \eta_{AL} = .0613$$
$$\eta_{LA} = .0308 \qquad \eta_{LL} = .9109$$

These values imply the following values for $\hat{\sigma}$:

(a) Change in $P_A$ only                    .37
(b) Change in $P_L$ only                    .96
(c) Equiproportional change in $P_A$ and $P_L$   .67

In the international comparisons the precise source of the change in the factor-price ratio is unknown. Equiproportionality of changes in the two prices involved will be assumed.

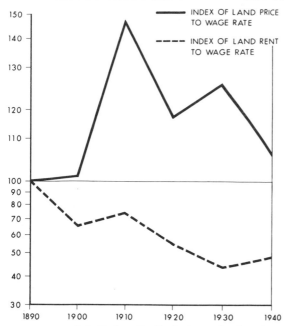

FIG. 3–8. Index of ratios between land costs and wage rates in Japan, based on land-price series and land-rent series. (Source: table 3–10. Note: 1890 = 100.)

DATA

Ideally, the test reported here should be based on wage-rate and land-rent data. Internationally comparable land-rent data are not available, however, and consequently land-price data are used. It should be noted that land-price data may also reflect valuations of land for purposes other than agriculture and thus may not really reflect opportunity cost of land in agriculture as accurately as one might wish. In a cross-sectional international comparison, with land–labor ratios and price ratios diverging by huge factors of up to 100, the errors involved may be small in relation to the observed differences.

On the other hand, when the test is used on a time series within a single country, the problems are greater. Table 3–10 presents data on wage rates, land prices, and land rents in Japan between 1890 and 1940, for which period both land-price and land-rent data are available. The corresponding land-price-to-wage ratio and land-rent-to-wage ratios are shown in the table and in figure 3–8. The divergence of the two series between 1890 and 1910 is extraordinary, but after that the trends are very similar.[23] From 1890 to

[23] It is not clear why the trends in the land-price series and land-rent series differ by so much. Over this early twenty-year period, interest rates were falling and the capital value of the land rent may have been rising. Furthermore, the growing power of tenant unions during this period may have brought about strong resistance to land-rent increases. See Yujiro Hayami, *Sources of Agricultural Productivity Growth in Japan* (Minneapolis: University of Minnesota Press, 1975).

1930, the series based on land prices is rising and the series based on land rents is falling. The tests for biases using the two series will clearly give different results.

For countries other than Japan, such a comparison of trends in land prices and land rents is not available. Therefore, a time series test will be performed using only the land-price series. For Japan, for the period 1890–1930, results with both series will be reported.

CROSS-SECTIONAL COMPARISON OF FACTOR INTENSITIES

The cross-sectional test is based entirely on the data of table 3–1. Table 3–7 presents the necessary elasticities of substitution $\sigma_N$ to explain the differences in factor ratios between any two countries in any given year in terms of shifts, along a common, homothetic isoquant map, that result from the ordinary substitution caused by corresponding factor-price differences. In order to compensate for possible estimation errors, for the errors that arise out of the use of land prices rather than land rents, and for bias in the method of computing the elasticity of substitution, a critical value of 1.34, which is double the estimated value, is utilized. Thus the hypothesis of neutral technical change is rejected only if $\sigma_N$, the elasticity of substitution that would be necessary to account for the observed differences in factor use by price ratios, exceeds the measured value for the United States by a factor of more than 2—that is, if it exceeds the critical value of 1.34. Even though the standard errors of the estimated factor demand elasticities do not warrant it, we must select such a large critical value because of the biases that may arise as a result of changes in the prices of "other" inputs. Throughout the period, the necessary elasticity of substitution exceeded the critical value of 1.34 in the United States–Japan comparison (table 3–7, row 1). From 2.08 in 1880, it declines to 1.35 in 1930 and then rises again to 1.93 and 3.12 in 1960 and 1970, respectively. There can be no doubt that the United States and Japan, throughout the period, were operating on agricultural production functions with clearly distinct factor-intensity characteristics.

In 1880, as we have noted earlier, the United States and the European countries were apparently on essentially the same production function.[24] This is not implausible, given the state of mechanical technology in the late nineteenth century. By 1930, however, differences between the European and United States production functions had clearly emerged, as indicated by the increases in the necessary elasticities of substitution. Even in 1930, however, the hypothesis of similar production functions cannot be rejected for the United States–Germany comparison. By 1960 and 1970, European technology differed very strongly from United States technology because

[24] The test was not performed for Denmark because the data for agricultural land prices in that country include buildings; similar data for the other countries do not include buildings.

technical change became extremely labor saving in the United States after 1930, as we shall see below.

The differences in factor ratios between United States and European agriculture in the twentieth century thus reflect not simply differences in relative factor prices but differences in the production functions available to United States and European farmers.

The results of the test for Europe versus Japan are presented in table 3–7, rows 5–7. In 1880, European technology was much less labor intensive than Japanese technology. However, by 1930 European technology and Japanese technology seem to have approached each other. By 1970, the technologies of the United Kingdom and France had again become clearly distinguishable from Japanese technology. It seems likely, however, that differences in factor ratios between Japanese and German agriculture in 1970 are accounted for primarily by differences in factor prices.

Rows 8 and 9 of table 3–9 show that British technology was almost always less labor intensive than French and German technology, except for Germany in 1930, when the test fails to show a clear technological difference. Row 10 shows that Germany and France were on the same technology until 1960. Thereafter, labor-saving technical change in France moved the two technologies apart, as will be shown below.

## THE TIME SERIES TEST

The intracountry time series test is again based on data of table 3–1, except for Japan between 1890 and 1930, for which period the data of table 3–10 are used. The results are shown in table 3–8.

In the United States, between 1880 and 1930, the land–labor ratio rose from 24.5 to 40.5, while the corresponding price ratio fell from 181 to 115. The necessary elasticity of substitution to explain the decline in $A/L$ by simple effects is 1.03. This falls short of the critical value of 1.34. Therefore, the hypothesis that technical change was neutral during this period cannot be rejected. However, the necessary elasticity of substitution jumps to 16.5 for the period 1930–1960, and in the 1960s the relative price ratio does not change, although the land–labor ratio continues to rise. Therefore, change has been strongly biased in a labor-saving direction since 1930.

In Great Britain, France, Germany, and Denmark the necessary elasticity was very low between 1880 and 1930, which implies neutral technical change. In Denmark, the changes in factor ratios and relative prices even imply labor-using technical change, and that may also be the case in the other European countries, where the necessary elasticities of substitution are exceedingly small.

Between 1930 and 1960 Great Britain experienced labor-saving technical change, although technical change remained neutral in the other European countries. In the 1960s, technical change in Great Britain, Denmark, and France was labor saving, but it remained neutral in Germany. Labor-saving technical change is therefore a recent phenomenon in Europe, and it never occurred at all in Germany.

In Japan, results for the period 1890 to 1930 depend on which series is used for the opportunity cost of land. The land-price series leads to the conclusion that technical change was labor saving, despite an apparent rise in the price of land in relation to the price of labor. This would be inconsistent with the induced innovation hypothesis. However, on a priori grounds, land rent is preferred over land price as a measure of the opportunity cost of land; thus, on the basis of land rent, technical change must have been either neutral or only slightly labor using. In any event, as the test for the subperiods 1880 to 1910 and 1910 to 1920 shows, the results are inconsistent with the hypothesis only up to 1910. From 1945 onward, no land rent data are available, and the test based on land prices shows slightly labor-saving technical change from 1930 to 1960. In the 1970s, technical change in Japan appears again to have been neutral.

APPENDIX 3–2

## Output, Factor Productivity, and Factor Price Data for Six Countries: 1880–1970

Notes that apply to all tables in this appendix (tables 3–11 through 3–16) follow. Notes that are specific to particular tables are appended thereto.

Sources:

Table 3–11: Yujiro Hayami et al., *A Century of Agricultural Growth in Japan* (Minneapolis and Tokyo: University of Minnesota Press and University of Tokyo Press, 1975). For output: Table A–1, column 8, spliced with 1958–1962 value of output in wheat units from Yujiro Hayami and Vernon W. Ruttan, *Agricultural Development: An International Perspective* (Baltimore: Johns Hopkins University Press, 1971), Table A–5. For agricultural land: Hayami et al., *Agricultural Growth*, Table A–4, column 3, multiplied by 1.14, the ratio of agricultural land to arable land in the 1960 Census of Agriculture. For male labor: Table A–3, column 1. For wage rate: Table A–8, column 2; 1890 value used for 1880. For land price: Table A–8, column 4; 1890 value used for 1880.

Table 3–12: For 1880–1968: Adolf Weber, "Productivity Growth in German Agriculture, 1850 to 1970," Staff Paper P73–1 (St. Paul: University of Minnesota, Department of Agricultural and Applied Economics, August 1973). For 1970: Adolf Weber, March 1974 and February 1975: personal communications; based on sources identified in Weber, "Productivity Growth."

Tables 3–13, 3–14, 3–15: For 1880–1960: William W. Wade, "Institutional Determinants of Technical Change and Agricultural Productivity Growth" (Ph.D. diss., University of Minnesota, 1973); for Denmark, Tables D–1, D–4; for France, Tables F–1, F–4; for United Kingdom, Tables G–1, G–4. For 1970: William W. Wade, Spring 1974: personal communication; based on sources identified in Wade, "Institutional Determinants."

Table 3–16: For 1880–1960: Hayami and Ruttan, *Agricultural Development*, Tables A–2 and C–2. For 1970: U.S. Department of Agriculture, *Agricultural Statistics*, 1973, Table 619, "Index of average value per acre," March value; idem, "Changes in Production and Efficiency, 1973," Table 2, "Index of output"; Table 21, "Index of total hours used for farmwork"; Table 25, "Index of farm real estate."

Notes:

Data on output are given in columns 1 and 2, on labor in columns 3 and 4, and on land in columns 5 and 6; columns 7–11 are derived from columns 1–6. Data on price of labor (wage rate) are given in column 12 and on price of land in column 13; column 14 is derived from columns 12 and 13.

One wheat unit is equivalent to the value of one ton of wheat valued at the geometric mean of 1957–62 farm gate prices in the United States, Japan, and India. For aggregation purposes, we have normalized the prices of other commodities by expressing them in terms of wheat-relatives. The method of constructing output measures in terms of wheat units is described in greater detail in Hayami and Ruttan, *Agricultural Development*, pp. 308–25.

M represents the monetary unit of the country described. Data in columns (12) and (13) are in current monetary units.

TABLE 3–11. Japan: Output, factor productivity, and factor price data, 1880–1970

| Year | Output (Y) Wheat Units (000) (1) | Index (1880 =100) (2) | Male Labor (L) Number (000) (3) | Index (1880 =100) (4) | Agricultural Land (A) Hectares (000) (5) | Index (1880 =100) (6) | Wheat Units per Male Year (Y/L) (7) |
|---|---|---|---|---|---|---|---|
| 1880 | 15,706 | 100.0 | 8,332 | 100.0 | 5,493 | 100.0 | 1.89 |
| 1890 | 18,795 | 119.7 | 8,354 | 100.3 | 5,712 | 104.0 | 2.25 |
| 1900 | 21,755 | 138.5 | 8,475 | 101.6 | 6,024 | 109.7 | 2.57 |
| 1910 | 26,755 | 170.3 | 8,527 | 102.3 | 6,466 | 117.7 | 3.14 |
| 1920 | 32,249 | 205.3 | 7,626 | 91.5 | 6,940 | 126.3 | 4.23 |
| 1925 | 32,674 | 208.0 | 7,386 | 88.6 | 6,875 | 125.2 | 4.42 |
| 1930 | 35,079 | 223.3 | 7,631 | 91.6 | 6,931 | 126.2 | 4.60 |
| 1940 | 37,060 | 236.0 | 6,263 | 75.2 | 7,088 | 129.0 | 5.92 |
| 1950 | 34,608 | 220.3 | 7,692 | 92.4 | 6,792 | 123.6 | 4.50 |
| 1960 | 52,436 | 333.9 | 6,232 | 74.8 | 7,048 | 128.3 | 8.41 |
| 1970 | 67,305 | 428.5 | 4,267 | 51.2 | 6,713 | 122.4 | 15.77 |

Note: All figures are five-year averages, centered on the years shown.

TABLE 3–12. Germany: Output, factor productivity, and factor price data, 1880–1970

| Year | Output (Y)[a] Wheat units (000) (1) | Index (1880 =100) (2) | Male Labor (L) Number (000) (3) | Index (1880 =100) (4) | Agricultural Land (A) Hectares (000) (5) | Index (1880 =100) (6) | Wheat Units per Male year (Y/L) (7) |
|---|---|---|---|---|---|---|---|
| 1880 | 45,137 | 100.0 | 5,684 | 100.0 | 36,040[b] | 100.0 | 7.94 |
| 1890 | 52,061 | 115.3 | 5,520 | 97.1 | 35,320 | 98.0 | 9.43 |
| 1900 | 65,927 | 146.1 | 5,452 | 95.9 | 35,094 | 97.4 | 12.09 |
| 1910 | 75,367 | 167.0 | 5,746 | 101.1 | 34,878 | 96.8 | 13.12 |
| 1920 | . . . | . . . | . . . | . . . | . . . | . . . | . . . |
| 1925[c] | 60,458 (72,103) | . . . (159.7) | 4,808 | 84.6 | 29,249 | 81.2 | 12.57 |
| 1930 | 72,688 (86,644) | . . . (192.0) | 4,547 | 80.0 | 29,375 | 81.5 | 15.99 |
| 1938[d] | 83,556 (99,599) | . . . (220.7) | 3,285 | 57.8 | 28,537 | 79.2 | 25.44 |
| 1950[e] | 39,248 (97,947) | . . . (217.0) | 2,258 | 39.7 | 14,033 | 38.9 | 17.38 |
| 1960 | 57,023 (142,550) | . . . (315.8) | 1,613 | 28.4 | 14,239 | 39.5 | 35.34 |
| 1968[f] | 72,073 (180,183) | . . . (399.2) | 1,214 | 21.4 | 13,871 | 38.5 | 59.37 |
| 1970[g] | 74,073 (185,964) | . . . (412.0) | 1,142 | 20.1 | 13,578 | 37.7 | 71.46 |

Note: All figures are five-year averages, centered on the years shown, except as indicated in footnotes (b)–(h).

a Wheat units and indexes shown in parentheses have been adjusted for changes in land area in order to provide a long-term output series for an "undivided Germany."

b For 1880–1882 only.

c For 1925 only.   d For 1938 only.   e For 1950 only.   f For 1968 only.   g For 1970 only.

h Based on five-year average; for the single year 1970, 64.9 (65.4) wheat units.

| Man Years per Wheat Unit $(L/Y)$ (8) | Wheat Units per Hectare $(Y/A)$ (9) | Hectares to Produce One Wheat Unit $(A/Y)$ (10) | Land (Hectares) per worker $(A/L)$ (11) | Wage Rate (M/day) $(P_L)$ (12) | Land Price (M/ha) $(P_A)$ (13) | Days Labor to Buy One Hectare $(P_A/P_L)$ (14) |
|---|---|---|---|---|---|---|
| .530 | 2.86 | .350 | .659 | (.183) | (343) | (1,874) |
| .444 | 3.29 | .304 | .684 | .183 | 343 | 1,874 |
| .390 | 3.61 | .277 | .711 | .371 | 968 | 2,609 |
| .319 | 4.14 | .242 | .758 | .469 | 1,613 | 3,439 |
| .236 | 4.65 | .215 | .910 | 1.472 | 3,882 | 2,637 |
| .226 | 4.75 | .210 | .931 | 1.424 | 3,822 | 2,683 |
| .218 | 5.06 | .198 | .908 | 1.098 | 3,206 | 2,920 |
| .169 | 5.23 | .191 | 1.132 | ... | ... | ... |
| .222 | 5.10 | .196 | .883 | ... | ... | ... |
| .119 | 7.44 | .134 | 1.131 | 484. | 1,429,528 | 2,954 |
| .0634 | 10.03 | .0997 | 1.573 | 1,794. | 2,358,431 | 1,315 |

| Man Years per Wheat Unit $(L/Y)$ (8) | Wheat Units per Hectare $(Y/A)$ (9) | Hectares to Produce One Wheat Unit $(A/Y)$ (10) | Land (Hectares) per worker $(A/L)$ (11) | Wage Rate (M/day) $(P_L)$ (12) | Land Price (M/ha) $(P_A)$ (13) | Days Labor to Buy One Hectare $(P_A/P_L)$ (14) |
|---|---|---|---|---|---|---|
| .1259 | 1.25 | .798 | 6.34 | 1.36 | 1,315 | 967 |
| .1060 | 1.47 | .678 | 6.40 | 1.38 | 1,315 | 953 |
| .0827 | 1.88 | .532 | 6.44 | 1.68 | 1,368 | 814 |
| .0762 | 2.16 | .463 | 6.07 | 2.07 | 1,869 | 903 |
| ... | ... | ... | ... | ... | ... | ... |
| .0795 | 2.07 | .484 | 6.08 | 3.07 | 2,730 | 889 |
| .0626 | 2.47 | .404 | 6.46 | 3.98 | 2,345 | 589 |
| .0393 | 2.93 | .342 | 8.69 | 3.50 | 2,188 | 625 |
| .0575 | 2.80 | .358 | 6.22 | 7.56 | 4,359 | 577 |
| .0283 | 4.01 | .250 | 8.83 | 18.00 | 6,812 | 378 |
| .0168 | 5.20 | .193 | 11.43 | 34.56 | 10,348 | 299 |
| .0140 | 5.40 | .185 | 12.20 | 42.12 | 11,448 | 244 |

TABLE 3–13. Denmark: Output, factor productivity, and factor price data, 1880–1970

| Year | Output (Y) | | Male Labor (L) | | Agricultural Land (A) | | Wheat Units per Man Year (Y/L) |
|---|---|---|---|---|---|---|---|
| | Wheat Units (000) (1) | Index (1880 =100) (2) | Number (000) (3) | Index (1880 =100) (4) | Hectares (000) (5) | Index (1880 =100) (6) | (7) |
| 1880 | 3,408 | 100.0 | 321 | 100.0 | 2,859 | 100.0 | 10.62 |
| 1890 | 3,882 | 113.9 | 326 | 101.6 | 2,913 | 101.9 | 11.91 |
| 1900 | 4,428 | 129.9 | 312 | 97.2 | 2,912 | 101.9 | 14.19 |
| 1910 | 5,837 | 171.3 | 346 | 107.8 | 2,883 | 100.8 | 16.87 |
| 1920 | 6,341 | 186.1 | 395 | 123.1 | 3,172 | 110.9 | 16.05 |
| 1925 | 6,830 | 200.4 | 404 | 125.9 | 3,217 | 112.5 | 16.91 |
| 1930 | 9,518 | 279.3 | 395 | 123.1 | 3,229 | 112.9 | 24.10 |
| 1940 | 9,015 | 264.5 | 391 | 121.8 | 3,218 | 112.6 | 23.06 |
| 1950 | 10,956 | 321.5 | 342 | 106.5 | 3,141 | 109.9 | 32.04 |
| 1960 | 14,378 | 421.9 | 303 | 94.4 | 3,094 | 108.2 | 47.45 |
| 1970 | 15,665 | 459.7 | 166 | 51.7 | 2,975[a] | 104.1 | 94.37 |

Note: All figures are five-year averages, centered on the years shown, except as indicated in footnote (a).

[a] For 1970 only.

TABLE 3–14. France: Output, factor productivity, and factor price data, 1880–1970

| Year | Output (Y) | | Male Labor (L) | | Agricultural Land (A) | | Wheat Units per Man Year (Y/L) |
|---|---|---|---|---|---|---|---|
| | Wheat Units (000) (1) | Index (1880 =100) (2) | Number (000) (3) | Index (1880 =100) (4) | Hectares (000) (5) | Index (1880 =100) (6) | (7) |
| 1880 | 36,589 | 100.0 | 4,970 | 100.0 | 34,594 | 100.0 | 7.36 |
| 1890 | 38,139 | 104.2 | 4,580 | 92.2 | 34,429 | 99.5 | 8.33 |
| 1900 | 40,636 | 111.1 | 5,020 | 101.0 | 35,200 | 101.8 | 8.09 |
| 1910 | 45,457 | 124.2 | 4,910 | 98.8 | 36,799 | 106.4 | 9.26 |
| 1920 | 46,146 | 126.1 | 4,540 | 91.3 | 36,219 | 104.7 | 10.16 |
| 1925 | 49,848 | 136.2 | 4,290 | 86.3 | 36,294 | 104.9 | 11.62 |
| 1930 | 53,464 | 146.1 | 4,040 | 81.3 | 35,566 | 102.8 | 13.23 |
| 1940 | 48,657 | 133.0 | 3,860 | 77.7 | 33,488 | 96.8 | 12.61 |
| 1950 | 51,311 | 140.2 | 3,300 | 66.4 | 33,562 | 97.0 | 15.55 |
| 1960 | 86,093 | 235.3 | 2,580 | 51.9 | 34,681 | 100.3 | 33.37 |
| 1970 | 122,346 | 334.4 | 2,041[b] | 41.1 | 33,035[b] | 95.5 | 59.94 |

Note: All figures are five-year averages, centered on the years shown, except as indicated in footnotes (b) and (c).

[a] Wage rate and land price are given in old Francs through 1960; only 1970 figures are given in new Francs. (One new Franc = 100 old Francs.)

[b] For 1968 only.

[c] For 1970 only.

| Man Years per Wheat Unit $(L/Y)$ (8) | Wheat Units per Hectare $(Y/A)$ (9) | Hectares to Produce One Wheat Unit $(A/Y)$ (10) | Land (Hectares) per Worker $(A/L)$ (11) | Wage Rate (M/day) $(P_L)$ (12) | Land Price (M/ha) $(P_A)$ (13) | Days Labor to Buy One Hectare $(P_A/P_L)$ (14) |
|---|---|---|---|---|---|---|
| .0942 | 1.192 | .839 | 8.91 | 1.6 | 611 | 382 |
| .0840 | 1.333 | .750 | 8.94 | 1.7 | 536 | 315 |
| .0705 | 1.521 | .658 | 9.33 | 2.1 | 536 | 255 |
| .0592 | 2.025 | .494 | 8.33 | 2.8 | 701 | 250 |
| .0623 | 1.999 | .500 | 8.03 | 5.9 | 1,413 | 240 |
| .0592 | 2.123 | .471 | 7.96 | 6.2 | . . . | . . . |
| .0415 | 2.948 | .339 | 8.18 | 5.2 | 1,186 | 228 |
| .0434 | 2.801 | .357 | 8.23 | 7.8 | 1,233 | 158 |
| .0312 | 3.488 | .287 | 9.18 | 21.5 | 2,459 | 114 |
| .0211 | 4.647 | .215 | 10.21 | 35.6 | 5,908 | 166 |
| .0106 | 5.266 | .190 | 17.92 | 71.9 | 12,743 | 177 |

| Man Years per Wheat Unit $(L/Y)$ (8) | Wheat Units per Hectare $(Y/A)$ (9) | Hectares to Produce One Wheat Unit $(A/Y)$ (10) | Land (Hectares) per Worker $(A/L)$ (11) | Wage Rate (M/day)[a] $(P_L)$ (12) | Land Price (M/ha) $(P_A)$ (13) | Days Labor to Buy One Hectare $(P_A/P_L)$ (14) |
|---|---|---|---|---|---|---|
| .1358 | 1.06 | .946 | 6.96 | 2.28 | 1,778 | 780 |
| .1201 | 1.11 | .903 | 7.52 | 2.43 | 1,674 | 689 |
| .1235 | 1.15 | .866 | 7.01 | 2.69 | 1,584 | 589 |
| .1080 | 1.24 | .810 | 7.49 | 3.00 | 1,583 | 528 |
| .0984 | 1.27 | .785 | 7.98 | 11.5 | 2,831 | 246 |
| .0861 | 1.37 | .723 | 8.45 | 14.9 | 4,055 | 272 |
| .0756 | 1.50 | .665 | 8.80 | 20.6 | 5,405 | 262 |
| .0793 | 1.45 | .688 | 8.68 | 33.1 | 5,200 | 157 |
| .0643 | 1.53 | .654 | 10.17 | 479.4 | 125,000 | 261 |
| .0300 | 2.48 | .403 | 13.44 | 1,508.0 | 250,000 | 166 |
| .0167 | 3.70 | .270 | 16.19 | 37.5[c] | 7,960[c] | 212 |

TABLE 3–15. United Kingdom: Output, factor productivity, and factor price data, 1880–1970

| Year | Output (Y) Wheat Units (000) (1) | Index (1880 =100) (2) | Male Labor (L) Number (000) (3) | Index (1880 =100) (4) | Agricultural Land (A) Hectares (000) (5) | Index (1880 =100) (6) | Wheat Units per Man Year (Y/L) (7) |
|---|---|---|---|---|---|---|---|
| 1880 | 20,847 | 100.0 | 1,288 | 100.0 | 18,949 | 100.0 | 16.19 |
| 1890 | 21,696 | 104.1 | 1,235 | 95.9 | 19,331 | 102.0 | 17.57 |
| 1900 | 21,040 | 100.9 | 1,178 | 91.5 | 19,602 | 103.4 | 17.86 |
| 1910 | 21,696 | 104.1 | 1,221 | 94.8 | 19,484 | 102.8 | 17.77 |
| 1920 | 21,696 | 104.1 | 1,154 | 89.4 | 19,121 | 100.9 | 18.80 |
| 1925 | 21,889 | 105.0 | 1,199 | 93.1 | 19,798 | 104.5 | 18.26 |
| 1930 | 23,163 | 111.1 | 1,151 | 89.4 | 19,611 | 103.5 | 20.12 |
| 1940 | 27,332 | 131.1 | 1,079 | 83.8 | 19,453 | 102.7 | 25.33 |
| 1950 | 31,502 | 151.1 | 985 | 76.5 | 19,518 | 103.0 | 31.98 |
| 1960 | 38,605 | 185.2 | 853 | 66.2 | 19,894 | 105.0 | 45.26 |
| 1970 | 49,203 | 236.0 | 562 | 43.6 | 18,831[a] | 99.4 | 87.55 |

Note: All figures are five-year averages, centered on the years shown, except as indicated in footnote (a).

[a] For 1970 only.

TABLE 3–16. United States: Output, factor productivity and factor price data, 1880–1970

| Year | Output (Y) Wheat Units (000) (1) | Index (1880 =100) (2) | Male Labor (L) Number (000) (3) | Index (1880 =100) (4) | Agricultural Land (A) Hectares (000) (5) | Index (1880 =100) (6) | Wheat Units per Man Year (Y/L) (7) |
|---|---|---|---|---|---|---|---|
| 1880 | 103,711 | 100.0 | 7,959 | 100.0 | 202,000 | 100.0 | 13.0 |
| 1890 | 123,416 | 119.0 | 9,142 | 115.0 | 235,000 | 116.4 | 13.5 |
| 1900 | 160,753 | 155.0 | 9,880 | 124.1 | 318,000 | 157.4 | 16.3 |
| 1910 | 170,087 | 164.0 | 10,359 | 130.2 | 333,000 | 164.9 | 16.4 |
| 1920 | 186,681 | 180.0 | 10,221 | 128.4 | 363,000 | 179.7 | 18.3 |
| 1925 | 199,126 | 192.0 | 9,818 | 123.4 | 350,000 | 173.3 | 20.3 |
| 1930 | 211,571 | 204.0 | 9,414 | 118.3 | 381,000 | 188.6 | 22.5 |
| 1940 | 240,611 | 232.0 | 8,487 | 106.6 | 411,000 | 203.5 | 28.4 |
| 1950 | 295,578 | 285.0 | 6,352 | 79.8 | 451,000 | 223.3 | 46.5 |
| 1960 | 352,619 | 340.0 | 3,973 | 49.9 | 435,000 | 215.3 | 88.8[a] |
| 1970 | 417,957 | 403.0 | 2,655 | 33.4 | 426,000 | 210.9 | 157.4 |

Note: All figures are five-year averages, centered on years shown.

[a] Differs from Hayami and Ruttan, *Agricultural Development*, Table B–1, column 6, p. 327: value in Table B–1 is incorrect. For 1960 U.S. agricultural output in wheat units, see Table A–5. For 1960 number of male workers, see Table C–2, column (U4).

| Man Years per Wheat Unit $(L/Y)$ (8) | Wheat Units per Hectare $(Y/A)$ (9) | Hectares to Produce One Wheat Unit $(A/Y)$ (10) | Land (hectares) per Worker $(A/L)$ (11) | Wage Rate (M/day) $(P_L)$ (12) | Land Price (M/ha) $(P_A)$ (13) | Days Labor to Buy One Hectare $(P_A/P_L)$ (14) |
|---|---|---|---|---|---|---|
| .0618 | 1.10 | .909 | 14.71 | 2.6 | 2,588 | 995 |
| .0569 | 1.12 | .891 | 15.65 | 2.5 | 2,174 | 870 |
| .0559 | 1.07 | .932 | 16.64 | 2.6 | 2,065 | 794 |
| .0563 | 1.11 | .898 | 15.96 | 2.8 | 2,065 | 738 |
| .0532 | 1.13 | .881 | 16.57 | 7.9 | 1,720 | 218 |
| .0548 | 1.11 | .904 | 16.51 | 5.5 | 1,512 | 275 |
| .0497 | 1.18 | .847 | 17.04 | 5.8 | 1,096 | 189 |
| .0395 | 1.41 | .712 | 18.03 | 7.2 | 1,730 | 240 |
| .0313 | 1.61 | .620 | 19.82 | 17.1 | 4,051 | 237 |
| .0221 | 1.94 | .515 | 23.32 | 28.8 | 6,076 | 211 |
| .0114 | 2.61 | .383 | 33.51 | 55.5[a] | 11,260 | 203 |

| Man Years per Wheat Unit $(L/Y)$ (8) | Wheat Units per Hectare $(Y/A)$ (9) | Hectares to Produce One Wheat Unit $(A/Y)$ (10) | Land (Hectares) per Worker $(A/L)$ (11) | Wage Rate (M/day) $(P_L)$ (12) | Land Price (M/ha) $(P_A)$ (13) | Days Labor to Buy One Hectare $(P_A/P_L)$ (14) |
|---|---|---|---|---|---|---|
| .07670 | .513 | 1.95 | 25.4 | .90 | 163 | 181 |
| .07410 | .526 | 1.90 | 25.7 | .95 | 132 | 139 |
| .06150 | .506 | 1.98 | 32.2 | 1.00 | 129 | 129 |
| .06090 | .511 | 1.96 | 32.1 | 1.35 | 213 | 158 |
| .05480 | .514 | 1.94 | 35.5 | 3.30 | 352 | 107 |
| .04930 | .569 | 1.76 | 35.6 | 2.35 | 269 | 114 |
| .04450 | .555 | 1.80 | 40.5 | 2.15 | 247 | 115 |
| .03530 | .585 | 1.71 | 48.4 | 1.60 | 180 | 113 |
| .02150 | .655 | 1.53 | 71.0 | 4.50 | 389 | 86 |
| .01130 | .811 | 1.23 | 109.5 | 6.60 | 711 | 108 |
| .00635 | .981 | 1.02 | 160.5 | 11.58 | 1,247 | 108 |

# II

*The Theory of Induced
Technical Change*

# FOUR

# The Microeconomics of Induced
# Technical Change

HANS P. BINSWANGER

IN this chapter we return to the task of building microfoundations for a theory of induced innovation that is subsumed under a broader theory of endogenous technical change that will be capable of answering the set of policy questions discussed in the first section of chapter 2. We will present a general discussion of the issues involved, together with a series of illustrative figures. The formal models that underlie and prove the statements of this chapter are presented in chapter 5, which concentrates on model-building questions.

The first section of this chapter discusses research issues: research as a sampling process and interactions between basic and applied research. The second section, on the role of factor prices, presents the basic induced innovation model. This model is very simple and provides answers to two questions that loomed large in chapter 2. The answer to the first question is yes: a society can gain in efficiency (that is, increase its economic growth) by deliberately choosing a technical change bias such as will save the progressively more expensive factor of production. It follows from this that from the society's point of view (and thus for all public sector research) it is desirable to take factor scarcities into account in determining the direction of technical change. And the answer to the second question follows as well: a private firm that undertakes research for its own production process will also have an incentive to take factor prices into account in determining the amount and direction of its research effort.

I would like to thank N. S. Jodha and J. G. Ryan for their very helpful comments on preliminary drafts of this chapter.
For an earlier attempt to deal with many of the issues discussed in this chapter see Hans P. Binswanger, "A Microeconomic Approach to Induced Innovation," *Economic Journal* 84 (December 1974): 940–58.

In the third section of this chapter, on the role of output prices, we ask the same two questions but with respect to the price of final output. The section shows that for both society and the individual firm it makes sense to concentrate research resources on commodities with higher prices and larger markets.

Sections 2 and 3 do not answer the question whether in a market economy the outcome of research decisions of all participants will in fact achieve, for all products and in the aggregate, a rate and bias of technical change consistent with maximizing production and growth. The fourth section, on research incentives and the role of market structure, addresses this question. First we examine the problem of how firm size, monopoly power, and patent laws affect the induced innovation mechanism. Then we consider the problem of how the mechanism works when research is not done by the user of the innovation but rather by a firm that supplies intermediate or capital inputs to the final producer, recovering its research expenditures through the sales price of such inputs.

Throughout the chapter, technologies are said to be efficient if they lead to an optimal increase in production measured by factor and goods prices that are assumed to reflect true factor and good scarcities. A few comments with respect to this procedure are in order. In the absence of price distortions resulting from policy interventions or market imperfections, existing factor and goods prices in a market economy reflect both their supply conditions and the way they are valued by consumers. The preferences of different consumers are reflected in proportion to their purchasing power. Hence prices are influenced by the distribution of income between countries, on the one hand, and within countries, on the other. Less developed countries (LDCs) are clearly not willing to accept the international distribution of income and may therefore object to international prices as a standard of valuation of commodities and factors of production. However, international prices still determine trading opportunities; a country can maximize different objective functions by first maximizing production with respect to these prices and then exchanging goods in the international market to adjust consumption to its own objective function.[1] Thus international prices are relevant in judging production efficiency even for the LDCs.[2]

### Research as a Sampling Process

In their chapter on "A Stochastic Model of Applied Research," Robert Evenson and Yoav Kislev treat applied research as a sampling

[1] For a review of these issues, see Partha Dasgupta, Amartya Sen, and Stephen Marglin, *Guidelines for Project Evaluation*, Project Formulation and Evaluation Series no. 2 (New York: United Nations Industrial Development Organization, 1972).

[2] If international prices fluctuate widely, some average value will have to be taken to evaluate efficiencies, and price stabilization policies around this level may be pursued nationally and/or internationally.

process, using seed research as an example.[3] They assume that at any given time, nature and the states of basic sciences and of plant breeding technology determine a probability distribution of potential yields. This distribution defines the potential payoffs to applied research. The applied researchers cannot affect the parameters of this distribution, but changes in basic knowledge or in plant breeding techniques can alter these parameters and will increase the potential payoffs to applied research.[4] Basic research, therefore, is *supportive* or *complementary* to applied research. Although it has no direct payoffs, it increases the potential payoffs of applied research.

Applied research is then viewed as drawing successive samples from a given distribution of potential yields.[5] Once a sample of size $m$ is drawn, the research payoff ($V$) is the difference between the sample point with the highest yield $Y_1$ and the yield of the currently used variety $\bar{Y}$, that is,

$$V|_m = Y_1 - \bar{Y} \tag{1}$$

All other sample points, except the highest yielding one, are immaterial and are disregarded. The *expected research payoff* is the first-order statistic, or the largest yield increase of the sample. The *ex ante* expected payoff can therefore be defined as the expected first-order statistic of a sample of size $m$. The payoff, therefore, is a function of the mean $\mu$ and the variance $\sigma^2$ of the distribution of potential yields and of the sample size $m$.

$$E(V) = h(\mu, \sigma^2, m) \tag{2}$$

The expected payoff $E(V)$ is an increasing function of the sample size (because the expected first-order statistic of a sample increases with its size), but the marginal payoffs decline as the sample size increases.[6] The research itself is subject to diminishing returns. Similarly, the research payoff rises with increases in the mean and the variance of the distribution of potential yields.[7]

[3] Robert Evenson & Yoav Kislev, *Agricultural Research and Productivity* (New Haven: Yale University Press, 1975).

[4] We do not deal here with the skill level of the researcher. However, the distribution that any researcher can expect does depend on his skills. His knowledge of the subject area determines the accuracy of his expectation and the efficiency of his sampling (experimental) techniques. The ways in which research skills affect research investment strategy are discussed in chapter 6.

[5] In plant breeding, selection occurs at several stages in the development of a new variety, a process which can take many years. In this simple model, the whole breeding cycle is considered as one single sampling process.

[6] This is true for all distributions with finite variance.

[7] Formally, these statements mean:

$$\partial E(V)/\partial m \geq 0 \quad , \quad \partial^2 E(V)/\partial m^2 \leq 0$$
$$\partial E(V)/\partial \mu \geq 0 \quad , \quad \partial^2 E(V)/\partial \sigma^2 \geq 0$$

Note that in this model the researcher cannot affect the distributional parameters $\mu$ and $\sigma^2$. Of course, when the researcher actually carries out his research, he may, in the process, form a new research payoff function with different parameters. However, this influences

The cost of research is the cost of drawing successive samples from the distribution. Suppose that sampling costs are constant, that is, that the price of each additional sample drawn is constant (this is not the assumption of the Evenson–Kislev model). A research administrator who disregards risk and simply wants to maximize the expected return from the research (i.e., maximize expected research benefits less research costs) will equate the marginal returns with the marginal cost of research. But now the scale of output to which the yield increase applies becomes important because the per-hectare yield increase is multiplied by the size of the area in which the crop is grown.

If one solves such a model of applied research, it is immediately clear that the optimal sample size will be larger, the larger the area planted to the variety, the larger the mean $\mu$ of the distribution of potential yields, and the larger the variance $\sigma^2$ of this distribution.[8] Thus, although research, as a process, is itself subject to diminishing returns, it is subject to increasing returns with respect to the size of the output to which it is applied. This is a common characteristic of investments in improved information.

There are two sources of uncertainty in a sampling approach to applied research. The distribution of potential yield increases may be well defined, but it is more likely that the decision maker will not know it with certainty. He may have formed expectations about it from his knowledge of previous research and of the state of the arts. It should therefore be viewed as a subjective probability distribution of potential yield increases whose parameters have an expected mean and variance. The other source of uncertainty is the variance of the expected first-order statistic, which would exist even if the underlying distribution were known with certainty. Evenson and Kislev took account of this second source of uncertainty by building their models as Markov chain models. However, they assumed that a distribution is known with certainty. Also, they did not incorporate the possibility of risk aversion by the decision makers.

In the models presented in the following two chapters, the above two sources of uncertainty will be largely neglected by assuming, as a first

---

not his *ex ante* decision but his research decision for the next period. This point is discussed further in chapter 5.

[8] Suppose the size of the region in which the new variety can be used is $S$, while the expected yield increase per hectare is $E(V)$. Then total expected benefits are $S \cdot E(V)$, and the research administrator maximizes the following for total benefits:

$$T = S \cdot E(V) - mP^m$$

where $P^m$ are research costs per sample unit. The first-order condition for this maximizing problem is:

$$S\delta \frac{E(V)}{\partial m} = P^m$$

which leads directly to the conclusions stated in the text.

approximation, that decision makers are risk neutral and maximize expected net returns from research over a subjective probability distribution.[9]

Another point should be noted here. In such an economic model of research, no researcher will ever attempt to achieve the highest yield in the distribution that is technically possible. With positive sampling costs, sampling will never be carried out to the point where expected marginal payoffs become zero, or $\partial E(V)/\partial m = 0$, a point that might be called the *scientific frontier*.[10] It is therefore inaccurate to describe a technology as being on a technological frontier in the sense that no further improvements are possible at the present time. How close a researcher will attempt to come to the scientific frontier depends on research costs and on the scale of output to which the innovation will apply.

Under constant costs of research, and with unchanging distributional parameters over time, the model presented above has no dynamic extension. If we assume, for the moment, that the expected yield advance $E(V)$ is realized in the sampling process, then no additional economic payoffs can be had from further sampling in the next period.[11]

Consider figure 4–1, where $\overline{Y}$ is the yield of the existing variety and $Y_1$ the yield found in the first period's research with the optimal sample size $m$. But $Y_1$ now becomes the reference yield with respect to which further yield improvements have to be found. Clearly, the probability of finding any yield increase beyond $Y_1$ is much smaller than the probability of finding an increase beyond $\overline{Y}$. A much larger sample will now be needed to find any yield increase at all. Although this is not technically impossible, it makes no economic sense to search further. A sample size identical to that used in the first period will (on the average) yield zero increase over and above the yield gain of the first period. And for any sample size the marginal total benefits of research will be less than research costs because of the diminishing returns to increas-

---

[9] Risk, however, is very important for research policy. If investors are risk averse, they will do less research than is socially optimal. Furthermore, they will prefer low to high risks and, thus, they will prefer applied to basic research. Risk aversion makes it attractive to pool research activities that have low covariances of outcomes in larger organizations, and as a result it affects market structure, among other things. For more detailed discussion of these issues see Kenneth J. Arrow, "Economic Welfare and the Allocation of Resources to Invention," in *The Rate and Direction of Inventive Activity: Economic and Social Factors* (Princeton: Princeton University Press, National Bureau of Economic Research, 1962), pp. 609–25, and Richard R. Nelson, "The Simple Economics of Basic Scientific Research," *Journal of Political Economy* 67 (June 1959): 297–306. [Both of these articles have been reprinted in Nathan Rosenberg, ed., *The Economics of Technological Change* (Harmondsworth, England: Penguin Books, 1971).]

[10] Such a point does not exist if the distribution approaches the horizontal axis asymptotically.

[11] Further benefits would exist only if the actual sampling did not lead to the expected yield increase but not if it exceeded it or met it precisely. Note also that the distribution is still assumed to be unaffected by actual research.

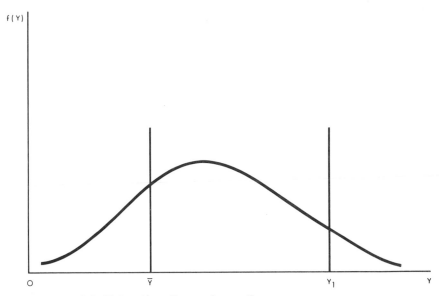

FIG. 4–1. Exhaustion of research payoffs.

ing a sample size beyond the $m$ of the last period. The research potential is therefore *exhausted* in the first period.

In the model of Evenson and Kislev, research costs are a rising function of the sample size in each period. The problem now becomes one of selecting an optimal research strategy for a number of periods, that is, determining a path of optimal $m$'s over time that will maximize the difference between the present values of the benefit stream and the cost stream. These authors show that, as long as the parameters of the yield distribution do not shift, the optimal number of trials will decline over time in such a model and will eventually become zero. Again, for a given distribution of potential yields the research payoffs are exhausted after a while.

The possibility that payoffs to applied research will be rapidly exhausted points to the importance of advances in basic or supporting research for continued research productivity. A scientific research station, therefore, often works on a spectrum of research projects, ranging from almost purely applied research to work on more basic problems. The supporting research can be aimed at changing the mean and/or the variances of the distributions sampled. For the same reason, a breakthrough in basic research or in experimental techniques is often followed by large investments in applied research to exploit the new distribution. It is precisely the gap between scientific knowledge and existing techniques that creates the payoffs to applied research.

In this context it should be noted that if we establish the response of applied research to economic factors, there is no reason why, at least to some extent, such responsiveness should not carry over to basic research as well. Some very basic research in physics is funded by governments because of the hope that a breakthrough will open new avenues for applied research and, thus, lead ultimately to increased productivity. Moreover, the recent energy crisis has led to substantial additional basic investigation of matters such as biological nitrogen fixation and alternative energy sources.[12]

Applied researchers who try to solve economically motivated problems, such as finding high-yielding varieties, do shift to more basic lines of inquiry when they find that they have reached a yield plateau with the given state of knowledge. But if one were to build a model of the accumulation of basic knowledge in a given field or industry, it would be very difficult to separate the basic advances into those directly motivated by economic factors in the industry and those that come about as the result of basic and applied research in other industries or in the fields of supporting and basic sciences. For this reason, the induced innovation models presented in the next few sections will be models of applied research that use Evenson and Kislev's perspective. Note, however, that responsiveness of basic research to economic factors would strengthen rather than weaken the theory. All the models to be presented are based on a simple comparative static framework. Reasons for not considering a full dynamic extension at this time are discussed in the last section of chapter 5.

## The Role of Factor Prices

Ahmad's model of induced innovation was discussed in chapter 2. Provided that the *innovation possibility curve* (IPC) depicted in figure 2–3 exists, the graph alone establishes, from either society's or an individual firm's point of view, the desirability of selecting the direction of technical change in accordance with factor scarcities. The models based on Kennedy's *innovation possibility frontier* (IPF) do the same thing, again, provided an IPF exists. However, the problem with the IPC and the IPF is that they describe innovation possibilities in such an abstract way that they seem very remote from research as it is actually carried out. They do not describe how a researcher can guide his work in a more or less labor-saving direction. If a model is to be used for policy purposes, this choice process has to be characterized. In addition, both models are based on the assumption that a fixed budget constraint exists for total research resources. As a result, the models cannot answer questions about how much of society's resources should be

[12] With respect to the increase in interest in biological nitrogen fixation, see Harold B. Evans, ed. *Enhancing Biological Nitrogen Fixation* (Washington, D.C.: National Science Foundation, June 1975).

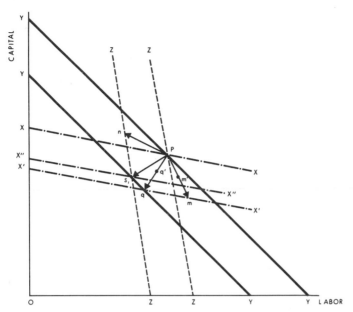

FIG. 4–2. Induced innovation with many possible research activities.

allocated to research and how these resources should be allocated to individual sectors of the economy.

These problems can be overcome if we build the model on the basis of research processes or activities that have a cost and that have specific implications for factor proportions. If we assume that research administrators or firms have a choice between several research activities, each of which affects the factor-intensity characteristics of the production process in a different way, we can set up the model as a portfolio–choice model of research projects. We can then ask how changes in factor prices, scale of output, research costs, goods prices, and market sizes affect the optimal research project mix and how these effects are related to the factor-intensity characteristics of the technology developed with the optimal research mix.[13]

When we are dealing with a fixed production function, a model like the above lends itself easily to graphic analysis. Consider figure 4–2. Point $P$ is the existing input–output combination, and the sets of parallel lines represent factor prices. $XX$ is the price line for relatively cheap labor and expensive

[13] The crucial assumption here is that different research projects have specific implications for factor intensities, that is, that some are clearly labor saving while others are clearly capital saving. In agriculture we can identify such lines relatively easily. Mechanical research usually tends to be labor saving. Research on weedicides is also clearly labor saving because it leads to the elimination of hand weeding. Research on new varieties or on pesticides is either neutral or land saving. Of course, even within the category of mechanical research, different research projects have different factor-saving characteristics; this is true of the other categories of research as well.

capital, and $ZZ$ is the price line for expensive labor and relatively cheap capital; $YY$ represents an intermediate factor price regime. In this graph it is assumed that the firm can alter the input–output ratio by undertaking any of four different research activities, represented by the arrows at $q$, $s$, $n$ and $m$. (In what follows, the letters $q$, $s$, $n$ and $m$ will stand both for the name of a research activity and for its intensity, or level.) These activities are the firm's innovation possibilities. The length of each arrow indicates the distance by which a given research effort moves the input–output combination. Activity $m$ is extremely capital saving, reducing capital requirements but increasing labor requirements. Activity $n$ is extremely labor saving and reduces labor requirements at the expense of increased capital requirements. The intermediate research activities $q$ and $s$ reduce capital and labor requirements respectively but in lesser degrees.

Suppose that for some reason the firm can pursue only one research activity at a time[14] and that the four alternatives described above are the only research approaches available. If labor is cheap (factor price line $XX$), it is quite clear that the relatively labor-using activities $q$ and $m$ will lead to a larger cost reduction than will the labor-saving activities $n$ and $s$. The graph is drawn such that, at $XX$, research activities $m$ and $q$ lead to an identical cost reduction. However, should wage rates fall further from $XX$, activity $m$ would lead to a larger cost reduction and would thus be preferred over $q$, despite the fact that moving from $q$ to $m$ will increase absolute labor requirements. When the relative wage rate rises from $X$ to $Y$, research approaches $s$ and $q$ lead to larger cost reduction than does $m$, that is, extremely labor-using research is eliminated as a possible choice. When the relative wage rate rises even further, to $ZZ$, the relatively less labor-saving activity $q$ is also superseded by $n$ and $s$, and should the relative wage rate rise beyond $ZZ$, $n$ will be preferred over $s$ because it leads to the largest cost reduction.[15]

The impact of changing relative factor prices on the choice of different research approaches is not surprising. After all, the expected benefit from a cost-reducing research project is the sum of reductions in input requirements weighted by the price of each factor, that is, it is the sum of the reduction in labor requirements, weighted by the wage rate, plus the reduction in capital requirements, weighted by the price of capital. Since these prices enter as weights, research projects that reduce primarily the high-priced factors will have higher benefits than those that reduce primarily the requirement of the

[14] In the formal models this assumption is not made.

[15] Note that $s$ and $q$ are technical improvements regardless of the level of factor prices. They always reduce costs, although the degree to which they reduce them depends on the level of factor prices. On the other hand, $n$ and $m$ are not always technical improvements but are technical retrogressions (they increase production costs) under extreme factor prices. When factor prices are $ZZ$, research approach $m$ increases costs rather than reducing them.

low-priced factors, and any research administrator who prefers large over small benefits will notice these differences.

Coming back to figure 4–2, suppose labor is cheap at $XX$ and a firm makes an incorrect decision by choosing research approach $s$ rather than $q$. It thus forfeits a possible cost reduction $X'X''$, measured in terms of capital. If such an error is made for an entire sector or for an economy as a whole, this forfeited cost reduction is a welfare loss.

In figure 4–2 the firm's innovation possibilities are extremely wide, and the direction of technical change is very responsive to factor prices. Suppose, however, that innovation possibilities are biased in a labor-saving direction. This could be either because research activities in the direction of $q$ and $m$ do not exist or because advances in these directions are more difficult to achieve than advances in the labor-saving directions. If research in the directions $q$ and $m$ were more difficult to achieve, then a given advance would require more research resources; the length of their arrows would be shorter. If the arrows ended at $q'$ and $m'$, respectively, the firm would not choose these activities even if wage rates were extremely low, because research activity $s$ would dominate $q'$ and $m'$ at all factor ratios.

In the mathematical models of the next chapter, innovation possibilities such as in figure 4–2 are built into a formal portfolio model of research.[16] To make it simple, the number of research possibilities is reduced to two, but the firm can pursue both of these at the same time and implement the research results of each independently. This will be referred to as the *independence assumption*. Changes in the bias of technical change are achieved by re-allocating research resources from one line to the other.

It is also assumed that returns to each research activity exhibit diminishing returns, which is consistent with the sampling perspective of the last section. In addition, a fixed budget constraint on the amount of research resources is no longer assumed.[17] Innovation possibilities corresponding to these assumptions are shown in figure 4–3.

The arrows $m$ and $n$ represent labor-using and labor-saving research activities, respectively. The advances possible with one unit of research resources allocated to a single line are shown by the length of the arrows from $P$ to $Q$ and $R$. Suppose marginal returns to each research eventually become zero. These points are represented by $U$ and $V$. In this situation, given the independence assumption, any point in the parallelogram $PUSV$ can be achieved, depending on the allocation of research resources to $m$ and $n$. The line $USV$ is the scientific frontier beyond which advances are not possible. Note, however, that a scientific frontier is never empirically observable, because in a model where each unit of research effort has a cost, a firm will

---

[16] The corresponding fixed-proportion model has also been presented in Binswanger, "Microeconomic Approach," pp. 940–58.

[17] All these assumptions are discussed in more detail in chapter 5, pp. 133–4.

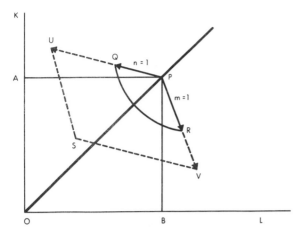

FIG. 4–3. Innovation possibilities of the formal model, with fixed proportions. [Adapted from Hans P. Binswanger, "A Microeconomic Approach to Induced Innovation," *Economic Journal* 84 (December 1974): 944].

never push research up to the point where marginal research payoffs become zero. At most, it will push research to the point where marginal returns from research are equal to marginal research costs. No firm, therefore, will ever be observed on a scientific frontier. If the research budget is constrained to, say, one unit, then the set of achievable points becomes a convex line between $Q$ and $R$. It is convex because of diminishing returns to each research activity. If only half the budget is allocated to each activity, both activities will be in a region of higher marginal returns than if the full budget were allocated to one single activity.

The relationship of this model to Ahmad's model is now fully apparent. A model based on research processes will be similar to Ahmad's model if a budget constraint is assumed. The line $QR$ is Ahmad's IPC with a research budget of one, except that it does not extend beyond $Q$ and $R$.[18] As the innovation possibilities of figure 4–3 can easily be expressed mathematically, it is now possible to approach the microtheory more rigorously.

In the next chapter a more general variable-proportion production function is admitted into the model. Both graphic and mathematical representations become more complex. However, the conclusions to be derived from a variable-proportion model do not differ from the fixed-proportion case. Figure 4–4 shows innovation possibilities with variable proportions graphically. The isoquant II′ represents the initial production function. Research activity $n$ pulls it into a labor-saving direction; $m$ pulls it into a labor-using direction.

[18] It can also be shown that Kennedy's IPF in single periods corresponds to such "isoquants" with fixed budget constraints. For a proof, see Binswanger, "Microeconomic Approach." Note further the $USV$ is not an IPC because at $S$ the research budget is much larger than at either $U$ or $V$.

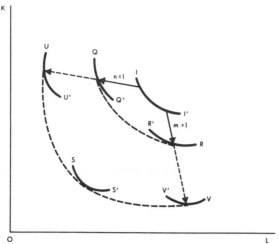

FIG. 4–4. Innovation possibilities of the formal model, with variable proportions.

The isoquants $QQ'$ and $RR'$ are the techniques achievable by allocating the
entire research budget to either one of the activities. Therefore the isoquant
that is the envelope of $QQ'$ and $RR'$ is again an IPC. The isoquants $UU'$ and
$VV'$ are the limiting techniques where marginal research payoffs become zero,
and $SS'$ is the isoquant that results from pushing both research activities up
to the point of zero marginal return simultaneously. The envelope around
the isoquants $UU'$, $SS'$, and $VV'$ is again the scientific frontier. It is not
comparable to an IPC because the research budget needed to achieve $SS'$
is much larger than the one needed to achieve either $UU'$ or $VV'$. Of course
the scientific frontier need not exist if marginal research payoffs never
become zero.

   Once innovation possibilities are described mathematically they can be
built into a model of an innovating firm (or a research institute doing research
for a sector of the economy or for an agricultural region). The first model
assumes the situation of a firm that wants to build a new plant to produce a
fixed output $Y$. The firm has the choice of building a plant of existing
design with an isoquant such as $II'$ or of improving the design by research
through research possibilities such as those of figure 4–4. The firm's research
budget is not fixed, that is, it is not constrained to an IPC such as $QR$ but
can obtain any isoquant within the scientific frontier. Research costs accrue
prior to the building of the plant, but the benefits of research, which are the
discounted expected cost reductions achievable by the project, accrue over
the lifetime of the plant.

   In this first model the output of the desired plant is fixed. (It is relaxed in
a later model.) Once the plant of given capacity is built, capital input is fixed

as well. This implies that labor input is also fixed at the necessary minimum level to produce the output determined by the capacity of the plant unless the plant shuts down. It is only before the plant is built that the firm has costless options of changing capital–labor ratios along isoquants such as $II'$. Thus the first model is similar to a putty-clay model.

Capital is assumed to be measurable in some physical unit whose price is given. Before and after research, the firm can build one unit of capital at a given purchase cost $R$. The expected cost of hiring one laborer, over the lifetime of the plant, is the discounted sum of expected wage payments over the lifetime of the plant. The lifetime of the plant is assumed to be fixed at $T$. Let this discounted stream of wage payments, henceforth simply called discounted wage rate, be

$$\tilde{W} = \sum_{t=0}^{T} W(t) \tag{3a}$$

or, in continuous time notation,

$$\tilde{W} = \int_0^T W(t)e^{-rt}\, dt \tag{3b}$$

where $W(t)$ is the expected wage rate at any given time.

It will be shown that corresponding to an isoquant such as $II'$ there exists a minimum cost function which relates the minimum cost of production $C_0^*$ to the purchase price of capital $R$, the expected discounted labor payments $\tilde{W}$, and the level of output $Y$. It can be written

$$C_0^* = YG_0(R, \tilde{W}) \tag{4}$$

where $Y$ enters multiplicatively if the production function is homogeneous of degree one.[19] The subscript zero refers to the initial isoquant possible without research. The minimum cost of production (exclusive of research costs) with any other isoquant developed by research can also be expressed as such a cost function. For example, we can write

$$C_1^* = YG_1(R, \tilde{W}) \tag{5}$$

where 1 denotes an isoquant after research.

[19] This is based on the theory of duality between cost and production function; see W. E. Diewert, "An Application of the Shephard Duality Theorem: A Generalized Leontief Production Function," *Journal of Political Economy* 79 (May–June 1971): 481–505; idem, "Functional Forms for Profit and Transformation Functions," *Journal of Economic Theory* 6 (June 1973): 284–316; Larry J. Lau, "Some Applications of Profit Functions," Memorandum no. 86–A and 86–B (Palo Alto: Stanford University, Research Center in Economic Growth, 1969); and H. P. Binswanger, "The Use of Duality Between Production, Profit and Cost Functions in Applied Econometric Research: A Didactic Note," Occasional Paper no. 10 (Hyderabad: International Crops Research Institute for the Semi-Arid Tropics, Economics Division, July 1975).

The research benefits exclusive of research costs are simply the difference of these two, namely

$$B = C_0^* - C_1^* \tag{6}$$

In the next chapter the innovation possibilities of figure 4–4 are built into this difference of cost functions such that the benefit of research becomes a function of $R$, $\tilde{W}$ and the levels of $m$ and $n$ research, that is,[20]

$$B = C_0^* - C_1^* = Y\psi(R, \tilde{W}, m, n) \tag{7}$$

Now the economic problem becomes that of maximizing total research payoffs less research cost, that is, of maximizing

$$V = Y\psi(R, \tilde{W}, m, n) - mP^m - nP^n \tag{8}$$

where $P^m$ and $P^n$ are the costs (or prices) per unit of the two research activities.

Similarly, it is possible to express the bias $Q$ of technical change [see equation (A–2), appendix to chapter 2] to the levels of $m$ and $n$, that is, to write

$$Q|_{R\tilde{W}} = \frac{\partial(K/L)}{\partial t} \cdot \frac{1}{K/L} = \psi(m, n) \tag{9}$$

Now it is a straightforward exercise in comparative statics to evaluate the effect of changes in the factor prices, the interest rate, and the output level on the research mix and on the bias corresponding to this mix. Four conclusions derived from this exercise follow.

> I. Given the research productivities of the two research activities, any rise in the *expected present value of total cost of a factor* will lead to an increased allocation of resources to that research activity, which saves the factor whose cost has risen. In general this will also lead to a more pronounced bias of technical change toward saving the factor whose factor cost has risen. This result is not affected by the size of the elasticity of substitution of the production function and holds regardless of whether or not a budget constraint on research resources is imposed.[21]

---

[20] Suitable restrictions on the functional forms of the research payoff functions of $m$ and $n$ research are necessary to ensure that $m$ is labor using while $n$ is labor saving.

[21] It is possible, however, to build models that do not always lead to this result. In a model without budget constraint on research resources, research possibilities can be restricted in such a way that both activities reduce the requirements of both factors. In such a model, under certain circumstances, a wage cost rise can lead to a more pronounced labor-using bias. This case is discussed in the next chapter, where it is argued that the restrictions on research possibilities necessary for it to occur are rather unlikely.

Expected discounted total cost of a factor can rise in several ways. First, either the purchase cost of capital or the expected wage rate can rise. The problem of whether higher wages themselves or only expected rises in the wage rate cause biases, discussed as Fellner's proposition in chapter 2, should now be put to rest.[22] It is the discounted expected future stream of wage rates, weighted by their demand in the production process, that is the relevant magnitude for the mechanism of induced innovation. This mechanism as such is not affected by the way in which firms form their expectations of future wage rates, that is, it does not matter whether they expect it to be constant at the existing level or whether they expect it to rise. Of course, if they expect it to rise, they will put more resources into labor-saving research activity than if they expect it to be constant, but this is a question of the magnitude of the induced bias and not of the mechanism by which it is induced.

Second, an increase in the discount rate raises the cost of capital relative to labor and, as a result, affects resource allocation as well. Third, if the initial production function is labor intensive, that is, if it requires large amounts of labor relative to capital, expected discounted wage costs will be higher than if the initial production function is capital intensive. Hence for given factor cost ratios and innovation possibilities, labor-saving research is more attractive if one starts from a labor-intensive point than if capital intensity is already high. This confirms the idea, which inspired the Kennedy approach to the problem, that the initial importance or share of a factor should have a role in guiding technical change. Indeed, once the model is limited by a budget constraint, the conclusions with respect to biases that can be reached on the basis of research processes are identical to those reached with an IPF in a one-period model.[23]

II. When the research budget is not limited by a budget constraint, a rise in the scale of output increases the total amount of research and hence increases the rate of productivity advance. This is the scale effect familiar from the section on research as a sampling process. However, the effect on the bias of an increase in plant size is not necessarily neutral and cannot be predicted on the basis of such a qualitative model.

III. Regardless of whether or not a research budget contraint exists, a rise in the cost of capital-saving research, or, alternatively, a reduction in the productivity of capital-saving research, will reduce the allocation of resources to such research and turn the bias in a more labor-saving direction and *vice versa*.

IV. If research is faced with a budget constraint on research resources, and if the constraint is binding, the effect of relaxing the

[22] William Fellner, "Two Propositions in the Theory of Induced Innovation," *Economic Journal* 71, no. 282 (June 1961): 305–8.

[23] For a formal proof, see Binswanger, "Microeconomic Approach."

research budget constraint is not necessarily neutral and cannot be predicted with a qualitative model alone.

These results may not be path breaking, but they do clarify a number of controversial points. The major gain is a much more realistic description of how factor prices affect the direction of technical change. Only with such an improved description of the process of induced innovation can questions of the allocation of research resources, economic policy issues in technical change, and empirical research on economic effects of factor scarcities be systematically investigated.

## The Role of Output Prices and the Allocation of Research Resources to Commodities

So far it has been assumed that firms are simply cost minimizers and that output is given. However, when firms are profit maximizers, a cost-saving technical improvement will not only alter their optimal input levels but will lead to an increase in their optimal output level because their average and marginal cost curves will have shifted downward. In a competitive environment they will expand output until marginal costs are equal to the output price again. This adds a further benefit to research projects as long as demand is elastic.[24]

In this section, we will first explore the effect of a change in output prices on the research decision of a firm that produces one output and faces an infinitely elastic demand; we will examine the ways in which output price and input prices interact in determining both total amount of research and the bias of technical change. This will be a formal model, corresponding to Schmookler's and Lucas's empirically verified statements of the relationship between increases in final demand on the one hand and increases in research activity and the rate of technical change on the other.[25] Then we extend the model to two commodities and assess the problem of the optimal allocation of research resources between them. A consideration of the problem of downward-sloping demand curves follows, and we conclude the section with a discussion of the determinants of an economy's aggregate labor intensity.

INFINITELY ELASTIC DEMAND CURVES. For a firm that faces an infinitely elastic demand for its output and has an infinitely elastic input supply, the benefit from research is the difference between profit before and after research. Consider again the problem of the firm that wants to build a

---

[24] When final demand is inelastic, technical improvements may actually reduce profits in the producer industry. This problem will be discussed later in this chapter and again in chapter 13.

[25] Jacob Schmookler, *Invention and Economic Growth* (Cambridge, Massachusetts: Harvard University Press, 1966); R. E. Lucas, Jr., "Tests of a Capital-Theoretic Model of Technological Change," *Review of Economic Studies* 34 (April 1967): 175–89.

plant of optimal size and optimal capital intensity with a given lifetime $T$. With the existing design, the expected profits of the firm will be

$$\pi_0^* = Y_0^*\tilde{P} - K_0^*R - L_0^*\tilde{W} = \pi_0^*(\tilde{P}, R, \tilde{W}) \tag{10}$$

where the asterisks refer to optimal average quantities over time.[26] $R$ is the purchase cost of capital while $\tilde{P}$ and $\tilde{W}$ are the discounted stream of expected output price and wage rate, that is,

$$\tilde{P} = \int_0^T P(t)e^{-rt}\,dt \quad \text{and} \quad \tilde{W} = \int_0^T W(t)e^{-rt}\,dt \tag{11}$$

Corresponding uniquely to the problem of maximizing these discounted profits subject to a production function (with diminishing returns to scale) is a *profit function* that expresses maximized discounted profits as a function of the expected prices $\tilde{P}$, $R$, $\tilde{W}$.[27]

Similarly, from any allocation of research resources a new *profit function* will emerge that relates post-research profits (from which research costs have not been deducted) to the factor and goods prices defined above and which can be written as

$$\pi_1^* = Y_1^*\tilde{P} - K_1^*R - L_1^*\tilde{W} = \pi_1^*(\tilde{P}, R, \tilde{W}) \tag{12}$$

Research payoffs $B$ (gross of research costs), therefore, are the *sum of the price-weighted increases and decreases in optimal output and input quantities:*

$$B = \pi_1^* - \pi_0^* = (Y_1^* - Y_0^*)\tilde{P} + (K_0^* - K_1^*)R + (L_0^* - L_1^*)\tilde{W} \tag{13}$$

Since output and input prices enter as weights in determining the benefits of any research plan, they naturally should enter the allocation of research resources to research activities with different implications for inputs and output. An example of how to specify such research payoffs in relation to the profit function and thus to the benefits of research $B$ is given in the next chapter. It is clear that only research activities that increase the optimal output level are admissible, because optimal output will always rise when costs are reduced, and cost-increasing technical changes are technological

[26] In fact, once a plant is built, actual output and labor input levels will be determined on the basis of current prices with respect to a restricted variable profit function. However, for the design decision and capacity determination, some constant average values are assumed in order to simplify the problem.

[27] Optimal input and output levels are derived from the profit function $\pi^*(\tilde{P}, R, \tilde{W})$ by Shephard's lemma

$$\frac{\partial\pi^*}{\partial\tilde{P}} = Y^*, \qquad -\frac{\partial\pi^*}{\partial R} = K^*, \qquad -\frac{\partial\pi^*}{\partial\tilde{W}} = L^*$$

and these relationships are used to derive output and input effects of research. See Diewert, "Functional Forms," Lau, "Some Applications of Profit Functions," or Binswanger, "Use of Duality."

retrogressions.[28] Furthermore, when biases are to be considered, at least two alternatives with different implications for optimal factor proportions at optimal output levels are needed.

The results of such a model are intuitively clear. The bias of technical change will, as before, respond to any change in total expected discounted factor costs, and the total amount of research will rise with rises in the expected discounted output price. But the effect on the bias of technical change of a rise in the output price cannot be predicted and depends on research possibilities and factor costs. Further evidence on the effect of final demand on the rate of technical change will be given in chapter 9.

Because of its three-dimensional nature, the one output–two inputs case above is not easy to present by means of a graph. The problem of allocating research resources to commodities, on the other hand, can be demonstrated graphically.

The case considered here is one of a region, or a small country, that has fixed resources and produces two commodities that face infinitely elastic demand. A thorough discussion of this problem has recently been worked out by Martin Abel and Delane Welsch, who also consider cases where final demand for the commodities is downward sloping.[29] The graphic discussion here borrows freely from their work.

In figure 4–5, the transformation curve $T_0T_0$ represents the output levels achievable with the initial technology. $T_1T_1$ represents a technology achieved by choosing research activities that favor primarily the output of commodity $X$, while $T_2T_2$ represents a technology achieved by primarily $Y$-favoring research. The $P_1$ lines are a price regime in which $X$ is expensive; the $P_2$ lines correspond to high prices of $Y$. When $Y$ is expensive, the commodity mix produced under technology zero is at point $S$, that is, relatively more of $Y$ is produced than of $X$. If $T_1$ is developed, the optimal commodity mix shifts to $Q^{**}$, which represents primarily an increase in the production of $X$ because the technology $T_1$ favors $X$. With technology $T_2$ the production point shifts to $S^*$, which is primarily an increase in $Y$ because both $T_2$ and the price ratio favor commodity $Y$.

It is clear from the graph that when $Y$ is expensive the income gain achieved by the technology $T_2$, which favors $Y$, is larger than the gain achieved by technology $T_1$. The income difference measured in commodity $X$ is the distance from $P_2^{**}$ to $P_2^*$. When the price ratio is in favor of $X$, the situation is exactly the reverse. Commodity prices then influence the payoffs

[28] A technical improvement, in the long run, must lower both average and marginal costs; otherwise, a given level of output cannot be produced at lower resource costs with the industry's firms in zero profit equilibrium.

[29] Martin E. Abel and Delane E. Welsch, "Environmental Constraints, Commodity Mix and Research Resource Allocation," in *Resource Allocation and Productivity in National and International Agricultural Research*, Thomas M. Arndt, Dana G. Dalrymple, and Vernon W. Ruttan, eds. (Minneapolis: University of Minnesota Press, 1977).

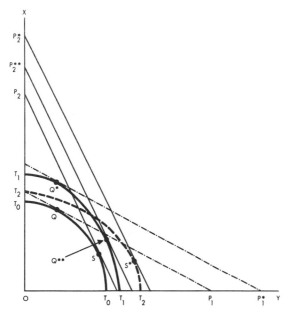

FIG. 4–5. Research resource allocation to commodities.

from research activities that increase the productivity of commodities differentially.

In this two-commodity case, the expected gains from the research (disregarding research costs) can again be expressed as the difference between optimal output quantities under pre-research and post-research technology:

$$B = (X_1^* - X_0^*)\tilde{P}_X + (Y_1^* - Y_0^*)\tilde{P}_Y \tag{14}$$

where $\tilde{P}$ again refers to discounted expected price streams and the asterisks refer to optimal quantities. If $\tilde{P}_X$ is high, an $X$-favoring research activity leads to a large increase in the optimal quantity of the expensive good, whereas a $Y$-favoring research activity leads to a large increase in the quantity of the inexpensive good (compare $S^*$ and $Q^{**}$); thus the benefits from the former are larger.

In chapter 5 the mathematics for the two-commodity case are shown to be identical to the mathematics for the cost-minimizing, two-factor case. Therefore the results of the cost-minimizing model can be directly applied here by replacing the words "labor" and "capital" with $X$ and $Y$, "factor prices" with "goods prices," and the term "factor-saving" with "$X$-favoring" or "$Y$-favoring technical change."

Using graphic techniques, Abel and Welsch[30] investigate how relative

[30] Abel and Welsch, "Environmental Constraints."

factor endowments of a region or a country are likely to affect research resource allocation to commodities with different factor intensities. Suppose two regions produce the same two outputs and face identical output prices. If one region has a factor endowment with a high capital–labor ratio and the other has an endowment with a low capital–labor ratio, according to trade theory the first region will produce relatively more of the capital-intensive commodity whereas the second will specialize in the labor-intensive commodity. Moreover, if research possibilities are not biased in favor of one commodity, the capital-intensive region should allocate more research resources to the capital-intensive commodity than to the labor-intensive one, and the reverse should be true for the labor-intensive region. This is simply because an equal rate of technical change leads to a higher total benefit in a large sector than in a small one. As a result, induced innovation will lead to strengthened regional specialization (at constant output prices).[31]

In the commodity model, the role of the fixed output level of the plant is taken by the size of the region. Benefits to research in a large homogeneous region are higher than benefits to research in a small region, a problem that strongly affects agricultural research resource allocation and one to which we will return in chapter 6. Also, in commodity research it is much easier to identify research activities that favor one specific commodity than it is to identify research activities that favor specific factors. Wheat research favors wheat, and rice research favors rice, of course. However, fertilizer research favors both commodities but gives greater emphasis to the one with the higher capacity for the efficient use of fertilizer. The same is true for research on all other intermediate factors common to both commodities.

The models have so far been restricted to two commodities or two factors at most. However, the theory of cost functions and profit functions, on which the models are built, is easily extended to the many-factor case. The next chapter sketches such an extension although it does not pursue the case in detail. It is clear that if researchers have many alternative research approaches open to them, some of which favor certain commodities and some of which favor certain factors, the effects of factor and goods prices on the commodity and factor direction will carry over into this more general case.

DOWNWARD-SLOPING DEMAND CURVES.    In a sense, the model of a firm doing research and facing an infinitely elastic demand is highly artificial because demand is infinitely elastic only in a purely competitive case with atomistic firms. But in such a situation no firm would have an incentive to

---

[31] This is fully consistent with United States agricultural experience. Experiment stations and private seed companies in the main corn-producing regions were the first to produce hybrid corn varieties, and experiment stations of dairy states allocate proportionately more research resources to dairy production than do the primarily crop-producing states.

pursue research, a problem to which we will return in the next section. (However, the model will still be valid for public research in a small trading country.)

When a downward-sloping demand curve is introduced, the model becomes more complicated and the simple cost function or profit function models can no longer be used. In a recent paper, Mitoshi Yamaguchi and I have used another approach to investigate the benefit side of the role of sectoral technical change and sectoral allocation of research resources.[32] An agricultural–nonagricultural two-sector model was built for a closed economy and applied to Japanese economic data from 1880 to 1965. Although much simpler, the model is in many ways similar to Allen C. Kelley and Jeffrey G. Williamson's[33] model of Japanese economic growth and reaches many conclusions similar to theirs. However, our model is not dynamic but is cast in general equilibrium, comparative static terms. The key difference between the Kelley–Williamson model and ours is that in our model rates of technical change can vary independently in the two sectors. This allows the investigation of the effects on growth and on resource transfer of differential rates of neutral technical change in the two sectors. One can therefore ask what would have happened at various stages of Japanese economic history if the policy had suddenly been directed at achieving a higher rate of technical change in one sector at the expense of the rate of technical change in the other. The demand side is modeled fairly simply; the main feature is that agricultural commodities face lower absolute price and income elasticities of demand than do nonagricultural commodities. The conclusions with respect to research resource allocation reached there are summarized briefly below.

The contribution to growth of a one percent increase in the rate of technical change is closely related to sector size. In 1880, agriculture produced 47 percent of the Japanese gross national product, and this share of the GNP declined rapidly, reaching 8 percent in 1965. As a consequence, the growth contributed by a one percent rise in the rate of agricultural technical change was always less than could be achieved by a corresponding rise in the rate of nonagricultural technical change, and the difference became larger as agriculture became less important.

The greater effect of nonagricultural technical change resulted also from the fact that agricultural labor was less productive than was labor in the nonagricultural sector. This is frequently assumed in such two-sector models, but it is also reflected empirically in sectoral allocations of output and inputs. In 1880, although, as we have already noted, agriculture pro-

[32] Mitoshi Yamaguchi and Hans Binswanger, "The Role of Sectoral Technical Change in Development, Japan 1880–1965," *American Journal of Agricultural Economics,* 58 (May 1975): 269–78.

[33] Allen C. Kelley and Jeffrey G. Williamson, *Lessons from Japanese Development: An Analytic Economic History* (Chicago: University of Chicago Press, 1974).

duced only 47 percent of the GNP, it engaged 75 percent of the total labor force and 63 percent of the capital stock of the economy. Furthermore, because of the elastic demand for nonagricultural goods and the inelastic demand for agricultural goods, technical change in agriculture resulted in declining resource use in that sector.

Agricultural technical change increases national income and turns terms of trade against agriculture, which increases demand for agricultural commodities. But the increase in demand for agricultural products caused by the income and price effect of technical change is not sufficient to offset the resource saving per unit of agricultural output made possible by the technical change. Therefore, technical change in agriculture pushes labor out of that sector into the nonagricultural sector, where its marginal productivity is higher.

Nonagricultural technical change, on the other hand, leads to a far stronger demand for nonagricultural goods because the price drop of these commodities and the income gain due to the technical change lead to a more than proportional rise in the demand for nonagricultural commodities which more than offsets the resource saving per unit of output made possible by the change. Nonagricultural technical change, therefore, strongly pulls resources out of relatively low-productivity agriculture into the higher productivity sector. These combined effects make nonagricultural technical change the stronger engine of growth even when the sectors are of equal size.

Nonagricultural technical change is thus seen as an important source of growth even in less developed countries with large agricultural sectors.[34] In addition, agricultural technical change cannot be expected to solve the unemployment problem of many less developed countries unless either technical change is highly labor using or the country faces a very elastic export demand for most of its agricultural commodities. While some small countries may be in such a favorable agricultural demand position, for most countries, the solution to the employment problem will have to be found in nonagricultural sectors with high demand elasticities. Of course these sectors will be able to absorb large additional amounts of labor only if technical change is not highly labor saving, which underlines the importance of the induced innovation mechanism.

The model just sketched cannot alone answer the question of how much of a country's, or a region's, resources should be allocated to given sectors of the economy. That depends not only on sector size and demand conditions but on the cost of achieving given rates of technical change in each sector. If

---

[34] Kelley and Williamson (*Japanese Development*, chapter 11) stress the same issue. Indeed, they point out that the prerequisite hypothesis (which, on the basis of European economic history states that an agricultural revolution and subsequent rise in agricultural productivity is a prerequisite to rapid industrialization and economic growth) is not supported by the development of Meiji Japan, in which nonagricultural productivity gains exceeded agricultural gains.

technical change is cheap in a small sector and expensive in a large one, one may want to invest heavily in technical change in the small sector. Moreover, the division in the model just sketched was between agriculture and the entire nonagricultural sector, but the latter is composed of many subsectors. In order to achieve a one percent rate of technical change in any one of these subsectors, we might have to utilize the same amount of research resources as would be required to achieve change in all of agriculture. Thus, total nonagricultural research expenditures to achieve a one percent gain in nonagriculture might well exceed expenditures necessary to achieve the same gain in agriculture.

THE AGGREGATE LABOR INTENSITY OF AN ECONOMY.  The traditional approach of trade theory to the problem of adjusting an economy's production processes to its labor, capital, and land endowments has stressed two mechanisms of adjustment: substitution of abundant factors of production for scarce ones along the production function of individual commodities, the *substitution effect*, and shift in output composition to commodities that use the abundant factors of production intensively, the *compositional effect*. To the extent that the profit-maximizing production mix differs from the utility-maximizing consumption mix, commodities are exchanged in international markets.

Price responsiveness of technical change broadens the possibilities for adjusting production relationships to the economy's factor endowments and makes unfavorable endowment ratios less of a constraint to economic growth than they would be in the absence of such responsiveness. Induced changes in factor intensities correspond to the substitution effect and result in the concentration of research resources, within each commodity, on research activities that save the progressively more scarce factors. Sensitivity of research resource allocation to output price leads to the concentration of research resources on commodities with large markets and/or rising relative prices, and this reinforces the compositional effect. If, for example, land becomes progressively more scarce, the prices of land-intensive commodities rise. The consumption mix is adjusted toward the more land-extensive commodities, which raises the potential research payoffs in these commodities. This is partially offset by the higher research payoffs in land-intensive commodities that arise out of their price increase (which in turn adds an incentive for land-saving research within these commodities).

In less developed countries, where overt unemployment or underemployment is widespread, it is doubly important to take advantage of the two traditional adjustment mechanisms and the corresponding induced innovation effects.[35] If technical change in the labor-intensive commodities lags

[35] John W. Mellor has recently stressed the compositional effect as one method of solving the employment problem. See John W. Mellor, "Relating Research Resource

behind change in capital-intensive commodities, employment problems will be aggravated and growth retarded in comparison with a situation in which technical change in these commodities is dynamic. Because similar reasoning will lead developed countries to concentrate research resources on capital-intensive commodities and on labor-saving research with these commodities, the less developed countries will be unable to rely exclusively on technology transfer from the developed world, a problem to which we will return in chapter 6.

## Market Structure and the Direction of Technical Change

Up to now we have neglected the institutional and market environment in which innovation takes place and have established only that, from the point of view of a society that wants to maximize income, it makes sense to allocate research resources on the basis of anticipated developments in goods and factor markets. It is also clear from our models that an individual firm that does research for its own use will have an incentive to behave in the same way.

This, however, is purely normative, and it does not tell us what will actually happen in the institutional and structural environment of a market economy. A firm's incentive structure depends on its institutional and structural environment, and we will have to see whether a given environment will actually lead to a research resource allocation consistent with maximizing income and growth.

Indeed, looking at the large income and productivity differentials between the developed world and the developing countries, it is quite clear that in the latter countries, the innovation process has not been efficient. It has not brought forth rates of technical change comparable to those experienced by the developed countries.[36] No doubt a latent demand for such rates of technical change was as strong in these countries as in the developed world, but somehow it did not express itself in a corresponding allocation of resources to research.

A basic difficulty in institutionalizing capacity for research is that of designing an efficient incentive system for the compensation of researchers and innovators. This has already been discussed in chapter 2. The demand of society for a cost-reducing innovation (or "the latent demand for technical change," in the terminology of part IV of this book) arises from the potential

Allocation to Multiple Goals," in *Resource Allocation and Productivity*, eds. Arndt, Dalrymple, and Ruttan, chapter 23. See also John W. Mellor and Uma Lele, "Growth Linkages of the New Foodgrain Technologies," *Indian Journal of Agricultural Economics* 28 (January–March 1973).

[36] Of course, the induced innovation process may not have worked as effectively as possible in the developed countries, but it certainly has worked better there than in the LDCs.

cost saving of the innovation over the total output of the industry that will use the innovation. However, in the absence of institutional arrangements to partially or fully transfer the benefits that accrue to imitators of the innovation back to the firm that bore the research expense, the benefits for any given firm from the research are only the cost savings that accrue on its own fraction of the industry's output. In competitive industries this is a very small fraction of the total benefits, and thus no firm would invest anywhere near the optimal amount in research.

Societies have developed four methods of combating this problem:

1. Creation of public, cooperative, or nonprofit research, the results and benefits of which are generally freely accessible to the entire industry served.

2. The granting of a proprietary or monopoly right to the innovator for a limited period of time, by means of patents or licenses.

3. Allowing the market structure to become oligopolistic or monopolistic (possibly through a publicly regulated monopoly). This will result in partial or total internalization of benefits, depending on the degree of monopoly.

4. Having research for competitive sectors carried out by input-supplying industries that are characterized by oligopolistic features.

Each of these arrangements for compensating innovators affects research incentives differently, and each of these effects can potentially interfere with the proper working of the induced innovation mechanisms described in the previous sections of this chapter.

When the first of these four methods is adopted and research is publicly funded, the research resource allocation process becomes as imperfect as any public allocation mechanism. The latent demand for technical change must be filtered through political institutions, and the outcome depends heavily on the political influence of various groups whose income position stands to be affected by the technical change. Efficiency considerations are not the only criteria by which choices will be made. Obviously the use of this method can partially or totally distort the induced innovation mechanism, directing it away from a simple income-maximizing goal, depending on the political structure of a society. This problem will be the central concern of part IV of the book. In this chapter only the roles of the second, third, and fourth methods above will be considered.

There is a voluminous literature on the effect of patent laws on incentives to do research.[37] Clearly, patents enable innovators to capture a large share

[37] For a recent review of this literature see F. M. Scherer, *Industrial Market Structure and Economic Performance* (Chicago: Rand McNally, 1970), chapters 15 and 16. See also William D. Nordhaus, *Invention, Growth and Welfare: A Theoretical Treatment of Technological Change* (Cambridge, Massachusetts: M.I.T. Press, 1969); F. M. Scherer,

of the benefits from an innovation, but, because by their very nature they slow down the process of diffusion, they may not be an optimal arrangement.

This is not the place to review the literature on patents. However, we do need to know whether existing patent laws can influence the bias and the sectoral distribution of technical change, apart from their impact on the aggregate rate of technical change. This could happen if the patent system were such that it transferred different shares of the benefits to the innovator depending on the nature of the innovation. Suppose that labor-saving innovations were patentable but capital-saving innovations were not. Such an extreme situation is most unlikely, but, quite clearly, it might bias technical change in a more labor-saving direction than might be warranted by the existing relative scarcity of labor and capital.

Framing the issue in this way leads immediately to the empirical question of whether the extent of patent protection varies among innovations that have different factor-saving characteristics. In this context it is important to realize that a large number of cost-saving innovations are embodied in goods that function as capital or as intermediate inputs in the production process of an industry but are produced by industries other than the user industry. The effectiveness of patent protection clearly differs for different product classes. One of the reasons for this is that with certain products it is easier than with others to innovate around the patents of a rival firm and thus to erode the benefits of the initial innovator.[38] This kind of situation could lead to biases if the extent of protection varied systematically with the factor-saving characteristic of the primary and intermediate inputs concerned; empirical research is needed on this question.

In agriculture, differential protection of innovators' or researchers' rights is conspicuous. With the exception of a few countries, seed varieties are not effectively protected by licenses. In the case of many varieties, once a farmer has bought a single lot he can reproduce the seed himself and sell it to neighbors without having to pay anything more to the plant-breeding firm—unless the genetic quality of the seeds decays rapidly with successive generations.[39] On the other hand, machines and chemicals are usually protected by patents. It was necessary to create a public agricultural research system to do research in the biological area in order to overcome the lack of incentive brought about

---

"Nordhaus Theory of Optimal Patent Life: A Geometric Reinterpretation," *American Economic Review* 62 (June 1972): 422–7; Morton I. Kamien and Nancy L. Schwartz, "Patent Life and R & D Rivalry," *American Economic Review* 64 (March 1974): 183–7 and Fritz Machlup, "Patents," *International Encyclopedia of the Social Sciences*, vol. 2 (London: Macmillan, 1968): 465.

[38] Scherer, *Industrial Market Structure*, chapter 16; William S. Comanor, "Research and Competitive Product Differentiation in the Pharmaceutical Industry in the United States," *Economica* 31 (November 1964): 372–84.

[39] It is precisely this sort of deterioration that occurs in hybrid seeds, and it is in the production of such seed that private companies are most active.

by this situation. Otherwise, technical change would have been slower and perhaps more strongly biased in a machinery and chemical-using direction. But this brings us back to the problem of the role of publicly funded research, the discussion of which we have deferred to part IV of the book.

In any case, it may not be easy to associate a particular factor-saving bias with particular product classes that receive more or less patent protection. Many agricultural innovations take the form of chemical products, such as pesticides and weedicides, which have similar patent protection. However, pesticides enable farmers to increase output by avoiding insect and fungus infestations, which in general cannot be prevented by hand labor, and no particular labor-saving bias is associated with these innovations. On the other hand, weed growth can be prevented by hand labor, and weedicides are therefore generally labor saving. Even within a given product or input class it will be difficult to establish clearly whether a particular bias is associated with the class as such.[40]

Related to the third method of providing research incentives is the question of how firm size and the degree of concentration in an industry affect the rate and bias of technical change. The Schumpeterian hypothesis assumes that large firms are much more efficient innovators because they can capture a larger share of the benefits from innovative activities and because they can achieve, according to Schumpeter, substantial economies of scale in the research process itself. The large body of literature that has emerged on this topic has recently been reviewed by Morton I. Kamien and Nancy L. Schwartz, whose conclusion that intermediate firms have the highest research intensities contradicts Schumpeter's hypothesis.[41] However, the review by

[40] Another problem is that cost-reducing management innovations and innovations like computer programs are not patentable; again the question arises whether these innovations as a class have a definite factor-saving character. A priori reasoning alone cannot answer this question.

[41] Morton I. Kamien and Nancy L. Schwartz, "Market Structure and Innovation: A Survey," *Journal of Economic Literature* 13 (March 1975): 3–4. "Put another way, these studies. . . indicate that by and large there are no economies of scale with respect to firm size in the invention process. . . . As will be seen, the bulk of the evidence indicates that among firms engaged in R & D, relative effort tends to increase with size up to a point and then decline, with middle size firms devoting the most effort relative to their size. . . . Roughly speaking, a combination of research efficiency that decreases beyond a quite moderate size and research input intensity that increases and then decreases beyond some point leads to anticipation that research output, relative to firm size, should increase with size but then decline with further increases in firm size. . . . In fact the evidence indicates that research output intensity does tend to increase and then decrease with increasing firm size. . . . Another major effort related to the Schumpeterian hypothesis has been determining the influence of market structure. . . . Measures of market structure commonly employed in these studies indicate at best something about the intensity of rivalry among the firms in a particularly defined industry. A major omission of the studies is the consequence of potential rivalry, so much stressed by Schumpeter, on inventive activity. Thus empirical definition and measurement of potential rivalry, and evaluation based thereon, remains a key element for our understanding of this phenomenon."

these authors of the ways in which monopolistic market structure affects research input and inventive output remains inconclusive. The answer to the question of whether the induced rate of technical change is accelerated or retarded by monopoly will have to wait for theoretical and empirical advances in this area of knowledge.

I am not aware of any literature that discusses whether size and market power could influence the bias (as distinct from the rate) of technical change.[42] If we look back at the models of the last section, it is clear that the cost-minimizing models of induced innovation apply well to a large or monopolistic firm that does its own process research. Indeed, regardless of the extent of market power and of its effect on a firm's price policy, a monopolistic firm will always be interested in reducing its cost of production. It therefore will have no incentive to choose more labor-saving innovations than a competitive firm would find profitable, as long as it purchases inputs in the same competitive market. For a given research budget it can still achieve the maximum cost reduction by taking factor prices into account in designing efficient technology. Although size and market power may affect the induced rate of technical change, it is reasonably safe to assume that market structure will not influence the bias of technical change originating in firms that do their own process research. But, in the absence of more thorough research, this remains a conjecture.

In market economies, a very substantial amount of the cost-reducing research for a given industry is not carried out by the firms of that industry nor by public or cooperative research institutes under its control, but rather by firms in other industries that supply inputs to the final goods producers. Innovations for the textile industry, such as synthetic fibers and colors, frequently come from the chemical industry or from the textile machinery industry. Mechanical research for agriculture is carried out mostly in the machinery industry, and the chemical industry develops most pesticides and other agricultural chemicals. Again, cost-reducing research in these intermediate goods industries frequently has the dual nature of product and process innovation.

One way to solve the problem of lack of research incentive in firms in a competitive industry is to get input suppliers to do the research. This can be done if the input-supplying industry is more concentrated than the final goods industry and/or if the input innovations can be patented.[43] However, the input-supplying industry's benefits from research do not arise out of the total

[42] V. Kerry Smith has shown that regulation of a public utility may induce it to search for labor-saving innovations as long as it has an incentive toward overcapitalization. V. Kerry Smith, "The Implications of Regulation for Induced Technical Change," *The Bell Journal of Economics and Management Science* 5 (Autumn 1974): 623–2.

[43] If an input innovation can be patented, the input-using firms in the final goods industry also have an incentive to do research and development. Indeed, a substantial number of inventions of agricultural machinery were developed by farmers.

cost reduction in the final goods industry but only from the sale of additional intermediate goods or from the increased price at which a new input innovation can be sold. Therefore, the question is whether the direction of the bias that arises out of the research by the input suppliers would differ from the bias that would result if the research were carried out under the principle of maximizing the cost reduction in the final goods industry.

As a concrete example, consider the case of the tractor industry and agriculture. The tractor producers want to maximize sales of tractors rather than to minimize agricultural production costs. Suppose that a tractor-embodied [44] innovation that would lead to maximum cost reduction were, at the same time, tractor saving. Wouldn't the tractor industry prefer to supply instead an innovation that would reduce costs less but that was tractor using? Per unit of agricultural output, the tractor-using innovation would certainly lead to higher tractor use than would the tractor-saving innovation.

It turns out, however, that this is not always the case. If the tractor industry is characterized by a reasonable degree of competition and rivalry among firms, each firm will attempt to get as large a share of the market as possible. Farmers will tend to buy those tractors that will make possible the largest cost reduction on their farms. Hence one tractor firm can expand its output at the expense of others if it supplies a tractor that reduces costs more than those of its competitors. This forces tractor producers to take the total agricultural cost situation into account in making research decisions, rather than only effects on the tractor-output ratio. If the market share of one firm rises sufficiently fast with respect to the cost differentials provided to agriculture by that firm's equipment, the firm will not care much about what happens to total market demand for tractors unless it anticipates becoming a monopolist. If all firms are aware of this situation, actual and potential rivalry will insure the proper working of the induced innovation mechanism.[45]

On the other hand, if the tractor industry is a monopoly, its concern will indeed be with the total derived demand for tractors. Should it not try to find innovations that are tractor-using or that at least do not reduce the share

[44] "Tractor-embodied" means that it is necessary to purchase the tractor to realize the technical advance.

[45] The role of potential and actual rivalry in the rate of inventive activity has become an important new source of insight into the process of technical change. Kamien and Schwartz, "Market Structure and Innovation," give a brief survey of this new field. Other important references are Morton I. Kamien and Nancy L. Schwartz, "Risky R & D with Rivalry," *Annals of Social and Economic Measurement* 3 (January 1974): 267–7; idem, "Timing of Innovation under Rivalry," *Econometrica* 40 (January 1972): 43–60; Yoram Bazel, "Optimal Timing of Innovations," *Review of Economics and Statistics* 50 (August 1968): 348–55; and F. M. Scherer, "Research and Development Resource Allocation under Rivalry," *Quarterly Journal of Economics* 81 (August 1967): 359–94.

of agricultural costs allocated to tractors? It clearly does have an incentive to do this, but the situation is more complicated.

The tractor monopoly does set the price of tractors above its production costs. This affects both the price of the tractors and the bias of technical change in agriculture by way of its research and development.[46] And the nature of the bias of technical change also affects the optimal price that the monopolist can charge. Assume that the monopolist can produce tractors at a constant cost but sells them at a higher price. If the elasticity of derived demand is $(\partial T/\partial R)(R/T) = \eta_{TR}$ where $R$ is the sales price and $T$ is the number of tractors sold, the optimal price markup over costs $\rho$ can be shown to be

$$\frac{R - \rho}{R} = \frac{1}{\eta_{TR}} \tag{15}$$

R. G. D. Allen shows that

$$|\eta_{TR}| = S_T|\eta_Y| + (1 - S_T)\sigma \tag{16}$$

where $\eta_Y$ is the elasticity of final demand for agricultural products, $S_T$ is the tractor share of the cost of agricultural production, and $\sigma$ is the elasticity of substitution between tractors and labor (or all other inputs combined).[47] Therefore, by implicit function rules,

$$\partial\left(\frac{R - \rho}{R}\right)/\partial S_T = -\frac{1}{\eta_{TR}^2}(|\eta_Y| - \sigma) \gtreqless 0 \leftrightarrow \sigma \gtreqless |\eta_Y| \tag{17}$$

Tractor-using technical change by definition raises the tractor share of production cost. Therefore, this equation implies that tractor-using technical changes will raise optimal price and profits if the elasticity of substitution is larger than the elasticity of demand for agricultural products and will decrease price and profits if the elasticity of substitution is less than the elasticity of final demand. If the elasticity of substitution is small enough, tractor-using technical change will reduce the markup of the monopolist, which to some extent affects his desire for tractor-using technical change. But if the elasticity of substitution is sufficiently large, tractor-using technical change will not only lead to more tractor use per unit of agricultural output than will neutral technical change but, in addition, will allow the monopolist to raise the

[46] In the textbook models of monopolistic and oligopolistic behavior, the firm is assumed to control the price or the quantity of the commodity it supplies, but not both. However, if the monopolist does any product innovation at all, he also controls the nature of the output he supplies and thus is free to set two of the three variables—price, quantity, and technology—independently. That this aspect of monopolistic behavior is indeed important is clear from the studies of potential rivalry discussed in the preceding footnote.

[47] R. G. D. Allen, *Mathematical Analysis for Economists* (New York: St. Martin's Press Inc., 1938): 373.

tractor price. This provides him with an additional incentive to seek tractor-using innovations.

Whether or not monopoly in the tractor industry tends to bias technical change in a tractor-using direction depends very much, therefore, on the size of the elasticity of final demand relative to the elasticity of substitution. Indeed, in the next chapter it is shown that, when the agricultural production function is of fixed proportion, the effects of tractor-saving technical change on both per-unit tractor demand and optimal price cancel each other out. In a case of that sort, the tractor monopoly has no incentive at all to seek more tractor-using technical change than would be optimal from the point of view of society. The available evidence seems to suggest that in a number of developing countries the elasticity of substitution exceeds the elasticity of final demand.[48] In that case the incentive structure for the monopolist creates a very real possibility that he may guide technical change in a direction that, from society's point of view, is inefficient.[49]

As the number of firms in the input-supplying industry rises, the likelihood of inefficient tractor-using biases is reduced. As we have already noted, each tractor firm can expand output at the expense of its rivals if it develops technologies that reduce its own agricultural production costs more than those of its rivals. Furthermore, even if it is still sufficiently large to have monopoly power ($R - \rho \geq 0$), the monopolistic markup is much more likely to be reduced than increased by tractor-using technical change. Consider equation (17). The elasticity of substitution in agriculture is not affected by the number of firms in the tractor industry, but for each firm the relevant $\eta_Y$ becomes the elasticity of that firm's part of the tractor demand with respect to the cost reduction provided by its equipment to agriculture.[50] This elasticity is, of

[48] The elasticity of substitution between tractor power and labor in several developing countries has been estimated to be in the 1.3 to 1.5 range. Elasticities of final demand for food grains are typically below 0.5. See V. Abraham, "Mechanization in Indian Agriculture: A Microanalysis," mimeographed (Waltair, India: Andhra University, Department of Applied Economics, 1975); Robert E. Evenson, "Labor in the Indian Agricultural Sector," mimeographed (New Haven: Yale University, Economic Growth Center, 1972); Gordon Gemmill and Carl Eicher, "The Economics of Farm Mechanization and Processing in Developing Countries," Research and Training Network Seminar Report (New York: Agricultural Development Council, December 1973). See also chapter 7.

[49] Note, however, that when $\sigma$ is very large, the elasticity of derived demand becomes very large, and monopoly power declines.

[50] We can define a function $Y^i(u_1, \ldots, u_i, \ldots, u_N)$ where $Y_i$ is the amount of agricultural output produced by the tractors of firm $i$, and $u_i$ is the unit cost of production in agriculture, using the tractor of firm $i$. Of course

$$\frac{\partial Y_i}{\partial u_i} < 0 \quad \text{and} \quad \frac{\partial Y_i}{\partial u_j} \geq 0 \quad \text{for } i \neq j$$

We can then write the total number of tractors demanded from firm $i$ ($T_i$) as

$$T_i = Y^i(u_1, \ldots, u_i, \ldots, u_N) K_i^*(R_i)$$

where $K_i^*(R_i)$ is the optimal number of tractors of firm $i$ per unit of output with the

course, much larger than the elasticity of demand for agricultural output as a whole. Thus $\sigma$ is much more likely to be smaller than $|\eta_Y|$ for each of the firms. But equation (17) says that if $\sigma$ is smaller than $\eta_Y$, a tractor-using technical change forces the tractor firm to reduce its price. This at least partially offsets the positive effect on tractor demand per unit of agricultural output that arises from tractor-using technical change.

It is important, therefore, that market structure in input-supplying industry should not become monopolistic. There should be a small enough number of firms so that each has an incentive to do research but not so small a number that rivalry among them disappears.[51] Refinement of models and empirical research will be necessary to ascertain whether monopolistic market structure has indeed contributed to biasing technical change in input-using and labor-saving directions.

In summarizing this section, it can be said that unless research is done in monopolistic input-supply industries, and unless elasticities of substitution in final production industries are large, it is unlikely that the institutional and structural features of private-sector research in modern market economies will prevent bias in the direction of technical change consistent with an economy's factor endowments.

The main question that remains unanswered is how public sector research or the lack thereof affects the mechanism of induced innovation and how it interacts with private research in determining the rate and bias of technical change. If the induced innovation mechanism had been working effectively with respect to the bias and amount of technical change in all countries, there would be no reason for the tremendous technological lag of the less developed countries. Therefore, something must have gone wrong in these countries. The discussion in this section indicates that the technology lag of developing countries is more likely to have resulted from the public decision-making process with respect to technical change than from structural and institutional features of private research in market economies.

## Induced Innovation and Economic Policy

For a planned economy, the relevance of induced innovation to planned resource allocation is easily stated. If their goal is to maximize

---

tractor price $R_i$. Note also that $u_i$ is a function of $R_i$ as well. The elasticity of demand for tractors by the $i$'th firm, given unit costs of all firms, is then

$$\eta_{TR}^i = S_T^i |\eta_Y^i| + (1 - S_T^i)\sigma$$

It is possible to separate $\eta_Y^i$ itself into one component that results from the final demand elasticity in agriculture and another that results from capturing tractor sales from other firms.

[51] In less developed countries it is sometimes argued that it is best to restrict the number of tractor producers so that problems of servicing and spare parts can be reduced. However, if there is no rivalry among firms in a less developed country, tractor

a given (normative) objective function, planners can use models of the allocation of research resources to different research activities that maximize the objective function, subject to the innovation possibilities as defined in the models of induced innovation. This can be handled, at least conceptually, with some of the recently developed mathematical models of research resource allocation.[52] If the objective function is not to maximize output, the weights attached to the reduction of particular factor requirements and to increases in production of particular commodities will not necessarily be international or market prices of factors of production and goods but their shadow prices, established by the objective function and by the planning process itself. International prices will still have an important influence on these shadow prices because they describe trading opportunities of the centrally planned economy that will have to be taken into account in maximizing the objective function, unless the country decides not to take advantage of trading opportunities at all. In such a planned economy, the problem that faces policy makers is how to achieve consistency of pricing and control policies, which should not be set so as to induce researchers or firms to allocate resources to research activities in a manner not consistent with the plan.

In this last section we are concerned primarily with the question of what the theory of induced innovation implies for the choice of economic policy tools to achieve any particular goal, such as the conservation of natural resources, or the prevention of pollution in market economies. From the work of Schmookler, Lucas, and Ben-Zion and Ruttan we know that the inducement effects are empirically verified with respect to goods prices and final demand.[53] With respect to factor prices and factor supplies, the empirical importance of the inducement effects will be further confirmed in part III of this book. Our question then becomes that of whether or not induced innovation fundamentally alters the approach to economic policy that arises out of traditional neoclassical welfare economics.

Paretian welfare economics relies on the market as a tool of allocation. Government intervention is advocated only in the presence of externalities, public goods, or increasing returns to scale. Furthermore, Paretian theory

---

producers will have little incentive to adapt their equipment to the country's factor endowments.

[52] Several papers in Arndt, Dalrymple and Ruttan, eds., *Resource Allocation and Productivity*, review and extend these models. See in particular C. R. Shumway, "Models and Methods Used to Allocate Resources in Agricultural Research: A Critical Review," chapter 21; Per Pinstrup-Andersen and David Franklin, "A Systems Approach to Agricultural Research Resource Allocation in Developing Countries," chapter 20; and Mellor, "Multiple Goals," chapter 23. See also Walter L. Fishel, ed., *Resource Allocation in Agricultural Research* (Minneapolis: University of Minnesota Press, 1971).

[53] Schmookler, *Invention and Economic Growth*; Lucas, "Capital–Theoretic Model"; Ben-Zion and Ruttan, chapter 9 of this volume.

requires that public policy deal with issues of income distribution by direct income or asset transfers rather than by market intervention through taxes, subsidies, or direct controls.[54]

The market mechanism relies on the positive output response of producers to output prices and on the adjustment of input mixes in a cost-minimizing way in response to changes in factor prices. Induced innovation reinforces both these mechanisms by directing the innovative effort of firms to goods and factors of production that are scarce or exhibit rising prices. In this sense the theory does strengthen the conclusions of welfare economics; it predicts an additional welfare loss if there is any interference with the adjustment process.

Again consider figure 2–3. Suppose the real opportunity cost ratio of capital and labor was $P_t$ and the choice of technologies was between $I_{t+1}$ and $I'_{t+1}$. If the factor prices were distorted to $P_{t+1}$, either by capital subsidies or labor "taxes," then entrepreneurs would choose $I'_{t+1}$ rather than the optimal technology $I_{t+1}$. The welfare cost of this move (or added unemployment per unit of output) would be the distance $P_{t+1}P'_{t+1}$. In the present example this would far exceed the static welfare cost of the price distortion with fixed technology, which would be only $P'_{t+1}P''_{t+1}$. Furthermore, the static welfare costs can rather easily be reversed by eliminating the price distortion, whereas

[54] The basis of this position is stated beautifully in the following quotation from Arrow: "(First Optimality Theorem). If a competitive equilibrium exists at all, and if all commodities relevant to costs or utilities are in fact priced in the market, then the equilibrium is necessarily *optimal* in the following precise sense (due to V. Pareto): There is no other allocation of resources to services which will make all participants in the market better off.

Both the conditions of this optimality theorem and the definition of optimality call for comment.... It is reasonable enough to assert that a change in allocation which makes all participants better off is one that certainly should be made.... From this it follows that it is not desirable to put up with a nonoptimal allocation. But it does not follow that if we are at an allocation which is optimal in the Pareto sense we should not change to any other. We cannot indeed make a change that does not hurt someone—but we can still desire to change to another allocation if the change makes enough participants better off and by so much that we feel that the injury to others is not enough to offset the benefits. Such interpersonal comparisons are, of course, value judgments. The change, however, by the previous argument ought to be an optimal state—of course there are many possible states, each of which is optimal in the sense here used.

With this in mind, the following statement can be made (Second Optimality Theorem): If there are no increasing returns in production, and if certain other minor conditions are satisfied, then every optimal state is a competitive equilibrium corresponding to some initial distribution of purchasing power. Operationally, the significance of this proposition is that if the conditions of the two optimality theorems are satisfied, and if the allocation mechanism in the real world satisfies the conditions for a competitive model, then social policy can confine itself to steps taken to alter the distribution of purchasing power." Kenneth J. Arrow, *Essays in the Theory of Risk Bearing* (Amsterdam: North Holland Publishing Company, 1974), chapter 8, "Uncertainty and the Welfare Economics of Medical Care," pp. 941–73.

For an exposition of the conditions for the second optimality theorem, see F. M. Bator, "The Anatomy of Market Failure," *Quarterly Journal of Economics* 72 (August 1958): 351–79.

the more dynamic, induced-technology effects cannot. Reverting from a nonoptimal capital-intensive technology path to a more labor-intensive path may require a long time.

A similar argument can be made if goods prices are distorted. Those goods whose relative prices rise as a result of the distortion will receive research resources in an amount that is disproportionate to their potential contribution to real national income.

If innovation is responsive to prices, the welfare cost of price distortions is likely to exceed the static welfare costs that are usually measured in empirical research and often found to be small.[55] The additional "dynamic" welfare loss that results from the inducement of inefficient technical changes must be added to other, more dynamic components of welfare losses of monopoly and quantitative restrictions, such as Harvey Liebenstein's loss of X-efficiency, Ann Krueger's welfare losses as a result of rent seeking, and the similar concept of partial or full *rent dissipation* of Steven Cheung.[56] However, contrary to the view of Paretian welfare economics, perfect competition cannot achieve the gains from induced innovation because an environment

[55] Christopher Dougherty and Marcelo Selowsky summarize eight studies on the welfare costs of tariffs and monopoly in developed countries, and none of these shows a welfare loss of more than one percent of GNP. They find a similarly negligible effect of misallocation of labor due to wage differentials among industries in Colombia ("Measuring the Effects of the Misallocation of Labor," *Review of Economics and Statistics* 55 (August 1973): 386–90). On the other hand, for selected less developed countries, Balassa and associates obtain values of static welfare losses that result from trade protection of up to 2.4 percent. Bela Balassa et al., *The Structure of Protection in Developing Countries* (Baltimore: Johns Hopkins University Press, 1971). Distortions are usually much higher in less developed countries, which explains the higher estimates. But large distortions seem to be necessary to cause large static welfare losses.

[56] Liebenstein states that firms that are protected from competition by quotas or by other means will generally produce commodities at higher costs than if the industry were competitive. This failure to achieve minimum cost production is called a loss in "X-efficiency." Harvey Liebenstein, "Allocative Efficiency vs. X-efficiency," *American Economic Review* 56, (June 1966): 392–415. Anne Krueger argues that quotas, licensing, and other quantitative controls create rents, which rational firms will try to capture by competing for them. In the process of competitive rent seeking, the firms will spend resources, for example, by investing in excess capacity to obtain quotas, or allocating resources to influence the licensing authorities and policy makers. Firms will stop investing further resources to obtain the rents when the marginal cost is equal to the marginal benefit of obtaining the rent. In this process the rent is exhausted by the resources spent to obtain it and becomes a welfare loss much larger than the usual welfare triangle. Anne O. Krueger, "The Political Economy of the Rent Seeking Society," *American Economic Review* 64 (June 1974): 291–303. Cheung calls the process of rent seeking *rent dissipation* and shows that the extent of dissipation (i.e., the proportion of the rent that is spent in resources to obtain it) depends on the allocation of property rights to the rent or to the asset that generates the rent. No rent is dissipated if the proprietary right to it is assigned exclusively and fully to specific owners, and dissipation is complete if no secure property rights to the rent or rent-generating asset exist. If the definition of property rights is somewhere in between, rent dissipation is only partial. Steven N. Cheung, "A Theory of Price Control," *Journal of Law and Economics* 17 (April 1974): 53–71.

of small firms cannot provide sufficient incentives for research. Taking this fact into account, we see that the theory of induced innovation cannot lead to a simple laissez-faire attitude. Government policy must be aimed at providing the right institutional environment, such as a set of patent laws and programs of publicly funded research, before induced innovation can take place. Some of these institutional issues are discussed further in part IV of the book.

Let us consider a few examples of the way in which the endogenous quality of technical change affects the policy prescriptions of static welfare analysis.

To accelerate capital accumulation and guide it in the direction desired by policy makers, many developing countries subsidize investment in plant and equipment both explicitly and implicitly by tax laws that allow rapid depreciation of capital goods. Sometimes foreign capital goods are further favored because foreign exchange allocations permit their importation at preferential exchange rates, whereas domestically produced capital goods must be purchased by potential users at prices that reflect domestic scarcities more closely. The general subsidization of capital, together with the preference sometimes given to foreign capital, leads to higher capital intensities than those that minimize cost at true scarcity values and provides an incentive to guide research in a more capital-using direction than is optimal.

Furthermore, if subsidization or taxation policies reduce the cost of imported capital sufficiently, the factor proportions of imported equipment that has been invented in the labor-scarce developed economies may be close to cost minimizing with respect to the distorted factor prices; thus incentives to do private adaptive research in a labor-using direction may be greatly reduced. As a consequence, the investment generated by these policies tends to result in less employment, for a given growth rate of capital, than where price distortions are absent. This strengthens the conclusion of the choice-of-techniques literature, which favors output price subsidies or subsidies on all input costs, including labor, as an approach to the protection of infant industries.

Consider the economics of pollution control.[57] Most economists advocate shifting the cost of pollution control to the industry that produces pollution, through effluent charges or direct controls. Effluent charges rather than controls are preferred in cases where charging on a quantitative basis is technically feasible and not very expensive. Associating a cost with these previously costless externalities has induced substantial research in techniques to reduce pollution or to prevent it by means of effluent treatments. And the theory of induced innovation strengthens the case for effluent charges as against quantitative controls. Under quantitative controls, once firms meet the control standards, any further incentive to reduce pollution

---

[57] For a review of this literature, see Vernon W. Ruttan, "Technology and the Environment," *American Journal of Agricultural Economics* 53 (December 1971): 707–17.

disappears. However, if a cost is associated with each unit of pollution, as long as it produces any pollution at all a firm has an incentive to find additional ways of reducing the cost of effluents.

Finally, the theory of induced innovation strengthens the view that market price can be an efficient means of allocation even for exhaustible resources. The theory implies that rises in the price of an exhaustible resource will induce innovations aimed at saving the resource or at finding close substitutes for it. This will reduce the likelihood that any one of the exhaustible resources will act as an ultimate constraint on growth.[58]

If this position is pushed to an extreme, it would imply that government policy in this area can be confined to ensuring the efficient working of the innovation process and the support of basic research. However, we have seen that the theory of induced innovation does not imply that technical change is possible in all directions and at all times. Innovation possibilities may be constrained, and for certain exhaustible resources it may not be possible to invent substitutes or to reduce their use substantially in most applications. Induced innovation theory alone, therefore, does not rule out the possibility that direct controls may eventually become necessary for certain raw materials. More knowledge about innovation possibilities is required. Nevertheless, the induced innovation perspective leads to a more optimistic assessment of future growth possibilities than the antigrowth proponents would predict.

The discussion in this chapter has focused on the process by which innovation is generated. It has not considered the issue of technology diffusion and transfer. The perspective of induced innovation is rich in policy implications for the allocation of research resources when technology transfer is possible and for a deeper understanding of the problems involved in technology transfer. To go into these matters, however, requires adaptations and extensions that we will undertake in chapter 6, after discussing the formal issues involved in modeling induced innovation in chapter 5.

[58] For an exhaustive review of the empirical evidence, see James P. Gander, *The Relationship of Technological Change and the Demand for and Supply of Raw Materials* (Salt Lake City: University of Utah, Bureau of Economic and Business Research, 1976).

# FIVE

# Issues in Modeling Induced
# Technical Change

HANS P. BINSWANGER

T HIS chapter follows closely the outline of the last chapter. It also presents mathematical models of the roles played by factor prices, goods prices, and market structure in research resource allocation when an industry has its research carried out by the industries that supply its inputs. Since the treatment is mathematical, more precise statements can be made and the conclusions of the last chapter can be enriched. The last section of the chapter discusses the problem of the dynamic extension of the models of induced innovation. Readers who are not interested in model-building issues may go on to chapter 6, which deals with issues of technology transfer.

## Cost-Minimizing Models and Factor Prices

This section presents extensions of my earlier work on modeling induced innovation, which was based on a production function with fixed proportions.[1] In the paragraphs that follow, these early models are extended to the case of production functions with variable proportions.

INVENTION POSSIBILITIES. As in chapter 4, the problem is to specify the relationships of different applied research processes to bias in the path of technical innovation and to changes in factor proportions. For this purpose, we will take basic knowledge as given. In the formal model we will consider

I owe a special intellectual debt to W. Erwin Diewert, Lawrence J. Lau and D. McFadden. Most of the models in this chapter are based on the relationships of duality between production and cost or profit functions which the work of these authors has made more amenable and accessible to both theoretical and empirical enquiries. Of course they are in no way responsible for errors that might have occurred in using these concepts.

[1] See Hans P. Binswanger, "A Microeconomic Approach to Induced Innovation," *Economic Journal* 84 (December 1974): 940–58.

only one relatively capital-saving research process $m$ and one labor-saving process $n$, with the choice of bias achieved by linear combinations of the two processes.

There are three possible ways of introducing research processes into a production function $Y = f(K, L)$ where $Y$ is output, $K$ is capital, and $L$ is labor input. The first is to choose a factor-augmenting form:

$$Y = f\left(\frac{K}{a}, \frac{L}{b}\right) \tag{1}$$

where $a$ and $b$ are factor-augmenting coefficients. If $a$ and $b$ are reduced at different rates, biases will result unless the elasticity of substitution is one. Therefore, we can make the rates at which $a$ and $b$ change functions of the research processes $m$ and $n$, with each of the latter having different "productivities" in reducing $a$ and $b$. This would be consistent with Kennedy's approach to induced innovation.[2]

The major disadvantage of this approach is that, when the production function is Cobb–Douglas, differing rates of change in $a$ and $b$ will *not* result in biases.[3] Any factor-augmenting technical change will be neutral. However, it is often empirically possible and convenient, in characterizing production functions in different countries, to use Cobb–Douglas functions with factor intensities that differ because of differences in their exponents. If the object of the theory is to explain cross-country differences in factor intensities such as those discussed in chapter 3, this approach is not attractive.

If it were true that capital-augmenting technical change is associated with improvements in physical capital and labor-augmenting technical change with increases in labor quality, factor augmentation would still be an excellent approach to our problem because the research lines and their effects could be associated with research on a specific factor of production. This would be a great advantage for empirical research on induced innovation. However, a technical change embodied in one factor does not necessarily augment only that particular factor. This is a point on which there is frequent confusion in the technical change literature. In fact, a new machine may reduce labor requirements while it leaves capital requirements unaffected or even increases them. Similarly, a new seed variety does not just reduce seed requirements per unit of output; it reduces the requirements of all factors of production. This issue is discussed further in appendix 5–1.

The second approach to our problem is to introduce research directly into the production function, just like a factor of production:

$$Y = f(K, L, m, n) \tag{2}$$

[2] Charles Kennedy, "Induced Bias in Innovation and the Theory of Distribution," *Economic Journal* 74, no. 295 (September 1964): 541–7.

[3] See appendix 2–1.

For comparative static purposes, this is entirely adequate. However, if dynamic extension were ever considered, we would have to use a stock of past research and the increments to the stock of new research in such a model. With constant parameters of $f$, this assumes that every unit of past research had the same effect on the production process as the newly contemplated research increment. This is not consistent with the notion of the exhaustibility of applied research discussed in the last chapter.[4]

A third approach is to assume that research affects the parameters of the production process. This assumption implies, however, that a specific functional form must be chosen for the production function (or the cost or profit function). Because of recent advances in production theory, this implication is less restrictive than it would appear at first. Diewert's generalized Leontief function and the *translog* functions provide approximations to twice-differentiable functions and are therefore not very restrictive.[5] In this framework, a dynamic extension would have to be handled as in Evenson and Kislev,[6] with a Markow process model in which the research payoffs in terms of the production parameters are redefined in each period, depending on the outcome of the previous period's research. The parameters in each period could be treated as state variables of the system, and their changes could be considered transition variables.

Assume that a firm with a variable-proportion, neoclassical production process does its own process research. The firm wants to build a new plant of fixed capacity $Y$ with a lifetime $T$. It can build a plant of existing design without doing any research, or it can improve the design of the plant by means of the research processes $m$ and $n$. Given factor prices and research costs, the firm must determine both optimal research levels and optimal input levels. And it must maximize with respect to four variables. The problem, however, can be reduced to choosing only optimal research levels by treating the input decision implicitly through the use of a minimum cost function $C^* = g(R, W)$ that relates minimized costs $C^*$ to factor prices.

In the problem above, output is given and, after construction, capital stock is given as well. Thus, labor input for the entire lifetime of the plant is also given, unless the plant shuts down. Even with variable proportions, therefore, the firm can choose the capital–labor ratio only once, and it does so on the

---

[4] However, introducing research into a production function in this way may sometimes be necessary in econometric research. As long as the period involved is not too long, or if the research activities considered cover whole classes of research rather than very narrowly defined research activities, this may still be appropriate.

[5] W. Erwin Diewert, "An Application of the Shephard Duality Theorem: A Generalized Leontief Production Function," *Journal of Political Economy* 79 (May–June 1971): 481–505; idem, "Functional Forms for Profit and Transformation Functions," *Journal of Economic Theory* 6 (June 1973): 284–316; Laurits R. Christensen, Dale W. Jorgenson and Lawrence J. Lau, "Transcendental Logarithmic Production Frontiers," *Review of Economics and Statistics* 55 (February 1973): 28–45.

[6] Robert Evenson and Yoav Kislev, *Agricultural Research and Productivity* (New Haven: Yale University, 1975).

basis of the discounted stream of wage rates over the entire period, instead of on the basis of the initial wage rate.

The firm knows that the capital purchase cost per unit of $K$ is $R$, and it expects the wage rate to be $W = W(t)$ for the period. Let the *discounted wage rate* per unit of labor be

$$\tilde{W} = \int_0^T W(t)e^{-rt}\,dt$$

and define the cost-minimizing problem as

$$\min C = KR + \tilde{W}L - \lambda(f[K, L] - Y) \tag{3}$$

Under the usual assumptions of production theory, a unique cost function corresponds to this problem:[7]

$$C^* = C^*(R, \tilde{W}) \tag{4}$$

By Shephard's lemma, for given parameters of the function we can always solve for optimal cost-minimizing input levels by taking first derivatives

$$K^* = \frac{\partial C^*}{\partial R} \quad \text{and} \quad L^* = \frac{\partial C^*}{\partial \tilde{W}} \tag{5}$$

where $K^*$ and $L^*$ are optimal input levels. It turns out that Diewert's generalized Leontief cost function is the easiest with which to work.[8] It has the following form:

$$C^* = Y(AR + B\tilde{W} + 2\gamma R^{1/2}\tilde{W}^{1/2}) \tag{6}$$

where output $Y$ enters multiplicatively into the function, if the production process is homogeneous of degree one,[9] and $A$, $B$, and $\gamma$ are the parameters of the function. If $\gamma$ is zero, then the cost function is additive, and an additive cost function corresponds to a fixed-proportion production function. By Shephard's lemma, the optimal input levels are

$$K^* = \frac{\partial C^*}{\partial R} = Y(A + \gamma R^{-1/2}\tilde{W}^{1/2})$$

---

[7] For an exposition of these properties of duality, see Lawrence J. Lau, "Applications of Profit Functions," Memorandum no 86-A and 86-B (Stanford: Stanford University, Research Center in Economic Growth, 1969). See also Diewert, "Shephard Duality Theorem," or Hans P. Binswanger, "The Use of Duality Between Production Profit and Cost Functions in Applied Econometric Research: A Didactic Note," Occasional Paper no. 10 (Hyderabad, India: International Crops Research Institute for the Semi-Arid Tropics, Economics Division, 1975).

[8] Diewert, "Shephard Duality Theorem."

[9] Constant returns to scale will be assumed throughout this and the next section of this chapter. A more general treatment would be to write $C^* = g(Y)(AR + B\tilde{W} + 2\gamma R^{1/2}\tilde{W}^{1/2})$ where $g'(Y) > 0$. This would have no real influence, however, on the results.

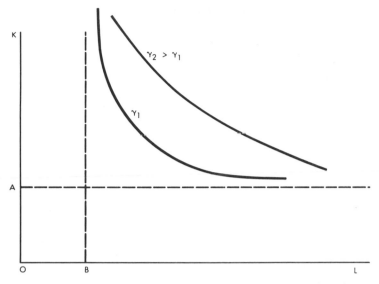

FIG. 5–1. Isoquants of the generalized Leontief cost function.

and

$$L^* = \frac{\partial C^*}{\partial \tilde{W}} = Y(B + \gamma R^{1/2} \tilde{W}^{-1/2}) \tag{7}$$

and the capital–labor ratio is

$$\frac{K^*}{L^*} = \frac{A + \gamma \tilde{W}^{1/2} R^{-1/2}}{B + \gamma \tilde{W}^{-1/2} R^{1/2}} \tag{8}$$

Both inputs are essential, and the function is globally concave if

$$A \geqq 0; \qquad B \geqq 0; \qquad \text{and} \qquad \gamma \geqq 0 \tag{9}$$

When (13) holds, the isoquant map of the function looks like that shown in figure 5–1. $A$ is the minimum level of $K$ necessary to produce one unit of output as $L$ moves toward zero; the relationship between $B$ and $L$ is analogous. The $\gamma$ parameter governs the curvature of the isoquant. The larger $\gamma$, the higher the elasticity of substitution $\sigma$. The elasticity of substitution is not constant but depends on price levels, as the following formula shows:[10]

$$\sigma = \frac{C^* Y}{2 K^* L^*} \gamma \tilde{W}^{1/2} R^{1/2} \tag{10}$$

[10] W. Erwin Diewert, "Application of Duality Theory," Discussion Paper no. 89 (Vancouver: University of British Columbia, Department of Economics, 1973).

Since $\gamma$ essentially governs the elasticity of substitution, this parameter is assumed constant. Differential changes in $A$ and $B$ are sufficient to create biased technical change, and therefore, changes in them will be made functions of the research processes $m$ and $n$.

Let $\hat{A} = (A_0 - A_1)/A_0$ and $\hat{B} = (B_0 - B_1)/B_0$ where the subscript 0 denotes the coefficients before research and the subscript 1 denotes the coefficients after research. $\hat{A}$ and $\hat{B}$ are, therefore, the percentage change in the coefficients attributable to research.

For reasons which will be explained below, it is necessary to make $\hat{A}$ and $\hat{B}$ functions of both research processes. To simplify as much as possible, the following assumptions are introduced:

(A) Research results are additive, that is, the results from one research process can be implemented independently of the research results from the other process.

(B) Research is subject to decreasing returns throughout its range.

(C) Only two research processes are considered, and they are subject to the same scale function.

(A), (B), and (C) combined lead to the following specification of invention possibilities:

$$\hat{A} = \mu(m)\alpha^m + \mu(n)\alpha^n$$
$$\hat{B} = \mu(m)\beta^m + \mu(n)\beta^n \tag{11}$$

where $\mu$ is the common scale function and

$$\mu \geqq 0$$
$$\mu_m, \mu_n \geqq 0 \tag{12}$$
$$\mu_{mm}, \mu_{nn} < 0$$

and where the $\alpha$ and $\beta$ parameters are the research productivity parameters that determine the factor-saving characteristics of each research line.

Assumption (A) is quite restrictive: Results from one research cannot affect the productivity of another. Nevertheless, many cases have been documented in which one research has had payoffs for another research activity. Such payoffs, however, have most often been unexpected; we are dealing here with subjective, *ex ante* functions. If *ex ante* research interactions are random, they will not affect a decision on the allocation of a research budget among various research lines. Two exceptions to this must be noted. First, large research establishments with many research activities will tend to increase their overall research budget if they know from experience that unexpected payoffs occur frequently, albeit in a random manner. Such an increase will be allocated in proportion among their various research activities. Second, supportive or basic research is pursued by profit-maximizing establishments precisely because of its interaction with more applied research activities.

Decreasing returns to research [Assumption (B)] are necessary to define a well-behaved maximization problem. They are also justified by the sampling nature of research. It may be argued that increasing returns to research are frequent because, after an initial period of investigation, a breakthrough sometimes occurs that substantially increases payoff to that particular research activity. In such a case, the *ex post* response curve may have exhibited increasing returns. But, again, the *ex ante* subjective research function may have exhibited diminishing returns because the breakthrough was not expected or because only a small probability was associated with it. Had it been otherwise, the decision maker would have made a large research investment in this activity right from the start. His initial investment, which led to the breakthrough, also led to the formulation of a new expected payoff function that again exhibits diminishing returns. Of course, if research requires an initial fixed investment, the response curve will have an initial range of increasing returns. Clearly a research establishment without budget constraint would not operate in this range. But such increasing returns would increase the probability of corner solutions in the models with budget constraint that are discussed below.

Assumption (C): This assumption is made only to simplify the mathematics, and its absence would not affect the basic results. Having the same scale function means that returns to research decrease at the same rate with the number of $m$ trials and the number of $n$ trials. If they become zero (which is not necessary for the model) they become zero at the same number of trials. Since the research productivities of $m$ and $n$ can differ according to the productivity coefficients $\alpha$ and $\beta$, this is not a very restrictive assumption.

The proportional changes in the cost function parameters $\hat{A}$ and $\hat{B}$ are treated as continuous functions of the research processes $m$ and $n$. Of course, trials in a research process are discrete. The functions must be interpreted, therefore, as continuous approximations of functions of discrete variables.

We now assume that the $m$ process is relatively capital saving and that the $n$ process is relatively labor saving. This places restrictions on the research productivity parameters $\alpha$ and $\beta$. The comparative static bias of technical change can be expressed as follows:

$$Q|_{R\tilde{W}} = \frac{K_0^* - K_1^*}{K_0^*} - \frac{L_0^* - L_1^*}{L_0^*} \gtreqless 0 \rightarrow \begin{cases} \text{capital saving} \\ \text{neutral} \\ \text{capital using} \end{cases} \qquad (13)$$

In the case of the generalized Leontief function, this becomes

$$Q = \frac{YA_0}{K_0^*} \hat{A} - \frac{YB_0}{L_0^*} \hat{B} \qquad (14)$$

In the fixed-proportion case, $YA_0 = K_0^*$ and $YB_0 = L_0^*$, and this reduces to $Q = \hat{A} - \hat{B}$. The change in the bias can be expressed as

$$dQ = \frac{YA_0}{K_0^*}\, d\hat{A} - \frac{YB_0}{L_0^*}\, d\hat{B} \tag{15}$$

After inserting the research payoff functions (11), the assumption that $m$ is capital saving and $n$ is labor saving implies that

$$\frac{\partial Q}{\partial m} = \frac{YA_0}{K_0^*}\, \hat{A}_m - \frac{YB_0}{L_0^*}\, \hat{B}_m = Y\mu_m\left(\frac{A_0}{K_0^*}\, \alpha^m - \frac{B_0}{L_0^*}\, \beta^m\right) > 0$$
$$\frac{\partial Q}{\partial n} = \frac{YA_0}{K_0^*}\, \hat{A}_n - \frac{YB_0}{L_0^*}\, \hat{B}_n = Y\mu_n\left(\frac{A_0}{K_0^*}\, \alpha^n - \frac{B_0}{L_0^*}\, \beta^n\right) < 0 \tag{16}$$

where $\hat{A}_m$, $\hat{A}_n$, $\hat{B}_m$, and $\hat{B}_n$ are the first derivatives of $\hat{A}$ and $\hat{B}$ with respect to $m$ and $n$.[11]

These constraints are automatically satisfied when the following constraint on $\alpha$ and $\beta$ holds:

$$\alpha^m > 0 > \beta^m$$
$$\beta^n > 0 > \alpha^n \tag{17}$$

This case can be called the *substitution* case, because the $m$ process reduces capital requirements but increases labor requirements, whereas the $n$ process reduces labor but increases capital requirements. But technical change possibilities need not always do this. It is possible that the $m$ and the $n$ process each reduce both capital and labor requirements, but that $m$ reduces capital requirements relatively more than $n$, whereas $n$ reduces labor requirements relatively more than $m$. We call this case the *pure technical change* case. In this case all $\alpha$'s and $\beta$'s are positive, and (16) is not automatically satisfied. But in this event, (17) can be transformed into the following condition:

$$\frac{\alpha^m}{\beta^m} > \frac{B_0 K_0^*}{A_0 L_0^*} > \frac{\alpha^n}{\beta^n} \geqq 0 \tag{18}$$

Note that in the fixed-proportion case this condition simplifies to:

$$\frac{\alpha^m}{\beta^m} > 1 > \frac{\alpha^n}{\beta^n} \geqq 0 \tag{19}$$

---

[11] In these comparisons for the biases we are interested in the optimal levels of $K$ and $L$ at constant factor prices. When we later investigate the effect of a change in the factor prices on the biases, that is, $\partial Q/\partial R$, the effects of the factor price changes on $K^*$ and $L^*$ will not be considered; only the effects through $\partial m/\partial R$ and $\partial n/\partial R$ will be examined. The total effect on factor ratios, of course, includes the effects $\partial K^*/\partial R$ and $\partial L^*/\partial R$.

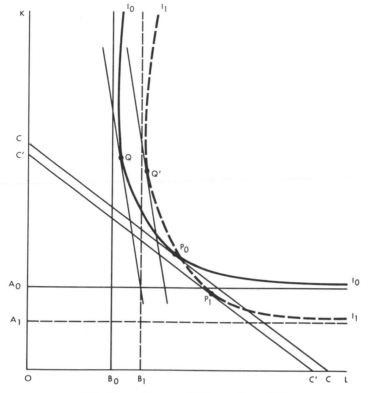

FIG. 5–2. Innovation possibilities with variable proportions.

Figure 4–3 in the last chapter illustrates the technical change possibilities for the fixed-proportion case when the substitution case holds.

In the pure technical change case, the arrows of the research activities $m$ and $n$ must point toward the inside of the quadrangle $OAPB$ of figure 4–3. The parallelogram $PUSV$, therefore, lies wholly inside the quadrangle $OAPB$.

Invention possibilities are neutral if

$$\alpha^m = \beta^n \qquad \alpha^n = \beta^m \tag{20}$$

The point $S$ of figure 4–3 then lies on the ray $OP$. Neutrality would be only a coincidence, however, and it is not assumed except in some special cases.

In figure 5–2 the effect of one research activity on the isoquant of the generalized Leontief function is shown graphically. $I_0$ is the isoquant before any $m$ research takes place, and the point $P_0$ is the initial cost-minimizing point for the factor prices $CC$. $A_0$ and $B_0$ are the coefficient levels before research. After a certain amount of $m$ research, $A_1$ and $B_1$ are reached, transforming the isoquant to $I_1$, with a cost-minimizing input combination $P_1$ at unchanged factor prices $C'C'$. In the case shown, technical change is relatively capital saving. It corresponds to the substitution case of constraint (17), that is, in equilibrium, the capital requirement is reduced at the expense of an absolute rise in the labor requirement.[12] In the pure technical change case, both the $A$ and $B$ lines (or coefficients) move toward the origin but at different proportional rates for the two research processes. Given the research functions, the set of potential technologies achievable with a research budget has an envelope such as the line $QR$ in figure 4–4 in the preceding chapter.

It can be argued that the model could be greatly simplified by having $m$ research just reduce the $A$ parameter and $n$ research just reduce the $B$ parameter, without $m$ entering into $B$ and $n$ entering into $A$. *This special case can be called the orthogonal case.* At least in the substitution case, even when the actual research lines indeed affect both $A$ and $B$, a suitable variable transformation could result in a transformed research process with orthogonal implications and an associated cost for each orthogonal direction.

This approach was rejected because most research processes do not have orthogonal factor-savings implications.[13] A new machine does not just reduce optimal factor requirements of capital or labor. Most of the time it affects both. And, as we shall see, an optimal research allocation may call for the use of only one research line. In that case there is no way to obtain a transformation that makes the outcome orthogonal.

The research productivity variables $\alpha$ and $\beta$ essentially summarize invention possibilities. Together with the $\mu$ function they reflect the parameters of the underlying distributions of $A$ and $B$ coefficients. Restricting ourselves to applied research and comparative static single-period models implies that the $\alpha$'s and $\beta$'s are constant. But that would not be true in a multi-period optimization model even without basic research. For each period these parameters would have to be redefined depending on the outcome of the last period's research because of the exhaustion argument of the last chapter. Building such extended models requires different techniques and, as we shall see, the marginal insight gained from such extensions is likely to be small.

THE COST FUNCTION AND THE FACTOR BIAS. The firm that wants to do research has to compare the cost of the plant of existing design with the cost of the plant that it might develop. The costs of the plant of existing design are:

$$C_0^* = YA_0R + YB_0\tilde{W} + 2\gamma Y R^{1/2}\tilde{W}^{1/2} \tag{21}$$

Note that $R$ is the purchase cost of capital, and $\tilde{W} = \int_0^T W(t)e^{-rt}\,dt$ is the discounted cost of one unit of labor over the lifetime of the project, so that

[12] Under very high labor costs this would be a technological retrogression, because the isoquants cross. But we are interested in a certain factor price range, and whether or not isoquants cross beyond it is immaterial.

[13] This absence of orthogonal factor-savings implications was discussed in connection with the factor-augmenting case, at the beginning of the chapter.

$C_0^*$ is the present value of the costs of the project. Present value of costs after research is:

$$C_1^* = YA_1R + YB_1\tilde{W} + 2\gamma YR^{1/2}\tilde{W}^{1/2} \tag{22}$$

The present value of the cost savings due to research is $C_0^* - C_1^*$. Taking this difference leads to:

$$C_0^* - C_1^* = YR(A_0 - A_1) + Y\tilde{W}(B_0 - B_1) \tag{23}$$

Transforming into $\hat{A}$ and $\hat{B}$ notations this can be written as:

$$C_0^* - C_1^* = YRA_0\hat{A} + Y\tilde{W}B_0\hat{B} = c_K\hat{A} + c_L\hat{B} \tag{24}$$

where

$$c_K = YRA_0 = \text{capital cost component}$$
$$c_L = Y\tilde{W}B_0 = YB_0\int_0^T W(t)e^{-rt}\,dt = \text{labor cost component}$$

Note first that when the production function is of fixed proportions, and when $A$ and $B$ are simply input–output ratios, then $c_K$ and $c_L$ are the present values of the capital and labor costs of the unimproved technology, respectively, because the $\gamma$ term is zero. However, in the case of a neoclassical production function when $\gamma$ is not zero, $c_K$ and $c_L$ do not exhaust total costs. Total costs also contain the $\gamma$ term, as can be seen in equation (21). It still is useful to think of $c_K$ and $c_L$ as the components of discounted capital costs and labor costs associated with the $A_0$ and $B_0$ terms of the initial unimproved technology.

Second, note that the $\gamma$ term is not part of the cost reduction that the firm will try to maximize. This implies that the size of the elasticity of substitution will not affect the firm's maximizing behavior with respect to research. This is in strong contrast to those induced innovation models that are based on factor-augmenting technical change and Kennedy's *innovation possibility frontier*. As has been shown in the appendix to chapter 2, in a factor-augmenting model, for equal differences in the rates of factor augmentation, the direction of the bias changes when the elasticity of substitution changes from less than one to more than one, and when it is one a bias cannot occur. But in the present model, what controls biases are the $A$ and $B$ parameters, and differential rates of change in them imply biases of equal sign regardless of whether the elasticity of substitution is less or more than one. Therefore, the substitution parameter has no influence on the inducement mechanism either.

NO BUDGET CONSTRAINT ON RESEARCH.    The behavior of the models is first examined without a constraint on the research budget.

We assume that research is undertaken at constant costs. The prices $P^m$

and $P^n$ are associated with each unit of research. The maximizing problem, therefore, is:[14]

$$V = C_0^* - C_1^* - mP^m - nP^n$$
$$= c_K \hat{A}(m, n) + c_L \hat{B}(m, n) - mP^m - nP^n \tag{25}$$

Substituting the research function (11) into (25) and rearranging terms leads to the following form of the maximizing problem:

$$V = \mu(m)(c_K \alpha^m + c_L \beta^m) + \mu(n)(c_K \alpha^n + c_L \beta^n)$$
$$- mP^m - nP^n \tag{26}$$

Investment in research will proceed up to the point where marginal research benefits are equal to marginal research costs; it will not proceed to the scientific frontier unless research costs are zero. This is shown by the first-order conditions:

$$\mu_m(c_K \alpha^m + c_L \beta^m) = P^m \quad (=1)$$
$$\mu_n(c_K \alpha^n + c_L \beta^n) = P^n \quad (=1) \tag{27}$$

The units of $m$ and $n$ are chosen such that their prices are equal to one. To trace the behavior of the optimal solution, differentiate totally:

$$\mu_{mm}(c_K \alpha^m + c_L \beta^m) \, dm = dP^m - \mu_m \alpha^m \, dc_K - \mu_m \beta^m \, dc_L$$
$$\mu_{nn}(c_K \alpha^n + c_L \beta^n) \, dn = dP^n - \mu_n \alpha^n \, dc_K - \mu_n \beta^n \, dc_L \tag{28}$$

Multiplying the left-hand side of the equations by $\mu_m/\mu_m$ and $\mu_n/\mu_n$, respectively, using the first-order conditions to eliminate the bracketed term, and multiplying all terms in $dc_K$ and $dc_L$ by $c_K/c_K$ and $c_L/c_L$, respectively, leads to equations in proportional or logarithmic changes of $c$ and $P$:

$$dm(\mu_{mm}/\mu_m) = d \ln P^m - c_K \mu_m \alpha^m d \ln c_K - c_L \mu_m \beta^m d \ln c_L$$
$$dn(\mu_{nn}/\mu_n) = d \ln P^n - c_K \mu_n \alpha^n d \ln c_K - c_L \mu_n \beta^n d \ln c_L \tag{29}$$

and solving for $dm$ and $dn$:

$$dm = \frac{d \ln P^m - c_K \mu_m \alpha^m d \ln c_K - c_L \mu_m \beta^m d \ln c_L}{\mu_{mm}/\mu_m}$$

$$dn = \frac{d \ln P^n - c_K \mu_n \alpha^n d \ln c_K - c_L \mu_n \beta^n d \ln c_L}{\mu_{nn}/\mu_n} \tag{30}$$

Equation (30) leads to the first observation: It is neither factor prices alone,

[14] Two minor points must be noted here. First, it is assumed that research occurs instantaneously, that is, that it does not take time. This is not a serious complication, however, because a time lag of research and the cost of lost output associated with it could be incorporated as a constant term into the maximizing problem. This would not affect the interior solutions to the problem but would make it necessary for the entrepreneur, after finding the optimal research mix, to check whether the present value of the cost reduction less the lost output were still positive. If it were not, he would do no research at all. Second, capital maintenance costs have been neglected. These could be integrated into the $c_K$ term, however, by discounting them and adding them to the purchase costs.

as in the Ahmad version of induced innovation, nor factor shares alone, as in the Kennedy–Weizsäcker–Samuelson version of induced innovation, that influence optimal research mix and hence rates and biases. Rather it is research costs and the discounted future labor and capital components $c_K$ and $c_L$ that are significant. Considering factor prices alone neglects the importance of factor quantity in factor costs; looking at factor shares alone neglects the impact of the scale of output on optimal research amounts. Both approaches, of course, fail to take account of research costs.

Given the signs of the derivatives of the functions in equations (12), one can show that research price has a negative effect on each research activity:

$$\frac{\partial m}{\partial \ln P^m} = \frac{\mu_m}{\mu_{mm}} \lesseqqgtr 0; \qquad \frac{\partial n}{\partial \ln P^n} = \frac{\mu_n}{\mu_{nn}} \lesseqqgtr 0 \tag{31}$$

The size of the negative effect depends on the curvature of the research functions. Because the amount of $m$ research is independent of the price of $n$ research (equation 31), it follows that total research (and hence the rate of technical change) declines if the price of either one or both research activities rises. If only the price of the more capital-saving activity rises, only $m$ research will decrease while $n$ research stays constant. Therefore, technical change will be more labor saving after a rise in the price of $m$ alone. This establishes the research cost effects on bias and rate of technical change.

Call the effect of the cost component of a factor on the research activity that tends to save it more strongly the "own-cost" effect (e.g., $\partial m/\partial \ln c_K$) and call the effect on the other research activity a "cross-cost" effect (e.g., $\partial n/\partial \ln c_K$). The own effects are positive.

$$\frac{\partial m}{\partial \ln c_K} = -\frac{c_K \mu_m^2 \alpha^m}{\mu_{mm}} \geqq 0$$

$$\frac{\partial n}{\partial \ln c_L} = -\frac{c_L \mu_n^2 \beta^n}{\mu_{nn}} \geqq 0 \tag{32}$$

The magnitude of the own effects depend on the own costs, the own research productivity $\alpha^n$ or $\beta^m$, and on how far the process of research has already been carried (indicated by the ratio $\mu_m^2/\mu_{mm}$).

As the logarithmic change of a product is the sum of the logarithmic changes of its components, we can write $d \ln c_K = d \ln R + d \ln Y + d \ln A_0$ and $d \ln c_L = d \ln Y + d \ln B_0 + d \ln \tilde{W}$.

$$\frac{\partial m}{\partial \ln c_K} = \frac{\partial m}{\partial \ln R} = \frac{\partial m}{\partial \ln A_0} \geqq 0$$

$$\frac{\partial n}{\partial \ln c_L} = \frac{\partial n}{\partial \ln \tilde{W}} = \frac{\partial n}{\partial \ln B_0} \geqq 0 \tag{33}$$

(The effect of $Y$ is discussed later.) Hence, equiportional rises in the two components of the cost components (discounted factor price or initial minimum factor requirements $A$ and $B$) have an effect of equal sign and size on the amount of research saving the particular factor. A higher minimum factor requirement (or input–output coefficient, in the fixed-proportion case) corresponds to a lower efficiency of the factors. Hence, the less efficient a factor, the more research resources will be devoted to it. This decomposition of the factor cost effects can always be carried out. Since all signs and magnitudes are identical, however, the decomposition will not be performed explicitly in this chapter.[15]

The cross-cost effects are as follows:

$$
\begin{aligned}
\frac{\partial m}{\partial \ln c_L} &= -\frac{c_L \mu_m^2 \beta^m}{\mu_{mm}} \gtreqless 0 \to \begin{cases} \text{pure technical change case} \\ \text{orthogonal case} \\ \text{substitution case} \end{cases} \\
\frac{\partial n}{\partial \ln c_K} &= -\frac{c_K \mu_n^2 \alpha^n}{\mu_{nn}} \gtreqless 0 \to \begin{cases} \text{pure technical change case} \\ \text{orthogonal case} \\ \text{substitution case} \end{cases}
\end{aligned}
\tag{34}
$$

The sign of these effects depends on whether we are in the substitution case (equation 17) or in the pure technical change case (equation 18). In the pure technical change case, $\alpha^n$ and $\beta^m$ are positive, that is, *the capital-saving research activity reduces labor requirements as well, and the research activity that saves labor also saves capital.* Therefore, the cross effects will be positive (in the absence of a research budget constraint), and a rise in the labor cost component will tend to increase research along the more capital-saving research activity as well as along the labor-saving activity.

In the substitution case, where $\alpha^n$ and $\beta^m$ are negative, a rise in labor costs will tend to decrease research along the capital-saving activity because that activity increases labor requirements, but the labor cost rise is a signal for more labor saving.

To derive the effects of interest rate and lifetime on the research mix, a further decomposition of the discounted wage rate can be carried out. Note that both $r$ and $T$ enter only through $\tilde{W}$.[16] Clearly a rise in $r$ would reduce the discounted wage rate $\tilde{W}$ because lower weights would be associated with the distant wage costs, while a rise in $T$ would increase $\tilde{W}$ because more periods with wage costs are added. Hence $\partial \tilde{W}/\partial r < 0$ and $\partial \tilde{W}/\partial T \geqq 0$. Therefore,

---

[15] At the microlevel at which this model is developed, initial efficiency is, of course, given. The relevant forces that alter costs are factor prices and scale of output.

[16] If capital maintenance costs were included in the model, $R$ would contain the integral of discounted maintenance costs and hence $r$ and $T$ as well. A slightly different method for finding $r$ and $T$ effects would have to be used. It is safe to assume, however, that maintenance costs are small relative to capital purchase costs and to the stream of wage costs, so that the results would not be modified substantially.

$\partial \ln c_L / \partial r < 0$ and $\partial \ln c_L / \partial T > 0$ while $\ln c_K$ is unaffected by $r$ and $T$. Using the chain rule on (34), therefore, leads to

$$\frac{\partial m}{\partial r} \lesseqgtr 0 \quad \text{and} \quad \frac{\partial m}{\partial T} \lesseqgtr 0 \qquad (34a)$$

depending on whether we are in the pure technical change or the substitution case. And by a similar operation on (33),

$$\frac{\partial n}{\partial r} \leqq 0 \qquad \frac{\partial n}{\partial t} \geqq 0 \qquad (33a)$$

This decomposition will also be taken for granted in the remainder, and only effects of $\tilde{W}$ will be discussed. But the effects of $r$ and $T$ on $\tilde{W}$ can be kept in mind.

It remains to establish the effects of capital and labor cost component rises on the bias of technical change. Recall the definition of the bias (14), its change (15), and its change in response to changes in $m$ and $n$ (16). Now,

$$\begin{aligned}
\frac{\partial Q}{\partial \ln c_K} &= \frac{\partial Q}{\partial m} \frac{\partial m}{\partial \ln c_K} + \frac{\partial Q}{\partial n} \frac{\partial n}{\partial \ln c_K} \\
&= Y\mu_m \left( \frac{A_0}{K_0^*} \alpha^m - \frac{B_0}{L_0^*} \beta^m \right) \frac{\partial m}{\partial \ln c_K} \\
&\quad + Y\mu_n \left( \frac{A_0}{K_0^*} \alpha^n - \frac{B_0}{L_0^*} \beta^n \right) \frac{\partial n}{\partial \ln c_K} \qquad (35)
\end{aligned}$$

In the substitution case, $\partial n / \partial \ln c_K$ is negative and the whole expression (35) is positive. Hence a rise in the capital cost component (owing to a rise in $R$) leads unequivocally to a more pronounced capital-saving bias. But in the pure technical change case the sign of (35) is undetermined. To understand the reason for this, first note again that both $m$ and $n$ reduce capital requirements in the pure technical change case. Therefore, a rise in the capital cost component is a signal to increase *both* research activities. But why is it that the increase in the labor-saving activity may be large enough to outweigh, in terms of the bias, the increase in the capital cost component? This is the result of diminishing returns to research. Suppose $R$ is initially zero and the capital cost component, therefore, is zero as well. As capital costs begin to rise, the more capital-saving activity is expanded more rapidly than the labor-saving activity. Hence, when capital costs continue to rise, the labor-saving research is in a range with smaller marginal returns than the capital-saving research. The absolute capital saving achievable through expanding labor-saving research may now be larger than that achievable by capital-saving research despite the fact that, at equal levels, the absolute capital reduction of the capital-saving activity exceeds the reduction brought about by the labor-saving activity. Suppose capital costs were to rise almost to infinity, and labor costs were zero. Because both activities actually save capital, it would be optimal to push both activities to the point where marginal payoffs are zero. At that point it is the shape of innovation possibilities that determines the bias and, apart from pushing research to that point, economic factors have no influence on the bias.

Not too much should be made of this odd behavior, because multiplicity of research activities weakens this conclusion. Suppose $m$ and $n$ initially are the only research activities that satisfy the condition that marginal benefits exceed research costs at zero level of research, and suppose that a research activity $k$ is more capital saving than $m$ but is initially dominated by $m$ and does not satisfy the marginal condition initially. Activity $k$ is therefore not activated. But if capital costs continue to rise, there comes a point where $k$ will satisfy this condition and will be activated. If any "substitution" activities exist at all they will eventually be activated, no matter how strongly dominated they are initially. However, in the range of factor prices where no substitution activities are activated, the indeterminacy of (35) still holds. Whether this case is of any importance is an empirical question.

To determine the effect of output on research levels, consider equation (30) and hold all prices and input coefficients constant. We can then simply replace $d \ln c_K$ and $d \ln c_L$ with $d \ln Y$ in (30). This leads to the following expressions:

$$\frac{\partial m}{\partial \ln Y} = -\frac{\mu_m}{\mu_{mm}} \mu_m(c_K \alpha^m + c_L \beta^m) = -\frac{\mu_m P^m}{\mu_{mm}} \geq 0$$

$$\frac{\partial n}{\partial \ln Y} = -\frac{\mu_n}{\mu_{nn}} \mu_n(c_K \alpha^n + c_L \beta^n) = -\frac{\mu_n P^n}{\mu_{nn}} \geq 0$$

(36)

Because by (27) the terms in the brackets times the first derivatives of the scale functions are positive and equal to research prices, the signs of (36) are easily established. An increase in the capacity of the plant increases both research levels and thus leads to a higher rate of technical change in both the substitution and the pure technical change cases.

The effect of an increase in output on the bias is not necessarily neutral.

$$\frac{\partial Q}{\partial Y} = \frac{\partial Q}{\partial m}\frac{\partial m}{\partial Y} + \frac{\partial Q}{\partial n}\frac{\partial n}{\partial Y} \gtreqless 0$$

(37)

Since by (36) $\partial n/\partial Y$ and $\partial m/\partial Y$ are positive, and by (16) $\partial Q/\partial m \geq 0$ and $\partial Q/\partial n \leq 0$, the sign of (37) cannot be established.

A BUDGET CONSTRAINT ON THE TOTAL AMOUNT OF RESEARCH. A research institute may have a fixed research budget to allocate among various research projects, or a firm may decide a priori how much it wants to spend on research. This type of case is important because, as can be seen in figures 4–3 and 4–4, it is particularly suitable to graphic interpretation.[17] At the same time, it must be noted that the determination of a research budget is certainly not independent of a priori knowledge about potential research payoffs. An experiment station has to justify its budget allocation with the legislature by showing that its research is potentially productive, and, similarly, the research department of a firm can increase its budget if it can show that its research is very productive.

The research budget can be written as:

$$mP^m + nP^n - F = 0 \qquad\qquad (38)$$

where $F$ is the research budget. Maximizing present value (equation 26) subject to (38) leads to the following first-order conditions:

$$
\begin{aligned}
&-mP^m - nP^n + F = 0 \\
&\mu_m(c_K\alpha^m + c_L\beta^m) = (1 + \lambda)P^m \qquad (=1 + \lambda) \\
&\mu_n(c_K\alpha^n + c_L\beta^n) = (1 + \lambda)P^n \qquad (=1 + \lambda)
\end{aligned}
\qquad (39)
$$

Totally differentiating these equations, setting $P^m = P^n = 1$, and going through the same transformations to proportional changes used to go from (25) to (26), the equations can be rewritten in the following matrix notation:

$$
\begin{bmatrix} 0 & 1 & 1 \\ 1 & -g_{11} & 0 \\ 1 & 0 & -g_{22} \end{bmatrix}
\begin{bmatrix} d\lambda^* \\ dm \\ dn \end{bmatrix}
=
\begin{bmatrix} S_0 \\ S_1 \\ S_2 \end{bmatrix}
$$

where $d\lambda^* = d\lambda/(1 + \lambda)$

$$g_{11} = \mu_m/\mu_{mm} < 0; \qquad g_{22} = \mu_n/\mu_{nn} < 0$$
$$S_0 = dF - md\ln P^m - nd\ln P^n$$

$$S_1 = \frac{c_K\mu_m\alpha^m}{1 + \lambda} d\ln c_K + \frac{c_L\mu_m\beta^m}{1 + \lambda} d\ln c_L - d\ln P^m$$

$$S_2 = \frac{c_K\mu_n\alpha^n}{1 + \lambda} d\ln c_K + \frac{c_L\mu_n\beta^n}{1 + \lambda} d\ln c_L - d\ln P^n$$

Hence, by inverting,

$$
\begin{bmatrix} d\lambda^* \\ dm \\ dn \end{bmatrix}
= \frac{1}{g_{11} + g_{22}}
\begin{bmatrix} g_{11}g_{22} & g_{22} & g_{11} \\ g_{22} & -1 & 1 \\ g_{11} & 1 & -1 \end{bmatrix}
\begin{bmatrix} S_0 \\ S_1 \\ S_2 \end{bmatrix}
\qquad (40)
$$

[17] In Binswanger, "Microeconomic Approach," conditions are discussed under which this case corresponds to the Kennedy approach as well.

and

$$dm = \frac{g_{22}S_0 - S_1 + S_2}{g_{11} + g_{22}}$$

$$dn = \frac{g_{11}S_0 + S_1 - S_2}{g_{11} + g_{22}} \tag{41}$$

The denominator is always negative because both $g_{11}$ and $g_{22}$ are negative. Assembling the terms in $d \ln c_K$ from $s_1$ and $s_2$, we have:

$$\frac{\partial m}{\partial \ln c_K} = -\frac{c_K(\mu_m \alpha^m - \mu_n \alpha^n)}{(g_{11} + g_{22})(1 + \lambda)} \geq 0 \tag{42}$$

Expression (51) is always positive if

$$\mu_m \alpha^m > \mu_n \alpha^n \tag{43}$$

Condition (43) always holds when $\alpha^n$ is negative (substitution case), but it also holds when $\alpha^n$ is positive. The proof is as follows: setting $P^m$ and $P^n = 1$, we solve the first-order conditions (39) for $\mu_m$, substitute into (43) and obtain the condition

$$\frac{\alpha^m}{c_K \alpha^m + c_L \beta^m} > \frac{\alpha^n}{c_K \alpha^n + c_L \beta^n}$$

$$\frac{1}{c_K + c_L(\beta^m/\alpha^m)} > \frac{1}{c_K + c_L(\beta^n/\alpha^n)} \tag{44}$$

Because under both conditions (17) and (18) $\beta^m/\alpha^m < \beta^n/\alpha^n$, the inequality in (53) is satisfied regardless of the signs of $\alpha^n$ and $\beta^m$. Similarly, it can be proved that the other own-cost effect is positive as well:

$$\frac{\partial n}{\partial \ln c_L} \geq 0 \tag{45}$$

When the budget constraint is binding and research prices are equal, $dm = -dn$. It follows then immediately that the cross-cost effects are equal to the own-cost effects.

$$\frac{\partial m}{\partial \ln c_K} = -\frac{\partial n}{\partial \ln c_K} \quad \text{and} \quad \frac{\partial n}{\partial \ln c_L} = -\frac{\partial m}{\partial \ln c_L} \tag{46}$$

In contrast to the unconstraint case, this allows us to prove monotonic relationships between biases and factor costs. Recalling that $\partial Q/\partial \ln c_K =$

$(\partial Q/\partial m)(\partial m/\partial \ln c_K) + (\partial Q/\partial n)(\partial n/\partial \ln c_K)$, we can simplify by using (46) to

$$\frac{\partial Q}{\partial \ln c_K} = \left(\frac{\partial Q}{\partial m} - \frac{\partial Q}{\partial n}\right)\frac{\partial m}{\partial \ln c_K} \geqq 0 \tag{47}$$

Because from (16), $\partial Q/\partial m \geqq 0$ and $\partial Q/\partial n \leqq 0$, the term in the brackets is positive and thus the whole expression is positive. A rise in the capital cost component will lead to a more capital-saving bias; a rise in the labor cost component will lead to a more labor-saving bias. The expressions $d \ln K$ and $d \ln L$ can, of course, be broken down into their components and each analyzed in turn. When the budget constraint is binding, an increase in one research activity is possible only at the expense of the other line. This is why it is now possible, even in the pure technical change case where it was not possible before, to predict that a rise in discounted labor costs will result in a stronger labor-saving bias.

Furthermore, it can be shown that a rise in the capital cost component has an effect of equal size but of opposite sign on research effort as does an equiproportional rise in discounted labor costs (as long as research prices are equal):

$$\frac{\partial m}{\partial \ln c_K} = -\frac{\partial m}{\partial \ln c_L} \tag{48}$$

From (42) and the equivalent equation for $\partial m/\partial \ln c_L$ we can obtain the following condition, which must hold in order for (48) to be satisfied:

$$-c_K(\mu_m \alpha^m - \mu_n \alpha^n) = +c_L(\mu_m \beta^m - \mu_n \beta^n)$$

or, rearranging terms,

$$\mu_n(c_K \alpha^n + c_L \beta^n) = \mu_m(c_K \alpha^m + c_L \beta^m)$$

Checking with the first order conditions (34), both sides are equal when research prices are equal.

The research prices affect research resource allocation and bias in the same way as in the unconstraint case. It cannot be proved that a change in the research budget has a neutral effect. Biases can result when one research activity is already so large that it encounters strongly diminishing returns. An increase in the research budget is then spent primarily on the previously neglected line of research.

A BUDGET CONSTRAINT ON TOTAL INVESTMENT RESOURCES.    A budget constraint on research alone is useful in tracing the allocation of research resources of a governmental research institute such as an experiment station, which most often has a fixed research budget in the short run. But a firm can borrow in order to do research or, if it has a borrowing constraint and if it finds research more profitable than physical investment, it can reallocate resources from the investment program to research. Similarly, a country can increase its savings rate or reallocate resources to research from physical investment if it faces a fixed saving rate. Establishing a budget constraint for research and physical investment separately does not maximize returns from total investment because rates of return of the two kinds of investments are not equated at the margin. Therefore, the previous model is only a narrow special case. And it turns out that a budget constraint on total investments alters the behavior of the model substantially.

The budget constraint is rewritten to allow the firm to use for research purposes what it saves in capital equipment.

$$mP^m + nP^n + c_K = F + c_K\hat{A} \tag{49}$$

The sum of search and initial capital expenditures is equal to the total budget plus the reduction in capital costs made possible by the research.

Unfortunately, this budget constraint considerably complicates the problem. Therefore, the specification of research possibilities is simplified such that $m$ affects only $A$ and $n$ only $B$. This is the *orthogonal* case discussed before, and the research productivity parameters $\alpha^n$ and $\beta^m$ are equal to zero in equations (11) and (26). $\hat{A}$ and $\hat{B}$, respectively, are functions of $m$ and $n$ alone. The first-order conditions of this problem, subject to (49), now become:

$$mP^m + nP^n + c_K = F + c_K\mu(m)\alpha^m$$
$$c_K\mu_m\alpha^m = P^m \qquad (=1) \tag{50}$$
$$c_L\mu_n\beta^n = (1 + \lambda)P^n \quad (=1 + \lambda)$$

If research possibilities are completely neutral, that is, if $\alpha = \beta$, the existence of the budget constraint alone biases technical change in a capital-saving direction. This can be proved as follows: If $\mu$ is quadratic [i.e., $\mu(m) = a_1m - \frac{1}{2}a_2m^2$] then $\mu_m = a_2(a_1/a_2 - m)$. Since $a_1/a_2$ is the level at which marginal returns to $m$ become zero, say $m^*$, we have $\mu_m = a_2(m^* - m)$. Also, since $m$ and $n$ have the same returns function, $m^* = n^*$. Using this specialization and setting $\alpha^m = \beta^n$, we can solve (50) for $m$ and $n$ explicitly:

$$m = m^* - \frac{1}{c_K a_2 \alpha^m}$$

$$n = m^* - \frac{1 + \lambda}{c_L a_2 \alpha^m} \tag{51}$$

Even if the capital and labor cost components are equal ($c_K = c_L$), $m$ will be larger than $n$ because when the constraint is binding, $\lambda$ is positive. Even when the cost components are not equal, a rise in $\lambda$, caused by a reduction in the overall capital constraint, leaves $m$ unaffected, but reduces $n$. In the orthogonal case, a reduction in $n$ is always a reduction in the labor-saving bias or an increase in the capital-saving bias. *Therefore, reducing the amount of total capital to the firm tends to lead to a capital-saving bias!*

The amount of capital-saving research in this formulation is independent of the capital constraint, because it generates the capital cost saving needed to do the research. Going through a procedure similar to that in the previous case, it is easily shown that

$$dn = dF - c_K(1 - \mu_m)\alpha^m \, d \ln c_K - md \ln P^m - nd \ln P^n$$

$$dm = \frac{\mu_m}{\mu_{mm}} (d \ln P^m - d \ln c_K) \tag{52}$$

These equations again show that capital-saving research is independent of the budget constraint and the level of $n$ research and depends only on what happens to the costs of capital and of capital research. Labor-saving research, on the other hand, simply gets the leftover budget and is adjusted upward as the capital constraint increases, downward as capital costs increase (because this leads to more budget allocation to capital-saving research), and downward when research costs increase. Again, a rise in $c_K$ increases the capital-saving bias.

The purpose of the model using this budget constraint is to show how important the specifications of the budget constraint are for the model. I myself find the model without budget constraint by far the most relevant.

### Profit-Maximizing Models and Goods and Factor Prices

In this section the research resource allocation model is generalized to include the effect of goods prices and market size. Furthermore, firms are assumed to maximize profits rather than simply to minimize costs.

THE ONE GOOD–TWO FACTOR CASE.    If the firm is maximizing profits rather than minimizing costs, the level of output is no longer given. Assume now that the firm faces infinitely elastic input and output markets, and that once it has built its plant it can no longer alter its size. All it can do is to vary its levels of labor input and output, depending on the current wage rates and output price. This situation can be described by a restricted variable profit function;[18]

$$\pi_{vt}^* = \pi_v^*(P_t, W_t, \bar{K}) \tag{53}$$

where $\pi_{vt}^* = Y_t^* P_t - L_t^* W_t$ is the maximized value of sales less labor costs in period $t$, $P$ is the price of the output, and $\bar{K}$ is the fixed capital stock.

[18] For a discussion of the profit function, see Lau, "Applications of Profit Functions," Binswanger, "Use of Duality," and Diewert, "Application of Duality Theory."

Optimal input and output levels are then, by Shephard's lemma, $Y_t^* = \partial\pi_v^*/\partial P_t$ and $L_t^* = -\partial\pi_v^*/\partial W_t$. Before the plant is built, however, the firm faces the problem of determining the optimal capital stock as well. In this case it must take into account the expected discounted value of output price and labor costs, assuming again that it knows $R$. In an analogy to the cost function, this problem can be described by a discounted profit function

$$\pi^* = \pi^*(\tilde{P}, R, \tilde{W}) \tag{54}$$

where

$$\tilde{P} = \int_0^T P(t)e^{-rt}\, dt \qquad \text{and} \qquad \tilde{W} = \int_0^T W(t)e^{-rt}\, dt$$

and $\pi^*$ is total discounted maximized profits. Optimal plant size, average output, and labor input then are $Y^* = \partial\pi^*/\partial\tilde{P}$, $K^* = -\partial\pi^*/\partial R$, and $L^* = -\partial\pi^*/\partial\tilde{W}$. Note, however, that once the plant is built the firm can improve on its profits by using the restricted profit function defined by the plant size and by taking current prices into account. The research decision, however, is based on the unrestricted profit function (54). Note also that the profit function (54) uniquely defines the restricted profit function (53).[19] Choose again a generalized Leontief form:[20]

$$\pi^* = A^1\tilde{P} - A^2 R - A^3\tilde{W}$$
$$+ 2\gamma_{12}\tilde{P}^{1/2}R^{1/2} + 2\gamma_{13}\tilde{P}^{1/2}\tilde{W}^{1/2} + 2\gamma_{23}\tilde{P}^{1/2}\tilde{W}^{1/2} \tag{55}$$

The $\gamma_{ij}$ parameters determine the transformation elasticities between the output and inputs, so that we leave them again constant. Research affects the parameters $A^i$.

Optimal input and output levels are

$$Y^* = A^1 + \gamma_{12}\tilde{P}^{-1/2}R^{1/2} + \gamma_{13}\tilde{P}^{-1/2}\tilde{W}^{1/2}$$
$$K^* = A^2 - \gamma_{12}\tilde{P}^{1/2}R^{-1/2} - \gamma_{23}R^{-1/2}\tilde{W}^{1/2} \tag{56}$$
$$L^* = A^3 - \gamma_{13}\tilde{P}^{1/2}\tilde{W}^{-1/2} - \gamma_{23}R^{1/2}\tilde{W}^{-1/2}$$

A concept of input biases before and after research can be defined as follows:

$$Q|_{\tilde{P},R,\tilde{w}} = \frac{K_0^* - K_1^*}{K_0^*} - \frac{L_0^* - L_1^*}{L_0^*} \tag{57}$$

It is easily seen that this bias depends only on what happens to $A^2$ and $A^3$, not on what happens to $A^1$.

One can define innovation possibilities in several ways. Again, it does not make much sense to have individual research processes affect only one of the three A's; most research processes will affect all optimal output and input

---

[19] The production process underlying (54) must be of a degree of homogeneity of less than one in $K$ and $L$.

[20] Diewert, "Functional Forms."

levels simultaneously. Proceeding again with two research processes, we can postulate $m$ to be capital saving and $n$ to be labor saving.

$$\hat{A}^i = \hat{A}^i(m, n) \tag{58}$$

Clearly, we want research to increase optimal output levels, to reduce optimal input levels, and to place suitable constraints on research productivity parameters in order to insure that $m$ is capital saving with respect to definition (57) and $n$ is labor saving. The research function can have the same form as those used before (equation 11).

It is not worthwhile to get into the details of this analysis here because the implications of factor prices for research levels and biases are the same in this model as in the cost-minimizing model. The new and predictable conclusion that emerges is that a rise in output prices will increase the optimal research levels and, consequently, the rate of technical change.

ALLOCATION OF RESEARCH RESOURCES TO COMMODITIES.   When a firm or a region produces several commodities from a given resource endowment, it must decide, on the basis of goods prices, how to allocate research resources to increase the efficiency of each product. This problem can be analyzed with a transformation function between the outputs:

$$\psi(X, Y) = 0 \tag{59}$$

If outputs can be sold at expected discounted prices $\tilde{P}_x$ and $\tilde{P}_y$, there exists a unique dual profit function which is convex in output prices:

$$\pi^* = \pi^*(\tilde{P}_x, \tilde{P}_y) \tag{60}$$

where $\tilde{P}_i = \int_0^T P_i(t)e^{-rt}\, dt$, $i = x, y$. Choose again a generalized Leontief function.

$$\pi^* = A\tilde{P}_x + B\tilde{P}_y + 2\gamma\tilde{P}_x^{1/2}\tilde{P}_y^{1/2} \tag{61}$$

A sufficient condition for convexity is that $\gamma \geqq 0$.

By Shephard's lemma, the optimal output levels are:

$$X^* = \frac{\partial \pi^*}{\partial \tilde{P}_x} = A + \gamma\tilde{P}_x^{-1/2}\tilde{P}_y^{1/2}$$

$$Y^* = \frac{\partial \pi^*}{\partial \tilde{P}_y} = B + \gamma\tilde{P}_x^{1/2}\tilde{P}_y^{-1/2} \tag{62}$$

In the fixed proportion case $\gamma = 0$, and for output quantities to be positive at all levels of $\gamma$ it is necessary that $A > 0$, $B > 0$.

Graphically, the transformation function appears as in figure 5–3. When $\gamma$ is equal to zero, the transformation function collapses to the point $P$. The

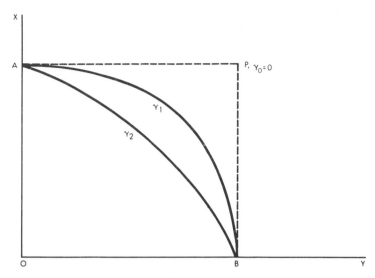

FIG. 5–3. The generalized Leontief transformation function.

smaller the value of $\gamma_1$, the flatter becomes the transformation curve. In figure 5–3 the constraint $\gamma_2 < \gamma_1 < \gamma_0 = 0$ must hold.[21]

The problem is to maximize the profit increase less research costs:

$$\max \pi_1^* - \pi_0^* - mP^m - nP^n = A_0 \tilde{P}_x \hat{A} + B_0 \tilde{P}_y \hat{B} - m\tilde{P}^m - n\tilde{P}^n$$
$$= c_x \hat{A} + c_y \hat{B} - m\tilde{P}^m - n\tilde{P}^n \qquad (63)$$

where $c_x = A_0 \tilde{P}_x$ and $c_y = B_0 \tilde{P}_y$ are the discounted *profit components* associated with the $A$ and $B$ terms at the initial levels of $A$ and $B$. Note that $c_x + c_y \geqq \pi^*$; these profit components are larger than total profits because the term $2\gamma \tilde{P}_x^{1/2} \tilde{P}_y^{1/2} < 0$. Because we want $A$ and $B$ to increase rather than decrease, we redefine $\hat{A} = (A_1 - A_0)/A_0$ and $\hat{B} = (B_1 - B_0)/B_0$; they are percentage *increases* rather than percentage *decreases*. After this redefinition the same research functions as in the cost-minimizing case can be used (equation 11).

Therefore the maximizing problem (63) has the same structure as the maximizing problems in the cost function case, and all results with respect to

---

[21] One inconvenient feature of the generalized Leontief function becomes apparent here: If the $m$ process increases the optimal amount of $Y_1$ but decreases the optimal amount of $Y_2$ at constant output-price ratios, it must follow that $B$ is a decreasing function of $m$. However, $B$ is the maximum amount of $Y$ that can be produced when $X$ is zero. If research is commodity specific, it would be better if that amount stayed constant. Therefore, the generalized Leontief transformation function is best viewed as a *local approximation* of the segment of the transformation function around the existing production point, it being recognized that at points far away the approximation may not really be good.

research allocation are analogous to those in the cost-minimizing case. We can also define a *commodity bias* $q$ to research as the change in the optimal output ratio at constant output prices.

$$q|_{\tilde{p}_x,\tilde{p}_y} = \frac{X_1^* - X_0^*}{X_0^*} - \frac{Y_1^* - Y_0^*}{Y_0^*} = \frac{A_0}{X_0^*}\hat{A} - \frac{B_0}{Y_0^*}\hat{B} \gtreqless 0 \begin{cases} X \text{ favoring} \\ \text{neutral} \\ Y \text{ favoring} \end{cases} \tag{64}$$

Because (64) has the same structure as (13), all results with respect to biases are analogous to the cost function case.

MULTIPLE OUTPUTS AND MULTIPLE INPUTS.    We now let $X_i$ stand for inputs or outputs and adopt the convention that inputs are negative $X_i$'s and outputs are positive $X_i$'s. There are $N$ outputs and $M$ inputs, and the total number of variables is $N + M$. Without research and with perfectly competitive input and output markets, the problem of the firm is to maximize:

$$\pi = \sum_{i=1}^{N+M} \tilde{P}_i X_i - \lambda f(X_i, \ldots, X_{N+M}) \tag{65}$$

where $f(X_i, \ldots, X_{N+M})$ is the strictly concave transformation function[22] and, again, $\tilde{P}_i = \int_0^T P_i(t)e^{-rt}\,dt$.

Corresponding uniquely to the problem (65) is a profit function[23]

$$\pi^* = \pi^*(\tilde{P}_1, \ldots, \tilde{P}_{N+M}) \tag{66}$$

which is strictly convex in prices. Choose again a generalized Leontief profit function:[24]

$$\pi^* = \sum_{i=1}^{N+M} \sum_{j=1}^{N+M} b_{ij}\tilde{P}_i^{1/2}\tilde{P}_j^{1/2} \tag{67}$$

A sufficient condition for $\pi^*$ to be strictly convex is that $b_{ij} \leq 0$ for all $i,j, i \neq j$. It is convenient to assume that $b_{ii} > 0$ for outputs $i = 1, \ldots, N$, and that $b_{ii} < 0$ for inputs $i = N + 1, \ldots, N + M$.

The factor demand and output supply functions are

$$X_i^* = \frac{\partial \pi^*}{\partial \tilde{P}_i} = \sum_{j=1}^{N+M} b_{ij}(\tilde{P}_j/\tilde{P}_i)^{1/2} \qquad i = 1, \ldots, N + M \tag{68}$$

If we have a set of research processes $(m, n, \ldots, k)$ that influence only the

---

[22] Owing to the sign convention, $f(X_1, \ldots, X_{N+M})$ is strictly concave in both inputs and outputs.

[23] See L. J. Lau, "Profit Functions of Technologies with Multiple Inputs and Outputs," *Review of Economics and Statistics* 59 (August 1972): 281–7.

[24] Diewert, "Functional Forms."

$b_{ii}$, then the increase in profits from research is

$$\pi_1^* - \pi_0^* = \sum_{i=1}^{N} b_{ii}^0 \tilde{P}_i \hat{b}_{ii} - \sum_{i=N+1}^{N+M} b_{ii}^0 \tilde{P}_i \hat{b}_{ii} \tag{69}$$

where $\hat{b}_{ii} = (b_{ii}^1 - b_{ii}^0)/|b_{ii}^0|$.

Note that we have to divide by the absolute level of $b_{ii}^0$ to define the $b_{ii}$ positively for a technological advance. As the $b_{ii}$ for the inputs are negative, however, the negative sign appears in (69) for the terms in $b_{ii}$ of the inputs. It is reasonable to assume that all research is either input specific or output specific. In an agricultural example, output-specific research might be plant breeding, whereas input-specific research might be research on machinery, soil chemistry, or pesticides. Unfortunately, this, again, does not imply that each $\hat{b}_{ii}$ is a function of just one research activity. Indeed, it is unreasonable even to assume that all output-specific research activities alter only the $b_{ii}$ for outputs and that input-specific research activities alter only those for inputs. To see this, consider the input demand and output supply functions (68), which can be rewritten as

$$X_i^* = b_{ii} + \sum_{j \neq 1} b_{ij}(\tilde{P}_j/\tilde{P}_i)^{1/2} \qquad i = 1, \ldots, N + M \tag{70}$$

Suppose $X_i$ is an output. Research on any one of the inputs can affect output supply only through $b_{ii}$. As long as $b_{ii}$ is constant, the output supply stays constant. But, in general, a firm that increases the efficiency of its inputs lowers its marginal cost curves for all of its outputs, and we would expect it to increase its output levels. Hence the $b_{ii}$ for the outputs have to be functions of the input-specific research lines as well.

Therefore, we write

$$\hat{b}_{ii} = \hat{b}_{ii}(m, n, \ldots, k) \qquad \text{for } (i = 1, \ldots, N + M) \tag{71}$$

The maximizing problem, therefore, takes the form

$$\max V = \sum_{i=1}^{N} b_{ii}^0 \tilde{P}_i \hat{b}_{ii}(m, n, \ldots, k) - \sum_{j=N+1}^{N+M} b_{ii}^0 \tilde{P}_i \hat{b}_{ii}(m, n, \ldots, k)$$
$$- mP^m - nP^n - \cdots - kP^k \tag{72}$$

Once appropriate restrictions are placed on the $b_{ii}$ functions, this problem can be resolved for the optimal research mix. This line of inquiry is not pursued further here. Clearly, the optimal amount of each research activity (say, $m$) is affected by all those input and output prices $P_i$ for which $\partial \hat{b}_{ii}/\partial m \neq 0$. And clearly a rise in the price of an output increases the optimal amounts of all those research activities for which $\partial \hat{b}_{ii}/\partial m > 0$, that is, for all those lines that favor the given output. And a rise in the price of an input $i$ will increase the optimal amounts of all those research activities that contribute to saving that particular factor, that is, the factor for which

$\partial \hat{b}_{ii}/\partial m > 0$. Also, the research levels will be affected by research productivities and initial efficiencies of factors of production.

## Market Structure in Intermediate Goods Industries and the Bias of Technical Change

In the last chapter we considered the problem of how the mechanism of induced innovation is affected if research is not carried out in the final goods industry but in an industry that supplies inputs in which innovations are embodied. We found that in the example of the tractor industry in its relationship to agriculture, the bias of technical change is likely to be more tractor using under this structural arrangement for research when the tractor industry is characterized by a high degree of monopoly. We also found that the tractor-using bias would be larger, the larger the elasticity of substitution between tractors and other factors of production in relation to the elasticity of final demand for agricultural output. However, it was stated that, if the elasticity of substitution were zero (fixed-proportion case) the bias of technical change would be unaffected by monopoly in the tractor industry. This proposition will be proved here.

Our approach is drastically simplified from the previous models. Suppose, first, that research for agriculture is carried out in an experiment station that tries to find the minimum cost for agriculture—that tries to minimize $YP$ plus research costs, where $Y$ is agricultural output and $P$ is the agricultural output price. Clearly, because agriculture is competitive, the price is unit costs, that is, $P = U(R, W)$, which we assume to be constant. Assume that the production function is of fixed proportion such that $U = RA + WB$ where $A$ is the capital–output ratio and $B$ is the labor–output ratio. Instead of making their proportional reductions $\hat{A}$ and $\hat{B}$ functions of research, we make $A$ and $B$ directly functions of research.[25] We also assume an orthogonal case in which each research activity reduces only one factor requirement, for example, $A = A(m)$ and $B = B(n)$.

Further, we assume that the innovation possibilities are neutral,[26] that is, $\partial A/\partial m = A_m = B_n$ if $m = n$. For reasons which will become apparent a little later, we use the symbol $\rho$ for the price of capital that is first supplied by a competitive industry at constant costs, and the price of each research activity is constant and equal to one. Hence the research station wants to minimize

$$
\begin{aligned}
V &= Y \cdot U(m, n) + m + n \\
&= Y \cdot [\rho A(m) + W B(n)] + m + n
\end{aligned}
\tag{73}
$$

where $m + n$ equals total research costs.

[25] The reason for this is that in order to determine total agricultural output, we need to know the effect of research on the absolute unit cost, not just its change. By making $A$ and $B$ functions of research we can easily do this. Of course, $\hat{A}$ and $\hat{B}$ research functions are related in a one-to-one relationship to $A$ and $B$ functions at any given point in time.

[26] This assumption is really not necessary, but it makes demonstration easier.

The following condition must hold at the optimum:

$$\frac{B_n}{A_m} = \frac{\rho}{W} \qquad (74)$$

$B_n/A_m$ is the ratio of marginal products of the research activities in a labor-saving direction ($B_n$) and a capital-saving direction ($A_m$), respectively. Since innovation possibilities are neutral, $B_n = A_m$ when $m = n$ or for all research allocations with neutral technical change. If $A_m$ is less than $B_n$, this means (because of diminishing returns to research) that $m$ exceeds $n$, or that technical change is labor using. Thus we can write[27]

$$\frac{B_n}{A_m} \gtreqless 1 \rightarrow \begin{cases} \text{labor-using (capital-saving) technical change} \\ \text{neutral technical change} \\ \text{labor-saving (capital-using) technical change} \end{cases} \qquad (75)$$

A rise in the ratio thus indicates a more pronounced capital-saving bias; a fall indicates a more pronounced labor-saving bias. Hence equation (75) shows the familiar fact that when $\rho$ (the price of capital) rises, technical change becomes more capital saving.

Now assume that technical change in agriculture can occur only by means of embodiment in tractors (measured in some physical unit, such as horsepower) and that horsepower can be produced at a constant cost $\rho$ by a monopolist before and after research (which amounts to assuming embodiment costs away).[28]

The monopolist has to decide what kind of research to do. But his benefits are derived only from the sale of tractors, not from agriculture's cost reduction. Thus one might suspect that the monopolist is not interested in total agricultural cost reductions but only in the effect of research on tractor sales. However, the monopolist controls both the sales price of tractors $R$ (which will be higher than his cost $\rho$) and the bias of the technology. So we have to see whether particular biases affect his pricing decision.

The monopolist's profits in this case are

$$\pi = (R - \rho) Y \cdot A \qquad (76)$$

where ($R - \rho$) is the markup over costs, $Y$ is agricultural output, and $A$ is the input of capital per unit of output. His benefits from research become

$$V = (R - \rho) Y[u(R, m, n)] A(m) - m - n \qquad (77)$$

where $u = AR + BW$.

---

[27] This holds only for neutral innovation possibilities. For nonneutral possibilities, neutrality would obtain at a ratio of $B_n/A_m$, which is different from one.

[28] Embodiment costs could be introduced also by making $\rho$ a function of research.

The first order conditions of this problem are

$$\frac{\partial V}{\partial m} = (R - \rho)Y_u RA_m A + YA_m - 1 = 0 \tag{78}$$

$$\frac{\partial V}{\partial n} = (R - \rho)Y_u WB_n A - 1 = 0 \tag{79}$$

$$\frac{\partial V}{\partial R} = YA + (R - \rho)Y_u A^2 = 0 \tag{80}$$

From dividing equation (79) by (80) we find the following condition:

$$\frac{Y_u RA_m A + YA_m}{Y_u WB_n A} = \frac{P^m}{P^n} \tag{81}$$

Solving (80) for the optimal price,

$$R = \rho - \frac{Y}{Y_u A} \tag{82}$$

Setting (82) into (81) leads to the condition for marginal research productivities

$$\frac{B_n}{A_m} = \frac{\rho}{W} \tag{83}$$

which is identical to the condition (74) for the agricultural research institute that follows a socially optimal rule.

In the fixed-proportion case, monopoly in the input-supplying industry that provides the technical change will therefore result in technical change taking precisely the same direction it would take in agriculture if the research were controlled by agriculture itself. This is remarkable, because the incentive to increase tractor input per unit of agricultural output is exactly offset by the reduction of the monopoly power that such an increase would entail. Of course we know that in the variable-proportion case the offsetting is incomplete and that when $\sigma$ becomes very large the price and input demand effects of capital-using technical change reinforce each other.

## The Problem of Dynamic Extensions

All the models presented so far are in comparative static terms. What are the prospects of pushing them into dynamic terms?

One of the first attempts to bring some dynamic considerations and expectations into the theory of induced innovation was Fellner's proposition, which we discussed in chapter 2.[29] However, it has been shown in the last two chapters that his proposition is not a question of the mechanism of inducement but of the magnitude of the induced bias.

One extension of the models that would be highly useful for future econometric work in this area would be the building of general equilibrium models in which both rates and biases can be induced. In particular, the roles of the size of the elasticities of supply of factors and of the size of the elasticities of demand for commodities (the latter was discussed to some extent in chapter 4) need attention.

The general equilibrium models could also be made dynamic for simulation purposes with actual economic data and for counter-factual historical analysis similar to that presented by Kelley and Williamson for Japanese economic history.[30] However, it is doubtful that using standard techniques of growth theory will provide any further insights than those that will come from dynamic simulations of general equilibrium models. The reason is that analysis of equilibrium properties of growth paths is of little value for empirical testing against history, because it is likely to take a very long time to reach such equilibrium paths from any disequilibrium position.[31] Given that actual economies are always subject to large exogenous shocks, such as wars or depressions, this implies that most recorded history does not trace equilibrium paths but rather phases of adjustment to disequilibria. And the behavior of economic variables in the adjustment phases differs strongly from their behavior on the equilibrium path.[32] When it comes to modeling

[29] William Fellner, "Two Propositions in the Theory of Induced Innovation," *Economic Journal* 71, no. 282 (June 1961): 305–8.

[30] Allan C. Kelley and Jeffrey C. Williamson, *Lessons from Japanese Development: An Analytic Economic History* (Chicago: University of Chicago Press, 1974).

[31] A. Dixit, "Growth Patterns in a Dual Economy," *Oxford Economic Papers* 3 (July 1970): 229–34.

[32] For a more thorough discussion of this issue see Kelly and Williamson, *Japanese Development*, pp. 86–91; see also Dixit, "Growth Patterns."

Equilibrium growth models are unable to capture many important features of the development process precisely because of their orientation toward equilibrium states and because they take as given so many things that will change in the development process itself, such as market structures, infrastructural equipment, technology, tastes, the structure of property rights, and many other institutions (see part IV). Development should rather be viewed as an iterative adjustment process to disequilibria caused by the development and production process itself and by exogenous shocks and influences. A fruitful approach might be to view development as a sequence of periods. At the beginning of each period, technology, tastes, capital stocks, and institutions are given and can be taken as parameters that enter the optimization problems of all the participants in the development process. Individuals and organizations then allocate resources to production, investment, technical change, and institutional change. In addition, exogenous shocks such as weather, developments in international markets, advances in basic and supporting sciences, and changes in ideas and tastes occur. Individual allocation decisions and exogenous shocks jointly determine production and consumption flows and changes in stocks, technology, institutions, and, possibly, tastes. New disequilibria emerge.

The next period's problem then starts with these newly created parameters, and a new

technical change endogenously, an additional and at least as important objection to asymptotic growth-model analysis arises, which is best illustrated by recalling the simple Evenson–Kislev model of applied research in chapter 4. Research is viewed as a sampling process over a given distribution of potential yields, and the research payoff is the difference between the highest yield found in the sample and the yield that has already been achieved. After each period, the highest sample yield of the last period becomes the reference yield over which improvements must be sought. Therefore, additional improvements in each period require larger and larger samples as long as the same distribution of yields is sampled. Since the research output is yield increments and not yields per se, research is a nonreproducible production process, and research potential is exhausted by research itself.

For a dynamic asymptotic growth model of induced innovation, however, it is necessary that a stable and reproducible relationship exist between research input and research output; otherwise, an equilibrium growth path cannot be achieved. It therefore is necessary to assume that the basic distribution from which yield samples are drawn shifts over time, thus replenishing opportunities for applied research. And there is no doubt that in the past, advances in supporting and basic sciences have fairly steadily opened up new profitable avenues for applied research in almost all fields, although in the next chapter we will show some examples where these advances were large but came rather intermittently.

In extending this model to a fully dynamic context, Evenson and Kislev have therefore assumed that the distribution of potential yields shifts exogenously at a constant rate over time. In the derived steady-state solution, the rate of yield increase (or technical change) turned out to be exactly equal to the rate of shifts in the distribution of potential yield increases, that is, the rate of technical change became equal to the rate of progress in the basic and supporting sciences. In such a model, applied technological research only determines the gap between techniques that exist and those that are scientifically possible.

Of course, it would be possible to incorporate the exogenously shifting potential distributions of the $A$ and $B$ parameters of the last chapter into our induced growth model. This has been done by Nordhaus for Kennedy's IPF.[33] However, Nordhaus shows that if such a model had a stable long-run growth path, the rates of change of the augmentation coefficients would be exactly equal to the rates of change of the parameters of the underlying distributions. This would also be the case if the above models were extended

---

round is initiated. In a way, this is a sort of dynamic programming model, except that individual actors have different objective functions. Such an approach lacks all the neatness of equilibrium growth models and will be extremely difficult to put into strict modeling frameworks. But thinking and looking at subproblems in these terms might allow us to learn more about development than we can learn from growth models.

[33] William D. Nordhaus, "Some Skeptical Thoughts on the Theory of Induced Innovation," *Quarterly Journal of Economics* 87, no. 2 (May 1973): 208–19.

in the same way. Rates and biases of technical change would be equal to the assumed rates and biases of basic and supporting scientific progress. This brings us straight back to a model of exogenous rates and biases of technical change.

Thus we arrive at a pessimistic conclusion. It is impossible to build a very long-term theory of economic growth that treats technical change in a truly endogenous way. This means that it is impossible to have a long-term theory of growth at all, because technical change is an essential part of growth. The fundamental problem is that it is impossible to know *ex ante* how basic and supporting sciences will develop in the future. Growth models cannot bridge that gap in our knowledge; they can only trace the consequences of various assumptions about the long-term development of basic knowledge.

It might of course be objected that it is possible to build a model of endogenous progress in supporting and basic sciences in which exhaustion of applied research possibilities or changes in economic variables will induce research in particular directions. Certainly basic research is responsive, to a limited extent, to economic factors. It must be recognized, however, that at the basic end of the continuum, a substantial part of scientific research is carried out without economic motives. Also, distributions of potential research payoff in one industry frequently shift, owing to advances in other industries, as when the invention of transistors led to productivity increases in many industries in which the application of transistors was never contemplated by the inventor. Furthermore, building more and more basic research into an induced innovation model would be going one layer deeper every time, so to speak, but it would not get us around the problem that for a meaningful growth model some exogenous shifts in the payoff distribution of the more and more basic lines of research must be assumed. And these assumed shifts will dominate the solution on the equilibrium growth path.

The usefulness of induced innovation models, therefore, should not be sought in their contribution to formal growth theory, but rather in what they imply for research policy: What are the institutions, and what is the market structure that will result in an optimal amount of technical change that minimizes the resource costs of production? And what are the implications of the theory for research resource allocation in the public sector and between basic and applied research? To answer these questions, comparative static models can carry us a long way, despite their simplicity and limitations.

APPENDIX 5–1
*A Note on Embodiment, Factor Quality,*
*and Factor Augmentation*

Technical change is said to be embodied in capital items if a firm must purchase a new machine in order to use the innovation. In this situation, only new machines embody the technical advance, which will be completely diffused throughout the economy only after the entire stock of existing capital equipment has been replaced by new machinery. This view of technical change has led to vintage models of economic growth, in which all technical change is embodied in capital. In such models, the rate of capital accumulation becomes a crucial variable in explaining the rate of technical change.[34] Technical change that is not embodied in machines, on the other hand, can increase the efficiency of the production process even if old machines are used. Examples of such technical change would be improvements in intermediate product quality, organizational improvements, and increases in labor quality.

It is clear that every technical change must be embodied in one factor of production in the following sense: To realize any technical change, a firm must purchase a factor of production that embodies it or must expend resources to embody it in the factors of production it has already purchased. A farmer who wants to make use of genetic advances in a crop must purchase the seeds in which they are embodied. Pesticides embody chemical advances. A firm that wants to use improved methods of organizing production must teach them to its employees. If the employees later leave, the firm must teach the methods again to new employees or hire others who have learned them elsewhere. Once this point is accepted, the question no longer is whether or not technical change is embodied but whether the embodiment costs are high or low and how fast embodiment can take place. Some organizational changes may be very easy to grasp; they may not require much time to learn and, therefore, they may be implemented rapidly. Intermediate inputs can be changed after improved inputs become available as soon as the unimproved stock is exhausted. Therefore, technical improvements embodied in intermediate inputs will spread rapidly and will depend less on the aggregate rate of investment than will technical change embodied in fixed-capital items.

Furthermore, it is clear that technical changes that increase the quality of a factor are embodied in that particular factor. However, the problem arises of measuring the quality changes and defining quality indexes for factors of production. The substantial literature on this issue has not yet produced a satisfactory solution to the problem.[35] Here I wish to point out only that changes in the quality of a factor can neither be viewed nor measured as rates of augmentation in a factor-augmenting production function:[36]

$$Y = f(X_1/a_1, \ldots, X_n/a_n) \tag{A-1}$$

[34] For a review of the embodiment hypothesis, see Murray Brown, *Theory and Measurement of Technical Change* (Cambridge: Cambridge University Press, 1966), pp. 77–92. Also Robert M. Solow, "Technical Progress, Capital Formation and Economic Growth," *American Economic Review* 52 (May 1962): 76–86; Dale W. Jorgenson, "The Embodiment Hypothesis," *Journal of Political Economy* 64 (February 1966): 1–17.

[35] Zvi Griliches, ed., *Price Indexes and Quality Change* (Cambridge, Mass.: Harvard University Press, 1971); Makoto Ohta, "Production Technologies of the U.S. Boiler and Turbogenerator Industries and Hedonic Price Indexes for their Projects: A Cost Function Approach," *Journal of Political Economy* 83 (February 1975): 1–26.

[36] Technical change affects only the variables, not the functional form of the production function. See also appendix 2–1 and footnote 1, chapter 2.

A given rate of labor augmentation cannot be linked to investment in human capital, and the rate of capital augmentation is not due solely to technical changes or quality improvements in machines or other capital items.[37]

In the case of a Cobb–Douglas function, any given rate of technical change can be viewed as a neutral shifter, as entirely labor augmenting, as entirely capital augmenting, or as an infinite number of combinations of these three.[38] However, if a technical change arises from a quality improvement in machines, that quality improvement cannot be assigned to any other factor in such an arbitrary way.

When a production function is of fixed proportions

$$Y = \min\left\{\frac{K}{a}, \frac{L}{b}\right\} \tag{A-2}$$

then the augmentation factors are simply the capital–output and the labor–output ratios.

Suppose, now, that the quality of a worker who operates a machine improves; he will be able to produce more output per machine-hour and per man-hour. Both the capital–output and the labor–output ratios are reduced, not just the latter. Both factors are augmented. Similarly, if a new machine that costs 10 percent more (but which is still operated by one man) is used, and if output rises by more than 10 percent per machine-hour, both the labor and machinery coefficients are reduced. If output per hour rises by only 10 percent, the capital–output ratio is unaffected and only the labor–output ratio falls by 10 percent. This would be an example of a technical change that is embodied in a machine but that augments only labor.

In agriculture, technical change is very frequently embodied in seeds. But the reduction in seed requirements per unit of output made possible by the new varieties is almost immaterial as compared to the reduction in land,

---

[37] The confusion of factor augmentation rates with quality indexes of factors is common in the technical change and development literature. Kelley and Williamson, *Japanese Development*, pp. 179–96, treat the rate of labor augmentation as the rate of human capital accumulation per worker and the rate of capital augmentation as the rate of improvement of the quality of purchased inputs from the nonagricultural sector. These authors identify the rate of land augmentation as the rate of development of irrigation facilities and propose to measure it by changes in the share of paddy fields in the total area planted to rice (p. 241). This they do despite the use of a Cobb–Douglas production function (see footnote 38). This error in interpretation in no way diminishes the importance of the counter-factual analyses of Japanese agriculture performed by the authors because the rationale for performing the analyses in no way depends on interpretation of augmentation rates as quality indexes.

[38] We can write

$$
\begin{aligned}
Q &= e^{\lambda t} L^{\alpha} K^{1-\alpha} && \text{neutral technical change} \\
  &= (e^{\lambda t/\alpha} L)^{\alpha} K^{1-\alpha} && \text{purely labor augmenting} \\
  &= L^{\alpha} (e^{\lambda t/1-\alpha} K)^{1-\alpha} && \text{purely capital augmenting} \\
  &= (e^{\lambda t/2\alpha} L)^{\alpha} (e^{\lambda t/2(1-\alpha)} K)^{1-\alpha} && \text{capital and labor augmenting.}
\end{aligned}
$$

labor, and capital requirements per unit of output. Most or all factors of production are augmented when seed quality is improved. Hence the augmentation rate of the seeds cannot measure the quality change of the seeds. This lack of correspondence between augmentation rates and investments in the quality of the corresponding factors by way of research, education, and training makes measured rates of factor augmentation very difficult to interpret in any economic sense. The only reason to measure them is that they have implications for the bias of technical change. But, as will be shown in chapter 7, it is possible to measure biases directly without measuring the corresponding factor augmentation rates, and the latter are not reported there because of their lack of economic interpretation.

Finally, factor-augmenting technical change is a special case of the more general framework used in this chapter. Call the change in per-unit factor demand that results from the technical change a *factoral rate of technical change*; for example,

$$\hat{K}^*|_{W,R} = \frac{\partial K^*}{\partial t}\frac{1}{K^*}\quad\left(= -\frac{K_0^* - K_1^*}{K_0^*} = -\frac{YA_0}{K_0^*}\hat{A}\right) \tag{A-3}$$

The parentheses enclose factoral rates of technical change for the general discrete case and for the special generalized Leontief function used throughout the chapter (see equations 13 and 14).

The bias is simply the difference between factoral rates:

$$B|_{W,R} = \hat{L}^* - \hat{K}^* \tag{A-4}$$

For production functions homogenous of degree one, the cost function corresponding to equation (1) of the factor-augmenting case can be written as $U = U[(Ra), (Wb)]$. Therefore $K^* = aU_R[(Ra), (Wb)]$. The observed change over time of $K^*$ is

$$\frac{\partial K^*}{\partial t}\frac{1}{K^*} = \eta_{KK}\hat{R} + \eta_{KL}\hat{W} - \hat{a} - \eta_{KK}\hat{a} - \eta_{KL}\hat{b} \tag{A-5}$$

where the hats denote rates of change over time in the variables and the $\eta$ are the factor demand elasticities with respect to the variables in the subscripts.

It is clear that the factoral rate of technical change for capital is

$$\hat{K}^* = \frac{\partial K^*}{\partial t}\frac{1}{K^*}\bigg|_{W,R} = -\hat{a} - \eta_{KK}\hat{a} - \eta_{KL}\hat{b} \tag{A-6}$$

Factoral rates are thus simply functions of factor augmentation rates. Note, however, that we can define and measure factoral rates of technical change, even when technical change is not factor augmenting but of a more general nature, as long as we have measured values of the factor demand elasticities or the cost function parameters that define the factor demand elasticities. (See chapter 7 for procedures.) Factor-augmenting technical change is thus a special case of factoral rates of technical change that needlessly complicates the analysis of biased technical change.

# SIX

# Technology Transfer and Research Resource Allocation

ROBERT E. EVENSON AND HANS P. BINSWANGER

I N this chapter we will attempt to integrate the findings of research in three areas of concern: research resource allocation, induced innovation, and technology transfer. In the preceding chapter, we explored the first two of these areas at some length. Here, however, it will be necessary to make some modifications in the theories we have developed in both chapters 4 and 5. For example, the problem of allocating research resources becomes more complicated when it must focus on not just one technology in a particular region but on several technologies employed in a variety of regions.

Economists have approached the problem of technology transfer from different angles. The Heckscher–Ohlin literature on factor proportions and comparative advantage advances the notion that labor-abundant countries should adopt the more labor-using of available techniques whereas countries where labor is scarce should adopt labor-saving techniques. Such "choice of technology" literature often fails to point out that a borrowing, and usually less developed, country must be careful to allocate research resources so as to develop techniques that are compatible with its resource endowments, and that techniques in use in advanced countries may often be inappropriate in this respect.[1]

Raymond Vernon's product-cycle model of international trade takes some

---

[1] A. K. Sen, *Choice of Techniques* (Oxford: Basil Blackwell, 1968). For some recent research conducted within the choice of technology framework, see James C. Pickett, D. J. C. Forsyth, and N. S. McBain, "The Choice of Technology, Economic Efficiency and Employment in Developing Countries," in *Employment in Developing Nations*, ed. Edgar O. Edwards (New York: Columbia University Press, 1974), pp. 209–21; John Woodward Thomas, "Employment Creating Public Works Programs: Observations on Political and Social Dimensions," in *Employment in Developing Nations*, ed. Edgar O. Edwards, pp. 297–312; C. Peter Timmer, "Choice of Technique in Rice Milling on Java," *Bulletin of Indonesian Economic Studies* 9 (July 1973): 57–76; and Amartya Sen, *Employment Technology and Development* (London: Oxford University Press, 1975).

account of research and development and traces feedback relationships between technical change, technology transfer, per capita income, and market size.[2] According to this model, consumer goods and labor-saving capital goods tend to be developed first in the United States, where market size, high income, and high labor costs provide a favorable climate for product innovations. At this stage, relative costs of factors and transportation are of less importance. Once the product is standardized and well accepted in U.S. and foreign markets, however, its producers may find it more profitable to supply the non-U.S. market from factories located abroad, thus taking advantage of other countries' lower labor costs and saving transportation costs as well. Eventually, when the new technology is widely adopted, indigenous producers abroad, as a function of their lower expenditures for labor, may begin to compete with U.S. producers in the U.S. market itself.

This model of technology transfer is of limited usefulness in agriculture, where standardization and economies of scale in production tend to play a minor role. Moreover, the model does not take into account the particular barriers to transfer in agriculture that are created by the fact that techniques of production exhibit *location specificity*. That is, variation in environmental factors produces variation in the performance of crops and livestock. An early attempt to incorporate location specificity and adaptive research in a diffusion model was undertaken by Zvi Griliches in his study of the diffusion of hybrid corn.[3] In this study, regional variation in the date of initial planting of hybrid corn is explained by the size and density of the potential hybrid-seed market, as estimated from the size of a region and from its density of corn production. Griliches hypothesized that private seed companies and research stations would initiate work on hybrid corn in regions where corn production was concentrated, that is, that innovative effort was a function of the potential rate of return to research investment.

At the same time, Griliches also explains the rate of adoption and level of acceptance of innovation in terms of the absolute profitability of the shift— in his example, from open-pollinated to hybrid corn. Other studies have offered this explanation as well.[4] In investigating international technology transfer, however, we must specify the technique as well as the factor and product prices involved in innovation, as these are likely to vary among countries.

The work of Vernon W. Ruttan and Yujiro Hayami not only incorporates

[2] Raymond Vernon, "International Investment and International Trade in the Product Cycle," *Quarterly Journal of Economics* 80 (May 1966): 107–207.

[3] Zvi Griliches, "Hybrid Corn: An Exploration of the Economics of Technological Change," *Econometrica* 25 (October 1957): 501–22.

[4] Edwin Mansfield, "Technical Change and the Rate of Imitation," *Econometrica* 29 (October 1961): 741–66; idem, "The Speed of Response of Firms to New Techniques," *Quarterly Journal of Economics* 77 (May 1963): 291–311; idem, "Intrafirm Rates of Diffusion of an Innovation," *Review of Economics and Statistics* 45 (November 1963): 348–59.

adaptive and basic research in the transfer framework but takes account of location specificity in agricultural technical change.[5] Citing examples of both biological and mechanical technology, they distinguish three phases in the process of technology transfer. The *material transfer* stage "is characterized by the simple transfer or import of new materials such as seed, plants, animals, machines, and techniques associated with these materials. Local adaptation is not conducted in an orderly and systematic fashion."[6] In the *design transfer* stage, technology is transferred primarily in the form of blueprints, formulas, and books. Some exotic materials may be imported but for the purpose of copying their designs rather than for use in actual production. Gradually, a systematic approach to the testing of foreign materials evolves. Finally, in the *capacity transfer* stage, "technology transfer occurs primarily through the transfer of scientific knowledge.... The effect is to create the capacity for the production of locally adapted technology according to the prototype technology existing abroad.... An important element in the process of capacity transfer is the migration of agricultural scientists."[7]

The sequence of technology transfer stages we have just described will be illustrated in our discussion of sugarcane research in the section on research-screening complementarity below. As later sections of this chapter demonstrate, however, these stages do not necessarily follow each other in the order described. With good reason, a country may choose, in respect to some sectors of its economy, to remain at the stage of material transfer considerably beyond the time when in other sectors it is accomplishing capacity transfer.

Whether a technology is scientifically sophisticated—that is, whether it incorporates the most recent findings of basic research or whether it is based on simpler and older scientific and engineering principles—is not the primary determinant of its appropriateness to the process of transfer. An *appropriate* technology, as we will use the term in this chapter, is one that enables minimum-cost production in any given country.

In deciding how to improve the productivity of a sector of its economy, a country has three primary options. Under the *direct transfer* option, a country simply screens and adopts the best of techniques from other countries without altering such technology through research of its own. Under a second option, a country can screen technology from abroad and, through a program of *adaptive research*, modify or redesign the borrowed techniques to suit its own resource endowments. Finally, a country may elect to screen not only technology but scientific knowledge from other countries and to undertake a *comprehensive research* program in order to produce its own techniques.[8]

[5] Vernon W. Ruttan and Yujiro Hayami, "Technology Transfer and Development," *Technology and Culture* 14 (April 1973): 119–51; see also Vernon W. Ruttan, "Technical and Institutional Transfer in Agricultural Development," *Research Policy* 4 (1975): 350–78.

[6] Ruttan and Hayami, "Technology Transfer," p. 124.

[7] Ruttan and Hayami, "Technology Transfer," p. 125.

[8] These three options are related to Hayami and Ruttan's three stages of technology transfer, outlined above. However, they do not coincide precisely because the direct

In this chapter we want to examine the factors that influence the choice among the direct transfer and research options. We will discuss these factors under the following five general headings: (1) the relative costs of direct transfer of technology and of adaptive and comprehensive research programs; (2) the complementarity between screening of existing technology and carrying out applied research; (3) the role of factor scarcity in determining the choice between adaptive and comprehensive research; (4) the degree to which the cost of a technology is sensitive to climatic, biological, and chemical variations in the environment; and (5) the issues involved in the allocation of resources in agricultural research systems. Following our discussion of these considerations, which we will illustrate with examples drawn primarily from agriculture, we will review some of the recent empirical studies of technology transfer and research productivity in agriculture. In a final section of the chapter we will present our conclusions.

In the discussions that follow it is important to keep in mind that the relative weights given each of the five sets of factors mentioned above in determining the choice among options will differ greatly among sectors of the economy and among countries, depending on the size of the country, its stage of development, economic endowment, and physical environment. The differences among sectors are such that at any given time the direct transfer option might be optimal in one sector while the comprehensive research option is best in another. And technologies in certain sectors are such that the majority of developed or developing countries will always depend on direct transfer rather than on one of the research options.

Furthermore, we do not put heavy emphasis on learning by doing. The problems of learning by doing affect all new technology, whether it is imported, adapted, or independently developed. It is likely that the period of learning by doing, or of achieving maximum efficiency with an imported technology, could be shortened by adaptive research or by the use of a locally developed technology that takes account of the human skill endowments specific to a given country. This would seem to tilt the choice toward the research options. However, there have as yet been no studies of the potential savings in time that selection of these options might achieve.

## The Costs of Direct Transfer, Adaptive Research, and Comprehensive Research

To understand the problems involved in the transfer of technology, it is important to know how the costs of new technology differ for the initial developer and the subsequent adopter.

The initial developer faces two classes of costs. Initial *research and development costs* are independent of the scale of output to which a production process

---

transfer option can involve either materials or designs and because both research options are predicated on capacity transfer.

is eventually applied. They do exhibit the familiar economies of scale with respect to output exhibited by all informational investments.

*Embodiment costs* of the new technology include the costs of embodiment of both physical and human capital. In the case of the former, we include only the additional costs per unit of capital of the new capital items versus the old capital items. If the new technology replaces machines that are not fully depreciated, the difference between undepreciated value and scrap value must be added to the embodiment costs.

The embodiment costs of human capital include time spent by instructors and by supervisors and workers in learning how to use the new technology efficiently. It is obvious, of course, that experimentation, a necessary part of technology development, increases its costs, as do errors during the start-up period.

Embodiment costs are essentially scale-dependent, that is, they depend on the numbers of workers trained or the size of the plant to be built. And the greater the change in technology, the higher these costs will be.

The adopter of technology that has already been developed faces a different set of costs. He must study the available alternatives and determine which one is best suited to his specific circumstances. These *information and screening costs*, like those of research and development, are scale-independent.

The embodiment costs faced by an adopter are approximately the same as for the initial developer, and they are scale-dependent. However, by avoiding some of the mistakes made by predecessors, the latecomer may be able to reduce his experimentation costs.

The adopter may sometimes also incur *license costs*, or fees for patented processes. These costs are usually scale-dependent.

The adopter's information and screening, embodiment, and license costs have in the past been lumped together as *transfer costs*.[9] This has had the unfortunate result of obscuring both the crucial difference between scale-dependent and scale-independent costs and the fact that embodiment costs may be only slightly lower for late adopters than for initial innovators.

Information and screening costs are low if the adopter's economic and physical environments are quite similar to those of the innovator. Let us suppose that a farmer has observed his neighbor begin to use a new wheat variety. If the neighbor's profit is greater than with the old variety, the farmer can be virtually certain that he too will be able to improve his profit by adopting the variety because the two farms operate in a similar economic, physical, biological, and climatic environment. All the information the farmer needs is his observation of his neighbor's higher profit with the new variety.

If a potential adopter is in a different agroclimatic region—of the same or

[9] For some empirical findings on transfer costs in industry, see Edwin Mansfield, "International Technology Transfer: Forms, Resource Requirements and Policies," *American Economic Review* 65 (May 1975): 372–6.

another country—the fact that a variety increases profit in its originating area is no longer sufficient information. The new variety may not suit economic, physical, and biological environmental conditions elsewhere. And the more these conditions differ, the greater the possibility that consumers in the adopter's area may not like the taste of the new variety. Moreover, the superiority of the new variety may depend on the amount of fertilizer used; thus if fertilizer is very expensive in the new area, the new variety may not be profitable. Clearly, the adopter in a region that differs markedly from the region in which a variety originated needs considerably more information than did our farmer-observer. The potential adopter may need to do some screening experiments in order to assess the local profitability of the new variety.

The costs of the transfer of technology may be quite considerable. In general, these costs are a function of the difference between the economic and physical environments of the area where a variety originates and those of a new area. To the degree that a given element of the environment varies between areas, the overall cost of transfer will rise. This is true for agricultural technology and generally for industrial technology as well, and it is an issue of importance to our considerations here. In a later section of this chapter we will introduce the concept of an *environmental sensitivity* index as a unified approach to measuring the effect of all environmental differences on the potential profitability in various locations of a given technology.

## Complementarity Between Screening and Research

Our discussion of the alternative methods for achieving technology transfer borrowing technology from abroad as against undertaking research to adapt such technology or to create new techniques—revealed that even the direct transfer option may be costly, as it requires sufficient screening activity to determine which among many technologies are best suited to particular local conditions.

Here we wish to point out that this screening activity necessary for direct transfer overlaps with the activities required for adaptive research and that the latter activities may also overlap with the work entailed in comprehensive research. Obviously, in order to adapt a foreign technique to local conditions it is necessary first to select, from among a variety of methods, the one technique that can be adapted most profitably. Similarly, in the process of making such a technique suitable to local conditions, information useful in developing wholly new techniques may be generated.

This complementarity between transfer options is probably great enough to lead to an efficient policy mix, one which includes both home-based and borrowing-based, or adaptive, research. The complementarity between screening and adaptive research, *ceteris paribus*, lowers the relative cost of adapting and tends to increase the probability that this will be the minimum-cost route to improvement. However, the adaptive part of the strategy may require a research design of sufficient similarity to the indigenous research design that a "parallel" research program, involving both adaptive and comprehensive research, may be efficient.[10]

That a great deal of research activity is itself screening is well illustrated by the history of varietal transfer in sugarcane production.[11] The earliest improved varieties of sugarcane were produced in a small set of experiment stations that were established prior to 1900. As the first new varieties were discovered in the Java and Barbados stations—and in stations in India, Mauritius, and Hawaii somewhat later—they were diffused quite rapidly to producers in many parts of the world. However, the simple screening performed by cane growers in most countries proved inadequate. The new varieties were susceptible to diseases prevalent in many new environments, and producers were forced to abandon them and to return to traditional varieties.

The screening of new sugarcane varieties ultimately required very systematic field testing based on an understanding of the various cane diseases and the development of methods of testing varieties for disease resistance. Sugarcane producers generally did not have the skills required to undertake this type of screening. In many countries the high incidence of diseases associated with the new varieties led growers to ban their use in order to protect native varieties from disease. The establishment of experiment stations in every country now had two objectives: to carry out varietal research programs, and to undertake the screening that had proven too difficult for the growers.

To pursue these objectives, in the early 1900s a number of experiment stations were established in South Africa, Mexico, Argentina, Australia, and several other countries. During the 1920s and 1930s these stations performed an important screening function. They selected those applied varieties suited to their growers' environmental conditions and facilitated international diffusion of the new varietal technologies. Their research programs in agronomy and cane breeding were dependent on their ability also to screen national and international genetic material as well as genetic and agronomic knowledge from other countries. The leading stations, notably those in Java and India,

---

[10] See the following section, as well as Richard R. Nelson, "Uncertainty, Learning, and the Economics of Parallel Research and Development Efforts," *Review of Economics and Statistics* 43 (November 1961): 351–64, for a further development of the parallel research concept.

[11] Robert Evenson, J. P. Houck, Jr., and V. W. Ruttan, "Technical Change and Agricultural Trade: Three Examples—Sugarcane, Banana and Rice," in *The Technology Factor in International Trade*, ed. Raymond Vernon (New York: Columbia University Press, National Bureau of Economic Research, 1970), pp. 418–33; Robert E. Evenson and Yoav Kislev, *Agricultural Research and Productivity* (New Haven: Yale University Press, 1975), pp. 34–57.

produced a new set of interspecific hybrid varieties which were rather rapidly diffused to countries with screening capabilities. By the late 1930s and the 1940s the new varieties developed and adapted specifically to local environmental conditions proved superior to the international stock of borrowable varieties. Research programs that were initially adaptive in character and based on international genetic material developed ultimately into truly indigenous, or comprehensive, research programs.

Similar examples of the transition from dependence on borrowed technology to the capacity to adopt and invest indigenous technology can be drawn from the history of the development of technology in the United States during the nineteenth century. Elting E. Morrison points out that "the fundamental ideas developed during the nineteenth century about heat, electricity, the strength of materials, the origin of the species, the structure of matter, and the nature of a variety of chemical reactions came from beyond our borders."[12] Even the basic processes that translated this knowledge into practice were largely imported. Yet the work of adapting ideas and processes into actual practice, utilizing the particular factor endowments of a new continent, contributed to the development of a capacity for both applied and fundamental supporting research. According to Morrison, the "school of engineering" that evolved out of the technological experimentation necessary to the construction of the Middlesex and Erie Canals "freed men who wanted to build and make things in this country from their dependence upon European advisors and European rules of thumb."[13]

## Adaptive Versus Comprehensive Research: The Role of Factor Scarcity

In order to understand the role played by factor scarcity in the decision as to research emphasis, let us assume that a country must choose between adaptive research on a capital-intensive technology or comprehensive research on its own labor-intensive home technology.[14] We will use the simplest version of the induced innovation model presented in chapter 3, on the assumptions that both technologies are initially of fixed proportions and that the country has a fixed budget of research for the sector involved. This model also sheds some light on the direct transfer option. We assume throughout that the objective of the research is to maximize the present value of cost-reducing advances in total factor productivity. Other possible

[12] Elting E. Morrison, *From Know-How to Nowhere: The Development of American Technology* (New York: Basic Books, 1974), pp. 110–11.

[13] Morrison, *From Know-How to Nowhere*, p. 44.

[14] This section borrows heavily from Hans P. Binswanger, "Borrowing of Technology, Adaptive Research and Research on Home Technology, A Conceptual Framework," *Pakistan Economic and Social Review* 12 (Summer 1974): 144–56.

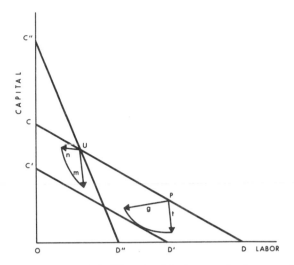

FIG. 6–1. The role of factor scarcity in research decision making.

social objectives can be considered separately, as the effects of decisions among alternatives on, say, employment are easily traceable.[15]

In figure 6–1, $CD$ is the importing country's factor price ratio, reflecting a low wage–rental rate. The point $U$ represents a particular foreign capital-intensive technology. $OD$ is the unit cost of production with this technology, measured in terms of labor, in the importing country. This cost of production differs from the unit cost of production with the technology $U$ in the country of origin because of differences in noneconomic, environmental factors. The point $U$ takes this into account. Costs differ also because of the differences in factor prices, but this is taken into account through the budget line $CD$.

The home technology $P$ is labor-using relative to $U$. A necessary condition for direct technology transfer without research is that unit costs of $U$ be lower than those of $P$ at the factor prices $CD$. This is not the case in the present example. Indeed, the figure is drawn such that on factor productivity considerations the country should be indifferent as between the $U$ and $P$ technologies. However, suppose that the receiving country subsidizes imported capital equipment either directly or through an overvalued exchange rate and the factor price line becomes steeper, moving to $C''D''$. On cost considerations, the imported technology is now preferred by entrepreneurs. This effect is well known and has two adverse consequences for employment. Per unit of output, less labor is used than if the home technology were used, and total output with $U$ for a given level of investment resources is smaller, thereby further reducing employment.

The fact that $U$ was developed in a higher labor-cost environment (budget

[15] Concern about employment, for example, strengthens the case for making decisions according to the proposed framework.

line $C''D''$) is reflected in the high capital–labor ratio of $U$ as well as in the possibilities for adaptive research. The two research-possibility frontiers with respect to $U$ and $P$ indicate the possible alternative technologies that can be developed by an applied research program if a fixed budget of research is allocated either to adaptive research on $U$ or to research on $P$.

It is likely that a country with relatively high-priced labor will have exploited the labor-saving research possibilities to such a degree that few profitable advances in that direction will now exist. It is also probable, however, that the country will have neglected the more capital-saving lines of research which, owing to relative factor prices, were not profitable. Therefore, in the adopting country there will be more opportunities to do research in a relatively capital-saving direction. Though not advantageous for the original developer, these research lines may become profitable under the receiver-country's factor prices. This is reflected in figure 6–1, where the length of the capital-saving line of research $m$ is longer than that of the labor-saving line $n$, that is, the research productivity parameters of $m$ exceed those of $n$.

Similarly, given the factor prices of the receiving country it is likely that opportunities for further labor-using improvements for $P$ will be small relative to those for capital-using inventions. This is reflected by the relative length of the arrows $g$ and $t$, which reflect higher research productivity in the capital-using than in the labor-using direction.

In the situation depicted in figure 6–1, a given level of research resources can improve the home technology by more than the imported technology $U$. With these resources, production costs can be reduced by $DD'$ in terms of labor. In such a case, the decision-maker will choose to do research on the home technology, if he decides to do research at all.

On the other hand, if the productivity of adaptive research on imported technology $U$ were larger—that is, if the arrows $m$ and $n$ were longer—so that the cost savings of adaptive research exceeded those of research on the home technology, then the decision maker would choose to do adaptive research and to use the modified technology $U$.

The decision maker will not conduct research at all but will either borrow the technology without adaptive research or continue to use the unimproved home technology if the discounted annual cost savings $CC'$ over the lifetime of the research result are less than the research costs. The decision to borrow outright should depend not only on the productivity of the foreign technology and on screening costs but also on the costs and productivities of adaptive research and research on home technology. The complementarity between screening and adaptive research, which we discussed in the preceding section, will lower the costs of adaptive research and will make the borrowing option less profitable.

Note also that if the decision maker makes his choice on the basis of distorted factor prices $C''D''$ he will often decide in favor of adaptive rather than home-technology research even if the growth contribution of the former is less than that of the latter. Moreover, the research will be biased in a more labor-saving direction than would be optimal with the true scarcity values of the factors of production.

In addition to the welfare loss that results from the misallocation of adaptive research resources to more labor-saving lines of research, the decision to pursue adaptive research on imported technology may have other serious effects. Since no research is done on the home technology, this technology will fall permanently behind in total factor productivity. At a later time, when the decision as to method of technology transfer presents itself again with respect to a new technology $U$, the home technology has even less chance to be considered as an alternative because its relative productivity position has further deteriorated.

It should be noted that the choice of adaptive research may be appropriate if the transfer *cum* research decision is taken with respect to the true scarcity value of factors *including the social costs of factor adjustments*.[16] In this case, home technology will be completely phased out over a number of years. However, if existing potential for improvement of home technology is not exploited because of policy-induced factor-price distortion, the policy maker may not only cause a purely economic welfare loss but may precipitate unnecessary social and income distribution disturbances when the sector in question is forced to switch to a foreign technology that requires different firm size and different factor proportions.

Note also that when research is superior to direct technology transfer there is often an added benefit for the sector of the economy that produces capital goods. Once adaptive research is undertaken it may become possible to build the new capital goods needed in order to utilize the adapted technology. Clearly such a development will strengthen the industrial structure of an economy.[17]

When the model depicted in figure 6–1 is generalized, by dropping the budget constraint on research resources, we come to the following decision framework for the technology *cum* research decision.

First, scientists and engineers need to determine what the potential research lines are, both for the foreign and the home technology. They should

---

[16] Obtaining public support for policy on adjustment costs may present a serious problem. Proper compensation to those who lose from social and economic change may be potentially lower than the gains from change, but few societies actually compensate the losers.

[17] See, for example, the cases reported in Amir U. Khan, "Appropriate Technologies: Do We Transfer, Adopt or Develop?" in *Employment in Developing Nations*, ed. Edgar O. Edwards (New York: Columbia University Press, 1974), pp. 223–33. In the field of mechanical technology, G. S. Aurora and Ward Morehouse offer a very useful case study of the problems involved in developing indigenous capital-goods industries that can utilize indigenous design capacity ("The Dilemma of Technological Choice in India: The Case of the Small Tractor," *Minerva* 12 (October 1974): 433–58).

attempt to determine for various research efforts the potential factor-saving achievable with respect to each factor. (Foreign-trained scientists and engineers are quite likely to develop biased estimates because they are more familiar with research and development possibilities and profitabilities in their own countries.)

Second, total factor costs of the foreign and the domestic technology in the receiving country's environment need to be estimated. True opportunity costs, not distorted factor prices, should be used.

Third, for each technology the optimal combinations of research activities must be determined. This optimum defines both the mix of research activities to be pursued and the total amount of resources to be devoted to research. The optimal amounts of research are reached when marginal, discounted, future cost-savings equal marginal research costs. The solution may imply zero research.

The technique with the lowest post-research costs is chosen in this simple model, but in a somewhat more complex model the possibility of parallel research should be considered. We have ignored uncertainty in this model. In fact, the research-possibilities frontier is only an "expected" frontier and is subject to variability in actual outcome. Nelson has shown that when a positive covariance between two research programs exists, it may be efficient to pursue both lines of research until one shows itself to be superior.[18] This possibility is somewhat more likely if two research programs complement one another. Consequently, it is possible that research on both home technology and imported technology might be pursued efficiently. On the whole, however, the results of the simple model are probably sufficient to force a choice.[19]

If the option of borrowing (or of adaptive research) lowers the cost of borrowing (or adapting) future foreign technology, as is likely to be the case, the expectation of future improvement by foreign technology will make abandonment of the home technology more likely.

*Direct Transfer and Adaptive Research in*
*the Context of Environmental Sensitivity*

In the preceding section, the choices between alternative development strategies were investigated in the context of factor prices. As we noted earlier, however, the superiority of one particular technology over another (including improvement prospects) depends not only on factor prices but also on the natural and reproducible environment. This has been well recognized in the case of agriculture, but it applies also to industrial technology. Differences in the quality of raw materials available locally can make

[18] Nelson, "Economics of Parallel Research and Development."

[19] Note that this refers to one type of production only. A country may undertake research on the improvement of home technology of some goods and adaptive research in the production of others.

a technology that is profitable in a foreign country unprofitable domestically; climatic differences, such as the rapid rate of corrosion in the tropics, may increase the costs of operating machines designed for other climates.

In this section we will begin by presenting a measure of *environmental sensitivity* which integrates the cost effects of both economic and noneconomic barriers to technology transfer. The measure is designed to provide a more systematic approach to understanding (1) the characteristics of a technology that facilitate its transfer among regions and (2) the characteristics of the environment that affect the transferability of a particular technology.

We will then discuss what it is that constitutes a real technology gap between two countries and the implications of the existence of real gaps for the choice between direct transfer, adaptive research, and comprehensive research.

The measure of environmental sensitivity (ES) is designed to reflect the differences in unit costs of a given technology between regions or countries. The measure is defined for all pairs of regions. For example, $ES_{AB}$ is a measure of the proportional difference in unit costs *with a given technology* between $A$ and $B$. The measure is defined separately for each technology. It is not based on cost differences of technologies actually in use in the two countries but on costs based on a technology that is a candidate for transfer. Furthermore, the measure is based on variable costs and does not account for pure rents to land or climatic characteristics. Let the economically relevant prices be $P_i$ $(i = 1, \ldots, n)$ and the noneconomic factors that influence costs be denoted by $Z_j$. For agriculture the $Z_j$ could be rainfall, soil quality, temperature, disease environment, or the like. We can now again use a minimum cost function to describe the minimum cost in each region, introduce the environmental characteristics as "fixed factors" of production, and write

$$C_A^* = g(P_{1A}, \ldots, P_{nA}, Z_{1A}, \ldots, Z_{mA}) \tag{1}$$

when the subscripts $A$ refer to the levels of the variables in region $A$. This function relates the minimum cost of production to the factor prices and the fixed environmental factors.[20]

The cost of production *with the same technology* in country $B$ would be

$$C_B^* = g(P_{1B}, \ldots, P_{nB}, Z_{1B}, \ldots, Z_{mB}) \tag{2}$$

The environmental sensitivity of the technology as between the two regions is measured by the proportional difference in costs:[21]

$$ES_{AB} = \hat{C}_{AB}^* = \sum_i \alpha_i \hat{P}_i + \sum_j \beta_j \hat{Z}_j \tag{3}$$

---

[20] Some of the environmental factors, such as level of irrigation or quality of raw material, are susceptible of change, but they are fixed at the amount of time for the potential adopter.

[21] This equation is derived as the discrete equivalent of the total differential
$$dC^* = \sum_i \{\partial C^*/\partial P_i\} \, dP_i + \sum_j \{\partial C^*/\partial Z_j\} \, dZ_j$$

where

$$\hat{C}^*_{AB} = (C^*_B - C^*_A)/\sqrt{C^*_A C^*_B}$$ represents proportional cost difference,

$$\hat{P} = (P_B - P_A)/\sqrt{P_A P_B}$$ represents proportional price difference,

$$\hat{Z} = (Z_B - Z_A)/\sqrt{Z_A Z_B}$$ represents proportional environmental factor difference,

$$\alpha_i = \frac{\partial C^*}{\partial P_i}\frac{P_i}{C^*}$$ represents elasticity of unit cost with respect to the prices, and

$$\beta_j = \frac{\partial C^*}{\partial Z_j}\frac{Z_j}{C^*}$$ represents elasticity of the unit cost with respect to environmental difference.

The proportional differences are computed with respect to geometric averages to make the measures symmetric. Country $A$ is the country of origin of the technology, while $B$ is the potential importer. Normally, we expect the index to be positive, that is, we expect costs to be higher in country $B$ because the technology was initially developed to provide maximum cost-reduction according to conditions in the country of origin.[22]

The ES measure contains a price, or economic, component $\sum_i \alpha_i \hat{P}_i$ and a noneconomic, environmental component $\sum_j \beta_j \hat{Z}_j$. The breakdown of the index into these economic and noneconomic components is useful in assessing their relative importance.

Each component in turn is composed of the effect of the environmental sensitivity characteristics specific to the technology (the $\alpha$ and $\beta$ parameters of its cost functions) and of the size of the environment differences specific to the countries compared ($\hat{P}$ and $\hat{Z}$). The transfer of a technology can therefore be difficult either because a technology is very sensitive to economic or noneconomic enviromental differences and/or because the environmental differences between which transfer is attempted are very large.

The relative importance of economic and noneconomic environmental differences will vary with the commodity, as reflected in the relative size of the $\alpha$ and the $\beta$ coefficients. Agricultural technologies will be much more sensitive to soil and climate conditions than will industrial technologies which, in turn, may be more sensitive to factor prices. Within agriculture, seed varieties will be more sensitive to the noneconomic environment than will mechanical innovations.

The environmental sensitivity measure can be used to predict where a given technology (fixed $\alpha$ and $\beta$ coefficients) is likely to be adopted. A technology that is sensitive primarily to factor prices can be relatively

[22] In the case of a new product, however, a learning-by-doing process (see Raymond Vernon, "International Investment and International Trade") takes place, after which country $B$, the importer of the technology, may have lower costs than country $A$. The manufacturing of components of electronic equipment in Korea, Taiwan, and Singapore illustrates this type of situation.

easily transferred to areas with similar factor prices but different non-economic environments; it is less easy to transfer such a technology to areas with different factor prices and similar economic environments.

Industrial technology is easily transferred between North America and Europe for precisely these reasons. On the other hand, seed varieties, which are quite insensitive to factor prices, can easily be transferred to areas with similar ecological environment, regardless of how large factor price differences are.[23] Hence the ES measure provides a way of estimating the barriers to technology transfer and helps in understanding whether these barriers derive from characteristics of the technology itself or from the magnitude of the environmental differences between the two regions involved in the transfer process.

Looking at the technology transfer problem from this angle shows that countries whose factor endowments and noneconomic environments differ substantially from those of developed countries are at a distinct disadvantage in modernizing their technologies (except in the case of labor-intensive, new products, mentioned above). The large differences between environments revealed by a high index of environmental sensitivity represents a very strong barrier to the diffusion of technology to those regions or countries with the most extreme factor endowment ratios, such as Java or Bangladesh.[24] Such countries or regions are frequently among the poorest and are in urgent need of efficiency increases. The high environmental barriers to technology transfer require that these countries devote more effort to indigenous research than countries with less extreme endowment ratios but equally low per capita income. Unfortunately, research skills at any level are currently very scarce in most of these countries.

The concept of environmental sensitivity is helpful also in understanding the nature of a real technology gap. Transfer decisions cannot be taken on the basis of observed cost differences alone. Suppose $C_A^*$ measures the unit cost of production with the most modern technology in use in the technically advanced country $A$, while $\tilde{C}_B^*$ is the cost of production with the existing technology in the less developed country $B$. The apparent technology gap can then be defined as

$$AG_{AB} = (\tilde{C}_B^* - C_A^*)/\sqrt{\tilde{C}_B^* C_A^*} \tag{4}$$

and is the observed proportional cost difference with respect to the geometric

[23] Hybrid corn developed in Iowa was rapidly accepted in northern Italy but not in the United States South. Mexican wheats were adopted by many different countries at different stages of economic development but only in those regions where ecological conditions were similar to those of Mexico.

[24] Bangladesh has not even been very successful in adopting the high-yielding rice varieties of the green revolution; these varieties require good water control, which is lacking in the country's flood plain conditions.

average.[25] However, the cost advantage of the new technology, once economic and noneconomic environmental differences are taken into account, is only

$$RG_{AB} = (\tilde{C}_B^* - C_B^*)/\sqrt{\tilde{C}_B^* C_B^*} \tag{5}$$

where $C_B^*$ is the cost of production with the new technology in country $B$. Hence the real gap is equal approximately to the difference between the apparent gap and the environmental sensitivity measure:[26]

$$RG_{AB} \cong AG_{AB} - \text{ES}_{ES} \tag{6}$$

It is clear that many apparent gaps are not in fact real, because the environmental sensitivity measure can easily exceed the apparent gap. Many unsuccessful attempts at technology transfer are undoubtedly due to an underestimation of environmental sensitivity and to a corresponding absence of real gaps before the transfer was attempted.

A region considering commodity development strategies will find the real technology gap measures useful. Region $B$, for example, even with imperfect measures of the real technology gaps $RG_{AB}$ for a particular commodity, could determine whether to pursue a thorough technology-screening program and from which countries or regions it might select technology for this purpose. It would probably pursue different programs for different commodities. For some commodities the apparent and real gaps may be very close; for others they may be quite different.

The gap measures are potentially useful in more dynamic contexts as well. Producers in a borrowing region may base policy on "anticipated gaps" in the near future. That is, with information about research programs in other regions, they may be able to predict changes in the cost of modern technology in the country of origin ($C_A^*$). In a long run context, we might note that a pure screening and borrowing strategy is profitable only if one or more of the gaps are expected to persist. Such persistence will occur only when the $\text{ES}_{AB}$ barrier is relatively low and when the donor region, because it is involved in research, can anticipate further technical innovation.

## Research Resource Allocation Issues in
## Agricultural Research Systems

Government as well as industry must take the ES concept into consideration when determining allocation of research resources. Consider a

[25] Apparent gaps cannot be measured for new products because they are not produced in country $B$.

[26] It is only approximately so because the gaps and the ES measure are normalized with respect to different geometric averages. If one gives up symmetry of the measures and computes them with respect to a single unit cost, then the real gap is exactly equal to the apparent gap less the ES.

political unit (a country or a group of countries) which, on the basis of differing microclimatic factors, can be divided into 100 small regions. Assume that these regions could be grouped into several macroregions, say 10, based on a more general classification of climatic factors. Now, will it be more efficient to undertake adaptive research in 100 regions, in 10, in one, or in none? Will it be efficient to support scientific research designed to produce knowledge (rather than specific technology), and to what level of climatic variation among regions should this work be directed?

The optimal size and location of research units will depend on the supply of research skills available, the degree to which environmental factors differ among regions, the proportion of the total production of a region devoted to a given commodity, and the availability from neighboring regions of transferable technology and scientific knowledge. There are three general patterns of research unit organization in agriculture:

1. A large number of independent units are established, each of which performs simple screening and minor adaptive research.

2. A small number of central institutions for adaptive research are organized, each of which is connected with several branch units that carry out screening and minor adaptive research.

3. A group of comprehensive research institutions are established, all of which undertake graduate teaching and scientific as well as adaptive research. Again, the work of these institutions is supplemented by the screening and minor adaptive research work performed by a number of branch units.

Because the supply of scientific skills is generally limited at the outset of research activity, most research systems have begun by following the first of these three patterns. In this initial stage, agricultural colleges may offer reasonably good bachelors' degree programs but are unable to provide graduate training. As a result, high-level skills must be either imported in the form of expatriate visitors or acquired through sending undergraduates abroad for further study.

In this early stage, research institutions have relatively few economies of size. Characteristically, large numbers of experiment stations are built in many different environmental niches, and quite often each station works exclusively on one commodity. For example, India, by the early 1960s, had established more than 500 agricultural experiment stations, most of which were very small and devoted to research on a single commodity.[27]

At a stage when there is little capacity for more than minor adaptive research, the spread of many research units over a wide area maximizes the transfer of existing technology. In fact, such research stations are often more

[27] Rakesh Mohan, Dayanath Jha and Robert E. Evenson, "The Indian Agricultural Research System," *Economic and Political Weekly* 8, no. 13 (March 31, 1973): A–21 to A–26.

concerned with diffusion of technology than with research itself. The more widely they are dispersed, the more easily such stations can attend to the needs of varying ecological niches.

If experiment stations were of the same minimum size (one or two senior staff plus junior staff), and if it were equally difficult or easy to screen and adapt across commodities (probably an untenable proposition), then each research station would serve environmental niches whose size would be determined by the distribution of production and the dispersion in ES factors. The "marginal value product" of screening and adapting activity depends upon the output of a particular commodity and the reduction in unit costs that results from the original selection and research. The more diverse the environmental features in a region and the greater the distance between the region and its potential sources of technology, the lower the marginal product.

Thus, in this simple case, the regions served by each station will not have equal production of the commodity or commodities in question. Large areas with relatively homogeneous environments and heavy production should have more stations per unit product affected than more diverse areas. Internationally, incidentally, this provides some insight into the difficulties faced by small countries with diverse environments, like Sri Lanka or Nepal, in improving agricultural production.

As their supplies of skilled research workers grow, most countries develop the main station–branch station organization of the second pattern. Scale economies, which result from the utilization of fixed-cost factors such as large-scale laboratory equipment and central library and administrative services, begin to take precedence over the benefits of decentralized tailoring of technology. Perhaps the most important factor in the movement toward centralization is the more complex nature of the screening required for full-fledged adaptive research. Screening activity becomes more demanding, but at the same time it is facilitated by the low-cost communication with other researchers that is possible in a more centralized system.

For any given research system, concentrating workers in fewer organizations entails some loss in the ability to tailor research effort closely to the environment. Delane Welsch discusses the trade-off between fine and more aggregate tailoring in research systems. He notes that plant breeders are keenly aware of their options in this regard.[28] A breeding program can be designed to produce varieties for two related but distinct niches, or it can attempt to produce varieties that are tailored to an average measure of the two niches' characteristics. The more important scale economies are, the less finely research can be tailored.

---

[28] Delane Welsch, "Relationship of Regional Agricultural Planning to International Agricultural Research Efforts" (Paper presented at the Agricultural Development Council Seminar on Regional Agricultural Development Planning, Los Baños, Philippines, April 17–19, 1973).

The latter point is important to an understanding of the role of the new international institutes for agricultural research, such as the International Rice Research Institute (IRRI), which are funded by the Consultative Group on International Agricultural Research (CGIAR) (see chapter 13). International research programs simply do not have the resources to make an effective contribution to technological development in the full range of environments in which a specific commodity is produced. For these programs the problem of the trade-off between economies of concentration and fine tailorability is crucial, yet international policy makers have not really begun to deal with this question.[29]

When an economy reaches the point where it is capable of producing research skills in substantial measure, it finds new complementarities between adaptive research, scientific research, and research training. These complementaries have often been exploited by developing institutions, such as the larger state experiment stations that are associated with state universities in the United States, where research is combined with graduate teaching. A combined orientation toward academic disciplines as well as agricultural commodities has made such institutions productive over long periods of time.[30] Scale economies in these institutions can be quite substantial, but they derive from the communication across disciplines, across commodity orientations, and between students and faculty. Where an institution only conducts research it does not appear to experience substantial scale economies.[31] In fact, the evidence suggests that many large governmental research institutes experience diseconomies of scale.

Although we cannot focus here on an institute's or a system's internal problems of organization and of optimizing research resource allocation, such issues are exceedingly important to the successful adaptation and creation of agricultural technology. A model of the internal structure of the agricultural experiment station, within which some of these problems can be considered, is presented in appendix 6–1. A thorough discussion of the structural problems of emerging systems may be found in Albert Moseman's *Building Agricultural Research Systems in the Developing Nations*.[32]

TRANSFER OF KNOWLEDGE.   In the formal models of induced innovation presented in chapters 4 and 5 we have shown that continued productivity

[29] However, the international institutes are currently attempting to reduce the non-economic component of the ES by focusing research efforts on the elimination of photoperiod sensitivity and the development of broad-spectrum disease resistance among plant varieties.

[30] Robert E. Evenson, "The Contribution of Agricultural Research and Extension to Agricultural Production" (Ph.D. diss., University of Chicago, 1968).

[31] See chapter 4 as well as Morton I. Kamien and Nancy L. Schwartz, "Market Structure and Innovation: A Survey," *Journal of Economic Literature* 13 (March 1975): 1–37.

[32] Albert H. Moseman, *Building Agricultural Research Systems in the Developing Nations* (New York: Agricultural Development Council, Inc., 1970).

of adaptive research depends on the degree to which an institute keeps abreast of advances in basic scientific knowledge. An institute can accomplish this either through its own research or by screening scientific research done elsewhere for applicability to its own particular problems. We will call the latter activity transfer of knowledge.

We noted earlier that for commodities with high environmental sensitivity indexes, efficient research systems are decentralized and stress the development of region-specific technology. As a consequence, diffusion of technology per se tends to be low. However, the diffusion of scientific knowledge is often quite significant in commodities with high ES indexes. In general we can say that in an efficiently organized system, the lower the degree of direct technology diffusion, the greater the amount of diffusion of knowledge.

At the same time, basic knowledge is not completely transferable; it confronts some of the same barriers to transfer as those encountered by direct technology diffusion. For example, knowledge of physiological characteristics of temperate-zone plants is not generally useful to scientists and farmers in the tropics. Because of this location specificity of knowledge, work directed to the discovery of new knowledge must be somewhat decentralized although less so than work aimed at technology discovery. Since the nature of the barriers to both knowledge and technology transfer is the same, similar methods can be used to determine how much decentralization is necessary and efficient in research focused on the discovery of either knowledge or technology.

It can also be noted that just as screening activity accomplishes the work of some of the necessary stages in carrying out adaptive research, so the latter endeavor develops information that the researcher in basic and supporting sciences must have in order to do his work. Thus both basic research and screening technology complement applied research in similar fashion.

EXTERNALITIES AND OPTIMAL INVESTMENT INCENTIVES. Because producers in a region are in general able to appropriate only part of the actual gain from regional investment in technology discovery, less research than is optimal will be conducted. The degree to which research gains can be appropriated is of course a function of ES factors: if new technology is easily transferred from one area to another, gains will be widely distributed. The situation, then, is the classic "externality" case, and the policy response requires some form of international cooperation. If several countries undertake a cooperative research program, they can appropriate, and "internalize," a high proportion of the gains.

There are, however, complicating factors. First, international trade factors have a great effect on the question of whether or not gains can be appropriated. Second, complementarity among regional or national research programs is usually sufficient to prevent the region that conducts the research from appropriating the entire gain.

International trade possibilities significantly affect the distribution of gains from research. In general we can distinguish between consumer or producer gains and consumer or producer losses that result from new technology. Producers will have an incentive to adopt new technology as long as it is available. In small-firm sectors like agriculture, however, individual producers will be unable to appropriate sufficient gains to justify high levels of research investment. The public sector will then undertake support of research systems based on the expectation that either producers or consumers (who are the public) will appropriate the gains. In a closed competitive economy, most gains will be appropriated through lower real prices to national consumers. Producer earnings will rise to the degree that factor prices in terms of goods increase. In an open trading economy, national consumers may capture few of the benefits from technology. Indeed, these gains may be appropriated by consumers in countries where no production of the good takes place (as with tropical fruits, for example).

Producers will gain from their research investment in comparison with other producers in the world market. If ES factors allow widespread transfer of technology or knowledge, however, these gains will be small since world prices may fall by as much or even more than costs. It can be seen, then, that new technologies in one region can actually impose losses on producers in other regions.

Further distributional analysis is beyond the scope of this chapter. Our major concern here has been to underline the importance of international factors to research investment incentives. It is easy to construct hypothetical cases in which consuming countries derive substantial benefits from the development of improved technology but where producing countries have very little incentive for investment in research.

Complementarity of national and regional research programs is an important factor in the appropriation of gains because it enables one or more regions to benefit from research done by another. A region would have a clear incentive to screen and adopt technology from other regions if this process were a simple matter. In general, however, ES factors prevent direct transfer except in cases where extraordinary improvements in technology have been made and where some regions lag very far behind other regions. The optimal investment strategy is to choose, rather than direct transfer of technology, the transfer of knowledge on which technology is built. It is in pursuit of this strategy that countries can take advantage of the complementarity between their own research and the stock of technology and knowledge available from other regions.

*Empirical Studies of Technology Transfer*
*in Agriculture*

The literature on technology transfer and diffusion is quite limited. Except in certain portions of the international trade literature, this subject has not attracted much formal economic analysis. And although the fundamental role of technology transfer in economic development has long been recognized, it is only recently that the phenomenon has been studied on an empirical basis.

Here we will attempt to review only a few studies of agricultural technology transfer. Although it is important to our general topic, the rich literature treating the industrial product cycle tends to stress learning by doing rather than environmental factors, and consequently we will not discuss it here.

EARLY RESEARCH.   In the mid 1960s, R. Latimer and D. Paarleburg studied the relationship between research activity and agricultural productivity and concluded that the pervasiveness of the knowledge generated by agricultural research was of such magnitude as to prevent the identification of a relationship between research investment and productivity in data on a number of representative U.S. states.[33] When a little later, both Zvi Griliches and Robert Evenson identified such a relationship but stressed the location-specific character of agricultural research, attention was diverted from the issue of pervasiveness.[34] However, the initiation of serious investigations of international patterns of productivity change in agriculture demanded that this issue be confronted squarely.

Prototypical of recent studies of technology transfer was the study of sugarcane variety history begun by Robert Evenson, J. P. Houck and Vernon W. Ruttan in 1969 and elaborated by Evenson a few years later. This study identified certain basic patterns of transfer and presented three findings that are of particular relevance to this discussion.[35]

> 1. International diffusion of varietal technology was found to be related to environmental factors (climate and incidence of disease), and the widespread diffusion of the 1930s was found to have occurred in association with an extraordinary advance in technology based on new scientific knowledge.
>
> 2. Research programs that were initiated in a number of countries in the 1920s and 1930s generally were not successful in developing new indigenous technology during the first fifteen to twenty years of their existence. They did develop very sophisticated screening techniques, however, and as a consequence were able to facilitate the transfer of interspecific hybrid varieties from Java and India to indigenous producing sectors.

[33] R. Latimer and D. Paarleburg, "Geographic Distribution of Research Costs and Benefits," *Journal of Farm Economics* 47 (May 1965): 234–41.

[34] Zvi Griliches, "Research Expenditures, Education and the Aggregate Agricultural Production Function," *American Economic Review* 54 (December 1974): 961–74; Evenson, "Agricultural Research and Extension."

[35] Evenson, Houck, and Ruttan, "Technical Change and Agricultural Trade"; Robert E. Evenson, "The 'Green Revolution' in Recent Development Experience," *American Journal of Agricultural Economics* 56 (May 1974): 387–95.

3. These indigenous research programs were found to have achieved wide success, after a period of time, in adapting the Javanese and Indian varieties to local environmental conditions. Moreover, by 1950, most cane-producing countries were found to have displaced the Javanese and Indian varieties with varieties produced in local stations.

The sugarcane experience of the 1920s and 1930s has much in common with the more recent experience in rice and wheat production in the tropical and sub-tropical countries. The dwarf wheat hybrids and the dwarf-plant rice varieties, widely diffused during the late 1960s, played a role very similar to that played by the interspecific hybrid sugarcane varieties of the 1920s. Initially, diffusion occurred through direct technology transfer, as Mexican wheats and IRRI rices were adopted in many countries. This was followed quite rapidly, however, by the diffusion of knowledge and basic genetic materials. These materials were quickly incorporated by most indigenous research institutions into breeding programs, the products of which are now displacing the earlier, adopted varieties.

Hayami and Ruttan have been instrumental in focusing attention on the subject of technology diffusion.[36] Their studies have demonstrated that international data can provide information about the agricultural growth process and the resources required to produce growth. This disclosure opened up new avenues for study of the technology transfer process.

THE CEREAL GRAINS STUDIES.    Two recent studies by Evenson and Yoav Kislev have utilized many of the findings of the sugarcane study and of Hayami and Ruttan's seminal work. Evenson and Kislev's studies incorporate many of the theoretical considerations that influence the transfer and research decisions we have discussed earlier in this chapter, and they provide empirical evidence for the importance of these considerations.[37] Both studies are based on an econometric analysis of cereal-grain yield data for more than 70 countries over a period of twenty-odd years.

Each of these studies used a production function framework that incorporates the effects of regional agroclimatic differences and of research on the products being studied. The basic idea that transfer of technology is easier within than across agroclimatic regions is incorporated by classifying countries into agroclimatic zones and regions and by assuming that a country

---

[36] Yujiro Hayami and Vernon W. Ruttan, *Agricultural Development: An International Perspective* (Baltimore: The Johns Hopkins University Press, 1971).

[37] Robert E. Evenson and Yoav Kislev, "Research and Productivity in Wheat and Maize," *Journal of Political Economy* 81 (November–December 1973): 1309–29; Robert E. Evenson, "Comparative Evidence on Returns to Investment in National and International Research Institutions," in *Research Resource Allocation and Productivity in National and International Agricultural Research*, eds. Thomas A. Arndt, Dana G. Dalrymple, and Vernon W. Ruttan (Minneapolis: University of Minnesota Press, 1977).

can benefit more from research done by ecological neighbors than from research done in different agroclimatic regions. Thus in an elementary way the studies do incorporate the concept of environmental sensitivity to noneconomic factors. However, because the production function framework and actual yield data were used, environmental sensitivity could not be measured precisely.[38]

For these econometric studies of the impact of research, measures of intensity had to be found for research within each country. The crucial problem was the availability and quality of data. Since the inception of these studies, a substantial effort has been devoted to the collection of an international inventory of agricultural research data including such categories as expenditures, manpower, and station distribution.[39] However, the data thus assembled by Evenson and his colleagues remain incomplete. Even the best figures suffer from comparability problems. The definition of "research worker" and "training" varies widely among countries, and the accuracy of expenditure data is impaired by exchange rate fluctuations and by varying accounting procedures. Moreover, research expenditure data cannot be divided either by sector within the agricultural industry or by type of research (e.g., basic or applied) performed.

Because of these difficulties, expenditure and manpower data were not used as intensity measures in the studies under discussion. Instead, an alternative measure of intensity was selected: the amount of research reported in the scientific literature. Published reports of scientific investigation in the fields of agriculture and biology were catalogued, utilizing relevant journals of abstracts. For the first study, for example, reports of research on wheat and maize were counted from *Plant Breeding Abstracts* and classified by country according to the first author's address.[40]

Although numbers of scientific reports are to some extent an indirect measure of research, this procedure has several clear advantages.[41] First, the large numbers of papers published assure a substantial degree of regularity. Second, most significant results of research work are published, although there may be some bias in favor of reports issuing from countries where

---

[38] The measurement of environmental sensitivity requires data on a single technique that will be used by farmers in some areas but not in others. Thus ES can be measured only on the basis of international yield trial data, an effort which we have begun.

[39] Robert E. Evenson and Yoav Kislev, "Investment in Agricultural Research and Extension: A Survey of International Data," *Economic Growth Center Discussion Paper* 124 (New Haven: Yale University, August 1971); James K. Boyce and Robert E. Evenson, *National and International Agricultural Research and Extension Programs* (New York: Agricultural Development Council, Inc., 1975).

[40] The scope of these *Abstracts* is international, and they endeavor to cover all significant work not only in plant breeding but in related subjects. The years examined for the present study were 1932–1969.

[41] Studies based on counts of published reports of scientific investigations are common in the area of the history of science; see, for example, Derek J. DeSolla Price, *Little Science, Big Science* (New York: Columbia University Press, 1963).

specific journals are edited. Third, there is a "floor" to the quality of articles accepted by journals of international standing, and further screening by journals of abstracts helps to secure homogeneity of quality. Fourth, published papers represent research output, and it is more appropriate to establish a connection between this output and agricultural productivity than it is to link productivity with the inputs of manpower and research expenditure. Finally, this method offers the only way of obtaining measures of crop-specific research, since expenditure and manpower data cannot be separated according to crop.

It is of course true that articles in scientific journals sometimes contain knowledge that is not directly applicable to production. Similarly, the total contribution of research effort to agricultural practice is not contained in published articles. Most often, however, the results of research of a competent scientific team doing innovative work in identifying and solving crucial problems will be published. Thus we can have some confidence that scientific papers can serve as proxies for scientific work.

*Research and Productivity in Wheat and Maize.* In the 1973 study by Evenson and Kislev, which used data on wheat and maize yields, countries were classified by geoclimatic region, according to a system developed by J. Papadakis.[42] As discussed earlier, this classification of regions by ecological characteristics was an early effort to incorporate the concept of environmental sensitivity.

The regression equations fitted in this study were as follows:

$$y_{jt} = \gamma_0 + \gamma_1 A_{jt} + \gamma_2 t + \gamma_3 \frac{K_{jt}}{d} + \gamma_4 \frac{B_{jt}}{d} + \gamma_5 S_j + u_{jt} \tag{7}$$

where $y_{jt}$ is yield in year $t$ in country $j$, $A_{jt}$ is the area planted to wheat or maize, $K_{jt}$ is the stock of indigenous research on the crop in country $j$, and $B_{jt}$ is the stock of borrowable research performed in other countries in the same geoclimatic region. Here borrowing can occur only within a geoclimatic region. A deflator of the research variables, $d$, depends either on the average area grown to the crop or on the number and homogeneity of growing regions within the country. Details of the construction of the research stock variables and the deflators are given in appendix 6–2.

The regressions were calculated in linear and in double-log (Cobb–Douglas) form. In the double-log form, all variables except time were replaced by their natural logarithms, and the value one was added to all stocks to avoid zeros.

Tables 6–1 and 6–2 report regression estimates for wheat and maize, respectively. The country-specific dummy variables $S_j$ make a major contribution to the explanation of these regressions. In the absence of variable

[42] Evenson and Kislev, *Agricultural Research and Productivity*; J. Papadakis, *Agricultural Geography of the World* (Buenos Aires: Avenida Córdoba 4564, 1952).

TABLE 6-1. Wheat yield regressions: Logistic borrowing function

| Regression Number | $R^2$ | Constant | Variables | | | |
|---|---|---|---|---|---|---|
| | | | Area[a] | Time[b] | Indigenous Research[c] | Borrowed Knowledge[d] |
| *Linear* | | | | | | |
| 1 | .923 | 24.515 | $1.2 \times 10^{-4}$ | 0.298 | 5.249 | |
| | | | (2.10) | (21.20) | (10.44) | |
| 2 | .923 | 24.990 | $-1.8 \times 10^{-4}$ | 0.267 | 0.001 | $7.2 \times 10^{-4}$ |
| | | | (2.79) | (16.63) | (0.50) | (9.31) |
| 3 | .928 | 23.650 | $-1.3 \times 10^{-4}$ | 0.230 | 4.646 | $6.4 \times 10^{-4}$ |
| | | | (2.35) | (14.76) | (9.45) | (9.01) |
| *Double Log* | | | | | | |
| 4 | .8978 | 2.9494 | 0.0386 | 0.0159 | 0.0359 | |
| | | | (2.21) | (9.68) | (3.33) | |
| 5 | .8980 | 3.0200 | 0.0389 | 0.0157 | 0.0199 | 0.0107 |
| | | | (1.95) | (9.51) | (1.30) | (1.49) |

Source: Robert E. Evenson and Yoav Kislev, "Research and Productivity in Wheat and Maize," *Journal of Political Economy* 81 (November–December 1973): 66.

Notes: The logistic borrowing function is described in greater detail in Appendix 6–2 to the present chapter; see particularly equation (A–7).

$N$ observations: 1,316 (64 countries, 21 years, 28 missing observations). Dependent variable: average yield = 100 kilos per hectare. Country dummy variables were included in all regressions to represent variable $S_j$ in equation (7). $\alpha$, $\beta$ values in the borrowed knowledge variable were estimated in regressions 2 and 5. The estimated values were: regression 2, $\alpha = 500$, $\beta = 6$; regression 5, $\alpha = 3000$, $\beta = 2$.

Parentheses enclose $t$ values.

[a] Wheat area in thousands of hectares.

[b] Year $t$, $t = 1, 2, \ldots, 21$.

[c] Sum of counts of *Plant Breeding Abstracts* from 1948 to year $t$ deflated by area in regressions 1 and 3 and by the adjusted number of subregions in regression 2.

[d] As defined in equations (A–7) and (A–8) in appendix 6–2. This variable was deflated by the adjusted number of subregions in regressions 2 and 3. No deflators were used in regressions 4 and 5.

$S_j$, $R^2$ is of the order of 0.4, which is to be expected when countries differ substantially in their yield potentials. The inclusion of this variable converts the regression into a covariance analysis, where the coefficients measure within-country effects. This in turn eliminates biases that could have been introduced by correlation between knowledge (own or borrowed) and yield-level potential.

The area and time variables were always significant, although the first varied in sign. The research and borrowing variables are positive in all and significant in most regressions.

All four estimates of the parameter $\alpha$ in tables 6–1 and 6–2 indicate intercepts $[1/(1 + \alpha)]$ of the borrowing function (see appendix 6–2) that are virtually zero. No borrowing takes place in the absence of indigenous research work. This somewhat surprising result is a striking empirical confirmation of the research-screening complementarity discussed earlier.

TABLE 6-2. Maize yield regressions: Logistic borrowing function

| Regression Number | $R^2$ | Constant | Variables | | | |
|---|---|---|---|---|---|---|
| | | | Area[a] | Time[b] | Indigenous Research[c] | Borrowed Knowledge[d] |
| Linear | | | | | | |
| 1 | .846 | 39.732 | $-4.8 \times 10^{-4}$ | 0.360 | 0.001 | |
| | | | (2.22) | (14.82) | (7.77) | |
| 2 | .848 | 39.994 | $-5.2 \times 10^{-4}$ | 0.337 | 0.010 | $1.5 \times 10^{0}$ |
| | | | (2.41) | (13.76) | (6.94) | (4.72) |
| 3 | .849 | 36.351 | $-1.1 \times 10^{-3}$ | 0.337 | 3.008 | $1.8 \times 10^{-3}$ |
| | | | (5.68) | (13.61) | (6.66) | (5.63) |
| Double Log | | | | | | |
| 4 | .8404 | 3.6322 | $-0.0613$ | 0.0153 | 0.0507 | |
| | | | (2.76) | (6.80) | (7.53) | |
| 5 | .8461 | 3.5846 | $-0.0414$ | 0.0149 | 0.0245 | 0.0562 |
| | | | (1.87) | (6.77) | (1.69) | (5.89) |

Source: Robert E. Evenson and Yoav Kislev, "Research and Productivity in Wheat and Maize," *Journal of Political Economy* 81 (November–December 1973): 66.

Notes: The logistic borrowing function is described in greater detail in appendix 6-2 to the present chapter; see particularly equation (A-7).

$N$ observations: 989 (49 countries, 21 years, 40 missing observations). Dependent variable: average yield = 100 kilos per hectare. Country dummy variables were included in all regressions to represent variable $S_j$ in equation (7). $\alpha$, $\beta$ values in the borrowed knowledge variable were estimated in regressions 2 and 5. The estimated values were: regression 2, $\alpha = 1,100$, $\beta = 2$; regression 5, $\alpha = 4,500$, $\beta = 0.4$.

Parentheses enclose $t$ values.

[a] Maize area in thousands of hectares.

[b] Year $t$, $t = 1, 2, \ldots, 21$.

[c] Sum of counts of *Plant Breeding Abstracts* from 1948 to year $t$ deflated by area in regressions 1 and 3 and by the adjusted number of subregions in regression 2.

[d] As defined in equations (A-7) and (A-8) in appendix 6-2. This variable was deflated by the adjusted number of subregions in regressions 2 and 3. No deflators were used in regressions 4 and 5.

The economic contribution of a scientific publication, according to the model, is composed of three parts: (a) the direct contribution of indigenous research to productivity—indicated by the coefficient of $K$ in tables 6-1 and 6-2; (b) the accelerating effect of indigenous work on borrowing—the contribution of a unit in the exponent of the borrowing function; and (c) the contribution of research in one country to productivity in others—the marginal contribution of a unit of borrowed knowledge $B$ times the transferability factor (also discussed in appendix 6-2), which indicates how many such units can be derived from a paper produced in one country, times the borrowing factor $1/(1 + \alpha e^{-\beta p})$. Estimates of these three components are listed in table 6-3.[43]

[43] In the linear model, the indigenous stocks were deflated both by area and by the regional deflators; estimates for both cases are reported in table 6-3. The unbiased estimate of $\gamma$ in the double-log model is its geometric mean. Accordingly, for such models marginal contributions are usually calculated at that point of the samples. However, the

TABLE 6–3. Estimates of marginal contribution of research

| Regression Number/Type | Direct Contribution (1) | Accelerating Borrowing (2) | Contribution to Others (3) |
|---|---|---|---|
| *Wheat*[a] | | | |
| 2   Yield, linear | 14,308 | 152,073 | 19,122 |
| 3   Yield, linear | 29,737 | . . . | . . . |
| 5   Yield, double-log (geometric averages) | 64,734 | 6,155 | 24,071 |
| 5   Yield, double-log (arithmetic averages) | 19,341 | 44,544 | 2,390 |
| *Maize*[b] | | | |
| 2   Yield, linear | 74,094 | 12,590 | 7,777 |
| 3   Yield, linear | 15,040 | . . . | . . . |
| 5   Yield, double-log (geometric averages) | 31,605 | 551 | 9,483 |
| 5   Yield, double-log (arithmetic averages) | 7,575 | 57,830 | 1,038 |

Source: Robert E. Evenson and Yoav Kislev, "Research and Productivity in Wheat and Maize," *Journal of Political Economy* 81 (November–December 1973); tables 6–1 and 6–2 of present chapter.

Notes: For details of calculations see appendix 6–2 to present chapter.

All figures are in dollars per year per publication.

[a] See table 6–1.

[b] See table 6–2.

The estimates in the last row in each of the "Wheat" and "Maize" sections of table 6–3 are probably the most accurate. They are based on a double-log model that incorporates the assumption of diminishing marginal products. The total value of the contribution of a publication is $66,285 for wheat and $66,443 for maize, which is surprisingly close. The distribution of the economic contributions among their components is also very similar for the two crops.

Elsewhere we have estimated that research expenditures associated with scientific publication range from U.S. $30,000 to $350,000 (1971 dollars) with an average value of approximately $100,000.[44] Without taking obsolescence into account, the figures in table 6–3 (for the yield regressions) are flow values

---

geometric mean will generally differ from the arithmetic, and this difference is a measure of the dispersion of the variable averaged (the arithmetic mean of the pair (5, 495) is 250; the geometric mean is 49.7). Yields per unit of land vary much less than the stocks of knowledge, which, by construction, start from small numbers for 1948 and continue to grow to 1968. Thus a better representation of the typical country is given by the arithmetic averages. For this reason, the estimates for the double-log model were calculated at these points of the sample as well. Since the logistic borrowing function discussed in appendix 6–2 is nonlinear, the estimates in column (2) of table 6–3 were prepared by calculating the marginal contribution for each point of the sample and averaging these values arithmetically or geometrically. The average borrowing factor values used in column (3) of this table were calculated in the same way.

[44] Evenson and Kislev, "Investment in Agricultural Research and Extension."

of permanent income streams, that is, they occur year after year. It would of course be unrealistic to assume that knowledge is not subject to obsolescence and depreciation, but even if these streams last for only twenty years (the present sample period), the values in table 6–3 imply substantial returns to investment in agricultural research.

*Contribution of Basic and Applied Research on Five Cereal Grains.* A more recent (1976) study of cereal grains production extends the work discussed above in several ways.[45] First, it adds a second factor of production (fertilizer) to the econometric specification and extends the analysis to five crops: wheat, maize, sorghum, barley, and rice. Second, and more important, it distinguishes between two types of research: applied, or technology-oriented (*A*-type), research and supporting, or science-oriented (*S*-type), research.[46] The study then attempts to identify the ways in which both types of knowledge may be produced and diffused.

As in the study of wheat and maize discussed above, research is measured by counting, in separate categories by crop, the publications that have been abstracted in a number of journals. *A*-type research on the cereal grains is carried out primarily in the fields of plant breeding and agronomy, which are

[45] The results of this study are reported in greater detail in Evenson, "Evidence on Returns to Investment."

[46] Discussion of research resource allocation has suffered from an excessive poverty in the language used to classify research. The following typology is adapted from Sterling Wortman, "The World Food Situation: A New Initiative" (Paper prepared for the Sub-Committee on Science, Research and Technology, U.S. House of Representatives, Washington, D.C., September 23, 1975):

*Operational* research is conducted at the firm level and is designed to adapt technology and resource management to local environments and to obtain information on constraints that limit factor productivity. Fertilizer experimentation in farmers' fields is an example of operational research.

*Tactical* research is undertaken specifically to identify improved components of production systems which operational researchers or managers can combine as required to meet the needs of firms that are located in particular areas or produce particular commodities. In agriculture, for example, tactical research is generally performed at regional experiment stations and includes such work as developing fertilizer-use practices, testing and developing methods for control of locally prevalent diseases and insect pests, and identifying new crop or animal production practices.

*Strategic* research is directed to the solution of broad-spectrum problems that affect entire agroclimatic regions or commodities produced therein or to the removal of major barriers to the improved production of a particular commodity or the performance of a particular function. The identification of materials that might serve as systemic insecticides is an example of strategic research in agriculture.

*Supporting* research seeks to develop new knowledge in areas where the probability is great that findings will be useful at the strategic, tactical, or operational level. Examples of supporting research in agriculture are work on nitrogen fixation and its potential application to the grasses and on photosynthesis, or the respiration processes of economic crop plants.

*Basic* research is undertaken to produce new knowledge of natural processes or behavior. Investigations in the general field of molecular biology represent an example of basic research that may in future give rise to agricultural research of the four above types.

covered by *Plant Breeding Abstracts. S*-type research, as defined here, is that performed not in pure science but in the basic agricultural sciences such as plant physiology, phytopathology, and soil science. These disciplines are covered in *Biological Abstracts.* Table 6–4 provides data on these two types of research for each of nine geoclimatic regions. (The data in this table are not in the form used in the regressions and are presented here simply to indicate the large regional differences in research activity and agricultural performance.)

A third way in which the present study differs from the earlier one is in the use of a finer geographic classification, which distinguishes between climate zones, regions, and subregions. The definition of these zones and regions, summarized in table 6–4, is based on a 1966 climate classification by Papadakis that is similar to the classification developed in the earlier study of wheat and maize.[47] The major climate regions in the 1966 classification are shown in table 6–4. A subregion is defined as a regional unit within a particular crop-producing region of a country. A country may produce wheat in several regions, and each of these will be considered a subregion. (An adjustment for size of subregions is made—see the footnotes to table 6–1 on area deflators.)

In the 1976 study of cereal grains (wheat, maize, sorghums, and millets, barley, and rice), data classified by crop, by country, and by year for the period 1948 to 1971 were subjected to regression analysis. The basic specification was

$$P = KL^{a_1}F^{a_2}A^{(a_3 + a_4 S)}RA^{(a_5 + a_6 ZS + a_7(A+S) + a_8(A+S)^2)}RY^{(a_9 + a_{10}A)} \qquad (8)$$

In this specification, $P$, $K$, $L$, and $F$ stand for the conventional determinants of production as follows:

> $P$ is production of grain in time period $t$ relative to average production in the three-year period 1949–1951;
>
> $L$ is acreage of each crop harvested in time period $t$ relative to average acreage in 1949–1951;
>
> $F$ is fertilizer consumption per acre of all grains in time period $t$ relative to average consumption in 1949–1951;
>
> $K$ is a constant term which, through the use of "dummy" variables, can take crop-specific factors into account.

Basically, the analysis is of changes in production over time. Because these variables are expressed relative to their 1949–1951 average levels, factors that accounted for differences in these levels are cancelled out. The assumption is that climatic, social, and other factors that determined the 1949–1951 differences in productivity did not affect production after those years (except through the research variables).

[47] J. Papadakis, *Agricultural Climates of the World* (Buenos Aires: Avenida Córdoba 4564, 1966).

TABLE 6—4. Research in cereal grains production by geoclimatic zones and regions

| Zones and Regions | Cumulated A-type Publications, 1942–70 | | | | | | Ratio of S-type Research to A-type Research | Adjusted Number of Subregions | Developing Country Share |
|---|---|---|---|---|---|---|---|---|---|
| | Wheat | Barley | Maize | Sorghum | Rice | All Cereals | | | |
| 1. Tropical Zone | | | | | | 48.3 | .90 | | |
| 1.1 Humid Equatorial | 1.5 | | 30.2 | 11.6 | 111.8 | 51.6 | 1.06 | 15.91 | 1.00 |
| 1.2 Humid Tropical | | .2 | 15.1 | 2.1 | 121.7 | 28.1 | .32 | 5.00 | .86 |
| 1.3 Dry Equatorial | | | 4.7 | 1.1 | 22.5 | 8.2 | 1.53 | 4.06 | 1.00 |
| 1.4 Hot Equatorial | 8.4 | | 19.3 | 13.6 | 224.5 | 68.7 | .96 | 10.22 | .95 |
| 1.5 Semi-Arid Equatorial | .0 | | 4.1 | 32.2 | 8.6 | 8.6 | .65 | 6.35 | 1.00 |
| 1.7 Humid Tierra | 20.4 | 20.4 | 30.6 | 26.0 | 20.8 | 24.1 | .85 | 16.19 | 1.00 |
| 1.8 Dry Tierra | | | 42.4 | | 18.1 | 52.8 | .50 | 2.06 | 1.00 |
| 1.9 Cool Winter Tropical | | | 18.5 | 87.4 | 353.1 | 144.9 | 1.00 | 5.58 | .86 |
| 2. Tierra Fria Zone | | | | | | 52.1 | .62 | | |
| 2.1 Tropical Highlands | 8.0 | 6.7 | 132.9 | 28.2 | | 52.1 | .62 | 8.72 | 1.00 |
| 3. Desert Zone | | | | | | 15.6 | 2.69 | | |
| 3.1 Hot Tropical | .0 | | 2.0 | | 4.5 | 2.3 | .22 | 3.00 | 1.00 |
| 3.2 Hot Subtropical | 20.9 | 11.8 | | | 6.7 | 15.8 | .76 | 16.94 | 1.00 |
| 3.7 Continental | 1.4 | 1.6 | .0 | .0 | 93.5 | 24.5 | 6.26 | 4.00 | .60 |
| 4. Subtropical Zone | | | | | | 54.9 | 1.18 | | |
| 4.1 Humid | 30.4 | 4.7 | 51.6 | 1.6 | 63.0 | 28.4 | 1.20 | 9.22 | .75 |
| 4.2 Monsoon | 116.6 | 128.1 | 69.7 | 144.9 | 52.0 | 102.7 | 1.31 | 6.91 | .66 |
| 4.3 Hot | 105.7 | 46.7 | 47.6 | 156.8 | 6.6 | 68.7 | .99 | 6.05 | 1.00 |
| 4.4 Semi-Arid | | | 10.0 | 5.0 | | 7.5 | .80 | 2.00 | 1.00 |

| | | | | | | | | | |
|---|---|---|---|---|---|---|---|---|---|
| 5. Pampean Zone | | | | | | 97.3 | 1.23 | | |
| 5.1 Pampean | 99.5 | 99.0 | 168.4 | 36.6 | | 97.3 | 1.23 | 4.53 | .20 |
| 6. Mediterranean Zone | | | | | | 39.6 | 1.95 | | |
| 6.1 Subtropical | 72.9 | 71.3 | 33.5 | 11.7 | 104.9 | 55.4 | 2.59 | 18.68 | .45 |
| 6.2 Marine | 14.0 | 2.2 | 34.4 | 12.0 | .0 | 16.8 | .80 | 7.24 | .25 |
| 6.5 Temperate | 77.3 | 18.9 | 45.5 | 4.0 | 23.5 | 37.4 | 1.90 | 11.27 | .17 |
| 6.7 Continental | 67.0 | 27.7 | 133.4 | 8.3 | 1.6 | 47.5 | 1.41 | 19.68 | .30 |
| 6.8 Subtropical Semi-Arid | 46.9 | 22.8 | 21.3 | 6.0 | | 26.7 | 1.68 | 14.26 | .50 |
| 6.9 Continental Semi-Arid | 4.6 | 3.0 | 9.0 | 1.0 | | 5.8 | .20 | 4.61 | .66 |
| 7. Marine Zone | | | | | | 120.1 | 2.02 | | |
| 7.1 Warm | 11.5 | 5.4 | | | | 8.4 | 2.00 | 2.00 | .00 |
| 7.2 Cool | 78.9 | 236.3 | 92.9 | | | 136.1 | 3.10 | 6.81 | .00 |
| 7.6 Cool Temperate | 97.1 | 145.8 | 158.9 | 20.3 | | 120.3 | 1.75 | 21.71 | .03 |
| 7.7 Cold Temperate | 90.6 | 144.8 | 187.9 | | | 133.9 | 1.46 | 8.00 | .00 |
| 8. Humid Continental Zone | | | | | | 256.2 | 2.79 | | |
| 8.1 Warm | 152.4 | 151.2 | 450.5 | 92.2 | 417.0 | 254.3 | 4.60 | 7.62 | .00 |
| 8.2 Semi-Warm | 164.3 | 124.1 | 703.0 | 283.5 | 622.3 | 291.5 | 1.50 | 12.16 | .00 |
| 8.3 Cold | 52.0 | 17.0 | | | | 34.5 | .63 | 2.00 | .00 |
| 9. Steppe Zone | | | | | | 357.9 | 1.35 | | |
| 9.2 Semi-Warm | 606.5 | 346.6 | 818.6 | 304.2 | 24.7 | 450.3 | 1.10 | 12.92 | .00 |
| 9.3 Cold | 636.4 | 348.5 | 111.9 | 12.0 | | 382.3 | 1.75 | 7.28 | .00 |
| 9.4 Temperate | 38.2 | 35.5 | | | | 36.9 | 1.96 | 4.34 | .00 |

Source: Robert E. Evenson, *Science and the World Food Problem*, Bulletin 758 (New Haven: Connecticut Agricultural Experiment Station. Based on author's Lockwood Lecture delivered April 18, 1974).

Note: Subregions are defined as $n(1 - d)$ where $n$ is the number of individual countries in the region and

$$d = \sum_{i=1}^{n} A_i - A/(2A_i - 2)A$$

$A_i$ is the acreage of the crop in country $i$. The term $d = 0$, when all countries in the region have the same acreage, approaches one as acreage in the region is concentrated in one country.

In the above specification, $A$ is cumulated $A$-type (technology-oriented) research investment (per subregion) in the country. A distributed lag is incorporated in this and all other research variables, that is,

$$A(t) = \sum_{1942}^{t-5} A_t + .8A_{t-4} + .6A_{t-3} + .4A_{t-2} + .2A_{t-1} \qquad (9)$$

The most recently completed studies are given low weights, because the full impact of research is not realized for 8 to 10 years after initial investment.

$S$ is cumulated $S$-type (science-oriented) research investment (per subregion) in the country. Note that because this variable enters only in the exponent, it does not affect productivity *directly* but only *indirectly*, through changing the productivity of $A$.

$RA$ measures $A$-type research conducted in *other* countries in the same geoclimatic *region*.

$ZS$ measures $S$-type research in *other* countries in the same geoclimatic *zone*.

$RY$ is an index of the yield of food grains per hectare in time period $t$ relative to the 1949–1951 yield averages in similar subregions outside the country.

The specifications thus introduce research benefits and transfer at four levels.

First, yield increases in similar subregions may be based on improvements in technology that can be directly adopted. The $RY$ index is designed to identify this effort.

Second, a country benefits not only from its own applied research investment $A$ but from the science-oriented research investment $S$ in the region within which it lies.

Third, a country can benefit from applied research done by other countries in the same geoclimatic region. Hence transfer of applied technology is admitted within but not across regions, and of course not across zones.

Fourth, a country can benefit from science-oriented research done by other countries in the same geoclimatic zone. Hence scientific knowledge is assumed to be transferable across regions within a given zone, but, again, not across zones. Thus, consistent with discussion earlier in this chapter, scientific knowledge is assumed to be more widely transferable than are the results of applied research.

The a priori expectations regarding the signs of the coefficients $a_1 a_2, \ldots, a_{10}$ are:

$a_1$ — Land coefficient: should be positive and should be approximately equal to one, since land is serving as a proxy for omitted inputs, chiefly labor and power.

$a_2$ — Fertilizer coefficient: should be positive and should approximately equal the share of fertilizer in total costs.

$(a_3 + a_4 S)$    Total coefficient of country $A$ research: should be positive for the mean value of $S$; to indicate that indigenous applied research has contributed to production, $a_3$ need not be positive if $a_4 S$ is sufficiently large to offset a negative $a_3$.

$(a_5 + a_6 ZS)$    Total regional applied research coefficient: should be positive if regional research has contributed to production; if zonal science research improves transferability of regional applied research, $a_6$ should also be positive.

$a_7$    Interaction coefficient $(A + S)$ between country $A$ and regional $S$ research: should be positive because regional research should complement, that is, raise the productivity of, country $A$ research.

$a_8$    Coefficient for the squared interaction term $(A + S)^2$: may be negative, indicating that when indigenous research is large relative to regional research it may be a net substitute for the latter.

$a_9$    Coefficient for the regional yield variable $RY$: should be positive; the size of the coefficient indicates the proportion of yield increases that are transferred between similar sub-regions as a consequence of activities unrelated to research.

$a_{10}$    Coefficient for the interaction between regional yields $(RY)$ and country $A$ research: should be negative; direct technology transfer becomes more difficult as a country's $A$ research increases because better alternatives are being discovered.

Regressions (1) and (2) in table 6–5 report the estimates of $a_1$ through $a_{10}$ for both developed country and developing country data. All coefficient signs are as expected, and all important coefficients have relatively low standard errors. The net contribution of both indigenous and regional, or borrowable, research to productivity is of high statistical significance. The values of the coefficients on the land and fertilizer variables are as expected.

The key technology transfer variables shown in table 6–5 are the inter-actions between $A$-type and $S$-type research. The $a_4$ coefficient gives evidence of a significant contribution by regional science research to a country's applied research productivity, indicating that $S$ knowledge is transferable within the region. Similarly, the $a_6$ coefficient indicates that zonal science research contributes significantly to the productivity of regional applied research and thus that $S$ knowledge can be transferred within the zone.

The terms that express interaction between country $A$ and regional $S$ research ($a_7$ and $a_8$) are designed to take account of both complementarity and substitutability between country and regional research (as differentiated from the wheat and maize study, which assessed complementarity only). In the developing countries it appears that where a great deal of indigenous research is undertaken it substitutes for the research of neighbors.

TABLE 6–5. Intercountry analysis of sources of cereal productivity growth

| Independent Variable | Developed Countries[a] Regression (1) | Developing Countries[b] Regression (2) | Developing Countries[b] Regression (3) |
|---|---|---|---|
| $a_1$ Land [ln $L$] | .965 (199.8) | 1.011 (228.7) | 1.083 (222.9) |
| $a_2$ Fertilizer [ln $F$] | .0333 (8.67) | .0318 (6.26) | .0273 (5.38) |
| $a_3$ Country $A$ Research [ln $A$] | .00707 (2.09) | .00231 (.75) | .0021 (.70) |
| $a_4$ Country $A$ × Country $S$ Research [(ln $A$) × $S$] | .00000404 (1.64) | .0000684 (7.33) | .0000524 (5.44) |
| $a_5$ Regional $A$ Research [ln $RA$] | .01611 (2.46) | −.00014 (.05) | −.00231 (.71) |
| $a_6$ Regional $A$ × Zonal $S$ Research [(ln $RA$) × $ZS$] | .0000639 (12.09) | .000147 (10.56) | .000157 (11.40) |
| $a_7$ Regional $A$ × Country $A + S$ Research [(ln $RA$) × $(A + S)$] | .0000093 (2.81) | .000095 (5.17) | .00010 (5.08) |
| $a_8$ Regional $A$ × Country $A + S$ Research Squared [(ln $RA$) × $(A + S)^2$] | .2306(−9) (1.46) | −.445(−7) (16.06) | −.646(−7) (7.49) |
| $a_9$ Regional Yield Index [ln $RY$] | .1753 (5.38) | .0627 (2.26) | .0026 (.09) |
| $a_{10}$ Regional Yield × Country $A$ Research [(ln $RY$) × $A$] | −.000215 (10.12) | −.00061 (8.94) | −.00036 (5.07) |
| $a_{11}$ Percentage Area Planted to High-Yielding Varieties [HYV] | | | .00574 (2.93) |
| $a_{12}$ Percentage Area Planted to High-Yielding Varieties, Squared [(HYV)$^2$] | | | −.00154 (3.67) |
| $a_{13}$ Percentage Area Planted to High-Yielding Varieties × Country $A$ Research [HYV × $A$] | | | .0000144 (5.81) |
| $a_{14}$ Dummy for Wheat | −.2233 (10.47) | −.018 (1.53) | −.060 (4.67) |
| $a_{15}$ Dummy for Barley | −.2777 (14.29) | −.081 (4.69) | .094 (5.46) |
| $a_{16}$ Dummy for Rice | −.3455 (12.57) | −.097 (7.29) | −.1164 (8.81) |
| $a_0$ Constant Term | .565 (10.55) | .026 (.51) | .087 (2.06) |
| $R^2$ (Adjusted) | .981 | .986 | .987 |

Notes: Dependent variable is cereal grains production index. Parentheses enclose $t$ ratios. Regressions were weighted by area and estimated by Baelestra–Nerlove technique of combining cross-section and time-series data. See P. Baelestra and Marc Nerlove, "Pooling Cross-Section and Time-Series Data in the Estimation of a Dynamic Model: The Demand for Natural Gas," *Econometrica* 34 (July 1966): 585–612.

[a] 87 crop-country combinations, 1948–1971: 2088 observations.

[b] 78 crop-country combinations, 1948–1971: 1872 observations.

The coefficients for the neighboring regional yield performance ($RY$) could be reflecting some direct technology diffusion between regions; however, alternative explanations are possible as well.

Regression (3) in table 6–5 adds the proportion of the crop planted to high-yielding varieties as an independent source of technology (HYV variables). It is of interest to note that the inclusion of the three HYV variables does not alter the basic results. It does appear that these variables are picking up a source of technology. The key HYV variable is the interaction between the availability of HYVs and investment in local adaptive research (coefficient $a_{13}$). In those countries with weak domestic research programs, the effect of green revolution technology is rapidly exhausted (see the negative sign for coefficient $a_{12}$). In countries with substantial indigenous research effort, the knowledge transfer process will convert the "borrowed" HYVs into locally adapted varieties, which will extend the green revolution to more environmental niches. Again, this confirms the strong research-screening complementarity we have discussed.

The economic implications of the results of the present study, as described in table 6–6, should be interpreted in the light of the statistical significance of the estimates and the fact that the basic model is subject to improvement. The computations in this table are based on the assumption that at time $t$ a $1,000 investment in research is added to the research stocks of time $t - 1$. The expected net increment to production from this investment is portrayed in figure 6–2.

An investment in time $t$ will not result in any discoveries that can be utilized by producers until at least 2 or 3 years after investment. The full impact of such investment is expected to be felt 8 or 10 years after initial investment, when production will rise to a maximum of $m$ dollars. The levels reported in table 6–6 are the estimated maximum levels to which production increases realized annually will rise. They represent the amount of real

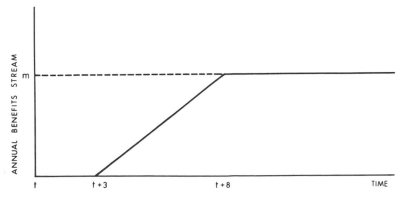

FIG. 6–2. Time profile of benefits from research investment.

TABLE 6–6. Estimated marginal benefit streams associated with research investment devoted to cereal grains improvement

| | Research Investment | | | |
|---|---|---|---|---|
| | Developed Countries | | Developing Countries | |
| Benefits | Technology-oriented | Science-oriented | Technology-oriented | Science-oriented |
| *Part 1*<br>Appropriated by investing country[a] | | | | |
| (a) Direct contribution | $630 | $12,300 | $3,710 | $35,600 |
| (b) Through complementarity with research in other countries | 1,620 | 1,620 | 7,200 | 7,200 |
| Total appropriable benefits | $2,250 | $13,920 | $10,910 | $42,800 |
| *Part 2*<br>Contributed to other countries[b] | 5,150 | 17,000 | 49,000 | 37,300 |
| Total international benefit stream (Part 1 + Part 2) | $7,400 | $30,920 | $59,910 | $80,100 |
| *Part 3*<br>Realized by a typical country from research investment by other countries in similar climate zones (or regions)[c] | | | | |
| (a) With average indigenous research capability | 8,580 | 520 | 55,000 | 1,700 |
| (b) With no indigenous research capability | 4,560 | 520 | 1,700 | 1,700 |

Source: All computations were made on the basis of regressions (1) and (2) in table 6–5 in the present chapter.

Notes: The figures in this table represent estimated levels (in 1973 dollars) to which benefit streams associated with a research investment of $1,000 will rise eight to ten years after initial investment.

Computations were based on mean values of variables in the derivatives from the two data sets. The derivatives are in terms of the effect on production of a change in the knowledge stock. The knowledge stock is converted from publications to dollars based on the data in Robert E. Evenson and Yoav Kislev, *Agricultural Research and Productivity* (New Haven: Yale University Press, 1975) chapter 2, Table 2.4. Cereal grain product is valued at $80 per metric ton (approximate 1971 prices).

[a] Computation 1(a) is based on the coefficient of variable $a_3$ only. Computation 1(b) is based on the coefficient of variables $a_4$, $a_7$, and $a_8$.

[b] Contribution to other countries is computed as 3(a) times the average number of other countries in similar regions for $A$ (.6 for developed countries, .9 for developing countries), and zones for $S$ (33 for developed countries, 23 for developing countries).

[c] Benefits realized from other countries are computed as the marginal products of $RA$ and $ZS$. 3(b) is computed setting $(A + S) = 0$.

economic "growth," or production, that can be purchased for a $1,000 investment. These are annual streams which continue year after year until the technology becomes obsolete.

Part 1 of the table shows the estimated appropriable benefits that can be purchased by investing in technology-oriented ($A$-type) or science-oriented ($S$-type) research. These benefits are as captured by the typical investing country. The estimates are based on the coefficients of the $A$ and $S$ variables in regressions (1) and (2) in table 6–5. The average cost of producing a publication is calculated according to a study by Evenson and Kislev.[48] A distinction is made between the direct contribution of research (derived from coefficients $a_3$ and $a_4$ in table 6–5) and complementarity between country and regional research (derived from $a_7$ and $a_8$).

Part 2 of table 6–6 reports the estimated contribution of research to countries (other than the investing country) that are in a position to benefit from the research investment. This is computed for a typical country (based on the $RA$ and $ZS$ coefficients, for which see discussion of basic specification above) and is not very meaningful for individual countries. However, it is important from an international perspective because the sum of the appropriated and the contributed benefits represents the total payoff of the investment. If the benefits rise to only $2,300 dollars, the internal rate of return realized on the investment is 15 percent, a rate that is realized on relatively few projects. Thus the amount of growth that can be purchased through investment in research appears to be several times greater than that obtainable through most other kinds of investments.

The implications of these data for investment in $S$-type research are particularly important. The literature on agricultural research policy in the developing countries stresses adaptive $A$-type research.[49] The results reported here indicate that policy makers may be persisting in making the same errors as in an earlier period when the emphasis was on direct technology transfer. The advocates of $A$-type research are counting on the transfer of scientific knowledge, but the high returns to $S$-type research indicate that this knowledge is not easily transferred.

These results strongly confirm the role of basic and supporting research, stressed in all models in this book, in generating the potential benefits of applied research.

Part 3 of table 6–6 shows the effect of indigenous research capability on the benefits a country can realize if another country in a similar geoclimatic region or zone invests $1,000 in $A$-type or $S$-type research. The benefits are

---

[48] Evenson and Kislev, *Agricultural Research and Productivity*. In 1973 dollars, the average cost of a publication, as defined in this study, was $140,000 in the developed countries and $125,000 in the developing countries. The cost differential in terms of scientists' time is much greater than this, but it is largely offset by a difference in production costs in the opposite direction.

[49] Albert H. Moseman, *Agricultural Research Systems*.

great for both developed and developing countries. However, in the absence of indigenous research ($A + S = 0$), as shown in 3(b), although the developed country can expect appreciable spillover from other countries, the developing country cannot. It is clear that a policy restricted to borrowing technology from neighbors simply does not work: little of such technology can be utilized unless an indigenous capacity for research exists. This suggests that if investment in international research centers is to bear fruit in countries which at present have minimal research capacity, high priority must be given to the support of national research systems.

The investigations of technology and knowledge transfer which we have discussed may be seen as pathfinders in a new field of study. As such, despite their limitations, they have disclosed a number of avenues for further work. The findings of these studies, together with some general considerations, provide us with a basis for a summary discussion of technology transfer.

*Conclusions*

Until very recently, the economic development literature as well as national policy in developing countries have emphasized the direct transfer of technology from developed nations; comparatively little attention has been given to the development of indigenous research. Only where enormous obstacles to direct transfer have been encountered or where the introduction of highly capital-intensive technologies into labor-abundant countries has led to undesirable social consequences has this emphasis shifted toward the development of intermediate, or appropriate, technologies. Where the shift to appropriate technology has occurred, policy recommendations have generally stressed applied and adaptive research and the dissemination among developing countries of information on existing technologies.

In this chapter we have discussed three primary obstacles to the direct transfer of technology. The first of these is the cost of activities such as acquiring information, screening technology, and training manpower to use the new methods. The costs of bringing an already existing technology to a developing country can be substantial, even when no adaptation of the technology is undertaken.

The second potential obstacle is the environmental sensitivity of a technology in terms of both economic and noneconomic factors. The ES index can be very high if factor scarcities and other noneconomic factors vary widely between environments. Although the economic components of environmental variation may be more important to industrial technology, in agriculture it is primarily the physical, biological, and climatic differences among regions that create barriers to the transfer of technology. Without adaptive research and development, technologies that are profitable in developed countries may not have an economic advantage over existing technologies in developing nations.

A third barrier to direct transfer is the frequent absence of research capacity at the applied level. As we have seen, there is a strong complementarity between the capacity for applied research and the ability to screen technology, and even direct transfer may be difficult without the former.

These three factors may often make direct technology transfer an unrewarding path to the development of productive technology in developing countries. In this context it is interesting to note that Japan, from the beginning of its modern economic development, complemented its direct transfer of technology by building indigenous research capabilities and undertaking adaptive and indigenous research.

In the context of the increased importance of adaptive and indigenous research we have also found that the returns to applied research and the dissemination of information are enhanced by a complementary investment in more basic research. There are a number of reasons why research of a more basic nature is essential to the productivity of an applied research program. First, in the absence of continuing basic research endeavors, new opportunities for applied research may cease to come about. Second, basic knowledge must in some degree reflect specific local variations. Third, as we have discussed, there is considerable complementarity between basic and applied research. Fourth, basic research is of great value in training researchers to do both basic and applied work. It should be noted that we are not advocating research emphasis on basic principles of sciences such as physics, chemistry, or mathematics but rather on those kinds of supporting research most relevant to agricultural technology.[50]

When it begins to put less emphasis on the direct transfer of technology, a country expands its options. First, it has the choice of how to allocate its research resources as between basic and applied research. Then it must decide whether adaptive research or research on the home technology is more attractive. The importance assigned to basic research will often depend on the state of development of research skills in a country. In early stages, when such skills, particularly those of a high level, are generally scarce, the choice will be forced by this fact alone toward more applied programs. As research skills develop, however, increasing emphasis will need to be placed on basic research work.

The choice between adaptive research and research on the home technology depends primarily on which strategy will lead to faster and more sustained

[50] Basic sciences are particularly important to biological technology. A good breeding program requires researchers who are thoroughly familiar with new knowledge in genetics, plant physiology, plant pathology, and related sciences. Biological research is thus close to basic research and requires skills that are not very different from the skills required for the latter. Mechanical research is not so closely tied to basic science, for engineering generally relies on long-established physical and metallurgical principles which, because they do not vary much across geographic regions, are rather widely diffused in developing nations.

success. The decision depends also on the magnitude of environmental differences; the greater these are, the more likely it is that home technology research will be chosen. Social and economic adjustment costs are some other factors that will enter into the decision. Frequently, of course, the new technology will combine elements of both the foreign and the home technology. For example, new varieties are often crosses between foreign and domestic varieties.

The transfer process is complex, and the picture we have sketched here is far from complete. We have as yet little evidence on the complementarities between technology screening and adaptive research and between basic and applied research in fields other than agriculture; indeed such evidence is minimal even in the field of mechanical agricultural technology. Further work will require both more and better data and improvements in methodology.

APPENDIX 6–1

*A Model of the Agricultural Research Institute*[51]

In attempting to understand the ways in which the modern agricultural research institute (or other research organization) responds to the institutional and physical environment in which it finds itself, it is helpful to conceptualize the institute along the lines suggested by Blase and Paulson in their model of agricultural experiment station performance (see figure 6–3). This figure attempts to show how the internal or intermediate processes and activities of the research station relate to the external environment in which it operates; we have touched on this relationship in our discussion of "institutional performance" in chapter 5.

Experiment station production processes, as outlined in figure 6–3, involve the transformation of *flow inputs* (e.g., budgeted funds) and *stock resources* (e.g., desire for change) into such *intermediate processes and activities* as program planning or building relationships with other institutions. These intermediate activities are then transformed into the three final *outputs* of *information, capacity,* and *influence.*

The most important and most visible output of an experiment station or a research laboratory is the *information* that is generated and released. In some fields, such as plant breeding, information, in the form of new technology, may be embodied in higher-yielding or pest-resistant crop varieties (cultivars). In other fields, information, in the form of new knowledge, may be embodied in published reports on farm management, cropping practices, or animal nutrition. The social science output of the experiment station may become a direct input into institutional innovations such as the design of cooperative

[51] This appendix draws on Melvin G. Blase and Arnold Paulson, "The Agricultural Experiment Station: An Institutional Development Perspective," *Agricultural Science Review* (Second Quarter 1972): 11–16.

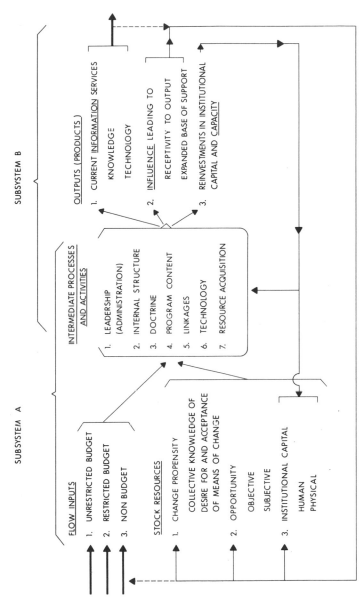

FIG. 6–3. Systems model of experiment station performance and development. [Adapted from Melvin G. Blase and Arnold Paulson, "The Agricultural Experiment Station: An Institutional Development Perspective," *Agricultural Science Review* 10 (2nd quarter, 1972): 11–16.]

marketing arrangements, commodity stabilization programs, or the revision of land tenure relationships. Over the long run, the use of resources for agricultural research must be justified in terms of the economic value of the new knowledge that such research produces.

If a research institution is to remain a valuable social asset, it must devote a portion of its resources to reinvestment in institutional capacity, that is, to the expansion of its physical and intellectual capital. This means, of course, that fewer resources can be allocated to the production of information that has immediate application. It means increasing the capacity of its scientific staff through graduate education, study leaves, and opportunities to conduct basic research. It also means modernizing the institute's facilities and administrative structure, as well as continually reviewing the philosophy that underlies its research program.

The frequent arguments about the relative emphasis that should be given to basic and applied research often reflect a deeper disagreement on the issue of expansion of capacity, particularly capacity as embodied in the professional staff. Such arguments may also reflect the fact that investment in expansion of intellectual capacity has a considerable spillover effect. Only a small portion of the returns may be realized by the research organization that bears the original cost of such investment. Moreover, the internal returns may be potentially negative if investment in staff capacity increases professional mobility.

All successful research institutions devote a significant portion of their resources to increasing their *influence*. In order to establish a successful claim on current and future resources, a research organization usually finds it necessary to maintain effective relationships with both public and private funding agencies. The organization may also find it useful to devote some of its resources to building a positive public image. Although such influence-building may have little direct value to society, it is essential to the continued effective operation of both public and private research institutions. It is of course true that occasionally institutions that have outlived their social function as producers of information devote a large portion of their resources to organizational maintenance activities.[52]

The intermediate processes and activities identified in figure 6–3 have little direct value to society, but they are indispensable to the institution itself. They may be seen as the research system's "engine," whose functioning determines the efficiency with which the system makes use of its resources. By and large, these intermediate services must be produced by the research institution itself rather than purchased from external sources. Their value is derived from their contribution to the output of the research institution.

[52] James T. Bonnen, "The Crisis in the Traditional Role of Agricultural Institutions," *Agricultural Policy in an Affluent Society*, eds. Vernon W. Ruttan, Arly D. Waldo, and James P. Houck (New York: W. W. Norton & Co., 1969), pp. 48–62.

*Linkages,* as referred to in figure 6–3, include contact and relationships with individuals and institutions outside the research station or laboratory— with other scientists, with the clients of the station, and with sources of support. The linkages carry messages in both directions. It is through these linkages that a research institution influences technical and institutional change within the field of its endeavor and is in turn influenced by changes in related science and technology and in society at large. The U.S. state agricultural experiment stations are characterized by a highly complex set of such linkages, including relationships with state crop-improvement associations, community and regional development councils, producer and consumer-interest groups, the extension service, and the entire hierarchy of local, state, and federal administrative and political institutions.[53] It is very difficult to maintain effective communication with such outside groups without becoming either a captive or an adversary.

The development of leadership is an extremely important intermediate activity. The notion that all a research director needs to do is to hire good men and let them "do their thing" is rapidly being displaced by the realization that the solutions to many significant technical and social problems require the careful coordination of research effort. Moreover, leaders must be sensitive to changing social goals and capable of transmitting the implications of such changes to the scientific staff.[54]

Leadership also involves *resource acquisition.* Leaders must be able to visualize and describe to others how the experiment station or research laboratory can contribute to the solution of current problems. And they must be capable of mobilizing and allocating both financial and scientific resources so as to produce the high returns to scientific and technological effort that society has come to expect. This means not only acquiring the necessary human and financial resources, but, what is even more difficult, creating an institutional environment where these resources can become productive.

The *technology,* or the methodology of research, is in continuous flux. A research program must be organized in such a way that the staff are aware of, and contribute to, advances in their own and in closely related fields. The allocation of resources to the production of research technology represents a capital investment in the capacity of the individual research worker, in the research institute that makes the investment, and in the broader research system or scientific community of which the institute is a part. Because research staff members are often willing to consider such investment in their

[53] It has been argued that the failure of many agricultural research institutions to maintain adequate links with the general scientific community has contributed to the sterility of many agricultural research efforts. See *The Report of the Committee on Research Advisory to the U.S. Department of Agriculture* (Washington, D.C.: National Research Council, 1972).

[54] See the discussion in chapters 12–20 in *Resource Allocation and Productivity,* eds. Arndt, Dalrymple, and Ruttan.

individual capacities as part of their remuneration, institutions that devote a relatively high proportion of their effort to basic, or other frontier-type supporting research are frequently able to pay salaries below the market level.

*Doctrine* is reflected both in an institution's articulation of its philosophy and goals and in its operating style. The operational manifestation of a change in doctrine is the reformulation of an institution's program.[55] Modifications in doctrine will be sterile, however, unless research resources are reallocated so as to contribute to the realization of the revised priorities. For example, the United States federal–state agricultural research system has been under increasing pressure to give greater emphasis, in establishing its research priorities, to environmental spillover effects of technical change in agriculture, to problems of human capital formation, and to institutional dimensions of community development.[56] Although the system's doctrine as stated has begun to reflect these altered emphases, in actual practice its traditional orientation toward production remains strong.

Modifications in program often imply drastic modifications in the *internal structure* of a research station. Problem-oriented interdisciplinary "centers" or "teams" tend to usurp the decision-making authority of discipline-oriented departments. During periods of stress, the reformulation of doctrine, the redirection of program, and the reorganization of internal structure may absorb substantial resources and seriously compete with the production of information. These efforts must be justified primarily in terms of their impact on the future productivity and viability of the experiment station.

APPENDIX 6–2

*A Model of Technology Development and Transfer in Wheat and Maize Production*

This appendix develops a model of crop technology improvement as applied to wheat and maize production. It is derived from a recent paper by Evenson and Kislev[57] and is intended to supplement the results reported in tables 6–1, 6–2, and 6–3 above.

A MODEL OF CROP TECHNOLOGY IMPROVEMENT

Crop yields are functions of soil, climate, and technology. Soil and climate determine yield potential with a given technology. Weather causes year-to-

---

[55] See, for example, the discussion of the changing role of the new international agricultural research institutes by Arthur T. Mosher, "Some Issues with Respect to the Role and Operations of the International Institutes," in *Resource Allocation and Productivity*, eds. Arndt, Dalrymple, and Ruttan.

[56] Vernon W. Ruttan, "Technology and the Environment," *American Journal of Agricultural Economics* 53, no. 5 (December 1971): 707–17.

[57] Evenson and Kislev, "Research and Productivity in Wheat and Maize."

year variations in yield. Shifting cultivation between different soils will also result in yield variations.[58]

$$y(t) = f\{S(t), T(t)\} + u(t) \tag{A-1}$$

where $y(t)$ = yield in year $t$, $S(t)$ = soil and climate (since the observations are made on countries, this variable can be taken as "country-specific conditions"), $T(t)$ = technology, and $u(t)$ = random weather effect. Technology is the form in which knowledge is revealed in production and is a function both of indigenously created $(K)$ and borrowed stocks $(B)$ of knowledge:

$$T(t) = T\{K(t), B(t)\} \tag{A-2}$$

$$K(t) = \int_0^t p(s)\, ds \tag{A-3}$$

$$B(t) = \int_0^t b(s)\, ds \tag{A-4}$$

where $p(s)$ = flow of indigenously created knowledge and $b(s)$ = flow of borrowed knowledge.

Because knowledge can be subject to depreciation and obsolescence, depreciation terms should be included in (A-3) and (A-4). Also, if $T$ is the best knowledge available—the "frontier of knowledge"—a lag operator may have to be included in (A-3) and (A-4) to account for the difference between actual and potential achievement.

A regional stock of knowledge is defined as

$$\tilde{R}_i(t) = \sum_j r_{ij} K_j(t) \tag{A-5}$$

where $r_{ij}$ is the share of country $j$'s wheat or maize area that belongs to region $i$. The pool of specific knowledge from which a country borrows, by hypothesis, is

$$R_{ij}(t) = \tilde{R}_i(t) - r_{ij} K_j(t) \tag{A-6}$$

that is, it is the stock of regional knowledge less the country's own contribution.

To formulate the borrowing activity, a *logistic borrowing function* was specified:

$$B_{ij}(t) = \int_0^t \left( \frac{R_{ij}(s)}{1 + \alpha e^{-\beta p_j(s)}} \right) ds \tag{A-7}$$

where $B_{ij}(t)$ is the borrowed stock and $\alpha$, $\beta$ are parameters. Note that borrowing is defined as a flow and is accumulated to a stock.

The borrowed stock of knowledge in a country is the weighted sum of the

[58] For notational convenience, in the general discussion $t$ is treated as a continuous variable. It appears as a subscript in regression equations. Similarly, integrals in the general discussion are represented by sums in the regressions.

stocks borrowed from the different regions with the regional shares, $r_{ij}$, as weights:

$$B_j(t) = \sum_j r_{ij} B_{ij}(t) \tag{A-8}$$

The parameter $1/(1 + \alpha)$, the intercept of the borrowing function, indicates the amount of borrowing a country can do in the absence of indigenous research. In the limit, as $p \to \infty$, the country borrows all of the regional pool. In the regressions, $\alpha$ and $\beta$ were estimated by searching for the value that will yield the highest $R^2$.

Production conditions are quite diversified, even in the smaller countries, and the measure of knowledge should be corrected to take account of this diversity. Two deflators are used to this end, and the numbers of publications in a country are divided by these deflators. The first deflator is the average crop (wheat or maize) area in the country over the period $\bar{a}_j$ in country $j$.

$$d_{1j} = \bar{a}_j \tag{A-9}$$

The use of this deflator is based on the assumption that crop production conditions vary with the area. This is not always a very good assumption— the United States and Soviet Russia lead the world in terms of the total number of papers, but with the use of this deflator they become relatively small producers of knowledge. Clearly, in some countries production conditions vary with small areas, while in other countries huge areas are homogeneous with respect to these conditions.[59]

Neglecting within-region diversification of production conditions, the number of regions in a country can also serve as a deflator. However, regions can vary a great deal in size, so the second deflator used was

$$d_{2j} = \frac{n_j}{\sum_i (r_{ij} - \bar{r}_j) + 1} \tag{A-10}$$

where $n_j$ is the number of regions in the country and $\bar{r}_j = 1/n_j$ is the average regional share. Thus,

$$\frac{1}{d_{2j}} = \frac{1}{n_j} + V_j \tag{A-11}$$

where $V_j$, like the variance, is a measure of dispersion. The inclusion of $V_j$ corrects for unequal size distribution of regions.

---

[59] In the absence of data on extension and other instruments of information dissemination or on the number of wheat or maize growers, the area deflators serve also as a proxy for the relative ease with which knowledge is spread over the countryside.

THE TRANSFERABILITY FACTOR

In the following equations, $i$ = region index, $j$ = country index, $J$ = number of countries in the sample, $I$ = number of regions, $n_i$ = number of countries in region $i$, and $r_{ij}$ = the share of country $j$ in region $i$.

A typical event (with probability $1/J$) is that a paper is produced in country $k$. Then $r_{ik}$ of it is contributed to region $i$. The total transfer potential of this part of the paper to the other countries in the region is

$$\left( \sum_i^{n_i} r_{ij} - r_{ik} \right) r_{ik} \tag{A-12}$$

To get the expected value of the borrowing potential for the region $i$, calculate

$$\frac{1}{J} \sum_k^{n_i} \left( \sum_j^{n_i} r_{ij} - r_{ik} \right) r_{ik} \tag{A-13}$$

and the expected value for the sample is

$$\frac{1}{J} \sum_i^I \sum_k^{n_i} \left( \sum_j^{n_i} r_{ij} - r_{ik} \right) r_{ik} = \text{the transferability factor} \tag{A-14}$$

Note that the term in parentheses is zero for regions with only one country.

*Some Cases and Tests*

# SEVEN

# Measured Biases of Technical Change: The United States

HANS P. BINSWANGER

T HE two-factor test of induced innovation performed in chapter 3 indicated that in general the experience of six countries studied was consistent with the induced innovation hypothesis. The paths of technical change of these countries were shown to be clearly different from each other. They are consistent with the separate countries' factor endowments, as hypothesized in the theory of induced innovation. Nevertheless, the test did cast doubt on the simple version of the induced innovation hypothesis, which assumes that innovation possibilities are neutral and that all biases are caused by factor price changes. The possibility of fundamental biases in a labor-saving direction or of biases arising out of the possibility of borrowing technology that has been developed under conditions characterized by different factor intensities must be admitted.

In this chapter the experience of United States agriculture from 1912 to 1964 is analyzed in much more detail than was presented in chapter 3. Specific attention is given to the problem of distinguishing between the separate roles played by fundamental biases and price-induced biases in technical change.

The work of Ryuzo Sato on measuring augmentation rates, and the development of the *translog* functional forms by Laurits R. Christensen, Dale W. Jorgenson, and Lawrence J. Lau provided the starting point for the econometric work in this chapter, and I would like to acknowledge a special intellectual debt to these authors. I am also indebted to Richard A. King, James A. Seagraves, and T. Dudley Wallace for guidance in respect to my dissertation, from which this chapter draws.

This chapter represents a revision and extension of material previously published in Hans P. Binswanger, "The Measurement of Technical Change Biases with Many Factors of Production," *American Economic Review* 64 (December 1974): 964–76, and Hans P. Binswanger, "A Cost Function Approach to the Measurement of Factor Demand Elasticities and Elasticities of Substitution," *American Journal of Agricultural Economics* 56 (May 1974): 377–86.

Tests of induced innovation must satisfy two basic requirements. First, a method must be found to separate observed factor-ratio or factor-share changes into a component that results from ordinary factor substitution along the isoquant of the production process and a component that derives from nonneutral shifts in the isoquant. This can be done by measuring biases of technical change. Second, once biases are measured, they must be related to the factor price changes to see whether factor-saving biases correspond to rising factor prices and vice versa. In this second task, all induced innovation tests are confronted with the following problem: Suppose technical change biases were very responsive to factor price changes, and suppose the land price had a tendency to increase. If such an increase were followed by technical change in a land-saving direction, the land price would then rise less than it would in the absence of technical change. In an extreme case it might not rise at all. This problem makes it difficult to show, from *ex post* empirical data, that it was the factor price that caused the bias and not some land-saving bias in the innovation possibilities. And the problem is impossible to overcome if aggregate, economy-wide data are used. However, at the level of individual industries, the prices of factors that are not specific to the industry can be regarded as exogenous, and thus a partial solution to the problem can be achieved.

The test performed in this chapter is based on directly measured biases of technical change. Biases are measured for the United States agricultural sector from 1912 to 1968 and for five factors (land, labor, machinery, fertilizer, and other inputs).[1] The price of land reflects the influence of some exogenous but of mostly endogenous elements. Prices of the other four factors, however, are governed in the long run primarily by the nonagricultural labor market and by cost conditions in the input-supplying industries. The biases of technical change in these four factors will be examined in comparison with the prices of the same factors in the following manner. Suppose, for example, that innovation possibilities are neutral and that factor prices are exogenous to the industry. In this case, a measured factor-saving bias should be associated with a rising factor price, and vice versa. Furthermore, turning points in trends of factor prices should be followed after some years by corresponding changes in the rates of biases. If, on the other hand, innovation possibilities are not neutral, then it is possible that a factor-using bias may be associated with a rise in the price of the corresponding factor. Indeed, such an occurrence can be used to test for the presence of a fundamental bias in innovation possibilities. Induced innovation may either offset or reinforce such a fundamental bias. But in the case of a factor-saving shift of prices, an acceleration of the price rise should, after some years, lead to a decrease in the rate of the factor-using bias. The measured series of biases and factor

---

[1] Because the test uses a many-factor framework, it does not require, as did the test in chapter 3, that separability restrictions be imposed on the production process.

prices will be inspected to check both for bias in innovation possibilities and for the sequence of turning points in prices and biases. As we shall see, the series provide remarkably strong evidence for the role of factor prices in inducing biases.

## The Measurement of Technical Change Biases with Many Factors of Production

The basic problem of measuring biases is most easily explained in a two-factor case. We define the Hicksian bias as the change in factor ratios that would have occurred had factor prices remained stable (see appendix to chapter 2):

$$B' = \frac{d(K/L)}{dt} \cdot \frac{1}{(K/L)}\bigg|_{\text{factor prices}} \gtreqless 0 \begin{cases} \text{labor saving} \\ \text{neutral} \\ \text{labor using} \end{cases} \tag{1}$$

The empirical difficulty of measuring biases arises from the fact that factor prices change over time, that is, the observed changes in the factor ratio have two causes: (1) ordinary factor substitution along a given production function and (2) biased technical change. Consider figure 3–1 (chapter 3); assume that the points $P$ and $Q$ represent the observed production points in period zero and period one and that the lines $BB$ and $CC$ represent the corresponding factor price ratios. If we knew that the production function was of fixed proportions, we would know that the entire change of the factor ratio between these periods was the result of technical change, and measuring biases according to equation (1) would be very simple. The move from $A$ to $B$ would have been a labor-saving technical change. But with a neoclassical production function, the observed data alone cannot tell us this. Suppose the elasticity of substitution were very large, as for the homothetic isoquant map $I_0^*$ and $I_1^*$. Then the entire change in factor ratios would be explained by ordinary factor substitution, and technical change would have been neutral. But if the elasticity of substitution is small, as for the isoquants $I_0$ and $I_1$, then the change in factor ratio is attributable partly to the ordinary price substitution effect and partly to a labor-saving technical change.

To measure biases, therefore, it is necessary to know the curvature parameters of the isoquants. In the two-factor *constant elasticity of substitution* (CES) case, we must know the elasticity of substitution in order to separate the observed factor ratio change into a component attributable to price changes and a component attributable to technical change. This approach leads to the following measurement equation:

$$Q' = (\hat{k} - \hat{\ell}) + \sigma(\hat{r} - \hat{w}) \tag{2}$$

where $\hat{k}$ and $\hat{\ell}$ are observed proportional rates of change of $K$ and $L$, and $\hat{r}$ and $\hat{w}$ are rates of change in the capital rental rate and the wage rate. The component of the capital–labor ratio change that derives from ordinary factor substitution is represented by $\sigma(\hat{r} - \hat{w})$.[2]

The measurement of biases thus consists of two steps:

I. Measure the elasticity of substitution in an independent sample.

II. Apply equation (2) to time-series data to measure the biases.

In the many-factor case the procedure is a similar two-step procedure. However, the biases are now defined in terms of factor shares (equation 3, chapter 2).

$$B_i = \frac{dS_i'}{dt} \cdot \frac{1}{S_i} \lessgtr 0 \rightarrow \begin{cases} i \text{ saving} \\ \text{neutral} \\ i \text{ using} \end{cases} \tag{3}$$

Also, the CES production function usually used in the two-factor case is inappropriate in the many-factor case, because then it implies the restriction that all partial elasticities of substitution are identical between all pairs of factors. This was considered to be too restrictive.

The *translog* function of Laurits R. Christensen, Dale W. Jorgenson, and Lawrence J. Lau,[3] does not imply such restrictive constraints on the production process, and it is very convenient to work with the translog cost function. In logarithms, this function can be written as

$$\ln C = \ln [h(Y)] + \ln \nu_0 + \sum_i \nu_i \ln W_i + \tfrac{1}{2} \sum_i \sum_j \gamma_{ij} \ln W_i \ln W_j \tag{4}$$

where $C$ is total cost and the $W$ are factor prices and where $h(Y)$ is a scale function of output and $\nu_0$, $\nu_i$, and $\gamma_{ij}$ are the parameters of the cost function. If the cost function were Cobb–Douglas, then the production function also would be Cobb–Douglas, as proved by Giora Hanoch.[4] Thus, we can think of the terms in the double summation as amendments to the Cobb–Douglas function that change the elasticities of substitution away from one (see also

---

[2] Proof of equation (2): Ryuzo Sato ["The Estimation of Biased Technical Progress," *International Economic Review* 11 (June 1970): 179–207] shows that rates of augmentation can be measured as follows:

$$\hat{a} = \frac{\sigma \hat{r} - \hat{y} + \hat{k}}{1 - \sigma}; \qquad \hat{b} = \frac{\sigma \hat{w} - \hat{y} + \hat{\ell}}{1 - \sigma}$$

Recalling equation (A–5) of chapter 2,

$$Q' = (1 - \sigma)(\hat{a} - \hat{b}),$$

and substituting the above expressions into this leads to equation (2).

[3] Laurits R. Christensen, Dale W. Jorgenson, and Lawrence J. Lau, "Transcendental Logarithmic Production Frontiers," *Review of Economics and Statistics* 55 (February 1973): 357–94.

[4] Giora Hanoch, "Generation of New Production Functions Through Duality," Discussion Paper 118 (Cambridge, Mass.: Harvard Institute of Economic Research, 1970).

appendix equations A–24 to A–27 below). The function allows arbitrary and variable elasticities of substitution among factors.

The function can be considered a functional form in its own right, or it can be regarded as a logarithmic, Taylor-series expansion to the second term of an arbitrary, twice-differentiable cost function around input prices of one. With the proper set of constraints on its parameters, therefore, it can be used as an approximation to any one of the known costs and production functions.

To measure biases, we need equations that explain factor shares in terms of factor prices. From Shephard's lemma, $\partial C / \partial W_i = X_i$, we find that the logarithmic derivatives of the cost function are factor shares.

$$\frac{\partial \ln C}{\partial \ln W_i} = \frac{W_i X_i}{C} = S_i \qquad i = 1, \ldots, n \tag{5}$$

Taking this derivative we have

$$S_i = \nu_i + \sum_j \gamma_{ij} \ln W_j \qquad i = 1, \ldots, n \tag{6}$$

If we differentiate these equations totally in logarithmic form we have

$$dS_i = \sum_j \gamma_{ij} d \ln W_j \qquad i = 1, \ldots, n \tag{7}$$

This represents the change in the share attributable to factor price changes alone. Now suppose that technical change over time alters the share by $dS_i'$, defined as the change which would have occurred without factor price changes.

Then we would rewrite (7) for technical change:

$$dS_i = \sum_j \gamma_{ij} d \ln W_j + dS_i' \tag{8}$$

where $dS_i$ is the observed change in shares and $d \ln W_j$ represents the observed factor price changes.

The share change due to technical change can therefore be measured as

$$dS_i' = dS_i - \sum_j \gamma_{ij} d \ln W_j \qquad i = 1, \ldots, n \tag{9}$$

Equation (9) can be interpreted as follows: To find out what the factor share changes would have been had factor prices remained constant, simply subtract from the observed factor share changes the part that was caused by changing factor prices. The $\gamma$ parameters contain the information by how much the changes in factor price ratios alone could have altered shares.

The two-step procedure to measure biases is therefore as follows:

     I. Measure the $\gamma_{ij}$ parameters of the translog cost function in an independent sample.

     II. Apply these parameters by means of equation (9) to time-series data on factor shares and factor prices.

The derivation of equation (9) has been entirely heuristic. Appendix 7–1 to this chapter gives a rigorous derivation of equation (9) in terms of a factor-augmenting, minimum-cost function. It should be noted, however, that equation (9) covers more general forms of technical change than the special case of factor-augmenting technical change. The approach of equation (9) is called "Model I". (Appendix 7–1 also reports a regression approach to measuring biases that assumes biases occur at a constant rate; this approach is called "Model II".)

### Results and Conclusions

The method of measuring biases described above was applied to United States agriculture from 1912 to 1962. Step I was performed with pooled cross-sectional data of most states for the years 1949, 1954, 1959, and 1964. The details of this estimation procedure and the data used are discussed in appendix 7–2.

The resulting $\gamma_{ij}$ estimates (see appendix table 7–4) were then used with aggregate United States time-series data to measure biases. The data and variable construction are discussed in detail in appendix 7–3.

The basic estimation equations for the biases are the equations

$$dS'_i = dS_i - \sum_j \hat{\gamma}_{ij} d \ln W_j \qquad i = 1, \ldots, n \tag{9'}$$

where the $dS'_i$ is the change in the share of factor $i$ in the absence of ordinary factor substitution owing to price changes; $dS_i$ is the actual total change in share $i$, which includes the effect of the price changes; and $d \ln W_j$ is the proportional change in the price of factor $i$. For actual estimation purposes, series of three-year moving averages of the shares and the factor prices were constructed. Then discrete differences of these moving averages at four-year intervals were taken and used in the discrete change equivalent of (9). The $\hat{\gamma}_{ij}$ coefficients are taken from table 7–4 in appendix 7–2. The resulting $dS'_i$ can be substituted into the discrete equivalent of equation (3) to compute rates of biases. Here, however, we compute the series $S'_i$, which show how the share would have developed after 1912 in the absence of factor price changes:

$$S'_{it} = S_{i,1912} + \sum_{\tau=0}^{t} \Delta S'_{it} \tag{10}$$

These series are presented in the first section of table 7–1. Series of standardized values, that is, $R_{it} = S'_{it}/S_{i,1912}$, are presented in figure 7–1. Because of the semilogarithmic scale of the figure, the slopes of the lines indicate biases according to equation (3), whereas the position of the line shows the cumulative bias since 1912.

How good are these series? The approach is not restrictive. Very few

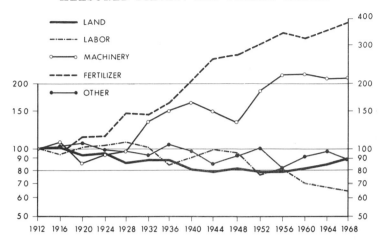

FIG. 7–1. Indices of biases in technical change: Model I estimates of $S'_{it}/S_{t,1912}$. (United States, $1912 = 100$.) [Adapted from Hans P. Binswarger, "The Measurement of Technical Change Biases with Many Factors of Production," *American Economic Review* 64 (December 1974): 972.]

constraints are imposed on the production process characterized by the translog cost function. The key assumption of the approach is the constancy of the $\gamma_{ij}$ parameters. When tested, this assumption was not supported as well as one might wish (see appendix 7–2). It would have been good to obtain a different set of $\gamma_{ij}$ estimates for the early 1900s. However, there are no data for such an estimation.

Some conclusions on the quality of the $S'$ series (which we call "Model I estimates") and the underlying $\gamma_{ij}$ estimates can be obtained by comparing them with different estimates. Appendix 7–1 reports a method for estimating constant rates of biases by means of regression (Model II). The regressions for estimating the $\gamma_{ij}$ parameters in appendix 7–2 contain time coefficients $\hat{\omega}_t$ (see table 7–4) that give an independent estimate of the biases for the period 1948–1964 by means of equation (A–21). Table 7–2 compares the two sets of estimates. The estimates agree in sign and in relative magnitude, and this strengthens our confidence in the models used in estimating the bias in factor shares.

Table 7–1 and figure 7–1 show the biases of all the inputs together. Over the whole period, the strongest was the fertilizer-using bias, followed by the machinery-using bias and by a very strong labor-saving bias after 1948. There was no pronounced long-term bias with respect to other inputs. Up to about 1940, technical change was slightly land-saving. It remained neutral till about 1956 and then was characterized by a land-using bias. Note also that biases frequently changed their rate and even their direction. Constancy of biases is definitely not a proper specification of technical change in United States agriculture.

In table 7–1, the index of agricultural input prices relative to output prices is also given. It shows a sustained rise in agricultural input prices from 1920 onward, interrupted only during the Great Depression. The benefits of the rate of technical change were thus reflected in a substantial drop in the prices of agricultural commodities relative to the prices of their inputs, and the

TABLE 7–1. Price-corrected shares $(S'_i)$, actual factor shares, and factor prices used in computing $(S'_i)$: United States agriculture, 1912–1968

| Year | Land | Labor | Machinery | Fertilizer | Other | Input/Output Price Index[a] |
|------|------|-------|-----------|------------|-------|------------------------------|
| *Price-corrected Factor Shares* $(S'_i)$[b] | | | | | | |
| 1912 | 21.0 | 38.3 | 10.9 | 1.9 | 28.0 | |
| 1916 | 21.2 | 36.7 | 11.6 | 1.8 | 28.7 | |
| 1920 | 19.6 | 39.3 | 9.3 | 2.1 | 29.7 | |
| 1924 | 20.0 | 39.7 | 10.3 | 2.2 | 27.8 | |
| 1928 | 18.1 | 41.4 | 10.4 | 2.7 | 27.4 | |
| 1932 | 18.8 | 40.3 | 14.3 | 2.7 | 24.0 | |
| 1936 | 18.9 | 32.5 | 16.3 | 3.0 | 29.3 | |
| 1940 | 16.8 | 34.3 | 17.6 | 3.9 | 27.5 | |
| 1944 | 16.5 | 38.4 | 16.1 | 4.8 | 24.2 | |
| 1948 | 17.1 | 37.2 | 13.9 | 5.1 | 26.7 | |
| 1952 | 16.5 | 29.8 | 19.7 | 5.7 | 28.3 | |
| 1956 | 16.3 | 30.6 | 23.1 | 6.5 | 23.4 | |
| 1960 | 17.1 | 27.2 | 23.4 | 6.1 | 26.1 | |
| 1964 | 17.8 | 25.8 | 22.4 | 6.7 | 27.3 | |
| 1968 | 19.1 | 25.3 | 23.1 | 7.2 | 25.3 | |
| *Actual Factor Shares* $(S'_i)$ | | | | | | |
| 1912 | 21.0 | 38.3 | 10.9 | 1.9 | 28.0 | |
| 1916 | 21.6 | 36.5 | 11.6 | 1.9 | 28.4 | |
| 1920 | 17.3 | 40.5 | 10.1 | 2.0 | 30.1 | |
| 1924 | 19.7 | 38.5 | 10.3 | 1.7 | 29.7 | |
| 1928 | 15.9 | 40.9 | 10.2 | 1.9 | 31.1 | |
| 1932 | 18.6 | 37.6 | 12.6 | 1.6 | 29.7 | |
| 1936 | 14.9 | 34.7 | 14.5 | 2.2 | 33.7 | |
| 1940 | 12.0 | 35.3 | 15.1 | 2.3 | 35.2 | |
| 1944 | 8.5 | 39.5 | 14.0 | 2.3 | 35.6 | |
| 1948 | 9.4 | 37.7 | 12.2 | 2.4 | 38.3 | |
| 1952 | 9.8 | 29.7 | 17.5 | 3.0 | 40.0 | |
| 1956 | 11.5 | 27.4 | 20.1 | 3.3 | 37.8 | |
| 1960 | 15.6 | 21.3 | 19.8 | 2.9 | 40.4 | |
| 1964 | 17.5 | 18.3 | 18.5 | 3.3 | 42.3 | |
| 1968 | 20.4 | 15.8 | 19.1 | 3.6 | 41.1 | |
| *Factor Prices Relative to Aggregate Input Prices*[c] | | | | | | |
| 1912 | 100.0 | 100.0 | 100.0 | 100.0 | 100.0 | 100.0 |
| 1916 | 105.2 | 99.2 | 102.1 | 98.1 | 96.4 | 107.7 |
| 1920 | 81.1 | 107.1 | 83.5 | 88.0 | 107.8 | 97.4 |
| 1924 | 99.2 | 112.1 | 93.1 | 77.6 | 88.8 | 120.0 |
| 1928 | 79.7 | 117.2 | 97.7 | 68.4 | 90.4 | 131.5 |
| 1932 | 97.8 | 118.4 | 140.7 | 78.2 | 61.7 | 164.5 |
| 1936 | 59.5 | 97.2 | 162.1 | 85.4 | 95.0 | 116.7 |

TABLE 7–1 (continued)

| Year | Land | Labor | Machinery | Fertilizer | Other | Input/Output Price Index[a] |
|------|------|-------|-----------|------------|-------|------------------------------|
| Factor Prices Relative to Aggregate Input Prices (continued) | | | | | | |
| 1940 | 49.6 | 101.7 | 164.1 | 58.8 | 91.0 | 176.0 |
| 1944 | 32.2 | 107.4 | 120.7 | 31.1 | 104.7 | 202.3 |
| 1948 | 34.0 | 115.5 | 105.6 | 23.5 | 103.9 | 214.5 |
| 1952 | 39.6 | 119.0 | 130.6 | 23.2 | 93.1 | 230.6 |
| 1956 | 48.2 | 134.8 | 140.0 | 21.8 | 75.9 | 302.7 |
| 1960 | 71.6 | 141.6 | 155.0 | 17.7 | 68.0 | 355.1 |
| 1964 | 82.9 | 149.6 | 159.9 | 15.5 | 66.4 | 407.9 |
| 1968 | 100.8 | 160.7 | 154.2 | 12.2 | 58.8 | 477.2 |

Source: See appendix 7–3.

[a] Share-weighted indexes of agricultural input prices relative to agricultural output prices. Source: Hans P. Binswanger, "The Measurement of Technical Change Biases with Many Factors of Production," *American Economic Review* 64 (December 1974), Table 3.

[b] Model I estimates.

[c] 1912 = 100.

benefits of technical change were passed along to consumers through this mechanism.[5] To test these biases against the induced innovation hypothesis, consider figures 7–2 to 7–5, in which indexes of the biases are plotted against the movements of their corresponding input prices (relative to agricultural input prices as a whole). Indexes of actual shares are also given.

In figure 7–2, note first that overall technical change was machinery-using, despite a substantial overall rise in the relative machinery price.[6] This clearly implies the presence of an exogenous, machinery-using bias. Had innovation possibilities been neutral, this bias could not have occurred in the presence of rising machinery prices.

TABLE 7–2. Comparison of Model I and Model II estimates of biases for the period 1948–1964 in the United States (in percent)

| Factor | 1948 Level of Shares | Estimated Share Change Owing to Technical Change Alone | |
|--------|----------------------|---------------------------------------------------------|---|
| | | Model I [equation (9)] | Model II [equation (A–21)] |
| Land | 9.4 | +2.3 | +.7 |
| Labor | 37.7 | −15.1 | −11.4 |
| Machinery | 12.2 | +6.9 | +8.5 |
| Fertilizer | 2.8 | +.5 | +1.6 |

[5] For evidence on the rate of agricultural technical change in United States agriculture, see Robert E. Evenson, "The Contribution of Agricultural Research and Extension to Agricultural Production" (Ph.D. diss., University of Chicago, 1968).

[6] This price is the price of machinery services, which includes interest charges, depreciation, fuel, and repair costs. Depreciation rates and repair costs have increased greatly over time.

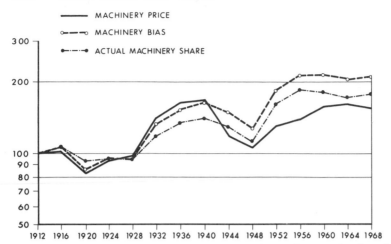

FIG. 7–2. Machinery bias, actual machinery share, and price of machinery inputs in relation to cost of all agricultural inputs.

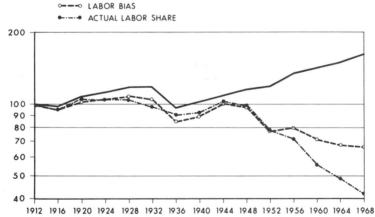

FIG. 7–3. Labor bias, actual labor share, and price of labor inputs in relation to cost of all agricultural inputs.

From table 7–1 it is also clear that the entire change in the machinery share is due to biases. The bias alone would have moved the machinery share from 10.9 percent in 1912 to 23.1 percent in 1968. The actual share rose only to 19.1 percent. The substitution effect against machinery owing to the machinery price rise had very little effect on the share because the elasticities of substitution of machinery with respect to other factors are close to unity on average (see table 7–5).

A remarkable feature of the bias and the price movements is the sequence of turning points. Between 1916 and 1920, relative machinery prices fell and

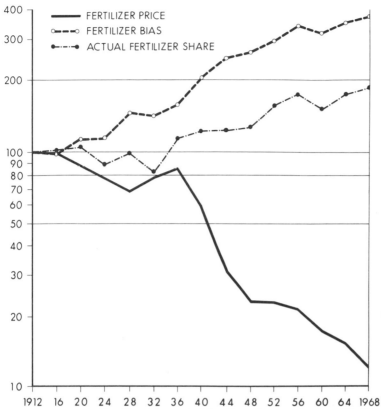

FERTILIZER PRICE
FERTILIZER BIAS
ACTUAL FERTILIZER SHARE

FIG. 7–4. Fertilizer bias, actual fertilizer share, and price of fertilizer inputs in relation to cost of all agricultural inputs.

then started to rise again.[7] From 1920 onward, a substantial machinery-using bias was in effect, and it operated at a particularly rapid rate after 1928. This is what the induced innovation hypothesis would predict. By 1928, relative machinery prices had returned to their 1912 level, but after that they rose rapidly till about 1940. Then in 1940 the bias changed from a machinery-using to a machinery-saving direction; this continued until 1948. From 1940 to 1948, machinery prices declined rapidly again, and in 1948 an eight-year period of rapid, machinery-using technical change began. In 1948 prices began to rise and continued to do so until 1960. Eight years after this change in price trend, in 1956, the machinery-using bias disappeared, and technical change became neutral with respect to machines.

The above sequence of turning points is fully consistent with the induced innovation hypothesis. Indeed, the price-responsiveness of the machinery

[7] It is not known whether the initial decline in machinery prices after 1912 was the continuation of a similar trend, begun earlier.

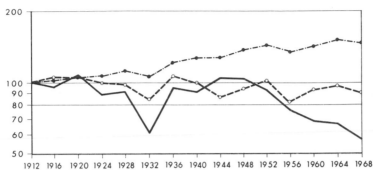

FIG. 7–5. "Other" input bias, actual share of "other" inputs, and price of "other" inputs in relation to cost of all agricultural inputs.

bias is quite remarkable. In addition, the occurrence of twelve to eight-year lags between the turning points is further evidence that prices influence the direction of technical change. A shorter lag would be more consistent with a choice-of-techniques hypothesis. Evenson has found a mean lag between the initiation and the impact of research on agricultural productivity of between five and one-half to eight and one-half years in the United States.[8] The lags of the turning points in biases with respect to turning points in the factor prices must be longer because it takes time for researchers and research administrators to become convinced that a new price trend will persist in the future. That the lags were shorter at the end of the period than at the beginning is also reasonable because both research effort and the rate of technical change were greater in the later half of the period than in the early half.

The comparison of the labor bias with labor price trends in figure 7–3 is also consistent with price-induced biases. Overall technical change was labor saving while labor prices were rising. There is thus no evidence of an exogenous bias with respect to labor.

The first period of labor price rise started in 1916 but it was not very long. It was followed, after 1932, by a short period of labor-saving bias at a very rapid pace. After 1936, the bias became almost neutral again and was relatively labor using between 1940 and 1944 (which, incidentally, is eight years after labor prices started to decline in 1932). The really sustained rise in labor prices, however, began only in 1936. And it was eight years later, in 1944, that United States agriculture started to enter a phase of rapid and sustained labor-saving technical change.[9]

[8] Evenson, "Agricultural Research and Extension."

[9] A similar labor-saving bias for agriculture was found by Theodore P. Lianos, "The Relative Share of Labor in the United States Agriculture," *American Journal of Agricultural Economics* 53 (August 1971): 411–22.

A comparison with the actual share shows that the latter dropped from 39.5 percent in 1944 to 15.8 percent in 1968, which is less than half its former value. The price-corrected share at the same time dropped from 38.4 to 25.3 percent. Of the total decline of the labor share in United States agriculture from 1944 to 1968, about 55 percent must be attributed to labor-saving technical change rather than to simple price effects. Technical change again is the most powerful source of changes in factor shares.

It should also be noted that the labor-saving bias was not wholly in favor of machinery. Up to 1956, these biases moved in opposite directions, but from then onward a machinery bias ceased to exist. In the last 12 years of the period, the labor-saving bias was offset by land, fertilizer, and other input-using biases and not by a machinery-using bias. The additional machinery use from 1956 onward should therefore be interpreted as a combination of substitution effects and neutral technical change with respect to this factor.

The fertilizer experience is shown in figure 7–4. Corresponding to a dramatic decline in the relative cost of fertilizer is a very substantial fertilizer-using bias. This is again consistent with the price inducement mechanism. However, the sharpest drop in relative fertilizer prices occurred between 1936 and 1948, and this was not followed by an acceleration of the fertilizer-using bias. It is possible, of course, that further intensification of the search for fertilizer-using innovations could simply not accelerate the bias because of the exhaustion phenomenon discussed in part II. Therefore, although this lack of response is not sufficient to disprove the induced innovation hypothesis, it does not support it either.

As for machinery and labor, the share change attributable to the bias greatly exceeds the share change that would have occurred as a result of simple price substitution.

Figure 7–5 shows the comparison for "other" inputs. Despite two periods of rapid rise in the prices of these inputs, biases occurred often, but they were almost immediately offset by contrary biases. Thus there is no support for price-responsiveness of the bias in this series. "Other" inputs, of course, are a conglomerate of all kinds of factors: agricultural products used as intermediate inputs, pesticides, costs of farm structures, taxes, interest charges, and so on. They were introduced in the analysis to obtain a full coverage of costs. Systematic behavior of any individual component of "other" inputs is likely to be obscured in the conglomerate.

Note also that neutral technical change and a decline in the price of other inputs led to an increase in the actual share despite the price rise. This is because of extremely large elasticities of substitution of other factors with respect to land, labor, machinery, and fertilizer (table 7–5).

It is not appropriate to compare the land price with the land bias because over most of the period studied the land price is largely endogenous to agriculture. Since land is the residual claimant and its price primarily reflects rents, it is likely to be strongly influenced by the biases themselves as well as by influences that derive from the rate of technical change and from movements in agricultural terms of trade.

In summary, the following conclusions stand out: In United States agriculture the biases of technical change with respect to machinery, labor, and fertilizers have been very responsive to changes in relative factor prices. In general, the direction of the biases has responded to changes in the factor prices with a lag from between sixteen to eight years, and the lags have become shorter over time. Both the long lags and their shortening over time are additional evidence that the biases arise out of a responsiveness of technical change and are not simply a choice-of-technique phenomenon. Furthermore, in the case of machinery, labor, and fertilizer, the observed biases and share changes were large and greatly exceeded the share changes that were attributable to simple substitution effects.

However, innovation possibilities are not always neutral. The overall machinery-using bias in the presence of an overall rise of machinery prices contradicts this. But even for machinery (and most clearly there), changes in factor prices have induced additional biases that offset or reinforced the bias in innovation possibilities according to the change in the trend in machinery prices.

APPENDIX 7–1

## Two Models for Measuring Biases

MODEL I. VARIABLE RATES OF BIASES: A STRICT DERIVATION OF EQUATION (9)

When I started working on measurements of biased technical changes, the only models for the measurement of bias that were available in the literature were in terms of factor-augmenting technical change such as Sato's procedure, which is discussed in equation (2).[10] Thus I derived equation (9) initially for the case of factor-augmenting technical change in the manner shown below. I also realized that the simpler derivation presented in the chapter proper was possible, but I did not realize that equation (9) in fact covers more general forms of biased technical change than factor augmentation. In particular, it is consistent with the factorial rates of technical change discussed in appendix 5–1, where I discuss at length the disadvantages of factor-augmenting technical change. In my *American Economic Review* paper on the measurement of biased technical change I still put substantial emphasis on factor augmentation.[11] I present the derivation of that early model here

---

[10] Sato, "Biased Technical Progress."
[11] Binswanger, "Technical Change Biases."

primarily for completeness but also to demonstrate the redundancy of measuring augmentation rates.

A minimum-cost function with technical change in factor-augmenting form and neutral economies or diseconomies of scale can be written

$$C = h(Y)\phi(W_1A_1, W_2A_2, \ldots, W_nA_n) \tag{A-1}$$

where $C$ is cost, $Y$ is the output level, and the $W$'s are the factor prices. The $A$'s are augmentation parameters corresponding to those in the dual production function in chapter 3. A proportional change in $A_i$ has the same effect on cost as a proportional change in the price of factor $i$.

Let $R_i = (W_iA_i)$, the factor price of the augmented factor unit $(X_i/A_i)$. The translog cost function can be written in logarithmic form as

$$\ln C = \ln[h(Y)] + \ln v_0 + \sum_i v_i \ln R_i + \tfrac{1}{2}\sum_i\sum_j \gamma_{ij} \ln R_i \ln R_j \tag{A-2}$$

where $h(Y)$ is a scale function of output and $v_0$, $v_i$, and $\gamma_{ij}$ are the parameters of the cost function. The following symmetry constraint holds for all translog functions (equality of the cross-derivatives):

$$\gamma_{ij} = \gamma_{ji} \qquad \text{for all } i, j, i \neq j \tag{A-3}$$

The function must satisfy the following conditions:

(1) *Linear homogeneity in prices:* When all factor prices double, the total cost must double. It can be shown that this implies

$$\sum_i v_i = 1; \qquad \sum_i \gamma_{ij} = 0; \qquad \sum_j \gamma_{ij} = 0 \qquad \text{for all } i, j \tag{A-4}$$

(2) *Monotonicity:* The function must be an increasing function of the input prices, that is,

$$\frac{\partial \ln C}{\partial \ln W_j} = v_i + \sum_j \gamma_{ij} \ln W_j \geq 0 \qquad i = 1, \ldots, n \tag{A-5}$$

(3) *Concavity in input prices:* This implies that the matrix

$$\frac{\partial^2 C}{\partial W_i\, \partial W_j} \tag{A-6}$$

must be negative semi-definite within the range of input prices.

In augmented units, Shephard's lemma, $\partial C/\partial W_i = X_i$, becomes

$$\frac{\partial C}{\partial R_i} = \frac{\partial C}{\partial W_i}\frac{dW_i}{dR_i} = X_i/A_i \tag{A-7}$$

The first derivatives of the translog function, with respect to the log of the factor prices, are equal to the shares:

$$\frac{\partial \ln C}{\partial \ln R_i} = \frac{\partial C}{\partial R} \frac{R_i}{C} = \frac{(X_i/A_i)R_i}{C} = \frac{(X_i/A_i)W_iA_i}{C} = \frac{W_iX_i}{C} = S_i \qquad \text{(A–8)}$$

Taking these derivatives, we have

$$S_i = \nu_i + \sum_j \gamma_{ij} \ln R_j \qquad i = 1,\ldots, n \qquad \text{(A–9)}$$

Differentiating (A–5) totally,

$$dS_i = \sum_{j=1}^{n} \gamma_{ij} d \ln R_j \qquad i = 1,\ldots, n \qquad \text{(A–10)}$$

The proportional (log) change of a product is the sum of the proportional changes of its components. Then

$$dS_i = \sum_{j=1}^{n} \gamma_{ij}(d \ln W_j + d \ln A_j) \qquad i = 1,\ldots, n \qquad \text{(A–11)}$$

Separating terms and using matrices,

$$\begin{bmatrix} dS_1 \\ \vdots \\ dS_n \end{bmatrix} = \begin{bmatrix} \gamma_{11} \cdots \gamma_{1n} \\ \vdots \quad \vdots \\ \gamma_{n1} \quad \gamma_{nn} \end{bmatrix} \begin{bmatrix} d \ln W_1 \\ \vdots \\ d \ln W_n \end{bmatrix} + \begin{bmatrix} \gamma_{11} \cdots \gamma_{1n} \\ \vdots \quad \vdots \\ \gamma_{n1} \quad \gamma_{nn} \end{bmatrix} \begin{bmatrix} d \ln A_1 \\ \vdots \\ d \ln A_n \end{bmatrix}$$

or

$$dS = \gamma(d \ln W) + \gamma(d \ln A) \qquad \text{(A–12)}$$

$\gamma$ is not of full rank due to the homogeneity constraint. But calling an arbitrary factor the $n$'th factor,

$$\gamma_{in} = -\sum_{i=1}^{n-1} \gamma_{ij} \qquad \text{(A–13)}$$

Using (A–9) to remove $\gamma_{in}$ from (A–8), we have

$$dS_i = \sum_{j=1}^{n-1} \gamma_{ij} dw_j + \sum_{j=1}^{n-1} \gamma_{ij} da_j \qquad \text{(A–14)}$$

where

$$dw_j = d \ln W_j - d \ln W_n = d \ln \left(\frac{W_j}{W_n}\right)$$

and

$$da_j = d \ln A_j - d \ln A_n = d \ln \left(\frac{A_j}{A_n}\right)$$

Let $\Gamma$ be the truncated $(n-1) \times (n-1)$ matrix of the $\gamma_{ij}$ which is of full rank. Then

$$dS_{(n-1)\times 1} = \Gamma\, dw + \Gamma\, da \qquad \text{(A–15)}$$

which gives us the solution for the changes in the $A$ ratios

$$da = \Gamma^{-1}\, dS - dw \qquad \text{(A–16)}$$

With the discrete time equivalent of (A–16), time series of the augmentation series can be estimated, provided reliable estimates of the $\Gamma^{-1}$ matrix are available. Going one step further, the share changes, which would have occurred in the absence of factor price changes, can be estimated directly. They are the share changes needed to estimate the biases according to equation (1). Call these changes $dS'$, which can be obtained from system (A–15) by setting $dw = 0$. Then

$$dS' = +\Gamma\, da \qquad \text{(A–17)}$$

And substituting $da$ from (A–16),

$$dS' = dS - \Gamma\, dw \qquad \text{(A–18)}$$

Equation (A–18) is the same thing as the text equation (9) converted to full rank and into matrix notation.

Thus we note that, even if technical change is factor augmenting, it is not necessary to estimate the factor-augmenting coefficients which, as shown in appendix 5–1, cannot be interpreted as changes in factor qualities anyway. Equation (A–18) directly measures biases, and the factor augmentation coefficients (A–16) are simply different transforms of the same variables and parameters used to measure biases. Thus they contain no independent information.

## MODEL II. A REGRESSION TECHNIQUE

Model I of equation (9) assumes that the rate of biases is not constant over time. For shorter time periods, however, it is possible to assume that the biases are constant. If this is done, biased technical change at constant exogenous rates can be introduced in the translog cost function in a way similar to that in which Christensen et al.[12] introduced it into the corresponding production function:

$$\ln C = \ln[h(Y)] + \ln \nu_0 + \sum_i \nu_i \ln W_i + \tfrac{1}{2} \sum_i \sum_j \gamma_{ij} \ln W_i \ln W_j$$
$$+ \nu_t \ln t + \omega_t (\ln t)^2 + \sum_i \omega_i \ln W_i \ln t \qquad \text{(A–19)}$$

where $t$ stands for time.

[12] Christensen et al., "Logarithmic Production Frontiers," pp. 28–45.

Upon differentiation, the share equations become

$$\frac{\partial \ln C}{\partial \ln W_i} = S_i = \nu_i + \sum_j \gamma_{ij} \ln W_j + \omega_i \ln t \qquad i = 1, \ldots, n \qquad \text{(A-20)}$$

which is estimation equation (A–23) with time entering as a variable. In this equation, $\omega_i$ is the constant exogenous rate of the bias of factor $i$.

If (A–20) is used as a regression equation with a time series or a combination of cross section and time series, the introduction of time in this way will ensure that biased technical change at constant rates will not bias the econometric estimates of the $\gamma_{ij}$'s. Furthermore, the coefficients $\hat{\omega}_i$ can be used to derive another set of price-corrected share series, say $dS_i''$, which can be used with text equation (3) to estimate the biases for the particular period:

$$dS_i'' = \hat{\omega}_i d \ln t \qquad i = 1, \ldots, n \qquad \text{(A-21)}$$

Of course, this model cannot be used to extrapolate outside of the short regression period because then the assumption of a constant exogenous rate of bias is tenuous.

### APPENDIX 7–2
#### *Cross-Sectional Measurement of Cost Function Parameters*

Before (A–18) or (9) can be used with time-series data, estimation of the coefficients of the gamma matrix is necessary. This must be done with cross-sectional data wherein, ideally, all units are on exactly the same production function. We can then assume that each $A_i$ is equal to one for all cross-sectional units, rewrite equation (A–9) with $R_i = W_i$,

$$S_i = \nu_i + \sum_j \gamma_{ij} \ln W_j + \epsilon_i \qquad i = 1, \ldots, n \qquad \text{(A-22)}$$

and use this system of equations to estimate the $\gamma_{ij}$ coefficients. Of course, we will never find a cross section where all units are on exactly the same production function. Ways of dealing with this problem are discussed below.

#### DATA

The cross-sectional estimation of the cost function used data from most states in the United States. A more detailed account of this estimation is given elsewhere.[13]

Four sets of cross-sectional data were obtained for 39 states or groups of states. The cross sections were derived from census and other agricultural statistics for the years 1949, 1954, 1958, and 1964.

---

[13] Binswanger, "Cost Function Approach."

In general, Zvi Griliches's definitions of factors were used.[14] He distinguishes the following five factors: land, labor, machinery, fertilizer, and all others. Intermediate inputs are included in this list, and the function fitted corresponds to a gross-output function rather than to a value-added function.

QUANTITY DATA. Except for "other" inputs, the quantity data were taken from Gideon Fishelson, who used Griliches's data with some changes.[15] For a detailed discussion of labor, land, and machinery, see Griliches or Binswanger.[16]

Fishelson's discussion of the construction of the land variable is as follows:

In this U.S. Census of Agriculture (U.S. Bureau of the Census, 1952, 1956, 1962, and 1966), the average value of land and buildings per farm in each state was reported. However, the land value represented not only the value of land to agricultural production but also included the site value of land. The value of buildings included both farm structures and dwellings. Hence, census data on value of land and buildings were inadequate for the purposes of this study. To measure land by the number of acres per farm (giving each acre a value of one) is also inadequate because of the diversity of soil quality, fertility and uses.

In this study the weighting procedure for measuring land value was based on a study by Hoover. The value of each acre in each state at each cross-section was measured by its 1940 price relative to that of an acre of pasture in the corresponding state. The value of an acre of pasture in each state in 1940 was calculated by dividing the total value of land in 1940 by the number of pasture equivalent units of the land in 1940. This value of an acre of pasture was kept constant over time. . . . The use of this method provided a measure of the stock of land in constant prices. According to this method, changes in the stock of land occurred only because of changes in the number of acres or their use. The stock of land was unaffected by changes in prices of agricultural products, site effects, or government programs.[17]

The only change made in the quantity data that were taken from Fishelson was that, whenever quantities per farm were used, the farm number was taken from various issues of the *Census of Agriculture* (U.S. Department of Commerce, 1950, 1954, 1959, 1964), rather than from *Farm Labor* (USDA, 1945–1972).[18]

[14] Zvi Griliches, "The Demand for Fertilizer: An Economic Interpretation of a Technical Change," *Journal of Farm Economics* 40 (August 1958): 591–606.

[15] Gideon Fishelson, "Returns to Human and Research Capital, United States Agriculture, 1949–1964" (Ph.D. diss., North Carolina State University, 1968).

[16] Zvi Griliches, "Research Expenditure, Education, and the Aggregate Agricultural Production Function," *American Economic Review* 54 (December 1964): 961–74; Hans P. Binswanger, "The Measurement of Biased Efficiency Gains in U.S. and Japanese Agriculture to Test the Induced Innovation Hypothesis" (Ph.D. diss., North Carolina State University, 1973).

[17] Fishelson, "Human and Research Capital."

[18] See table 7–3.

Because expenditure data corresponding to Fishelson's quantity data could not be constructed for "other" inputs, new quantity data were defined as follows: The quantity of other inputs is the sum of the explicit and implicit annual expenditures on all other material inputs used in production. The explicit expenditures were the cash expenditures on purchases of livestock, poultry, feed, seeds, plants, and bulbs, on operation and repairs of farm structures, and for other miscellaneous items. The implicit expenditures were interest on livestock and crop inventories (8%), depreciation (4.2%), interest on the value of farm structures (5%), and the share of real estate taxes assigned to buildings. Each of the expenditures was separately deflated to its 1949 price level in order to arrive at a quantity measurement (for taxes, the agricultural output price index was used).

EXPENDITURES AND FACTOR SHARES. The expenditure variables were defined, as far as possible, to correspond to the quantity variables. Expenditure shares were obtained by dividing the expenditures of each factor by the sum of the expenditures.

Expenditures on land are computed simply as 6 percent of the value of land plus the share of real estate taxes assigned to land.

Expenditures for labor are computed as the number of man-days of labor, from Fishelson, multiplied by a daily wage rate without room and board (see table 7-3). This assumes that the opportunity cost of farm operators is the wage rate they could earn as workers on other farms.

Expenditures for machinery are assumed to be 15 percent of the value

TABLE 7-3. Sources for expenditure data

| Variables | Source |
| --- | --- |
| Farm income, change in inventories, rental value of dwellings, all explicit current operating expenditures. | *Farm Income Situation* for the years 1954–1972, July supplements (Washington, D.C.: U.S. Department of Agriculture). |
| Annual average daily wage rate without board or room. | *Farm Labor*, various issues from 1945–1972 (Washington, D.C.: U.S. Department of Agriculture). |
| Farm number. | *Census of Agriculture*, various issues for the years 1950, 1954, 1959, 1964 (Washington, D.C.: U.S. Department of Commerce). |
| Input and output price indexes. | *Agricultural Statistics*, various issues from 1936–1972 (Washington, D.C.: U.S. Department of Agriculture). |
| Repairs and operation of farm dwellings and service structures; depreciation of dwellings, service buildings, motor vehicles, other machinery and equipment; value of farm machinery and equipment; value of crop inventories. | Unpublished material, U.S. Department of Agriculture. |

assigned to farm machinery and equipment for purposes of interest and depreciation plus current expenditures for operation and repairs.

Fertilizer expenditures are directly reported by the USDA.

Other expenditures were computed exactly as the quantity of other inputs, except that the individual items were not deflated. Aggregate expenditures estimated in this way had a tendency to exceed aggregate income by as much as 10 percent.

Prices were taken to be the expenditures divided by the quantities. Prices were then deflated to the 1949 price level, using the United States agricultural output price index. Note that this procedure implies that the price of other inputs is equal to one for all states in the year 1949. Table 7–3 lists all the data sources.

ESTIMATION PROCEDURE

The estimation equations are[19]

$$S_{ikt} = \nu_i + \sum_j \gamma_{ij} \ln W_{jkt} + \omega_i \ln t + \sum_r \delta_{ir} d_r + \epsilon_{ikt} \tag{A-23}$$

where   $i, j = 1, \ldots, 4$ are the indices for the factors of production,
  $k = 1, \ldots, 39$ are the indices for the states,
  $t = 1, \ldots, 4$ are the indices for the time periods,
  $\delta_{ir}$ are share-specific regional dummies for $r = 1, \ldots, 4$, and
  $d_r = 1$   if $k \in r$,
    $0$   if $k \notin r$.

That equation (A–23) measures the $\gamma_{ij}$ parameters of the functional form (A–2) can be seen as follows: If there is only one cross section, and if all cross-sectional units have the same $A_i$ parameters (no efficiency differences), factors can be rescaled to make all $A_i$ equal to one. Hence $W_{jk} = R_{jk}$. If there are neutral efficiency differences among the cross-sectional units, all the $A_i$ will differ by the same proportion among the two units. This proportion can be absorbed in a separate intercept term for each unit. These intercepts drop out upon differentiation so that we can again set all $A_i = 1$. If more than one cross section is used, (A–23) still gives the correct estimates for (A–2), provided that for all cross-sectional units each $A_i$ changes at the constant rate $\omega_i$ during the period under investigation. If any omitted factor, such as education or research and extension, affects efficiency neutrally, leaving such factor out of the estimation equation will not bias the results.

The estimation equations are unaltered if neutral efficiency differences exist among states or time periods. Neutral differences would alter only the intercept $\nu_0$ of the cost function, which drops out upon differentiation.

Nonneutral efficiency differences among the observational units will have

---

[19] Because of the homogeneity constraint (6), only $n - 1$ equations are linearly independent and can be estimated simultaneously.

the effect that the true $S_i$ will differ for each observational unit; at equal factor prices, shares will not be equal.[20] If such differences occur among all units, the estimates of the coefficients of (A–20) will be biased. However, if such differences occur only among groups of states, the proper set of regional dummies will again lead to unbiased estimators. Regional dummies distinguishing five regions were, therefore, included in the regression equations. Nonneutral differences might arise due to educational differences, differences in research and extension, or differences in product mix.

If (A–20) is estimated with time-series data, a time trend in the estimation equation will solve the problem of estimation of biases over time, as explained in Model II, provided the rates of biases stayed reasonably constant over the estimation period.

A detailed account of the error specification problem is given in an earlier article of mine.[21] Problems arise from the fact that (1) time-series and cross-sectional data are combined, and (2) that, within each cross section, the error terms of the shares equations are not independent.[22]

Both problems could not be handled simultaneously. For estimation purposes, all cross sections were combined and restricted generalized least squares (RGLS) was applied to the four-shares equation, as if there were no problem of error interdependence over time. While this leads to consistent estimates of the $\gamma_{ij}$ coefficients, there is an efficiency loss, and $t$-ratios of the estimates will be overstated to some extent.[23]

Prior to the estimation, several constraints were tested by applying the model to the four cross sections individually, using restricted generalized least squares. These tests, therefore, did have the desired asymptotic properties. The homogeneity constraint was not rejected in any of the four

---

[20] Nonneutral efficiency differences between two states imply that, at equal factor prices, the states will use factors in differing proportions. Factor shares, therefore, will differ even at equal factor prices.

[21] Binswanger, "Cost Function Approach."

[22] Problem (1): For each share equation, data from four cross sections are combined. This poses the familiar problem of combining cross-sectional and time-series data. Despite the five-year interval between the cross sections, this problem is still important: The correlation coefficients of the ordinary least squares (OLS) residuals of the share equations between the cross sections of 1949 and 1965 ranged between 0.62 and 0.87. If first-order autocorrelation were the true error specification over time, this would imply first-order autocorrelation coefficients larger than 0.9.

Problem (2): Within each of the four cross sections, the error terms of the $n - 1$ estimation equations are not independent. This is because for each state the same variables that might affect the shares as well as the prices were left out of the model. If restrictions across equations ($\gamma_{ij} = \gamma_{ji}$) are imposed, OLS estimators are no longer efficient, despite the fact that all equations contain the same explanatory variables on the right-hand side. Therefore, the seemingly unrelated regression problem applies. See Henri Theil, *Principles of Econometrics* (New York: John Wiley & Sons, Inc., 1971).

[23] The computer program used was the Triangle Universities Computing Center's *Two and Three Stage Least Squares* (*TTLS*).

cross sections (.05 significance level). The symmetry constraint was rejected only in the 1964 data set. However, the Cobb–Douglas constraint ($\gamma_{ij} = 0$ for all $i, j$) was rejected in all cross sections.[24] Hence, homogeneity and symmetry were imposed in the estimation where all data were pooled.

Pooling the cross sections implies constancy of the $\gamma_{ij}$ coefficients over time. This was tested as follows: a two-equation generalized least squares (GLS) model is fitted for each share, with the 1949 data used for the first equation and the 1959 data for the second. The homogeneity constraint was imposed on the data. The hypothesis is never rejected at the .01 level of significance, although it is rejected in two equations at the .05 level.

Table 7–4 reports the estimates of the pooled regressions. The $t$-ratios of the price coefficients appear to be low, despite the fact that they may be overstated to some extent. However, $\gamma_{ij} = 0$ implies that the corresponding partial elasticity of substitution is equal to one [see equations (A–24) and (A–25)]. Therefore, we would expect, a priori, that some of the $\gamma_{ij}$ coefficients would be zero.

In the labor and the machinery equations the coefficients of time are significant. They imply that technical change has been labor saving and machinery using. Significant coefficients of regional dummies imply non-neutral regional efficiency differences.

The estimates of the $\gamma_{ij}$ coefficients can be converted into point estimates of Allen partial elasticities of substitution ($\sigma_{ij}$) and of elasticities and cross elasticities of factor demand ($\eta_{ij}$) according to the following equations:[25]

$$\sigma_{ij} = \frac{\gamma_{ij}}{S_i S_j} + 1 \qquad \text{for all } i \neq j \qquad \text{(A–24)}$$

$$\sigma_{ii} = \frac{1}{S_i^2}(\gamma_{ii} + S_i^2 - S_i) \qquad \text{for all } i \qquad \text{(A–25)}$$

$$\eta_{ij} = \frac{\gamma_{ij}}{S_i} + S_j \qquad \text{for all } i \neq j \qquad \text{(A–26)}$$

$$\eta_{ii} = \frac{\gamma_{ii}}{S_i} + S_i - 1 \qquad \text{for all } i \qquad \text{(A–27)}$$

The $\gamma_{ij}$ coefficients have little intuitive meaning, and therefore it is easier to evaluate them by what they imply for these elasticities. Table 7–5 shows the results using the unweighted average factor shares of the 39 states in the period 1949–1964.

The matrix of elasticities of substitution is negative semi-definite, which

[24] All three tests were performed against a completely unconstrained model.
[25] Proofs of these equations are given in Binswanger, "Cost Function Approach."

TABLE 7–4. Restricted estimates of the coefficients of the *translog* cost function and *t*-ratios

| Factor | Independent Variables | | | | | | Regional Classifications[b] | | | | |
|---|---|---|---|---|---|---|---|---|---|---|---|
| | Land | Labor | Machinery | Fertilizer | Other[a] | Year | Intercept | MN | GF | SE | GS |
| Land | .07747 | −.03613 | .00478 | .01066 | −.05678 | .00847 | .2603 | −.1021 | −.0394 | −.1073 | −.0577 |
| | (6.02) | (3.25) | (.47) | (2.14) | | (1.47) | (9.96) | (10.2) | (4.1) | (8.9) | (4.7) |
| Labor | | −.06367 | −.00661 | −.02805 | −.13446 | −.05482 | .5218 | .0194 | −.0016 | .0169 | .0246 |
| | | (3.67) | (.59) | (4.97) | | (9.08) | (14.91) | (1.63) | (.15) | (1.09) | (1.63) |
| Machinery | | | −.03485 | −.00877 | .04545 | .02498 | .0926 | −.0033 | .0369 | −.0186 | .0072 |
| | | | (1.31) | (.97) | | (4.66) | (3.46) | (.41) | (5.08) | (1.86) | (.73) |
| Fertilizer | | | | .00068 | .02548 | .00178 | .0745 | .0104 | −.0041 | .0370 | −.0024 |
| | | | | (.12) | | (.63) | (5.6) | (2.5) | (1.10) | (7.24) | (.49) |
| Other | | | | | −.14861 | | | | | | |

Note:

Restrictions imposed were $\gamma_{ij} = \gamma_{ji}$ and $\sum_{j=1}^{n} \gamma_{ij} = 0$ for all $i, j$.

Critical values with 578 degrees of freedom are $t.05 = 1.96$ and $t.01 = 1.65$. The *t*-ratios may be overstated because of error interdependence over time.

GLS methods were used here. Because of the ambiguous interpretation of these statistics in GLS models, no $R^2$ are reported. For shares' equations in individual years estimated by OLS methods, the $R^2$ ranged from 0.5 to 0.9.

[a] These implied estimates were computed using the homogeneity constraint.

[b] "Intercept" stands for western states. MN, GF, SE, and GS are dummies for mixed northern agriculture, grain farming states, the Southeast, and Gulf states, respectively, and their coefficients are deviations from the intercept.

TABLE 7–5. Estimates of the partial elasticities of substitution and of factor demand with respect to own price

| | Land | Labor | Machinery | Fertilizer | Other[a] |
|---|---|---|---|---|---|
| *Elasticities of Substitution* | | | | | |
| Land | −2.225 | .204 | 1.215 | 2.987 | −.031 |
| | (.57) | (.24) | (.46) | (.93) | |
| Labor | | −3.028 | .851 | −1.622 | 2.224 |
| | | (.19) | (.25) | (.53) | |
| Machinery | | | −7.379 | −.672 | 1.844 |
| | | | (1.23) | (1.72) | |
| Fertilizer | | | | −26.573 | 2.961 |
| | | | | (4.61) | |
| Other | | | | | −2.852 |
| *Elasticities of Factor Demand* ($\eta_{ii}$) | | | | | |
| Land | −.3356 | .0613 | .1792 | .1062 | −.0112 |
| | (.09) | (.07) | (.07) | (.03) | |
| Labor | .0308 | −.9109 | .1256 | −.0577 | .8122 |
| | (.04) | (.06) | (.04) | (.02) | |
| Machinery | .1833 | .2560 | −1.0886 | −.0239 | .6733 |
| | (.07) | (.08) | (.18) | (.06) | |
| Fertilizer | .4506 | −.4878 | −.0991 | −.9452 | 1.0815 |
| | (.10) | (.20) | (.30) | (.16) | |
| Other | −.0046 | .6690 | .2720 | .1053 | −1.0417 |

Note: Standard errors, in parentheses, were computed as follows:

$$SE(\sigma_{ij}) = \frac{SE(\gamma_{ij})}{S_i S_j} \; ; \qquad SE(\eta_{ij}) = \frac{SE(\gamma_{ij})}{S_i}$$

[a] These implied estimates were computed using the homogeneity constraint.

implies that the matrix of cross derivatives of the cost function is negative semi-definite, that is, that the cost function is concave.[26]

All own demand elasticities have the correct sign. The demand for land appears very inelastic. The demand elasticities for machinery and other inputs are larger than one, a fact to keep in mind since it implies that a rise in the corresponding prices will, other things being equal, lead to a decline in the factor share.

APPENDIX 7–3

*United States Time-Series Data*

The same basic approach was applied to these data as to the cross-sectional data discussed in appendix 7–2. The differences are described below.

[26] The elasticities of substitution also show that the production process is not separable between primary and intermediate inputs. Separability would imply, *inter alia*, that the partial elasticities of substitution of fertilizer with the primary factors land, labor, and

LAND

The total quantity of land for the United States for the census years 1910–1954 was taken from Hoover.[27] His approach was followed in computing the data for 1959 and 1964. For the missing years, interpolation was used. The approach is as described in appendix 7–2, except that the units were changed to 1910–1914 prices.

Expenditures on land are composed of the interest charged on the value of land plus the portion of real estate taxes assigned to land. The interest rate used is the average rate on new loans made by the Federal Land Bank. For the years 1910–1916, this was approximated by subtracting 0.8 percent from the Federal Land Bank's interest rate on mortgage loans.

LABOR

The quantity of labor is computed as the United States Department of Agriculture (USDA) series of man-hours of labor used for farm work multiplied by 1.06. The adjustment was made because the series does not account for standby time but is computed simply as hours needed to do the job (USDA, personal communication). The labor price is the 1970 composite rate per hour from farm labor divided by the composite index of farm wage rates for each year. This treatment is better than the one used with the cross-sectional data. There are no hour-of-work statistics for states, however.

MACHINERY

The stock of machinery was estimated by deflating the value of motor vehicles and the value of other farm machinery and equipment by their respective price indices. Included in farm machinery stock was the constant value of horses and mules, derived by multiplying their total number by their average 1910–1914 price. This price was found by dividing the value of horses and mules by their number. Neglecting animal power in a time series starting in 1910 would have been inappropriate because animals were an important power source in the early years. The drawback is that horses were dropped from the compilations of agricultural statistics in 1962, which introduces a small break in the series.

Machinery expenditures are composed of the total operating expenditures on machinery and equipment, depreciation thereon as computed by the USDA, 12 percent of the current value of horses and mules for depreciation and operating costs, plus the current value of horses and mules times the interest rate on new loans increased by two percent.

---

machinery are equal [Ernst R. Berndt and Laurits R. Christensen, "The Internal Structure of Functional Relationships: Separability, Substitution, and Aggregation," *Review of Economic Studies* 3, no. 123 (July 1973): 403–10]. This is obviously not the case.

[27] D. Hoover, "Land Prices in United States Agriculture, 1910–1950" (Ph.D. diss., University of Chicago, 1961).

FERTILIZER

Expenditure data are published, as well as a price index for fertilizer. Therefore, a quantity index of fertilizer is derived as expenditures divided by the price index.

OTHER INPUTS

Expenditures are computed as the sum of current expenditures (feed, livestock purchases, seed, lime, miscellaneous, repairs and operation of buildings), and implicit expenditures (building depreciation, accidental damage to buildings, the share of real estate taxes assigned to buildings, the value of buildings times the interest rate, and the value of livestock and crop inventory times the interest rate increased by two percent). From this total were subtracted the estimated operating expenditures and depreciation of horses and mules.

The quantity was derived as the sum of the individually deflated current expenditures plus the implicit expenditures deflated by the output price index. The final data used were three-year moving averages of the above series.

TABLE 7–6. Sources for United States time-series data

| Variables | Source |
| --- | --- |
| Farm income, rental value of dwellings, all current expenditures, depreciation of all capital items, accidental damage, taxes. | *Farm Income Situation*, July 1971 (Washington, D.C.: U.S. Department of Agriculture). |
| All price indices; value of land, buildings, livestock and crop inventories; interest rates, number and value of horses and mules. | *Agricultural Statistics*, various issues from 1936–1972 (Washington, D.C.: U.S. Department of Agriculture). |
| Hours of work. | 1964 and 1971 issues of *Statistical Bulletin 233, Changes in Farm Production and Efficiency* (Washington, D.C.; U.S. Department of Agriculture). |
| Value of buildings. | *Farm Real Estate Market* (May 1959) (Washington, D.C.: U.S. Department of Agriculture). Later years: various issues of *Farm Real Estate Market Developments* (Washington, D.C.: U.S. Department of Agriculture, 1961–1972). |
| Quantity of land, land class data. | Up to 1954: Hoover, *Land Prices in United States Agriculture* (Washington, D.C.: U.S. Department of Agriculture, 1961); 1959 and 1964 data constructed from land data series in *Census of Agriculture 1964* (Washington, D.C.: Bureau of the Census). |

For reporting purposes only, the price and quantity variables were transformed into indices. The quantity indices are indices of inputs per unit of output; the price indices are derived by deflating all prices by the output price index. The absolute magnitudes of these index numbers may be questionable, but they are unimportant. It is the trends of these index numbers in relation to one another that is important. The data sources for the U.S. time-series data are summarized in table 7–6.

# EIGHT

# A CES Test of Induced Technical Change: Japan

PATRICK YEUNG AND TERRY L. ROE

$\mathbf{I}$N chapter 7 Binswanger has presented a test of the induced innovation hypothesis based on the direct measurement of the effect of factor-augmenting bias on factor shares. Here we introduce a different approach, which involves an attempt to extend the *constant elasticity of substitution* (CES) production function. A review of the literature on alternative models of induced innovation and empirical tests of the hypothesis can be found in chapters 2, 4, and 5.

In the first two sections of this chapter we formulate and discuss a factor-augmenting CES production function with separate augmentation coefficients for labor and land. In the third section we present a test for *hysteresis*, the tendency for a firm, an industry, or an economy to remain locked into a particular path of technical change. In the fourth section of the chapter we develop an empirical test of the induced innovation hypothesis itself. This test is couched within the framework of the adapted CES model and uses data on the development of Japanese agriculture from 1880 to 1940, or from the early years of the Meiji period to the outbreak of the Pacific war. Finally, in appendix 8–1, we discuss the procedures for making parameter estimates of the CES production function.

## A CES-Type Metaproduction Function

A dynamic two-factor production function of the general form

$$Y = F(K, L; t)$$

The authors are indebted to Hans P. Binswanger, William Griffiths, Vernon W. Ruttan, and William W. Wade for suggestions and comments on drafts of this chapter. The research on which the chapter is based was supported partially by the University of Minnesota Economic Development Center. The authors assume responsibility for any shortcomings in the material presented here.

can be made explicit in the CES form

$$Y_t = [\alpha(K_t e^{\delta t})^{-\rho} + \beta(L_t e^{\lambda t})^{-\rho}]^{-1/\rho} \tag{1}$$

where $Y$, $K$, $L$, and $t$ represent output, capital, labor, and time respectively; $\alpha$ and $\beta$ are traditionally referred to as the distribution parameters, $\delta$ and $\lambda$ as the rates of factor augmentation over time, and $\rho$ as the substitution parameter.[1] A particular feature of this approach is that the factors are expressed in efficiency units.

There are certain weaknesses inherent in this approach. First, the rates of factor augmentation are assumed to be fixed over time. There is, however, no a priori reason why this should be true. Second, the model does not identify the origins of efficiency growth. Because the source of innovation is not specified, we cannot know whether a given technical change is induced or autonomous.

To compensate for these weaknesses, equation (1) can be improved upon by postulating that the innovation is induced by relative input price changes that reflect changes in relative input scarcities. In dealing with agricultural output ($Q$), and stipulating that the primary factors be land ($A$) and labor ($L$), a metaproduction function may be written as

$$Q_t = [\alpha(A_t e^{\delta I_t})^{-\rho} + \beta(L_t e^{\lambda I_t})^{-\rho}]^{-1/\rho} \tag{2}$$

where $I_t$ represents an index of relative factor prices for labor and land. Like equation (1), equation (2) is homogeneous in the inputs. It differs from (1) essentially in the replacement of time $t$ with the labor–land index $I_t$. In equation (2), factor augmentation is assumed to be induced by changes in $I_t$. Even though constant factor-augmentation parameters, $\delta$ and $\lambda$, are still postulated, the rates of factor augmentation need not be constant over time. (In fact, they would not be constant unless $I_t$ were perfectly correlated with time.)

In both equations (1) and (2) it can be observed that if the factor-augmentation coefficients are equal and different from zero, technical change is neutral. When $\delta$ is different from $\lambda$, the innovation is nonneutral in character. It is shown below that in equation (2), if the substitution parameter $\rho$ and $dI_t/dt$ are both positive and $\delta$ exceeds $\lambda$, the case is land saving (labor using), and if $\lambda$ exceeds $\delta$, the case is labor saving (land using). If $dI_t/dt$ is negative, then $\delta$, $\lambda$ must be negative in order to be consistent with technical change. In this case, if $\delta > \lambda$, technical change is labor saving and if $\lambda > \delta$, technical change is land saving.

The mean estimates of $\delta$ and $\lambda$ from a time series of observations on $I_t$ reflect measured factor augmentation over a period of time. Thus, in the

---

[1] For an application of this model, see Y. Kotowitz, "On the Estimation of a Non-Neutral CES-Production Function," *Canadian Journal of Economics* 1 (May 1968): 429–39.

making of predictions based on these estimates, occasional reversed directional changes in $I_t$ imply that previous efficiency gains are undone.

To make equation (1) operational, let us define the relative factor price index as

$$I_t = (w/r)_t/(w/r)_{t_0} \tag{3}$$

where $(w/r)_t$ represents the relative prices of labor and land in the $t$th year and $t_0$ is the base year.

Assuming that factors are paid according to their marginal productivities,

$$r_t = \left(\frac{\partial Q}{\partial A}\right)_t = \alpha\left(\frac{Q}{A}\right)^{1+\rho} e^{-\delta\rho I_t} \tag{4}$$

and

$$w_t = \left(\frac{\partial Q}{\partial L}\right)_t = \beta\left(\frac{Q}{L}\right)^{1+\rho}_t e^{-\lambda\rho I_t} \tag{5}$$

Dividing (5) by (4) yields

$$\left(\frac{w}{r}\right)_t = \frac{\beta}{\alpha}\left(\frac{A}{L}\right)^{1+\rho}_t e^{(\delta-\lambda)\rho I_t} \tag{6}$$

Taking logarithms and rearranging terms,

$$\ln\left(\frac{A}{L}\right)_t = -\frac{1}{1+\rho}\ln\frac{\beta}{\alpha} + \frac{1}{1+\rho}\ln\left(\frac{w}{r}\right)_t + \frac{(\lambda-\delta)\rho}{1+\rho}I_t \tag{6a}$$

from which we can obtain the elasticity of factor substitution $\sigma_t$:

$$\sigma_t = \frac{d\ln(A/L)_t}{d\ln(w/r)_t} = \frac{1}{1+\rho} + \frac{(\lambda-\delta)\rho}{1+\rho}I_t = \frac{1}{1+\rho}[1 + (\lambda-\delta)\rho I_t] \tag{7}$$

This elasticity may not be constant over time. Assuming that $(\lambda - \delta) \neq 0$ and $\rho \neq 0$, $\sigma$ would change as $I_t$ changes. In this case, $\sigma_t$ may be referred to as the *meta-elasticity of factor substitution* in order to associate it with the metaproduction function. Note also that from the derivation $d\ln(A/L)/d\ln(w/r)$ of equation (6a), if $I_t$ is taken as exogenously given, then $\sigma_t$ equals the traditional form of $1/(1 + \rho)$ in equation (7).

*Some Variations of the CES Approach*

In model (1), factor augmentation is assumed to be induced by changes in $I_t$, so that the rates of factor augmentation depend on the rate of change of $I_t$. Model (1) therefore considers factor-price change to be the only induce-ment mechanism. It follows also that if $I_t$ does not change over time, the rate of factor augmentation will become zero.

Additional variables can be specified to remove this shortcoming, as follows:[2]

$$Q_t = e^{\gamma t}[\alpha(A_t e^{\delta I_t})^{-\rho} + \beta(L_t e^{\lambda I_t})^{-\rho}]^{-1/\rho} \tag{8}$$

In this case, and in the absence of changes in $I_t$, time causes a neutral shift in the production function. The function can also be specified to allow for nonneutral shifts in technical change that are associated with the time variable, as follows:

$$Q_t = [\alpha(A_t e^{\delta I_t + \theta t})^{-\rho} + \beta(L_t e^{\lambda I_t + \phi t})^{-\rho}]^{-1/\rho} \tag{9}$$

When $\theta \neq \phi$, time causes a nonneutral shift of the production function at constant rates. Factor efficiency influences that are correlated with time might include advancements in the state of the basic and supporting sciences that affect the rate and bias of technical change. This does not imply a constant rate of efficiency gain, because additional efficiency changes may be obtained through variations in $I_t$.

Production functions (2), (8), and (9) are homogeneous of degree one in $A$ and $L$, implying constant returns to scale. If inputs other than $A$ and $L$ are considered in order to deal with the problem of variable returns to scale, (8), for instance, may be modified to include a scale parameter $\nu$:

$$Q_t = e^{\gamma t}[\alpha(A e^{\delta I})^{-\rho} + \beta(L e^{\lambda I})^{-\rho}]^{-\nu/\rho} \qquad 0 \leqq \nu \leqq 1 \tag{8a}$$

This is slightly more general than (8). Assuming that factors are paid accord-ing to their marginal productivities, the first derivatives, $\partial Q_t/\partial L_t$ and $\partial Q_t/\partial A_t$, of (8a) can be equated with $w_t$ and $r_t$, respectively. Then, dividing $w_t$ by $r_t$ yields

$$\left(\frac{w}{r}\right)_t = \frac{\beta}{\alpha}\left(\frac{A}{L}\right)_t^{1+\rho} e^{(\delta - \lambda)\rho I_t}$$

which is the same result as in (6). It follows that the elasticity of substitution of (8a) also has the same form as (7).

Similarly, the marginal productivity conditions of equation (9) are

$$w_t = \frac{\partial Q_t}{\partial L_t} = \beta\left(\frac{Q}{L}\right)_t^{1+\rho} e^{-\rho(\lambda I_t + \phi t)}$$

---

[2] Further modifications, such as the specification of additional factor-augmenting terms, the specification of $I_t$ as a distributive lag, or varying the degree of homogeneity can also be undertaken.

and

$$r_t = \frac{\partial Q_t}{\partial A_t} = \alpha \left(\frac{Q}{A}\right)_t^{1+\rho} e^{-\rho(\delta I_t + \theta t)}$$

yielding

$$\left(\frac{w}{r}\right)_t = \frac{\beta}{\alpha} \left(\frac{A}{L}\right)_t^{1+\rho} \left(\frac{H_A}{H_L}\right)^{\rho} \tag{10}$$

where

$$H_A \equiv e^{\delta I_t + \theta t}$$

and

$$H_L \equiv e^{\lambda I_t + \phi t}$$

It can be seen from (10) that given the factor augmentation values, the sign of the substitution parameter $\rho$ influences the direction of change in the land–labor ratio and the direction of factor augmentation bias (see also the appendix to chapter 2). Furthermore, since $dI_t/dt$ can be positive or negative, the values of $\delta$ and $\lambda$ must have the appropriate sign; otherwise, technical change is negative or undone. Following E. Drandakis and E. Phelps,[3] the direction of Hicks' bias can be defined in terms of a change in the marginal rates of substitution at constant factor prices, which yields the following three cases for (9):

(i) $\rho = 0$, technical change is always neutral;

(ii) $\rho > 0$, technical change is labor saving if $h_L > h_A$ and land saving if $h_L < h_A$;

(iii) $\rho < 0$, technical change is always labor saving if $h_L < h_A$ and land saving if $h_L > h_A$

where

$$\begin{aligned} h_A &\equiv d \ln H_A/dt = \delta \, dI_t/dt + \theta \\ h_L &\equiv d \ln H_L/dt = \lambda \, dI_t/dt + \phi \end{aligned} \tag{11}$$

When $\theta = \phi$, it can be seen from these conditions that if $dI_t/dt$ is positive, technical change is positive if $\delta$, $\lambda$ are also positive. In this case, if $h_L > h_A$, $\delta < \lambda$, and the reverse is true if $h_L < h_A$. If $dI_t/dt$ is negative, the factor augmentation parameters $\delta$, $\lambda$ must be negative in order to be consistent with technical change. In this case if $h_L > h_A$, $\delta > \lambda$, that is, $|\delta| < |\lambda|$. The reverse exists if $h_L < h_A$.

[3] E. Drandakis and E. Phelps, "A Model of Induced Invention, Growth and Distribution," *Economic Journal* 76 (December 1966): 823–40.

It can also be verified that the elasticity of substitution derived from (10) takes the same form as that in models (2) and (8).

The above variations of model (2) are intended to show the flexibility of the CES approach. In the next section we will consider the issue of hysteresis and its implications for our approach. This will lead us into the fourth section of the chapter, where we discuss the results of applying alternative models to the Japanese experience.

### A Test for Hysteresis

Hysteresis suggests that biases of technical change tend to develop inertia, that is, they tend to continue in the same direction beyond the time when economic factors have indicated that other paths would be more efficient. The phenomenon of hysteresis has certain implications for changes in the elasticity of factor substitution over time. Since the elasticity of substitution of the model presented here is dynamic, it will be helpful to give brief consideration to the concept of hysteresis and to ascertain whether it may be broadened by knowledge gained from the application of our model.

The theoretical argument for the exhaustibility of technical change in one direction presented in chapters 4 and 5 above disputes the notion of hysteresis. In his recent work on technical change in nineteenth-century America, Paul A. David develops a theory of induced innovation that incorporates this concept.[4] The aspects of David's theory that are of interest to us here are illustrated in figure 8–1.

The discrete unit isoquants $TT$ and $T'T'$ represent two processes, with capital intensities $\gamma$ and $\alpha$, that have been adopted from an available process frontier ($APF^o$).[5] The linear nature of the $APF^o$ implies that the techniques $TT$ and $T'T'$ could be employed in linear combinations. The fundamental production frontier ($FPF^o$) represents the currently existing state of knowledge.

According to David, a substantial factor-price change could induce changes

---

[4] Paul A. David, *Labor Scarcity and the Problem of Technological Practice and Progress in Nineteenth Century America*, Memorandum no. 162 (Palo Alto: Stanford University, Center for Research in Economic Growth, 1974). See also Paul A. David, *Technical Choice, Innovation and Economic Growth* (London: Cambridge University Press, 1975), pp. 57–91.

[5] Here we employ David's terminology. Isoquant $FPF^o$ represents the broader array of potential (latent) processes that could be designed and developed within the current—existing—state of knowledge with a high probability of success. The available process frontier ($APF^o$) represents the range of techniques that have been selected from the set defined by $FPF^o$ and that are available to producers. These techniques are described in machinery catalogues, in engineers' and architects' blueprints, and by the formal systems and rules of thumb that managers, supervisors, and craftsmen have derived for operating existing facilities. (See David, *Technical Choice*.) David's $FPF^o$ appears to be similar to the innovation possibility curve and his $APF^o$ seems similar to the meta-production function as these are defined in footnote 4 in chapter 3.

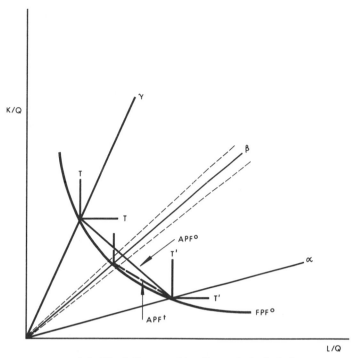

FIG. 8–1. The influence of inertia on technical change.

in capital intensity in two ways. Given an initial factor-price tangency at the
vertex of $T'T'$, for example, a decrease in the relative price of capital could
induce a movement on the $APF^o$ toward the vertex of $TT$. Or, an alternative
response could be the development of a new technique at the upper vertex of
$APF^t$, with a capital intensity of $\beta$.[6]

With this background, David argues that a price disturbance that results
in a movement from $\alpha$ to $\beta$ "is clearly sufficient to launch an incidental,
myopic exploration of the $\beta$-ray."[7] He states that once the point of the $\beta$-
ray's intersection with the upper vertex of $APF^t$ is reached, a mere restoration of the status quo ante in the factor markets would not draw even the
most myopic producer back to the $\alpha$-technique.

According to David, the new variations of production methods generated
by the experience with the $\beta$ technique would show a frequency distribution
whose density is greatest in the region immediately surrounding the $\beta$-ray,
graphically suggesting the area between the dotted lines, which are referred
to as *elastic barriers*. Technical progress now occurs as a movement down the

---

[6] In an international context, according to David, the bias could also be caused by a
foreign-generated shift in $FPF$.

[7] David, *Labor Scarcity*, p. 81.

$\beta$-ray. David refers to this as localized technical progress due purely to learning by doing and describes it as resembling the outcome of a random walk between the elastic barriers.[8] "Eventually, even with progress down the $\beta$-ray occurring at a retarded rate—as we generally expect to happen on a learning curve—the $APF$ could become approximately L-shaped."[9]

An important accompaniment of technical change, according to David's theory, is the narrowing over time of the range of observed factor substitutions. In other words, the elasticity of factor substitution decreases over time as the $APF$ becomes L-shaped. In any event, the range of observed factor substitutions will not broaden. Thus our model will support the existence of hysteresis if $\sigma_t$ decreases but will be inconsistent with hysteresis if $\sigma$ is found to increase over time.

## Empirical Model: The Case of Japanese Agriculture, 1880–1940

Parameter estimates of the CES-type metaproduction function developed earlier in this chapter are derived by estimating the coefficients of their corresponding profit-maximizing equations. The estimating equations and the data used to estimate them are presented in appendix 8–1. Initially, model (9) was fitted to the Japanese data. The results suggested that technical change in Japan was not consistent with the induced innovation

TABLE 8–1. Estimates of equations (A–6) and (A–7) of model (9) with two dependent-variable transformations

| Dependent Variable | Estimates of Coefficients | | | |
|---|---|---|---|---|
| | $b_1$ | $b_2$ | $b_3$ | $b_4$ |
| $Q_1'$ | $-.21042$ (.15089) | 1.76609 (.1451) | .26683 (.01587) | $-.01298$ (.01365) |
| $Q_2'$ | $-.22662$ (.18218) | 1.74260 (.17520) | .26790 (.01916) | $-.00752$ (.01649) |

| Dependent Variable | $b_5$ | $b_6$ | $b_7$ | $R^2$ | $d$ |
|---|---|---|---|---|---|
| $Q_1'$ | $-.00248$ (.00155) | $-.07070$ (.01315) | .00547 (.00120) | .990 | 1.202 |
| $Q_2'$ | $-.00534$ (.00187) | $-.06936$ (.01588) | .00021 (.00145) | .982 | .913 |

Note: All values in parentheses are standard error estimates.

[8] As such, according to David, no theory of "inducements," no mechanism responsive to market signals need be found to explain the not infrequent appearance of extended innovation sequences.

[9] David, *Labor Scarcity*, p. 81.

TABLE 8–2. Parameter estimates of model (9) based on two estimations of the statistical model

| Dependent Variable | Estimates of Parameters | | | |
|---|---|---|---|---|
| | $\alpha$ | $\beta$ | $\rho$ | $\delta$ |
| $Q_1'$ | 2.20030 | .00136 | 2.74771 | −.01771 |
| | (1.14137) | (.00120) | (.22287) | (.01837) |
| $Q_2'$ | 2.33810 | .00151 | 2.73274 | −.01028 |
| | (1.44732) | (.00163) | (.26696) | (.02230) |

| Dependent Variable | $\theta$ | $\lambda$ | $\phi$ |
|---|---|---|---|
| $Q_1'$ | −.00338 | −.09644 | +.00746 |
| | (.00206) | (.01876) | (.00156) |
| $Q_2'$ | −.00730 | −.09474 | +.00029 |
| | (.00241) | (.02266) | (.00193) |

Notes: All values in parentheses are standard error estimates.
Relationships for estimating the variances of above parameters are as follows:
$\text{Var}(\alpha, \beta) = e \exp(-2b_j/b_3)(1/b_3^2) \text{Var } b_3 + (b_j/b_3)^2 \text{Var } b_3 - (2b_j/b_3) \text{Cov } b_j b_3$, for $j = 1, 2$
$\text{Var}(\rho) = (1/b_3^4) \text{Var } b_3$
$\text{Var}(\delta, \theta, \lambda, \phi) = (1/1 - b_3)^2 (b_j/1 - b_3)^2 \text{Var } b_3 + \text{Var } b_j - (2b_j/1 - b_3) \text{Cov } b_j b_3$, for $j = 4, 5, 6, 7$

hypothesis. In an attempt to eliminate some of the statistical shortcomings of this model, several of the other models described above were also fitted to the data. The results of the several analyses are presented below.

MODEL (9). The fit of the statistical model, which is derived by combining equations (A–6) and (A–7) in the manner of (A–3) (these equations can be found in appendix 8–1) appears to be reasonably good overall, although some serial correlation may be present (table 8–1). Small variance estimates and consistent signs were obtained for the coefficients of factor prices, $1/(1 + \rho)$, and for the coefficients of the labor–land index, $I_t$.

The parameter estimates of model (9) and their respective variances are derived from the estimated statistical model (table 8–2). The derivation of the parameter estimates is straightforward. The estimated parameter variance is based on the large-sample property relationships of the asymptotic distribution of a function of sample moments.[10]

The estimates of the distribution parameters $\alpha$ and $\beta$ are similar in terms of both magnitude and relative variance. It follows from the relationship for estimating their variances that these estimates are sensitive to the magnitude and the signs of intercepts $b_1$ and $b_2$.[11] Therefore, if the assumptions that

[10] Henri Theil, *Principles of Econometrics* (New York: John Wiley and Sons, Inc., 1971), pp. 373–4.
[11] The relationships for estimating the variances of these parameters are given in the footnote to table 8–2. It should be noted that each of these equations contains a remainder term that approaches zero as sample size increases.

guarantee consistent estimates of the intercepts $b_1$ and $b_2$ are not valid, the variances of $\alpha$ and $\beta$ may be overestimated.

The estimates of the substitution and factor-augmentation parameters are of primary importance here. The estimates of the substitution parameter $\rho$ are positive and strongly different from zero. Thus, except for the land-augmentation parameter $\phi$ associated with time, all factor-augmentation parameters are of the expected sign, that is, their signs are consistent with technical change. The next step is to test for a significant difference between the augmentation parameters in order to assess the direction of change.

To test the hypothesis of difference between the augmentation parameters in table 8–2 it is necessary to estimate the covariances of these parameters, because only the covariances of the coefficients in table 8–1 are given directly.[12] The hypothesis that $\theta$ is different from $\phi$ is accepted at the 95 percent level of confidence in the case of equation $Q'_1$ but not in the case of equation $Q'_2$. Thus, on the basis of the estimation of model (9) we cannot tell whether factors correlated with time alone have induced a labor-saving or a labor-using bias in the direction of technical change in Japan.

Although the parameters $\delta$ and $\lambda$ are negative, as predicted, they are not of the expected relative magnitude, even though the estimated variance of $\delta$ is relatively large. Thus the test of the hypothesis that $\delta$ is not different from $\lambda$ is rejected in both cases. This implies that $\delta > \lambda$, which is not consistent with the Hicks–Ahmad version of the induced innovation hypothesis.

The rates of labor augmentation $(\hat{h}_L)$ computed from equation (11) exceed the rates of land augmentation $(\hat{h}_A)$ for the entire period 1880–1940. Because of the magnitudes of $\theta$, the augmentation to land is slightly negative when $\hat{h}_L$ is positive. The exception to this rule is exemplified by the years 1920 and 1925, when wages increased substantially in comparison with the value of land. Labor-augmented technical change was greater for the period 1880–1910 than for the period 1915–1940. We conclude that the results of fitting model (9) to the Japanese data suggest that technical change did occur during the period 1880–1940, that this change was biased in the direction of saving labor

---

[12] The estimates of the covariances of $\delta\lambda$ and $\theta\phi$ are based on Theil, *Principles of Econometrics*, and are of the form

$$\text{Cov } \delta\lambda = \frac{b_6 b_4}{(1 - b_3)^4} \text{ Var } b_3 - \frac{b_6}{(1 - b_3)^3} \text{ Cov } b_4 b_3 - \frac{b_4}{(1 - b_3)^3} \text{ Cov } b_3 b_6$$

$$+ \frac{1}{(1 - b_3)^2} \text{ Cov } b_4 b_6 \, ;$$

$$\text{Cov } \theta\phi = \frac{b_7 b_5}{(1 - b_3)^4} \text{ Var } b_3 - \frac{b_7}{(1 - b_3)^3} \text{ Cov } b_5 b_3 - \frac{b_5}{(1 - b_3)^3} \text{ Cov } b_3 b_7$$

$$+ \frac{1}{(1 - b_3)^2} \text{ Cov } b_5 b_7$$

TABLE 8-3. Estimates of elasticity of factor substitution derived from models (9), (8), and (2) for the periods 1880–1890, 1880–1940, 1930–1940

| Dependent Variable | Model (9) | | | Model (8) | | | Model (2) | | |
|---|---|---|---|---|---|---|---|---|---|
| | 1880–1890 | 1880–1940 | 1930–1940 | 1880–1890 | 1880–1940 | 1930–1940 | 1880–1890 | 1880–1940 | 1930–1940 |
| $Q'_1$ | .2232 | .2325 | .2350 | .1818 | .1962 | .1985 | .2461 | .2594 | .2613 |
| $Q'_2$ | .2212 | .2322 | .2338 | .1768 | .1929 | .1939 | .1541 | .1645 | .1661 |

and using land, and that this change occurred despite the fact that the price of labor declined relative to the price of land.[13]

The estimates of the elasticity of factor substitution obtained from model (9) are of particular interest in the light of the theory of technical change suggested by David.[14] Estimates of the elasticity of substitution are obtained by substituting the estimates from table 8–2 into equation (7) for the years 1880–1890, 1880–1940, 1930–1940. These estimates appear in the left-hand panel of table 8–3. The estimates range from a low of .2212 in 1880–1890 to a high of .2338 in 1930–1940, suggesting that the elasticity of substitution was essentially constant, with perhaps a slight tendency to increase.

These results appear to be inconsistent with the theory advanced by David, which suggests that the elasticity of factor substitution should decrease over time. The David model implies that as producers gain familiarity with the technique, technical progress will occur and factor intensity ratios will remain unchanged, even though changes occur in relative factor scarcity.

The results obtained from estimating model (9) appear to be consistent with the direction of technical change as estimated by using the two-factor test (chapter 3). They are not consistent with the induced innovation hypothesis. That is, while the results indicate that $h_L > h_A$, consistency with the induced innovation hypothesis would require that $\lambda \geqq \delta$, $\lambda$, $\delta \leqq 0$, and $\phi > \theta$, $\phi$, $\theta > 0$ where their magnitudes are such that $h_L > h_A$. Because of this inconsistency, model (8) was estimated.

MODEL (8).    The results obtained from estimating model (8) yielded no appreciable change in the distribution parameters $\alpha$, $\beta$ or in the substitution parameter $\rho$. The estimates of $\delta$ are $-.00165$ and $.0074$, and in both equations $Q'_1$ and $Q'_2$ these estimates do not differ significantly from zero. The estimated magnitudes of $\lambda$ are somewhat greater than in the case of model (9). The estimates of $\lambda$ are $-.10958$ and $-.10552$ for equations $Q'_1$ and

[13] It is shown in chapter 7 that a general decline in the Japanese labor–land price ratio matched with an increase in the land–labor ratio is inconsistent with labor-using technical change. Thus, with respect to the direction of change, Binswanger's conclusions and ours appear to be in agreement.

[14] David, *Labor Scarcity.*

$Q_2'$ respectively, and their corresponding variance estimates are small. The estimate of the augmentation parameter $\gamma$ associated with time is .00461, and it is significant in the case of equation $Q_1'$ but small and insignificant in the case of $Q_2'$.

As in the case of model (9), no definite statement can be made as to the neutrality of the technical changes that are correlated with time. The estimates of the parameters $\delta$, $\lambda$ are significantly different, and therefore $h_L > h_A$. This is consistent with a labor-saving direction of technical change and inconsistent with the induced innovation hypothesis. While the elasticity estimates are somewhat smaller than in the case of model (9), they also show a tendency to increase over the period 1880–1940 (table 8–3).

Since the time variable is highly correlated with factor prices, and since no definite statement can be made as to its impact on the rates of factor augmentation, this variable was removed, and model (2) was estimated.

MODEL (2).   The results from fitting model (2) to the data appear to be good, with less evidence for serial correlation than in the previous models (table 8–4). Also, the coefficient estimates appear to be reasonably consistent with those shown in table 8–1, although the estimates of the substitution parameter are generally somewhat larger and, as a result, the estimates of the elasticity of factor substitution are generally somewhat smaller. The lowest estimates of $\sigma_t$ for the years 1880–1890, 1880–1940, and 1930–1940 are .1541, .1645, and .1661, respectively (table 8–3). As in the case of model (9), this

TABLE 8–4.   Estimates of equation (14), model (2), with two dependent-variable transformations

| Dependent Variable | Estimates of Coefficients[a] | | | | |
|---|---|---|---|---|---|
| | $b_3$ | $b_4$ | $b_5$ | $R^2$ | $d$ |
| $Q_1'$ | .30251 | −.01169 | −.08638 | .921 | 1.082 |
| | (.02241) | (.01915) | (.01861) | | |
| $Q_2'$ | .19864 | −.00578 | −.06478 | .888 | .831 |
| | (.02049) | (.01751) | (.01701) | | |

| Dependent Variable | Estimates of Parameters | | | | |
|---|---|---|---|---|---|
| | $\alpha$ | $\beta$ | $\rho$ | $\delta$ | $\lambda$ |
| $Q_1'$ | 11.0323 | .00269 | 2.30571 | −.01676 | −.12384 |
| | (11.3237) | (.00268) | (.24493) | (.02751) | (.02692) |
| $Q_2'$ | .0644 | .00002 | 4.03413 | −.00721 | −.08084 |
| | (.1236) | (.00004) | (.51931) | (.02185) | (.02136) |

Note: All values in parentheses are standard error estimates.
[a] Estimates of $b_1$ and $b_2$ are not listed in order to conserve space.

TABLE 8–5. Parameter and elasticity of factor substitution estimates of model (2) where the labor–land index $(I_t)$ is divided into two series for $t = 1880, \ldots, 1910$ and $t = 1915, \ldots, 1940$

| Dependent Variable | $I_{1880}, \ldots, I_{1910}$ | | | $I_{1915}, \ldots, I_{1940}$ | | |
|---|---|---|---|---|---|---|
| | $\delta$ | $\lambda$ | $\sigma_t$ | $\delta$ | $\lambda$ | $\sigma_t$ |
| $Q_1'$ | −.02503 | −.12355 | .2154 | −.02855 | −.08061 | .2373 |
| | (.00917) | (.01075) | | (.01235) | (.01363) | |
| $Q_2'$ | .01173 | −.09199 | .2034 | −.02812 | −.08583 | .2263 |
| | (.01140) | (.01152) | | (.01283) | (.01210) | |

Note: All values in parentheses are standard error estimates.

suggests that technical change did not increase the difficulty of substituting labor for land. In fact, the evidence here, as in the previous cases, appears to suggest that the kind of technical change experienced by Japan slightly increased the ease of substitution between labor and land. As before, the hypothesis is accepted that $\delta$ is larger than $\lambda$ (table 8–4).[15]

While Japanese land values generally increased relative to wages throughout the period 1880–1940, the period from about 1915 to 1940 is characterized only intermittently by this phenomenon. That is, $dI_t/dt < 0$ for $t = 1800, \ldots, 1910$ and $dI_t/dt \gtrless 0$ for $t = 1915, \ldots, 1940$. This suggests that, unless factor augmentation develops inertia, both land and labor should be augmented during the latter period. But it also means that the overall direction of factor bias for the latter period is difficult to predict on an a priori basis. Furthermore, if hysteresis is present, no increase in the elasticity of factor substitution can be expected.

Although the data series is perhaps too short for a supportable probability statement, the augmentation parameters of model (2) were nevertheless estimated for these two periods (table 8–5). The results for the period 1880–1910 are consistent with the results reported above, that is, $h_L > h_A$. For the period 1915–1940, however, the direction of technical change appears to be nearly neutral. The estimates of the elasticity of factor substitution are consistent with those above and suggest that the ease of substituting labor for land may have increased (table 8–5).

*Conclusions*

In this chapter we have developed a dynamic CES-type function that incorporates the Hicksian induced innovation hypothesis into a

[15] For purposes of comparison, model (1) was estimated, but it did not fit the data nearly as well as model (2). Serial correlation appeared to exist, and the variance estimates of the elasticity of factor substitution $[1/(1 + \rho)]$ were large. This precluded our tests of the augmentation parameters $\theta$, $\phi$. The elasticity estimates ranged from 1.017 to −.0099, while the estimates of the time augmentation parameter of land ranged from .0116 to .0016. The estimate of the augmentation parameter for labor ranged from .0185 to .0144. The variance estimates of these parameters were also large.

meta-production function. This function was postulated within a two-dimensional input space and, in this study, utilized a relative input-price index as its shift variable. The addition of this variable resulted in the function having the desirable property of a variable elasticity of factor substitution. The study used only a partial equilibrium approach, in that changes in the relative price index were assumed to be exogenously determined.

In the present study, which used data on land prices (rather than data on land rents, as in the study reported in appendix 3–1, chapter 3), it was found that technical progress that was labor saving and land using took place in Japan during the period 1880–1940. This bias, which appeared to be stronger during the period 1880–1910 than during the period 1915–1940, is contrary to expectation because wages generally declined while land increased in price throughout the entire sixty-year period. The results of fitting the models described in this chapter to the above data are therefore not consistent with the Hicks–Ahmad version of the induced innovation hypothesis. This unforeseen bias in the direction of technical change may reflect some fundamental bias in innovation possibilities or it may imply that transfer of technology took place only from countries or regions that were endowed with land and other agricultural resources of greater quantity and quality than was Japan. Whatever its source, the bias more than offset any influence that increases in the price of land relative to labor might have had on the direction of technical change. It may be that the extreme labor intensity that characterized Japanese agriculture at the beginning of the modern period precluded any further shift in the labor-using direction of technical change, even though the price of labor continued to decline relative to land for several decades.

It is possible that the use of a relative price series based on land-rental rates rather than on land prices would lead to findings consistent with the results of the research reported in chapter 3 (appendix 3–1) and with the general implications of the induced innovation hypothesis. No final statement about the nature of the technical change bias in Meiji Japan can be made until further investigation has revealed whether land price or land-rental rate more accurately reflects the opportunity cost of land during that period.

In this study estimates of the elasticity of factor substitution for the period 1880–1940 ranged from a low of .1645 to a high of .2594. Changes in the elasticity of factor substitution over time were slightly positive, suggesting that the kind of technical change that occurred did not increase the difficulty of substitution between labor and land. Thus the Japanese experience appears not to have been consistent with the hysteresis model of technical change postulated by David.

There remain two serious specification problems in the use of the CES test introduced in this chapter. First, although the price of land, at least during the earlier part of the time period examined, was almost totally endogenous to agriculture, our specification treats the prices of both labor and land as exogenous. This could have caused statistical biases in our estimates of the augmentation parameters. A second and more serious problem is that there are obviously more than two factors of production involved in the Japanese agricultural economy. The CES production function limitation to two factors of production, without providing a separability assumption, prevents us from considering other inputs, such as machinery. It seems likely that more progress in perfecting a test for induced innovation will be made along the lines suggested in chapter 7 than through further development of the CES model.

APPENDIX 8–1

*Estimation Procedures*

Parameter estimates of the CES-type metaproduction function developed above are derived from estimating the coefficients of their corresponding profit-maximizing equations. These estimating equations, together with a discussion of the data used to calculate them, are presented below.

STATISTICAL MODELS

MODEL (2). In principle, a test of the direction of bias in induced innovation may be obtained directly from equation (6a). This is basically the Moroney method of estimating the elasticity of substitution. The statistical significance of the difference between $\lambda$ and $\delta$ may be found by testing the statistical significance of the difference of coefficient $(\lambda - \delta)\rho/(1 + \rho)$ from zero in equation (6a). This must be predicated on the prior test of significance of the difference of $\rho$ from the coefficients $1/(1 + \rho)$ in the same equation. This procedure has been abandoned, however, because, as $I_t$ is the index of $(w/r)_t$, a high degree of multicollinearity exists between $\ln (w/r)_t$ and $I_t$.

An alternative procedure is therefore used. The estimation of the unknown parameters of model (2) is obtained by converting equations (4) and (5) to ln form as follows:

$$\ln \left(\frac{Q}{A}\right)_t = -\frac{1}{1 + \rho} \ln \alpha + \frac{1}{1 + \rho} \ln r_t + \frac{\delta\rho}{1 + \rho} I_t \qquad \text{(A–1)}$$

and

$$\ln \left(\frac{Q}{L}\right)_t = -\frac{1}{1 + \rho} \ln \beta + \frac{1}{1 + \rho} \ln w_t + \frac{\lambda\rho}{1 + \rho} I_t \qquad \text{(A–2)}$$

Because the coefficient $1/(1 + \rho)$ is common to both variables $r_t$ and $w_t$, these equations were combined to yield the estimating equation

$$Q' = XB + \mathbf{u} \tag{A-3}$$

where

$$Q' = \begin{vmatrix} \ln (Q/A)_{t_o} \\ \vdots \\ \ln (Q/A)_{t_n} \\ \ln (Q/L)_{t_o} \\ \vdots \\ \ln (Q/L)_{t_n} \end{vmatrix} \qquad X = \begin{vmatrix} 1 & 0 & \ln & r_{t_o} & I_{t_o} & 0 \\ \vdots & \vdots & & \vdots & \vdots & \vdots \\ 1 & 0 & \ln & r_{t_n} & I_{t_n} & 0 \\ 0 & 1 & \ln & w_{t_o} & 0 & I_{t_o} \\ \vdots & \vdots & & \vdots & \vdots & \vdots \\ 0 & 1 & \ln & w_{t_n} & 0 & I_{t_n} \end{vmatrix}$$

$$B = \begin{vmatrix} b_1 \\ \vdots \\ b_5 \end{vmatrix} = \left| -\frac{1}{1 + \rho} \ln \alpha, \; -\frac{1}{1 + \rho} \ln \beta, \; \frac{1}{1 + \rho}, \; \frac{\delta\rho}{1 + \rho}, \; \frac{\lambda\rho}{1 + \rho} \right|$$

and $\mathbf{u}$ is a $2n$ component vector of disturbances that are assumed to be randomly, log-normally, and independently distributed with a zero mean and a constant variance. This formulation allows for the restricted estimation of $1/(1 + \rho)$ by ordinary least squares and, consequently, for the derivation of unique estimates of the parameters of model (2).

MODEL (8).   From the first derivatives of equation (8) with respect to $A$ and $L$, the estimation equations of model (8) are

$$\ln \left(\frac{Q}{A}\right)_t = -\frac{1}{1 + \rho} \ln \alpha + \frac{1}{1 + \rho} \ln r_t + \frac{\delta\rho}{1 + \rho} I_t + \frac{\gamma\rho}{1 + \rho} t \tag{A-4}$$

and

$$\ln \left(\frac{Q}{L}\right)_t = -\frac{1}{1 + \rho} \ln \beta + \frac{1}{1 + \rho} \ln w_t + \frac{\lambda\rho}{1 + \rho} I_t + \frac{\gamma\rho}{1 + \rho} t \tag{A-5}$$

Because the coefficient $1/(1 + \rho)$ is common to both the variables $\ln r_t$ and $\ln w_t$ in (A-4) and (A-5), and $\gamma\rho/(1 + \rho)$ is common to the $t$-term in both equations, these equations can be combined in the manner of equation (A-3) by constraining the coefficient of time to be equal in both equations as well.

MODEL (9).   From the first derivatives of equation (9) with respect to $A$ and $L$, the estimation equations of model (9) become:

$$\ln \left(\frac{Q}{A}\right)_t = -\frac{1}{1 + \rho} \ln \alpha + \frac{1}{1 + \rho} \ln r_t + \frac{\delta\rho}{1 + \rho} I_t + \frac{\theta\rho}{1 + \rho} t \tag{A-6}$$

and

$$\ln\left(\frac{Q}{L}\right)_t = -\frac{1}{1+\rho}\ln\beta + \frac{1}{1+\rho}\ln w_t + \frac{\lambda\rho}{1+\rho}I_t + \frac{\phi\rho}{1+\rho}t \quad \text{(A–7)}$$

Because the coefficient $1/(1+\rho)$ is common to both variables $r_t$ and $w_t$, these equations can again be combined in the manner of equation (A–3) but without constraining the time coefficient in the two equations to be equal.

It has been observed in this chapter that during the period 1880 to 1940, Japanese agricultural production increased as wages generally declined relative to land values. Thus in the present study of Japan, $dI_t/dt$ is generally negative. From equation (11) it then follows that to be consistent with technical progress, the augmentation coefficients $\delta$, $\lambda$ should be equal to or less than zero. Ahmad's induced innovation hypothesis suggests that the decline in wages relative to land price should have encouraged technical progress that was biased in a land-saving and labor-using direction.[16] The null hypothesis is that $\delta$ is not different from $\lambda$, that is, that relative factor scarcity did not bias the direction of technical change. The alternative hypothesis is that $\delta$ is different from $\lambda$, and to be consistent with a land-saving and labor-using direction of technical change, it follows from equation (11) that $\delta < \lambda$ where, as stated above, $\delta$, $\lambda \leq 0$. This test is predicated on the prior test that $\rho > 0$. Notice that in the case of model (9), if $\delta < \lambda$ and $\delta$, $\lambda \leq 0$, the direction of technical change in Japan can still be labor-saving if the augmentation coefficients $(\theta, \phi)$ associated with the time variable dominate the augmentation coefficients $(\delta, \lambda)$ associated with $I_t$.

## DATA

Time series data on agricultural output, land and labor inputs, and input prices, together with a discussion of the derivation of these data, are available for Japan for the period 1880 to 1960.[17] Because data were not uniformly available for the war and postwar years, however, in the present study we used the cutoff date of 1940.

All observations are quinquennial. Observations on land and labor were made at each five-year interval beginning with 1880. Prices (rents and wages) were also measured every five years starting in 1880; in this case, however, five-year averages were computed. This procedure lags prices in comparison with the land and labor data and takes into account the effect of expectation and adjustment lags on the adoption of technical change.

With the present model it is difficult to make an a priori selection of the "best" measures of agricultural output, as Hayami and Ruttan have done,

[16] Syed Ahmad, "On the Theory of Induced Invention," *Economic Journal* 76, no. 302 (June 1966): 344–57.

[17] Yujiro Hayami and Vernon W. Ruttan, *Agricultural Development: An International Perspective* (Baltimore: Johns Hopkins University Press, 1971).

for several measures appear equally accurate. The two data series that were used as measures of agricultural output are gross agricultural output (all commodities net of intermediate goods supplied within agriculture) and gross crop output. The land area measure is hectares of arable land, and the measure for labor is agricultural male workers. Accordingly, the following two transformations were made with regard to measures of the dependent variable $(Q')$ in equation (A–3):

$$Q'_1 = \left| \begin{array}{l} \ln \text{ (all commodities/arable land)} \\ \ln \text{ (all commodities/male workers)} \end{array} \right|$$

$$Q'_2 = \left| \begin{array}{l} \ln \text{ (all crops/arable land)} \\ \ln \text{ (all crops/male workers)} \end{array} \right|$$

Land value is the weighted average of the prices of paddy fields and upland fields where the areas of each are used as weights. The specification of the functional form of the CES-type metaproduction function developed above offers a direct test of the Hicks–Ahmad version of the induced innovation hypothesis.

NINE

# Aggregate Demand and the Rate
# of Technical Change

URI BEN-ZION AND VERNON W. RUTTAN

$T$HE theory of induced innovation has been applied primarily in efforts to understand the roles played by resource endowments and factor prices in determining the direction of technical change. This chapter represents an attempt to establish, on an empirical basis, the degree to which the rate of technical change is responsive to final demand forces. Demand-induced innovation was first studied empirically at the firm and industry levels by Jacob Schmookler and Zvi Griliches (see discussions in chapters 2 and 6, respectively).[1] At the macroeconomic level, the responsiveness of technical change to final demand was first tested and confirmed by R. E. Lucas (see chapter 2).[2]

The factors that condition the responsiveness of technical change to final demand at both microlevel and macrolevel have been elaborated in the models discussed in chapters 4 and 5. These factors include the higher prices and/or higher output levels of commodities that obtain in periods of expanding demand and lead to greater profitability of research.

The helpful comments of Martin Abel, Hans P. Binswanger, James M. Henderson, Edi Karni, T. Paul Schultz, Theodore W. Schultz, Robert Shiller, and Christopher Sims, and of participants in workshops at the University of Minnesota, the University of Tel Aviv, and the Technion Israel Institute of Technology, are gratefully acknowledged. We also wish to thank Yash P. Mehra, Dan Peled, and Jim Spitzer for their valuable research assistance, and to express our appreciation of the financial support provided us by the U.S. Agency for International Development through the University of Minnesota Center of Economic Development and by the Ford Foundation (grant no. 8) through the Israel Foundation Trustees.

[1] Jacob Schmookler, *Invention and Economic Growth* (Cambridge, Mass.: Harvard University Press, 1966); Zvi Griliches, "Hybrid Corn: An Explanation in the Economics of Technical Change," *Econometrica* 25 (1957): 501–22.

[2] R. E. Lucas, "Tests of a Capital-Theoretic Model of Technological Change," *Review of Economic Studies* 34 (1967): 175–90.

The model we develop in the first section of this chapter explains the relationship between aggregate demand and the rate of technical change. We show that the value of input-saving technical change is greater in periods of growing demand than in periods of stable or falling demand. Our discussion leads us to conclude that because higher profitability induces a higher rate of technical change, it also leads to a positive relationship between the rate of technical progress and changes in aggregate demand. An important assumption which we add to the analysis is that because labor and capital are quasi-fixed factors of production, their relevant marginal price is not constant over time. Specifically, the relevant marginal price is higher in a period of expansion and lower in a period of declining output. In making this assumption we follow the resource-fixity approach introduced by Glen L. Johnson and Clark Edwards.[3] We use this approach to analyze the relationship between changes in the demand for a product and choice of optimal inputs by producing firms.

In the second section of the chapter we present an aggregate model that relates the gain from technical change to the fluctuation of aggregate demand and uses the result to analyze the demand for technical change over the business cycle.

A model that tests the responsiveness of technical change to final demand is presented in the third section of this chapter. This model cannot distinguish between inducements to innovation which arise out of the price and quantity effects of increases in commodity demand and those inducements which arise out of factor price changes described in the model based on the concept of resource fixity. The model in this third section should thus be viewed as an empirical verification of both these effects.

Finally, in the last two sections of the chapter we discuss results, policy implications, and possible extensions of the model presented.

*Quasi-Fixed Factors of Production and*
*the Choice of Inputs by Firms*

In simple price theory, and in the short run, factors of production are classified as either fixed or variable. Inputs used up in a current accounting period, such as raw materials or electricity, are usually classified as variable inputs. Inputs that provide services over a series of accounting periods, like a machine or a building, are usually classified as fixed inputs.

Kenneth J. Arrow has shown that the irreversibility of investment affects the firm's choice of the optimal path of inputs to satisfy a given vector of

[3] Glen L. Johnson, "Supply Functions, Some Facts and Notions," in *Agricultural Problems in a Growing Economy*, ed. Earl O. Heady (Ames: Iowa State College Press, 1958); Glen L. Johnson, "The State of Agricultural Supply Analysis," *Journal of Farm Economics* 42 (1960): 175–90: Clark Edwards, "Resource Fixity and Farm Organization," *Journal of Farm Economics* 41 (1959): 747–59.

output over time.[4] This is because, in a time-series context, irreversible input is a quasi-fixed input that is variable with respect to an increase in production but fixed with respect to a decline in production.[5]

In general, a factor of production is a quasi-fixed factor when the purchase of the durable factor is associated with an irreversible payment. Consequently, a quasi-fixed factor of production is not necessarily a fixed factor in price-theory terminology. Consider, for example, a case in which there is a market for used capital and in which a machine is defined as a quasi-fixed factor if there are transaction costs in the market for used machines. The result is that the market price is below the net value of the machine.

In the special case of no-depreciation, the existence of transaction costs simply means that the price that must be paid for a new piece of equipment is higher than the price at which an identical machine can be sold once it has been installed in a plant, even though it has not been used and, as a consequence, performs on a level with the new equipment. When a firm increases capital stock in a period of expansion, therefore, it must pay higher prices than the marginal price for which it can sell a "used" asset in a period of contraction.[6]

Let $K_0$ be the stock of the quasi-fixed factor that the firm has on hand. For a level of input below $K_0$, the relevant cost per unit is $P^1$, which is the selling price of returned assets. For a level of input above $K_0$ the relevant price is $P^0$, which is the purchase price of a new unit. This is shown diagrammatically in figure 9–1.[7]

With regard to the firm's labor input, the transaction costs in the market are determined in several ways.

First, it seems reasonable to assume that there are costs involved both in hiring and in firing workers. Thus, layoff decisions will be determined by balancing the savings that can be realized by reducing a firm's labor force during a period of low-level economic activity against the costs involved in rehiring workers when economic activity revives.

Second, as Gary S. Becker suggests, part of the human capital that is embodied in a worker is *firm-specific* and affects that worker's marginal product only in a particular firm or job.[8] The cost of obtaining this specific human capital is shared by the firm and the worker. The worker's wage rate is below the value of his marginal product in the firm but above the value of

---

[4] Kenneth J. Arrow, "Optimal Capital Policy with Irreversible Investment," in *Value, Capital and Growth, Papers in Honor of Sir John Hicks,* ed. J. N. Wolfe (Edinburgh: Edinburgh University Press, 1968).

[5] If the asset is depreciable, reduction in the input is limited by the rate of depreciation.

[6] This assumes that the purchase prices of new assets are constant over the relevant time horizon.

[7] For a similar diagram and analysis, see Edwards, "Resource Fixity."

[8] Gary S. Becker, *Human Capital* (New York: Columbia University Press, National Bureau of Economic Research, 1964). Of course, a good portion of human capital—that is, general human capital—affects a worker's marginal product in other firms as well.

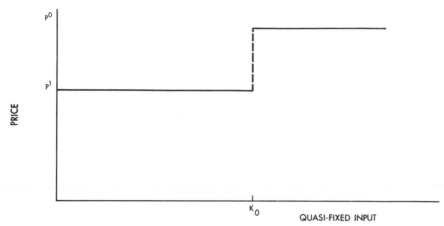

FIG. 9–1. Relevant supply curve of a quasi-fixed factor (for a firm with stock on hand $K_0$).

the marginal product that he can achieve in another firm. If the firm fires an employee, it loses the return on its share of the investment in that worker's specific human capital.

Walter Oi elaborated this approach and emphasized the view that labor input is a quasi-fixed factor of production.[9] R. L. Miller developed a model of the firm's demand for labor over time which took into account the specific investment in human capital.[10] In his model, Miller used an *inventory approach* to the demand for labor, which "consists of a dichotomized (peak, off-peak) system of equations that attempts to capture the relevant differences in decision-making by firms during peak and off-peak periods in the production cycle."[11] The model suggests a systematic relationship between the choice of inputs by firms and fluctuations in demand.

In the following analysis, we will assume that a firm has three inputs: labor $L$, capital $K$, and material $M$, which are combined in a production function of product $X$:

$$X = f(L, K, M) \tag{1}$$

The purchase prices of the input and output are $P_L^0$, $P_K^0$, $P_M^0$, and $P_X$, which are assumed for simplicity to be constant over time.[12] Following our earlier discussion, we assume that labor and capital are quasi-fixed factors

---

[9] Walter Oi, "Labor as a Quasi-fixed Factor," *Journal of Political Economy* 70 (1962): 538–55.

[10] R. L. Miller, "A Short Term Econometric Model of Textile Industries," *American Economic Review* 61 (1971): 279–89.

[11] Miller, "Econometric Model," p. 279.

[12] If prices are rising in an inflationary process, this assumption implies that all prices of inputs and output change at the same rate, so that "real prices" are constant.

of production with the selling prices of $P_L^1$ and $P_K^1$ respectively,[13] where

$$P_L^1 < P_L^0 \quad \text{and} \quad P_K^1 < P_K^0$$

The analysis above suggests that when firms expand their output they face higher prices for labor and capital than during a period of reduction in output. The marginal product of labor and capital will be $P_L^1$ and $P_K^1$, respectively, in a period of falling demand and $P_L^0$ and $P_K^0$ in a period of rising demand.[14] In a period of falling demand the firm will evaluate the labor and capital inputs at their lower selling prices $(P_L^1, P_K^1)$, while in a period of rising demand the firm will evaluate the quasi-fixed factors at their purchase prices $(P_L^0, P_K^0)$.

It should be noted that the recorded market prices are always the purchase prices $P_L^0$, $P_K^0$ in which transactions are made. The selling prices $P_L^1$ and $P_K^1$, which are the relevant marginal prices in periods of falling demand, are not recorded or measured in the national income accounts.[15]

### Aggregate Demand and the Profitability of Technical Change

Economic theory suggests that there is a direct relationship between level of investment and the expected profitability of investment. According to Schmookler, a firm's incentive to invent is also dependent on expected profit: "The essential point is that the incentive to make an invention, like the incentive to produce any other goods, is affected by the excess of expected return over expected costs."[16] Similar models of endogenous technical change were developed and tested by Lucas and by J. A. Rasmussen.[17]

We assume that investment by a firm in research and development is expected to reduce the levels of input needed to obtain a given output $X$. The expected saving per unit of output $S$ that results from an investment $R$

[13] For simplicity, we assume that $P_L$ and $P_K$ each represent a price per unit of flow of labor and capital services.

[14] This analysis also suggests that the firm will choose different combinations of quasi-fixed inputs and material in different phases of the business cycle. In particular, in periods of rising output the firm will use lower ratios of quasi-fixed factors to the variable factor than in periods of falling demand.

[15] The idea that from the firm's point of view measured market prices and observed profits are not appropriate variables in a period of falling demand was suggested more than a decade ago by Ruttan. Vernon W. Ruttan, "Technological Changes in the Agricultural and Non-Agricultural Sector of the U.S. Economy" (Paper presented to Seminar on Measurement of Technical Change, Giannini Foundation for Agricultural Economics, University of California, Berkeley, April 1959).

[16] Jacob Schmookler, "Economic Sources of Inventive Activity," *Journal of Economic History* 20 (March 1962): 1–20.

[17] Lucas, "Capital-Theoretic Model"; J. A. Rasmussen, "Application of a Model of Endogenous Technical Change to U.S. Industry Data," *Review of Economic Studies* 40 (1973): 225–93. See also chapter 2 for a rigorous formulation of this approach.

in technology can be measured by the reduction in the cost of producing a given output that is expected to result from the investment.

$$S = (C(X, 0) - C(X, R)/X) \tag{2}$$

where $C(X, 0)$ is the minimum cost of producing output $X$ with a given technology $(R = 0)$, and $C(X, R)$ is the expected minimum cost of producing $X$ with an improved technology to be obtained by the investment $R$.

The savings in cost per unit of output is achieved by a reduction in input requirement per unit and can be written

$$S = (\sum_{i=1}^{n} \Delta a_i P_{a_i}) \tag{3}$$

where $\Delta a_i$ is the reduction of input $a_i$ per unit of output and $P_{a_i}$ is the relevant price at which the input is evaluated.

In the case of three-factor input, described by equation (1), we can write (3) as

$$S = (\Delta m \cdot P_M + \Delta k \cdot P_K + \Delta l \cdot P_L) \tag{4}$$

where $m$, $k$, and $l$ are the inputs of material, capital, and labor *per unit of output* at the level of $X$. Here $P_M$, $P_K$, and $P_L$ are the prices at which the input saving is evaluated.[18]

According to the model developed in the first section, the relevant prices of labor and capital in a period of rising demand are the purchase prices of input services $P_K$ and $P_L$, respectively, and the value of a given reduction in inputs per unit of output is determined as follows:

$$S^0 = \Delta m \cdot P_M + \Delta k \cdot P_K^0 + \Delta l \cdot P_L^0 \tag{5a}$$

In a period of falling demand, the saving per unit is determined by the selling price of quasi-fixed inputs:

$$S^1 = \Delta m \cdot P_M + \Delta k \cdot P_K^1 + \Delta l \cdot P_L^1 \tag{5b}$$

Because the relevant prices of the quasi-fixed factors in periods of rising demand $(P_K^0, P_L^0)$ are higher than the relevant prices in periods of falling demand $(P_K^1, P_L^1)$, the saving brought about by a technical change will be higher in a rising market than in a falling market. Also, as the price of the variable input is assumed to be constant over the business cycle, the input is relatively more expensive in a falling market than in a rising market. As a result, technical change may be biased toward saving of materials in periods of falling demand and toward saving of quasi-fixed factors in periods of rising demand.

[18] Note that in general an investment in research and development $R$ can be used to achieve different combinations of reductions in factor inputs per unit of output. In this case, the induced innovation approach suggests that it is optimal for the firm to choose a technical change that will maximize the value of saving $S$. We assume that $(\Delta a_i)$ in (3) is already chosen, such that the value of $S$ is maximized for a given $R$.

Now let $S_t$ be the saving that is expected to result from a technical change brought about by the firm's investment $R_t$ in research and development. The firm will make the investment if the rate of return is above the firm's cost of capital. In other words, the investment is profitable if the present value of the expected savings exceeds the cost of investment. Thus

$$\sum_{i=1}^{n} \frac{S_{t+i}}{(1+r)^t} > R_t \tag{6}$$

where $r$ is the interest rate and $S_{t+i}$ is the savings expected to result, in period $t+1$, from the investment in new knowledge or technology made in period $t$. The savings expected in period $t+1$ is estimated at time $t$ on the basis of information available at that time.

Assuming that the marginal productivity of investment diminishes (in a manner similar to Keynes' marginal efficiency of capital), we predict a direct relationship between the level of investment in technical progress and the expected savings from the investment. In other words, firms will spend more on investment in technology in periods when the expected rate of return from investment is higher than when it is lower. Both the expected size of the savings from a given investment and the expected rate of return realized from the savings over time will be higher if the firm projects a rising demand for its product than if it projects a declining demand.

One variable that commonly affects changes in demand for the product of a particular firm or industry is fluctuation in aggregate demand, or the movement of the business cycle for the entire economy. A period of rising aggregate demand is not necessarily a period of rising demand for a particular firm. However, we assume that in general, as aggregate demand rises, the percentage of firms that experience increased demand for their products will rise also. Similarly, we would expect that as aggregate demand falls, the percentage of firms and industries that also face falling demand will increase.

Considering all firms together, we can conclude that the greater the change in aggregate demand, the higher will be the expected return on technical investment and, as a result of the latter, the higher the level of investment will be. In other words, investment in technical progress will be higher in the rising phase of the business cycle and lower in the declining phase.[19] The relationship between aggregate investment in technical improvement and changes in aggregate demand can be written

$$R_t = f(D_{t-z}^{t+v}, D_{t-z}^{t+v+1}, D_{t-z}^{t+v+2}, \ldots, D_{t-z}^{t+v+k}) \tag{7}$$

[19] Our analysis was based on the assumption that market price of output is constant (at least in terms of the prices of purchased inputs). If the price of output rises with the business cycle, this will strengthen the relationship between aggregate demand and investment in technical change. For a more detailed discussion of this point see especially chapter 2, as well as Yoram Barzel, "Optimal Timing of Innovation," *Review of Economics and Statistics* 50 (1969): 348–55.

where $D_{t-z}^{t+v}$ represents the prediction, made in period $(t - z)$, of changes in aggregate demand in future period $t + v$; $z$ represents a lag between the time at which the investment appropriation was made and the time at which the actual investment takes place; and $v$ represents the lag between the actual investment outlay and the realization of savings in cost due to the technical change that results from the investment.[20]

Although (7) represents a simplified model of investment decision in technical progress, it is not written in terms of observable variables. In particular, the expectations of firms' managers are not directly observable. However, we can assume that managers use both current and past data in predicting future changes in aggregate demand, and thus, expected aggregate demand can be written as

$$D_{t-z}^{t+v+i} = f(E_{t-z}, E_{t-z-1}, \ldots, E_{t-z-n}) \tag{8}$$

where $E_{t-z-n}$ represents sets of variables which are observable at time $t - z$ and which firms use to predict the future trends of aggregate demand.

Using (8) we can write $R_t$ as a function of observable variables that serve as business cycle indicators:

$$R_t = f(E_{t-z}, \ldots, E_{t-z-n}) \tag{9}$$

We assume that investments in research and development will be embodied in more productive capital equipment and will lead to a rise in the index that is employed to measure technical change. Thus we can view changes in the index of technical progress TG in a given period as a distributed lag function of previous expenditures on technical progress.

$$(\Delta \text{TG})_t = f(R_{t-z}, R_{t-z-1}, \ldots, R_{t-z-j}) \tag{10}$$

By substituting (9) into (10), we can write technical progress as a function of observed indicators that are regarded as proxy to the future direction of aggregate demand:

$$(\Delta \text{TG})_t = f(E_{t-z}, E_{t-z-1}, \ldots, E_{t-m}) \tag{11}$$

The model can be tested empirically by using estimates of either (9) or (11). Because data on aggregate investment in technical progress are not easily available, we concentrate our empirical work on a test of the later equation. In other words, in our empirical work, we will test the relationship between technical change and variables that can be used as business cycle indicators.[21]

---

[20] Studies of general investment behavior by firms emphasize the lag between investment decision and the actual "realized" investment. See Dale W. Jorgenson, "Capital Theory and Investment Behavior," *American Economic Review* 53 (May 1963: Papers and Proceedings): 247–59. One would expect a similar lag between decision and realization in investment in research and development.

[21] It should be noted that investment in research and development may have exogenous components which cannot be described as functions of changes in the level of

The model developed in this section uses the profit variable to relate technical change to change in aggregate demand. The model's main implication is that the rate of technical change is higher in periods of rising demand than in periods of falling demand. This proposal clarifies the relationship between the *timing of innovation* and various economic factors, and it strengthens the view that the rate of technical change is an induced, endogenous variable.

The classical theory of induced innovation of John R. Hicks, William Fellner, Syed Ahmad and others has suggested that in a given time period, innovations are biased toward inputs that become scarce and more expensive.[22] In our model, we see that over time, the rate of innovation is higher in periods of rising aggregate demand. During such periods the demand for primary factors rises more rapidly than the supply, and prices rise relative to periods of slower growth in demand. This comparison between technical change at a given point in time and the timing of a technical change which is in a time-series context suggests that the model can be viewed as a clear extension of the classical theory of induced innovation.

### The Empirical Model

One important implication of the model developed in the preceding section is the direct link between change in aggregate demand and technical changes. The link is based on the profitability of, or expected return to, investment in technical progress. We show that the greater the expected increase in aggregate demand, the higher will be the expected return to investments in technical change and, consequently, the higher will be the level of investment.

We conclude that the realized technical change can be viewed as a distributed lag function of the actual (or expected) changes. In the aggregate demand, this relationship can be written as follows:

$$\left(\frac{\Delta TG}{TG}\right)_t = \alpha_0 + \alpha_1\left(\frac{\Delta D}{D}\right)_{t-1} + \alpha_2\left(\frac{\Delta D}{D}\right)_{t-2} + \cdots + \alpha_k\left(\frac{\Delta D}{D}\right)_{t-k} \quad (12)$$

where $(\Delta TG/TG)_t$ is the relative change in the level of technology (or the rate of technical progress) in period $t$. $(\Delta D/D)_t$ is the percentage change in aggregate demand in period $t$.

---

aggregate demand. Individual expenditures on education and direct government expenditures on research and development may be two important components; their influence is regarded as a part of the stochastic term in (11).

[22] J. R. Hicks, *The Theory of Wages* (London: Macmillan and Co., Ltd., 1st ed. 1932. 2nd ed. 1963); William Fellner, "Two Propositions in the Theory of Induced Innovation," *Economic Journal* 71, no. 282 (1961): 305–8: Syed Ahmad, "On the Theory of Induced Invention," *Economic Journal* 76, no. 302 (1966): 344–57.

According to equation (12), the rate of technical change is given in the form of a distributed lag function of the change in output. The lag distribution of length $k$ is determined by two types of lags: the lag between change in aggregate demand and investment in technical progress; and the lag between investment in research and development and realized technical change. The second lag reflects the time that elapses between actual investment in a technical improvement and the realized technical change. This lag, which depends on the production process of new technical knowledge, may be a "quiet" variable, because a breakthrough in research can come after a relatively short or a relatively long period. For example, the rate of technical progress and the number of patents in year $t$ may result from an investment made two or ten years ago.

The high variability of the lag in patents was recognized by Schmookler, who used a seven-year moving average of the annual patent series in his empirical work on patents.[23] Following a similar procedure, we assume that there is a trend in the level of technology in the economy and that changes in aggregate demand affect changes in the realized index of technical progress around the line of this trend. Thus, we write (12) in a "level" form as follows:

$$\ln \mathrm{TG} = \beta_0 + \beta_1 t + \beta_2 \ln D + \sum_{i=0}^{k} \alpha_i \left(\frac{\Delta D}{D}\right)_{t-i} \tag{13}$$

where the time period $t$ and the level of aggregate demand $D$ represent the long run *trend line*, the changes in aggregate demand $(\Delta D/D)_{t-i}$ explain the short-run effect of deviation from the trend line, and ln represents the natural logarithm of the variable.

In order to estimate (13), we must specify a measure of the technical index as well as a measure of aggregate demand. Technical change is usually measured as a residual—as the change in output that is not explained by changes in labor and capital inputs. Thus,

$$\left(\frac{\Delta \mathrm{TG}}{\mathrm{TG}}\right)_t = \left(\frac{\Delta X}{X}\right)_t - W_1 \left(\frac{\Delta L}{L}\right)_t - W_2 \left(\frac{\Delta K}{K}\right)_t \tag{14}$$

where $(\Delta X/X)_t$, $(\Delta L/L)_t$, and $(\Delta K/K)_t$ are the relative changes of output, labor input and capital input, respectively, and $W_1$ and $W_2$ are the shares of labor and capital in the total output.[24]

Because (14) defines technical change as a function of change in output, it is inappropriate to use output as a measure of aggregate demand in (13) for purposes of estimation. Also, because firms will try to predict changes in aggregate demand by using observable variables, we can choose exogenous

[23] Schmookler, "Sources of Inventive Activity"; idem, *Invention and Economic Growth*.
[24] Since we use only a two-factor model, the term *output* in this context refers to value added.

variables which may be used by firms to predict output level and changes in output. Such variables are regarded as proxy variables for predicting the direction of aggregate demand.

Two variables commonly used in the literature to explain and predict changes in aggregate demand are change in money supply and change in the level of government expenditure. These two variables are of course closely associated with the monetary and fiscal policies of the overall economy.[25]

In addition to change in the money supply we have also used the level and changes in real money balances in the economy as the monetary variable. The relationship between monetary variables and aggregate demand has been analyzed by Milton Friedman, Christopher A. Sims and others.[26] We have also used these monetary variables in an analysis of the role of money in the production function.[27]

In order to analyze the effect of fiscal policy on the level and direction of aggregate demand we use the level and changes in real government expenditure on goods and services.

Finally, because the current level of a variable and recent changes in the level of that variable are not independent, we have used the lag level of both real money balances and real government expenditures, together with the recent rates of change of these two variables. The final empirical version of the model is written as follows:

$$\ln (TG)_t = \alpha_0 + \alpha_1 t + \alpha_2 \ln (RMPC)_{t-k} + \alpha_3 \ln (RGPC)_{t-k}$$
$$+ \sum_{t=0}^{k} \beta_i \left(\frac{\Delta M}{M}\right)_{t-i} + \sum_{t=0}^{k} \gamma_i \left(\frac{\Delta G}{G}\right)_{t-i} \tag{15}$$

where $t$ is the time trend variable, $RMPC$ is the level of real money balances per capita, $RGPC$ is real government expenditure per capita, $(\Delta M/M)$ and $(\Delta G/G)$ are the rates of change in $RMPC$ and $RGPC$, and $k$ is the number of periods of lags used in the regression. As $k$ has no specific theoretical value, we have used alternative values of $k$.

[25] For some discussion and a test of monetary and fiscal actions see Leonoll C. Andersen and Jerry L. Jordan, "Monetary and Fiscal Actions: A Test of their Relative Importance in Economic Stabilization," *Review of the Federal Reserve Bank of St. Louis* 50 (November 1968): 11–24.

[26] Milton Friedman, "A Monetary Theory of Nominal Income," *Journal of Political Economy* 79 (1971): 323–37: Christopher A. Sims, "Money, Income and Causality," *American Economic Review* 62 (1972): 540–52.

[27] Uri Ben-Zion and Vernon W. Ruttan, "Money in the Production Function: An Interpretation of Empirical Results," *Review of Economics and Statistics* 57, no. 2 (May 1975): 246–7. We can use nominal money balances to explain nominal income. This is advantageous because nominal money balances can be regarded as exogenous (see Sims, "Money, Income and Causality"). However, since nominal money supply affects both prices and real output, we use real money balances to approximate the effect on real output.

*Data and Results*

The empirical model suggested in the preceding section was tested using United States annual data for the period 1929–1969.

Technical change in a given period was calculated, according to equation (14), as the difference between actual rate of growth of real output and the explained measure of output. In this work we have used the *index of technological progress* (TG) that was calculated by L. R. Christensen and Dale W. Jorgensen.[28] The index is based on corrected measures of capital and labor inputs.

Data on money supply are taken from Milton Friedman and Anna Schwartz[29] (for 1925–1968) and from the survey of current business[30] (for 1968–1969). The population is that used in the *National Income and Product Accounts of the United States* (for 1929–1965)[31] and in *Business Statistics* for the later years.[32] As a price index we have used the implicit GNP deflator from Christensen and Jorgenson.[33]

The results of the estimation of (15), which are corrected for the first-order serial correlation, are given in table 9–1.[34] These results show that the levels and rates of growth of real balances have a significant positive effect on technical change. The variables associated with government expenditure are less significant, and only current change in government expenditure has a significant coefficient. In summary, however, the results support the prediction of the model with regard to the relationship between technical progress and changes in aggregate demand.

The data on the rate of change in monetary and fiscal variables indicate a significant correlation between these variables in a given period. Therefore, we have estimated (14) twice using first monetary and then fiscal variables as proxies for changes in aggregate demand.

Using the fiscal and monetary variables separately we have also extended the length of the lag from 3 to 7 years. The long lag is based on our assumption of the long and variable lag between the derived demand for invention and its realization in the form of technical progress. The results of the estimation, corrected for serial correlation, are given in tables 9–2 and 9–3, for monetary variables and for fiscal variables, respectively.

[28] L. R. Christensen and Dale W. Jorgenson, "Measuring the Performance of the Private Sector in the U.S. Economy 1929–1969," in *Measurement of Economic and Social Performance*, ed. M. Moss, Studies of Income and Wealth, vol. 38 (New York: Columbia University Press, 1973), pp. 233–351.

[29] Milton Friedman and Anna Schwartz, *Monetary Statistics of the United States* (New York: National Bureau of Economic Research, 1970).

[30] *Business Statistics* (Washington, D.C.: U.S. Department of Commerce, 1971).

[31] *The National Income and Product Accounts of the United States 1929–1965* (Washington, D.C.: U.S. Department of Commerce, 1966).

[32] *Business Statistics.*

[33] Christensen and Jorgenson, "Measuring the Performance of the Private Sector."

[34] The results in tables 9–1 and 9–2 were corrected for the first-order serial correlation using the Cochran–Orcutt iteration procedure.

TABLE 9-1. Relationship between index of technical change (TG) and monetary and fiscal variables in the United States, 1929-1969

| Independent Variable | Coefficients and $t$ Values |
|---|---|
| Constant | 0.398 |
| | (30.66) |
| Time | $0.265 \times 10^{-1}$ |
| | (22.07) |
| Real money per capita | 0.2201 |
| [ln $RMPC_{t-4}$] | (3.54) |
| Real government expenditures per capita | $0.156 \times 10^{-2}$ |
| [ln $RGPC_{t-4}$] | (−0.06) |
| Rates of changes in real money per capita | |
| [$DM0$][a] | 0.268 |
| | (2.72) |
| [$DM1$] | 0.375 |
| | (3.80) |
| [$DM2$] | 0.124 |
| | (1.15) |
| [$DM3$] | 0.124 |
| | (2.06) |
| Rates of changes in real government expenditures per capita | |
| [$DG0$][b] | $0.226 \times 10^{-1}$ |
| | (2.00) |
| [$DG1$] | $0.505 \times 10^{-2}$ |
| | (0.0327) |
| [$DG2$] | $-0.731 \times 10^{-2}$ |
| | (−0.38) |
| [$DG3$] | $0.129 \times 10^{-7}$ |
| | (0.56) |
| $R^2$ | 0.997 |
| $D.W.$ | 2.183 |

Note: Parentheses enclose $t$ values of coefficients.

[a] $DM0, \ldots, DM3$ denote $\left(\dfrac{\Delta M}{M}\right)_t, \ldots, \left(\dfrac{\Delta M}{M}\right)_{t-3}$

[b] $DG0, \ldots, DG3$ denote $\left(\dfrac{\Delta G}{G}\right)_t, \ldots, \left(\dfrac{\Delta G}{G}\right)_{t-3}$

The results indicate that both monetary and fiscal variables seem to have a strong influence on the rate of technical change and that the length of the lag between change in aggregate demand and technical progress is quite long. These results are consistent with our analysis.[35]

### Summary and Conclusion

In this chapter we have analyzed the relationship between growth in aggregate demand and the rate of technical change. Schmookler suggested

[35] While the results in the table indicate that monetary variables are more important than fiscal variables in determining technical change, more work may be necessary to justify such a conclusion.

TABLE 9–2. Relationship between index of technical change (TG) and monetary variables in the United States, 1929–1969

| Independent Variable | Coefficients and $t$ Values | Independent Variable | Coefficients and $t$ Values |
|---|---|---|---|
| Constant | 0.367 (100.68) | DM3 | 0.274 (3.91) |
| Time | $0.260 \times 10^{-1}$ (86.36) | DM4 | $0.966 \times 10^{-2}$ (0.16) |
| ln $RMPC_{t-8}$ | 0.208 (16.92) | DM5 | 0.209 (13.78) |
| $DM0^a$ | 0.390 (6.29) | DM6 | 0.198 (16.68) |
| DM1 | 0.320 (4.64) | DM7 | 0.213 (18.03) |
| DM2 | 0.142 (1.96) | $R^2$ D.W. | 0.9985 1.9421 |

Note: Parentheses enclose $t$ values of coefficients.

$^a$ $DM0, \ldots, DM7$ denote $\left(\dfrac{\Delta M}{M}\right)_t, \ldots, \left(\dfrac{\Delta M}{M}\right)_{t-7}$

TABLE 9–3. Relationship between index of technical change (TG) and fiscal variables in the United States, 1929–1969

| Independent Variable | Coefficients and $t$ Values | Independent Variable | Coefficients and $t$ Values |
|---|---|---|---|
| Constant | $-0.480$ (85.87) | DG3 | $0.7859 \times 10^{-1}$ (5.75) |
| Time | $0.2423 \times 10^{-1}$ (22.55) | DG4 | $0.7537 \times 10^{-1}$ (5.87) |
| ln $RGPC_{t-8}$ | $0.7839 \times 10^{-1}$ (4.82) | DG5 | $0.7106 \times 10^{-1}$ (5.08) |
| $DG0^a$ | $0.3502 \times 10^{-1}$ (2.48) | DG6 | $0.7515 \times 10^{-1}$ (5.05) |
| DG1 | $0.5162 \times 10^{-1}$ (4.20) | DG7 | $0.7693 \times 10^{-1}$ (4.91) |
| DG2 | $0.5114 \times 10^{-1}$ (3.86) | $R^2$ D.W. | 0.9957 1.4749 |

Note: Parentheses enclose $t$ values of coefficients.

$^a$ $DG0, \ldots, DG7$ denote $\left(\dfrac{\Delta G}{G}\right)_t, \ldots, \left(\dfrac{\Delta G}{G}\right)_{t-7}$

that the rate of technical change is responsive to the rate of growth in aggregate demand.[36] We first developed a formal model to test the Schmookler hypothesis. We then tested the model against United States data for the period 1929–1969. The results are consistent with the Schmookler hypothesis.

[36] Schmookler, *Invention and Economic Growth*; Schmookler, "Sources of Inventive Activity."

The rate of growth of aggregate demand explains a relatively large share of the variation in the rate of technical change in the United States economy. We did not test the effects of the rate of growth in aggregate demand on factor choice or on factor-saving bias in technical change. The manner in which labor and capital are conceptualized, as quasi-fixed factors of production, may have important implications with regard to the demand for factors of production and the inducement of factor-saving bias in technical change. We have not been able to explore these implications in this chapter.

TEN

# Biased Choice of Technology
# in Brazilian Agriculture

JOHN H. SANDERS AND VERNON W. RUTTAN

THIS chapter deals with the consequences of mechanization policy in
Brazil. The problems that arise in the transfer of mechanical technology are different from those encountered in transferring biological
technology. In chapter 6 it was stated that mechanical technology is far less
sensitive than biological technology to noneconomic environmental conditions. At the same time, because it requires sizeable capital investment and
because it is generally labor saving, mechanical technology is much more
sensitive to factor prices than are seed varieties and other components of
biological technology. For these reasons, it is appropriate to view mechanization as a process of diffusion that is responsive to changes in the relative
prices of capital and labor. This means that it is often more appropriate to
analyze the process of mechanization within the framework of a choice of
technology model than within the framework of an induced innovation
model.

It was the increasing price of labor that induced the invention of the
tractor and other mechanical equipment in the United States and Canada
during the first half of this century. In Europe, however, widespread use and
further development of the tractor were delayed until after the Second World
War, when rising wage rates led to a very rapid rate of technology diffusion.
This diffusion required only the adaptation of United States technology to

The research on which this chapter is based was supported by a Foreign Area Fellowship
and by a United States Agency for International Development grant to the Economic
Development Center of the University of Minnesota. The material presented here does
not necessarily reflect the view of either of these institutions. We are indebted to H. P.
Binswanger, J. L. Dillon, J. Ryan, R. G. Saylor, and A. Weber for substantive and
editorial suggestions.

European conditions and the establishment of local industrial capacity for the production of tractors.[1]

Today in less developed countries (LDCs) the situation is similar. Because of widespread diffusion of automobiles, buses, and trucks, most of these countries are capable of servicing mechanical equipment, and many have the capacity to produce it. Moreover, owing to the fairly low sensitivity of mechanical technology to noneconomic environmental conditions, in general only adaptive research and engineering are required. Adaptive research is not dependent on high-level scientific skills but, rather, on mechanical principles that have long been known and on skills that are widely diffused even in less developed countries.

As a consequence of the foregoing, the modest advances of mechanical technology in the LDCs can be explained not by a supply constraint but rather by the fact that low wage rates provide little incentive to adapt and adopt mechanical technology. Where mechanical innovations have been introduced in environments characterized by low wage rates, they have usually been of the yield-increasing type, such as irrigation and post-harvest processing or storage equipment. In the absence of large subsidies, the use of tractors has diffused rapidly only when induced by high or rising wage rates. Such rises are due either to the higher opportunity cost of labor in agriculture that arises from the more intensive cropping made possible by biological and irrigation advances—as in the Punjab—or to an increasingly strong urban demand for labor—as in Western Europe and Japan.

Since the Second World War, mechanization has taken place in Latin America at a more rapid rate than in most of the LDCs.[2] The resource allocation issues that arise in connection with the diffusion of mechanical technology are well illustrated by the case of Brazil. Government resources used to subsidize tractors and to subsidize domestic industrial capacity to produce tractors must be diverted from other uses such as the creation of yield-increasing biological technology. A decision to subsidize tractors and to protect the tractor industry, therefore, often represents an implicit decision to forego the benefits of yield-increasing investments.

This chapter is an attempt to describe the consequences of the price-distorting mechanization policies that have been followed by Brazil particularly since 1960. In the first section, the responsiveness of tractor adoption

[1] This time sequence of original and adaptive mechanical research is substantiated by patent statistics from North America and Europe presented in James K. Boyce and Robert E. Evenson, *National and International Agricultural Research & Extension Programs* (New York: Agricultural Development Council, Inc., 1975).

In Japan the spread of tractor use occurred only in the mid-1950s. Here more adaptive research and engineering were required in order to fit the new technology to Japan's typically small farms.

[2] For a broader description of Latin American mechanization, see K. C. Abercrombie, "Agricultural Mechanization in Latin America," *International Labor Review* 106 (July 1972): 11–45.

to prices and subsidized credit is tested empirically. The second section develops a model of resource allocation for the benefit of the country's larger farms and its industrial center that appears to be consistent with policies pursued by Brazil. It is shown that one effect of the subsidization of tractor mechanization was to facilitate a shift in the comparative advantage in sugarcane production from the depressed Northeast region, which had low wage rates, to the more developed regions of the South, where wages were rising. A similar shift in comparative advantage from small to large farms is discussed.

Mechanization on the Brazilian frontier raises some special issues, and for this reason we devote the third section of this chapter to a discussion of its effects and future implications. Mechanization has been occurring more rapidly on the frontier than anywhere else in the country. Moreover, besides substituting for labor, mechanization may increase yields in regions where land preparation is extremely difficult. The frontier has abundant land for potential crop expansion, and in many areas its heavy soils require high levels of power input for effective land preparation. The chapter concludes with a discussion of the policy implications of all the above aspects of the mechanization process in Brazil.

*Factor Price Distortions, Tractor Sales, and Labor Use*

The rapid increase in the use of tractors in Brazil is a post-World War II phenomenon. In 1950 there were only 8,372 operative tractors in Brazil, although tractors had been used in Rio Grande do Sul and São Paulo as early as the 1920s. Since the 1950s Brazilian mechanization has proceeded at a rapid rate. By 1970 the number of operative tractors had reached 165,870.[3]

The government has stimulated mechanization in various ways, including the support of preferential exchange rates during the 1950s. However, the primary governmental instrument has been subsidized credit with long repayment periods and interest rates below the inflation rates (see table 10–1). These credits to stimulate tractor purchases were especially important after 1960, when a Brazilian tractor industry was established and imports were gradually reduced to very small numbers. The close relationship between subsidized credit and tractor sales is illustrated in figure 10–1. This relationship was tested statistically, using a demand-for-tractors equation that

[3] John H. Sanders, "Mechanization and Employment in Brazilian Agriculture, 1950–1971" (Ph.D. diss., University of Minnesota, 1973), pp. 10, 12. For the 1970 data, see *Censo Agropecuario Brasil, VIII Recenseamento Geral–1970*, vol. 3 (Rio de Janeiro: Fundação Instituto Brasileiro de Geografia e Estatistica, 1975), p. 44. Note that all 1970 tractor data reported in Sanders, "Mechanization and Employment" (which were taken from the Preliminary Census), were revised for the present chapter in accordance with the foregoing final Census.

TABLE 10-1. Tractor financing and terms, 1960–1971

| Year | Tractor Financing by Bank of Brazil[a] Real Value (million 1971 cruzeiros) | Interest Rate | Commercial Bank Interest Rate[b] | Rate of Inflation[c] |
|---|---|---|---|---|
| 1960 | ... | ... | 19.6 | 26.3 |
| 1961 | 90.2 | 8 | 22.3 | 33.3 |
| 1962 | 186 | 9 | 25.1 | 54.8 |
| 1963 | 205 | 11 | 30.5 | 78.0 |
| 1964 | 248 | 11 | 33.3 | 87.8 |
| 1965 | 192 | 17.25 | 34.7 | 55.4 |
| 1966 | 256 | 17 | 34.9 | 38.8 |
| 1967 | 206 | 18 | 34.1 | 27.0 |
| 1968 | 249 | 15 | 33.7 | 28.1 |
| 1969 | 219 | 15 | 30.9 | 21.7 |
| 1970 | 255 | 15 | ... | 19.8 |
| 1971 | 349 | 15 | ... | 19.5 |

Source: John H. Sanders, "Mechanization and Employment in Brazilian Agriculture, 1950–1971" (Ph.D. diss., University of Minnesota, 1973), pp. 11, 32, 33.

[a] The Bank of Brazil was the predominant lender at subsidized rates, although a limited amount of credit was provided by several other banks in which federal or state governments were shareholders. The nominal value of credits was deflated with the Getulio Vargas Institute Index of Domestic Prices (Index no. 2), with 1971 as the base year.

[b] These data on real commercial bank interest rates were estimated in L. E. Christoffersen, "Taxas de juros e a estrutura de um sistema de bancos commerçiais em condições inflacionarios, o caso do Brasil," *Revista Brasileira de Economia* 23 (June 1969). Christoffersen made these estimates for the International Bank for Reconstruction and Development based upon his interviews with various banks.

[c] GDP Implicit Price Deflator.

included tractor prices relative to crop prices, tractor prices relative to the wage rate, the real value of the interest rate of the Bank of Brazil adjusted for inflation, and tractor stock lagged by one year. In a number of model specifications, the tractor finance variable was always highly significant.[4]

It is clear from the above that government policy, especially when it reduced the price of capital, must have had an important effect upon the mechanization process. If the elasticity of substitution between machinery and labor in Brazilian agriculture were low, the primary effect of this policy would be to reduce production costs at the farm level and to increase output at the sector level. Conversely, if the elasticity of substitution between machinery and labor were high, then subsidizing credit would have a significant labor replacement effect.

[4] See Sanders, "Mechanization and Employment," pp. 12–29. The original equation was modified in later unpublished work by Fernando Homen de Melo, in which the specification of the tractor finance variable was improved. The results show an increased tractor price elasticity as compared with that discussed in Sanders, "Mechanization and Employment."

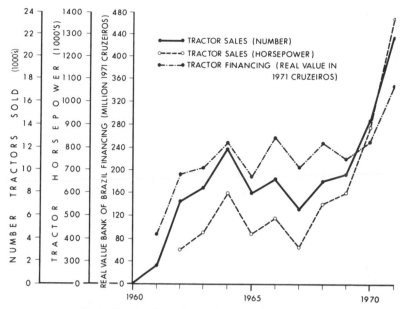

FIG. 10–1. Tractor financing and domestic tractor sales in Brazil, 1960–1971. [Source: John H. Sanders, "Mechanization and Employment in Brazilian Agriculture, 1950–1971" (Ph.D. diss., University of Minnesota, 1973), pp. 32, 139, 140, 190. Note: "Tractor sales" includes domestic production only. Tractor imports were permitted when there was no "national similar"; thus only a small number of imports were financed. Imports declined very rapidly after 1961.]

The tests for the availability of alternative technologies are both intuitive and of a more rigorous, quantitative nature. Agricultural production practices encountered in Brazil range from planting with only a stick or a hoe to the highly mechanized, wheat-soybean operations of Rio Grande do Sul, Paraná, São Paulo, and Mato Grosso. At a more formal level we can test the sensitivity of the farm-level choice of technologies (or the capital–labor ratios) to changes in the price of machinery relative to labor. This sensitivity was ascertained in the present study by estimating the elasticity of substitution between machinery and labor. Tractors were used as proxy for all machinery. The elasticity of substitution was found to be very high, ranging from 1.5 in 1950 to 1.9 in 1960.[5] The observation units were the Brazilian

[5] The estimated demand function was derived from a two-stage CES production function of the following type:

$$Y = a[\alpha(E_L L)^{-p} + (1 - \alpha)(E_K K)^{-p}]^{-1/p}$$

In this equation, $L$ and $K$ are labor and land, respectively, and $E_L$ and $E_K$ are labor-substituting and land-substituting inputs. The labor-substituting inputs were principally machinery; the primary land-substituting inputs were fertilizer, fertilizer-responsive varieties, and other agricultural chemicals, excluding herbicides. The potential yield

TABLE 10–2. Average horsepower per four-wheel tractor in Brazil and the United States, 1960–1971

| Year | Brazil | United States | Year | Brazil | United States |
|------|--------|---------------|------|--------|---------------|
| 1960 | 54.1 | 50.5 | 1966 | 53.2 | 65.9 |
| 1961 | 52.9 | 53.8 | 1967 | 55.5 | 68.2 |
| 1962 | 48.0 | 56.0 | 1968 | 60.4 | 69.5 |
| 1963 | 46.5 | 58.0 | 1969 | 62.3 | 72.8 |
| 1964 | 50.2 | 59.3 | 1970 | 62.3 | 72.4 |
| 1965 | 53.5 | 63.1 | 1971 | 63.1 | 76.9 |

Sources: Brazil: Associação Nacional dos Fabricantes de Veículos Automotores (ANFAVEA), "A racionalização da industria de tratores e fundamental para a tecnifição da nossa agricultura—passo decisivo na retomada do desenvolvimento economico do Pais," *Separata de Industria Automotiva*, no. 106 (April 1968), and other industry data. United States: Paul E. Strickler, Agricultural Economist, Production Resources Branch, Farm Production Economics Division, Economic Research Service, U.S. Department of Agriculture, July 1971.

Notes: These data exclude microtractors. For Brazil, data are based on production figures; for the United States, data are based on sales figures. However, the difference between the two types of data is negligible because there is little holding of inventory in the industry.

states. These high elasticity estimates were not only intuitively plausible but also remarkably consistent with those of other studies that used farm-level and regional data.[6]

There has also been a rapid increase in Brazil in the proportion of tractors with higher horsepower. Table 10–2 shows that, with a slight lag, Brazilian use of tractors closely followed the shift to heavier machines in American agriculture during the 1960s. Brazilian production of light tractors (less than 40 horsepower) declined steadily from 1963 and ceased entirely in 1970.[7]

In summary, it is clear that in Brazil farmers confronted tractor prices that were distorted by the negative price of credit. There is also evidence that labor prices were biased upward by minimum-wage policies.[8] Since capital–labor ratios in Brazilian agriculture were very sensitive to relative prices, a substantial impetus toward labor substitution was created. Moreover, at the

effect of machinery, that is, its possible land-substituting effect, will be discussed later in the chapter. For more details on the derivation of the above equation and its estimation, see Sanders, "Mechanization and Employment," pp. 39–63.

[6] Wayne R. Thirsk, "Factor Substitution in Colombian Agriculture," *American Journal of Agricultural Economics* 56, no. 1 (February 1974): 73–85. See also the other studies cited by Thirsk.

[7] See Sanders, "Mechanization and Employment," p. 189. Production of microtractors and motorized cultivators was continued. These are used principally for vegetable and grape production, particularly in São Paulo. Manufacture of tractors of low horsepower began again, however, when in December 1975 Agrale began producing light tractors. See *Noticias de Associação Nacional dos Fabricantes de Veículos Automotores*, São Paulo, Brazil, December 1975.

[8] See R. Gerald Saylor, "An Analysis of the Demand for and Supply of Farm Labor in the State of São Paulo" (Paper presented at the Ohio State University Conference on Brazilian Agricultural Development, Columbus, Ohio, January 1975), p. 12.

same time a shift toward heavier tractors occurred within the tractor industry. In a country where a large percentage of the labor force is employed in agriculture (44 percent in 1970)[9] and where rates of migration from rural to urban areas are high, these two substitutions seem to be inefficient policy choices. In the next two sections two hypotheses to explain these choices will be suggested and evaluated.

### Political Power and Technology Choice

The substitution of machinery or power for labor and for land in Brazilian agriculture has been influenced by both regional and farm-size factors. We will consider the regional factor first. As table 10–3 indicates, Brazilian mechanization has been concentrated most heavily in the southern and central western states, especially in São Paulo and Rio Grande do Sul. In 1970, almost two-thirds of total tractor stock was located in these two states.

In the Brazilian Northeast, with its concentration of low-income inhabitants and scarcity of land with adequate, regular rainfall, there has been little mechanization. In the South, especially in the rural areas of the Belo Horizonte–Rio de Janeiro–São Paulo industrial center, rapid industrial growth has encouraged both substantial rural–urban migration within and into this area and an increasing demand for agricultural products for food and for industrial use. There has been large-scale migration from the Northeast to the South. This has partially replaced the stream of rural emigrants from the older agricultural areas such as São Paulo and Minas Gerais and has facilitated the settlement of agricultural frontier areas that have access to this industrial center, especially in Paraná, Goiás, and Mato Grosso.[10]

There are certain inefficiencies in the migration process. The industrial center has felt burdened by an imported work force that has very low levels of human capital investment in terms of health and of basic and applied education. In the advanced industrial area and at its frontier there has been a tendency in agriculture to substitute machines for this labor force, leaving the Northeast to resolve its own human capital problems. Why? Much of the progress that has occurred in agriculture in São Paulo, Rio Grande do Sul,

[9] Calculated from "O censo demografico de 1970," *Conjuntura Economica* 26 (February 1972): 151.

[10] D. H. Graham, "Divergent and Convergent Regional Income Growth and Internal Migration in Brazil—1940–1960," *Economic Development and Cultural Change* 18, no. 3 (April 1970): 370; G. Edward Schuh, "Algumas observações sobre o desenvolvimento da agricultura no Brasil," *Revista Brasileira de Economia* 26, no. 4 (October–December 1972): 204–26; John H. Sanders and Frederick L. Bein, "Agricultural Development on the Brazilian Frontier, Southern Mato Grosso," *Economic Development and Cultural Change* 24, (April 1976): 593–610: William H. Nicholls, "The Brazilian Food Supply: Problems and Prospects," *Economic Development and Cultural Change* 19, no. 3 (April 1971): 378–90.

TABLE 10–3. Tractor–labor ratios and distribution of tractor stock in Brazilian states, 1950–1970

| State[a] | Numbers of Tractors per 1,000 Agricultural Workers[b] | | | Percentage of Total Tractor Stock in Brazil | | |
|---|---|---|---|---|---|---|
| | 1950 | 1960 | 1970 | 1950 | 1960 | 1970 |
| *South and Central West Regions* | | | | | | |
| São Paulo | 2.5 | 15.7 | 43.5 | 45.6 | 44.3 | 39.6 |
| Rio Grande do Sul | 2.10 | 11.4 | 27.6 | 26.8 | 24.7 | 24.1 |
| Rio de Janeiro | 1.7 | 6.3 | 15.7 | 6.2 | 2.7 | 2.3 |
| Mato Grosso | 0.6 | 4.5 | 11.8 | 0.6 | 1.4 | 2.6 |
| Goiás[c] | 0.3 | 2.7 | 10.4 | 1.1 | 2.2 | 3.4 |
| Guanabara | 3.5 | 6.0 | 9.7 | n.s. | n.s. | n.s. |
| Paraná | 0.6 | 4.0 | 9.4 | 3.3 | 8.4 | 11.2 |
| Santa Catarina | 0.1 | 1.9 | 7.9 | 0.5 | 1.8 | 3.7 |
| Minas Gerais | 0.4 | 2.3 | 4.4 | 9.1 | 7.8 | 5.6 |
| *Northeast Region* | | | | | | |
| Alagoas | 0.1 | 0.9 | 2.2 | n.s. | n.s. | n.s. |
| Rio Grande do Norte | 0.07 | 1.1 | 1.9 | n.s. | n.s. | n.s. |
| Sergipe | 0.3 | 0.3 | 1.6 | n.s. | n.s. | n s. |
| Pernambuco | 0.2 | 0.8 | 1.15 | 1.7 | 1.6 | 0.8 |
| Paraiba | 0.1 | 0.8 | 1.4 | n.s. | n.s. | n.s. |
| Bahía | 0.06 | 0.3 | 0.9 | 1.0 | 0.9 | 1.1 |
| Ceará | 0.06 | 0.3 | 0.8 | n.s. | n.s. | n.s. |
| Piaui | 0.1 | 0.2 | 0.5 | n.s. | n.s. | n.s. |
| Maranhão | 0.04 | 0.05 | 0.1 | n.s. | n.s. | n.s. |

Source: *Censo Agropecuario, VIII Recenseamento Geral–1970* (Rio de Janeiro: Fundação Instituto Brasileiro de Geografia e Estatistica, 1975). Separate, by-state volumes of this reference were used for all states except São Paulo, Minas Gerais, Pernambuco, and Maranhão. At the last revision of this paper, because the volumes for the latter states had not yet been published, it was necessary to utilize *Dados Preliminares Gerais do Censo Agropecuario–VIII Recenseamento Geral–1970, Região Centro-Oeste* (Rio de Janeiro: Fundação Instituto Brasileiro de Geografia e Estatistica, April 1972), pp. 18, 31. The preliminary census material included tractor and labor data for the 1950 and 1960 Censuses.

Note: n.s. = not significant. Data on the percentage of tractor stock are presented for the 10 most mechanized states only. For each of the remaining 8 states the relevant figures are less than one percent. The total numbers of tractors in Brazil for the years 1950, 1960 and 1970 were 8,372, 61,324, and 165,870, respectively.

[a] From the states traditionally considered the East, only Espírito Santo has been deleted. Because of their proximity to the major industrial center of the South, Rio de Janeiro, Guanabara, and Minas Gerais were included in the South Region. Pará and Amazonas of the North have been excluded.

[b] "Agricultural workers" means total agricultural labor force.

[c] Includes the Federal District.

and on the frontier has been characterized by a large-farm development pattern. Obtaining and using seasonal labor is much more difficult for the large than for the small farm unit because the latter is better able to rely on family labor. Evidence in support of this greater difficulty of substitution of labor for capital, by transferring labor from small farms to large farms,

TABLE 10-4. Sugarcane production costs and labor use in two regions of Brazil

| Region | Production Costs per Ton (in cruzeiros) | Labor Costs per Hectare (in cruzeiros) | Labor Use per Hectare (in man-days) |
|---|---|---|---|
| São Paulo (South) | 3,341 | 631 | 37.4 |
| Pernambuco (Northeast) | 4,541 | 997 | 98.2 |

Source: "Pesquisa sobre condições e custos de produção de lavoura canavieira," *Revista Brasileira de Economia* 19 (October–December 1965): 37–40.

is provided by the lower elasticity of substitution between labor and capital in regions where large farms are concentrated. In 1960, the São Paulo estimate of the elasticity of substitution was 0.4, whereas the all-Brazil estimate was 1.9.[11] Because of this low elasticity of substitution, large farms can be expected to be much more interested in subsidies to mechanization than in governmental measures to facilitate the efficiency of labor migration between regions.

Thus, one explanation for the rapid growth of mechanization in the South is that this region has been able, through its substantial political power, to influence the government to subsidize mechanical technology as a substitute for labor, the region's—and especially the large farm's—relatively scarce factor. Subsidizing agricultural machinery in the industrial area would be expected to offset the lower labor costs in the depressed region, the Northeast. Consider the case of the Northeast's most important crops, sugarcane and cotton, which have traditionally been produced in that region in a labor-intensive manner. We hypothesize that one effect of subsidized mechanization has been to facilitate a shift of the comparative advantage in the production of these crops from the Northeast to the South.[12] Table 10-4 shows that in Pernambuco, in the Northeast, labor was a more important component of the

[11] See Sanders, "Mechanization and Employment," p. 61. This tendency of large farmers to prefer machinery over labor imported from other regions has been observed also in the Punjab, where agricultural development has been occurring recently at a rapid rate. See C. H. Hanumantha Rao, "Farm Mechanization in a Labour Abundant Economy," *Economic and Political Weekly* 7, no. 5–7 (February 1972): 397.

[12] The rise in importance of cane and cotton in the economy of the South preceded the Second World War. Between 1920 and 1940 the number of coffee trees in São Paulo increased from 823 to 1,093 million, but cotton and cane production increased at an even faster rate, from 105 to 841 thousand tons of cotton, and from 1.1 to 2.2 million tons of sugar. See *Censo Agricola, VI Recenseamento Geral do Brasil, 1950* (Rio de Janeiro: Fundação Instituto Brasileira de Estatistica e Geografia, 1956), pp. 134, 135.

Werner Baer reported a similar regional income-distribution effect of Brazilian industrialization policy operating in favor of the South to the detriment of the Northeast. "The industrialization policy of the government has thus caused a substantial transfer of assets to the South, mitigating the amount of regional income distribution achieved through the fiscal system." W. Baer, "Regional Inequality and Economic Growth in Brazil," *Economic Development and Cultural Change* 12, no. 3 (April 1964), p. 284. The tax incentive programs of SUDENE (Superintendencia do Desenvolvimento do Nordeste), intended to encourage capital formation for Northeastern industry, may have modified this situation during the last several years.

TABLE 10–5. Shifts in concentration of sugarcane and cotton production between the Northeast and the South, 1950–1973 (in thousand tons)

| | Sugarcane | | | Cotton | | |
|---|---|---|---|---|---|---|
| | | South | | | South | |
| Year | Northeast | All | São Paulo | Northeast | All | São Paulo |
| 1950 | 13,727 | 12,981 | 6,914 | 477 | 691 | 405 |
| 1955 | 16,819 | 18,017 | 10,936 | 493 | 755 | 387 |
| 1960 | 20,235 | 29,206 | 19,896 | 718 | 885 | 641 |
| 1965 | 24,886 | 42,014 | 29,476 | 853 | 1,128 | 626 |
| 1970 | 26,900 | 40,146 | 30,357 | 517[a] | 1,436 | 708 |
| 1973 | 37,147 | 46,424 | 38,296 | 884 | 1,370 | 612 |

Source: *Anuario Estatistico do Brasil* (Rio de Janeiro: Instituto Brasileiro de Estatistica e Geografia), various years. For the Northeast: unpublished data from the Bank of the Northeast for all years except 1973, for which *Anuario Estatistico* was used.

Note: "Northeast" here includes Maranhão, as it does by conventional definition. "South" includes the Central Western frontier as well as São Paulo, Paraná, Minas Gerais, Mato Grosso, and Goiás. Because of climatic restrictions on the expansion of sugarcane and cotton production, states south of Paraná are not included.

[a] Although most of the sugarcane crop is grown outside of the area typically affected by severe lack of rainfall, or the "drought polygon," most cotton is grown within this area. As a result, cotton production has declined abruptly in years of drought, such as 1970.

total cost of sugarcane production and fewer operations were mechanized than in São Paulo. Table 10–5 illustrates a continuing shift in the concentration of production of sugarcane from the Northeast to the South since 1950. In 1950, sugarcane production in São Paulo was half that in the Northeast. By 1973, São Paulo alone was producing more sugarcane than the entire Northeast region. This shift in production advantage occurred at the same time that the South, especially the São Paulo sugar-producing region, was experiencing rapid agricultural mechanization.[13]

In cotton production, the relative and absolute growth of the South was also faster than that of the Northeast, but the difference is not so dramatic as in the case of sugarcane. This slower shift of the comparative advantage in cotton production from North to South probably reflects both difficulties

[13] Production of sugar for export is controlled by the Brazilian Sugar Institute [Instituto do Açúcar e do Álcool (IAA)]. Recently, a higher price has been maintained for Northeastern than for São Paulo sugar. This price differential has not been sufficient to compensate for the differences in subsidies received and in other advantages of production between the South and the Northeast.

The following studies document the importance of mechanization in the large-scale sugar operations of São Paulo: H. G. Hughes, "Economic Analysis of Sugarcane Production in São Paulo, Brazil" (Ph.D. diss., University of Missouri, 1971); R. Alcantara and A. A. Prato, "Returns to Scale and Input Elasticities for Sugarcane: The Case of São Paulo, Brazil," *American Journal of Agricultural Economics* 55, no. 4 (November 1973): 577–83; and O. J. T. Ettori et al., "Custo de produção de cana industrial pelos fornecedores cotistas em São Paulo," *Agricultura em São Paulo* 15 (1949): 33–54. The latter two studies report lower per-unit production costs for the larger mechanized farms. Neither mentions the preferential subsidies, particularly on machinery but on other inputs as well, that are received by the larger, more mechanized producers.

in mechanizing the harvest and unstable international markets. Goiás cotton production, which is largely mechanized, soared from 26,000 to 302,000 tons between 1968 and 1972 and then fell again to 60,000 tons in 1975; during this same period, cotton production in Northeastern states such as Ceará and Rio Grande do Norte, where traditional methods are used, has declined.[14]

We would expect a shift in production advantage similar to the shift among regions to occur between farms of different sizes. The smaller farm is likely to have an advantage over the larger in the production of labor-intensive commodities. On large farms the real cost of labor would be expected to be above the current wage rate because of the extra cost of finding and managing a large temporary labor force, especially for critical seasonal operations that must be performed rapidly.[15] Moreover, in good years large farmers face the risk of substantially increased seasonal wage rates in areas where they depend upon hired labor from small farms for harvesting. When the harvest of all is increased, the marginal value product of small farmers on their own properties is increased. The large producer must either pay premium rates or wait until small farmers finish their own harvest. If he chooses to wait, he increases his risks in the event climatic conditions necessitate rapid harvesting. The implications of the above are repeatedly seen in rural Brazil. In the absence of mechanization, medium and large farmers devote more of their land and other inputs to extensive activities, such as raising beef cattle, than do small farmers.[16] In years of good cotton harvests in the Northeast, daily wage rates increase rapidly, and medium to

[14] Goiás has been producing annual cotton, with high input use and, generally, a mechanized harvest. Since the United States Civil War, Ceará and Rio Grande do Norte have been producing mainly tree cotton, at very low input levels. If cotton had been more profitable, and if more effort had been devoted to varietal development with the aim of achieving uniform maturation and defoliation, the regional shift in cotton would probably have been as dramatic as that in sugarcane. (Unpublished data from the Brazilian Ministry of Agriculture.)

[15] Rao makes the same observation for Indian agriculture: "Unlike for a small farmer, who contributes own labour on the farm, labour forms a paid-out cost for a large farmer. The real cost of draft power for large farms is higher still, owing to managerial and supervisory costs." Rao, "Farm Mechanization," p. 397.

Note that if a large farmer attempts to resolve this problem by hiring a large, permanent workforce, he will be faced with an excess labor situation in nonpeak periods. His ability to level out labor demand is often constrained by weather conditions. Scott and Smyth found a positive correlation between farm size and wage rates in their study of mechanization in Western Europe. See H. G. Scott and D. J. Smyth, *Demand for Farm Machinery—Western Europe*, Study no. 9 (Ottawa: Royal Commission on Farm Machinery, Queens Printer, 1970).

Cline argues that in many developing countries there is a dualistic labor market. Because of the cost of a job search, the small farmer utilizes his family labor beyond the point at which the marginal value product equals the going wage. See W. R. Cline, "Interrelationships Between Agricultural Strategy and Rural Income Distribution," *Food Research Institute Studies in Agricultural Economics, Trade and Development* 12, no. 2 (1973): 144–7.

[16] J. J. de C. Engler, "Alternative Enterprise Combinations Under Various Price Policies on Wheat and Cattle Farms in Southern Brazil" (Ph.D. diss., Ohio State University, 1971); J. N. Stitzlein, "The Economics of Agricultural Mechanization in

large farmers complain of labor shortages and talk of the necessity to mechanize.

In this section we have discussed the differential impact of credit subsidies for tractors among regions and between farm sizes. The resultant factor-price distortions[17] have encouraged the substitution of capital for labor and a shift in production from the more labor-intensive farms and regions to those farms and regions where labor costs were originally much higher. These policies have also contributed to the widening of income disparities among regions and income groups.[18] In the next section of this chapter we will examine the farm-level effects of mechanization on the frontier region, where the rate of mechanization is more rapid than anywhere else in Brazil.

## Mechanization on the Brazilian Frontier*

In discussing the effects of mechanization policy in the South and Northeast regions of Brazil we have considered the Central West an extension of the South. It is on the fast-developing frontier of this Central West region

Southern Brazil" (Ph.D. diss., Ohio State University 1974); R. L. Baur, "Description of Capital and Technology Changes at the Farm Level in Four Southern Brazil Regions: 1960–1969" (Ph.D. diss., Ohio State University, 1974).

[17] See G. W. Smith, "Brazilian Agricultural Policy, 1950–1967," *The Economy of Brazil*, ed. H. S. Ellis (Berkeley: University of California Press, 1969), pp. 226–41 for a summary of the various types of subsidies employed in Brazilian agricultural policy.

[18] Direct confirmation of this effect of mechanization on income distribution in Brazil is lacking even though there have been many studies of income distribution. For an elaboration of the argument and for reports of several Asian empirical studies document-ing these effects, see W. R. Cline, "Rural Income Distribution," pp. 151, 154, 155.

The United Nations and other sources have reported that in 1960 income concentra-tion in Brazil was greater than it was in many other Latin American countries and in most developed countries. From 1960 to 1970, although income concentration increased in Brazil, it decreased in agriculture. However, sectoral income differences between agricultural and nonagricultural activities increased. These findings are consistent with the results we would expect from the release of labor from agriculture by increased mechanization. Extensive rural-rural migration throughout the decade led to increased income for many migrants. Rural-rural and rural-urban migration would explain in part the decrease in income concentration within agriculture during this period.

See Economic Commission for Latin America, *Income Distribution in Latin America* (New York: United Nations, 1971), pp. 69–78; A. Fishlow, "Brazilian Size Distribution of Income," *American Economic Review* 62 (May 1972): 391–403; R. Hoffman and J. C. Duarte, "A distribuição da renda no Brasil," *Revista da Administração de Empresas* 12 (June 1972): 46–67; Graham, "Regional Income Growth," pp. 376–9; D. H. Graham and S. B. de Holanda Filho, *Migration, Regional and Urban Growth and Development in Brazil: A Selective Analysis of the Historical Record: 1872–1970*, vol. 1 (São Paulo: Universidade de São Paulo, Instituto de Pesquisas Economicas, 1971); C. G. Langoni, *Distribuição da renda e desenvolvimento economico do Brasil* (Rio de Janeiro: Editora Expressão e Cultura, 1973); G. F. Patrick and J. J. de Carvalho Filho, *Low Income Groups in Brazilian Agriculture: A Progress Report*, Station Bulletin no. 79 (Lafayette, Indiana: Purdue University, Department of Agricultural Economics, April 1975); and G. E. Schuh, "The Income Problem in Brazilian Agriculture," mimeographed (Lafayette, Indiana: Purdue University, Department of Agricultural Economics, 1974).

* This section has been adapated from John H. Sanders and Frederick L. Bein,

that the most rapid mechanization in Brazil has occurred. In order to explore the possibility that on the frontier the labor-substituting effect of mechanization may be less important than the output-expanding effect, we need to examine these effects at the firm level. Specifically, does machinery increase yields and thereby eliminate a bottleneck that has held back an increase in production in regions with difficult soil preparation?

The three states that had agricultural frontiers in 1950 and in which the highest immigration rates occurred between 1950 and 1970 are Paraná, Goiás, and Mato Grosso. In table 10–6, mechanization in these states is compared with that of São Paulo and Rio Grande do Sul, the states in which agriculture is most highly mechanized. The most rapid rates of growth in mechanization, crop production, and area cultivated in Brazil during the period 1950–1970 occurred in these frontier states.[19]

In order to evaluate the farm-level explanations for mechanization we will look at two specific regions on the frontier in Mato Grosso. In this state the number of tractors increased from 50 in 1950 to 4,386 in 1970. The most common explanations for mechanization on the frontier are a shortage of labor, generally in one or more critical seasonal operations, and a large power requirement for land preparation, particularly of soils with heavier texture. In the early process of agricultural development, when a large proportion of the work force is still in agriculture, the first of these explanations holds primarily for the large farms. For these larger farms, as we have already noted, the possibility of substituting labor and animal power for machinery is more limited. Because there has been large-scale immigration of labor into the frontier region, and because wages still vary considerably among regions,[20] the long-run supply elasticity of low-wage labor is expected to be relatively high for the region. Our interest here is in evaluating the importance of the second reason for mechanization—its yield effect—rather than the seasonal labor bottleneck confronted by medium and large farmers. Thus our sample was drawn from two groups of small farmers who worked different soil types. It is hypothesized that mechanization (1) will have a high rate of return per hectare in areas with heavier-texture soils and (2) will be less used in areas with lighter-texture soils. Note that because returns are considered on a per hectare basis, area expansion per worker—the primary effect associated with mechanization—is held constant.

---

"Agricultural Development on the Brazilian Frontier, Southern Mato Grosso," *Economic Development and Cultural Change* 24 (April 1976): 593–610, and appears here by permission of The University of Chicago Press. (© 1976 by the University of Chicago Press. All rights reserved.)

[19] Because aggregate yields declined in these states, the output increases came from expansion of the area cultivated. This area expansion resulted from both mechanization and rapid immigration. See Sanders and Bein, "Agricultural Development," pp. 593–5.

[20] See Sanders, "Mechanization and Employment," pp. 146–52. For 1970 wage data see *Censo Agropecuario*.

TABLE 10-6. Mechanization in the frontier and capital-intensive states of Brazil and a comparison of tractor-labor ratios in Brazil and the United States

| State/Country | Number of Tractors in State | | | Percent of Total Number of Tractors in Country | | | Tractor/Labor Ratio[a] | | |
|---|---|---|---|---|---|---|---|---|---|
| | 1950 | 1960 | 1970 | 1950 | 1960 | 1970 | 1950 | 1960 | 1970 |
| *Frontier states* | | | | | | | | | |
| Paraná | 280 | 5,181 | 18,619 | 3.3 | 8.4 | 11.2 | 0.6 | 4.0 | 9.4 |
| Goiás | 89 | 1,356 | 5,692 | 1.1 | 2.2 | 3.4 | 0.3 | 2.7 | 10.4 |
| Mato Grosso | 50 | 838 | 4,386 | 0.6 | 1.4 | 2.6 | 0.6 | 4.5 | 11.8 |
| *Capital-intensive agricultural states* | | | | | | | | | |
| São Paulo | 3,819 | 27,176 | 65,731 | 45.6 | 44.3 | 39.6 | 2.5 | 15.7 | 43.5 |
| Rio Grande do Sul | 2,245 | 15,169 | 39,993 | 26.8 | 24.7 | 24.1 | 2.1 | 11.4 | 27.6 |
| Brazil | | | | | | | 0.7 | 3.9 | 9.4 |
| United States | | | | | | | 360 | 720 | 1,205 |

Sources: Brazil, all states except São Paulo: *Censo Agropecuario, Brasil, VIII Recenseamento Geral–1970* (Rio de Janeiro: Fundação Instituto Brasileiro de Geografia e Estatistica, 1975), pp. 26, 44. São Paulo: Preliminary census results. United States: *Changes in Farm Production and Efficiency: A Summary Report*, Statistical Bulletin no. 233 (Washington, D.C.: U.S. Department of Agriculture, Economic Research Service, June 1972), pp. 22, 29.

Note: Tractors include all tractors used in agriculture, with no weighting by type of tractor. Labor is defined as the entire agricultural labor force, including seasonal labor.

[a] Determined by dividing the total number of tractors by 1,000 agricultural workers.

The test of these interrelated hypotheses proceeds in two stages. First, farmers' reasons for mechanizing are summarized and the rate of return estimated for a *cerrado* (heavier-texture soil) area. Then a comparison is made between the mechanization levels of two similar agricultural areas that have substantial differences in soil quality. Farm interview data used are from two agricultural colonies in southern Mato Grosso that have similar land-holding systems and cropping patterns.

Of the 66 farmers in Terenos, Mato Grosso, and the surrounding area who work an average crop area of 10.9 hectares, only four used animal power for land preparation. The rest used machinery on a custom rental basis or machinery lent by the landlord. Only the land preparation operation was mechanized. In Terenos, farmers stated that mechanized land preparation was necessary owing to the difficulty of working the *cerrado* after the long, dry season. The planting season stretches from October through December, after five to seven months of dry season. Because animal power cannot be used until after the first rains, one advantage of mechanical land preparation is that soil can be broken prior to the rains, thus improving water absorption and facilitating more rapid planting.

Before using animal power it is necessary to cut or burn the weeds and to remove some roots and clods. Both of these operations can be avoided by using mechanical power. Moreover, the farmers of Terenos claimed that animals, with the implements used locally, did not plough deeply enough for cotton. For rice, the depth of animal ploughing was sufficient, but germination was reduced by failure to break up the soil adequately. Furthermore, farmers reported that mechanized land preparation, and particularly the disking, reduced the weed problem by turning over the soil and preparing it better so that fewer cultivations were required. This turning and disking was considered equivalent to a second cultivation. Finally, farmers reported a risk element in using animals for land preparation. The difficult land preparation activities occur at a time when the animals are weakest, immediately after the dry season. Supplementary feeding is not generally given to work animals during the dry season, and an overworked, weakened animal may die.

The most striking advantage of mechanical power over animal power is the reduction in time required for basic preparation operations. Using animal power, these operations require an average of 5 days per hectare, but using mechanical power they require an average of only 5 hours (see table 10–7).[21] Note that this reduction in per-hectare labor requirements apparently made possible a substantial expansion of the area cultivated. Producers who used animal power worked 6.5 hectares of crops on the average, but farmers

[21] Oxen are generally worked only half days after the dry season. It is possible to achieve similar time savings with mechanized cultivation, but none of the farmers in the sample did so.

TABLE 10–7. Rates of return to mechanized land preparation per hectare of upland rice in Terenos, Mato Grosso, 1971/72 crop year

A. Land preparation parameters

| | Animal Power | Mechanized Power |
|---|---|---|
| Preparation of one hectare of land:[a] | | |
| Time required for | | |
| Ploughing | 5 days | 3 hours |
| Disking or breaking | | 2 hours |
| Cost[b] (in cruzeiros) of | | |
| Basic preparation | 58.60 | 77.00 |
| Additional cultivation[c] | 35.00 | |
| Savings[d] (in cruzeiros) achieved by mechanized land preparation at yield advantages of | | |
| 10% | | 72.00 |
| 15% | | 108.00 |
| 20% | | 144.00 |

B. Rates of return

| | At Yield Advantage[e] of | | |
|---|---|---|---|
| | 10% | 15% | 20% |
| Where elimination of additional cultivation results in cost savings | 15 | 62 | 109 |
| Where additional cultivation continues to be performed | −33 | 16 | 63 |

Source: John H. Sanders, "Mechanization and Employment in Brazilian Agriculture, 1950–1971" (Ph.D. diss., University of Minnesota, 1973), pp. 105, 196. Data were obtained from Frederick Bein's field interviews.

[a] Furrowing was sometimes also done.

[b] Cost of mechanical power was taken as the average of 22 observed custom rental prices. Cost of animal power was calculated by summing the costs of labor, animals, and implements. Labor was priced at the minimum wage. The method of calculating costs of animals and implements is illustrated in Sanders, "Mechanization and Employment," pp. 111–14. Data for Mato Grosso labor and other costs were provided by the Instituto de Pesquisa Agropecuaria de Oeste, Campo Grande, Mato Grosso.

[c] See Sanders, "Mechanization and Employment," p. 114.

[d] Calculated on the basis of mean yields and mean price received. See Sanders, "Mechanization and Employment," pp. 112–13.

[e] These yield advantages were taken from estimates in Sanders, "Mechanization and Employment," pp. 239–40. They varied from 9 to 20 percent, depending upon the crop.

who employed mechanized power worked 11.2 hectares. As expected, the principal effect of mechanization was to facilitate the expansion of cultivated area. On the frontier, even for the small farmer, there is still considerable potential to increase area cultivated either through more intensive utilization of existent land holdings or through the purchase of land at prices lower than those in the prime agricultural areas of the South.

Note than on a per-hectare basis, land can be prepared more cheaply by animal than by mechanical power (see table 10–7). Mechanical power, on a per-hectare basis, becomes advantageous only when the cost savings from one less cultivation and/or the yield advantage of mechanized land preparation are considered as well.[22] These facts were combined to estimate the internal rate of return to the hiring of custom rental services for land preparation. In this analysis, neither the reduced risks nor the effect of expanding crop area per worker were considered. The rate of return per hectare for mechanized land preparation was

$$\frac{C_1 + C_2 + Y - K}{K} \tag{1}$$

where

$C_1$ was the cost saving from reduced labor and animal-time;
$C_2$ was the cost saving due to the decreased number of cultivations;
$Y$ was the value of the yield difference resulting from mechanization; and
$K$ was the cost of machinery custom-rental.

Adjusting for time passed between operations, this becomes

$$C_1 + \frac{C_2}{(1 + r)^{0.17}} + \frac{Y}{(1 + r)^{0.5}} = K \tag{2}$$

where

$r$ is the internal rate of return.[23]

Table 10–7 indicates that the rate of return *per hectare* from mechanized land preparation was positive, except where there were no savings in cultivation costs and a yield differential of only 10 percent.

In contrast to the farmers of Terenos, only 16 percent of the 49 farmers in the Fatima do Sul, Mato Grosso, sample used mechanical power for land

[22] Four Terenos farmers who used animal power were observed to have substantially lower yields. Three of these experienced crop failures, and the fourth achieved below average rice yields. However, this sample is very small, and it is unlikely that these disastrous yields can be attributed entirely to the failure to use mechanical power. The yield advantages of mechanical power shown in table 10–7 were based on calculations that utilized São Paulo data (see Sanders, "Mechanization and Employment," pp. 239, 240). In this study, factors other than mechanization that affected yields, particularly the use of biochemical inputs, were held constant. The yield differentials varied among crops, ranging from 10 to 20 percent.

[23] The simplification of the rate of return equation (1) used for calculations in table 10–7 assumes that all costs and returns occur at the same time. Owing to the short time period between planting and sale, this simplification should not affect the estimated internal rate of return significantly. The discounting is based on the following pattern of activities. Cultivation occurs one-and-a-half to two months after planting, and sale takes place approximately six months after planting. For further details see Sanders and Bein, "Agricultural Development," pp. 609, 610.

preparation. This sample was also composed of small farmers in an area of fertile soil, or *terra roxa*. Our explanation for the wide gap between the two areas in degree of mechanization of land preparation is the difference between the areas in soil texture. In better-texture soil, power requirements for land-preparation operations are lower. Thus the superior texture of the *terra roxa* of Fatima do Sul made mechanized land preparation less important. In Terenos, mechanization, by improving the land preparation on *cerrado*, appeared to have helped overcome a barrier to production increase. As a consequence, almost all farmers in the sample (94%) used tractors for this operation, although they continued to rely upon animal power for all other operations.

In summary, our examination of two frontier regions has indicated that on heavier-texture soils there is a reasonably high rate of return to mechanization. In the frontier area, mechanization not only facilitated the expansion of cultivated area but also had a substitution, or yield-increasing, relationship with land. In areas where soil texture makes preparation difficult, mechanization helped overcome a bottleneck that held back an increase in production even for small farmers. Because animal power could not provide sufficient force for adequate soil preparation in the *cerrado* area, mechanization was necessary to expand the crop area cultivated and to increase yields. Moreover, the tractors with heavier horsepower have a comparative advantage in performing this operation.

Not all Brazilian soils require so much power for their preparation as do the *cerrado* soils, nor is there as much potential for expansion of crop area in all agricultural regions as on the frontier. Mechanization levels were much lower in the *terra roxa* soil than in the *cerrado* area. Thus the present analysis supports the hypothesis that mechanization facilitated the cropping of poorer soil areas.[24] Since there is substantial *cerrado* area in Brazil, mechanization is expected to continue at rapid rates, especially in the South and the Central West, and to hasten the settlement and cropping of these areas. There is an alternative to extensive cropping of these marginal soil areas by means of subsidized mechanization. That is to improve yields in better soil areas, both on the frontier and in the older agricultural areas, through developing better varieties. If frontier settlement objectives are to include increased absorption of labor from other depressed regions of Brazil that have less agricultural potential, it will be particularly important to focus on such varietal improvement.

*Developing a Selective Mechanization Policy*

The importance of factor price distortions in stimulating tractor sales has been shown. When a government actively intervenes in its factor markets

[24] The heavier-texture soil of *cerrado* regions is less fertile than the soil of *terra roxa* areas.

it is not surprising to see factor substitution take place. One effect of subsidization in Brazil was to increase the rate of substitution of tractor power for labor. The primary beneficiary has been the agricultural sector of the greater South, including the Central West frontier, and particularly that part of the sector composed of the larger farmers. Given the sizeable agricultural population of the Northeast and the large segment of the labor force still engaged in agriculture, the increased inequality of income that has resulted from the rapid introduction of heavy agricultural tractors may be a high price to pay for the growth in output that has been achieved. In order to obtain a rate of technical change more consistent with factor endowments and a less skewed income distribution between regions and within agriculture, it may be desirable to reduce subsidies to mechanization and to establish a policy in support of smaller scale mechanization, especially, in the Northeast, mechanization using animal power.[25] Other strategies for increasing agricultural output that may allow for a more favorable distribution of income by region and per capita are the development of new varieties of sugarcane and tree cotton in the Northeast and the introduction there of sorghum and other drought-resistant crops.

However, on the frontier and in other areas where the soil has a heavy texture there is a yield effect from mechanization. In such areas, heavier tractors are necessary, and the Brazilian frontier offers substantial potential for a continuing expansion of area cultivated. The farm-size effect of mechanization could be minimized in these areas by developing selective mechanization strategies. Policies that would facilitate private or govern-

[25] Several studies in Ceará have suggested that the small farmer's seasonal labor problem with respect to weeding can be eased by the use of animal cultivators. These studies report an increase in yields, in area cultivated, and in employment when the animal cultivator is introduced. See J. H. Sanders, J. A. Pereira, and M. B. Gondim, "Mudança tecnologica e desenvolvimento agricola do estado de Ceará" (Paper presented at the annual meeting of the Brazilian Agricultural Economics Association, Porto Alegre, Rio Grande do Sul, July 1974), and D. M. de Albuquerque Lima and J. H. Sanders, "Selecting and Evaluating New Technology for Small Farmers in the Central Sertão of Ceará" (Paper presented at the Ohio State University Conference on Brazilian Agricultural Development, Columbus, Ohio, January 1975).

Other studies have reached similar conclusions as to appropriate mechanization policies for other regions. See W. R. Cline, "Rural Income Distribution," pp. 151, 152; B. F. Johnston and J. B. Cownie, "The Seed-Fertilizer Revolution and Labor Force Absorption," *American Economic Review* (September 1969). See also Montague Yudelman, Gavan Butler, and Ranadev Banerji, *Technological Change in Agriculture and Employment in Developing Countries* (Paris: Organization for Economic Cooperation and Development, 1971); Don Winkelman, *The Traditional Farmer: Maximization and Mechanization* (Paris: Organization for Economic Cooperation and Development, 1972); Carl H. Gotsch, "Tractor Mechanization and Rural Development in Pakistan," *International Labour Review* 107, no. 2 (February 1973): 133–66. For a review of various studies, see Gordon Gemill and Carl Eicher, "The Economics of Farm Mechanization and Processing in Developing Countries," Research and Training Network Seminar Report no. 4 (New York: Agricultural Development Council, Inc., December 1973).

mental tractor rental could help offset the high fixed costs of heavy tractors. Unless further income concentration within agriculture is a policy objective, mechanization policy needs to be designed to overcome difficulties of soil preparation for all farm sizes without shifting the comparative advantage in crop production to large farmers. Moreover, research emphasis on increasing yields on better lands of the frontier may have a larger social return, through increased labor absorption in that region, than would further subsidizing of mechanization to promote settlement in the less fertile, *cerrado* region.

Factor price distortions that result in implicit subsidies received primarily by large farmers not only worsen regional and personal income distribution in Brazil but also reduce the potential labor-absorption effect of frontier settlement. The type of factor substitution experienced in Brazil—rapid mechanization on a small sector of large farms—has been responsive to the distorted factor prices. The primary public benefit appears to have been the cost saving achieved in the administration of extension and credit programs by concentrating agricultural development efforts on a relatively small group of large farmers. The issue faced by government has not been a choice between improved income distribution or increased production and exports, as has frequently been suggested. Small and medium farmers can increase production and contribute to foreign exchange earnings. The technical change package needed by such farmers may be different from that required by large farmers. Nevertheless, because it would allow participation of a greater number of Brazilian farmers in the adoption of new technology, removing factor price subsidies and investing in the capacity to produce new agricultural technology could bring about a higher output payoff and an improved distribution of income than the present strategy can effect.[26]

Brazil's mechanization policy illustrates a Latin American phenomenon: the use of selective subsidies to ease the adjustment problems of a small sector of large farmers. There are other technical change alternatives that are more consistent with Brazilian factor endowments than these subsidies for heavy mechanization. The argument for more public investment in alternative technologies—such as animal mechanization and new varieties—especially for the Northeast and the frontier is analogous to the argument in support of subsidies for labor use rather than capital in the industralization process of developing countries. The Brazilian observations may well be relevant for many other countries in which small sectors of large farm owners dominate agricultural policy and attempt to shape technical change to release the constraints of their relative factor endowments rather than the constraints on

[26] For an excellent review of mechanization policy decisions in developing countries, see G. F. Donaldson and J. P. McInerney, "Changing Machinery Technology and Agricultural Adjustment," *American Journal of Agricultural Economics* 55 (December 1973): 829–39.

the agricultural sector and on society in general. Brazil is thus a classic example of the need for institutional evolution as an accompaniment to the process of technical change. Recent efforts by the Brazilian National Agricultural Research Enterprise (EMBRAPA) to develop new agricultural technology for the Northeast encourage the authors to be cautiously optimistic about the potential for such evolution in Brazil.

ELEVEN

# Social Structure and Biased Technical
# Change in Argentine Agriculture
ALAIN DE JANVRY

W H Y has agricultural production stagnated in comparison with
population growth in Latin America over the last forty years? It
is crucial that we find an answer to this question, for stagnation in the output
of food has had a dramatic effect both on the economic performance of Latin
American nations and on the welfare of their people. Increasing importation
of food by these nations is correlated with growing deficits in the balance
of payments, with inflationary pressures, and with higher labor costs. Unchanging per capita output, combined with a rise in income for some members
of society, has led to a deteriorating nutritional situation for a majority of
people and to severe hardship for the large masses of subsistence peasants. In
recent years, the reduced availability of food surpluses from the United States
and the rising cost of energy have placed in sharp focus the high economic
and human costs of agricultural underdevelopment.

Several conflicting explanations of the poor performance of Latin American
agriculture have been advanced over the last few years. These views fall into
three major categories: the monetarist, the structuralist, and the unequal
development theories. From a review of these theses we can draw three basic
questions: (1) why are the terms of trade unfavorable for agriculture in Latin
America; (2) why is technical change biased against yield-increasing innovations; and (3) why does a land tenure system that is dominated by the
traditional landed elite impede the supply response under prevailing market
conditions?

After answering the first of these questions we will develop a model for the
inducement of technical and institutional change that will help us obtain

This chapter represents a revised version of Alain de Janvry, "A Socioeconomic Model of
Induced Innovation for Argentine Agricultural Development," *Quarterly Journal of
Economics* 87 (August 1973): 410–35.

answers to the remaining two questions. We will then use this model to analyze the case of Argentine agriculture in some detail.

### Theories of Agricultural Stagnation

The collapse of the international market in the late 1920s marked the beginning of a long period of stagnation in agricultural production in Latin America. During the 1950s and 1960s only Mexico showed sustained high growth rates, and by the end of the 1960s agriculture was stagnating in that country as well. In Argentina growth rates have continued to be below two percent yearly, barely matching a slow population growth.

To understand this phenomenon, we must first understand its historical and structural context. Before 1930, Latin American social structure was dominated by traditional landed elites who monopolized agricultural production and exports. A triple coincidence favored this agroexporter model: an active external market, cheap servile labor, and the availability of land for expansion of the frontier. The characteristic form of land tenure was the *latifundio*, which maintained capitalist relations with the market while it held labor in a semifeudal relationship with respect to the conditions of production. With labor tied to the land through debt and through payment of wages in land, the *latifundio* secured the cheap labor it required. It prevented workers from capturing their own opportunity cost in the labor market in spite of labor shortages in the mining and industrial sectors.

After 1930, the situation changed drastically in two ways. First, the terms of trade for agriculture deteriorated sharply. Second, horizontal expansion was no longer possible without considerable infrastructure investment. Growth came to depend upon increasing the average productivity of the land which, in turn, required technical change. Yet growth accountancy studies and inspection of the evolution of yields over time reveal a dearth of land-saving technical changes in the Latin American nations, with the general exception of Mexico.

For the monetarists, stagnation in the post-1930s was the result of governmental promotion of "cheap food policies" that stifled the profitability of agricultural investments.[1] These policies were introduced in the context of promoting import-substitution industrialization—which is achieved by over-valuing exchange rates in order to cheapen imported capital goods and by imposing tariffs to protect nationally produced industrial goods. The resulting net effective protective tariff on agriculture has been highly negative.[2]

Although they correctly identify one of the major determinants of agri-

[1] Theodore W. Schultz, *Economic Growth and Agriculture* (New York: McGraw-Hill Book Company, Inc. 1968), p. 175.

[2] Bela Balassa, "Effective Protection in Developing Countries," in *Trade, Balance of Payments, and Growth*, ed. J. Bhagwati et al. (Amsterdam: North-Holland Publishing Co., 1970), pp. 300–23.

cultural stagnation—cheap food—the monetarists confuse phenomenon and essence for they are unable to explain the rationale for cheap food in terms of the political economy of the social system that promotes it. Thus, T. W. Schultz and H. G. Johnson attribute the observed discrepancies between market and efficiency prices to policy mistakes that must be stricken out by restoration of the rules of the competitive game.[3] Their analysis also fails to explain the fact that, in spite of deterioration in prices, real prices of land have increased steadily, which indicates increasing ground rents. As S. Aranda and A. Martinez point out, "the relative decline in agricultural prices did not result at all in the bankruptcy of the *latifundists*."[4] "*Latifundismo* is '*un grande negocio*'."[5]

For the structuralists, agricultural stagnation is the inevitable outcome of the operation of a land tenure system characterized by the *latifundio-minifundio* binomial. Under this kind of system, the monopoly of land and water and the barring of labor from access to the means of production permit the dominant class to derive enormous economic and social advantages even while they use land extensively. As a result, the behavior of *latifundists* is oriented more to the maintenance of the economic and social status quo than to profit maximization and capital accumulation.[6] The main empirical defense of this thesis lies in observing that intensity of land use declines as farm size increases. Yet it turns out the yield differences between multifamily and single family farms are not so great. In spite of the management absenteeism and land speculation that occur on their large farms, the *latifundists* have privileged access to credit, technology, and information. Thus in spite of their extensive (by international standards) land use, the *latifundists* are still the prime innovators in the countryside. By taking an overly agrarian view, the structuralists, like the monetarists, confuse phenomenon and essence by giving excessive importance to land tenure as a production system while failing to identify the broader determinants of the establishment and perpetuation of that system. By attributing stagnation to the economic behavior of *latifundists*, the structuralists fail to recognize that this behavior (absenteeism, extensive land use, horizontal instead of vertical expansion) is, in fact, individually optimal for profit maximization under the economic system in which it occurs.

The unequal development theory sees the process of capital accumulation occurring in the context of the center–periphery dichotomy popularized by

[3] Schultz, *Economic Growth*, and Harry Gordon Johnson, *Economic Policies Toward Less Developed Countries* (London: Allen & Unwin, Ltd., 1967); see also Markos Mamalakis and Clark Winton Reynolds, *Essays on the Chilean Economy* (Homewood, Illinois: Richard D. Irwin, Inc., 1965), p. 148.

[4] S. Aranda and A. Martinez, "Estructura Económica: Algunas características fundamentales," in *Chile Hoy* (Mexico: Siglo XXI, 1970), p. 132.

[5] Solon Barraclough, ed., *Agrarian Structure in Latin America* (Lexington, Massachusetts: Lexington Books, 1973), p. 101.

[6] Ibid., p. xxiv.

Raul Prebisch.[7] Through historical analysis, proponents of this theory establish a sharp contrast between the processes of accumulation as they take place in these two areas of the world capitalist system. For growth to occur in any economic system, the capacity to consume must be developed on a par with the capacity to produce. To satisfy the needs for market expansion that occur in the center, income needs to be redistributed in such a way as to benefit labor. Thus wages become closely tied to increases in the productivity of labor. In S. Amin's view, labor, in the center, is both a cost and a benefit to capital—it is a cost because wages are a liability against profits, but it is also a benefit because wages create the market that permits sustained accumulation.[8] In the periphery, links of dependency have established a production system that finds its markets abroad (in the case of plantations and mining) or among the upper classes (in the case of durable goods produced by import substitution) but not in the greater affluence of labor. Wages are a cost only, and the logic of profit making requires that costs be minimized. The easiest way to achieve this is by promoting cheap food.

According to this third theory, enormous productivity gains in U.S. agriculture and the dumping of food surpluses on the world market provide the conditions under which cheap food can be promoted in the periphery. The world price of food falls: in the center, food expenditures are reduced and the market size for industry increases; in the periphery, the price of labor falls, which leads to a decline in the prices of raw materials, agricultural products specific to the periphery, and manufactured products exported to the center. Cheap food in turn requires cheap agricultural labor in order to maintain the rate of profit. This labor is obtained from the large sector of subsistence peasants. Wages paid to workers from this subsistence economy can be set below the needs of the worker and his family because some of the family's subsistence needs are met through traditional production in the *minifundio*. And maintenance of such a subsistence economy does not impede growth of the modern sector, as the latter does not find its market among labor. The unequal development thesis is thus able to provide a more satisfactory answer to the question (that the monetarists view as a determinant of stagnation) as to why the terms of trade are unfavorable for agriculture.[9]

Given the price situation we have described, why has there been no green revolution in the countries of Latin America? Why has technical change been biased, not only in Brazil (see chapter 10) but throughout Latin America,

[7] Raul Prebisch, "Commercial Policy in Underdeveloped Countries," *America Economic Review* 49 (Supplement) (May, 1959): 251–73.

[8] S. Amin, *Accumulation on a World Scale* (New York: Monthly Review Press, 1974).

[9] For a full development of this point, see Alain de Janvry, "The Political Economy of Rural Development in Latin America: An Interpretation," *American Journal of Agricultural Economics* 57, no. 3 (August 1975); and Alain de Janvry and Carlos Garramón, "The Dynamics of Rural Poverty in Latin America," *The Journal of Peasant Studies* 4, no. 3 (April 1977): 206–16.

toward labor-saving and against land-saving technologies? To answer these questions we must first conceptualize the process through which technical and institutional innovations are developed.

## The Inducement of Technical and Institutional Innovations

The process through which the public sector is induced to generate technical and institutional innovations has been examined in a study by Hayami and Ruttan.[10] In the model proposed by these authors, the starting points are the stock of scientific knowledge—conceptualized as defining the *innovation possibility curve* in the factor space—and the relative factor scarcities. Through functioning of the market, changes in relative factor scarcities determine changes in relative factor prices which, in turn, lead to the search within the innovation possibility curve for new, cost-minimizing technologies. These technologies will be biased toward saving the most expensive factor. The new technological opportunities may, in turn, induce institutional changes that will make it easier for society to capture the benefits of these opportunities. In this model causality runs in linear fashion from technical to institutional change.

Causation clearly does not always run in linear fashion from technical to institutional change. Equally often, and perhaps even more importantly, it runs in the opposite direction; the two types of changes occur in interaction with each other. And this interaction cannot be reduced to a purely economic, market phenomenon but must be understood as a social process that operates within the political economy.

By contrast, the model we use here is one in which the generation of technical and institutional innovations by the public sector is conceptualized as a dynamic, interactive process involving both demand and supply. In this process the socioeconomic structure, the politico-bureaucratic structure, and the innovation-producing institutions are given explicit roles (figure 11–1). The central node of the model is a *payoff matrix* that specifies *ex ante* the net economic gains and losses that any set of particular interest groups expect to result from the implementation of any set of alternative latent public goods (technical and institutional innovations). Alternative technical innovations offer options among commodities (for example, food versus cash crops, cereals versus livestock), among regions (irrigated versus dry land, fertile versus marginal lands), and among technological biases (land-saving bio-chemicals versus labor-saving mechanical devices, modern versus intermediate mechanical techniques). Alternative institutional innovations require

[10] Yujiro Hayami and Vernon W. Ruttan, *Agricultural Development: An International Perspective* (Baltimore: Johns Hopkins University Press, 1971). Binswanger has developed a more rigorous model of induced technical change than the earlier Hayami-Ruttan model (see chapters 2 and 4).

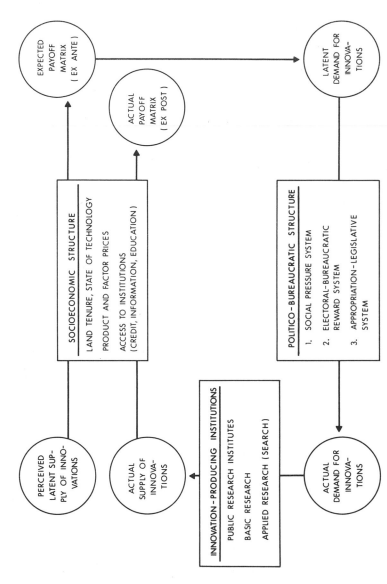

FIG. 11–1. Supply and demand for technological and institutional innovations.

decisions on monetary policies (prices, tariffs, exchange rates, and interest rates), fiscal policies (taxes and subsidies), and structural policies (land tenure and market organization). Particularly important among interest groups are commercial farmers, traditional landed elites, subsistence farmers, landless agricultural workers, industrial employers, urban workers at varying income levels, exporters, and the government. Each social group expects to derive a specific income gain or loss from each particular latent public good. These income effects are the expected payoffs that constitute the arguments in the *ex ante* matrix of public goods and social groups. In this model the economic base of society determines its evolution.

The supply-and-demand mechanism for public goods is centered on the payoff matrix and conditioned by the socioeconomic structure, the politico-bureaucratic structure, and the innovation-producing institutions. Specifically, the demand for new public goods originates from the matrix of expected payoffs. Each social group has a latent demand for particular public goods; this demand arises from the payoffs the group expects to derive. All groups' latent demands are translated into a set of actual demands through the functioning of the politico-bureaucratic system. Of particular importance in this process are (1) the social pressure system whereby social groups produce vote commitments and exert direct pressure on bureaucrats to promote interest in and support for their particular latent demands; (2) the electoral system and the bureaucratic reward system that translate vote commitments and direct pressure into specific political and bureaucratic commitments; and (3) the legislative system that transposes these commitments into specific budget appropriations and laws. The actual demands for innovations that emerge from this filtering process are thus those latent demands that have succeeded in bringing about allocation of public resources for particular innovations.

The relative power over the politico-bureaucratic structure wielded by different social groups is the determining factor in whether or not such groups' specific latent demands are eventually translated into actual demands. These actual demands are then transformed into an actual supply of innovations by the innovation-producing institutions. Within these institutions, the store of scientific knowledge and the size of allocations of physical and human capital to basic research will determine the position of the innovation possibility curve. The amount of physical and human capital allocated to applied research will determine the intensity of the search for new, cost-minimizing techniques along the innovation possibility curve. Hence, the nature of the organization of national and international research systems determines the intensity and bias of their response to the set of actual demands brought to bear on them. And the resulting actual supply of innovations, through its effect on components of the socioeconomic structure, produces specific actual payoffs for each social group.

### The Payoff from Technical Innovation

The neoclassical theory of induced innovation is useful in identifying both the payoff from and the latent demand for technical innovation. We will extend the theory here to describe the determination of a new sector equilibrium with generation of technology occurring in response to a change in product or factor prices. This will facilitate our analysis of the way in which the payoffs from innovations change as market forces restore a competitive equilibrium.

We use the *ex ante* concept of a *scientific frontier* (as we may call it to be consistent with part I of this book) in which isoquants shift with changes in the stock of scientific knowledge and envelop all known or potentially discoverable technical blueprints at one stage of scientific knowledge. Following Ahmad, different levels of research budgets then define a set of *innovation possibility curves* (IPCs), which lie above the isoquant defined by the scientific frontier and which envelop all technologies discoverable with a given research budget.[11]

In the Schumpeterian tradition, technical change can then result either from expansions of scientific knowledge (which shift the isoquants of the scientific frontier and the set of IPCs) or from discovery of new production techniques within the same IPC.

Consider the determination of a new sectoral equilibrium for agriculture in response to a change in factor price ratios, with costless generation of technological innovations (see figure 11–2). Say that there are only two factors of production—land ($T$) and all other factors ($X$). In the initial period ($t - 1$), the unit isoquant of the IPC is $IPC_{t-1}$, the unit cost line is $AB$,[12] and the unit isoquant of the production function used is $I_1$. The sector is in equilibrium at 1, where Schumpeterian profits are zero.

Now assume that land prices increase while the prices of all other inputs decrease (product prices may have changed also) and that the net effect is to shift the unit cost line to $CD$. Without innovations, individual farmers may adjust to the new factor price ratio through factor substitution from 1 to 2 on $I_1$, but at 2 profits are still negative. In order for profits to be nonnegative, a unit level of output must be produced on or below $CD$. Given $IPC_t$, as in figure 11–2, there exists a *latent demand* for the innovation of isoquant $I_2$, at which individual profits will be maximized. Since at 3 Schumpeterian profits are positive, further price and innovation adjustments are necessary to bring the sector to a new equilibrium. If demand is inelastic and factor supplies elastic, product prices will drop until a sectoral equilibrium is obtained at 3. If final demand is elastic, the supply of land inelastic, and the

---

[11] Syed Ahmad, "On the Theory of Induced Invention," *Economic Journal* 76, no. 302 (June 1966): 344–57. See also chapter 2, pp, 20–25.

[12] The unit cost line is $P_T T + P_X X = 1$ where $P_T$ and $P_X$ are the factor prices relative to product price. It is, hence, the locus of points where profit per unit of output is zero.

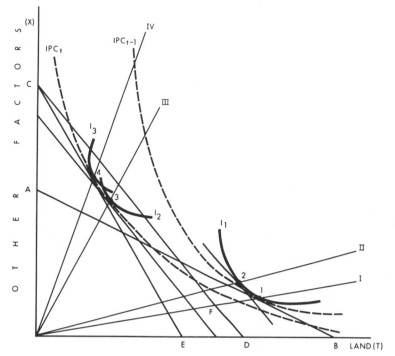

FIG. 11–2. Sectoral equilibrium with costless innovations.

supply of other inputs elastic, land prices will rise until they internalize all
non-zero profits, shifting the unit cost line to $CE$ and establishing a new
sectoral equilibrium at 4 with technology $I_3$. Intermediate cases, where there
is some inelasticity of demand and some inelasticity of supply of other inputs,
will lead to sectoral equilibria between 3 and 4. In the adjustment process,
factor ratios have changed from I to II because of factor substitution and
from II to III or IV because of technical innovations.

Research costs can be introduced into the solution by postulating, for
example, that the cost of innovating increases as the factor ratios of the new
techniques diverge from the factor ratios of the traditional, well-known
technologies. Then, if research costs are internalized in product prices, $CD$
pivots around $F$, and the optimum latent demand shifts toward traditional
technologies.

Isoquant $I_1$ corresponds to traditional resource-based technologies where
land is used extensively, while $I_2$ and $I_3$ are modern technologies that are in
latent demand. If market prices are socially optimal, so will be this latent
demand. With the problem of underdevelopment and technological back-
wardness in mind, we are interested in specifying the factors that shift
the latent demand for innovations in such a way that the final sectoral

equilibrium is achieved at a distance from the socially optimal, advanced technologies. Of these factors the most important are as follows:

1. *The size of the implicit tariff, or the discrepancy between internal prices of products and inputs, on the one hand, and the price levels that prevail in the world market valued at the equilibrium exchange rate, on the other.* Most significant is the industrial protectionism that arises from import substitution policies and both raises the price of new capital inputs for agriculture and shifts the latent demand toward traditional technologies. The same shift results from lowering product prices through overvaluation of the exchange rate, export retentions, and other instruments of cheap food policy.

2. *The risk attached to the price levels of input X and of products that will shift the latent demand toward traditional technologies if there is aversion toward such risk.* In this case, risk aversion implies basing innovation decisions on an expected relative price of $X$ that is sufficiently high to have a strong probability of not being exceeded. Hence, risk aversion has the same effect as a rise in the price of $X$, and it shifts latent demand away from socially optimal modern technologies. Variability of product prices also has these effects.

3. *Higher research costs per unit of output that also, when internalized in product prices, shift the latent demand toward traditional technologies.* Because of both learning by doing and economies of scale in research, costs will tend to be higher in less-developed countries. If there is a fixed, predetermined research budget, the size of the budget will determine an interval of inventable factor ratios around the traditional technology, and the optimum latent demand for technology may lie outside the interval. In this event, the budget allocated for research will be incompatible with a socially optimal use of agricultural resources.

4. *The stock of scientific knowledge that determines the position of $IPC_t$ and also displaces latent demand.* Note that the previous three shifters affect latent demand through displacement of the unit cost line. Developed countries and international agricultural research centers tend to have scientific frontiers that lie closer to the origin in the factor space than do less-developed countries. This is because basic agricultural sciences are to some extent location-specific and because developed countries have devoted more resources to the discovery of such knowledge (see chapter 6). Even if the historical IPC is neutral, the latent demand for innovations in less-developed countries, more often than in developed countries, will be for traditional technologies.

In shifting latent demand away from its socially optimal position, the prevailing economic and scientific conditions can determine a technological path remote from a socially optimal use of agricultural resources.

*Rationality of the Actual Demand for Innovation*

Since the payoffs from technology differ among social groups according to the nature of technology, it is necessary first to categorize the different types of agricultural technology and then to identify their corresponding payoff vectors. We must then describe the nature of the actual demands for innovations in terms of the existing social class structure.

A CLASSIFICATION OF TECHNOLOGY. For purposes of characterizing the demand for innovations, technologies can be classified very broadly into four categories: (1) mechanical—tractors, harvesters, and windmills; (2) biological—hybrid seeds and cattle breeds; (3) chemical—fertilizers, insecticides, and pesticides; and (4) agronomic—cultural practices and management techniques (crop rotation, permanent pastures, forage reserves, fertility tests, etc.)[13] These technologies can be further characterized in terms of their own impact both on the marginal rates of technical substitution among capital, labor, land, and management and on yield level. As Seckler suggests, it is useful to distinguish between "on line" management, which consists of the actual direction of farm activities, and "staff" management, which deals with decision making as to choice of activities and techniques (principally investment decisions, financial and fiscal administrative work, and commercial activities).[14]

Mechanical innovations raise the productivity of labor mainly by making it possible for a given area of land to be worked by fewer people. By thus reducing labor costs, they substantially reduce on-line management requirements. And as a firm becomes more capital-intensive, the allocation of resources will tend to change. Less labor, more capital, less on-line management, and more staff management per unit of land will be required. As pointed out by Sen[15] and other writers, while mechanization considerably raises yield per unit of labor, it generally does not lead to yield increases per unit of land unless it is accompanied by investment in land-saving capital goods such as advanced biological, chemical, or agronomic techniques.

Biological innovations have relatively little effect on labor and management requirements. They are slightly capital using and moderately yield increasing when used outside of complete packages of techniques.

The returns from research on mechanical techniques can, in great part, be captured by the innovating firm. This is less commonly so in the case of biological innovations since, after the first sale, the new seeds and breeds can be reproduced and disseminated by farmers themselves.[16] Also, seed companies will tend to work on the development of new varieties that perform best under prevailing production conditions, such as declining soil

[13] In the earlier work of Hayami and Ruttan and in chapter 3 of this book, categories (2), (3), and (4) are combined under "biological technology."

[14] David William Seckler, "Reflections on Management, Scale, and Mechanization of Agriculture," *Proceedings of the Western Agricultural Economics Association*, 43rd annual meeting, Tucson, Arizona, July 1970 (Corvallis: Oregon State University), pp. 80–4.

[15] Amartya Kumar Sen, *Choice of Techniques: An Aspect of the Theory of Planned Economic Development* (Oxford: Basil Blackwell, 1968), p. 82.

[16] For this reason, private seed companies typically have concentrated their efforts on true hybrids, which cannot be reproduced.

fertility where the fertilizer package is not used (as in Argentina), or heavy fertilization once high-yielding varieties have been introduced (as in the countries that have experienced the green revolution).[17] Because it is costly to develop modern biological-chemical-agronomic packages, and because seed or chemical companies can appropriate only a small fraction of the returns to such research, private firms generally will not engage in research on these types of innovations.

Chemical innovations aim at increasing yield. They are fundamentally land saving in that they permit the substitution of capital and labor for land. To intensify the use of capital and labor, however, requires both more on-line and more staff management per unit of land.

Finally, agronomic innovations use both labor and on-line management and they save land. Like chemicals, they are strongly yield increasing.

The returns from chemical and agronomic innovations generally cannot be captured by the innovating firm and as a result, research on these kinds of innovations must be performed by the public sector.[18]

Packages of biological, chemical, and agronomic technologies combine the factor biases of their components and tend to use both labor and on-line management and to be very strongly yield increasing.

We have categorized technologies as either land or labor saving, and this has led to categorizing capital in the same manner. We can now write an aggregate production function for the agricultural sector in the following separable form where the degree of substitutability among inputs is high within but quite low between subfunctions:

$$Y = F[f(K_T, T), g(K_L, L)]$$

where

$$Y = \text{aggregate output,}$$
$$T \text{ and } L = \text{land and labor inputs,}$$
$$K_T = \text{landesque capital (chemicals and other capital associated with biological inputs and agronomic practices), and}$$
$$K_L = \text{laboresque capital machinery.}$$

One can conceptualize, as Owen does, the dynamic contribution of agriculture to economic development as resulting from a "double developmental squeeze on agriculture" composed of a "production squeeze," which causes output to increase, and an "expenditure squeeze," which causes

---

[17] See S. M. Sehgal, "Private Sector International Agricultural Research: The Genetic Supply Industry," in *Resource Allocation and Productivity in National and International Agricultural Research*, eds. Thomas M. Arndt, Dana G. Dalrymple, and Vernon W. Ruttan (Minneapolis: University of Minnesota Press, 1977), pp. 404–15.

[18] Among chemical innovations, those having to do with insecticides and pesticides tend to produce returns that are more capable of being captured than are the returns from research on fertilizers.

agriculture to release labor resources.[19] Then, since the output-increasing capital investments are accounted for in the landesque subfunction $f(K_T, T)$, the production squeeze can be analyzed (assuming an elastic labor supply) from that portion of the production function alone. Similarly, for fixed $K_T$, labor use is dealt with through the laboresque subfunction $g(K_L, L)$, and (assuming an inelastic supply of land) the labor contribution of agriculture can be analyzed from that subfunction. This separation of subfunctions also facilitates the comparison of processes by which innovations are generated. The returns from research on $g(K_L, L)$ are appropriable, and as a result such research will be carried on largely by private firms. The returns from research on $f(K_T, T)$ generally are not appropriable, and consequently this type of research will require public sector intervention. In the following model of agricultural development, we will confine ourselves to the factor space $(K_T, T)$, in analyzing the inducement of yield-increasing, technological innovations by the public sector, and to the factor space $(K_L, L)$, in analyzing the inducement of labor-saving innovations by the private sector.

THE ACTUAL DEMAND FOR INNOVATION.   The first step in the specification of a socioeconomic model of induced innovation consists of distinguishing between latent and actual demands for innovation. If expected profits are being maximized, a change in prices or a change in the IPC from $t - 1$ to $t$ will create a *latent demand* for innovations corresponding to the neoclassical production function tangent at 3 or 4 to IPC$_t$ in figure 11–2. As shown earlier, higher and more variable prices of capital inputs, lower and more variable product prices, higher costs of innovations, and lower stocks of scientific knowledge will all shift the latent demand toward the more traditional technologies and away from a socially optimal use of agricultural resources.

The second step in outlining our model consists of specifying the decision processes that underlie the *actual demand* for innovations. This demand will materialize in essentially two forms: (1) research budgets, in terms both of their overall size and their specific allocations, and (2) a flow of information to the agricultural experiment stations with respect to the types of innovations currently needed. The crucial question, then, is from what group or groups do these demands arise? The answer is, the economic agents to whom the payoffs from technical change accrue. In Argentina, where there is a highly elastic long-run demand for exportable agricultural products (mainly meat, corn, and sorghum), the direct welfare gains from technical change accrue largely to the agricultural sector in the form of greater producer surpluses.[20] And because the increase in gross income results from larger

---

[19] W. F. Owen, "The Double Developmental Squeeze on Agriculture," *American Economic Review* 56, no. 1 (March 1966): 43–70.

[20] For the sake of simplicity, our analysis will be carried out as though this demand were infinitely elastic.

exportable surpluses, welfare gains also accrue indirectly to the entire economy through a very high import multiplier.[21] Thus two demands for technical innovation come from these two recipients of welfare gains—the agricultural sector, which voices its demand through the dominant farm organizations, and the public at large, which expresses its demand through the government. Because there exist a variety of forms of technical change, and because these forms can differentially affect producer and exportable surpluses, the two demands may conflict.

Almost universally, the demand for innovation that has dominated the course of agricultural research has originated in the agricultural sector. This can seem paradoxical in situations of inelastic demand because welfare gains that result from yield-increasing innovations may be negative for agriculture unless rationalized in the dynamic context of the "agricultural treadmill," as discussed below.[22] On the other hand, welfare gains attributable to non-yield-increasing technologies—usually those which involve mechanization—will increase producer surplus but will not have any major effect on prices or on consumer surplus. In Argentina, in the absence of government policy toward technical change in agriculture, the actual demand for innovation originates almost exclusively in the agricultural sector.[23] Since agricultural interests have traditionally been dominated by large landowners, the demand for innovation that determines the amount and allocation of public research funds derives from this group. And the same group conveys information to the scientists, since it is the educated, large farmers who are in closest contact with the experiment stations.[24]

From the foregoing it is postulated that the actual demand for public innovations results from the maximization of the objective function of the dominant farm interests. Specification of this objective function is now in order. Unfortunately, little is known of its structure because in analyzing technical change economists and sociologists have focused on the adoption mechanism rather than on the nature of innovation, on the occurrence rather than on the demand for innovation (*ex post* growth accountancy), on innovation by private firms rather than by public institutions, and on the normative latent demand instead of on the actual demand. Yet, important clues can be derived by turning to history.

To maintain the land rent in the face of unfavorable terms of trade, the traditional landed elites use their social power over the institutions to derive

[21] E. Bee de Dagum, "Le Multiplicateur Dynamique d'Exportation: Un Modèle pour l'Argentine," *Economie Appliquée* 22 (1969): 89–112.

[22] Williard Wesley Cochrane, *Farm Prices: Myth and Reality* (Minneapolis: University of Minnesota Press, 1958), Section III.

[23] Darrell F. Fienup et al., *The Agricultural Development of Argentina* (New York: Frederick A. Praeger, 1969).

[24] Edith S. Obschatko and Alain de Janvry, "Factores limitantes del cambio tecnológico en el sector agropecuario Argentino," *Desarrollo Económico* 11 (March 1972): 263–85.

from them privileged economic advantages. This "discriminatory institutional rent" takes the form of quasi-subsidies that are captured principally through a low fiscal burden relative to other sectors of the economy; through monopolization of institutional credit, with negative real interest rates and partial recovery of loans; and through privileged access to the public services of research, information, marketing, education, and infrastructure investments. Even though this rent is captured mainly by the traditional elites, it becomes internalized in the price of all land, as there is only one market, and this further drives down the profitability of farm investments for the nonelites (who do *not* have privileged access to credit and other farm inputs.) [25] Thus, the key to the class behavior of the traditional landed elites is that if monopolization of the institutional process permits deriving socially selective compensations to maintain profitability of the *latifundio* under an unfavorable and largely uncontrolled economic situation, perpetuation of this profitability requires that institutional control prevent the generation of institutional services that jeopardize perpetuation of that control. It is this economic constraint of the *perpetuation of institutional control* that gives real significance to the class objective of social status quo—the social status quo *is* what permits the perpetuation of institutional control by the traditional landed elites.

The next question is, how can the institutional process be managed in order to simultaneously generate compensatory economic advantages and insure reproduction of institutional control? To answer this question we must identify the basis of the social power of the traditional elites and the kinds of institutional services that, though they might provide short-run economic advantages, constitute a threat to this basis of power. Clearly the traditional elites derive their social power from their monopoly over the land. As the Inter-American Committee for Agricultural Development (CIDA) observes, "land tenure relationships tend to coincide with power relationships." [26] The types of institutional services that jeopardize the perpetuation of institutional control, therefore, are those that generate sources of growth that are substitutes for land. In particular, the diffusion of land-saving technologies (the green revolution) and the opening of new lands through infrastructure public works (particularly irrigation projects), when these activities constitute the major potential sources of agricultural growth, erode the social power basis of traditional elites. [27] The economic necessity of perpetuating institutional control by the traditional elites, in order to deal with unfavorable terms of trade, results in a class Malthusianism toward the sources of

[25] This is one of the major reasons why family farms are practically nonexistent in Latin America.

[26] Barraclough, *Agrarian Structure*, p. 14.

[27] The green revolution and accompanying irrigation programs have made a spectacular contribution to output growth in Mexico. See Folke Dovring, "Land Reform and Productivity in Mexico," *Land Economics* 46 (August 1970), pp. 264–74.

growth. Institutional control resulting in agricultural stagnation is, thus, a contradiction of coercive unequal exchange in the peripheral economy dominated by the traditional landed elites. This element that enters into the decision process from which an actual demand for technical innovation is derived can be conceptualized as the maximization of congruence with the prevailing factor ratio in the $(T, K_T)$ space.

Yet profit maximization under a congruence constraint cannot be a sufficient specification of the landed elites' objective function, as congruence will have to be sacrificed when profits are negative. Hence, if stress is defined here as negative or falling profits, stress would appear as a powerful inducer of innovations that do not satisfy congruence requirements. This is consistent with the conclusion of Rosenberg's historical review of the inducement of innovations, according to which "it is clear that threats to an established position have often served as powerful inducements to technical change."[28]

There are three elements that seem to enter into the decision mechanism of the inducement of innovations by the traditional landed elites. Congruence dominates expected profit ($\Pi$) maximization lexicographically, and stress dominates congruence, also lexicographically.[29] If a risk-aversion goal in the form of a survival constraint, like $P_r (\Pi \geq 0) = \alpha$, that also dominates congruence is introduced, the lexicographic objective function for innovations is:

$$LU \{P_r(\Pi \geq 0) = \alpha; \; E(\Pi) \geq 0; \; \text{Max congruence}; \; \text{Max } E(\Pi)\}$$
$$\text{(survival)} \qquad \text{(stress)} \qquad \text{(congruence)} \qquad \text{(profits)}$$

Before we investigate the kind of actual demand for technical innovation that this decision mechanism implies, we need to analyze the process of adoption of new technologies. This is because innovation and adoption mechanisms interact in generating an adjustment path of actual to latent demand.

### The Adoption of New Technologies

The adoption of new and profitable agricultural techniques—once they have been made available by private business firms or public research institutions or by importation from other countries—is determined essentially by the profit objectives of the individual farm entrepreneur. The rate at which new techniques are adopted is conditioned by a set of economic, institutional, and structural factors that tend to introduce severely regressive biases.

[28] N. Rosenberg, "The Direction of Technological Change: Inducement Mechanisms and Focusing Devices," *Economic Development and Cultural Change* 18 (October 1969): 23.

[29] In a lexicographic objective function, objectives are preordered or ranked, and higher order objectives are not considered until all lower-order objectives have been satisfied.

In specifying the decision process that leads to innovation by the public sector, we have emphasized the interplay between the stress produced by negative, or falling, profits and the search for higher profits. The same situation obtains in the case of adoption. Economic coercion of farmers to adopt new techniques has been characterized as the "technological treadmill" by Cochrane.[30]

Cochrane has described the dynamics of the technological treadmill in the context of an inelastic demand for farm products. Output-increasing, cost-reducing technical changes are adopted by alert, profit-seeking farmers, and aggregate supply shifts to the right. Prices drop, and so do the profits of all other farmers, who are then forced to adopt the new technology in order to lower their costs and to maintain their income position. This eliminates the quasi-rents of the early adopters, and they must again look for new technological opportunities. They do this by pressing the agribusiness firms and the agricultural experiment stations to innovate further. In this model, a minority of active profit seekers can put the entire sector on a permanent disequilibrium course of rapid technological change.

Countries like Argentina are largely open on the world market of beef and cereals, where they face highly elastic demand schedules. Nevertheless, although there is no demand-induced treadmill, the coercive mechanism that brings about adoption of new technologies develops in response to a *land market induced treadmill*. This mechanism has dynamic properties that are very distinct from those of the product market (or demand) induced treadmill.

Assume that new techniques are available and that they are adopted by some farmers. For these farmers, the rate of return on resources increases. If the capital market has been in equilibrium, this increase in rate of return must be capitalized in land values in order for the capital market to return to a state of equilibrium. Adopters will bid up the price of land, of which there is an inelastic aggregate supply, until rates of return are again on a par with opportunity costs. As land values increase, both the opportunity cost of holding land and the flow of capital gains increase. The net effect on profits depends upon the magnitudes of the rate of increase in land values $\Delta$ relative to the opportunity costs of capital $r$. If, as is usually the case, $r > \Delta$, profits of owner-operators and of tenants who do not modify their allocation of resources are reduced.

Adoption of new technologies by some farmers raises the price of land and depresses the income position of nonadopters. However, the basic difference between product market and land market treadmills is that, whereas a product treadmill affects the cash income position of nonadopters, a land treadmill affects only the noncash income position of owner-operators.

[30] Cochrane, *Farm Prices*, p. 85.

Increases in the cost of land are changes in opportunity costs, not in cash costs. And the perception of a deterioration in noncash income will indeed take much longer to develop than the perception of changes in cash income. There are only two categories of farmers on whom the impact of the land treadmill is immediate: recent entrants into the farm sector, who must buy their land at the inflated values, and tenants, who are forced to rent their lands at the increased user costs.

In summary, it has been argued that a technological treadmill effect exists even when product demand is elastic. This treadmill operates through the land market rather than through product markets (provided land is in fixed aggregate supply), and it is of much longer run in its impact on the rate of adoption even though it is ultimately as inescapable as Cochrane's treadmill.

There are several other important differences between these two treadmill mechanisms in terms of their impact on agricultural development.

1. Under the influence of a land treadmill there will be much greater variation in the degree to which new techniques are employed on farms than under the influence of a product treadmill.

2. Although a product treadmill may create a latent demand for land-saving technologies (if the decline in price is not sufficient to offset profits and, as a result, land values increase—see figure 11–2), a land market treadmill will produce a much stronger latent demand for land-saving technologies. The United States experience of the last 15 years supports this argument. As a consequence of government intervention to maintain product prices through land allotments that served to control production, a large portion of the returns from technical change—and from intervention as well—were capitalized in land values, and this led to the development of land-saving technologies. In fact, the concept of the land market treadmill may describe recent technical progress in United States agriculture more accurately than does the product market treadmill.

3. Under the land market treadmill, welfare gains from yield-increasing technical changes accrue wholly to producers; they are not transmitted to consumers through lower food prices and higher consumer surpluses as they would be under a product treadmill mechanism. Hence, the extractive squeeze in Owen's Mill–Marshallian model is no longer existent. In the open economy, welfare gains from technological change that accrue to the entire economy exist only through the generation of foreign exchange and the import multiplier. If an appropriation of the agricultural surplus is desired, non-market mechanisms such as taxation must be used.

Whatever the form of the treadmill, market forces impose a dynamic, coercive mechanism of change upon the agricultural sector. Hence, new technology appears as a powerful agent of structural and behavioral changes. In the Argentine context, the generation of highly profitable technological packages could, in turn, generate diseconomies of large scale and force direct

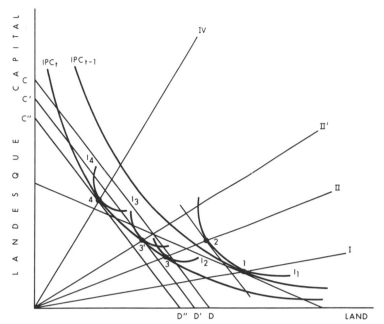

FIG. 11–3. Actual demand for land-saving technical innovations.

management of farms, thus acting to encourage a land reform process that could be accelerated by land taxation schemes and by the revival of the land rental market.

### The Adjustment Path of Actual to Latent Demand

Coming back to the lexicographic objective function previously specified as the structural model from which the actual demand for innovations is derived, it was shown that nonnegative Schumpeterian profits constitute a priority goal. Hence, in figure 11–3, the area of the $IPC_t$, which satisfies this dominant goal, is on or below the unit cost line $CD$. This segment of the $IPC_t$ may be further restricted to meet the goal of risk aversion. Once survival is insured and stress is eliminated, maximum congruence with prevailing factor ratio II becomes the implicit priority goal. Once this is done, expected profits are maximized.

If the unit cost line is $CD$, stress is eliminated, congruence with II is maintained, and expected profits are maximized by innovation of the isoquant $I_2$ tangent at 3 to $IPC_t$. Hence, the actual demand for innovations applies to isoquant $I_2$. If, on the other hand, the unit cost line is at $C'D'$, elimination of stress requires changing the factor ratio to II'. The actual demand for innovation concerns $I_3$ which satisfies the postulated utility

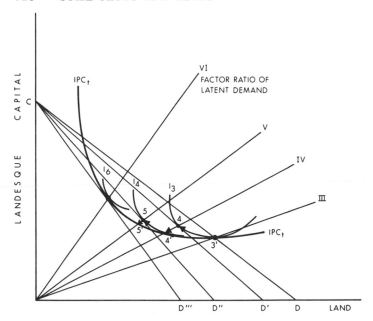

FIG. 11–4. Dynamic adjustment path between actual and latent demands.

function. Hence, stress shifts the actual demand away from congruence with prevailing production structures and focuses innovative effort on more advanced technologies. Only if the unit cost line is at $C''D''$ (which is the most stressful among the three possibilities considered in figure 11–3) are the actual and latent demands coincident in aiming at technology $I_4$.

A feature of the decision mechanism just specified is that, although it usually generates a lag between actual and latent demands and therefore implies a social cost, the interplay between innovation decisions and adoption decisions generates a dynamic adjustment path in actual demand such that actual demand converges toward latent demand. This path is described in figure 11–4.

Say that the unit cost line is $CD$ and that isoquant $I_3$ has been generated as described in figure 11–3. Once technology $I_3$ is available for adoption, individual profit maximizers will use it at 4 where profits are positive. If, as in Argentina, product demand and supply of landesque capital $K_T$ are elastic while that of land $T$ is inelastic, land values will increase to $CD'$ in order to internalize profits. But then, technology $I_4$ will be innovated because it is congruent with prevailing factor ratios and because it maximizes expected profits. In time, $I_4$ will be used at 5, and land values will adjust to $CD''$. Step by step, actual demand converges toward latent demand for technology $I_6$, at which the sector reaches a stable equilibrium. The introduction of stress and congruence in the decision-making process for innovations creates a lag between actual and latent demands, but this lag tends to disappear through the interplay of individual profit-maximization behavior in the adoption and use of available technologies, of social innovation decisions, and of market mechanisms.

All the shifters of latent demand that move demand away from a social optimum are also shifters of actual demand, but the latter will further diverge from the optimum latent demand as they are affected by the following:

1. *The representativeness of the farm interests from whose objective function the actual demand for innovations is derived.* The more representative these interests are, the wider will be the spectrum of prevailing production structures that they include and thus the weaker the congruence goal will be. If, by contrast, farm interests are dominated by large landowners, both congruence requirements with low landesque capital-to-land ratios $K_T/T$ and traditional technologies will prevail. The influence on the budgeting of agricultural research of nonfarm interests, voiced through government, will also shift actual demand, presumably toward latent demand, which is closer to a social optimum.

2. *The intensity of the dialectic interactions between interest groups and research scientists.* Most particularly, informing farm interest groups about potential technical innovations will orient actual demand toward economically optimal latent demand as the real cost of myopic congruence requirements becomes better known. According to Hayami and Ruttan:

> The dialectic interaction among farmers and research scientists and administrators is likely to be most effective when farmers are organized into politically effective local and regional farm "bureaus" or farmers associations. The response of the public sector research and extension programs to farmers' demand is likely to be greatest when the agricultural research system is highly decentralized, as in the United States.[31]

3. *Ease of entry into the farm sector for either owner-operator or tenant; the easier this entry, the lower the congruence requirement.*

Mechanical and biological innovations have been in high demand because they are not bound by congruence requirements, and they are not so bound because, rather than endanger the power basis of the traditional elites from whom institutional rents are derived, they actually strengthen that basis. In addition, because the returns from research on machinery, seed, and breeds can be internalized by private firms, new mechanical and biological techniques spread rapidly in Argentine agriculture without a research contribution by the public sector. Because they are strongly cost-reducing, these technologies have led to substantial increases in producer surpluses. This is evidenced by a violent upsurge in real land values, which have more

[31] Hayami and Ruttan, *Agricultural Development*, p. 57.

than doubled in the last twenty years. However, because these technologies do little to increase yields, they could not help to maintain exportable surpluses nor could they have any appreciable effect on national economic welfare.

As no government demand and only a weak farmer demand for chemical and agronomic technologies was directed to Argentinian public research stations, the supply of such technologies was severely limited by the overall size and specific allocations of existing research budgets.

Moreover, the use of research budgets reflects scientists' concerns with social relevance as well as with their own personal advancement. For example, at the National Institute of Agronomic Research (INTA) in Argentina, a system for recognizing individual achievement that is based largely on pure scientific endeavor and biased in favor of persons with foreign training tends to promote research that is not responsive to local demands. A similar situation apparently obtains in the national research network of India. In contrast, as exemplified at the international agricultural research centers, perceptive scientists who are concerned that their work be socially relevant and who want and can utilize freedom in allocating research funds can sometimes bypass actual demand and focus their efforts directly on latent demand.[32]

## The Gap Between Actual and Latent Demand for Innovation in Argentina

In order to explain, within the framework of the above model of induced innovation, the nature of technological progress in the cereal (corn and wheat) and beef-breeding sectors of Argentina, and in order to understand why the production of these sectors has stagnated, we must determine whether the following statements are true.

1. Current price ratios generate a *latent demand* for land-saving, yield-increasing technologies.

2. This latent demand eventually diverges substantially from its socially optimal position as a result of cheap food and import substitution policies (and particularly policies that support overvalued exchange rates).

3. The new land-saving technologies are incongruent with the current factor ratios of dominant farm interests. Hence, because there is no stress, the *actual demand* for these innovations, as directed to the public sector, is weak. Funds for research on those technologies are scarce, and research tends to be oriented toward satisfying other interests.

[32] Di Tella Institute, "Determinación de objectivos y asignación de recursos en el INTA" (Buenos Aires: Centro de Investigaciones en Administración Pública (CIAP), 1971); Theodore W. Schultz, "The Allocation of Resources to Research," in *Resource Allocation in Agricultural Research*, ed. Walter L. Fishel (Minneapolis: University of Minnesota Press, 1971).

4. Because the new technologies are not accompanied by technical and economic research and information, they are, in effect, not available for adoption by individual farmers and thus are not used.

First let us turn to the cereal sector, where Argentine yields are about half present United States levels, though before the 1930s they were equal in both countries. Technical change as embodied in the genetic characteristics of seeds spread remarkably fast—in fact about as rapidly as in the United States. The same is true for machinery. Since the returns from research on seed and machinery can be appropriated, private firms supplied these innovations, sometimes—as in the case of machinery—through mere importation of technology. Once these techniques were available, their high profitability, enhanced in the case of machinery by capital subsidies provided by cut-rate credits and tax write-offs, brought about their quick adoption. Mechanization increased the movement of labor from the agricultural sector to other sectors of the economy and transformed Argentine agriculture, via labor-saving technological change, into a labor-surplus economy. It had little effect, however, on output level and exportable surpluses. Because the new seed developed in Argentina was designed to work in traditional production contexts and not within packages of new techniques that include fertilizers, it also failed to affect yield appreciably.

Although major yield increases can be expected with the use of fertilizers, insecticides, and herbicides—and with the new, high-yielding varieties to go along with these inputs—at present, such chemicals are rarely used on cereals. To assess the potential for fertilizer use, production functions were fitted to experimental data on fertilizer response, allowing for an interaction between fertilizer on the one hand and the natural fertility of the soil on the other.[33] Since these two elements substitute for one another, lower levels of fertilizer response are expected when land is more fertile. The estimated production functions are thus of the type

$$Y = f(F, F \times M, M, L, X)$$

where

$$Y = \text{yield},$$
$$F = \text{fertilizer},$$
$$M = \text{soil fertility before fertilization},$$
$$L = \text{stochastic composite weather index},$$
$$F \times M = \text{interaction between fertilizer and soil fertility, and}$$
$$X = \text{other variables such as varietal dummies and cultural practices.}$$

[33] Empirical results are given in A. de Janvry, "Optimal Levels of Fertilization Under Risk: The Potential for Corn and Wheat Fertilization Under Alternative Price Policies in Argentina," *American Journal of Agricultural Economics* 54, no. 1 (February 1972): 1–10.

Maximum expected profits are given by:

$$E(\Pi) = g\left(\frac{P_F}{P}, M, X\right)$$

where $P_F$ is the price of fertilizer and $P$ is the price of the cereal considered. Since, for nitrogen, $P_F/P = 8$ at the farm level in Argentina when it would be equal to 3 at United States prices of nitrogen, latent demand is shifted away from its socially optimal position. It is thus of interest to measure the social loss that results from the current fertilizer price policy.

A *fertilization possibility frontier* can be defined as the locus of points

$$\frac{P_F}{P} = h(M/X, E(\Pi) = 0), \qquad h' < 0, h'' < 0$$

where $E(\Pi) = 0$. Profits are positive within this frontier and negative outside of it. Because $M$ is a good proxy for the ratio that measures extensiveness of land use, $T/K_T$, the frontier also identifies the set of such factor ratios that are congruent with fertilizer use at each price level. This frontier would shift to the right with more responsive varieties and, generally, with all the cultural practices $X$ that are positively related to $Y$ in the production function. More intensive use of the land would also decrease $M$ and would allow the use of fertilizer on a greater percentage of the total area planted to cereal.

Ultimately, as is probably already the case in the United States and Europe, all of the land would lie within the fertilization possibility frontier and would be receptive to fertilizer use. At present, however, our results indicate that only about half of the corn and wheat acreage in the traditional production areas of these cereals lies within the fertilization possibility frontier at current prices. Since low $T/K_T$ ratios are observed in the smaller farms that use the land intensively, half of the cereal acreage would mean more than 75 percent of the farms in those regions. Thus even at present prices there is a latent demand for fertilizer technology and, clearly, a greater potential demand at higher prices. But large farms with high $T/K_T$ ratios have no potential for fertilizer use until their land is cropped more intensively and the fertilization possibility frontier is shifted to the right. For this reason, where there is no stress, and where congruence with prevailing factor ratios is a dominant goal, no actual demand for fertilizer technology emanates from the dominant farm interests.

As a result of the foregoing, INTA initiated systematic research on fertilizers only in 1962 and then gave it low priority. Even after the establishment of the cooperative INTA-CIMMYT-Ford Foundation program, which began to produce results in 1969, there continued to be a lack of interest in fertilizer research.[34] And even now, because of a firm belief that trials must

[34] "CIMMYT" is the acronym for the International Maize and Wheat Improvement Center, in El Batán, Mexico.

be conducted under conditions that correspond to practices actually followed by farmers (that is, without insecticides and herbicides), the results are poorly controlled, often unusable, and generally biased toward an underestimation of fertilizer response. This belief of farmers and researchers gives further evidence of the subtle action of congruence requirements in generating a gap between actual and latent demands for innovations.

An *ex post* inspection of the location of the fertilizer trials we have described indicates that a high percentage of the trials were on the wrong side of the fertilization possibility frontier. This was so mainly because it was easier for scientists to work with the educated, large farmers who have contacts with the research station and who also have land to spare for experiments. Since land fertility was not taken into account in the analysis of the data, the conclusion was inevitably reached that fertilizer use is indeed of dubious economic worth in Argentina and, eventually, an "insult to the land." Hence, failure to adopt fertilizer technology is not the result solely of unfavorable prices or of perverse individual attitudes toward profit maximization, or change. It is also—perhaps primarily—the result of the real unavailability of the techniques for adoption at the farm level, owing to lack of information and lack of both agronomic and economic research.

In summary, there is a latent demand for fertilizer in Argentina, but it has been substantially shifted from its socially optimal position by unfavorable terms of trade. Because new fertilizer techniques are not wholly available to individual farmers they cannot be adopted. And finally, under the present land tenure system, the actual demand for research on fertilizers is so weak as to be almost nonexistent.

Similar conclusions can be drawn from an analysis of technological progress in beef breeding, a sector of agriculture that is dominated by large absentee landowners. The quantity of beef produced per acre has remained constant since 1935. Very few yield-increasing, management-intensive animal husbandry and breeding techniques—such as permanent pastures, forage reserves and pregnancy tests—are used. On the other hand, the industry has made advances in the genetic improvements of breeds. Winsberg describes the quick diffusion of new breeds in response to economic incentives.[35] Just as in corn and wheat, genetic improvements, once available, have been quickly adopted. They have been generated through both private and public research, presumably because they were congruent with the existing farm scale and management production patterns.

Only in the last few years has public research on intensive breeding techniques been undertaken. Economic analyses of the few experimental data currently available all underline the high profitability of these

---

[35] M. Winsberg, "Modern Cattle Breeds in Argentina: Origin, Diffusion, and Change," Occasional Publication no. 13 (Lawrence, Kansas: University of Kansas, Center for Latin American Studies, 1968).

techniques, especially when they are combined appropriately into packages.[36] There is, therefore, a latent demand for such innovations.

On the other hand, an analysis of profit functions based on farm surveys made in 1968 and 1969 illustrates the incongruence of these mangement-intensive techniques with large-scale farms and absenteeism. Including real capital gains from increases in land values (which have been more than 5 percent yearly in the last 20 years) in the definition of net income per acre, the function was estimated as

$$NI = f(A, D, S, A \times D, A \times S)$$

where

$A$ = index of technical progress
$D$ = number of days spent on the farm by the staff manager,
$S$ = farm size in hectares, and

$A \times D$
and
$A \times S$ = interactions between $A$ and $D$ and between $A$ and $S$.

The predicted iso-net return functions show that, while management dedication and the use of new, modern techniques are profitable on small farms, this is not the case on large farms. They also show that the highest profits per acre are still obtained by large absentee and traditional landowners. As a result, there has not been and is not now any strong demand for research on these new technologies. In line with this, most farmers interviewed in these surveys preferred horizontal to vertical expansion with available capital, and 53 percent of the owners of farms larger than 2,000 hectares had more than one farm.

The failure of small and medium farmers to adopt the new breeding techniques reflects, in part, the serious lack of technical and economic information on their uses, particularly when they are combined in packages of techniques. It also reflects the existence of a strong, regressive social bias against small farmers in respect to access to credit, information, and education, all of which are clearly important in the adoption of new technologies. Thus, failure to adopt new techniques results from lack of profitability for large farmers and from institutional biases against small farmers; in all cases it reflects the actual unavailability of these techniques for individual adoption, not perverse economic behavior. This is important, because it refutes the traditional structuralist arguments according to which absenteeism and large scale operations hinder technological progress and lead to stagnation. Quite to the contrary, we find that causality runs from the control of institutions by the landed elites, to the unavailability of profitable techniques for

---

[36] Empirical results of this analysis of the beef-breeding sector are given in Obschatko and de Janvry, "Factores limitantes del cambio tecnológico."

adoption by farmers, and only then to absenteeism and large scale operations—which are the most rational forms of economic behavior, given the former conditions.

In summary, we find that a latent demand for research on modern breeding techniques exists, although actual demand is weak. Lack of adoption is due to the real unavailability of these techniques for adoption by individual farmers.

*Conclusion*

The model of dialectical interaction between technical change and institutional organization outlined in this chapter provides a means to interpret the failure of technical change to emerge as an important source of growth in Argentine agriculture. Analysis of the modern agricultural history of Argentina, based on this model, has also revealed why the modest technological change that has occurred in Argentine agriculture has been excessively biased toward labor-saving technologies and why there has been only limited response to the latent demand for land-saving technologies. Our analysis underlines the need for a more thorough examination of the ways in which social structures determine technical biases and for an exploration of the kinds of social and institutional changes that can resolve the current situation of stagnation in food production.

# IV

*Induced Institutional*
*Change*

# TWELVE

# Induced Institutional Change

VERNON W. RUTTAN

I N the preceding chapters of this book we have presented a new investment model of induced technical change, and we have tested this model against the experience of agricultural development in both western and nonwestern economies. We have demonstrated, on the basis of both theory and empirical evidence, that the rate and the direction of technical change are responsive to the rate of growth in demand and to relative resource endowments. We have also shown that the transfer of technology among regions and countries is responsive to essentially the same autonomous processes that induce the evolution of technical change from new knowledge.

The demonstration that technical change can be treated as endogenous to the development process does not imply that the progress of either agricultural or industrial technology can be left to an "invisible hand" that directs technology along an "efficient" path determined by "original" resource endowments or by the growth of demand. The production of the new knowledge that leads to technical change is the result of a process of institutional development.[1] And technical change, in turn, represents a powerful source of demand for institutional change. However, we know a great deal more about the process by which new knowledge is used to alter

I am indebted to the following persons, who participated in the January 20, 1975 ADC/RTN Seminar on Institutional Innovation, for comments and suggestions on an earlier draft of this chapter: Peter Dorner, Donald Kanel, Kenneth McDermott, John D. Montgomery, Douglas North, Mancur Olson, Jr., James C. Roumasset, William Siffin, Russell Stevenson, and Abraham Weisblat. I have also benefited from comments by Edgar S. Dunn, Jr., G. Parthasarthy, and Nathan Rosenberg.

[1] The development of institutions capable of producing a continuous stream of new knowledge is a relatively recent phenomenon. According to Alfred North Whitehead, "the great invention of the nineteenth century was the invention of the method of invention." Alfred North Whitehead, *Science and the Modern World* (New York: Macmillan, 1925), p. 96.

the rate and direction of technical change and of technology transfer than we do about the ways in which resources are applied to bring about institutional innovation and transfer.

We have already introduced the notions that institutions play an important role in the generation and diffusion of technical change and that they are a source of bias in the direction of both technical effort and productivity growth. Binswanger, in chapter 5, has discussed the impact of market structure on research resource allocation. In chapter 10, Sanders and Ruttan have discussed public policy, particularly the subsidization of interest rates, as a source of bias in the direction of technical change in Brazilian agriculture. And in chapter 11, de Janvry has outlined a model of dynamic interaction between technical change and institutional organization.

In the present chapter we will elaborate the elements of a theory of institutional change in which shifts in the demand for institutional change are induced by changes both in the relative prices of factors and products and in the technology associated with economic growth, and in which shifts in the supply of institutional change are induced by advances in knowledge in the social sciences and in fields such as law, business, social service, and planning. We will then consider the implications of imperfections in the organization of the markets in which economic and political resources are exchanged for institutional innovation and for improvements in institutional efficiency.

*Theories of Institutional Change*

During the last two decades we have greatly improved our analytical capacities and accumulated a substantial amount of empirical knowledge—and we need both knowledge and the ability to analyze if we are to achieve a complete understanding of the role of technical change in economic development. However, as already noted, we have far to go in understanding the processes that enable a society to generate a continuous stream of institutional innovations in response to technical and economic opportunities or constraints.

WHAT IS INSTITUTIONAL CHANGE? A distinction is often made between the institution and the organization.[2] An institution is usually defined as the

___

[2] "The term 'institution' has two meanings.... One type...may be said to be created by the 'invisible hand'. The extreme example is language, in the growth and changes of which deliberate action hardly figures: ...law is in varying...degree of the same kind. The other type is of course the deliberately made, of which our Federal Reserve System and this [American Economic] Association itself are examples. With age, the second type tends to approximate the first." Frank H. Knight, "Institutionalism and Empiricism in Economics," *American Economic Review* 42 (May 1952): 51. Knight's view is consistent with that of Samuel P. Huntington: "Institutions are stable, valued, recurring patterns

set of behavioral rules that govern a particular pattern of action and relationships. An organization is generally seen as a decision-making unit—a family, a firm, a bureau—that exercises control of resources. For our purposes, this is a distinction without a difference. What one organization—a household or a firm, for example—accepts as an externally given behavioral rule is the product of tradition or decision by another organization, such as organized labor, a nation's court system, or a religion.[3]

In this chapter the concept of institution will include that of organization. Thus the term *institutional innovation*, or *institutional development*, will be used to refer to a change (1) in the behavior of a particular organization, (2) in the relationship between such an organization and its environment, or (3) in the rules that govern behavior and relationships in an organization's environment.[4]

A clear understanding of the nature of the relationship between technical and institutional change has continued to elude economists and other social scientists interested in the historical and institutional dimensions of development. Researchers in this area, however, have tended to take one or the other of two opposing views: that institutional change depends on technical change, or that technical change depends on institutional change.

TECHNOLOGICAL DETERMINISM. Marx had far greater insight into the historical relationships between technical and institutional change than his contemporaries. He viewed invention as a social process rather than as a

---

of behavior. Organizations and procedures vary in their degree of institutionalization.... Institutionalization is the process by which organizations and procedures acquire value and stability." Samuel P. Huntington, "Political Development and Political Decay," *World Politics* 17 (April 1965): p. 394.

[3] A useful analogy can be drawn between these concepts of the institution and the organization, on the one hand, and external and internal scale economies, on the other. Jacob Viner insisted that the external economies of scale enjoyed by one firm or industry come about as a result of internal economies in some other firm or industry. Jacob Viner, "Cost Curves and Supply Curves," *Zeitschrift für Nationalökonomie* 3 (1932): 23–46.

[4] This definition is broader than Veblen's but consistent with that used by Commons. See John R. Commons, *The Economics of Collective Action* (New York: Macmillan, 1950), p. 26; David Seckler, *Thorstein Veblen and the Institutionalists* (London: Macmillan, 1975), p. 61. The definition used here encompasses the classification employed by Lance E. Davis and Douglass C. North in *Institutional Change and American Economic Growth* (New York: Cambridge University Press, 1971). These authors distinguish five categories of institutional entities and behaviors: (1) *institutional environment:* "the set of fundamental political, social and legal ground rules that establishes the basis for production, exchange and distribution" (p. 6); (2) *institutional arrangement:* "an arrangement between economic units that governs the ways in which these units can cooperate and/or compete" (p. 7); (3) *primary action group:* "a decision-making unit whose decisions govern the process of arrangemental innovation" (p. 8); (4) *secondary action group:* "a decision-making unit that has been established by some change in the institutional arrangement to help effect the capture of income for the primary action group" (p. 8); (5) *institutional instruments:* "documents or devices employed by action groups to effect the capture of income external to the existing arrangemental structures" (p. 9).

result of the transcendental insight or inspiration of the occasional genius.[5] Within the Marxian system, the class struggle reflects the continuing "contradiction" between the evolution of economic institutions and progress in the technology of production.[6] Although Marx stressed the dialectical relationship between changes in modes of production (technical change) and changes in production relationships (institutional change), he believed the former provided the more dynamic source of change in social organization.[7] His view continues to dominate much of Marxian thought on the relationships between technical and institutional change.[8]

Technological determinism has been a dominant theme in the work of the American institutional school. Veblen and his followers regarded technology as the dynamic factor in economic progress and growth; institutions were static factors. Ervin K. Zingler points out that in Veblen's system "it was the . . . dialectical struggle and conflict between dynamic technology and static institutionalism which caused economic and political institutions slowly to be displaced and replaced, and systems of economic organization to undergo historical change and adjustment."[9] And Simon Kuznets has discussed his quantitative investigations into the sources of modern economic growth in terminology that is strikingly similar to that employed by Veblen.[10]

[5] Nathan Rosenberg, "Karl Marx on the Economic Role of Science," *Journal of Political Economy* 82 (July–August, 1974): 713–28; idem, "Marx as a Student of Technology," mimeographed (Palo Alto: Stanford University, Department of Economics, 1975).

[6] This view is expressed in a number of Marx's works, among them, Karl Marx, *A Contribution to the Critique of Political Economy*, trans. N. I. Stone (Chicago: Charles H. Kerr, 1918). For reviews of the Marxian historical perspective see Mandell Morton Bober, *Karl Marx's Interpretation of History*, 2nd ed. rev. (Cambridge, Mass.: Harvard University Press, 1948) and David McLellan, *Karl Marx: His Life and Thought* (New York: Harper and Row, 1973), pp. 137–67.

[7] Karl Marx, *Capital, A Critique of Political Economy*, ed. Friedrich Engels (New York: The Modern Library, copyright 1906, by Charles H. Kerr and Company). According to Marx, "Technology discloses man's mode of dealing with Nature, the process of production by which he sustains his life, and thereby also lays bare the mode of formation of his social relations and the mental conceptions that flow from them." (p. 406n).

[8] See, for example, A. Nikolayev, *R & D in Social Reproduction* (Moscow: Progress Publishers, 1975). According to Nikolayev, "Along with other productive forces scientific knowledge determines the development of the socio-economic system" (p. 181).

[9] Ervin K. Zingler, "Veblen vs. Commons: A Comparative Evaluation," *Kyklos* 17 (1974): 331; Seckler, *Thorstein Veblen*, pp. 68–77; Allan G. Gruchy, "Economic Thought: The Institutional School," *International Encyclopedia of the Social Sciences*, vol. 4 (New York: Macmillan and Free Press, 1968), pp. 462–7; C. E. Ayres, *The Theory of Economic Progress*, 2nd ed. (New York: Schocken Books, 1962). According to Ayres, "the technological revolution spreads in inverse proportion to institutional resistance" (p. xix) and "technological development forces change upon the institutional structure by changing the material setting in which it operates" (p. 187).

[10] Simon Kuznets, "Modern Economic Growth: Findings and Reflections," *American Economic Review* 63 (June 1973): 237–58; idem, *Modern Economic Growth: Rate, Structure and Spread* (New Haven: Yale University Press, 1966), p. 9. For a similar view, see William Parker, "Economic Development in Historical Perspective," in *Economics of Technological Change*, ed. Nathan Rosenberg (Harmondsworth: Penguin Books, 1971): 137–47.

It is interesting to note that research on the diffusion of technology in sociology and anthropology has also been strongly influenced by the view that modernization involves overcoming the irrational forces of custom, culture, and personality in order to take advantage of the opportunities opened up by technical advances.[11] In the field of development economics, however, there is a tendency to de-emphasize the notion of resistance and to place primary emphasis on the size of the income stream generated by technical change. Institutional innovation has thus been viewed as a lagged response to the rising economic value of man and to the growth of productivity.[12]

Among the neo-institutionalists, the theme of the modernizing impact of technology on institutions has been abandoned in favor of a concern for the design of institutions that can manage the "dehumanizing forces" of technical change. While they differ sharply on the welfare implications of technical change, both the old and the new institutionalists seem to share a view of technical change as the product of an autonomous inner logic of scientific discovery and technical innovation.[13]

---

[11] For sociological views, see Elihu Katz, Herbert Hamilton, and Martin L. Levin, "Traditions of Research on the Diffusion of Innovation," *American Sociological Review* 23 (April 1963): 237–52; Everett M. Rogers, *Diffusion of Innovations* (New York: The Free Press of Glencoe, 1962); Thorsten Hagerstrand, *Innovation Diffusion as a Spatial Process* (Chicago: University of Chicago Press, 1976), pp. 299–324; Everett M. Rogers (with F. Floyd Shoemaker), *Communication of Innovations: A Cross Cultural Approach*, 2nd ed. (New York: The Free Press, 1971), pp. 44–97.

Among works in anthropology are George M. Foster, *Traditional Societies and Technological Change*, 2nd ed. (New York: Harper and Row, 1973) and Edward H. Spicer, ed., *Human Problems in Technological Change* (New York: Russell Sage Foundation, 1952). For a critical review, see Glynn Cochrane, *Development Anthropology* (New York: Oxford University Press, 1971).

[12] This view has been emphasized by Theodore W. Schultz, in *Transforming Traditional Agriculture* (New Haven: Yale University Press, 1964), and in "Institutions and the Rising Economic Value of Man," *American Journal of Agricultural Economics* 50 (December 1968): 1113–22. See also Kazushi Ohkawa, "Policy Implications of the Asian Agricultural Survey—Personal Notes," *Regional Seminar on Agriculture: Papers and Proceedings* (Makatí, Philippines: Asian Development Bank, 1969): 23–29.

I have expressed a similar perspective in an earlier work: "A major source of institutional change has been an effort by society to internalize the benefits of innovative activity.... The modernization of land tenure relationships, involving a shift from share tenure to lease tenure and owner–operator systems of cultivation in much of western agriculture, can be explained, in part, as a shift in property rights designed to internalize the gains of entrepreneurial innovation by individual farmers." Yujiro Hayami and Vernon W. Ruttan, *Agricultural Development: An International Perspective* (Baltimore: Johns Hopkins University Press, 1971), p. 60. For a criticism of this perspective, see Peter Dorner, "Institutions as Aids to Development," Paper presented to the Fifteenth International Congress of Agricultural Economists, São Paulo, Brazil, August 20–29, 1973. Dorner seems to argue that the prospect of economic gain has not been a significant inducement to agrarian reform.

[13] "Science is not guided by any social purpose. As with technology, the effects on humanity are simply the by-products of its own self-seeking. As a collective enterprise science has no more social conscience than the problem-solving computers it employs. Indeed, like some ponderous multipurpose robot that is powered by its own insatiable

INSTITUTIONAL DETERMINISM.    A somewhat less vigorous tradition, exemplified by Polanyi's analysis of the sources of the industrial revolution, maintains that institutional rather than technical change is the dynamic source of economic development.[14] Following this line of thought, Douglass C. North and Robert P. Thomas attribute the major sources of Western economic growth to changes, brought about by the pressure of population against increasingly scarce resource endowments, in the institutions whose rules govern property rights.[15] These authors attempt to demonstrate that technical innovation and productivity growth represent a lagged response both to institutional changes induced by long-run changes in relative factor and product prices and to changes in the size of the market.

Growth, according to North and Thomas, can occur only if the economic organization is efficient.[16] Efficient economic organization may require the modification of property rights in order to reduce the differential between private and social returns to innovative activity. Improvements in the organization of factor markets, which involve the redefinition of property rights for both land and labor, occur primarily in response to changing relative prices (that is, changes in the relative scarcity) of land and labor. Later, the demands of an expanding market economy impose pressure to improve the organization of the product market and induce an expansion in the size of political units. The fact that between 1500 and 1700 Holland and England developed more rapidly than France and Spain is seen by North and Thomas as the result of the particular kinds of property rights created by the emerging national states in response to continuing fiscal crises.

North and Thomas repeatedly emphasize their commitment to the view that institutional change precedes, and is more fundamental than, technical

---

curiosity science lurches onward." E. J. Mishan, *The Costs of Economic Growth* (New York: Praeger, 1967), p. 129. For a similar but less extreme view, see Allan G. Gruchy, *Contemporary Economic Thought: The Contribution of Neo-Institutional Economics* (Clifton, New Jersey: Augustus M. Kelley, 1972), pp. 296–7.

[14] Karl Polanyi, *The Great Transformation* (Boston: Beacon Press, 1957), p. 119.

[15] Douglass C. North and Robert Paul Thomas, *The Rise of the Western World* (London: Cambridge University Press, 1973) and idem, "An Economic Theory of the Growth of the Western World," *The Economic History Review* 22 (1970): 1–17. For a criticism of the North-Thomas point of view, see the review by W. W. Rostow, *Journal of Economic Literature* 12 (June 1974): 493–6.

[16] According to North and Thomas, "the government is primarily an institutional arrangement that sells protection and justice to its constituents. It does so by monopolizing the definition and enforcement of property rights over goods and resources and the granting of rights to the transfer of these assets. In return for this service, the state receives payment in the form of taxes. Since economies of scale in the provision of protection and justice make this transaction potentially worthwhile to the constituents, a basis exists for a mutually advantageous trade between the governed and the government. So long as economies of scale continue, the state's evident protection and enforcement of property rights increases the income of all constituents and this saving is divided in some manner between the constituents and the state." North and Thomas, *Rise of the Western World*, p. 97.

change. They regard the rise of the more intensive systems of cultivation, such as the replacement of the two-field system by the three-field system, as involving an institutional response to changing relative factor prices rather than to technical change.[17] Moreover, they emphasize that an expanding market economy contributes to rising per capita income even in the absence of technical change.[18]

Working on a less cosmic scale, Alfred D. Chandler, Jr. has argued that the managerial revolution that took place in American industry in the 1950s and 1960s was more the product of institutional changes induced by expanding market opportunities than a response to the economic gains from potential scale economies that may be realized from technical change.[19] This revolution had its inception in the 1920s, when new patterns of organization began to develop at DuPont, General Motors, Standard Oil (of New Jersey), and Sears. From a system that was composed of, on the one hand, operating companies in which decision making for all departments was highly centralized, and, on the other, loosely held, decentralized holding companies, a new system evolved wherein operating decisions for a group of multi-divisional structures were highly decentralized whereas strategic planning and financial control for the whole group remained under the jurisdiction of central offices.[20] The "systematization of strategic decisions through the building of a general office and the routinizing of product development . . . institutionalized the strategy of diversification" in leading firms.[21] Chandler argues that the gains in institutional efficiency that resulted from these structural innovations created, in turn, an environment conducive to technical innovation. In his view, the economies of scale in American industry are far more a product of institutional innovation than a product of technical change.

## A Model of Institutional Change

Within modern analytical economics there is a tendency to either abstract from institutional change[22] or to treat institutional change as

[17] North and Thomas, *Rise of the Western World*, p. 43.

[18] Ibid, p. 93.

[19] Alfred D. Chandler, Jr., *Strategy and Structure: Chapters in the History of American Industrial Enterprise* (Cambridge, Mass.: M.I.T. Press, 1972).

[20] "The inherent weakness in the centralized, functionally departmentalized holding company became critical only when the administrative load on the senior executive officers increased to such an extreme that they were unable to handle their entrepreneurial responsibilities efficiently." Chandler, *Strategy and Structure*, p. 299.

[21] Chandler, *Strategy and Structure*, p. 394.

[22] According to Paul A. Samuelson, *Foundations of Economic Analysis* (Cambridge, Mass.: Harvard University Press, 1948), "the auxiliary constraints imposed upon the variables are not themselves the proper subject matter of welfare economics but must be taken as given" (pp. 221–2). For an excellent critical review of the welfare economics approach to institutional change, see James C. Roumasset, "Induced Institutional Change, Welfare Economics, and the Science of Public Policy," Working Paper Series no. 46 (Davis: University of California, Department of Economics, October

exogenous to the economic system.[23] Neither of these approaches is adequate. In the real world, property rights are costly to enforce, market exchange consumes resources, and information is scarce.[24] To ignore the fact that institutional change not only affects resources use but is itself a resource-using activity is to leave our understanding of the process of institutional change and our capacity to incorporate institutional change into the analytical framework of modern economics in the same unsatisfactory condition that characterized our approach to the treatment of technical change in economics prior to the mid-1950s.

We hypothesize here that institutional change may be induced by the *demand* for more effective institutional performance that is associated with economic growth. And we hypothesize also that institutional change may occur as a result of advances in the *supply* of knowledge about social and economic behavior, organization, and change.

THE DEMAND FOR INSTITUTIONAL CHANGE.   There are available in the literature several elements of a theory of the demand for institutional change. As we have noted earlier, North and Thomas explain the economic growth of Western Europe between 900 and 1700 primarily in terms of changes in the institutions whose rules govern property rights. These institutional changes, in their view, were induced by the pressure of population against increasingly scarce resource endowments. Theodore W. Schultz, focusing on more recent economic history, has identified the rising economic value of man during the process of economic development as the primary

---

1974). For a critique of general equilibrium theory in respect to its lack of focus on institutional matters, see Martin Shubik, "Beyond General Equilibrium," Discussion Paper 417 (New Haven: Cowles Foundation for Research in Economics at Yale University, January 14, 1976).

[23] The approach to institutional change that is characteristic of much of the reform tradition is illustrated in Abba P. Lerner, *The Economics of Control* (New York: Macmillan, 1944): "In this study...we shall assume a government that wishes to run society in the general social interest and is strong enough to override the opposition afforded by any sectional interest" (p. 6). Harry G. Johnson has commented, "The main tradition of welfare economics takes a Benthamite or Fabian view of the state as a dispassionate and all-wise modern equivalent of Plato's philosopher-king, correcting the errors of his subject society by appropriate taxes, subsidies, and lump sum transfers of income." Harry G. Johnson, "The Current and Prospective State of Economics," *Australian Economic Papers* 13 (June 1974): 1–27. This point has been made even more succinctly by Irving Louis Horowitz, *Three Worlds of Development*, 2nd ed. (New York: Oxford University Press, 1972): "In the planning ideology all planning is done by a dedicated development oriented elite supported by loyal, self sacrificing masses" (p. 49).

[24] Mancur Olson, Jr., "Some Historic Variations in Property Institutions," mimeographed (College Park: University of Maryland, Department of Economics, 1974). Olson argues that property rights in a good or a service will not be claimed unless it is profitable to claim them. "The hypothesis...is applicable at two levels. There cannot be property rights in any social setting unless individuals find it profitable to claim a property right and the government of a community also finds it in its interest to allow that property right" (p. 7).

source of institutional change.[25] There seems little doubt that North and Thomas would agree with Schultz that, "It is hard to imagine any secular economic movement that would have more profound influence in altering institutions than would the movement of wages relative to that of rents."[26]

During the high Middle Ages (1000–1300) in Europe, "land was becoming scarce and rising in value."[27] As land scarcity became general, the pressure to limit common-property uses increased. More effective control over land use was consistent with the introduction of more intensive systems of agricultural production. The three-field system began to replace the traditional biennial rotation.

In the early modern period, continuing pressure of population on the land led to the elimination of the commons and to a transition from a system of cultivation based on the use of servile labor to a system based on either owner-operatorship of land by peasant proprietors or the use of wage labor by capitalist land owners.[28] The result was the evolution of even more intensive systems of crop production, particularly in the low countries and England. These same systems later became dominant in Germany, Denmark, and France. During the 20th century, as land has become a less serious constraint on the growth of agricultural production, the thrust of institutional evolution in respect to property rights in agricultural land has been to reduce the private rights of the individual producer.[29]

More recently, the demand that the environment absorb the residuals from both agricultural and industrial production and from transportation has come into intense conflict with the demand for environmental services and amenities.[30] This competition has resulted in a dramatic rise in the economic value of common property resources that had previously been regarded as free goods.[31] The result has been the emergence of new institutions designed to clarify the property rights of individuals, firms, and communities in respect to these increasingly valuable common property resources.

North and Thomas also identify periods of substantial economic progress

[25] Schultz, "Rising Economic Value of Man," pp. 1113–22.

[26] Ibid., p. 1120.

[27] North and Thomas, *Rise of the Western World*, p. 23.

[28] Olson, "Some Historic Variations."

[29] Leonard A. Salter, Jr., *A Critical Review of Research in Land Economics* (Madison: University of Wisconsin Press, 1967), pp. 5–38; Folke Dovring, *Land and Labor in Europe in the Twentieth Century* (The Hague: Martinus Nijhoff, 1965).

[30] See Allen V. Kneese and Blair T. Bower, eds., *Environmental Quality Analysis* (Baltimore: Johns Hopkins University Press, 1972).

[31] Garett Hardin, "The Tragedy of the Commons," *Science* 162 (December 1968): 1243–8; Beryl L. Crowe, "The Tragedy of the Commons Revisited," *Science* 166 (November 1969): 1103–7; Vernon W. Ruttan, "Technology and the Environment," *American Journal of Agricultural Economics* 53 (December 1971): 707–17; V. Kerry Smith, *Technical Change, Relative Prices, and Environmental Resource Evaluation* (Baltimore: Johns Hopkins University Press, 1974).

when wages were rising relative to the value of land. They find that during such periods, institutional changes occurred that gave the peasant or the freeholder greater control over the use of his own labor. Institutional change induced by the rising economic value of man has been rapid, indeed dramatic, during the last century and a half. We have moved from a state in which slavery, which denies man the opportunity or the incentive to invest in himself, was predominant to our present state, where both private and public investment in the human agent, in terms of both the promotion of health and education, have become institutionalized.

The same sequence that North and Thomas observed in European development, wherein institutional change occurs in response to changes in labor–land price ratios, has been reported in contemporary developing countries. In Indonesia between 1868 and 1928, a period of generally rapid economic growth, patron–client obligations were modified in favor of tenants and landless laborers. Since the late 1920s, as land prices have risen against wage rates, the balance has again shifted, to favor land owners rather than tenants and laborers.[32] In a number of developing countries, the use of more intensive farming systems has led to an increase in the economic value of water. And this increased value has induced institutional changes that have led to more precise definitions of property rights in respect to irrigation water and to greater use of market mechanisms in the allocation of water.[33]

There can be little question that the new income streams released by technical change do represent an important source of demand for institutional change. Potential gains from new and more efficient technologies represent a powerful motivation for private-sector research and development and for public-sector investment in the exploration of natural resources and the development of science and technology. The development of modern corporate organization, from a stage in which permission to form a limited-liability joint stock corporation was granted by the state as a monopoly privilege, to the present day, when enactment of general incorporation laws has established the right of association for the purpose of conducting economic activity, represents an institutional response to the economic opportunities opened up by advances in the technology of transportation, communications, and manufacturing in the nineteenth century.[34]

[32] Benjamin White, "Agricultural Involution: A Critical Note," mimeographed (Jakarta: Agro-Economic Survey, October 1974), p. 14. White refers to G. H. Van der Kolff, "The Historical Development of Labor Relations in a Remote Corner of Java as they Apply to the Cultivation of Rice" (Batavia: IPR International Research Series, Report C, 1937), and to D. H. Burger, "Laporan mengenai desa Pekalongan dalam Tahun, 1868 to 1928," *Tindjauan Ekonomic* (Jakarta 1971).

[33] Robert R. Jay, *Javanese Villagers: Social Relations in Rural Modjokuto* (Cambridge, Mass.: M.I.T. Press, 1969).

[34] Oscar Handlin and Mary F. Handlin, "Origins of the American Business Corporation," *Journal of Economic History* (March, 1945): 1–23. Reprinted in Frederic C. Lane and Jelle C. Riemarsma, eds., *Enterprise and Secular Change: Readings in Economic History* (Homewood, Ill.: Richard D. Irwin, 1953): 102–24.

The partitioning of the new income streams that result from the efficiency gains associated with technical change or improvements in institutional performance represents a major incentive for further institutional change.[35] In a classical or neo-classical world, unencumbered by the use of political resources to achieve economic objectives, the new income streams generated by technical change would be distributed to factors according to the Ricardian model of distribution.[36] The gains would flow to owners of the factors that are characterized by relatively inelastic supply functions. It is easy to see, however, that the only function served by the capture of the new income streams by the suppliers of inelastic factors—and these are the factors that act as a constraint on, rather than as a source of, growth—is to establish a claim on the social product. As a result, advances in technology can be expected to set in motion attempts by individuals to reallocate their personal resources and to organize and initiate collective action for the purpose of redefining property rights so as to achieve greater equity in the partitioning of the new income streams.[37] Advances in institutional efficiency that are associated with the rise of the corporate (or cooperative) form of organization give rise to growth dividends that induce a demand for the corporate organization of labor, in the form of unions, and of farmers, in the form of cooperatives, so that each group may participate more effectively in the partitioning of the new income streams.[38]

THE SUPPLY OF INSTITUTIONAL CHANGE. Change in relative factor prices plays a role in the North–Thomas and the Schultz models of induced

[35] Fred Cottrell, "Technology and Social Change on American Railroads," in George K. Zollschan and Walter Hirsch, eds., *Explorations in Social Change* (New York: Houghton Mifflin, 1964). For example, Cottrell points out that technical change in the communication industry "may disrupt the functions of family and community, undermine the authority of the religious, result in the destruction of old economic arrangements, and destroy the ability of a government . . . to rule legitimately" (p. 73).

[36] For a graphic exposition of the Ricardian model of distribution, see Harry G. Johnson, *The Two Sector Model of General Equilibrium* (Chicago: Aldine-Atherton, 1971), pp. 10–12.

[37] Theodore W. Schultz, "The Value of the Ability to Deal with Disequilibria," *Journal of Economic Literature* 13 (September 1975): 822–46. Schultz argues that "the ability to deal with economic disequilibria is enhanced by education, and this ability is one of the major benefits to people privately in a modernizing economy" (p. 843). He confines his discussion to individual responses to disequilibria.

[38] Commons' work seems to have focused largely on the role of institutions, or of collective action, in the reallocation of the ownership of material and human resources and on the associated changes in the distribution of income in the process of economic growth. His concentration on the *transaction* as the primary unit of investigation, his taxonomy of transactions (bargaining, managerial, rationing) based on power relationships, his concept of *reasonableness* in his theory of value, and his concern with social choice and control all seem to derive from an acute insight into the inability of partial equilibrium analysis to provide a rationale for the distribution of income that is socially acceptable (ethical) rather than formal in a society capable of generating a continuous stream of growth dividends. See Kenneth H. Parsons, "John R. Commons' Point of View," *Journal of Land and Public Utility Economics* 17 (August 1942): 245–66 (reprinted in Commons, *Economics of Collective Action*, pp. 341–75).

institutional change that is quite similar to the role it plays in the model of induced technical change outlined in chapters 2 through 4. However, neither North and Thomas nor Schultz attempt to provide a theory of the supply of institutional change. And we find little help in either the older institutional literature or the newer, neo-institutional literature.

It seems reasonable to hypothesize an analogy between the supply of institutional change and the supply of technical change. Just as the supply curve for technical change shifts to the right as a result of advances in scientific and technological knowledge, so the supply curve for institutional change shifts to the right as a result of advances in knowledge in the social sciences and related professions such as business, planning, law, and social service. Moreover, advances in knowledge in the social sciences and related professions reduce the cost of institutional change just as advances in knowledge in the natural sciences and engineering reduce the cost of technical change.

This is not to argue that institutional change is entirely dependent on formal research that leads to new knowledge in the social sciences and related professions. Technical change did not wait for research in the natural sciences and technology to become institutionalized. Similarly, institutional change may occur as a result of the exercise of innovative effort by politicians, bureaucrats, entrepreneurs, and others as they conduct their daily activities.[39] The timing or pace of institutional innovation may be influenced by external contact or internal stress. One of the objectives of institutionalizing social science research capacity is the achievement of greater efficiency in the allocation of social science research resources. Better allocation of these resources will make it possible (a) to speed up the production of new knowledge designed to be used as input in those areas of institutional change given high priority by society and (b) to apply the new knowledge so as to bring about a more precise linkage between the objectives of institutional change and the institutional changes that are actually implemented.

If the effect of advances in knowledge in the social sciences and related professions is to shift the supply curve for institutional change to the right, or to move the institutional innovation possibility curve closer to the origin,

---

[39] "Those who take a Marxian rather than a Keynesian view of the relation between the power of ideas and *praxis* see evidence that solutions to social problems are worked out by men and women going about their daily work...and that the grand theories distill these practical experiences." Paul P. Streeten, "Social Science Research on Development: Some Problems in the Use and Transfer of an Intellectual Technology." *Journal of Economic Literature* 12 (December 1974), pp. 1290–1300. The same point is made by P. C. Joshi: "The circumstances which gave an initial stimulus to intellectual inquiry into the land question...preceded the professionalization of Indian economic studies.... Enquiries into the land problem were thus initiated by those concerned directly with the formulation of land and revenue policies (or the critique of these policies) and not by professional social scientists." P. C. Joshi, *Land Reforms in India* (New Delhi: Allied Publishers, 1975), p. 7.

the question of the elasticity of supply of knowledge in the social sciences emerges as an important issue. The implicit presumption in the modern tradition of analytical economics seems to be that the supply of institutional change itself is, with appropriate allowance for time lags, reasonably elastic. This view seems inconsistent with the view, held by a number of historians of economic thought, that the supply of knowledge in economics is relatively impervious to the impact of external events.[40]

We cannot, at this time, resolve the issue of the elasticity of supply of knowledge in economics or in the other social sciences. We would hypothesize that, within the framework of a particular paradigm, the supply of knowledge about the economy is more elastic than the supply of disciplinary knowledge itself.[41] In any event there would seem to be little question that both "paradigm shifts" and advances in disciplinary knowledge within the framework of a particular paradigm do have the effect of shifting the supply curve for knowledge about the economy to the right and hence of reducing the cost of institutional change.

One of the most dramatic examples of the effect of new knowledge in the social sciences on institutional innovation and efficiency can be seen in the new understanding of macroeconomic relationships associated with the Keynesian revolution.[42] No effort has been made to estimate the economic gains generated by the new knowledge in enabling the developed economies of the West to operate at close to full employment since World War II. We do, however, have estimates, made by Arthur M. Okun, of the contributions to United States economic growth of the reductions in personal and

---

[40] George J. Stigler, *Essays in the History of Economics* (Chicago: University of Chicago Press, 1965), chapter entitled "The Influence of Events and Policies in Economic Theory," pp. 16–30. According to Stigler, "The dominant influence upon the working range of economic theorists is the set of internal values and the pressure of the discipline" (p. 22). For further support of this view, see Joseph J. Spengler, "Exogenous and Endogenous Influences in the Formation of Post-1870 Economic Thought: A Sociology of Knowledge Approach," in Robert V. Eagly, ed., *Events, Ideology and Economic Theory* (Detroit: Wayne State University Press, 1968), pp. 159–205. For an example of an opposing view, see James R. Simpson, "The Origin of United States Academic Interest in Foreign Economic Development," *Economic Development and Cultural Change* 24 (April 1976): 633–44.

[41] Thomas S. Kuhn, *The Structure of Scientific Revolutions* (Chicago: University of Chicago Press, 1962), uses the term "paradigm" to refer to the basic set of assumptions adopted within a scientific discipline in a particular historical phase or by a particular school. Thus we can refer to the "neo-classical paradigm" or the "Keynesian paradigm."

This hypothesis is consistent with the view of Robert K. Merton, *Social Theory and Social Structure* (New York: The Free Press, 1968): 39–72. See also idem, *On Theoretical Sociology* (New York: The Free Press, 1967).

[42] John M. Keynes, *The General Theory of Employment, Interest and Money* (New York: Harcourt and Brace, 1936). For an early evaluation of Keynes' theories, see S. E. Harris, ed., *The New Economics* (New York: Knopf, 1947). For a more recent evaluation, see Harry G. Johnson, "The Keynesian Revolution and the Monetarist Counter-Revolution," *American Economic Review* 61 (May 1971): 1–14.

corporate income taxes under the Revenue Act of 1964.[43] Tax cuts amounting to $13 billion in 1964 and 1965 were made with the explicit objective of reducing the gap between actual and potential GNP. These tax cuts were recommended by the Council of Economic Advisors as a result of quantitative projections based on estimates of disposable income, consumption, investment, and inventory relationships. Okun's *ex post* estimates indicate that during the first two years after the tax cut the tax reduction contributed $25 billion to the growth of the GNP and, ultimately, $36 billion to its growth. In retrospect, these estimated gains should be partially discounted to the extent that they contributed to the inflation of the late 1960s.[44]

Neither the analytical capacity, the statistical data, nor the institutional responsibility necessary for such quantitatively based policy interventions were available until after World War II. The institutionalization of statistical capacity, in the Commerce Department's Office of Business Economics, and analytical capacity, in the President's Council of Economic Advisors, was a direct product of the advances in economic knowledge associated with the Keynesian revolution.[45]

Neither the United States nor any other country has yet been as successful in other social sciences as in economics in institutionalizing capacity to provide the new knowledge that can help reduce the economic and human costs of social change. Nevertheless, as governments begin to concern themselves with the more complex problems of social change, they create incentives for finding better ways to utilize the full capacities of the other social sciences in solving problems of public policy.[46]

A SYNTHESIS.    Arguments over the relative priority of technical or institutional change are generally unproductive. Technical and institutional change, as de Janvry argues in chapter 11, are highly interdependent and therefore must be analyzed within a context of continuing interaction.

The sources of *demand* for technical and institutional change are very similar. A rise in the price of land (or natural resources) in relation to the price of labor induces technical changes designed to release the constraints on

[43] Arthur M. Okun, "Measuring the Impact of the 1964 Tax Reduction," in *Perspectives on Economic Growth*, ed. Walter W. Heller (New York: Random House, 1968), pp. 27–49.

[44] The Council urged an income tax surcharge well before President Johnson recommended it to Congress in 1967. However, the surcharge was not acted on by Congress until June 1968. James Tobin, *The New Economics One Decade Older* (Princeton: Princeton University Press, 1974), p. 36.

[45] Stephen K. Bailey, *Congress Makes a Law: The Story Behind the Employment Act of 1946* (New York: Columbia University Press, 1950).

[46] For a review of the development of the social sciences in the public sector in the United States, see Gene M. Lyons, *The Uneasy Partnership: Social Science and the Federal Government in the Twentieth Century* (New York: The Russell Sage Foundation, 1969).

production that result from the inelastic supply of land and, at the same time, induces institutional changes that lead to greater precision in the definition and allocation of property rights in land. A rise in the price of labor relative to the price of land (or natural resources) induces technical changes designed to permit the substitution of capital for labor and, at the same time, induces institutional changes designed to enhance the productive capacity of the human agent and to increase the worker's control of the conditions of his own employment. The new income streams generated by technical change and by gains in institutional efficiency induce change in the relative demand for products and open up new and more profitable opportunities for product innovations. This leads to greater diversity in consumption patterns. And the new income streams generated by either technical or institutional change induce further institutional changes designed to modify the way the new income streams are partitioned among factor owners and to alter the distribution of income among individuals and classes.

Shifts in the *supply* of technical and institutional change are generated by similar forces. Advances in knowledge in science and technology reduce the cost of the new income streams that are generated by technical change. Advances in knowledge in the social sciences and related professions reduce the cost of the new income streams that are generated by gains in institutional efficiency, including improved skills in conflict resolution.

The significance of the model of institutional change proposed in this section is that it suggests a theory of induced institutional change that is capable of generating testable hypotheses regarding alternative patterns of institutional change (a) for a particular society over time and (b) for a number of countries at a given time.[47] It is possible to build on the model outlined in this section to develop a theory of induced institutional change that is both explanatory and predictive. Such a theory not only can explain events up to the present time but can generate hypotheses regarding the future direction of institutional change and can offer a guide for research in economics and other social sciences aimed at achieving more effective institutional performance and more rapid institutional innovation.

---

[47] Schultz has suggested several hypotheses as to the effect of economic growth on the demand for institutional change: (1) Economic growth results in a shift to the right of the demand for market institutions that facilitate the monetization of economic activity. (2) As economic growth becomes increasingly dependent on advances in knowledge, the demand for institutions to produce and distribute knowledge shifts to the right. (3) In an economy where growth increases the economic value of human agents, there will be a shift in the character of the institutions that govern property rights in material and human resources. Schultz, "Rising Economic Value of Man," pp. 1118, 1119. For an attempt to test these three hypotheses against development experience in Mexico and Indonesia, see Elam K. Stauffer and Melvin G. Blase, "Institutional Disequilibria in the Development Process," *Economic Development and Cultural Change* 22 (January 1974): 265–78.

*Institutional Performance*

In the preceding section we have elaborated a theory of the demand and supply of institutional change. We have presented examples that suggest that empirical counterparts to the theory are to be found in the economic history of both western and nonwestern societies.

How effective are the economic and political markets that translate the latent sources of demand and supply of institutional change into effective institutional innovation? The forces that affect the demand and the supply of institutional innovation appear to operate through relatively imperfect markets. The economic and political resources needed to generate shifts in the demand and the supply of institutional change are distributed unequally among individuals and institutions. The new income streams generated by technical and institutional innovation provide incentives for the use of political resources to partition the gains. The resources devoted to shifting the demand and supply of institutional change and to partitioning the gains from institutional change among resource owners and social classes are allocated through relatively inefficient markets for political resources.[48]

In this section we will explore the ways in which the structure of these economic and political markets affects the efficiency with which shifts in latent demand for and supply of institutional innovation are translated into actual changes in institutional organization and performance. Attention will be focused on the issues of bureaucratic behavior and collective action. These issues are particularly significant in determining the degree to which the markets for institutional innovation and for more effective institutional performance approximate the process of induced institutional innovation suggested in the preceding section.

MARKET STRUCTURE AND EFFICIENCY. In economics, the formal analysis of institutional performance has evolved primarily out of an attempt to understand the implications of market structure for the behavior of the firm. Much of the early work in the field of economic organization was directed toward analyzing the effects of the structure of factor and product markets on the conduct and performance of the firm.[49] This concern with the impact of the external environment on firm behavior has been complemented by a

---

[48] For an elaboration of the concept of political markets, see Warren F. Ilchman and Norman Thomas Uphoff, *The Political Economy of Change* (Berkeley: University of California Press, 1971): 30–32. For a discussion of the limitations of the "political market" approach to the modeling of historical development processes, see Joseph O. Reid, Jr., "Understanding Political Events in the New Economic History," mimeographed (Chicago: University of Chicago, Department of Economics, April 1976).

[49] Joan Robinson, *The Economics of Imperfect Competition* (London: Macmillan, 1933); Edward H. Chamberlain, *The Theory of Monopolistic Competition* (Cambridge, Mass.: Harvard University Press, 1948); Joel S. Bane, *Industrial Organization* (New York: John Wiley, 1959).

newer body of research on administrative behavior that focuses on the implications of bureaucratic organization for resource allocation and for the growth of the firm.[50]

There is also a long tradition in economics that focuses on the organization of production in a socialist system. This has involved an effort to specify the rules that would guide managers of public enterprises to approximate the equilibrium resource-allocation and output levels that would characterize a private firm, or an economy, under perfect competition.[51] As the production of both public and private goods by public sector institutions has expanded, even in nonsocialist economies, a burgeoning literature on the theory and practice of public investment decision making has emerged.[52]

A major weakness of both the literature on the economics of socialism and the research within the tradition of benefit-cost analysis is that neither contains an explicit theory of political or bureaucratic behavior. For a time, an implicit "altruistic," or "organic," theory of bureaucratic behavior assumed that if politicians and bureaucrats were provided with optimization rules, such rules would be adopted and implemented.[53] It has become increasingly apparent, however, that the effectiveness of legislative bodies in translating individual preferences into public policy—that is, the efficiency with which votes are exchanged for policies—depends on the institutions a society employs in making its choices.[54] It has also become clear that the management of public sector enterprises—including government bureaus, university departments or research institutes, regional or local development authorities, and nationalized industries—cannot be expected to follow the maximization rules or objective functions specified by enabling or funding legislation or by planning agencies. The behavior of the managers of such institutions is influenced by the structure of the economic and political factor and product markets in which they operate.[55]

As a result of the foregoing, both economists and political scientists, over

[50] Herbert A. Simon, "New Developments in the Theory of the Firm," *American Economic Review* 52 (May 1962): 1–15.

[51] Oscar Lange and Fred M. Taylor, *On the Economic Theory of Socialism* (Minneapolis: University of Minnesota Press, 1938); Lerner, *Economics of Control.*

[52] The early cost–benefit literature is reviewed in John V. Krutilla and Otto Eckstein, *Multiple Purpose River Development* (Baltimore: Johns Hopkins University Press, 1957), and in Otto Eckstein, *Water Resource Development: The Economics of Project Evaluation* (Cambridge, Mass.: Harvard University Press, 1958).

[53] See Lerner, Johnson, and Horowitz, as cited in footnote 23.

[54] Anthony Downs, *An Economic Theory of Democracy* (New York: Harper & Row, 1957); James M. Buchanan and Gordon Tullock, *The Calculus of Consent* (Ann Arbor: University of Michigan Press, 1962); Kenneth Arrow, *Social Choice and Individual Values* (New York: John Wiley 1963); Edwin T. Haefele, *Representative Government and Environmental Management* (Baltimore: Johns Hopkins University Press, 1973).

[55] William A. Niskanen, "The Peculiar Economics of Bureaucracy," *American Economic Review* 58 (May 1968): 293–305; William A. Niskanen, Jr., *Bureaucracy and Representative Government* (Chicago: Aldine-Atherton, 1971); Huntington, "Political Development."

the last two decades, have made an increasingly intensive effort to develop more formal approaches to the analysis of collective choice and action. In this effort they have attempted to bring more powerful analytical tools to bear on a set of issues that had been of primary interest to an earlier generation of institutional economists, political scientists interested in pluralism, and sociologists concerned with organization theory.[56] In many respects, this effort to understand the behavior of public-sector institutions is analogous to the efforts in the field of economic organization and administrative behavior to understand the external and internal forces that govern the behavior of bureaucratically organized enterprises in the private sector.

According to Albert Breton, the new lines of research on the problems of collective choice and action are encompassed in four bodies of theory: the theories of public goods, democracy, decision rules, and transaction costs.[57] Breton regards the work on the theory of public goods as inadequate to explain the forces that determine the allocation of resources between public and private goods because there is no institutional counterpart to the formal theory. The theory of democracy does, in Breton's view, incorporate essential elements of observable political systems—political parties, decision rules, and information cost—but it tends to underestimate the returns to participation in political activity.[58] Work on the theory of decision rules has focused primarily on problems of individual choice and is only beginning to incorporate the processes of institutional decision making. The theory of transaction costs focuses on the implications of the costs, in terms of both resources and time, of market and nonmarket transactions; it is just now being formalized.

In development, we are particularly concerned with collective action that leads to the technical and institutional changes that expand a society's capacity for growth and development. These capacity-expanding technical and institutional innovations are developed primarily as a result of actions by individuals working within, or attempting to influence the behavior of, private or public-sector bureaucracies. In the next two sections we will look at Niskanen's investigations of bureaucratic behavior and Olson's

---

[56] See the earlier references in this chapter to the work of John R. Commons on the role of institutions in economic growth. For a review of the pluralist tradition in political science, see Theodore J. Lowi, *The End of Liberalism* (New York: Norton, 1969), and Mancur Olson, Jr., *The Logic of Collective Action; Public Goods and the Theory of Groups* (Cambridge, Mass.: Harvard University Press, 1965). For a classic example of organization theory, see Philip Selznick, *TVA and the Grass Roots: A Study in the Sociology of Formal Organization* (Berkeley: University of California Press, 1949).

[57] Albert Breton, *The Economic Theory of Representative Government* (Chicago: Aldine, 1974), pp. 3–9. See also the review of the literature on public choice by Dennis C. Mueller, "Public Choice: A Survey," *Journal of Economic Literature* 14 (June 1976): 395–433.

[58] "It is difficult to believe, when one observes the large amount of political activity that exists in democratic societies, the large flow of political news put out by media,... and the large number of individuals who vote, that political information exists in very small amounts." Breton, *Representative Government*, p. 6.

work on the transaction costs of collective action as we attempt to analyze the processes by which latent demand for institutional innovation is transated into effective demand for institutional change.[59]

BUREAUCRATIC BEHAVIOR.    The significance of the new work on the economics of bureaucratic behavior is that it provides an approach to the modeling of the maximizing behavior of bureaucratic entrepreneurs on the budget and output of the bureau. A bureau, as defined by Niskanen, is any nonprofit organization that is financed at least in part by a periodic appropriation or grant.[60]

The behavior of most bureaus, in Niskanen's view, is conditioned by the fact that they acquire their factors of production primarily in competitive markets but they market most of their services, or output, in monopoly or monopsony markets. Most bureaus are financed by a single, dominant collective organization—a national or provincial legislative body, for example —which, in turn, is financed by tax revenues. Similarly, the sponsoring organization or clientele group that benefits from the bureau's program is usually dependent on a specific bureau to supply the service it needs, and the bureau depends on the clientele group for its political support. Under these conditions, the relationship between the bureau and its sponsoring organization is that of a "bilateral monopoly."

In order to construct what might be called the "pure theory" of bureaucratic behavior, Niskanen combines the above observation with the argument that the utility function of the bureaucratic entrepreneur–manager is a monotonic function of the total budget of the bureau.[61] Three very significant hypotheses are generated by the Niskanen model:

---

[59] Niskanen, *Bureaucracy and Representative Government*; Olson, *Logic of Collective Action*.

[60] This includes "all nonprofit organizations, such as all government agencies and enterprises, most educational institutions and hospitals, and the many forms of social, charitable, and religious organizations.... Some component units in profit-seeking organizations...providing such services as advertising, public relations, and research have...the critical characteristics of bureaus. Thus, the more difficult it is to identify a component's contribution to corporate profits, the more likely that the component will act like a bureau." Niskanen, *Bureaucracy and Representative Government*, pp. 16, 17.

[61] "Among the several variables that may enter the bureaucrat's utility function are the following: salary, perquisites of the office, public reputation, power, patronage, output of the bureau, ease of making changes, and ease of managing the bureau. All of these variables except the last two...are a positive monotonic function of the total budget of the bureau during the bureaucrat's tenure in office. The problems of making changes and the personal burdens of managing a bureau are often higher at higher budget levels but both are reduced by increases in the total budget. This effect creates a treadmill phenomenon inducing bureaucrats to strive for increased budgets until they can turn over the management burdens of a stable higher budget to a new bureaucrat." Ibid., p. 38. In response to criticism, Niskanen has modified the utility function proposed in *Bureaucracy and Representative Government*. His modified model still generates the hypotheses that follow. See also idem, "Bureaucrats and Politicians," *The Journal of Law and Economics* 18 (December 1975): 617–44.

(1) A bureau will supply a larger output than either a competitive industry or a profit-seeking monopoly. This suggests that the owners of the specific factors used to produce the bureau's output will be in favor of a bureaucratic form of organization: educators will prefer public schools; postal workers will resist the formation of a national postal corporation.[62]

(2) As long as budget represents a constraint on output, a bureau will have an incentive to engage in promotional activities that both increase the demand and decrease the elasticity of demand for its services.[63]

(3) A bureau that faces a highly elastic demand for its services will supply the service at or near the cost that would prevail in a competitively organized industry. Conversely, an inelastic demand enables the bureau to capture a higher share of the economic rents generated by its activities. These rents may take the form of personnel expansions or more impressive facilities.[64]

Except in a few areas, such as national defense, the bureaucratic model specified in the "pure theory" is difficult to observe. Bureaus typically supply a mix of services to several clientele groups. In the United States a college of agriculture supplies a mix of teaching, research, and extension to widely varied clientele groups (see chapter 6, appendix 6–1). It derives revenue from both state and federal legislatures as well as from tuition payments and from the sale of commodities. However, there are alternative options open to the legislative bodies that appropriate funds and to the clientele groups that support legislative appropriations. The U.S. Congress can, for example, appropriate research funds for the U.S. Department of Agriculture rather than for the state experiment stations. Farmers can obtain information from neighboring states' experiment station publications and extension services as well as from the farm press. Students can enroll in colleges of agriculture in states other than their own or pursue curricula other than agriculture at public or private universities in their own states. The effect of these modifications is to make the demand for the services of the college of agriculture, including its teaching, research, and extension units, more elastic than implied in the pure bilateral monopoly model of bureaucratic behavior, as well as to induce institutional behavior similar to that seen in a competitive industry.[65]

The Niskanen model, however, does have substantial predictive power. The prediction of a tendency toward excess production under conditions of elastic demand and the generation of excessive rents under conditions of

---

[62] Niskanen, *Bureaucracy and Representative Government*, p. 58.

[63] Ibid., p. 77.

[64] Ibid., p. 130.

[65] Niskanen does discuss the behavior of the "mixed" bureau, which receives part of its financing from a grant and part from the sale of a service, and the multi-service bureau, which supplies two or more services. He concludes that "the broadening of the service line of one bureau is an essential condition for reducing the monopoly power of other bureaus supplying the same service. Competition in a bureaucracy is as important a condition for social efficiency as it is among profit-seeking firms." Ibid., p. 111.

inelastic demand seems consistent with empirical knowledge of bureaucratic behavior. The tendency to produce a level of output that exceeds the equilibrium level in a competitive market has been demonstrated by W. Keith Bryant in an analysis of the United States food stamp program.[66] And Anne O. Krueger has estimated that the resources directed to such rent-seeking or rent-generating activities as the effort to obtain legal or illegal access to national (or licensed) employment, commodities, and services represent a significant share of GNP in a number of developing countries.[67]

Modeling bureaucratic behavior by means of the neoclassical theory of the firm has clearly produced a number of powerful insights into the efficient supply of bureaucratic services. In this body of work, however, little explicit consideration is given to institutional innovation. Thus it is difficult to relate the constipated behavior that is implied by the partial equilibrium models of bureaucratic behavior to the invention of new institutional alternatives that have been described by the historians of political and economic development.

COLLECTIVE ACTION. The generation of growth dividends as a result either of technical advance or of more effective institutional performance opens up a second source of demand for institutional change. The very significance of technical change is that it permits the substitution of knowledge for resources, or of less expensive and more abundant resources for more expensive resources—that is, it releases the constraints on growth imposed by inelastic resource supplies. Similarly, improvements in institutional performance reduce the costs of economic organization.

The effect of institutional innovation is to reduce the costs of new income streams. These new income streams become available to factor owners at lower prices than the prices of new income streams in sectors of the economy that have failed to achieve rapid technical or institutional change. The innovative organizations (households, firms, bureaus) seek to externalize the costs and internalize the gains from innovative activity. The effect, in any progressive society, is to induce a continuous stream of institutional changes that are designed to modify the way gains from advances in technology and institutional performance are partitioned among owners of factors and among social classes.

Historical examples of this process are numerous. Demand for changes in land tenure systems has at times been induced by potential gains from the application of new technology, as in the enclosure movement in England.

[66] W. Keith Bryant, "An Analysis of the Market for Food Stamps," *American Journal of Agricultural Economics* 54 (May 1972): 305–25; idem, "An Analysis of the Market for Food Stamps: Correction and Extension," *American Journal of Agricultural Economics* 54 (November 1972): 689–93.

[67] Anne O. Krueger, "The Political Economy of the Rent Seeking Society," *American Economic Review* 64 (June 1974): 291–303.

Such demand has sometimes been exerted through political pressure by tenants, who wish to participate in the gains from productivity growth.[68] In the United States, labor unions were organized to create the political power necessary to assure workers' participation in the growth dividends generated by industrial development.[69] The development of the agricultural research and extension system represented an effort by both farmers and the general public to realize the new income streams that were potentially available to society through the application of advances in biological and mechanical technology in agricultural production.[70] The political effort that has been devoted to the development of the price support programs for agricultural commodities from the mid-1920s to the present can be viewed as an effort by agricultural producers to capture a higher share of the gains that have resulted from the institutionalization of agricultural research. In the absence of these price programs, a higher share of the gains from technical advance would have been passed on to consumers, in the form of lower food prices.[71]

Efforts to modify the partitioning of the growth dividends generated by technical or institutional change are the product of collective action. Both the Commons tradition in institutional economics and the pluralist tradition in political science have emphasized that voluntary associations that share common economic interests play a constructive role in repairing inequities in the distribution of income associated with rapid economic growth.[72]

Recent efforts to extend the microeconomic theory of firm and consumer behavior to the analysis of collective action have seriously challenged the assumption that collective action represents a rational pursuit of individual self-interest. Olson's work is a particularly creative attempt to extend the implications of the theory of the firm, or the industrial organization, to the analysis of collective action.[73]

Olson emphasizes that both organizational costs and conflict between

[68] Hayami and Ruttan, *Agricultural Development*, pp. 259–64.

[69] Selig Perlman, *A Theory of the Labor Movement*, 1928 (Reprint. New York: Augustus M. Kelley, 1966).

[70] Joseph C. Fitzharris, "Science for the Farmer: The Development of the Minnesota Agricultural Experiment Station: 1868–1910," *Agricultural History* 48 (January 1974): 202–14; also, Roy V. Scott, "Science for the Farmer: Comment," *Agricultural History* 48 (January 1974): 215–20.

[71] Commons, *Economics of Collective Action*, pp. 209–38; Willard W. Cochrane, *Farm Prices: Myth and Reality* (Minneapolis: University of Minnesota Press, 1958); Ross B. Talbot and Don F. Hadwiger, *The Policy Process in American Agriculture* (San Francisco: Chandler, 1968).

[72] For a vigorous criticism of the pluralist tradition of "interest-group liberalism," see Lowi, *End of Liberalism*, and Charles M. Hardin, *Presidential Power and Accountability* (Chicago: University of Chicago Press, 1974).

[73] Olson, *Logic of Collective Action*. See also Mancur Olson, Jr. and David McFarland, "The Restoration of Pure Monopoly and the Concept of the Industry," *Quarterly Journal of Economics* 76 (November 1962): 613–31.

individual and group interest are constraints on the mobilization of political resources to achieve economic objectives. "If members of a large group rationally seek to maximize their personal welfare, they will not act to advance their common or group objectives unless there is coercion to force them to do so, or unless some separate incentive, distinct from the achievement of the common or group interest, is offered to the members of the group individually on the condition that they help bear the costs or burdens involved in the achievement of the group objectives.[74]

Olson identifies factors that keep larger groups from furthering their own interests: "First, the larger the group, the smaller the fraction of the total group benefit that any person acting in the group interest receives. . . . Second, . . . the larger the group . . . the less likelihood that any small subset of members . . . will gain enough from getting the collective good to bear the burden of providing even a small amount of it. . . . Third, the larger the number of members in the group, the greater the organization costs and thus the higher the hurdle that must be jumped before any of the collective good at all can be obtained."[75] As a result, there is good reason for each potential group member to wait for others to make the organizational effort or to bear the costs of maintaining the organization.

There are two ways of dealing with these barriers to group action. Members of a latent group may be coerced into participation or they may be provided with incentives beyond the usual economic interest required for the mobilization of political resources. For example, when the agricultural extension service was being developed in the United States, farmers typically were forced to organize local "farm bureaus," or associations, in order to gain access to the educational services of an extension agent. These local farm associations were later joined in the national Farm Bureau, which became an important political force, and as this political role expanded, the federal government and the states began a movement to "divorce" the extension service from the Bureau. The Farm Bureau then compensated for this diminishing public support by organizing cooperative marketing, purchasing, and insurance companies that either made their services available only to Farm Bureau members or limited their patronage dividends to Bureau members.[76]

The pattern described above has been followed by other United States farm organizations as well, such as the Farmers Union and the National Farmers Organization. Perhaps the most tightly organized farm groups in the United States at the present time are the marketing cooperatives for specific commodities such as those for dairy products, citrus fruits, peaches,

---

[74] Olson, *Logic of Collective Action*, p. 2.
[75] Ibid.
[76] O. M. Kyle, *The Farm Bureau Through Three Decades* (Baltimore: The Waverly Press, 1948).

cranberries, and grapes. These organizations have the advantage of smaller numbers, geographic concentration, monopoly or near-monopoly access to markets, and influence on federal and state legislation that supports the establishment and enforcement of marketing orders. The combination of coercion and related services provided the agricultural base on which programs of political action could be built.[77]

When we compare the strength of farmers' organizations in developed and developing countries, we see an inverse relationship between size of farm population and farmers' political power: in developed countries, farm populations are typically small and power considerable; in developing nations, farm populations are large and political power almost nonexistent. In countries where industrial labor represents a small portion of the total labor force and where organized labor is small in comparison with the entire industrial labor force (usually developing countries), there is a greater difference between the wages of organized and unorganized labor than in countries where industrial and organized segments are larger (usually developed countries). Olson's approach to the theory of collective action also provides powerful insights into the failure of both the most disadvantaged and the most broadly based group in a society—for example, farmers in developing countries and consumers in developed countries—to achieve effective organization and sufficient political influence to pursue their group interests.

The barriers to voluntary collective action have led to efforts to design public agencies that could enforce workable competition or could exercise countervailing power against organized producers on behalf of consumers.[78] Experience with antitrust and other consumer-oriented regulatory agencies, however, has been interpreted as consistent with the Niskanen model of bureaucratic behavior and the Olson model of collective action.[79] For example, the interests of producers have often dominated those of consumers in the enabling legislation that has established regulatory agencies. And even when consumer interests have initially been dominant the regulators have tended, over time, to become instruments of the regulated.[80]

### Dynamics of Institutional Innovation

The inferences that can be drawn from the theories of bureaucratic behavior and collective action are profoundly pessimistic. Both theories

[77] Charles M. Hardin, *The Politics of Agriculture* (Glencoe: Free Press, 1952); Olson, *Logic of Collective Action*, pp. 153–9; Lowi, *End of Liberalism*, pp. 102–15.

[78] John Kenneth Galbraith, *American Capitalism: The Concept of Countervailing Power* (Boston: Houghton Mifflin, 1952).

[79] Roumasset, *Induced Institutional Change*, pp. 15–20.

[80] George J. Stigler, "The Theory of Economic Regulation," *Bell Journal of Economics and Management Science* 2 (Spring 1971): 3–21.

suggest that the markets for economic and political resources wherein the demand for institutional change is expressed are so imperfect as to create fundamental biases in the direction of institutional change. These biases generally favor organized producers over consumers. Among producers, the biases favor those who must make the greatest investment in either capital goods or human resources. Thus the market for institutional change will work better for organized oil producers than for organized farmers; it will be more effective for organized medical practitioners than for organized industrial workers.

On the other hand, the evidence does not support the proposition that we can realize large gains by eliminating structural imperfections.[81] Nor do the data suggest that wages have risen more rapidly in the organized than in the unorganized sectors of the labor market.[82] We hypothesize that the explanation of the apparent inconsistency in these inferences from the theories of bureaucratic behavior and collective action will be found on the supply side of the market for institutional change. More specifically, *we hypothesize that shifts to the right of the supply curve for institutional change, or shifts in the institutional innovation possibility curve, tend to reduce the cost of institutional change and to make the market for institutional change more efficient.*

BUREAUCRATIC ENTREPRENEURSHIP. We can explain some of the apparent incompatibility between the theories of bureaucratic behavior and collective action by considering the joint implications of these theories. The theory of collective action suggests that there are many constraints on the ability and the motivation of large groups to organize formally in order to pursue their special interests. At the same time, a major implication of the theory of bureaucratic behavior is that bureaucratic entrepreneurs, in the pursuit of larger budgets and larger staffs, will find it in their interest to organize clientele groups who have a latent demand for their services. Thus the effect of bureaucratic entrepreneurship, when it is directed to building a larger producer or consumer clientele in order to create a demand for bureaucratic services, is to reduce the costs of organization.[83] This explains why, when Olson began to examine the history of labor, agricultural, and professional organizations that act as pressure groups, he frequently discovered the "hidden hand" of bureaucratic entrepreneurship.

[81] Christopher Dougherty and Marcelo Selowsky, "Measuring the Effects of the Misallocation of Labor," *The Review of Economics and Statistics* 55 (August 1973): 386–90.

[82] For evidence on the earnings experience of both organized and unorganized labor, see H. Gregg Lewis, *Unionism and Relative Wages in the United States* (Chicago: University of Chicago Press, 1963); see also R. A. Kessel and A. A. Alchian, "The Meaning and Validity of the Inflation Induced Lag of Wages Behind Prices," *American Economic Review* 50 (March 1960): 43–67.

[83] Albert Breton and Raymond Breton, "An Economic Theory of Social Movements," *The American Economic Review* 59 (May 1969): 198–205.

The cost of organizing a latent group may decline sharply during a period of economic and social stress. Under such circumstances, the latent demand for social change "creates opportunities for social profit which social entrepreneurs will want to reap [,] and in so doing [they] will 'supply' or provide social movements to those who want them."[84] Olson and Niskanen appear to have underestimated the degree to which those who supply and those who demand a public good may cooperate in order to achieve access to current or latent gains from technical or institutional innovation.[85] Furthermore, a society's tolerance for inequity in the distribution of income may decline over time, thus further reducing the costs of organization.[86] This leads us to conclude that size may be a less significant constraint to organization than Olson implies.

INSTITUTIONAL DIFFUSION AND TRANSFER. The possibility of borrowing institutional innovations, either through processes of diffusion or through organized programs designed to transfer institutions across social, economic, and political constituencies, further reduces the cost of institutional change. Throughout modern history, imperialistic, nationalistic, and altruistic policies have resulted in a massive transfer of institutional forms among countries. After independence, many of the new Latin American republics followed the United States pattern in establishing the forms of constitutional democracy and presidential leadership. In a number of countries, the English, French, and Dutch legal systems were superimposed on systems of law and custom that had long been in existence. Germany and Japan deliberately

[84] Ibid., p. 201.

[85] See Jan Smith, "Communities, Associations and the Supply of Collective Goods," *American Journal of Sociology* 82 (September 1976): 291–308; John Chamberlin, "Provision of Collective Goods as a Function of Group Size," *American Political Science Review* 65 (June 1974): 707–16. It has also been argued that formal organization is less important in effective group action then presumed by Olson. See Joel M. Guttman, *The Demand for Publicly Financed Agricultural Research: An Application of A Theory of Collective Action* (Ph.D. diss., University of Chicago, August 1976). Guttman presents an interest-group theory of collective action that encompasses the utilization of political resources by unorganized or latent groups in order to influence public policy on behalf of their economic interests; the formation and maintenance of group organization in pursuit of group interests; and the effect of group size and geographic distribution. The theory is employed to explain differences among states (in the U.S.) in levels of state expenditures for agricultural research.

[86] "In the early stages of rapid economic development, when inequities in the distribution of income among different classes, sectors and regions are apt to increase sharply, it can happen that societies' tolerance for such disparities will be substantial. To the extent that such tolerance comes into being, it accommodates, as it were, the increasing inequities in an almost providential fashion. But this tolerance is like a credit that falls due at a certain date. It is extended in the expectation that eventually the disparities will narrow again. If this does not occur, there is bound to be trouble and, perhaps, disaster." Albert O. Hirschman, "The Changing Tolerance for Income Inequality in the Course of Economic Development," *The Quarterly Journal of Economics* 87 (November 1973): 545.

imported liberal institutional forms as part of their programs of economic nationalism. In recent decades, bilateral and multilateral technical assistance agencies have been an important source of institutional transfer. Developing countries continue to view the process of institutional transfer as a natural complement to their efforts to develop the capacity for technical innovation. In agriculture, both the experiment station and the extension service have become pervasive.

Inappropriate institutional transfer results in biases in the supply of institutional change that are similar to the biases that inappropriate technology transfer introduces into the supply of technical change. There is an extensive literature on the inappropriate transfer of institutions and on the distorting impact of such transfer on institutional development.[87]

One body of literature that has contributed to our understanding of the institutional transfer process is the collection of material on institution building. This body of knowledge has evolved out of an effort, primarily in the field of public administration, to provide technical assistance agencies with an effective methodology for intervention to induce more effective institutional performance.[88] The institution-building literature has typically adopted an explicitly normative orientation toward institutional change. The test of effective institutionalization is the normative impact of the organization on its setting. Thus, the effectiveness of the institutionalization of experiment station capacity for rice research is appropriately assessed by the impact that the new knowledge derived from rice research has on rice yields, on the incomes of rice producers, or on the price of rice to urban consumers. The institution-building literature exhibits a pervasive concern

[87] For a review of some of this literature, see John D. Montgomery, *Technology and Civic Life* (Cambridge, Mass.: M.I.T. Press, 1974), pp. 117–37.

[88] The institution-building literature is largely a product of two programs. The first of these was the Inter-University Research Program on Institution Building, which was staffed by researchers from Indiana, Michigan State, and Syracuse Universities and the University of Pittsburgh and was headquartered at the Graduate School of Public and International Affairs at Pittsburgh. The guiding concepts for this project have been summarized by J. Esman, "The Elements of Institution Building," in *Institution Building and Development*, ed. Joseph W. Eaton (Beverly Hills: Sage Publications, 1972): 21–39. The second project was undertaken by the Committee on Institutional Cooperation–Agency for International Development Rural Development Research Project, which was staffed by people from the Universities of Wisconsin, Minnesota, Illinois, Missouri, Indiana, North Carolina, Ohio, Utah State, and Purdue. The objective of this project was to examine and evaluate the results of AID–university cooperative programs designed to assist in the development of agricultural education and research institutions in developing countries.

For a review and appraisal of the results achieved by the two research programs, see William J. Siffin, "The Institution Building Perspective: Properties, Problems and Promise," in *Institution Building: A Model for Applied Social Change*, eds. D. Woods Thomas, et al. (Cambridge, Mass.: Schenkman, 1972), pp. 113–48. For an annotated bibliography of the institution building literature, see Melvin G. Blase, *Institution Building: A Source Book* (East Lansing: Midwest Universities Consortium for International Activities, Inc. 1973).

with the problem of transferring particular organizational forms from the developed to the developing nations and with the institutionalization of capacity for technology transfer and innovation.[89]

At the same time, the institution-building approach has been criticized for not giving more explicit attention to the development of a typology by which opportunities for appropriate institutional change can be differentiated on the basis of both technological and environmental characteristics.[90] Siffin argues, for example, that it is easier to institutionalize an organization that focuses on developing technology than an organization that is not technology-centered. He points out that the relatively "closed-system" quality of many technologies means that the behaviors they require are quite particular to their operations and not common to the sociocultural system at large. On the other hand, where there is no closed-system technology, as in community development efforts, effective institutionalization may be exceedingly difficult to achieve.[91]

NEW KNOWLEDGE IN THE SOCIAL SCIENCES.   The relative ease with which closed-system techniques can be transferred across geographic or political boundaries and institutionalized in societies with quite different resource and cultural endowments than those of the societies in which such techniques were initially developed constitutes an important source of bias in the direction of institutional as well as of technical change.[92] The availability of such transfer possibilities diverts resources from the process by which institutional innovations that are consistent with national or regional cultural endowments can be developed. Institutional forms that are trans-

[89] In the more recent institution-building literature there is a good deal of rhetoric to the effect that technical assistance involves more than the simple transfer of resources, knowledge, or institutions and that emphasis should be placed on institution-building activities that have a greater experimental content. See, for example, Milton J. Esman and John D. Montgomery, "Systems Approaches to Technical Cooperation: The Role of Development Administration," *Public Administration* 29 (September–October 1969): 507–39.

[90] Siffin, "Institution Building Perspective," pp. 123–7. Siffin's approach to the role of technology in institution building draws very heavily on James D. Thompson, *Organizations in Action* (New York: McGraw-Hill, 1967). The Thompson conception can be summarized as follows: the design, structure and behavior of organizations will vary systematically with (a) differences in technologies, and (b) variations in task environments.

[91] A. T. Mosher, "Administrative Experimentation as the Way of Life for Developmental Projects," *International Development Review* 9 (June 1967); Vernon W. Ruttan, "Integrated Rural Development Programs: A Skeptical Perspective," *International Development Review* 17, no. 4 (1975): 9–16.

[92] "The conscious and efficient practice of physical science and the design of physical systems has been perfected to the point where normal system problem solving is dominated by the reorganizations associated with new physical technology—the redesign of machine subsystems and control. This has had the effect of accelerating the rate at which organizational crises occur." Edgar S. Dunn, *Economic and Social Development, A Process of Social Learning* (Baltimore: Johns Hopkins University Press, 1971), p. 243.

ferred from rich to poor countries rarely make efficient contributions to development without substantial adaptation. Indeed, institutional innovations are probably even more location-specific than are technical innovations. The attempt to transfer European and North American models of producer cooperatives to developing countries represents one of the more conspicuous examples of an unproductive use of resources in the field of institutional development.

Throughout most of history, the *social learning*[93] that has given rise to improvements in institutional performance and to institutional innovation has occurred primarily through the slow accumulation of successful precedent or as a by-product of administrative or managerial expertise or experience. Within the last century, advances in knowledge in the social sciences have opened up new possibilities for efficiency in institutional innovation. We have suggested earlier in this chapter that the demand for knowledge in the social sciences is derived from the demand for more efficient institutional performance. Advances in knowledge in the social sciences can lead to more efficient performance by existing institutions and to innovations that promote the development of new and more effective institutions. For example, research leading to the quantification of commodity supply and demand relationships has led to the more efficient functioning of supply management, food procurement, and food distribution programs; research on the social and psychological factors affecting the diffusion of new technology has led to more efficient performance by agricultural extension services and to the more effective design of agricultural production campaigns; and research on the effects of land tenure or group farming arrangements has led to institutional innovations that have brought about greater equity in access to natural resources and greater productivity in the utilization of resources in rural areas.

The effect of advances in social science knowledge has been to shift the supply function for institutional change to the right. That is, the substitution of social science knowledge and analytical skill for the more expensive process of learning by trial and error reduces the cost of institutional innovation. It seems clear, however, that a society can realize the new income streams made possible by these more efficient sources of institutional innovation only if it can develop the capacity to generate indigenous social science knowledge as well as to adapt to its own resource and cultural conditions the social science learning of other societies.

Few nations have yet begun to realize the gains that are made possible by the institutionalization of social science research capacity. Alexander

[93] The term *social learning* is used by Dunn to refer to the process by which both the individual and the group attain new knowledge and achieve new behaviors through interaction. In the earliest stage of development, this process occurs through mimicry. As organisms gain in complexity and sophistication, it occurs through the sharing of experience. See Dunn, *Economic and Social Development.*

Gerschenkron has argued that advances in social science knowledge have contributed to institutional change more by reinforcing ideology than by advancing analytical capacity.[94] Edgar S. Dunn, Jr., insists that scientific effort in the social sciences has focused more on research designed to maintain existing patterns of institutional organization than on research aimed at transforming such patterns.[95] Karl Polanyi, however, has expressed a much more optimistic view of the contribution of social science knowledge to institutional innovation.[96]

Regardless of how one interprets historical experience, it does seem clear that during the second half of this century, advances in the social sciences have been making a major contribution to reducing the cost of institutional change. Social science research capacity and institutional design and management capacity, which draws on social science knowledge, have become effectively institutionalized in many countries. The planning agency and the planner have emerged as leading actors in the design and implementation of policies aimed at achieving more effective institutional performance.

Researchers and planners have recently been giving an increasing amount of attention to the design of institutions that will achieve greater equity in institutional performance. The inability of the relatively disadvantaged—who are the majority in many societies—to gain access to either economic or political resources remains a serious constraint on the realization of the improved institutional performance that is made possible by advances in social science knowledge.

*Perspective*

The theory of induced institutional change as it is outlined in this chapter is incomplete. Clearly, the theory takes an incrementalist approach to the concept of institutional innovation. We have not responded fully to the criticisms of the incrementalist approach.[97] We have yet to analyze the

[94] Alexander Gerschenkron, "History of Economic Doctrines and Economic History," *The American Economic Review* 59 (May 1969): 1–17. Gerschenkron comments: "Had the theories been more operational, primarily in the narrow, pragmatic sense of the word, had there been, that is, a sufficiently large stock of empirical knowledge to support them, their impact upon events would have been much larger" (pp. 16, 17).

[95] Dunn, *Economic and Social Development*, pp. 207–17, 245–61.

[96] "Social, not technical, invention was the intellectual mainspring of the Industrial Revolution.... The triumphs of natural science had been theoretical in the true sense, and could not compare in practical importance with those of the social sciences of the day.... The discovery of economics was an astounding revelation which hastened greatly the transformation of society...while the decisive machines had been the inventions of uneducated artisans some of whom could hardly read or write. It was both just and appropriate that not the natural but the social sciences should work as the intellectual powers of the mechanical revolution which subjected the powers of nature to man." Polanyi, *Great Transformation*, p. 119.

[97] "The new liberal public philosophy was corrupted by the weakness of its primary intellectual component, pluralism. The corrupting element was the myth of the automatic society." Lowi, *End of Liberalism*, p. 54.

efficiency and equity implications of institutional performance from a social learning viewpoint. And we have not yet provided the induced institutional innovation hypothesis with an empirical test as rigorous as the induced technical innovation tests that have already been developed and implemented.

It is clear that there is a severe bias in the markets through which the forces of demand for and supply of institutional change operate—through which economic and political resources are utilized in the effort to achieve institutional innovation and efficiency. And we see no intellectual or political system that suggests how to eliminate this bias.

The theory of induced institutional change that we described in the initial pages of this chapter, however, does open up the possibility of using resources in the social sciences and related professions to develop innovations that are more consistent with particular resource and cultural endowments of societies than such innovations have been in the past. In the next chapter we will examine the history of the technical and institutional changes associated with the green revolution—the major effort at expanding food production in developing countries that took place in the 1960s and 1970s—within the context of the theoretical concepts of induced technical and institutional innovation. Thus the test of the theory that we have presented in this chapter will be the degree to which the theory facilitates our understanding of the roles played by both technical and institutional change in the process of economic development.

# THIRTEEN

# Induced Innovation and the Green Revolution

VERNON W. RUTTAN AND HANS P. BINSWANGER

IT is useful to test the theories of induced technical and institutional change outlined in earlier chapters against the history of technical and institutional change in agriculture during the 1965–75 decade. This is the decade of the green revolution in grain production in the agriculture of many developing countries. The green revolution has produced dramatic increases in grain production in some localities. It has also induced complacency in high places, and it has contributed to an escalation of interdisciplinary aggression among development professionals. At a more fundamental level, there has been a close interaction between institutional and technical change in both the generation and the diffusion of the new cereals technology.

The theory of induced innovation implies a dynamic, dialectical interaction between technical and institutional change. In this chapter the green revolution experience is used as an organizing theme to illustrate the interrelated complex of institutional and technical changes implied by the theory of induced innovation.

There are both advantages and disadvantages in utilizing the experience of the green revolution in this manner. A major advantage is the opportunity to draw on contemporary development experience rather than on the earlier, historical experience of countries that are now developed. The fact that the changes associated with the green revolution are still in the process of working themselves out constitutes a disadvantage: the complete record has not been written. Furthermore, the impact and significance of the changes

We are indebted to John Duewel, Peter Dorner, Michael Lipton, Norman K. Nicholson, Ralph H. Retzlaff, and Abraham M. Weisblat for comments and criticism of an earlier draft of this chapter.

that have occurred are still the subject of considerable debate, some of which is ideologically motivated.[1]

*What Is the Green Revolution?*

The term "green revolution," as used in this chapter, refers to the development and diffusion of high-yielding cereal varieties, primarily wheat and rice, in the developing countries of the tropics and semitropics, beginning in the mid-1960s.[2]

These new high-yielding cereal varieties are the culmination of a significant advance in biological technology. This advance led to the production of seeds that embody a greater genetic potential for response to increased amounts of plant nutrition. Many of the new varieties were developed at what is now the International Maize and Wheat Improvement Center (CIMMYT) in Mexico and at the International Rice Research Institute (IRRI) in the Philippines; some are products of national crop improvement programs in other countries.[3]

The research that led to the new varieties that were first released in the mid-1960s was based on work of much earlier origin. Semidwarf wheats had been developed in Japan by 1873. Early in the twentieth century, several of these Japanese varieties were used in wheat breeding work in Italy. Breeders in Japan crossed Japanese varieties with American varieties to produce the *Norin* varieties. These were brought to the United States in 1946, developed further, and taken to Mexico in the early 1950s. There Norman Borlaug and his associates used them, together with some of the Italian varieties, to develop the Mexican wheat varieties that have since served as the dominant model in wheat improvement.

Early-maturing rice varieties were known in China as early as 1000 A.D. The first new varieties released by IRRI were based on genetic materials

[1] Much of the discussion has been consistent with an observation by Barrington Moore, Jr., *Social Origins of Dictatorship and Democracy: Land and Peasant in the Making of the Modern World* (Boston: Beacon Press, 1966): "In all ages and countries, reactionaries, liberals, and radicals have painted their own portraits of small rural folk to suit their own theories" (p. 117).

[2] Use of the term "green revolution" to describe the new, "seed–fertilizer" technology was apparently first suggested in a speech by USAID administrator William Gaud. See "The Green Revolution: Accomplishments and Apprehensions" (Washington: Society for International Development, 1968).

[3] For a concise review of the institutional and technical background of the green revolution, see Dana G. Dalrymple, *Development and Spread of High-Yielding Varieties of Wheat and Rice in the Less Developed Nations*, Foreign Agricultural Economic Report no. 95 (Washington, D.C.: U.S. Department of Agriculture, Economic Research Service, in cooperation with U.S. Agency for International Development, August, 1976). These developments are described in greater detail in E. C. Stakman, Richard Bradfield, and Paul C. Mangelsdorf, *Campaigns Against Hunger* (Cambridge, Mass.: Harvard University Press, 1967), and in Yujiro Hayami, "Elements of Induced Innovation: A Historical Perspective for the Green Revolution," *Explorations in Economic History* 8 (Summer 1971): 445–72.

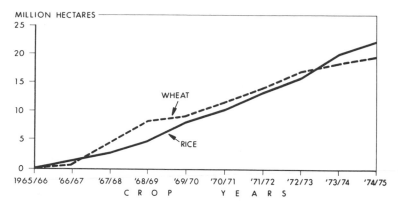

FIG. 13–1. Estimated area of high-yielding varieties of wheat and rice, Asia and Near East. [Source: Dana G. Dalrymple, *Development and Spread of High-Yielding Varieties of Wheat and Rice in the Less Developed Nations*, Foreign Agricultural Economic Report no. 95, 5th ed. (Washington, D.C.: U.S. Department of Agriculture, Economic Research Service, Foreign Development Division, in cooperation with U.S. Agency for International Development, August 1976), p. ix.]

drawn from China, Taiwan, and Indonesia. However, the model of the biologically efficient rice plant for areas with well developed irrigation systems—the short, stiff-strawed, fertilizer-responsive plant—was based very heavily on experience in developing the *Norin* rice varieties in Japan and the *Ponlai* varieties in Taiwan.[4] Indeed, the green revolution technology that has become available to farmers in South and Southeast Asia since the mid-1960's is essentially the same technology that contributed to the growth of productivity in Japan and Taiwan earlier in this century.[5] It is also clear that the innovations in biological technology that led to the rapid diffusion of the green revolution, or seed-fertilizer technology, in South and Southeast Asia after the mid-1960s were induced by changes in relative resource endowments and factor prices similar to changes that had occurred earlier in Japan and Taiwan.[6]

[4] Yujiro Hayami, in association with Masakatsu Akino, Masahiko Shintani and Saburo Yamada, *A Century of Agricultural Growth in Japan: Its Relevance to Asian Development* (Minneapolis: University of Minnesota Press, and Tokyo: University of Tokyo Press, 1975), pp. 64–6; S. C. Hsieh and V. W. Ruttan, "Environmental, Technological and Institutional Factors in the Growth of Rice Production: Philippines, Thailand and Taiwan," *Food Research Institute Studies* 7 (1967): 307–41.

[5] Even authors who ought to know better continue to identify green revolution technology as "western." See, for example, Nicholas Wade, "Green Revolution (I): A Just Technology, Often Unjust in Use," *Science* 186 (December 27, 1974): 1186–92. See also Keith Griffin, *The Political Economy of Agrarian Change: An Essay on the Green Revolution* (Cambridge, Mass.: Harvard University Press, 1974), pp. 51–2. Griffin appears to deliberately obscure the fact that the technical improvements associated with the introduction of the *Ponlai* varieties in Taiwan embodied the same kind of technology that became available to rice producers in South and Southeast Asia after the mid 1960s.

[6] Hayami, "Elements of Induced Innovation." See also chapter 3.

The expansion of area devoted to the new wheat and rice varieties since the mid-1960s, in Asia and the Near East, has been documented by Dana G. Dalrymple (see figure 13-1 and footnote 3). The roles played by technology transfer and indigenous research in the diffusion process have been analyzed, in chapter 6 of this book, by Evenson and Binswanger. Although the rate of diffusion has been approximately the same for wheat and rice, the yield impact of the new wheat varieties has been somewhat more dramatic than the yield impact of the new rice varieties.[7]

The higher yields that have accompanied the introduction of the new cereal varieties have typically been achieved by using higher levels of fertilizer, by controlling the spread of weeds, insects, and disease more effectively, and by managing the delivery and use of water more efficiently. In some areas the introduction of the new varieties has been associated with intensified mechanization.

It is consistent with the available evidence to view the mechanization of land preparation and harvesting operations that is sometimes associated with the green revolution as responsive to changes in the relative prices of mechanical power, animal power, and labor rather than as a technical complement to the green revolution seed-fertilizer package.[8] In some

---

[7] T. N. Srinivasan, "The Green Revolution or the Wheat Revolution," in *Agricultural Development in Developing Countries: Comparative Experience*, ed. M. L. Dantwala (Bombay: Indian Society of Agricultural Economics, 1972): 404–16; Andrew Pearse, *The Social and Economic Implications of Large-Scale Introduction of New Varieties of Food Grain* (Geneva: United Nations Research Institute for Social Development, 1974).

[8] Data from the Indian and Pakistani Punjab on the complementarity between use of tractor power and use of high-yielding varieties in respect to intensification of crop production are particularly instructive. Among the many helpful studies are Bashir Ahmed, "The Economics of Tractor Mechanization in the Pakistan Punjab," *Food Research Institute Studies* 14, no. 1 (1975): 47–64; William H. Bartsch, "Employment Effects of Alternative Technologies and Techniques in Asian Crop Production: A Survey of Evidence," provisional draft (Geneva: International Labor Office, 1973); Carl H. Gotsch and Walter P. Falcon, "The Green Revolution and the Economics of Punjab Agriculture," *Food Research Institute Studies* 14, no. 1 (1975): 27–46; Hiramitsu Kaneda, "Economic Implications of the 'Green Revolution' and the Strategy of Agricultural Development in West Pakistan," *The Pakistan Development Review* 9 (Summer 1969): 111–43; John P. McInereny and Graham F. Donaldson, *The Consequences of Farm Tractors in Pakistan*, Staff Working Paper no. 210 (Washington: International Bank for Reconstruction and Development, February 1975); C. H. Hanumantha Rao, *Technological Change and Distribution of Gains in Indian Agriculture* (Delhi: Macmillan Company of India, 1975), pp. 23–90; Inderjit Singh and Richard H. Day, "Factor Utilization and Substitution in Economic Development: A Green Revolution Case Study," *The Journal of Development Studies* 11 (April 1975): 155–77; Montague Yudelman, Gavin Butler, and Ranaa Banerji, *Technological Change in Agriculture and Employment in Developing Countries* (Paris: Organization for Economic Cooperation and Development, 1971), pp. 69–100. The general effect of these studies is to question whether there is any substantial technical complementarity between the use of tractors and high-yielding varieties. In the Pakistani Punjab, for example, McInereny and Donaldson find that the subsidization of tractor technology was associated with a more than doubling of farm size and with a

countries that are characterized by highly labor-intensive systems of crop production—for example, Japan in the mid-1950s and Taiwan in the mid-1960s—mechanization was induced by a decrease in the rural labor force and by the rising wage rates for agricultural labor that were associated with growing demand for labor in the urban industrial sector.[9] In other areas, where cereal yields were relatively low from the start, intensification of crop production resulted in rapid growth in the seasonal demand for labor and/or power on larger farms during the land preparation and harvesting seasons.[10] In some areas, public policies have contributed to price distortions in factor and product markets that have induced inefficient substitution of mechanical power for animal power and for labor. This view of tractor mechanization is consistent with the data presented in chapter 3, with the analysis of mechanization in Brazilian agriculture in chapter 10, and with the data presented in table 13–1. At present it seems more appropriate to analyze the mechanization of motive power in agriculture within the context of a choice-of-technology model than within the framework of an induced innovation model.

Before attempting to test the induced innovation hypothesis against the experience of the green revolution, it will be useful to outline, more formally than in chapters 11 and 12, a model of the sources of demand for technical and institutional innovation and of the sources of biases in such demand. It will also be useful to refer briefly to the history of the agricultural experiment station, the institutional innovation that has generated much of the new biological technology underlying the green revolution.

---

decrease in labor use per cultivated acre of 40 percent but with an increase in cropping intensity of only 7 percent. In the Indian Punjab, Rao finds no evidence of technical complementarity between tractors and high-yielding varieties. His analysis indicates that the growth in the use of tractors in the Indian Punjab was a function of (1) increases in the price of food grains relative to tractor capital and operating costs, (2) a rise in the cost of labor and animal power relative to tractor capital and operating costs, and (3) the unequal structure of land holdings. A major puzzle in this body of literature is the fact that different results have been obtained from the simulation and from the *ex post* studies of complementarity between use of tractors and of high-yielding varieties. Although the simulation studies, such as those of Bartsch and of Singh and Day, typically demonstrate substantial complementarity between use of tractors and use of the high-yielding varieties, the *ex post* studies have failed to provide convincing evidence of such complementarity.

[9] Keizo Tsuchiya, *Productivity and Technological Progress in Japanese Agriculture* (Tokyo: University of Tokyo Press, 1976): 168–179; idem, "Economics of Mechanization in Small-Scale Agriculture," in *Agriculture and Economic Growth: Japan's Experience*, eds. Kazushi Ohkawa, Bruce F. Johnston, and Hiromitsu Kaneda (Tokyo: University of Tokyo Press, 1969): 155–72. See also Herman Southworth, ed., *Farm Mechanization in East Asia* (Singapore: The Agricultural Development Council, 1972).

[10] See for example the very careful analysis by Edward J. Clay, "Equity and Productivity Effects of a Package of Technical Innovations and Changes in Social Institutions: Tubewells, Tractors and High Yielding Varieties," *Indian Journal of Agricultural Economics* 30 (October–December 1975): 74–87.

TABLE 13-1. Selected indicators of factor use and factor prices in the Philippines, Thailand, Taiwan, and Japan in the mid-1960s

| Indicators | Philippines | Thailand | Taiwan | Japan |
|---|---|---|---|---|
| Cultivated land in hectares (000s) | 6,042 | 11,267 | 890 | 5,996 |
| Agricultural workers (000s) | 5,824 | 10,200 | 1,867 | 15,238 |
| Numbers of draft animals (000s) | 2,052 | 5,174 | 360 | 1,782 |
| Mechanical horsepower (hp) | 278,900 | 605,200 | 130,253 | 15,997,300 |
| Power tillers | 12,560 | 5,200 | 110,103 | 15,516,910 |
| Tractors | 266,340 | 600,000 | 20,150 | 480,390 |
| Price of mechanical power ($/hp) | 129 | 67 | 112 | 68 |
| Power tillers | 154 | 133 | 112 | 68 |
| Tractors | 128 | 66 | | |
| Farm wages ($/day) | 0.88[a] | 0.53 | 1.04 | 2.60[a] |
| Factor price ratio[b] | 147 | 126 | 108 | 26 |
| Horsepower per agricultural worker | 0.048 | 0.059 | 0.070 | 1.05 |

Source: Randolph Barker, William H. Meyers, Cristina M. Crisostomo, and Bart Duff, "Employment and Technological Change in Philippine Agriculture," *International Labor Review* 106 (August–September 1972): 17.

[a] Because in the Philippines and in Japan wages included meals, money wages reported for these countries were raised by 33 percent and 10 percent, respectively.

[b] Price of mechanical power divided by farm wages.

*Sources of Demand for Technical and Institutional Innovation*

The models developed in chapters 11 and 12 imply that different groups in society emerge as demanders of technical and institutional change only if they perceive that such change will result in a payoff to them. Thus, in order to formulate public policy with respect to technical and institutional innovation, we need to understand how the new income streams that arise from technical or institutional change are partitioned among regions and between producers and consumers, between farmers and laborers, and between large and small farmers.

PRODUCERS VERSUS CONSUMERS.    The manner in which the gains from technical change are partitioned between producers and consumers of a particular commodity depends on the slopes of the demand and supply curves for the product and on the rates at which these curves are shifting over time.[11] In a market characterized by a highly elastic demand, or by rapid growth in demand, producers will be able to retain a relatively large share of the gains from technical change. In a market characterized by inelastic demand, or by slow growth of demand, most of the gains from technical change will be passed on to consumers in the form of lower product prices.

*Producers surplus.*    The analytical basis for the above conclusions can be illustrated by means of the conventional Marshallian concepts of producers and consumers surplus.[12] In figure 13–2, let $dd$ be the domestic demand curve for a commodity such as rice, in a country such as the Philippines, which normally imports part of the rice it consumes. Let $s_n$ represent the supply function for rice prior to technical change. If it is government policy to stabilize the price of rice at $P_o$, domestic producers will supply an amount $OQ'_n$. It will be necessary for the government to import an amount $Q'_nQ_o$ in order to satisfy consumer demand. Now assume that it is possible, for a

[11] Willard W. Cochrane, *Farm Prices, Myth and Reality* (Minneapolis: University of Minnesota Press, 1958).

[12] John Martin Currie, John A. Murphy, and Andrew Schmitz, "The Concept of Economic Surplus and Its Use in Economic Analysis," *The Economic Journal* 81 (December 1971): 741–99. The example presented here is drawn from Yujiro Hayami and Masakatsu Akino, "Organization and Productivity of Agricultural Research Systems in Japan," in *Resource Allocation and Productivity in National and International Agricultural Research*, eds. Thomas M. Arndt, Dana G. Dalrymple, and Vernon W. Ruttan (Minneapolis: University of Minnesota Press, 1977): 29–54. See also Yujiro Hayami and Robert W. Herdt, *The Impact of Technological Change in Subsistence Agriculture on Income Distribution* (Manila: International Rice Research Institute, December 1975). R. K. Linder and F. G. Jarrett, "Measurement and Distribution of Research Benefits," Discussion Paper (Adelaide, Australia: University of Adelaide, Economics Department, November 1976), point out that the size of the benefits from research and the distribution of these benefits between producers and consumers depend on both the origins and the slopes of the $s_n$ and $s_o$ curves (see figure 13–2).

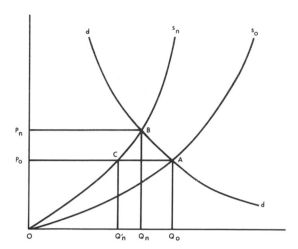

FIG. 13–2. Effect of a change in technology on producers and consumers surplus.

relatively modest investment, for the national rice experiment station to adapt or develop a new rice production technology that has the effect of shifting the supply function to $s_o$. As long as the supply function does not shift to the right by more than $s_o$, the additional rice can be used to replace rice that was formerly imported. The price to producers will remain unchanged, and producers as a group (landowners and laborers) will, after paying for any inputs purchased from the nonagricultural sector, gain by an amount equivalent to $CAO$. In this case the entire social return to the investment in rice research is captured by producers.

The same analysis would apply in the case of a country that is a small enough exporter to face a perfectly elastic demand curve for its product. Assume, for example, that the Philippines is self-sufficient in rice at the world price level $P_o$ and at output level $Q_o$. A shift in the supply function further to the right from $s_o$ would permit the additional production to the right of $Q_o$ to be exported at the world market price $P_o$. If Philippine exports are too small to affect the world price, the entire gain will be captured by producers.

In such a situation, producers would probably be willing to impose a tax or a cess on their production in order to support the research needed to shift the supply function. The Minister of Agriculture could increase his popularity among rice producers by securing public funding for the research. The Ministers of Trade and Finance and the Chairman of the National Economic Council would not find it difficult to support the Minister of Agriculture in this effort because the productivity gains from the agricultural research would improve the country's balance of payment accounts.

*Consumers surplus.* Figure 13–2 can also be used to illustrate a situation in which the gains from technical change accrue primarily to consumers. Assume that we are dealing with a country that is almost self-sufficient when rice sells in the domestic market at a protected price that is somewhat above the world price. Assume, for example, that the price is $P_n$ and the level of output is $Q_n$. If we introduce a technical change that results in a shift of the supply function from $s_n$ to $s_o$, output will rise to $Q_o$, and the price will fall to $P_o$. Consumers will gain by an amount equal to $ABC + BP_nP_oC$. The net social benefit is $ABC + ACO$. We could use the same analysis to examine the effect for a country like Thailand, whose rice exports are sufficiently large to affect the world price. In such a case, the gains to consumers would be shared between domestic and foreign consumers.

The transfer to consumers of the benefits of technical change in food production has a clearly progressive impact on a country's income distribution because poor people spend a larger proportion of their budgets on food than do rich people. This impact will be most progressive for those staple foods that form the major portion of the diets of the poorest groups. It will be less progressive in the case of foods characterized by high income elasticities, such as dairy products and beef.

In an economy faced by inelastic commodity demand, the institutional changes that are associated with advances in technology can be expected to be different from those changes that occur in cases where all of the gains are captured by producers. In the former situation, urban political leaders will find it easier to support appropriations for research than they will when most of the gains are captured by producers. Even agricultural laborers, if they are politically organized, may favor the kind of technical change characterized by a shift in the supply curve from $s_n$ to $s_o$ because they will gain from the lower price of rice. Such a gain can sometimes outweigh the loss in employment that occurs as a result of (neutral) technical change in cases of inelastic demand for output. Producers or their representatives can be expected to press for price supports and/or production controls in order to enlarge the size of the producers surplus (and to reduce the size of the consumers surplus).

The more progressive farmers—the specialized seed producers and the early adopters—are able to take advantage of elastic commodity demand schedules for their production early in the adoption cycle. By always being ahead of others they reap substantial gains from sequences of technical changes.[13] Furthermore, individual regions that supply national markets

---

[13] Adoption lags that systematically favor the larger producers occur because it is more profitable for large farms than for small farms to invest in information and because extension agents and salesmen derive a higher payoff from convincing large farmers to adopt innovations than from convincing small farmers to do this. A regressive element in the income distribution is thus introduced by a continuous sequence of technical changes. This point is discussed more fully in Finis Welch, "Some Income Distributional Effects of Technical Change" (Paper presented at the Agricultural Development Council Workshop on Technology and Factor Markets, Singapore, August 9 and 10, 1976).

face elastic commodity demand even if national demand is inelastic. As a consequence, every region has an incentive to achieve faster technical progress than the rest of the country, and lagging regions may experience real losses as a result of technical changes in progressive regions.[14]

It should be noted that we can extend our analysis to include the simultaneous effects of shifts in both demand and supply. If the demand function *dd*, as a result of population and/or income growth, is shifting to the right more rapidly than the supply curve, as a result of technical change, is shifting to the right, prices will rise but by a smaller amount than if there had been no shift in the supply curve.[15]

In general, consumer interests play a relatively modest role in the expansion of agricultural research capacity that occurs in response to rising food prices.[16] A period of food shortage or of high prices, such as occurred between 1972 and 1974, often creates an environment in which research entrepreneurs are encouraged to persuade budget officials and legislative bodies that funds invested in agricultural research will have a relatively high payoff. Because of the very inelastic demand for most basic foods, the social return to the measures undertaken to eliminate even mild food shortages or to maintain modest food surpluses may be quite high.

Shifts in the demand for technical change in the production of agricultural commodities may be generated by either producers or consumers. Typically, however, agricultural research is carried out by organized producers, by suppliers of purchased inputs, or by the public sector. Under what conditions may the public sector emerge as a supplier of agricultural research? We

[14] For an in-depth analysis of this problem, see Robert E. Evenson, "Technology Access and Factor Markets in Agriculture" (Paper presented at the Agricultural Development Council Workshop on Technology and Factor Markets, Singapore, August 9 and 10, 1976). Technical change that is limited to the more prosperous areas of a country has a regressive impact on that country's income distribution; the reverse is true for technical change that is limited to backward areas.

[15] A model similar to that employed in this section has been used to apportion the gains and losses from rice research between consumers and producers, to explore the distributional effects on different consumer income strata and on producer groups, and to analyze the changing sources of political support for rice research over time in Colombia. See G. M. Scobie and R. Posada T., *The Impact of High-Yielding Rice Varieties in Latin America with Special Emphasis on Colombia* (Cali, Colombia: Centro Internacional de Agricultura Tropical, 1976) and Grant M. Scobie, "Costs and Returns to Rice Research" (Paper delivered at Conference on Economic Consequences of New Rice Technology, Los Baños, Laguna, Philippines, International Rice Research Institute, December 1976). Shigeru Ishikawa has employed a similar approach to explain the emergence of a labor market in which cash transactions replace payments in kind, when wages are no longer determined by sharing arrangements but, rather, by market forces. See Shigeru Ishikawa, "Peasant Families and the Agrarian Community in the Process of Economic Development," in *Agriculture in Development Theory*, ed. Lloyd G. Reynolds (New Haven and London: Yale University Press, 1975): 451–96. See also Timothy Josling, "Agricultural Trade: Implications for the Distribution of the Gains from Technical Progress," in *Trade, Agriculture and Development*, eds. George S. Tolley and Peter A. Zadrozny (Cambridge: Ballinger, 1975): 165–80.

[16] See the discussion of "Collective Action" in chapter 12.

hypothesize two general conditions that are likely to induce a supply response by the public sector:

(1) Under conditions of elastic demand that result from import substitution or export possibilities it may be fairly easy for organized producers to identify their own interests with those of the nation and to establish a claim on public sector support for agricultural research. In a decentralized political system, smaller political units—states or provinces or even smaller political subdivisions—that "export" agricultural commodities to the rest of the economy may rationally view public investment in agricultural research as an investment in regional economic development.

(2) Public-sector investment that is designed to expand the supply of agricultural research may also be induced by a shift in the domestic terms of trade in favor of agriculture. Such a shift results in a rise in the price of wage goods, which increases real cost in other sectors of the economy. If a shift in the terms of trade toward agriculture persists for too long or emerges too rapidly it may generate consumer unrest.

The history of irrigation investment in the Philippines represents a particularly interesting case of induced institutional innovation along the lines suggested in the producer–consumer surplus model outlined above.[17] Yujiro Hayami and Masao Kikuchi have demonstrated that acceleration in irrigation investment in the Philippines since the late 1950s represents a response to the rising cost of bringing new land into cultivation and to the increase in the benefit-cost ratio for irrigation investment that is associated with the introduction of higher-yielding rice varieties. These authors also demonstrate that short-run fluctuations in the flow of funds for irrigation investment in the Philippines were associated with movements in world rice prices—that is, with fluctuations in the price of imported rice.

Numerous other examples of induced institutional or policy responses can be cited. The 1918 rice riots in Japan were a major factor in the Japanese government's decision to intensify its efforts to increase rice productivity in Korea and Taiwan.[18] In the United States, the long-term rise in food prices from the mid-1890s to the early 1920s was associated with rapid growth in federal and state expenditures on agricultural research. And in many developing countries the food crises of the mid-1960s and the early 1970s tended to reinforce efforts to achieve self-sufficiency in basic food commodities.[19] They also stimulated international aid efforts in support of

[17] Yujiro Hayami and Masao Kikuchi, "Investment Inducements to Public Infrastructure: Irrigation in the Philippines," mimeographed (Los Baños: International Rice Research Institute, Agricultural Economics Department, November 1975).

[18] Yujiro Hayami and Vernon W. Ruttan, *Agricultural Development: An International Perspective* (Baltimore and London: Johns Hopkins University Press, 1971), pp. 201–5.

[19] Mahar Mangahas, "Philippine Rice Policy Reconsidered in Terms of Urban Bias," *The Philippine Review of Business and Economics* 9 (June 1972): 57–77; idem, *The Political Economy of Rice in the New Society* (Diliman: University of the Philippines, Institute of Economic Development and Research, July 1974).

both the new international agricultural research system and a number of national agricultural and rural development efforts.[20]

BIASED DEMAND FOR TECHNICAL AND INSTITUTIONAL INNOVATIONS. If the agricultural sector gains as a whole, the partitioning of the gains among different producer groups and among landowners and laborers depends on the scale and factor biases of the technical and institutional changes and on the elasticities of supply of land and labor.

In the literature on the economics of technical change, the concept of *neutrality* has acquired, over time, a relatively precise analytical content.[21] Neutrality is typically defined as the condition in which a given technical change has the same degree of impact on the demand for all factors of production. A labor-saving technical change, on the other hand, shifts the labor demand per unit of output backward at a faster rate than the other factor demands per unit of output. *Scale neutrality* may be defined as the absence of any impact by a technical change on scale economies.

The concept of neutrality in institutional change has not been explored with the same degree of analytical rigor as has neutrality of technical change. In the present study we are concerned with institutional neutrality or non-neutrality with respect to both relative factor demand and scale. We define an institutional innovation as biased in a labor-saving direction if its effect is to decrease the labor demand relative to the demand for other factors; we define it as biased in a labor-using direction if its effect is to increase the demand for labor as compared with demand for other factors. And we define an institutional innovation as biased toward large scale if it increases the marginal productivity of factors employed on large units more than the productivity of factors used on small units; we define it as biased toward small scale if it leads to a greater increase in marginal productivity of factors utilized on small units than of those used on large units.

It is important, for purposes of both analysis and policy formulation, to distinguish between the impact of technical change and the impact of institutional change on factor demands or scale. Suppose it is observed that the introduction of a technical innovation has been associated with a greater

[20] Where the sources of demand are primarily external or latent, the political and economic costs of a response are often minimized by a symbolic response. President Johnson responded to the world food crisis of the mid-1960s by directing his science advisors' office to conduct a study. See Presidents Science Advisory Committee, *The World Food Problem* (Washington: U.S. Government Printing Office, May 1967). In 1974, President Ford responded to the pressures generated by the World Food Conference by requesting the National Academy of Sciences–National Research Council to study the capacity of the U.S. agricultural research system to contribute to expanding world food production. In both of these situations the real volume of U.S. aid in support of agricultural development continued to decline. However, there was a reallocation of aid effort toward more support for agricultural research.

[21] See the discussion by Binswanger in chapters 2 and 7.

increase in the marginal productivity of factors employed on large farms than on small farms. This could occur as a result of a scale bias in the technology in favor of large (and against small) farms. In the cases of Brazil (chapter 10) and Argentina (chapter 11), institutional environments that were biased against small farmers induced additional bias in the direction of technical change. The path of technical change would have been less capital intensive if factor prices had accurately reflected relative resource endowments.

If the objective of social policy is to assure equity with respect to scale, two possible alternatives are available. One is to attempt to design technologies that are sufficiently biased in the direction of small scale to offset the institutional bias toward large scale. The other alternative is to introduce institutional innovations that eliminate the scale biases of existing institutions.[22]

It is unlikely that bias in either institutional or technical innovation can be avoided. It is extremely difficult, at the micro level, to imagine many individual technical or institutional innovations that are neutral with respect either to scale or to factor demand. Our primary interest, from the viewpoint of both analysis and policy, is in the direction of bias at a more macro level— the regional, sectoral, or national level. At these broader levels it is possible to examine analytically some of the ways in which economic and political forces interact to condition the demand for technical and institutional change and to partition the new income streams made available to society through growth of productivity.

In chapter 10, we presented a case study of a situation where institutions were biased in favor of the development and introduction of labor-saving technology that had a clear scale bias. The support for a scale bias in technical and institutional change came primarily from the large-farmer groups. Larger farmers will typically represent the primary sources of demand for both labor-saving technical changes and for institutions to support such changes, because the changes will benefit employers of hired labor regardless of the elasticity of final demand.

To understand the demand for biased technical change or for institutional innovation that supports technical change, we must understand the distributional consequences of technical change for factors of production. In the absence of biases, the gains from technical change are distributed among factors according to such factors' supply elasticities. If the producing sector gains as a whole (elastic-output demand case), the factor in most inelastic supply gains most. But this same factor also sustains the largest losses when the sector as a whole loses from technical change (low elasticity of final demand). Biases of technical change in all cases inflict losses on the factor

[22] The complexities involved in such choices are discussed within the context of public health technologies and institutions in Amitai Etzioni and Richard Remp, *Technological Shortcuts to Social Change* (New York: Russell Sage Foundation, 1973).

against which the bias occurs, as compared with a situation of neutral technical change.[23]

## The Institutional Sources of Technical Change: The Agricultural Experiment Station

The development of the modern agricultural experiment station is a particularly instructive example of a demand-induced institutional innovation that became itself an efficient supplier of technical innovation. The socialization of agricultural research was the institutional innovation that enabled agriculture, in the developed countries, to become one of the first modern, science-based industries.[24] The scientific and technical innovations generated by the experiment station have, in turn, induced further institutional changes in the organization of developing societies. In this section, we will review the history of the experiment station movement and present an analytical interpretation of the interrelated scientific, economic, and political roles of the agricultural experiment station in agricultural development.

HISTORICAL ORIGINS OF THE AGRICULTURAL EXPERIMENT STATION.[25] Agricultural science emerged in England as an organized field of inquiry in the latter years of the English agricultural revolution, from the late eighteenth to the early nineteenth centuries. During this period, an intensive, integrated, crop-and-livestock husbandry system, which had been evolving over several centuries, was analyzed and made popular by Arthur Young

[23] This partial equilibrium model of the distribution of the benefits from technical change has been formalized by Robert E. Evenson, based on earlier joint work with Finis Welch (Evenson, "Technology Access").

The partial equilibrium model neglects general equilibrium feedback loops via the overall factor availability in an economy, and via the demand effects arising from the income effects due to technical change. Taking those into account can lead to distributional implications of technical changes that differ from those derived in partial equilibrium models [Hans P. Binswanger, "Distributional Consequences of Neutral Technical Changes: Partial Versus General Equilibrium Analysis" (Paper presented at the Agricultural Development Council Workshop on Technology and Factor Markets, Singapore, August 9 and 10, 1976)].

However, different potential demander groups for technical or institutional changes will usually express demand for individual technical changes, the factor demand and income effects of which will be small in relation to the size of the economy and which therefore cannot be expected to behave on the basis of the knowledge of second-order general equilibrium effects that may be small and difficult to trace.

[24] In the science-based industries, formal research and development represents the primary source of technical innovation. In the older, engineering-based industries, which were the primary focus of the industrial revolution, the link between technical innovation and advances in science was much more tenuous; formal research and development was institutionalized relatively late in the development of these industries.

[25] This section draws on Hayami and Ruttan, Agricultural Development, pp. 27–30, 136–44, and on Vernon W. Ruttan, "Technical and Institutional Transfer in Agricultural Development," Research Policy 4 (1975): 350–78.

and other exponents of agricultural science. The system was refined and improved by a number of large estate owners who practiced scientific agriculture and experimented with improved agricultural practices.

The history of the modern agricultural experiment station traces back to the establishment of the Edinburgh Laboratory in 1842 and the Rothamsted Experimental Station in 1843. The Edinburgh Laboratory was supported by the voluntary contributions of members of the Agricultural Chemistry Association of Scotland. Unsatisfied demands for immediate practical results led to the dissolution of the Laboratory in 1848. The Rothamsted station, in England, was financed personally by Sir J. B. Lawes and his family throughout the nineteenth century.

A more viable funding pattern emerged in 1852, when the first publicly supported agricultural experiment station was established in Germany, at Möckern, in Saxony. The British "new husbandry" doctrine had been transferred to Germany in the early years of the nineteenth century. The demonstration of the relation of soil minerals to plant growth by Justus von Liebig and others during the second quarter of the nineteenth century established a firmer scientific foundation for advances in agricultural technology than had existed up to that time. The stagnation of German agriculture combined with the newly perceived potential for agricultural productivity growth (resulting from publication of Liebig's work) led to pressures for the state to implement a more formal organization of support for the development of methods of applying the new scientific knowledge to agriculture. Saxon farmers drafted a charter for a publicly supported agricultural experiment station, and the charter was legalized by statute and funded by appropriations from the government of Saxony.

Although the German system of agricultural research evolved later than the British, it provided a more effective environment than the latter for the "enlargement" of new scientific and technical knowledge. As a specialized institution, operating under its own charter and supported by the state, it was not as subject to pressures for immediate practical results as was the privately supported research of the English landowners or even the cooperatively organized Edinburgh Laboratory.

The German institutional innovation—the socialization of agricultural research—diffused to the United States and Japan. In both countries this innovation evolved rapidly beyond the German model. However, in response to the enormous differences between the United States and Japan in respect to resource endowments and social and economic traditions, development followed distinctive paths in each country.[26]

The institutionalization of public-sector responsibility for research in the

[26] See Hayami, *Agricultural Growth in Japan* for a brief history of the development of agricultural research institutions in Japan.

agricultural sciences and technology in the United States can be dated from the 1860s. The Act of May 15, 1862, which created the United States Department of Agriculture, and the Act of July 2, 1862, which donated "public lands to the several states and territories which may provide colleges for the benefit of American agriculture and the mechanic arts," became the first federal, legal authority for the development of a nationwide agricultural research system.

The institutional pattern for the organization of agricultural research that emerged in the United States drew heavily on the German experience. A number of the leaders in the movement to establish state experiment stations in the United States had studied in Germany. There was a substantial traffic of young Americans to European, and particularly German, centers of graduate education in the agricultural sciences. This foreign training, however, sometimes resulted in behavior and events similar to those often observed today among trainees from underdeveloped countries: "European professors were puzzled by American students who, after beginning well abroad, lapsed into mediocrity upon returning home. And one recalls cases in which Americans, inspired by European science, actually began to make basic contributions; but never went on to a fulfillment of the potentialities so revealed."[27]

In institutionalizing agricultural research, the United States created a dual, federal-state system. Although the federal system developed more rapidly than the state system, it was not until the later years of the nineteenth century that the U.S. Department of Agriculture achieved any significant capacity to provide the scientific knowledge needed to deal with urgent problems of agricultural development. The emergence, toward the end of the century, of a viable pattern of organization required breaking away from a discipline-oriented system and organizing a number of scientific bureaus, each of which focused on a particular set of problems or commodities. Dupree cites the Bureau of Animal Industry, established in 1884, as an example: "The Bureau of Animal Industry thus had most of the attributes of the new scientific agency at its birth—an organic act, a set of problems, outside groups pressing for its interests, and extensive regulatory powers."[28]

[27] Richard Harrison Shryock, "American Indifference to Basic Science During the Nineteenth Century," in *The Sociology of Science*, eds. Bernard Barber and Walter Hirsch (New York: The Free Press of Glencoe, 1962), pp. 104–5. Shryock attributes this lack of accomplishment in basic science to an orientation toward applied science, which "seems to promise most for utility in the near future" (p. 110). It is also clear that the role of science "entrepreneurship" occupied a major share of the attention of the men who established the U.S. agricultural experiment station system.

[28] "The department [of Agriculture] gradually evolved an adequate social and political mechanism, the government bureau.... The ideal new scientific bureau had clearly defined characteristics. In the first place, the center of interest was a problem, not a scientific discipline.... Thus the ideal bureau chief sought continuity by means of a grant of power in the organic act of Congress.... In the second place, the ideal bureau

The capacity of the land-grant colleges to produce new scientific and technical knowledge for purposes of agricultural development was even more limited than that of the Department of Agriculture. The first state experiment station, the Connecticut State Agricultural Experiment Station, was not established until 1877. And until 1887, when the Hatch Act, which provided federal funding for the support of land-grant college experiment stations, was passed, only a few states were providing any significant financial support for agricultural research at the state level.

The initial emphasis of the new national experiment station system was on the testing and diffusion of available technology, that is, on the transfer of technology among regions and farmers.[29] The institutionalization of agricultural research capacity in the United States proceeded slowly until after the closing of the land frontier in the late 1880s. When the domestic terms of trade began to shift in favor of agriculture after the mid-1890s, resources devoted to agricultural research began to increase rapidly. It was well after the turn of the century, however, before the new state experiment stations could be regarded as productive sources of new knowledge. And it was not until 1914, with the passage of the Smith-Lever Act, that a firm institutional basis for the educational functions of the Department of Agriculture and the land-grant colleges was established, in the form of a cooperative federal–state extension service. By the early 1920s a national agricultural research and extension system had been effectively institutionalized at both the federal and state levels.

INTERNATIONAL DIFFUSION OF AGRICULTURAL RESEARCH CAPACITY. Institutionalization of the capacity to produce a continuous sequence of technical change leading to productivity growth in agriculture has proceeded slowly in most countries. There have typically been substantial time lags relative to the changes in factor endowments and prices and to shifts in the domestic terms of trade. In the United States and Japan the dual, national–state responsibility for agricultural development created a reasonably "efficient" market for the allocation of political resources to institutional innovation and development in the field of agricultural research and extension. In many developing countries, however, the markets for the allocation of political resources are relatively inefficient. Control over the access to limited political resources has slowed down the process of institutional

---

aimed at a stable corps of scientific personnel which was not only competent but also loyal to the bureau and confident that its work was important to the country.... In the third place, the ideal bureau established as harmonious relations as possible with many groups outside itself." A. Hunter Dupree, *Science in the Federal Government: A History of Policies and Activities to 1940* (Cambridge, Mass.: Harvard University Press, 1957), pp. 158–9.

[29] Robert E. Evenson, "Comparative Evidence on Returns to Investment in National and International Research Institutions," in *Resource Allocation and Productivity*, eds. Arndt, Dalrymple, and Ruttan.

innovation. The restrictions placed on political organization in rural areas have dampened the generation and biased the use of political resources.[30] The result, in countries where these conditions obtain, has been the under-representation of peasant cultivators, compared with the political elite, with organized urban workers, and with the plantation sector, in the formulation of agricultural policies and in the administration of agricultural and rural development programs.[31]

These political constraints on the evolution of viable rural organizations are particularly critical for the progress of agricultural research because the private sector has only limited incentives to develop a scale-neutral technology that is appropriate in an agricultural system characterized by small operating units. Even in the more developed western societies, the homogeneity of agricultural products, the small size of the farm firm, the difficulty of maintaining proprietary control, and the close linkage between biological science and technology have made it difficult for the individual agricultural producer to capture the gains from innovations that have led to advances in biological technology. In a very few cases, agricultural producers have organized themselves to provide private funding—often through a self-imposed tax or cess on production—to support agricultural research. Efforts of this sort have been most successful in situations where the production of a commodity has been dominated by a limited number of relatively large firms that produce primarily for export: for example, in the pineapple and sugar industries in Hawaii and the rubber industry in Malaysia.

Failure to institutionalize public-sector agricultural research has, at times, seriously distorted the pattern of technological change and resource use (see chapters 10 and 11). Mechanical technology has been much more responsive than biological technology to the inducement mechanisms that operate in the private sector. Institutionalization of public-sector capacity to provide a continuous stream of new agricultural technology that is consistent with resource endowments has generally been most effective when the political environment encouraged the organization of local and regional farm "bureaus" or farmers' associations. The political will of the elite can be mobilized in the interest of rural development best when it is guided by an organized rural constituency.

Yet by 1900, nearly fifty years after the Saxon invention of "socialized" agricultural research, very few countries had made substantial progress toward the establishment of productive national agricultural research systems. Even as late as 1950, effective national agricultural research

[30] Warren F. Ilchman and Norman Thomas Uphoff, *The Political Economy of Change* (Berkeley: University of California Press, 1971).

[31] The importance of decentralization is illustrated in John D. Montgomery, *Allocation of Authority in Land Reform Programs: A Comparative Study of Administrative Processes and Outputs*, Research and Training Network Reprint (New York: The Agricultural Development Council, 1974). Reprinted from *Administrative Science Quarterly* (March 1972): 62–75.

systems had been established in only a small number of countries, primarily in Western Europe, North America, Oceania, and the USSR. In Latin America, Africa, and Asia (except for Japan), investment in agricultural research was confined primarily to major export crops: sugar, rubber, tea, coffee, cotton, and a few others. Both in the former colonial areas and in the export-dependent national economies, the commodities used by domestic consumers or produced primarily by smallholders were typically bypassed in the allocation of resources to agricultural research.[32]

This bias in research allocation in former colonial areas is, of course, consistent with the model of induced institutional innovation developed in chapters 11 and 12. The major gains of technical change in plantation crop production could be expected to accrue either to consumers in the metropolitan country, or to expatriate plantation owners, depending on the elasticity of demand for the plantation crop. As a result, there were strong pressures for colonial administrators to allocate resources for research on the export commodities. Benefits from technical change in domestically consumed food crops would accrue primarily to smallholder-producers and local consumers. However, these groups were generally not organized in such a way as to exert real influence on colonial administrators. The failure of colonial and many postcolonial political systems to reflect the latent demands of agricultural producers adequately has been an important factor in the lag in the institutionalization of effective agricultural research systems in many developing countries.[33]

During the three decades since World War II, investment in agricultural research has risen dramatically. National agricultural research and training programs have become effectively institutionalized in a number of developing countries. Annual expenditures on agricultural research by governments in Latin America, Africa, and Asia rose from approximately $140 million in 1951 to $960 million in 1974 (in 1971 constant U.S. dollars).[34] By the mid 1970s a new set of international crop and animal research institutes had been established in Latin America, Africa, and Asia (see table 13–2). These institutions are developing a capacity to link the emerging national systems

[32] Even the resources that were devoted to agricultural research on the commercial crops produced for export under colonial administrations were extremely limited. See, for example, G. B. Masefield, *A History of Colonial Agricultural Service* (Oxford: Clarendon Press, 1972).

[33] It is of interest to note that since the change from colonial to national administration, the Rubber Research Institute of Malaysia has shifted the emphasis of its research program toward the development of technologies that are more appropriate for smallholder cultivation. See Colin Barlow, "Development and Equity in the Natural Rubber Industry," mimeographed (Canberra: Research School of Pacific Studies, Department of Economics, 1975).

[34] James K. Boyce and Robert E. Evenson, *National and International Agricultural Research and Extension Systems* (New York: The Agricultural Development Council, 1975), Table 1.1.

into an international network capable of developing, communicating, and diffusing research methodology and its results and of mobilizing a coordinated effort to produce a continuous stream of agricultural technology suited to the environment of the developing countries of Asia, Africa, and Latin America.[35]

The effectiveness of the new international crop research institutes in the transfer of agricultural research capacity is the result, to a substantial degree, of the organization of research effort around the objective of developing high-yielding varieties (HYVs). The institutionalization of research programs around closely articulated bodies of biological theory and method was also instrumental in the rapid transfer of the skills of "genetic engineering" or "biological architecture" to national research systems.[36] The history of the development and diffusion of agricultural research capacity provides support for Siffin's observation that it is easier to institutionalize an organization whose operations are primarily concerned with a well-developed technology than an organization that is not technology (or methodology) centered.[37]

The new international agricultural research institutes are funded by a consortium of private foundations, national aid agencies, and international development banks. They are governed by boards of trustees which, in turn, are responsible to the Consultative Group on International Agricultural Research (CGIAR). The Consultative Group's secretariat is headquartered at the offices of the World Bank, in Washington, D.C. The Group's Technical Advisory Committee (TAC) has its secretariat in the offices of the United Nations Food and Agriculture Organization, in Rome.

It is not entirely clear what factors have induced the developed countries to support the new international agricultural research system. During the 1950s and 1960s, the several developed countries transferred to a number of developing countries substantial quantities of food grains as concessional imports. Although this did represent a substantial resource transfer to a number of poor countries, it also had a depressing effect on domestic production incentives in those countries. Support for the development of the international agricultural research system, and for the development of national

[35] For a more detailed discussion of the international agricultural research system, see J. G. Crawford, "International Agricultural Research: An Encouraging Venture in International Collaboration," in *Resource Allocation and Productivity*, eds. Arndt, Dalrymple and Ruttan. See also Consultative Group on International Agricultural Research, *International Research in Agriculture* (New York: The Ford Foundation, 1974).

[36] Burton E. Swanson, "Impact of the International System on National Research Capacity: The IRRI and CIMMYT Training Programs," in *Resource Allocation and Productivity*, eds. Arndt, Dalrymple, and Ruttan. See also Burton E. Swanson, *Organizing Agricultural Technology Transfer: The Effects of Alternative Arrangements* (Bloomington: Indiana University, Program of Advanced Studies in Institution Building and Technical Assistance Methodology, 1975).

[37] William J. Siffin, "The Institution Building Perspective: Properties, Problems and Promise," in *Institution Building: A Model for Applied Social Change*, eds. D. Woods Thomas et al. (Cambridge, Mass.: Schenkman, 1972), pp. 123–7.

TABLE 13-2. Present structure of the international agricultural research network

| Center | Location | Research | Coverage | Date of Initiation | Proposed Budget for 1976 ($000) |
|---|---|---|---|---|---|
| IRRI (International Rice Research Institute) | Los Baños, Philippines | Rice under irrigation; multiple cropping systems; upland rice | Worldwide, special emphasis in Asia | 1959 | 9,588 |
| CIMMYT (International Maize and Wheat Improvement Center) | El Batán, Mexico | Wheat (also triticale, barley); maize (also high-altitude sorghum) | Worldwide | 1964 | 10,506 |
| IITA (International Institute of Tropical Agriculture) | Ibadan, Nigeria | Farming systems; cereals (rice and maize, as regional relay stations for IRRI and CIMMYT); grain legumes (cowpeas, soybeans, lima beans, pigeon peas); root and tuber crops (cassava, sweet potatoes, yams) | Worldwide in lowland tropics, special emphasis in Africa | 1965 | 10,759 |
| CIAT (International Center for Tropical Agriculture) | Palmira, Colombia | Beef; cassava; field beans; swine (minor); maize and rice (regional relay stations for CIMMYT and IRRI) | Worldwide in lowland tropics, special emphasis in Latin America | 1968 | 7,916 |
| WARDA (West African Rice Development Association) | Monrovia, Liberia | Regional cooperative effort in adaptive rice research among 13 nations with IITA and IRRI support | West Africa | 1971 | 850 |
| CIP (International Potato Center) | Lima, Peru | Potatoes (for both tropics and temperate regions) | Worldwide, including linkages with developed countries | 1972 | 4,044 |
| ICRISAT (International Crops Research Institute for the Semi-Arid Tropics) | Hyderabad, India | Sorghum; pearl millet; pigeon peas; chickpeas; farming systems; groundnuts | Worldwide, special emphasis on dry semiarid tropics, nonirrigated farming. Special relay stations in Africa under negotiation | 1972 | 13,800 |

| | | | | | |
|---|---|---|---|---|---|
| IBPGR (International Board for Plant Genetic Resources) | FAO, Rome, Italy | Conservation of plant genetic material, with special reference to crops of economic importance | Worldwide | 1973 | 939 |
| ILRAD (International Laboratory for Research on Animal Diseases) | Nairobi, Kenya | Trypanosomiasis; theileriasis (mainly east coast fever) | Africa | 1974 | 4,573 |
| ILCA (International Livestock Center for Africa) | Addis Ababa, Ethiopia | Livestock production systems | Major ecological regions in tropical zones of Africa | 1974 | 6,400 |
| ICARDA (International Center for Agricultural Research in Dry Areas) | Lebanon, Syria, and Iran | Crop and mixed farming systems research, with a focus on sheep, barley, wheat, broad beans, and lentils | Worldwide, emphasis on the semiarid winter precipitation zone | 1976 | 3,300 |
| *Associate Centers* | | | | | |
| AVRDC (Asian Vegetable Research and Development Centre) | Shanhua, Taiwan | Vegetable improvement (Mung bean, soybean, tomato, sweet potato, Chinese cabbage, white potato); cropping systems | South, Southeast, and South Asia | 1971 | 1,954 |
| IFDC (International Fertilizer Development Center) | Muscle Shoals, United States | Development of new, and improvement of existing, fertilizer materials and processes | Worldwide | 1975 | 2,348[a] |
| IFPRI (International Food Policy Research Institute) | Washington, D.C., United States | Food policy | Worldwide | 1975 | 1,000 |

Source: J. G. Crawford, "Development of the International Agricultural Research System," in *Resource Allocation and Productivity in National and International Agricultural Research*, eds. Thomas M. Arndt, Dana G. Dalrymple, and Vernon W. Ruttan (Minneapolis: University of Minnesota, 1977), pp. 282–3. Crawford's basic material was reproduced in Nicholas Wade, "International Agricultural Research," *Science* 188 (May 9, 1975): 587. Budget data for 1976 were obtained from the Secretariat of the Consultative Group on International Agricultural Research, World Bank, Washington, D.C.
[a] Operating budget only.

agricultural research systems, has been regarded, in the 1970s, as a more productive use of aid resources than direct commodity assistance.

We have documented the productivity of the new international institutes in chapter 6. It would be inaccurate to argue that the new seed–fertilizer technology would not have emerged had the new international system of agricultural research institutes not been established. Prototype green-revolution rice varieties capable of responding to higher levels of fertilizer inputs and to more intensive methods of cultivation were being developed in the early and mid-1960s in the Philippines, Indonesia, Malaysia, and India. Similar varieties were developed in the early 1960s in China. At the same time, it is clear that the new institutions were responsible for speeding up both the development of the new varieties and the development of research capacity. The effect of institutionalizing an international network of research institutes was to focus additional scientific capacity on the development of the new cereals technologies. In addition, the new institutes served as effective communication links among the developing national research systems. In the United States and Japan, the national research systems served a similar function in relation to the state and prefectural systems.

It is also clear that the success of the first two international institutes (IRRI and CIMMYT) has had an important "demonstration effect" that has led many national governments to accelerate the development of their agricultural research systems. The strong interaction effect between national and international research that we have demonstrated in chapter 6 implies that the returns to investment in agricultural research have been high compared with returns from other investment alternatives.[38]

In retrospect, the institutional innovations that led to the organization of the international agricultural research institute system can be seen as comparable in significance to the Saxon invention of socialized agricultural research. It is possible that the complexities of funding and management will become a source of weakness that could jeopardize the future viability of the international institute system. It does seem clear, however, that in today's world even the largest nations cannot expect to achieve scientific and technical self-sufficiency in the fields related to agricultural development without imposing heavy costs on their development effort.

Of more immediate concern than a premature termination of the new international research system is the problem of developing efficient "steering" mechanisms that will enable the new system to respond efficiently in contributing to technical and institutional innovations that are adapted to the resource and cultural endowments of poor countries. The international

[38] Boyce and Evenson, *Agricultural Research and Extension Programs*, pp. 101–21; Robert E. Evenson and Yoav Kislev, *Agricultural Research and Productivity* (New Haven: Yale University Press, 1975).

agricultural research institutes and centers operate in an even more complex environment than do national or state (provincial) agricultural experiment stations. The functions of leadership, resource acquisition, and maintenance of linkages are particularly complex. The specific responsibilities of the institute directors and of the Consultative Group on International Agricultural Research in the generation of support for core budgets, special projects, and outreach activities have not been clearly delineated. Linkages with scientists and other professional workers, with other research institutions, and with funding sources in both developed and developing countries are often characterized by political as well as scientific and economic considerations. The institute leadership and staff must establish working relationships in an environment characterized by widely different perceptions of the roles played in this endeavor by political, administrative, and scientific considerations.

In the United States and Japan, the decentralized pattern of state, or provincial, funding of agricultural research was an important factor in inducing the agricultural research system to allocate its scientific and technical resources in a manner consistent with national and regional resource endowments.[39] A comparable mechanism to assure that the technical efforts of the new international system will be responsive to the interests of agricultural producers and consumers in the LDCs rather than to the particular interests of developed-country donors has not yet emerged. One development that would assure a more effective balancing of supply and demand forces in the international market for agricultural research capacity would be the financial participation of LDCs in the Consultative Group on International Agricultural Research. An initial step in this direction was taken in 1974, when Nigeria joined the Consultative Group.

## The Institutional Consequences of Technical Change

Technical change in modern agriculture depends primarily on capacity for institutional innovation. It is a product of public and private investment in experiment station capacity. The technical innovations, and the new income streams that become available as these innovations are adopted, become themselves sources of institutional change.

THE INSTITUTIONAL IMPACT HYPOTHESIS. The manner in which the income streams that result from the introduction of new technology are partitioned among producers and consumers depends on the institutional relationships that govern behavior in factor and product markets. And

[39] For the United States, see Joel Morris Guttman, "The Demand for Publicly Financed Agricultural Research: An Application of a Theory of Collective Action" (Ph.D. diss., University of Chicago, August 1976). For Japan, see Hayami et al., *Agricultural Growth in Japan.*

realization of new income streams, in turn, induces further institutional changes designed to modify the partitioning of the new consumers and producers surpluses among factor owners, social classes, and economic sectors.[40]

Within the agricultural sector, the production surpluses generated by the new technology can be expected to modify the factor shares that are captured by the suppliers of labor and the suppliers of land. These changes in the functional distribution of income will be associated with changes in the personal distribution of income among the social classes engaged in agricultural production—landless laborers, tenants, and landowners. As these changes in the distribution of income among factor owners and classes occur, we can expect social and political stress to lead to institutional innovations designed to bring about further modifications of income distribution.

The partitioning of the new income streams between agricultural producers and other economic groups can also be expected to change. The new agricultural technology is typically embodied in inputs purchased either from the industrial sector or from specialized agricultural firms, such as producers of improved seed. Adoption of the new technology leads to a rise in the demand for capital equipment and for credit. And diffusion of the new technology increases the surpluses that pass through market channels. The effect is to increase both the factor shares going to suppliers of technical inputs and credit and the flow of income to suppliers of marketing services. The redirection of income flows becomes, in turn, a source of social and political stress, which induces institutional change in the organization of factor and product markets.

Earlier in this chapter (see section on "Producers vs. Consumers") we examined the implications of changes in the demand and supply relationship for the partitioning, among producers and consumers, of the new income streams that result from technical change. Changes in the rates of growth of demand or supply alter the partitioning of income streams between producers and consumers. These changes, in turn, lead to demands by producers and/or consumers for changes in the organization of product markets.

Finally, the growth of producer and consumer income results in the modification of both private and public-sector consumption, as well as of savings and of investment. The effect is to induce political and social stress over the partitioning of the new income stream between the private and the public sectors. And within the public sector the effect is to induce competition

---

[40] See for example Mancur Olson, Jr., "Rapid Growth and Destabilizing Force," *Journal of Economic History* 23 (December 1963): 529–52: Albert O. Hirschman, "The Changing Tolerance for Income Inequality in the Course of Economic Development," *Quarterly Journal of Economics* 87 (November 1973): 544–62; Simon Kuznets, "Modern Economic Growth: Findings and Reflections," *American Economic Review* 63 (June 1973): 247–58.

between the development and the control bureaucracies for control over the allocation of increments to public revenue.

The foregoing discussion of the pervasive impact of advances in productivity on institutional change is consistent with much historical experience. The struggle between landlords and peasants over the establishment of property rights in land and labor has been a persistent theme in European economic history.[41] In midwestern United States, populist sentiment against the suppliers of transportation and marketing services led to the regulation of the railroads and to legislation that was designed to encourage the cooperative as an alternative to corporate enterprise in agricultural factor and product markets.[42] The history of farm price support programs in the United States, from the mid-1920s to the present, can be viewed as a struggle between agricultural producers and the rest of society in the partitioning of the new income streams that have resulted from technical progress in agriculture.

The success of Meiji Japan in transforming agricultural surpluses into public revenue and private savings, which in turn became sources of investment in the nonagricultural sector, provided the historical evidence for the credibility of the dynamic dual economy models of the early 1960s.[43] In recent years, India has employed a complex, zonal pricing system for food grains in order to transfer income from agricultural producers in surplus-producing regions to consumers in deficit-producing regions.[44]

In the Thanjavur district of India, the green revolution led to an increase in demand for both labor and land. This resulted in steep rises in the incomes of landowners owing to the inelastic supply of land. However, elastic supply of labor from surrounding districts prevented wage rates from rising substantially. This unequal impact led to labor unrest and to attempts by laborers to restrict immigration. Landowners were more successful in organizing themselves, however, and formed an association by means of which they prevented the labor unions from gaining effective control over the labor supply in the district.[45]

[41] In England, "capitalist" landlords were successful in capturing rights to the commons from the peasantry. In France "capitalist" peasants were successful in dispossessing feudal landlords. Moore, *Social Origins*, pp. 3–100.

[42] Carl C. Taylor, *The Farmers Movement: 1620–1920* (New York: American Book Company, 1953).

[43] Dale W. Jorgenson, "The Development of a Dual Economy," *Economic Journal* 70 (June 1961): 309–34; Gustav Ranis and J. C. H. Fei, "A Theory of Economic Development," *American Economic Review* 51 (September 1961): 533–65; J. C. H. Fei and Gustav Ranis, *Development of Labor Surplus Economy: Theory and Policy* (Homewood, Ill.: Irwin, 1964).

[44] John W. Mellor, "The Function of Agricultural Prices in Economic Development," in *Agricultural Development in Developing Countries—Comparative Experience*, ed. M. L. Dantwala (Bombay: Indian Society of Agricultural Economics, 1971), pp. 122–40.

[45] K. C. Alexander, *Agrarian Tension in Thanjavur* (Hyderabad: National Institute of Community Development, 1975); Andre Beteille, *Studies in Agrarian Social Structure* (Delhi: Oxford University Press, 1974), chapter 5.

The impact of the new income streams generated by technical change can be expected to extend beyond the institutions normally identified as responsive to changes in factor-product prices. According to T. Scarlett Epstein, the new income streams that result from advances in agricultural productivity, together with the declining participation of women in economic activity, are bringing about changes in marriage practices. In the South India villages that Epstein studied, the bride price has been customary among lower-caste families while the dowry has been customary among Brahmans. As the wives of the more successful lower-caste families have become economically inactive, the dowry has tended to replace the bride price.[46]

SEVEN GENERALIZATIONS: THE DIRECT IMPACT OF THE GREEN REVOLUTION. The effects of the new "fertilizer-consuming" wheat and rice varieties on the distribution of income in Asian agriculture have been the subject of casual empiricism, interdisciplinary competition, and ideological conflict almost from their introduction in the mid 1960s.[47] The green revolution has clearly not lived up to the more extravagant claims that have been made for it.[48] It is more accurately viewed as part of the continuing evolution of more intensive systems of agricultural production, based on advances in biological and chemical technology.

Some of the early critical evaluations appeared to reflect little more than interdisciplinary pique or aggression. The green revolution shifted attention from the earlier architects of development—planners, economists, and other social scientists—to geneticists, plant breeders, and agronomists, all of whom had been producing development without thinking about it. Social scientists rushed in to explore the second and third generation problems

[46] "Where formerly a peasant wife was an economic asset, she has now become a liability. Accordingly, the groom's family now wants to be paid for taking over the responsibility of keeping her, where previously they had been prepared to compensate her father for the loss of her productive contribution." T. Scarlett Epstein, *South India: Yesterday, Today and Tomorrow: Mysore Villages Revisited* (New York: Holms and Meier, 1973), p. 199. See also the review of Epstein's book by Michael Lipton in the *Journal of Peasant Studies* 2 (January 1975): 236–41.

[47] Among the early evaluations that were most thoroughly grounded on personal experience or empirical evidence are: Wolf Ladejinsky, "The Green Revolution in the Punjab: A Field Trip," *Economic and Political Weekly* 4 (June 28, 1969): A73–A83; idem, "Green Revolution in Bihar, The Kosi Area: A Field Trip," *Economic and Political Weekly* 4 (September 27, 1969): 1–14; Clifton R. Wharton, Jr., "The Green Revolution: Cornucopia or Pandora's Box," *Foreign Affairs* 47 (April 1969): 464–76; Bruce F. Johnston and John Cownie, "The Seed–Fertilizer Revolution and Labor Force Absorption," *American Economic Review* 59 (September 1969): 569–82; Walter P. Falcon, "The Green Revolution: Generations of Problems," *American Journal of Agricultural Economics* 52 (December 1970): 698–710; Brian Lockwood, P. K. Mukherjee, and R. T. Shand, *The High Yielding Varieties Programme in India, Part I* (New Delhi: The Planning Commission of the Government of India, and Canberra: The Australian National University, 1971).

[48] Lester R. Brown, *Seeds of Change* (New York: Praeger, 1970).

before establishing whether the initial impact on production had been adequate to meet the problem of lagging food supplies.[49]

A second set of criticisms clearly has been more ideologically motivated. Hope for the radicalization of the lower peasantry and landless laborers has been viewed as dependent on the continuation of the process of immiserizing growth.[50] The radical critics have welcomed the green revolution in socialist economies like those of Cuba and China. In nonsocialist economies, the introduction of the high-yielding varieties is viewed as raising the cost of radical change by channeling new income to the middle and upper peasantry. It is assumed that continued stagnation would lower the cost of radical change by identifying the interests of the middle peasants with the landless workers. The technically neutral green revolution technology, which could improve the economic viability of the small farmer, has been viewed as increasing the political cost of revolutionary change. Because it offers the prospect of improvement in the welfare of rural people without revolution, the seed–fertilizer technology has become the focus of a great deal of radical rhetoric.

However, as a consequence of the accumulation, by the mid-1970s, of a substantial body of empirical evidence, we are now in a position to throw some light on the nature of the impact of the adoption of new varieties on functional and personal distribution of income.[51] We can summarize the

[49] See the literature review by T. Byres, "The Dialectic of India's Green Revolution," *South Asian Review* 5, no 2 (January 1972): 99–116.

[50] See, for example, Ali M. S. Fatemi, "The Green Revolution: An Appraisal," *The Monthly Review* (June 1972): 112–20. See also Harry M. Cleaver, Jr., "The Contradictions of the Green Revolution," *The American Economic Review* 72 (May 1972): 177–188; Griffin, *Economy of Agrarian Change*, and the literature referred to in Richard Franke, "A Guide to Radical Literature on Economic Development with Special Reference to Asian Agricultural Development," *Bulletin of Concerned Asian Scholars* 6, no. 4 (1974): 14–16.

[51] Among a number of particularly useful studies that review and evaluate this literature are the following: Clive Bell, "The Acquisition of Agricultural Technology: Its Determinants and Effects," *The Journal of Development Studies* 9 (October 1972): 124–59; K. M. Azam, "The Future of the Green Revolution in West Pakistan: A Choice of Strategy," *International Journal of Agrarian Affairs* 5 (March 1973): 404–29; Bandhudas Sen, *The Green Revolution in India: A Perspective* (New Delhi: Wiley Eastern, 1974); Carl H. Gotsch (with Bashir Ahmad, Walter P. Falcon, Muhammad Naseem, and Shahid Yusuf) *Linear Programming and Agricultural Policy: Micro Studies of the Pakistan Punjab*, Food Research Institute Studies 14, no. 1, special issue (1975); Rao, *Technological Change and Distribution of Gains;* and Gelia T. Castillo, *All in A Grain of Rice: Review of Philippine Studies on the Social and Economic Implications of the New Rice Technology* (College, Laguna, Philippines: Southeast Asian Regional Center for Graduate Study and Research on Agriculture, 1974). Castillo is particularly critical of Griffin (*Economy of Agrarian Change*), terming his comments on the Philippine experience superficial (pp. 212–30).

One limitation of the green revolution literature is its overwhelming "South Asian" bias. For a comparison of the factors affecting adoption of the new technology among villages throughout the rice-growing regions of Asia, see Randolph Barker, ed., *Changes in Rice Farming in Selected Areas of Asia* (Los Baños, Philippines: International Rice Research Institute, 1975).

conclusions that emerge from the studies that provide this data in a series of seven generalizations.

I. *The new wheat and rice varieties were adopted at exceptionally rapid rates in those areas where they were technically and economically superior to local varieties.* In the Indian Punjab, the proportion of total wheat area planted to the new high-yielding varieties of wheat rose from 3.6 percent in 1966/67, the year in which the HYVs were introduced, to 65.6 percent in 1969/70.[52] In three important wheat-producing districts in the Pakistan Punjab, 73 percent of wheat acreage was sown with Mexican wheats during the 1969/70 post-monsoon season.[53] In the Philippines, 95 percent of the farmers in the barrios and almost 60 percent of the farmers in the entire municipality where the new rice varieties were first planted (Gaspan, Nueva Ecija) had adopted the new varieties by 1969, four years after introduction.[54] These rates compare favorably with the diffusion rates of new crop varieties in developed countries.[55]

The rate of adoption of the new wheat and rice varieties has declined since the early 1970s (figure 13–1). In the case of the new wheat varieties, the largest yield increments have been achieved in relatively arid areas where farmers have had access to effective tubewell or gravity irrigation systems. In the case of rice, the largest yield increments have been achieved on irrigated land during the dry season in areas such as Central Luzon (Philippines) or Western Uttar Pradesh (India). The agroclimatic regions to which the wheat varieties developed at CIMMYT and the rice varieties developed at IRRI were best adapted have achieved relatively rapid and high levels of adoption. In other regions, where these varieties have had to be adapted or where it has been necessary to develop even newer varieties that are suited to different environmental conditions—or even to modify such conditions—the rate of

[52] Surjit S. Sidhu, "Economics of Technical Change in Wheat Production in the Indian Punjab," *American Journal of Agricultural Economics* 56 (May 1974): 221. For a more complete account, see Surjit Singh Sidhu, "Economics of Technical Changes in Wheat Production Punjab, India" (Ph.D. diss., University of Minnesota, 1972). The Sidhu study utilized farm-level survey data for the four years 1967/68, 1968/69, 1969/70, 1970/71. For a very interesting extension of the Sidhu study, see Siddanaik Bisaliah, "Effects of Technological Change on Output, Employment and Functional Income Distribution in Indian Agriculture: A Case Study of the Punjab Wheat Economy" (Ph.D. diss., University of Minnesota, 1975). For empirical evidence on the diffusion and impact of the high-yielding wheat varieties in India, see V. S. Vyas, *India's High Yielding Varieties Program in Wheat, 1966–67 to 1971–72* [El Batán, Mexico: Centro Internacional de Mejoramiento de Maíz y Trigo (CIMMYT), 1975].

[53] Azam, "Green Revolution in West Pakistan," p. 408.

[54] Castillo, *All in a Grain of Rice*, pp. 32–96. See also Robert E. Huke and James Duncan, "Spatial Aspects of HYV Diffusion," in *Seminar Workshop on the Economics of Rice Production* (Los Baños: International Rice Research Institute, December 1969), pp. 2–1 to 2–40.

[55] Everett M. Rogers, *Diffusion of Innovations* (New York: The Free Press, 1962), p. 106.

TABLE 13–3. Mexican-type wheat acreage as percentage of all wheat acreage, by size and tenure of holdings: 1969/70 post-monsoon season in Lyallpur, Sahiwal, and Sheikhupura Districts, Pakistan

| Number of Acres in Holding | Owner Holdings | Owner-cum-Tenants | Tenant Holdings | All Holdings |
|---|---|---|---|---|
| Less than 12½ | 71.0 | 80.4 | 66.7 | 72.5 |
| 12½ to 25 | 63.3 | 71.7 | 69.2 | 68.0 |
| 25 to 50 | 71.9 | 92.7 | 81.9 | 82.0 |
| 50 | 73.2 | 87.3 | 57.3 | 78.6 |
| All sizes | 69.4 | 80.5 | 70.0 | 73.4 |

Source: K. M. Azam, "The Future of the Green Revolution in West Pakistan: A Choice of Strategy," *International Journal of Agrarian Affairs* 5, no. 6 (March 1973): 408. Original source: Government of the Punjab, Planning and Development Department, Statistical Survey Unit, *Fertilizer and Mexican Wheat Survey Report* (Lahore, 1970), p. 38.

diffusion has been slower, and the yield impact has been lower.[56] Diffusion to yet other areas will depend, to a very substantial degree, on the development of varieties of wheat and rice that are suited to other ecological niches and on investment in irrigation and drainage in those areas where well-adapted varieties are available. It will also depend on the successful development of high-yielding varieties of other food grains, coarse grains, and grain legumes.[57]

II. *Neither farm size nor farm tenure has been a serious constraint on the adoption of new high-yielding grain varieties.* Differential rates of adoption by farm size and tenure have, of course, been observed. What the available data seem to imply, however, is that within a relatively few years after introduction, lags in adoption rates owing to size or tenure have typically disappeared. The data on adoption of new wheat varieties from the Pakistan Punjab, presented in table 13–3, are fairly typical of the data available from other areas where the high-yielding varieties are technically well adapted. Essentially similar results have been reported for wheat in India, for rice in the Philippines and Indonesia, and for maize in Kenya.[58] A stylized model of the

[56] Francine R. Frankel, *India's Green Revolution: Economic Gains and Political Costs* (Princeton: Princeton University Press, 1971); Randolph Barker and Mahar Mangahas, "Environmental and Other Factors Influencing the Performance of New High Yielding Varieties of Wheat and Rice in Asia," in *Agricultural Development in Developing Countries*, ed. Dantwala, pp. 225–36. In the case of rice, the environmental constraints that limit the yields of the new high-yielding varieties are the same as those that limited yields in the pre-green-revolution period. See Hsieh and Ruttan, "Growth of Rice Production," pp. 307–41.

[57] It seems likely that the data shown in figure 13–1 underestimate the rate of diffusion of HYVs during the 1970s. The data do not reflect the diffusion of high-yielding varieties of maize, sorghum, millet, and some other grains that have had a substantial impact on grain production in some areas.

[58] See Sen, *Green Revolution in India*, pp. 32–54; Mahar Mangahas, Virginia A. Miralao, Romona P. de los Reyes (with Normando de Leon), *Tenants, Lessees, Owners: Welfare Implications of Tenure Change* (Quezon City: Ateneo de Manila University

ADOPTION LEVEL (%)

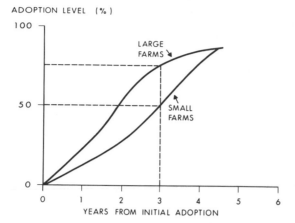

FIG. 13-3. Stylized model of HYV diffusion process.

diffusion process similar to that in figure 13-3 would describe the results of a very large number of diffusion studies that have attempted to measure the association between farm size and level of adoption from the time HYVs are introduced.

III. *Neither farm size nor farm tenure has been an important source of differential growth in productivity.* Sidhu's evidence from the Indian Punjab indicates that the new wheat technology has been approximately neutral with respect to scale—it has not been strongly biased in either a labor-saving or a capital-saving direction—and that small and large farmers have achieved approximately equal gains in efficiency.[59] Azam interprets the data that are available from a number of studies in the Pakistan Punjab to indicate that "while a number of smaller farmers do face relatively more severe constraints of irrigation water and credit, the differences in the severity of these constraints [are] . . . not serious enough to have caused any significant differences in the yields obtained by the small farmers as compared with the large

Press, 1976), pp. 23–43; Mahar Mangahas, "Economic Aspects of Agrarian Reform under the New Society," *The Philippine Review of Business and Economics* 11 (December 1974): 175–87; Irlan Soejono, "Growth and Distributional Changes of Paddy Farm Income in Central Java, 1968–1974" (Ph.D. diss., Iowa State University, 1976); idem. "Growth and Distributional Changes in Paddy Farm Income in Central Java," *Prisma— Indonesian Journal of Social and Economic Affairs*, no. 3 (May 1976): 26–32; John Gerhart, *The Diffusion of Hybrid Maize in Western Kenya* (Mexico, D.F.: Centro Internacional de Mejoramiento de Maíz y Trigo, 1975).

[59] Surjit S. Sidhu, "Relative Efficiency in Wheat Production in the Indian Punjab," *The American Economic Review* 64 (September 1974): 742–51. Sidhu concludes "(1) that small and large wheat producing farms have equal relative *economic efficiency* and equal relative *price efficiency* and (2) that tractor-operated and non-tractor operated wheat producing farms have equal *economic efficiency* and equal relative *price efficiency*. . . . This implies that these farms also have equal technical efficiency" (p. 746).

farmers."[60] Mangahas has obtained similar results from an analysis of rice-producing farms in the Philippines.[61]

IV. *The introduction of the new high-yielding wheat and rice technology has resulted in an increase in the demand for labor.* Sidhu's results indicated a very substantial shift to the right in the labor demand function on wheat-producing farms as a result of the introduction of the new wheat varieties in the Indian Punjab.[62] Using Sidhu's data to analyze the sources of growth in the demand for labor in the Punjab, Bisaliah found that the direct output effect of the new technology on the demand for labor was partially offset by substitution effects.[63] The net effect of the increase in demand for labor has been a significant rise in real wages in the Punjab and in other parts of Northwest India at a time when real wages were constant or declining in most states in India.[64]

An extensive review of the literature by Bartsch indicates that the introduction of high-yielding varieties into traditional wheat and rice production systems has typically resulted in substantial increases in annual labor use per hectare.[65] This increase in labor use has stemmed from greater utilization of labor per unit of cropped area and, in some cases, from higher cropping intensity.[66] Even mechanized farms typically were utilizing increased labor inputs per hectare, although simulation results conducted by Bartsch and others indicate that labor input per hectare might be expected to decline substantially under fully mechanized techniques combined with adoption of the HYV technology. At this stage it seems more accurate to view the growth of tractor mechanization of farm operations in areas like the Punjab as an economic response to the rising demand for labor associated with intensification of crop production rather than as an autonomous source of labor displacement.[67] The process of mechanization was under way prior to the

---

[60] Azam, "Green Revolution in West Pakistan," p. 418.

[61] Mangahas et al., *Welfare Implications of Tenure Change*, pp. 23–43.

[62] Sidhu, "Economics of Technical Change," p. 221. See also William Staub, *Agricultural Development and Farm Employment in India*, Foreign Agricultural Economic Report no. 84 (Washington, D.C.: U.S. Department of Agriculture, Economic Research Service, September 1973).

[63] Bisaliah, "Effects of Technological Change," pp. 53–84, 115–43, 154–68.

[64] Deepak Lal, "Agricultural Growth, Real Wages, and The Rural Poor in India," *Economic and Political Weekly* 11 (June 1976): A47–61; G. Parthasarthy, "Wages and Incomes of the Weaker Sectors in Rural India," *Indian Journal of Agricultural Economics* 29 (July–September, 1974): 78–91; Edward Allen Baker, "Agricultural Wages and Production in India" (M.S. thesis, University of Illinois, 1971).

[65] Bartsch, "Employment Effects of Alternative Technologies."

[66] In some areas the demand for tractors is strongly influenced by their utility for transportation as well as in farm operations. The substitution of tractor for animal power may also release land that has been devoted to forage production for other uses.

[67] Inderjit Singh and Richard H. Day, "Factor Substitution in Economic Development: A Green Revolution Case Study," *Journal of Development Studies* 11 (April 1975): 155–77. In interpreting the several studies based on budgeting or simulation methodology, it is useful to keep in mind an observation made by M. L. Dantwala: "Studies based

introduction of the new wheat varieties, and it has been reinforced by the more rapid growth in demand for labor since their introduction.

V. *Landowners have gained more than tenants and laborers from the adoption of the higher-yielding grain varieties.* Data assembled by Mellor indicate that although the percentage increase in labor earnings from increased employment and wages is often fairly large, the percentage of the increased output allocated to labor is relatively small (table 13–4).[68] Data reported by Dayanath Jha indicate that the factor share to land rose in every state in India between 1960/61 and 1970/71.[69] For example, in Aligarh district, where 10 percent of the increased output went to labor, 67 percent went to land and capital and 23 percent went to other costs (including 8 percent to fertilizer).[70] While the technical change increased the demand for labor and land in a neutral way in the areas where it occured, the neutral shift was often translated into an unequal distributional outcome (a) as a result of the high elasticity of the supply of labor in relation to the supply of land faced by many regions that experienced the green revolution and (b) by the rapid shift to the left of the supply curve for labor as a result of population growth.

In the Philippines, Mangahas found that the effect of land tenure on productivity was neutral. There were no significant differences among owner operators, lease-holders, and share tenants in respect to either adoption of the high-yielding varieties or efficiency in the use of inputs.[71] However, differences in tenure remain, as before the introduction of the high-yielding varieties, a major source of income disparity in rural areas.

on field investigations of what had actually happened or was happening are less pessimistic about the labor absorption capacity of the new technology than the findings based on econometric models and attempted projections." M. L. Dantwala, "Poverty and Unemployment in Rural India," draft (Ottawa: International Development Research Centre, September 1973), p. 189.

[68] Mellor provides a particularly useful review of the literature and exposition of the complex interrelationships between increased production, product prices, real wages, and employment. See John W. Mellor, *The New Economics of Growth* (Ithaca and London: Cornell University Press, 1976), chapter entitled "Agricultural Modernization and the Rural Poor," pp. 76–106.

Mellor's method of standardizing the results of the several studies reported in table 13–4 underestimates the factor share to labor in situations where wage rates are rising. Nevertheless, even fairly liberal allowances for potential gains in wage rates would not reverse the conclusion that during the period the data cover, the increase in return to land was greater than the increase in return to labor.

[69] Dayanath Jha, "Agricultural Growth, Technology and Equity," *Indian Journal of Agricultural Economics* 29 (July–September 1974): 211. See also Rao, *Technological Change and Distribution of Gains*, pp. 91–180.

[70] Considerable caution should be exercised in interpreting these results. The data presented in the article by Jha cited above indicated that the factor share to land rose more rapidly in states with slow growth in output than in states with rapid growth in output. The implication is that in many areas in India the rise in the factor share to land must be explained along classical Ricardian lines, that is, as a result of rising pressure of labor against land.

[71] Mangahas, "Economic Aspects of Agrarian Reform," pp. 175–87. See also Mangahas et al., *Welfare Implications of Tenure Change*.

Much of the literature on the green revolution has failed to distinguish between its absolute and relative effects on income distribution. Many authors who refer to the worsening position of the smaller owners and tenants or of the landless laborers are apparently referring to the widening absolute gap in the income distribution rather than to an actual decline in the income of those who occupy the lower end of the income distribution in rural communities. This point is effectively illustrated by data from a study by C. Geoffrey Swenson in the Thanjavur district in South India.[72] Similar results have been reported by Soejono in Indonesia.[73] Swenson's results are of interest because of extreme inequity in the distribution of income in the villages he studied (table 13–5). Between 1965/66 and 1970/71, paddy (rough rice) production increased by approximately 22 percent. Median and mean household real income from all sources rose by 12 percent. The distribution of income among income and tenure classes remained essentially unchanged. Owner–operators' real income rose by 14 percent, tenants' by 17 percent, and landless laborers' by 14 percent.[74] In 1965/66 the Gini ratio for all households was 0.707, and in 1970/71 it was 0.700.[75] This recitation of the essentially neutral effect of the initial impact of the new technology does tend to obscure what is perhaps the most important observation to be made in respect to Swenson's data: that there was an extreme disparity of income among classes, both in 1965/66 and in 1970/71. Almost 60 percent of the increase in income, which derived primarily from increases in rice production, went to the 5 percent of households that had the highest income in 1965/66.

[72] C. Geoffrey Swenson, "The Effect of Increased Rice Production on Employment and Income Distribution in Thanjavur District, South India" (Ph.D. diss., Michigan State University, 1973). See also C. Geoffrey Swenson, "The Distribution of Benefits from Increased Rice Production in Thanjavur District, South India," *Indian Journal of Agricultural Economics* 31 (January–March 1976): 1–12.

[73] Soejono, "Paddy Farm Income in Central Java, 1968–1974." Soejono reports a decline in income inequality among rice producers between 1968/69 and 1973/74 in eight intensive rice-growing areas that had experienced rapid growth in the use of the new high-yielding varieties. He also reports that the HYV growers used 30 percent more pre-harvest labor than did traditional variety growers.

[74] Real income of owner-tenants declined by 3 percent. This decline in the group average was the result primarily of a very large decline in the income of two medium-size owner-tenants.

[75] An indication of the extreme bias in income distribution in the Thanjavur districts studied by Swenson is that in India as a whole the Gini ratios for the distribution of rural and agricultural incomes are 0.41 and 0.49, respectively. See Sen, *Green Revolution in India*, p. 46. In the Aligarh District in Western Uttar Pradesh, the Gini ratio for farm families declined from 0.514 in 1963/64 to 0.428 in 1968/69. See Katar Singh, "The Impact of New Agricultural Technology on Farm Income Distribution in the Aligarh District of Uttar Pradesh," *Indian Journal of Agricultural Economics* 28 (April–June 1973): 5,6. In the Philippines scattered data from village studies suggests Gini ratios for farm families in the 0.35–0.40 range. See Castillo, *All in a Grain of Rice*, p. 220. The Gini ratios for the size distribution of farm operating units compiled in Barker, *Changes in Rice Farming*, also suggest a more equal distribution of resources among farm families in Southeast Asia than in South Asia.

TABLE 13–4. Division of increased "payments" between labor and other inputs, various high-yielding varieties and areas, India

| Area | Increase in Gross Value of Output | | Increase in Labor "Payments" | | Percent of Increased Output to Labor[a] | Percent of Increased Output to Other Inputs[b] | Percentage Increase in Labor "Payments" for a One Percent Increase in Gross Value of Output |
|---|---|---|---|---|---|---|---|
| | Rupees per Acre | Percentage Increase | Rupees per Acre | Percentage Increase | | | |
| *Wheat* | | | | | | | |
| Aligarh, U.P.[c] | 462 | 71 | 46 | 58 | 10 | 90 | 0.8 |
| Varanasi, U.P.[d] | 620 | 65 | 11 | 15 | 2 | 98 | 0.2 |
| Udaipur, Rajasthan[e] | 343 | 43 | 18 | 13 | 5 | 95 | 0.3 |
| Punjab[f] | 450 | 100 | 56 | 42 | 12 | 88 | 0.4 |
| *Monsoon-season Paddy* | | | | | | | |
| West Godavari, Andhra Pradesh[g] | 269 | 38 | 32 | 17 | 12 | 88 | 0.4 |
| East Godavari, Andhra Pradesh[g] | 216 | 33 | 20 | 13 | 10 | 90 | 0.4 |
| Uttar Pradesh[d] | 1,100 | 200 | 67 | 92 | 6 | 94 | 0.5 |
| Tamil Nadu[h] | 550 | 100 | 33 | 20 | 6 | 94 | 0.2 |
| Laguna, Philippines[i] | 374 | 72 | 3 | 3 | 1 | 99 | 0.0 |
| Sambalpur, Orissa[j] | 404 | 95 | 36 | 28 | 11 | 89 | 0.3 |
| *Post-monsoon Season Paddy* | | | | | | | |
| West Godavari, Andhra Pradesh[g] | 562 | 86 | 39 | 16 | 7 | 93 | 0.2 |
| East Godavari, Andhra Pradesh[g] | 761 | 153 | 39 | 30 | 5 | 95 | 0.2 |
| Tamil Nadu[h] | 625 | 100 | 46 | 21 | 7 | 93 | 0.2 |
| Gumai Bil, Bangladesh[k] | 948 | 208 | 302 | 125 | 32 | 68 | 0.6 |
| *Pearl millet* | | | | | | | |
| Kaira, Gujarat[l] | 300 | 85 | 39 | 27 | 13 | 87 | 0.3 |
| Average | 532 | 97 | 52 | 35 | 9 | 91 | 0.3 |

Source: John W. Mellor, *The New Economics of Growth: A Strategy for India and the Developing World* (Ithaca: Cornell University Press, 1976), p. 81. Adapted from data given in the sources listed in footnotes (c) through (1) below.

[a] Labor "payment" is defined as physical labor input (family and hired) in man-days at a constant wage.

[b] Other input "payments" are defined as gross value of output minus share to labor.

[c] R. S. Dixit and P. P. Singh, "Impact of High Yielding Varieties on Human Labor Inputs," *Agricultural Situation in India* 24, no. 12 (March 1970).

[d] J. P. Mishra and B. D. Shukla, "A Study on the Economics of High Yielding Varieties Programme," *Agricultural Situation in India* 24, no. 2 (May 1969).

[e] S. S. Acharya, "Comparative Efficiency of High Yielding Varieties Programme—Case Study of Udaipur District," *Economic and Political Weekly* 4, no. 44 (November 1, 1969).

[f] *Evaluation Study of the High Yielding Varieties Programme, Rabi 1967–68, Wheat* (New Delhi: Government of India, Programme Evaluation Organization, Planning Commission).

[g] *Report on the Study of High Yielding Varieties Programme, Kharif and Rabi, 1968–69*, Phase II (Waltair: Andhra University, Agro-Economic Research Centre).

[h] *Evaluation Study of the High Yielding Varieties Programme, Kharif and Rabi, 1968–69* (New Delhi: Government of India, Programme Evaluation Organization, Planning Commission).

[i] C. M. Crisostomo, W. H. Meyers, T. B. Paris, Jr., B. Duff, and R. Barker, "The New Rice Technology and Labor/Absorption in Philippine Agriculture" (Paper presented at the Conference on Manpower Problems in East and Southeast Asia, Singapore, May 1971).

[j] R. N. Tripathy and B. Samal, "Economics of High Yielding Varieties in LADP: A Study of Sambalput in Orissa," *Economic and Political Weekly* 4, no. 43 (October 25, 1969).

[k] Sharif Md. Masud and F. L. Underwood, *Gumai Bil Boro Paddy Profits and Losses, 1967–68 Season*, F. M. Research Report no. 5 (Mymensingh: East Pakistan Agricultural University, Bureau of Agricultural Economics, Statistical and Sociological Research, April 1970).

[l] B. M. Desai and M. D. Desai, *New Strategy of Agricultural Development in Operation* (Vallabh Vidyanagar: Sadar Patel University, Agro-Economic Research Centre, 1968).

TABLE 13–5. Patterns of distribution of total value income among all agricultural households in survey villages:    Shares of ordinal groups of households, 1965/66 and 1970/71

|  | Percent of Total Value Income | |
|---|---|---|
| Household Income Groups[a] | 1965/66 | 1970/71 |
| Top 5 percent | 56.4 | 58.0 |
| Top 10 percent | 66.7 | 67.1 |
| Top 20 percent | 75.7 | 75.8 |
| Second 20 percent | 10.2 | 9.3 |
| Third 20 percent | 6.7 | 6.6 |
| Fourth 20 percent | 5.0 | 5.4 |
| Bottom 20 percent | 2.3 | 2.9 |
| Gini ratio | 0.707 | 0.700 |

Source: C. Geoffrey Swenson, "The Distribution of Benefits from Increased Rice Production in Thanjavur District, South India," *Indian Journal of Agricultural Economics* 31 (January–March 1976): 1–12.

[a] The observations for landless labor households were adjusted by a factor of 3.43 to represent the ratio of landless labor households to farm operator households.

VI. *The introduction of the new high-yielding varieties has contributed to a widening of wage and income differentials among regions.* As mentioned in the first generalization, these varieties have been developed to respond most favorably to those elements in the environment that are subject to man's control. They are more responsive than the varieties they have replaced to higher levels of fertilization, to more effective irrigation and drainage and to more effective control of pathogens, insects, and weeds. Reductions in sensitivity to certain natural variations, such as day length and temperature, make these new varieties more adaptable to intensive systems of crop production. Thus, the contribution of the new varieties to productivity growth has been greatest in those regions where there has been substantial investment in physical and institutional infrastructure development.[76] And this pattern has been reinforced by the location-specific character of agricultural technology.

In India, increased productivity has been concentrated in a rather limited number of districts.[77] This differential regional impact is seen quite clearly in data from several states and regions of India (table 13–6). The differing rates of productivity growth have been associated with the widening of wage rate differences among regions. Edward A. Baker indicates that in India during the period from 1954/55 to 1968/69 the supply curve for labor in the agricultural sector appears to have been perfectly elastic in all areas except

[76] C. H. Hanumantha Rao, "Factor Endowments, Technology and Farm Employment: Comparison of East Uttar Pradesh with West Uttar Pradesh and Punjab," *Economic and Political Weekly* 2 (September 25, 1976): A117–23. See also Srinath Singh, *Modernization of Agriculture* (New Delhi: Heritage Publishers, 1976).

[77] G. Parthasarthy, "Dilemmas of Marketable Surplus: The Indian Case," mimeographed (Ithaca: Cornell University, February 1976).

TABLE 13–6.  Annual linear growth rates of agricultural output and residual productivity, 1958–1961 to 1963–1965 and 1963–1965 to 1969–1971

| Region/State | 1958–1961 to 1963–1965 | | 1963–1965 to 1969–1971 | |
|---|---|---|---|---|
| | Output | Residual productivity | Output | Residual productivity |
| *North West India* | | | | |
| Gujarat | 4.71 | 2.81 | 7.13 | 4.78 |
| Haryana | 1.23 | −0.70 | 20.40 | 16.10 |
| Punjab | 3.60 | 0.52 | 19.20 | 13.40 |
| Rajasthan | 0.06 | −0.99 | 13.60 | 12.70 |
| *North Central and Eastern India* | | | | |
| Andhra Pradesh | 2.63 | 0.11 | −0.24 | −1.05 |
| Assam | 1.48 | −0.18 | 5.45 | 3.98 |
| Bihar | 2.36 | 0.32 | 1.57 | −0.82 |
| Madhya Pradesh | 0.76 | 0.05 | 3.00 | −1.52 |
| Maharashtra | 0.85 | −0.93 | 0.08 | −2.13 |
| Orissa | 4.80 | 1.93 | 3.15 | 1.30 |
| Uttar Pradesh[a] | 2.47 | 0.66 | 4.87 | 1.43 |
| West Bengal | 4.66 | 2.67 | 2.18 | −0.36 |
| *South India* | | | | |
| Kerala | 1.30 | −1.25 | 2.15 | −0.67 |
| Mysore | 2.96 | 0.69 | 1.93 | 0.27 |
| Tamil Nadu | 1.77 | −1.43 | 3.08 | 0.61 |

Source: R. E. Evenson and D. Jha, "The Contribution of Agricultural Research Systems to Agricultural Production in India," *Indian Journal of Agricultural Economics* 28 (October–December 1973): 216, 217.

[a] District-level data suggest that output and productivity growth rates for Eastern Uttar Pradesh during the period 1963–1965 to 1969–1971 may have been in the same range as for Haryana and Punjab.

Punjab–Haryana and a few intensive wheat-producing districts in other states. During this period average annual daily real wages decreased in all states except Punjab–Haryana, Uttar Pradesh, Kerala and, possibly, Tamil Nadu.[78]

The contribution of the new seed–fertilizer technology to the widening of regional income disparities has apparently been greater than the technology's impact on disparities in income within communities and regions.[79] The widening regional disparities in income and the associated changes in the regional distribution of political resources can be expected to provide a more important source of institutional stress and institutional change than the stress at the community level that has received so much attention in recent literature.

[78] Baker, "Agricultural Wages and Production"; A. V. Jose, "Trends in Real Wages of Agricultural Labourers," *Economic and Political Weekly* (March 30, 1974): A25–A30; Lal, "Agricultural Growth."
[79] Rao, *Technological Change and Distribution of Gains*, p. 178.

VII. *The effect of the introduction of the new high-yielding varieties has been to slow the rate of increase in food grain prices at the consumer level.* During the 1974/75 crop year the new higher-yielding, or modern, varieties of wheat were planted on close to 50 million acres and the new high-yielding varieties of rice were planted on over 53 million acres in Asia and the Near East (figure 13–1). In Asia, over 60 percent of the wheat area and over one-quarter of the rice area is planted to the modern varieties developed since the mid-1960s. Evenson has estimated that in crop year 1974/75 the supply of rice in all developing countries was approximately 12 percent higher than it would have been if the same total resources had been devoted to production of rice using only the traditional rice varieties available prior to the mid-1960s.[80]

The impact of a shift to the right in the supply of food grain is particularly significant for both the urban and rural poor. The distribution of gains among consumers depends primarily on the relative amount of a particular commodity that is consumed by each income group and on the price elasticity of demand in each group. The larger the quantity consumed and the higher the absolute value of the price elasticity of demand in the lower income strata in relation to the higher income strata, the more favorable will be the distributional benefits. This is illustrated quite dramatically by the impact of the new rice technology and consumer welfare in Colombia since the mid-1960s. Between 1966 and 1974 the proportion of the total rice area that was planted to modern varieties rose from 10 to 99 percent. Yields on irrigated land rose from 3.1 to 5.4 metric tons per hectare, and total rice production increased from 600 thousand to 1,570 thousand metric tons. Most of the increased production was absorbed in the local market. The benefits were transmitted to consumers through lower prices and increased per capita consumption. The benefits were strongly biased in favor of low income consumers. The lowest income quartile of Colombian households, which received only 4 percent of household income, captured 28 percent of the consumer benefits that resulted from the shift to the right in the supply curve for rice.[81]

In most countries, increases in food grain production have generally not been adequate to prevent substantial increases in food grain prices, when

[80] Robert E. Evenson, "Comparative Evidence on Returns to Investment in National and International Research Institutions," in *Resource Allocation and Productivity*, eds. Arndt, Dalrymple, and Ruttan, pp. 237–65. See also R. E. Evenson, P. M. Flores, and Y. Hayami, "Costs and Returns to Rice Research" (Paper delivered at Conference on Economic Consequences of New Rice Technology, Los Baños, Laguna, Philippines, International Rice Research Institute, December 13–16, 1976).

[81] Scobie and Posada T., *Impact of High Yielding Rice Varieties*; Scobie, "Costs and Returns to Rice Research"; and Per Pinstrup-Andersen, "Decision-Making on Food and Agricultural Research Policy: The Distribution of Benefits from New Agricultural Technology Among Consumer Income Strata," *Agricultural Administration* 4, no. 1 (January 1977): 13–28, show that in Colombia, if commodity priorities for research were established in terms of a criterion of consumer benefits for the low income strata, the priority ranking should be cassava, maize, plantain, rice, potatoes, and beans.

measured in current dollars, in the face of the general inflationary pressures that have dominated world commodity markets between the late 1960s and the early 1970s. It is clear, however, that in the absence of the contribution of the new high-yielding varieties, food grain prices would be even higher in many countries of Asia, Africa, and Latin America. Part of the new income streams generated by the new varieties have been transferred from producers to consumers either through the market or through administered distribution schemes. Thus while there may be some ambiguity regarding the distribution of the gains by size of farm or by economic or social class within the agricultural sector, there can be little question that the distributional effect on the consumption side has been positive. And among those who have gained on the consumption side have been the landless and near-landless workers in rural areas.

In respect to issues revolving around the distribution of gains between producers and consumers, the literature has given less attention to the developing countries that have benefitted from the new high-yielding varieties than to the developed countries. This may be in part because the rapid growth of demand, which has stemmed primarily from population growth, has tended to equal or exceed the rate of growth of supply, even when the latter has been augmented by rapid technical change. Perhaps the more important factor is that with relatively few exceptions, the peasant producers of food crops in Asia are not effectively organized to reflect their economic interests at the policy level. Resistance to low price levels tends to take the form of attempts to adjust the crop mix to relative price shifts rather than to influence price policy directly.[82]

The picture that emerges from this review of the evidence on the initial impact of the green revolution can be summarized as follows: A technology that is essentially neutral with respect to scale has been introduced into environments in which the economic, social, and political institutions have varied widely with respect to their neutrality.[83] This view has been eloquently

[82] Timmer reports, for example, that in the early 1970s Indonesian policy makers had to learn again the lesson "that farmers do not like to repay debts with stalk paddy at below market prices." C. Peter Timmer, "The Political Economy of Rice in Asia: Indonesia," *Food Research Institute Studies* 14, no. 3 (1975): 216. In India, organized producer groups have been more effective in exerting pressure on the policy-making process. See, for example, Arun Chowdhury, "Buying Off the Large Farmers," *Economic and Political Weekly* 9 (October 5, 1974): 1690-1.

[83] By the mid-1970s, the essential neutrality of scale of the new cereals technology had been conceded even by the more outspoken critics of the effects of the green revolution. "The new technology for producing food is not characterized by important economies of scale, and the growth of inequality which has in practice accompanied technical change is not a necessary consequence of attempts to raise yields. The problem arises not from the nature of the most appropriate technology, but from the bias of government policy and the fact that public institutions clearly are not scale-neutral." Griffin, *Economy of Agrarian Change*, p. 69.

expressed by Wolf Ladejinsky: "When all is said and done, it is not the fault of the new technology that the credit service doesn't serve those for whom it was originally intended; that the extension service is not living up to expectations; that the panchayats are essentially political rather than development bodies; that security of tenure is a luxury of the few; that rentals are exorbitant; that ceilings on land are merely notational; that for the greater part tenurial legislation is deliberately miscarried, or wage scales are hardly sufficient to keep soul and body together."[84]

Where the technology has been introduced in areas characterized by a reasonable degree of equity in the distribution of resources, the effect has been favorable in terms of both productivity and equity. When the technology has been introduced in areas characterized by great inequity in the distribution of resources, the productivity impact has been weak, and the pattern of inequity has been reinforced. The differential impact of the technology on income growth has apparently been greater among regions than among economic factors or among social classes within regions.

It should be pointed out at this stage that it is very dangerous to conclude from the type of evidence now available on the green revolution that future technical change of a similar type would lead to patterns of distribution that are similar to those we have observed to date. If technical change were to occur in less favored regions, or if the producers who experienced it were to be faced with inelastic demand conditions owing to more widespread technical change or lower population growth, the distributional outcomes could be substantially different from those observed in the past.

THE DYNAMICS OF INSTITUTIONAL IMPACT.    It is apparent that one must look beyond the immediate impact of the new high-yielding technology on productivity and income to observe the longer-run institutional changes suggested by the institutional impact hypothesis in terms of its implications for (a) stress on communal institutions and (b) stress on intersector relationships.

It is useful at this point to differentiate the perspective that has emerged in this chapter from that presented by some of the literature that has focused on the secondary impact of the green revolution. Some authors tend to argue simultaneously that (a) the production impact has been barely perceptible and (b) the effects on rural income and social organization have been both pervasive and severely regressive.[85] In part, this reflects a failure to analyze the changing sources of growth in agricultural production in areas where the new technology has been adopted. In areas of adoption there has typically been a very substantial shift in the sources of growth of grain output. Increases in

---

[84] Ladejinsky, "Green Revolution in Bihar."
[85] Griffin, *Economy of Agrarian Change*, pp. xii, xiii, 1–14.

output per unit area have become increasingly important in comparison with increases in area cultivated.[86]

The new income streams that result from productivity growth can be expected to impose stress on the institutions that determine the way in which income is partitioned among factor owners and economic classes at the community level. The new income streams can also be expected to impose stress on the institutions that partition the gains from productivity growth between the agricultural and nonagricultural sectors. In this section we draw on the green revolution literature to illustrate the effect of both *communal stress* and *intersector stress* on institutional change at the community level and on the institutions that govern the relationships between the agricultural and nonagricultural sectors.

*Stress on communal institutions.*   Advances in agricultural productivity can be expected to impose stress on the relationships among factor owners and social classes and thus to lead to substantial changes in the institutions that govern property rights in factors of production and in relationships among social and economic classes.

Evidence of communal unrest in rural areas of India during the late 1960s was interpreted at that time to strengthen the communal stress hypothesis.[87] The number of reports of communal conflict rose from 19 cases in 1967 to 43 cases in 1968. A study by the Home Ministry found that "over 80 percent of the agitations were led by the landless against landowners, and concerned demands for increased agricultural wages, security of tenure, larger crop shares, and...redistribution of land."[88] Francine Frankel's view that "the 'proximate' causes which actually converted latent discontent into open conflict were located in the new agricultural strategy" was widely shared.[89] Yet events moved much more slowly than anticipated. The green revolution in India did not turn "red." And evidence of changing institutional relationships within rural communities is more difficult to come by now than appeared likely a few years ago.

Some observers attribute the decline in the numbers of reported cases of agrarian unrest to the use of "volunteer" forces organized by landowners and to the use of police and military units to suppress organized farm workers.[90] Others have questioned the relationship between the green revolution

---

[86] For the Philippines, see Cristina Crisostomo and Randolph Barker, "Growth Rates of Philippine Agriculture, 1948–1971," in *Agricultural Growth in Japan, Korea, Taiwan, and the Philippines*, eds. Yujiro Hayami, Vernon W. Ruttan, and Herman Southworth (Honolulu: The University Press of Hawaii, 1978). For India, see R. E. Evenson and P. Jha, "The Contribution of Agricultural Research Systems," *Indian Journal of Agricultural Economics* 28 (October–December 1973): 216–17.

[87] For a history of peasant unrest in India, see Kathleen Gough, "Indian Peasant Uprising," *Economic and Political Weekly* 9 (August 1974): 1391–412.

[88] Frankel, *India's Green Revolution*, p. 9.

[89] Ibid., p. 10.

[90] Ibid., pp. 109–18, 203–8.

and the observed unrest.[91] Regardless of the weight we give either explanation, it does seem clear that political leadership on the left was inadequate to the task of organizing the latent unrest in rural areas that occasionally manifested itself in communal violence in the late 1960s. Middle and upper peasants have had some success in presenting organized resistance to government measures—land ceilings, grain levies, and taxes—that limit the gains from productivity growth. Lower peasants and landless workers, however, have not organized effectively to achieve greater participation in the gains from productivity growth.[92]

Although the institutional changes that have occurred since the green revolution are clearly less dramatic than anticipated a decade ago, it is generally agreed that changes that will modify the balance of economic and political power in rural areas are in process. The effect of growth in agricultural production, whether this growth is more aptly termed revolution or evolution, has been to loosen traditional caste and patron-client relationships. The trend away from paying for harvest labor in kind—that is, giving the laborer a percentage of the crop harvested—to paying for such labor in money wages has accelerated. The landless laborers' traditional property right to a share of the harvest is being expropriated. Increasingly, the income of the landless laborer is based on a wage rate that is determined in the labor market rather than on a property right that derives from the laborer's residence in a particular village.

The shift from a pattern of communal relationships based on customary rules governing land rights and use and on traditional patterns of labor exchange to a system in which the prices of land and labor are established by the forces of supply and demand operating through land and labor markets has been under way in many areas of Asia for over a century.[93] The effect of the sharply higher yields that have resulted from the introduction of the new cereal varieties has been to create a disequilibrium in the traditional balance of customary relationships that had evolved under conditions of static agricultural technology.[94]

[91] "In areas of fastest change, namely Punjab, Haryana and West Uttar Pradesh, there is little evidence of growth in tensions between different classes in the rural sector...even in Thanjavur, technological changes led to tensions between classes, not so much in the New Delta where the change was rapid as in the lagging Old Delta where the inequalities in land ownership and status are conspicuous." Rao, *Technological Change and Distribution of Gains*, p. 179. See also André Béteille, *Studies in Agrarian Social Structure* (Delhi, Oxford University Press, 1974), p. 169; Sen, *Green Revolution in India*, pp. 103–5.

[92] D. A. Low, "The Radical Left in South Asia," *South Asian Review* 8 (April 1975): 241–8. See also Ghanshyam Shah, "The Upsurge in Gujarat," *Economic and Political Weekly* 9 (August 1974): 1429–54.

[93] James C. Scott, "The Erosion of Patron-Client Bonds and Social Change in Rural Southeast Asia," *The Journal of Asian Studies* 33 (November 1972): 5–37.

[94] In discussing these changing relationships, Scott employs a model similar to the model of induced institutional change outlined in the preceding chapter. According to

The shift from customary to market determination of harvest shares that is now under way in Java provides a particularly striking illustration of the effect of productivity growth on institutional change.[95] Throughout the history of colonial development, and despite rapid population growth, traditional relationships have continued to control the allocation of resources and the distribution of production in Javanese villages. Clifford Geertz, in what is now a classic study, has described as *agricultural involution* the process by which these villages have accommodated ever larger populations on unchanging areas of land, "redistributing poverty" in such a way that every family has a niche.[96]

According to Geertz, "in addition to land tenure and land use, the involutional process also worked its peculiar patterns of changeless change on the distribution side. With the steady growth of population came also the elaboration and extension of mechanisms through which the agricultural product was spread, if not altogether evenly, at least relatively so, throughout the huge human board which was obliged to subsist on it."[97] As this process began to reach its technological limits in wet rice production, calorie consumption levels, but not the quality of the diet, were maintained by extending the same processes to the production of dry-field crops (maize, soybeans, peanuts, cassava). The technical and institutional changes that Geertz associates with agricultural involution enabled the community to survive through a process of "shared poverty."[98] Until rather recently, communal control over the allocation and use of resources and income was adequate to prevent serious deterioration in levels of living. But indigenous forms of communal control were not adequate, in the face of Dutch colonial

---

Scott, "it is possible in a given agrarian context, to view changes in the legitimacy or approval given a class of patrons largely as a function of changes in the objective balance of goods and services exchanged individually and collectively between the strata.... The peasants have some implicit notion of the balance of exchange—of what it costs them to get the patrons' services—and that any substantial change in that balance is likely to lead to a corresponding change in the legitimacy of the exchange relationship." Ibid., p. 10. Scott's observation can also be applied to the landowner. The patron has some implicit notion of the balance of exchange, that is, of what it costs him to get the service of tenants and laborers.

[95] See William L. Collier, Gunawan Wiradi, and Soentoro, "Recent Changes in Rice Harvesting Methods," *Bulletin of Indonesian Economic Studies* 9 (July 1973): 36–45; William L. Collier, Soentoro, Gunawan Wiradi, and Mahali, "Agricultural Technology and Institutional Change in Java," *Food Research Institute Studies* 13 (1974): 169–94; and Bodhisantoso, "Rice Harvesting in the Krawong Region (West Java) in Relation to High Yielding Varieties," *Centre of Southeast Asian Studies Working Papers* 6 (Melbourne, Australia: Monash University, 1975).

[96] Clifford Geertz, *Agricultural Involution: The Process of Ecological Change in Indonesia* (Berkeley: University of California Press, 1966).

[97] Ibid., p. 97.

[98] The process of agricultural involution described by Geertz in Java resembles very closely a process that T. Scarlett Epstein describes as having occurred in the village of Wangala in South India (Epstein, *South India*).

administrations, to organize communal resources in order to reverse the process of involution and to improve the welfare of the rural population.[99]

By the late 1960s, there were indications that the closely articulated system of communal control over production and distribution described by Geertz was beginning to break down. The process of expanding production by means of increasingly labor-intensive systems of cultivation under the conditions of static technology was reaching its upper limit. Javanese farmers were already operating along the upper ranges of the available labor-output response function. Furthermore, the breakdown of administrative capacity that accompanied nationalist ascendency made it very difficult for local institutions to continue to mobilize labor resources for the maintenance and regulation of the irrigation system.

The Bimas and Bimas Gotong Royong rice intensification programs of 1963–70 can be viewed as institutional innovations designed to centralize the mobilization of resources to meet rice production goals.[100] By 1970 it was apparent, even to the Indonesian government, that achievement of the program targets exceeded the administrative capacity of the central and provincial governments. The Bimas programs were not without effect, however. The new fertilizer-responsive crop varieties imported from the Philippines and developed in Indonesia had been widely diffused, and peasants had become familiar with the use of fertilizer and insecticides.

The new income streams that have been generated by the diffusion of new rice-production and processing technology have had the effect of further weakening the communal control over the allocation of resources and the partitioning of income streams. Yet the new income streams generated by the productivity gains appear to be inadequate to support the growth of employment opportunities that would stabilize or reverse the growing pressure of labor against land resources. Downward pressure on rural wage rates and levels of living is continuing. If the induced institutional innovation model suggested earlier is valid, we would expect, under these conditions, a renewed effort to achieve communal control over the allocation of resources and the partitioning of income streams in Java.

Where the higher-yielding rice varieties (IR8, IR5, C4, and *pelita*) were adopted in Java, opportunities for sharply higher returns to harvest labor under prevailing sharing arrangements were created. The higher yields also

[99] George M. Foster argues that what he terms the "cognitive orientation" or "world view," of peasant societies precludes effective organization for communal development. George M. Foster, "Peasant Society and the Limited Good," *American Anthropologist* 67 (1965): 301.

[100] Gary E. Hansen, *The Politics and Administration of Rural Development in Indonesia: The Case of Agriculture*, Monograph no. 9 (Berkeley: University of California, Center for South and Southeast Asia Studies, April 1973); idem, "Rural Administration and Agricultural Development in Indonesia," *Pacific Affairs* 44 (Fall 1971): 390–400; idem, "Indonesia's Green Revolution: The Abandonment of a Non-Market Strategy Toward Change," *Asian Survey* 12 (November 1972): 932–46; Timmer, "Rice in Asia."

induced landowners to seek ways of reducing the size of the shares traditionally allotted to harvesters. In some areas, landowners have been successful in
reducing the share of the rice crop that is paid to workers for harvesting.
In other areas, where the harvest share has been more firmly fixed by tradition or by threats of retaliation by landless workers, landlords have attempted
to limit rights to the harvest share to laborers who undertake additional
services, such as weeding or threshing. As a result, large numbers of rural
people are being squeezed out of rice cultivation and the activities associated
with harvesting and processing and into other activities in which the returns
are even lower.[101]

Under an alternative procedure that has emerged in some villages in Java,
the landowner sells his crop while it is still standing to a contractor (*penebas*),
who harvests the crop with his own crew of hired laborers. Usually the
contractor and his laborers are from a different village. Apparently the
contractor is considered to be a middleman and thus not constrained by
traditional village obligations. In several villages studied by Collier and his
associates, this change in institutional arrangements has reduced the share of
the crop that covers harvest costs from one-sixth to one-eleventh or one-
twelfth. This institutional change in harvest arrangements is accompanied by
technical changes in harvest methods, which in turn lead to further reductions
in the use of labor for harvesting.[102] In other areas of Java the institutional
constraints on the elasticity of the labor supply that derive from the tradition of restricting harvesting rights to village residents have been weakened.
In some areas where yields have risen sharply, the number of migrant
workers has increased, and the amount of rice earned from harvesting by
local laborers has declined.

The effect of the institutional changes that have occurred thus far has
been to enable the owners of the factor that is most inelastic in supply—
in this case, land—to collect a higher share of the rents that are generated by
the technical change.

[101] Collier et al., "Agricultural Technology"; Benjamin White, "Population, Involu-
tion and Employment in Rural Java," *Development and Change* 7 (1976): 276–90:
C. Peter Timmer, "Choice of Technique in Rice Milling on Java," *Bulletin of Indonesian
Economic Studies* 9 (July 1973): 57–76; William Collier, Jusuf Colter, Sinarhadi, and
Robert d'A. Shaw, "Choice of Techniques in Rice Milling on Java," *Bulletin of
Indonesian Economic Studies* 10 (March 1974): 106–20; C. Peter Timmer, "A Reply,"
*Bulletin of Indonesian Economic Studies* 10 (March 1974): 121–6. John Duewel has
cautioned against assuming that these institutional changes have been induced entirely
by technical change. He argues that intravillage exchange relationships had already
begun to break down as a result of the ideological conflicts that occurred at the village
level in the late 1950s and early 1960s. Thus, in his view, the effect of the technical
changes was to speed up institutional changes that were already under way. John
Duewel 1976: personal communication.

[102] "Under the new system, the penebas limits the number of harvesters, insists that
they use the sickle (rather than the hand knife or ani-ani), reduces the traditional harvest
share, weighs the amount each harvester cuts, and pays in money." Collier et al.,
"Agricultural Technology," p. 170.

As noted earlier in this chapter, the initial impact of the introduction of the new higher-yielding crop varieties was an increase in the demand for labor. The secondary effect, however, at least in some areas, has been to induce technical and institutional changes that serve to offset this increased demand for labor. It seems unlikely that the secondary changes that have been set in motion in Java, India, and elsewhere by advances in agricultural productivity have yet run their course. The reduction in employment opportunities in an environment where as many as half of the village residents are landless laborers can be expected to induce further institutional changes that will lead to a new pattern of patron-client relationships based on nontraditional leadership.[103]

*Intersector stress.*   Advances in agricultural productivity can be expected to induce substantial stress between the agricultural and the nonagricultural sectors. This stress emerges as political resources are utilized in modifying the institutions that partition the new income flows between agricultural producers (landowners, tenants, laborers), on the one hand, and the suppliers of marketing services, consumers, and the public sector, on the other.

The major tradition in postwar development theory has emphasized the role played by agriculture in capital formation during the early stages of economic development.[104] In these formulations, a major function of development policy is the design of market and nonmarket institutions that are capable of transferring control over the agricultural surpluses generated by advances in agricultural productivity to urban workers, entrepreneurs, and bureaucrats.[105]

The most carefully documented examples of the successful transfer of

[103] By the early 1970s, this process had apparently gone much farther in the Philippines than in Indonesia. Thomas C. Nowak and Kay A. Snyder, "Economic Concentration and Political Change in the Philippines," in *Political Change in the Philippines: Studies of Local Politics Preceding Martial Law*, ed. Benedict J. Kerkvliet (Honolulu: The University Press of Hawaii, 1974). For a discussion of the changes in labor market institutions that occurred under somewhat similar conditions in prewar Japan and precommunist China, see Ishikawa, "Peasant Families," pp. 461–70, 488–90. For a discussion of the process in India, see V. S. Vyas, "Structural Change in Agriculture and the Small Farm Sector," Presidential Address to the Gujarat Economic Association (Ahmedabad: Indian Institute of Management, November 15, 1975).

[104] This tradition draws much of its inspiration from W. Arthur Lewis's now classic paper, "Economic Development with Unlimited Supplies of Labor," *Manchester School of Economics and Social Studies* 72 (May 1954): 139–91. See also Dale W. Jorgenson, "The Development of a Dual Economy," *Economic Journal* 71 (June 1961): 309–34; Gustav Ranis and J. C. H. Fei, "A Theory of Economic Development," *American Economic Review* 51 (September 1961): 533–65, and Fei and Ranis, *Labor Surplus Economy.*

[105] One of the criticisms made of the green revolution is that it has enabled the agricultural sector to perform this traditional function too efficiently. "The introduction of high yielding varieties of food grains in regions which already are relatively well endowed with irrigation facilities has enabled the marketable surplus to be increased, and the resource transfer to continue, at a negligible cost in terms of investment in rural areas. The significance of the 'green revolution' is not so much that it has resulted in an improved livelihood in rural areas. . . as that it has allowed governments to persist with industrial policies which have taken many governments to the brink of catastrophe." Griffin, *Economy of Agrarian Change*, p. 128.

agricultural surpluses into capital formation in the nonagricultural sector are drawn from the development experience of Japan and Taiwan. In Japan, increased agricultural output and productivity represented a major source of capital accumulation in the nonagricultural sector during the period from 1880 to 1920.[106] This contribution by agriculture to the general economy was made in three ways. Heavy agricultural taxes constituted the principal means of siphoning off the increment in agricultural productivity. In the first decades of the Meiji period, the agricultural sector accounted for over 85 percent of public revenue, and this share did not fall to below 50 percent until after World War I. Throughout the same period the public sector's share of total investment ranged between 30 to 50 percent. A second way in which the gains from the agricultural sector were translated into capital investment in other sectors of the economy was through an increase in the share of agricultural output that accrued to landlords. There is evidence to show that in Japan a relatively high share of such increased rents did flow into capital formation. Finally, growth in farm output and productivity facilitated capital formation in the nonagricultural sector by limiting the rise in food prices during a period when expansion of the money supply performed an important role in financing new investment. Even after 1920, when agriculture's relative contribution to economic growth in the rest of the economy had declined, the social rate of return from investment in research on rice remained high.[107]

In Taiwan, increased output and productivity in agriculture has been an important source of capital formation in the nonagricultural sector since 1895. During the period 1895/1930, payments to landlords and taxes represented the major institutional means employed to transfer resources from the agricultural sector. Since 1930, financial institutions have become an important institutional device for mobilizing farmers' savings for investment in the nonagricultural sector. Direct transfers to consumers, through a shift against agriculture in the domestic terms of trade, have been important only since 1950.[108]

[106] Bruce F. Johnston, "Agricultural Development and Economic Transformation: A Comparative Study of the Japanese Experience," *Food Research Institute Studies* 3 (November 1962): 224–76. Johnston draws on Henry Rosovsky, "Japanese Capital Formation: The Role of the Public Sector," *Journal of Economic History* (September 1959), and on Gustav Ranis, "The Financing of Japanese Economic Development," *Economic History Review* (September 1961).

[107] Hayami et al., *Agricultural Growth in Japan*, pp. 135–69. See also Masakatsu Akino and Yujiro Hayami, "Efficiency and Equity in Public Research: Rice Breeding in Japan's Economic Development," *American Journal of Agricultural Economics* 57 (February 1975): 1–10: Mitoshi Yamaguchi and Hans P. Binswanger, "The Role of Sectoral Technical Change in Development, Japan 1880–1965," *American Journal of Agricultural Economics* (May 1975): 269–78.

[108] Teng-hui Lee, *Intersectoral Capital Flows in the Economic Development of Taiwan* (Ithaca: Cornell University Press, 1971). See also T. H. Shen, ed., *Agriculture's Place in the Strategy of Development: The Taiwan Experience* (Taipei: Joint Commission on Rural Reconstruction, 1974).

The intersector resource transfers from the agricultural to the nonagricultural sector that were so important in the historical development of Japan and Taiwan have not been as carefully documented in contemporary development experiences. Tolerance for disparity in the distribution of income among classes, sectors, and regions has declined.[109] As a result, there is a tendency for intersector stress over the partitioning of new income streams to be greater in contemporary developing countries than it was in Japan and Taiwan during comparable stages in their development history.

Events that occurred in Pakistan in the 1960s provide what is perhaps the most dramatic example of intersector and interregional stress resulting from rising economic disparity. During the 1950s and 1960s, Pakistan followed a development policy that resulted in intensified disparities among regions, sectors, and classes. The development of industry, infrastructure, and commerce was concentrated in West Pakistan. Moreover, the new wheat and rice varieties were transferred directly from Mexico and the Philippines to the relatively well-endowed, irrigated farms of the West Pakistan Punjab. Without further adaptive research, these varieties were not as well suited to the less adequately irrigated and floodprone areas of East Pakistan (Bangladesh). Within West Pakistan, agricultural development efforts emphasized providing institutional support to those farmers who already possessed a relatively favorable resource base. Although disparities in adoption rates among farm-size groups disappeared almost entirely within four or five years after introduction, they were widespread at the outset.[110] In the mid-1960s, Pakistan was widely cited as an example of successful development strategy.[111] More recently it has been cited as an example of "development disaster."[112] Both views are overdrawn. However, there can be little doubt that the stress that resulted from widening disparities among regions, sectors, and classes did contribute to the traumatic divorce of the two wings of the country.

A more typical source of intersector stress is created by attempts to use a command rather than a market approach to the transfer of marketable surpluses from producers to consumers. The use of such a command approach is illustrated by the 1973 rice procurement effort of the rice procurement agency (Bulog) in Indonesia. From 1969 to 1972, rice prices remained relatively stable in the face of a rising general price level. In spite of a 20

[109] Hirschman, "Changing Tolerance for Income Inequality," pp. 544–66. For an interesting discussion of ideological factors in reducing the tolerance for inequality, see K. C. Alexander, "Emerging Farmer–Labor Relations in Kuttanad," *Economic and Political Weekly* 8 (August 25, 1973): 1551–60.

[110] Azam, "Green Revolution in West Pakistan."

[111] Gustav F. Papanek, *Pakistan's Development: Social Goals and Private Incentives* (Cambridge, Mass.: Harvard University Press, 1967).

[112] Hirschman, "Changing Tolerance For Income Inequality."

percent increase in rice production, real incomes in rice-producing areas failed to rise. As a result of poor harvests and inadequate imports, rice prices rose sharply in late 1972 and early 1973. The procurement agency tried to meet its targets by requiring that the cooperatives (BUUD) that had only recently been established deliver quotas to the government procurement agency at the floor price that had been in effect since 1970. Farmers resisted the program in spite of strong efforts by some regional governors to reinforce the Bulog procurement effort with military support. By the time the program was discontinued, in August of 1973, the cooperatives had lost whatever limited credibility they possessed. Some observers have argued that the procurement targets could have been met with reasonable price incentives.[113]

India employed a much more sophisticated, mixed command-market system to extract surpluses from food grain producers. Market prices in surplus-producing states were held down by limiting the interstate movement of grain. In addition, farmers were required in some years to deliver quotas for government procurement at prices below the depressed market price. In late 1975, the procurement price for wheat in the Punjab was 105 rupees per quintal. The black market price was almost twice this amount.

The burden of the zonal system fell on cultivators in the surplus states in proportion to their marketing and on the high-income consumers in the deficit states (who purchase at market prices rather than in government fair-price shops). The gains went to consumers in the surplus states and to producers in the deficit states.[114] Although Indian administrative capacity has been able to operate the zonal price and levy system relatively successfully, these operations have been a source of substantial unrest in surplus areas.[115]

In the Philippines, an attempt has been made to diffuse the gains from agricultural productivity growth more broadly in rural areas by speeding up the implementation of the 1963 Agricultural Land Reform Code. In addition to the economic gains to former tenants, enforcement of the land reform code was expected to bring important political gains. The modernizing urban elite would be able to weaken the political power of the traditional rural elite and would find increasing support from an expanded class of peasant proprietors, who could be expected to be more interested in liberal reform than in radical change. As in the earlier land reforms of the 1950s and 1960s, the effort of the mid-1970s has dissipated some of these gains through sluggish and inept

[113] Peter McCawley, "Survey of Recent Developments," *Bulletin of Indonesian Economic Studies* 9 (November 1973): 1–8; Gary E. Hansen, *Rural Local Government and Agricultural Development in Indonesia* (Ithaca: Cornell University, Center for International Studies, November 1974): 56–78; Timmer, "Rice in Asia," pp. 196–231.
[114] Mellor, "Function of Agricultural Prices," pp. 23–37.
[115] See, for example, Chowdhury, "Buying Off the Large Farmers," pp. 1690–1.

management.[116] Furthermore, the potential gains to the peasant producers from agricultural productivity growth have been eroded by efforts to inhibit increases in food prices during a period of rapid inflation. During the 1974/75 crop year, the fertilizer-rice price relationship became so unfavorable that production was adversely affected. Tensions between landlords and tenants and between urban and rural areas remain unresolved.[117]

The evidence, which we have presented in this chapter, of the role of technical change in inducing institutional innovations is far from clear. It has been difficult to separate the effects of technical change from the other dynamic changes that have also impinged on the countries that have experienced the green revolution. Many of these countries have experienced rapid rates of growth in nonagricultural income and employment. Almost all have experienced unprecedented rates of population growth.

It does seem clear, however, that the contribution of the new seed–fertilizer technology to food grain production has weakened the potential for revolutionary change in political and economic institutions in rural areas in many countries in Asia and in other parts of the developing world. In spite of widening income differentials, the gains of productivity growth, in those areas where the new seed–fertilizer technology has been effective, have been sufficiently diffused to preserve the vested interests of most classes in an evolutionary rather than a revolutionary pattern of rural development.

By the mid-1970s, however, the productivity gains that had been achieved during the previous decade were coming more slowly and with greater difficulty in many areas. Perhaps the revolutionary changes in rural institutions that the radical critics of the green revolution have been predicting for the past ten years will occur as a result of increasing immizerization in the rural areas of many developing countries during the coming decade.

[116] The Philippine political leadership, from Magsaysay to Marcos, has been quite skillful in responding to the threat of rural unrest with just enough reform (or promise of reform) to weaken the momentum of peasant unrest while simultaneously it offers other political concessions designed to weaken the leadership of the peasant movements. See Gerrit J. Huizer, "Philippine Peasant Organizations," *Solidarity* 7 (June 1972): 17–32.

[117] "Antagonism between landowners and tenants...[has] become more intense and open since Presidential Decree No. 27 (on land reform) was issued on October 21, 1972." Jose E. Medina, Jr., *The Philippine Experience With Land Reform Since 1972: An Overview* (New York: Asia Society, Southeast Asia Development Advisory Group, 1975), p. 17.

FOURTEEN

# A Postscript on Alternative Paths
# of Induced Institutional Change

VERNON W. RUTTAN

I N chapter 13 we illustrated the dialectical process of technical and institutional change with data from the experience of the green revolution in Asian agriculture. We saw that an institutional innovation—the socialization of agricultural research—had been widely diffused and, as a consequence, had become an efficient source of technical change. The new income streams that have been generated by technical change have, in turn, become a powerful source of further institutional change. The economic expansion brought about by these forces has led to an imbalance among the economic, political, and social statuses of households, sectors, and classes. The resulting stress is modifying property rights in land as well as many other institutional arrangements for partitioning the gains from productivity growth in agriculture among classes, factors, and sectors. The outcome of all this has been the establishment of new incentives for technical and institutional innovation in response to new patterns in the distribution of economic and political resources. In this brief, final chapter we offer some preliminary suggestions as to the implications of the material presented in earlier chapters (particularly chapters 11, 12, and 13) for the development of a set of testable hypotheses with respect to the sources of alternative paths of induced institutional change.

As we have seen, there is a large normative literature in economics on institutional change. But the radical and reformist thrust of this literature has been a barrier to analytical consideration of the effects of natural and cultural endowments on the direction of institutional change. The tools of formal economic analysis have only occasionally been utilized in explaining alternative historical paths of institutional change or in exploring alternative future paths of such change. When economists have employed these tools in considering the issue of institutional change, they have typically focused on such grand themes as revolution, not on the incremental changes in institutional performance or the gradual cumulation of institutional innovations with which history is more familiar.[1]

Our review of the green revolution experience and of the historical process of agricultural and rural development leads us to suggest that it is possible to distinguish between two broad paths of institutional change: One path weakens, another strengthens the control of the community, or of society, over the allocation of resources and over the partitioning of income streams.[2]

In the cases we have examined, institutional change has followed both of the above paths. The socialization of agricultural research was dependent on the ability of the state to generate public revenue, and thus it involved the expansion of social control over the allocation of research resources. The effect of institutionalizing agricultural research in the public sector has been the development of an institution—the agricultural experiment station —that is capable of supplying new sources of productivity growth at a relatively low cost. This in turn has resulted in an expansion of the resources available to society. The institutional changes that have followed this expansion of resources have had the effect of reducing the control of the community over the allocation of resources and over the partitioning of income streams.

It is possible to generalize these observations in the form of two broad hypotheses with respect to the direction of institutional change.

*First, the effect of growth in the income flows available to a community or society is to induce institutional changes that weaken the control of the community*

[1] See, for example, Mancur Olson, Jr., "Rapid Growth as a Destabilizing Force," *Journal of Economic History* 23 (December 1963): 529–52. See also James C. Davis: "Toward a Theory of Revolution," *American Sociological Review* 27 (February 1962): 5–19, and Ronald G. Ridker, "The Economic Determinants of Discontent: An Empirical Investigation," *The Journal of Development Studies* 4 (January 1968): 174–219. Ridker interprets the earlier literature as consistent with the empirical generalization that "the relationship between discontent and the rate of economic growth turns out to be U-shaped, high levels of discontent associated with both low and high rates of economic growth with a minimum point occurring somewhere between" (p. 179).

For a review and extension of the sociological literature on agrarian revolution, see Jeffrey M. Paige, *Agrarian Revolution: Social Movements and Export Agriculture* (New York: The Free Press, 1975). Sociological theories, as well as Paige's own theory, tend to utilize the structural characteristics or economic organization of agricultural commodity production as explanatory factors affecting the intensity and political success of rural social and political movements.

[2] The terms "community" and "society" are employed in a broad context to include the diverse elements of even a fragmented social structure. See, for example, Irving Louis Horowitz, *Three Worlds of Development*, 2nd ed. (New York: Oxford University Press, 1972): "A social structure might be considered a dynamic balance of disharmonious parts. If we start from the real position of societies, it is evident that conflict situations are intrinsic and organic to social structure. Considered in this manner, the group, the community, or the nation are particularized areas of social activity in which conflicts arise and are resolved" (p. 489).

*or of society over the allocation of resources and the partitioning of income flows.*
New income flows may be generated by geographic or geologic discovery, by
technical change, or by prior institutional change.

*Second, the effect of stagnation or decline in the income flows available to a*
*society is to induce institutional changes that expand the control of the community*
*or the society over the allocation of resources and the partitioning of income flows.*
Stagnation or decline in income flows may occur as a result of increased
pressure of population against resource endowments, technological stagnation
or retrogression, or institutional changes such as colonial or other external
intervention into a society.

These hypotheses appear consistent both with historical experience and
with our understanding of the processes of dialectical interaction between
technical and institutional change. Institutional change occurs (*a*) as a result
of the efforts of economic units—households, firms, bureaus—to internalize
the gains from economic activity and to externalize the costs of economic
activity and (*b*) as a result of efforts by the broader society to force economic
units to internalize the costs and externalize the gains from economic
activity.[3]

The hypotheses suggest that during periods when new income flows are
being generated at a rapid rate, innovating units are relatively successful in
loosening the social constraints that limit their ability to capture the gains
from economic growth and in transferring the costs of growth to other
economic units and to the community—or society—at large. Thus the plantation sector was relatively successful in capturing the gains from expansion in
the production and export of staple commodities in both the colonial and
noncolonial economies of South and Southeast Asia.[4] Plantation owners were
also relatively successful in transferring the costs of growth to the smallholder, peasant, and public sectors. As a result, the peasant sector was unable
to develop the mass purchasing power necessary to sustain economic growth
in the nonagricultural sectors. Moreover, the public sector was prevented
from developing the capacity to provide the institutional and physical
infrastructures in rural areas that were needed to enable the economy to
break out of an enclave pattern of development. Much of the experimentation
with political systems in which South and Southeast Asian governments
have engaged during the last several decades can be viewed as an attempt to
evolve a system of political and economic organization that is capable of

[3] Edgar S. Dunn, Jr., "Heilbroner's Historicism versus Evolutionary Possibilities,"
*Zygon* 10 (September 1975): 272–98. See also Vernon W. Ruttan, "Technology and the
Environment," *American Journal of Agricultural Economics* 53 (December 1971): 707–
717.

[4] J. S. Furnivall, *Colonial Policy and Practice* (New York: New York University Press,
1956); Thomas B. Birnberg and Stephen A. Resnik, *An Econometric Study of Colonial*
*Development* (New Haven: Yale University Press, 1975).

mobilizing the region's natural and human resources to achieve more rapid development.

In contrast, a period of economic stagnation or decline can be expected to induce institutional changes that will enable the community, or the society, to force innovating units both to bear the costs of technical or institutional change and to transfer the gains to other economic units or to the community or society generally. Thus, the long period of secular economic stagnation in China during the latter half of the nineteenth and early half of the twentieth centuries induced a set of revolutionary institutional changes that gave both the local community and the broader society more effective control over local and national resources.[5]

The most dramatic of these institutional changes involved the development of China's capacity to mobilize its labor resources to produce an economic surplus that could be channeled into developing the nonagricultural sectors. As the long period of stagnation is reversed and new growth dividends become available, it seems reasonable to anticipate a set of institutional innovations that will weaken social control over allocation of the growth dividends. Control over these dividends will be captured by the enterprises and individuals who provide the sources of growth, as has occurred in the more mature socialist societies of Eastern Europe and the USSR.

The process of technical and institutional change that has been described in this and in the last three chapters is dialectical rather than linear. The impact of technical and institutional innovations that open up new sources of growth—that generate new income streams—in traditional societies can be expected to induce further institutional innovations that weaken communal and social control over the allocation and use of resources.

A period of rapid growth, followed by a period of relative decline or stagnation resulting from the exhaustion of either resource endowments or technological potential or from a failure of institutional innovation, can be expected to induce institutional innovations that give society greater social control over the allocation and use of resources. If this greater social control is utilized to mobilize the resources of the society, and if these resources are directed to the generation of technical and institutional innovations that are consistent with the resource and cultural endowments of the society, a new period of growth will be induced.

We now have the elements of an integrated theory of technical and institutional innovation that has both explanatory and predictive power with respect to the direction of technical and institutional change. The two hypo-

---

[5] Barrington Moore, Jr., *Social Origins of Dictatorship and Democracy: Land and Peasant in the Making of the Modern World* (Boston: Beacon Press, 1966), pp. 162–227. For a more qualified appraisal, see Ramon H. Myers, *The Chinese Peasant Economy: Agricultural Development in Hopei and Shantung, 1890–1949* (Cambridge, Mass.: Harvard University Press, 1970).

theses suggested in this chapter are inferences drawn from very specific historical materials. Their generality can be determined only by testing them against a broader body of historical experience. Such a test should include periods of stagnation and decline as well as periods of growth. If the elements suggested here are to be fused into a more general theory, the models of induced technical and institutional innovation must be complemented by a more adequate understanding of technical and institutional stagnation and decline.

The direction of change in the economic value of man in many parts of the developing world remains unclear. Although great progress is being made in urban and industrial development, there is disturbing evidence that the return to labor in the rural areas of many countries is stagnant and that real wages earned by landless laborers have declined. The failure to achieve gains in real income over the last several decades is inducing a set of institutional changes that are tending to give the community greater control over the use of human labor. In China, these efforts to mobilize the labor force for development have, by most reports, been relatively successful. In Tanzania, as in most developing countries, these efforts are still going through a period of costly trial and error. The effort to expand communal control over man's economic and cultural activity is often accompanied by institutional innovation designed to increase the precision with which property rights in physical resources such as land and water are defined.

In contrast, the developed countries of the West have experienced a sharp rise in the economic value of man over the last century and a half. The effect has been to induce institutional changes that have led to a loosening of communal control over the individual's investment in his own capacity and over his economic and cultural activity. As the contribution of property, particularly land, has declined in relative importance as a source of growth, the institutions of private property have weakened. At the same time, institutions designed to achieve greater consistency between individual and communal objectives in the use of physical resources have been strengthened.

It should be emphasized again that we are not suggesting that the future course of a nation's history will be fully determined either by its resource endowments or by its cultural and institutional endowments. We do insist that analysis of a nation's resource and cultural endowments, within the framework of the theory of induced innovation, can provide guidelines to efficient paths of technical and institutional change. Or, put somewhat differently, such an analysis can suggest ways of allocating resources so as to remove those resource constraints that are most inelastic and those institutional constraints that are most restrictive of growth and development.

# Contributors

URI BEN-ZION, Senior Lecturer, Technion Israel Institute of Technology, Haifa, Israel

HANS P. BINSWANGER, Associate, The Agricultural Development Council, New York City; Agricultural Economist, International Crops Research Institute for the Semi-Arid Tropics (ICRISAT), Hyderabad, India

ALAIN DE JANVRY, Associate Professor, Department of Agricultural Economics, University of California, Berkeley, California

ROBERT E. EVENSON, Associate, The Agricultural Development Council, New York City; Visiting Professor, Department of Agricultural Economics, University of the Philippines, Los Baños, Philippines

YUJIRO HAYAMI, Professor, Faculty of Economics, Tokyo Metropolitan University, Tokyo, Japan

TERRY L. ROE, Associate Professor, Department of Agricultural and Applied Economics, University of Minnesota, St. Paul, Minnesota

VERNON W. RUTTAN, President, The Agricultural Development Council, New York City and Singapore

JOHN H. SANDERS, Economist, Centro Internacional de Agricultura Tropical (CIAT), Cali, Colombia

WILLIAM W. WADE, Economist, Standard Oil of California, San Francisco, California

ADOLF WEBER, Professor, Institut für Agrarpolitik und Marktlehre der Christian-Albrechts-Universität Kiel, Kiel, Germany

PATRICK YEUNG, Staff Economist, World Bank, Washington, D.C.; formerly Assistant Professor, Department of Economics, University of Illinois, Urbana, Illinois

# Index

Abel, Martin E., 108, 109

Achievement distribution, 5

Agricultural experiment stations: in Germany, 372; origins of, 372; in Scotland, 372; as source of technical change, 371–81; in the U.S., 372–4

Agricultural involution, 401

Agricultural Land Reform Code (Philippines), 407

Agricultural output, 50–59, 69–70; constraints on growth of, 71

Agricultural research institute, model of, 204–8

Agricultural research systems, 179–82; development of national and international, 374–81

Agricultural stagnation, theories of, 298–301

Agricultural technology. See Technology, agricultural

Agriculture: biased technology in Brazilian, 276–96; biases in U.S., 215–42; factor substitution and, 45–9; innovation in, in Argentina, 309–12; Japanese, 1880–1940, 250–55; location specificity and, 165, 166; mechanization and, 362; monopoly and, 119–22; patent protection and, 116–17; research in, 15, 29, 188, 202, 371–81; resource endowments and, 49–59; technology transfer in, 184–8

Ahmad, Syed, 6. See also Hicks–Ahmad model of technical change

Allen, R. G. D., 120

Amin, S., 300

Animal power, 290–91

Aranda, S., 299

Argentina: adoption of new technologies in, 312–15; agricultural stagnation in, 298–301; demand for innovation in, 309–12, 315–23; inducement of technical change in, 301–4; land tenure in, 311–12; payoff from technical innovation in, 304–6

Arrow, Kenneth, 14, 262

Azam, K. M., 388

Baker, Edward A., 394

Bangladesh, 406

Bartsch, William H., 361, 389

Becker, Gary S., 263

Beef, elastic demand for, 313

Ben-Zion, Uri, 24, 126

Bias: factor, and cost function, 137–43; Fellner's evidence on induced, 39–41; intermediate goods industries and, 154–6; labor-saving, 63–4, 69; of technical change in the U.S., 215–42; scale, 370; and technology choices in Brazilian agriculture, 276–96; variable rates of, 228–31

Bimas Gotong Royong rice intensification program, 402

Binswanger, Hans P., 6, 7, 76, 91, 100, 111; two-factor test of induced innovation of, 66, 73–80

Biological technology. See Technology, biological

Bisaliah, Siddanaik, 386, 399

Borlaug, Norman, 359

Brazil: capital–labor ratio in, 284; cotton production in, 285–6; labor in, 283, 286; mechanization in, 278, 279, 284, 287–96; migration in, 282; price-distorting policies in, 277–95; soil preparation in, 293, 294; use of tractors in, 278–82

Breton, Albert, 344

Bureaucratic behavior, theory of, 343, 345–7

Bureaucratic entrepreneurship, 351–2

Bureau of Animal Industry (U.S.), 373

417

THE JOHNS HOPKINS UNIVERSITY PRESS

*This book was composed in Monotype Modern Extended text*
*and Victoria Condensed Titling type by William Clowes & Sons Ltd.*
*from a design by Susan Bishop. It was printed on 50-lb*
*Publishers Eggshell Wove paper and bound in Joanna Arrestox*
*cloth and Kivar 5 by Universal Lithographers, Inc.*

LIBRARY OF CONGRESS CATALOGING IN PUBLICATION DATA

Binswanger, Hans P
   Induced innovation.

    1. Technological innovations. 2. Economic development. I. Ruttan, Vernon W.,
joint author. II. Title. HC79.T4B54    301.24'3    77–23387
ISBN 0–8018–2027–8